PENGUIN BOOKS

A VOYAGE ROUND JOHN MORTIMER

'Excellent, a perceptive and affectionate biography of a national monument and treasure' *Sunday Times*

'Candid and conscientious . . . It sails as close in-shore as is possible for anyone but the subject himself to get' *Daily Mail*

'A finely written story' *Sunday Herald*

'Beautifully written' *Evening Standard*

'Grove . . . has presented a pretty unflinching portrait of this clever man with an apparently impenetrable carapace . . . yet you do leave the book with a better sense of him' *Observer*

'Seldom have author and subject been so well met. She has captured exactly his air of the raffish flaneur [in] this gripping biography of a life well lived' *Country Life*

'There is everything you could want in this funny, engaging, very well-written book in terms of fact and anecdote' *Spectator*

'A terrific biography' *Irish Independent*

D0681949

ABOUT THE AUTHOR

Valerie Grove is a journalist who for the last twenty years has written interviews for the *Sunday Times* and *The Times*. She was born in South Shields, and read English at Girton College, Cambridge. She has written two highly acclaimed biographies, of the writers Dodie Smith and Laurie Lee. She is married with four children and lives in London.

A Voyage Round John Mortimer

VALERIE GROVE

PENGUIN BOOKS

PENGUIN BOOKS

Published by the Penguin Group
Penguin Books Ltd, 80 Strand, London WC2R ORL, England
Penguin Group (USA) Inc., 375 Hudson Street, New York, New York 10014, USA
Penguin Group (Canada), 90 Eglinton Avenue East, Suite 700, Toronto, Ontario, Canada M4P 2Y3
(a division of Pearson Penguin Canada Inc.)
Penguin Ireland, 25 St Stephen's Green, Dublin 2, Ireland
(a division of Penguin Books Ltd)
Penguin Group (Australia), 250 Camberwell Road, Camberwell, Victoria 3124, Australia
(a division of Pearson Australia Group Pty Ltd)
Penguin Books India Pvt Ltd, 11 Community Centre, Panchsheel Park, New Delhi – 110 017, India
Penguin Group (NZ), 67 Apollo Drive, Rosedale, North Shore 0632, New Zealand
(a division of Pearson New Zealand Ltd)
Penguin Books (South Africa) (Pty) Ltd, 24 Sturdee Avenue, Rosebank, Johannesburg 2196, South Africa

Penguin Books Ltd, Registered Offices: 80 Strand, London WC2R ORL, England

www.penguin.com

First published by Viking 2007
Published in Penguin Books 2008

2

Copyright © Valerie Grove, 2007

The moral right of the author has been asserted

The permissions listed on page 501 constitute an extension of this copyright page

Typeset by Rowland Phototypesetting Ltd, Bury St Edmunds, Suffolk
Printed in Great Britain by Clays Ltd, St Ives plc

A CIP catalogue record for this book is available from the British Library

ISBN: 978–0–141–01954–3

www.greenpenguin.co.uk

Penguin Books is committed to a sustainable future
for our business, our readers and our planet.
The book in your hands is made from paper
certified by the Forest Stewardship Council.

To Lucy, Emma and Victoria,
my three girls,
and Oliver,
the oh-thank-God

Contents

List of Illustrations

All images are courtesy of John and Penny Mortimer unless stated otherwise.

Author's Note

I have distinguished John Mortimer's two wives in the same way as they tended to be identified in life: the first Mrs Mortimer, Penelope, is invariably referred to as Penelope; the second Mrs Mortimer, later Lady Mortimer, is always Penny.

I envied my subject his freedom to produce two volumes of memoirs without including an index or notes. My own notes are minimal. Most of the information about John's life, if the source is not specified in the text, comes from the dozens of conversations I have had with him since April 2004, and with the friends listed in the Acknowledgements; also from his father's diaries, and his own scrapbooks, notebooks and manuscripts kept at Turville Heath Cottage.

Penelope Mortimer wrote, like her husband, two volumes of memoirs. When writing these she depended on the detailed diary she had always kept, and which she distilled into a résumé she referred to as her 'Chronology'. To Jeremy Mortimer, Penelope's literary executor, and to his sisters, who allowed me to use and quote from the Chronology, as well as from her published works, I am deeply indebted.

1. An Only Child

I am sure you would love John and I do wish he could know you; he will be 17 next April and he is the most cheerful and entertaining of companions so that Mother and I feel very glum when he is at school – I think him a genius, though Kathleen won't have it so. I have never known a boy of his age so deeply read in English literature and he has a decided talent for writing verse. He is also very interested in painting and very clever in designing stage sets & costumes and spends endless time designing settings for different plays on a miniature stage with scenery lighting and figures complete. He paints a good deal at Harrow and contributes to the Harrow weekly paper & won a prize in the reading aloud competition & passed his school certificate with seven credits – there's a paragon for you! With all this he is a dear boy with a great sense of fun . . .

Clifford Mortimer, who wrote these words in 1939 to his sister Gertie, would have been gratified to know that, by the end of the century, the British public agreed with him that his boy was a lovable genius. He would perhaps be amazed to have become his son's prime source of material. The author of *Mortimer on Probate* had steered his son, an aspiring writer, towards the legal profession. Obediently the only child followed him into the same Probate, Divorce and Admiralty division of the High Court, and shared his father's gloomy chambers at 1 Dr Johnson's Buildings in the Temple. Being a barrister was to prove John Mortimer's unique selling point. The law would give him cachet among authors, as the only playwright-QC. And he chose, in his work, to celebrate Clifford Mortimer by recreating him, time and again.

Every opinion he held came from his father, with the notable exception of Clifford's aversion to music. He absorbed Clifford's literary enthusiasms. He inherited his retentive memory, his atheism, his terror of boredom; also his asthma and glaucoma. He continued to live in the house Clifford built, unable to consider changing anything in it, and expanding its surrounding acres. The garden became for him, as it had been for his father, the basis of his affection for the English countryside, a symbol of stability and permanence, a refuge, 'a solace and a kind of drug'. He even replicated, eventually, his father's ability to carry on working in spite of physical dependence on others. Indeed, he most admired his father's ability to rise above his blindness, never complaining or referring to it at all, and applied the same stoicism to his own immobility. 'I miss him all the time, and I'm terribly overshadowed by him,' John said. 'And I do find myself with the feeling that I'm repeating his life.'

Many authors have used their characterful fathers as an inspiration, theme and scourge: Charles Dickens and his debt-ridden, Micawberesque father, John; V. S. Pritchett and the feckless Walter; Auberon Waugh and the irascible Evelyn. But John Mortimer went further: he rarely conducted a public conversation without a reference to Clifford as the major influence on his life. Auberon Waugh, trying to interrogate John for the *New York Times* about the televising of Evelyn Waugh's *Brideshead Revisited*, could not steer him from the subject. 'Whenever John Mortimer talks about himself – or about Rumpole or almost any of his characters – the conversation always returns to his father.' By then the father he had so touchingly dramatized in his best play, *A Voyage Round My Father*, had eclipsed the original in vividness. His wife Penelope wrote, of his 1957 play *The Dock Brief*, that the character of Morgenhall was 'inspired by his father who, in slightly different guises, would serve him indefatigably for the rest of his career'. But he would sometimes wonder if he had truthfully represented his father, or invented him. The public Clifford seemed to have become 'a sort of fictional character . . . the effect has been perhaps that my father has vanished or turned into a different character from what he really was'. To cite a random example from 1981: 'I don't know who he is any more . . . I've written so much dialogue for him to say that I can't remember what he said and what I've made up. When I wrote the play, I wrote many lines for him which he never said in his life.'

How to disentangle the factual Clifford from the fictional, theatricalized version? By all accounts he was remarkably clever (he got to Cambridge at sixteen) and a skilled advocate. His most enduring published writing, the preface to *Mortimer on Probate*, the standard textbook on the validity of wills, is – even allowing for the turgid legalese – quite impenetrable. One of John's stepdaughters found Clifford Mortimer daunting, another found him lovable. Laurence Olivier's portrayal of him (in *A Voyage Round My Father*) came closest, John said, because Clifford was 'alarming', while Alec Guinness 'wasn't angry enough'. He writes of Clifford's terrifying rages, directed at others but never at his son. Clifford's favourite literary quotations suggest someone drily sardonic, with a sense of the absurdity of life, coupled with a determination to be stoical about it. He would cite Swinburne's 'raptures and roses of vice' and add, helpfully, 'The roses and raptures of vice are damned uncomfortable, as you'll certainly find out. You have to get into such ridiculous positions.'

Whole scenes of Shakespeare's plays had lodged in Clifford's head, and choice phrases were deployed in various circumstances: 'Nymph, in thy orisons be all my sins remember'd' from *Hamlet*, a general address to a lady; 'Is execution done on Cawdor?' from *Macbeth*, a disconcerting inquiry to throw at a boy aged four; and 'rush forth and bind the boy' from *King John*, which sounded like a firm of solicitors, so in the Law Courts Clifford could perplex a solicitor by greeting him with, 'Are you from Rushforth and Bindtheboy?'

John's Clifford specializes in mischievous aphorisms: 'Love has been greatly overestimated by the poets', 'No one could possibly get the slightest pleasure out of music', 'All schoolmasters have second-rate minds', 'Immortality would be a terrible bore, like living in some great transcendental hotel with nothing to do in the evenings', 'Lot of damned dull stuff in old Proust', 'Travel limits the mind.' He sent his sayings out like challenges, into the darkness around him.

But Clifford's diaries indicate a less dramatic personality altogether, neither irascible nor particularly comical.

In the nine volumes Clifford dictated to his wife between 1946 and 1961, there is scarcely a half-ironical comment or even a bemused reaction to his son's early plays and novels. There is an occasional Pooterish element: 'Just as we were preparing for tea unexpected visitors arrived who turned out to be the widow of Harry Mortimer, Lizzie's nephew and two friends of hers who live in Henley, Mr and Mrs Morris. I was wearing a ragged coat.' That Clifford did possess a sense of comedy is suggested by the excellent cartoons he drew and the verse parodies he wrote as a young man. (He had had a story, 'The Little Bright Star', published in *Pearson's Magazine* in 1901 when he was only sixteen.) But no witty remark enlivens the diary: it is an exhaustive factual log of herbaceous cultivation, peppered with minor domestic incident. For instance, on the day his only grandson was born in 1955, he dictated: 'John telephoned us to say that Penelope had a baby boy born at 8am. Smith has made up a hotbed in the cucumber frame and sown grass on the old rose beds. We . . . went on planting our rhododendron seedlings.'

By the time John had fulfilled his father's aspirations and more – taking silk, achieving a knighthood, creating an amusing old barrister figure based partly on Clifford – John himself had begun to turn into the old boy reincarnate. In old age, he too required the devoted care of others. When he could still walk, he would reach for one of Clifford's walking canes, kept by Clifford's desk. The televised image of the old blind Clifford in a neatly darned tweed suit and damaged straw hat, making amusingly perverse remarks, was replaced in the public mind by an equally familiar image of the octogenarian John, in immaculate grey suit and waistcoat, wheeled through the throng at public events such as the wedding of Charles and Camilla, or the première of a new film starring his daughter Emily. The media's insatiable appetite for another Mortimer interview was part of the 'national treasure' persona that attached itself to him: the status conferred on a handful of enduring personalities who, by dint of longevity, easy familiarity, undemanding dependability, invoke almost universal feelings of fondness in the nation's heart. He was 'a man whose private and professional lives float on a tide of affection', as one profile put it. Sir John Mortimer, white hair beautifully brushed, face dominated by owlish glasses, emanated a genial willingness to hail a fellow celebrity or supply a passing gossip columnist with a usable quote.

Biographies whose early pages are peopled with distant ancestry bored John – always easily bored – and the voyage he took round his father did not venture further back than the paternal grandfather who had emigrated to Pietermaritzburg before the Boer War. (Of his other grandfather, Henry Bartlett Smith, who committed suicide in Leamington Spa, he knew little.) John was the sixth John Mortimer in the recorded family tree that started with the birth of a John Mortimer in Crediton, Devon, in 1794. Clifford Mortimer's father, John Mortimer III, born 1850, was a Bristol spirit merchant with a company named Mortimer & Clune. He converted to Methodism, signed the Pledge and sailed off to South Africa, because he had been to the Transvaal in 1871 on a doctor's recommendation to relieve his asthma. So Clifford was English-born, in 1885, but emigrated at five and attended a prep school in Pietermaritzburg named Merchiston, followed by Michaelhouse, Natal's version of an English public school.

At Merchiston, Clifford was 'Dux of the school' (head boy) in 1897, aged twelve. At the annual prize-giving, music and drama were performed. In 1894, Master Clifford Mortimer played Hubert (who said 'rush forth and bind the boy') in a scene from *King John*, while Master Jim Sisson played the Prince. The two boys, reported the *Natal Witness*, 'displayed no lack of spirit and no little elocutionary power'. The following year, Clifford and his best friend Sisson did a scene from *The Merchant of Venice*, with Clifford as Shylock and Sisson as Portia. 'At breakings-up we used to hurl speeches out of Shakespeare at each other,' Clifford told the author of the school's history fifty-seven years later. 'That is how I come to remember so much of the Immortal Bard.' The significance for

John was that Clifford had a prodigious memory: not just for Shakespeare, but for Conan Doyle, H. Rider Haggard (creator of 'She Who Must Be Obeyed'), P. G. Wodehouse and Mark Twain. Theirs were stories Clifford knew almost by heart.

In 1992, while writing volume two of his memoirs, John made a trip to South Africa, *à la recherche du temps perdu*, accompanied by his son Jeremy, visiting Clifford's sister's family, the Lovell-Shippeys. But what John could relate of Clifford's boyhood amounts to little more than a single story. In his memoirs, John described how Clifford would be sent up-country in his school holidays, to 'run wild', staying at some small, lonely hotel where he put his birthday cake in a tin under his bed and, on the proper day, ate it in solitary celebration. John had previously used this story in *A Voyage Round My Father* in 1969:

FATHER: I said – the boy's probably running wild.
MOTHER: Oh, I don't think so.
FATHER: Oh yes he is. And a good thing too. When I was a young boy in Africa, they sent me off – all by myself – to a small hotel up country to run wild for three months. I took my birthday cake with me and kept it under my bed. I well remember . . . (*He laughs*) when my birthday came round I took the cake out, sat on my bed, and ate it. That was my celebration!

The curious recollection of the cake under the camp bed had already been aired in an earlier play. In *What Shall We Tell Caroline?* (1958) Arthur, the headmaster, reminisces:

When I was a boy my birthday always fell when I was away from home at Cadet camp. My old aunt gave me my cake to take in a tin. I had to keep it under my bed until the day came, then I'd get it out and eat it.

Plainly, Clifford had been sent away to a school summer camp in the month of his birthday, January. John chose to see this as a symptom of parental detachment. 'Both his and my mother's family, it seems,' he wrote, 'were determined to avoid any situation in which they could sniff the danger of an emotional display.'

But in the letter to his sister already quoted, Clifford waxes lyrical about memories of their childhood: of playing in the wattle plantation, when Gertie would make 'glorious little hot cakes for tea, or ginger beer in screwtop bottles':

> Do you remember the night when we arranged the cards so that Father got all the hearts? I had the declaration. He said, looking at his hand, 'I'll tell you something at the end of the game' & I kept him on tenterhooks, pretending to consider my bid. Presently I said, 'leave it to you Partner', & he pounced and with hearts so that he could hardly keep a straight face.

Clifford grew up to be tall and fair, with a high, balding brow and long, slim legs. Photographs show, to my mind, a good-looking man, but John writes boldly that his father's combination of thick nose, fat chin and protruding lower jaw meant that he 'couldn't be called handsome'. At Trinity College, Cambridge, Clifford Mortimer read law, got a second-class degree in 1904, and was called to the Bar in Natal. But he was practising both in the Supreme Court there and in the High Court in London soon afterwards, and was involved in prominent divorce and probate cases from 1909.

While taking part in these cases, Clifford was also writing his magnum opus, *Mortimer on Probate*, the law textbook which supplanted *Executors*, by Sir Edward Vaughan Williams, and a previous volume by Tristram and Coote. Indeed, *Mortimer on Probate* remains the standard today. It was published in 1911, when Clifford was only twenty-six: a voluminous 1,363 pages (at 42 shillings) of thorough exposition – 'a work of infinite pains,' said the *Law Journal*; 'an excellent treatise,' said the *Law Magazine* – including an examination of 'unsoundness of mind' and an appendix on precedents of pleading. The frontispiece bore a line from Richard II's 'let's talk of graves, of worms, and epitaphs' speech: 'Let's choose executors and talk of wills.'

The book's immense size was reduced by Clifford for the revised edition in 1916, the year he met his future wife, at thirty-one.

Kathleen May Smith was a tall, slender, dark-haired, brown-eyed beauty who looks not unlike photographs of Katherine Mansfield. John would cite the fact that she had read Shaw's *The Intelligent Woman's Guide to Socialism and Capitalism* as evidence of an independent streak: he wrote of her as a spirited Shavian 'New Woman' who had set out alone at the age of seventeen on the sea voyage to South Africa in 1914. She was one of three clever daughters of Henry Bartlett Smith, the bum-bailey, as Clifford Mortimer referred to him, and his wife, Eleanor, née Langford. Smith had succeeded his father as High Bailiff (debt collector) of Warwickshire; but in John's childhood he was rarely spoken of, because one morning in August 1915, at the age of sixty-four and suffering from overwork and depression, he had taken his gun into his garden and shot himself in the head. It was an extremely sad story. Kathleen heard about her father's suicide while in South Africa: the family sent her a clipping from the local paper, with no covering letter. But the newspaper gave the full text of her father's farewell letters to his wife and his friends, explaining that he had suffered forty years of hell from 'Bridgeman', auditor of the bailiff's accounts. Henry's salary had been reduced; he had no assistant; he could not endure the anxiety and insomnia, and besides, he dreaded the onset of blindness of which he had been warned. 'The cruel treatment I have received from the Treasury after 49 years' service has completely broken me down,' he wrote. He thanked his friends for their kindness, adding, 'It is an awful ending, but I cannot fight against it any longer. May God in his mercy be kinder to me than Bridgeman has been. PS The money is all right – to a penny.' To his wife he wrote that his life had truly been hell for years and he could no longer hide it: 'I am beaten. I cannot go on. I do not want to be an incubus to you as I should be if I lived.' It was his eldest daughter, Evelyn, who found him, unconscious, in a garden shed; he died in Warneford hospital that evening. The coroner said the county of Warwickshire had lost a very old servant who had faithfully discharged his duties for many years.

The three Smith daughters were all exemplary, prize-winning students at Leamington High School (now the Kingsley School, after its founder Rose Kingsley, daughter of Charles). Kathleen and her sister Evelyn, who became head girl, co-edited the school magazine; Evelyn then took a first-class degree in London, became an English mistress and later a full-time writer. She lived on a houseboat on Loch Lomond with her friend Dorothea Mohr, and wrote girls' school novels with more originality than their for-mulaic titles – *Binkie of IIIB*, *Milly in the Fifth*, *Phyllida in Form III* and *The Right Head Girl* – might suggest. The youngest of the sisters, Marjorie, known as Daisy, was the cleverest: she got a scholarship in 1914 to Lady Margaret Hall, Oxford. By that time, Kathleen was in South Africa. She had won a scholarship in 1907 to Birmingham School of Art; then took herself to Paris, where she taught drawing at a lycée in Versailles and in 1912 had a painting exhibited in the Paris Salon, before answering an advertisement for an art teacher at St Anne's, a girls' school in Natal.

Eighty years later, when John visited Natal, he read what his mother had written in the school magazine, urging pupils to strive for excellence with this firm prescription: 'We must be very stern judges of our own productions, always careful to realize the differ-ence between what we do and what we would do, and each time more anxious to get nearer to our own idea of perfection.' As well as a perfectionist she must have been a brave girl, John thought: she had ridden bareback across the veldt and swum naked under waterfalls. Back in England in 1915, Kathleen wrote to Clifford Mortimer at the request of his parents, whom she had met in South Africa. As his family had clearly hoped, he took Kathleen for a picnic on the bank of the Thames at Chiswick and in due course proposed. By then he wore the uniform of a second lieutenant in the Inns of Court Volunteer Rifles, and was about to be posted to France, but a sympathetic senior officer intervened and arranged for him to become legal adviser to the Inland Waterways instead. Hence Clifford's advice to John in 1938: 'If they give us war again, get yourself a job in the Inland Waterways.'

John writes that Kathleen, whom he cast in a self-effacing role, was revered as a heroine and a saint in her middle age 'for putting up with my father, an almost impossible task'. Only with hindsight had he appreciated her qualities, her integrity, and often said he regretted his neglect of her. But she never complained of neglect (at any rate, no more so than any widowed mother of a very busy only son). And in a perceptive comment, John said that behind the blushing gentleness, his mother was 'a stronger character than my father'.

Clifford and Kathleen were married on 1 February 1917, in the parish church of Summertown, Oxford, because Kathleen's sister Marjorie (Daisy) was then an undergraduate at Lady Margaret Hall. The witnesses were Daisy and Evelyn. After the war, Clifford resumed his work at the Bar, and by the time John was born, on 21 April 1923, the Mortimers were renting an apartment on the western edge of Hampstead Heath, in the Pryors, an Edwardian Gothic block of mansion flats built by Paul Waterhouse, son of the great Victorian architect Alfred. When John was five, Clifford began renting a pretty Georgian house nearby in Downshire Hill and took a flat in Harcourt Buildings in the Temple. In their Hampstead days, John went to his first kindergarten in Belsize Park. Clifford, in his black jacket and waistcoat, striped trousers and spats, with cigar ash on the watch-chain (the outfit John later adopted for Rumpole), would be driven each morning to the Law Courts in a hearse-like Morris Oxford by his clerk, 'Leonard'. Leonard's real name was Henry. All Clifford's clerks were known as Leonard, after the first one, who was killed on the Somme.

John's tale of his father coming home and saying, 'Remarkable win today, old boy. Only evidence of adultery we had was a pair of footprints upside down on the dashboard of an Austin Seven parked in Hampstead Garden Suburb,' became one of his most oft-told anecdotes, vastly enjoyed by audiences, whether true or not. What is certain is that Clifford was involved almost daily in extramarital dramas, which are chronicled in a handsome cuttings volume dated 1905–24. Since divorce was still uncommon, the Law Courts in London heard divorce petitions from all over the land. 'Actress as Respondent'; 'Dentist as Co-Respondent'; 'Passionate Love letters found in trunk'; 'Wife's Secret Friendship'; 'Melancholy story of Married Man's Intrigue'; 'Woman's Pitiful Confession. Touching Letters Pinned to Curtain'. Such are the headlines that animate Clifford Mortimer's scrapbook, with its tales of stolen wills, servant-girls caught sitting on employers' knees, policemen climbing ladders to spy on adulterous bedrooms, lodgers who kiss their landlady in the kitchen, illicit assignations in fields and hotel rooms, a bride who 'has been brought up like a hot-house plant, ignorant of everything', a wife who 'made herself thoroughly obnoxious to her husband's people' and a husband who threw the marble top of a washstand at his wife.

Clifford's cuttings-book is a fascinating relic of the days when the Law Courts were fully reported in *The Times* and the *Daily Mail*, complete with descriptions ('he is a little man with sharp features and piercing eyes') and dramatic disclosures. In *Parmeggiani* v. *Sweeney*, for example: '"Were you engaged by Parmeggiani as his servant?" asked Mr Shearman. "No," cried Madame, emphatically. "I was his companion in misery."' A witness in the same case was asked, 'When you were in Paris, did you have dynamite in your possession?' And later: 'The witness added that he went to Walsall to manufacture bombs.'

Letters told all, in that era, and were produced as exhibits in court to provide graphic evidence of tragic misalliances:

You took me when I was 19 and darkened my whole life . . . Now after seven long years, you are going to change, and for whom – Alice? Had she been at least as goodlooking as I am my pain would not be so great.

Dear Ted – You have known for years I have not had a wife's love for you . . . Will you act as a good man, and let me try a fresh life with a man who I know will be absolutely my master as regards my way of life? I have got to part from my dear children . . . You will have all the sympathy; I all the condemnation.

'My passionate love for you is dead and can never live again,' wrote Captain Bernard Treleaven Taperell to his wife, Isabel, in 1919. The name is typical. Clifford's clients' names – in *Wolfenden* v. *Wolfenden, Samborne-Palmer* v. *Samborne-Palmer, Venables* v. *Venables, Fenwick* v. *Fenwick, Bonham-Carter* v. *Bonham-Carter* (in which the wife, 'Imp', wrote to her husband 'My dear Tush', imploring him to 'let bygones by bygones') – reflect the fact that divorce was then a luxury available chiefly to the upper or professional classes. Such cases Clifford could infuse with Shakespearian references. 'Oh, beware, my lord, of jealousy,' he would intone. 'It is the green-eyed monster which doth mock the meat it feeds on.'

In April 1922 an account of a divorce case in *The Times* shows Clifford encountering one of those judges of the 'Who is Mick Jagger?' type.

Mr Justice Hill, when counsel recalled the husband's remark to the wife, 'Stop your grizzling', said: 'I am not sufficiently up in modern slang to know whether "Stop your grizzling" is an affectionate term or not.'

Mr Mortimer: 'I can assure your lordship it is not a term of endearment.' (Laughter.)

The Times reported:

Counsel rarely get into the public eye, or receive much space in the Press, through their addresses to juries; but it is generally agreed that Mr Clifford Mortimer's address in the girl bride case was a particularly brilliant one. His epigram, 'Snobbery is not a matrimonial offence, for women marry snobs every day,' was one of those shrewd thrusts which have a wider appeal than is usually found in counsel's speeches.

Divorce work, Clifford told his son, offered unique insights into the human panorama. Newspaper reports referred to heartbreak, to sweethearts and 'conjugal rights', and husbands who gave their wives' lovers 'a good thrashing'. Letters were found in a wife's desk, addressed to 'My Dearest Girlie'. One respondent 'told his wife that it was necessary for his literary work that he should descend into the depths of society'. A husband discovered that 'his wife was a woman of dreadful temper, who said she would make him grovel at her feet and horsewhip him, as she had done her first husband'. John was absolutely truthful when he told his audiences that he was raised, fed, sheltered, clothed and educated on the proceeds of adultery, cruelty, desertion and 'wilful refusal to consummate'.

An only child can derive great benefit, not only from his parents' sole attention, but from hours spent on his own. In the past at least, an only child in a house well stocked with books would read far more than one surrounded by siblings. John, like Wordsworth, 'was taught to feel, perhaps too much / The self-sufficing power of Solitude'. He became a constant reader. He also felt compelled to perform and entertain his parents. His conviction grew that he had another self, alongside: he could watch this alter ego, daring him to be mischievous, wondering what he could get away with. 'Being alone was easier, I had long ago discovered, if you became two people, the actor and the observer.' When he was four, his mother anxiously confided to her sister his preference for solitary activities. Only-child status infused John's behaviour from infancy into old age, when he needed peace in which to write, but had to be sure that the solitude was finite, that he would soon be surrounded by people again – preferably admirers, eager to hear his racontage, otherwise melancholia would set in. In John's boyhood, his mother's chief emotional attachment was to Clifford, who demanded most of her time and care. For a while, Leonard's wife, Elsie, was engaged as John's nanny: 'my nurse, governess and friend'. He was left with Elsie when his parents went to Scotland in May 1926, to Aunt Evelyn's houseboat; and later, when the Mortimers went to the seaside, they stayed at a four-star hotel, while Elsie and the boy were billeted at a boarding house along the promenade – a normal practice among the upper middle classes of their generation.

The details of John's life before the age of ten are like 'the snapshots of an only child who had, in those slow-moving days, much time to notice things'. Letters to Kathleen from her sister Evelyn (who died of pneumonia in 1928, aged forty-two) conjure up a cosseted nephew, 'darling Johnkin', who looked adorable in his striped pyjamas and dressing gown, who went tobogganing and to children's parties, and caught whooping cough. Evelyn advised Kathleen not to worry unduly 'about his attitude to other snippets . . . The social age doesn't begin till about five, does it? Then I expect you'll wish it hadn't begun!' As he was so short-sighted, the world was for him 'an Impressionist haze', the blackboard 'a chalky confusion'. At five, he got his wire spectacles and 'the world sprang at me in hideous reality'. In 1929, by which time his parents were living in their Temple flat, he sat an exam and was admitted to a costly little pre-prep school, Mr Charles Gibbs's establishment occupying two Georgian houses at 134–5 Sloane Street, where the boys wore blazers and peaked caps in Post Office red. The other mothers were affluent ladies-about-town. Kathleen delivered him on the first day, but it was Elsie who took him there daily from the Temple. Over lunch, Mr Gibbs would read aloud to the boys from narrative poems about the Empire and heroic ballads, leaving gaps, they noticed, at unsuitable passages. One fellow pupil was Peter Ustinov, another only child with a penchant for performance and anecdote: Ustinov was bullied, until he performed a humorous cabaret and vanquished the bullies. There was also Nicholas Mosley, son of Sir Oswald and his first wife, who were low in funds thanks to Mosley's founding the British Union of Fascists; young Mosley and his sister had to live with their nanny, Hyslop, in their former chauffeur's flat behind Ebury Street. The school's forte, boxing, was taught by a cauliflower-eared pugilist known as 'Mr 'It-Me'. His lessons were for John a weekly appointment with terror ('like playing Russian roulette with an earthquake'). Many years later he wrote a play, *David and Broccoli*, about a boxing instructor (' 'It me. 'Arder') and his impact on a studious, sensitive boy; by then John had learned that a writer can exorcize demons by writing about them. The play caused Mr 'It Me 'to melt, in my memory, into a fictional character'.

John's one fond memory of Mr Gibbs's school was of Miss

Bellamy ('Miss Boustead' in *Clinging to the Wreckage*), the Cub mistress, who would take her Sloane Square Wolf Cubs by tube to Wimbledon Common, where she would stand in a clearing while the Cubs scattered and then, in a variation of Grandmother's Footsteps, tried to crawl unnoticed between her legs, for the prize, a box of Cadbury's chocolates: 'the only form of competitive sport I have ever enjoyed'.

Every Christmas was spent at Battle, East Sussex, with Aunt Daisy and Uncle Harold. Daisy had married Harold Heal, younger brother of the more famous Ambrose, in 1922. Ambrose inherited the family business, Heal's, the furniture emporium that had stood in Tottenham Court Road since 1840. Ambrose had become the Terence Conran of his day and made Heal's a byword for modern design. Harold, who designed the desk at which John wrote so many of his books, had inherited the family's patented bed-spring and became a manufacturer of fine beds under the company name of Staples. This made Harold far richer than Clifford, but his under-heated, over-furnished manor house was referred to by the Mortimers as 'the North Pole'. On Christmas Day they would all go and deliver tins of biscuits or tea to the estate gardeners and woodmen, and later put on black-tie evening dress for Christmas dinner. Harold and Daisy were childless, so again John was the sole child, surrounded at the feast by local colonels and neighbours. On Boxing Day they would go, in Harold's Lagonda, to the pantomime at White Rock Pavilion on the pier at Hastings, 'a magical place' for John, to see the Crazy Gang and other music-hall acts.

For weekends and holidays after 1929, Clifford began to rent a Thames Valley cottage: Summer Cottage at Summer's Heath, between Turville Heath and Southend, close to the fine Elizabethan manor of Stonor. In 1936 the artist John Nash described it as 'one of the most beautiful and still unspoilt corners of the country' and so it remains. The location proved important, for in this valley John Mortimer put down roots, and was bound for life. Lit by oil lamps, its tin bath filled with water from the well, the cottage cost a shilling a week to rent, payable to Lilias Hoare

Nairne, lady of the manor. According to John, she had taken an axe, gift of her husband the General, and razed the beech trees on the common, the wood supplying the furniture factories of High Wycombe. John made friends and playmates not only of Victor Hoare Nairne, the lady's son, but of the boys in the poky cottage next door, Sam and Willie Rockall, sons of a 'bodger', who made chair legs from beech logs. One Christmas, Clifford proposed an outing for all three boys to see the pantomime in Reading. Mr Rockall would not hear of it: once they had been to the theatre, who knew where it would end? There was also Elsie Cross ('Iris Jones' in his memoirs), the gardener's daughter from along the common, who taught him to whistle, and with whom he made houses out of bracken, furnished with old crocks. He envied Elsie and the Rockall boys their freedom to play in the bracken on long, light evenings after their days at the village school. When John went away to prep school, a wedge was driven between them so 'holidays were a solitary pleasure'.

Like most sensitive writers, he could always evoke childhood sensations: the smell of his pet white mice in the garage; the icy walk through the garden to the earth-closet by the vegetable patch, the stone hot-water bottle in the cold bed. 'I know exactly how it felt to be sitting alone on a radiator, unwrapping the blue bag of salt and shaking it into a packet of crisps, my eyes pricking with tears, apparently abandoned by my parents in the first week at prep school.'

In 1932, when John was nine, Clifford bought twenty acres of land nearby and built Turville Heath Cottage. John recalled walking under the scaffolding, climbing ladders and smelling freshly sawn wood as the new house emerged, deliberately cottage-sized. Clifford would quote Abraham Cowley's seventeenth-century poem 'The Garden', whose dedication to John Evelyn related his lifelong desire 'that I might be Master at last of a small House and large Garden . . . and there dedicate the Remainder of my Life to the Culture of them, and study of nature'. So the dimensions and scope of the garden were far grander and more dramatic than those of the house, blending with the superb beech woods all around. The small house bears the stamp of the 1930s, with white clapboard walls and a roof of green pantiles; the window frames are yellow metal, and a door on to the terrace, decorated with yellow and white chevrons in the art deco manner, was the gateway to Clifford's true pride and joy. Two long herbaceous borders at either side of a wide central grass avenue were the only formal note. Halfway down the walk is a circle with paths leading off behind each border, and at the end of the avenue are two seats, either side of a statue backed by dark yew. The rhododendrons, camellias, azaleas and shrub roses have a backdrop of rare and beautiful trees – eucryphias, *Acer griseum, Fothergilla monticola*, Indian horse chestnut and flowering cherries, a tulip tree, and a blue cedar planted in celebration of King George V's silver jubilee. In the beech copses are strange deep flint burial pits, in spring full of daffodils and narcissi, and beyond them a field where rare trees, cherries and crab apples grow. In his kitchen garden Clifford grew peaches and nectarines, melons and asparagus.

The cost of the land and the construction of the house, by a builder named Hepworth, came to £4,000, which is what Clifford then earned in a year. At one end of the house was the cavernous garage for the Morris Oxford, and a shed containing the generator, as there was no mains electricity (and no main drains). The garage later became John's writing room, and the shed his bathroom, where his abundance of awards and caricatures hang, and a book room containing editions, in many languages, of his works.

The house was furnished in Kathleen's taste: unpolished Windsor chairs and gate-legged dining table in pale bleached oak, the 1930s favourite; the polished floors scattered with homespun rugs. There were plain covers on the armchairs, and a winged armchair by the fireplace in the sitting room where Clifford, and later John, would preside. Kathleen's paintings of Parisian roofscapes in misty shades of grey and blue hang on the walls. In John's day they were joined by John Piper, a Matisse lithograph, Walter Sickert, Jacob Epstein, Augustus John and Gaudier-Brzeska.

In the largest of the three upstairs bedrooms, which were heated by paraffin stoves, french windows opened on to a balcony looking out over the garden. It was in this bedroom that John watched his father die and heard him reply, when he asked him not to be angry because he couldn't have a bath, 'I'm always angry when I'm dying.' Twenty years later he watched Olivier performing this deathbed scene in that very room and uttering those words. 'Such incidents,' he wrote, 'add deeply to the part the house has played in my life.'

In 1932 the villages of Turville, Turville Heath and Northend still had two churches, a chapel, a school, two shops and several pubs. The butcher, the baker and the fishmonger delivered provisions; a milkmaid arrived daily, carrying two pails of creamy milk on a yoke. By 1950, a gradual gentrification had begun. Today the chapel and the shop have gone; two pubs are desirable private residences. 'Now,' wrote John in 2004, 'the cottages contain businessmen and women, and television personalities' – neighbours such as Melvyn Bragg, Jeremy Paxman, David Sainsbury – 'and the grander houses around us are the homes of members of famous rock groups', two Deep Purple musicians being among John's closest friends. The area remains a densely green part of rural England undisfigured by petrol station or housing estate. Its proximity to two motorways carrying commuters to London, an hour away, is reflected in the property prices. But John said, in 2007, he had no idea of the value of his house 'and no desire ever to sell it'.

In 1932, the same year as Clifford built their home, they sent John to board at the Dragon School in Bardwell Road, North Oxford. 'I blamed my mother,' John used to say. 'I was very resentful of that.' Strange, to resent a practice that was accepted for boys of his age and class. Until he was eight, he said, he had been happy. But he had a recurring dream, in which 'at the age of nine I should be taken out and hanged', which he interpreted as a dread of being sent away. He told his father, who seemed not to hear, and his mother, who said all small boys felt this. Even when nearing sixty, he expressed a lingering resentment. 'At no time did my mother ever explain satisfactorily why she was determined to get me out of the house for the best part of the year,' he wrote, 'to send me off to face the gloom and discomfort of icy dormitories, terrible fish which wore a sort of black mackintosh and was eaten with tinned peas, and shell-shocked masters who either confused us with the Huns or fell embarrassingly in love with us.'

'Fish in black mackintosh' is a succinct summary of the horrors of school dinners. But this view of events is odd. When he wrote these words John was conveniently forgetting that he had sent his own first two children 'out of the house for the best part of the year' as boarders, not always happily. Later he excused himself for having done so – 'But that was when I was young and busy and less thoughtful, less considerate perhaps.' By then, John had begun to revise his resentment and to allow that the Dragon had served him well. In 1995 he sent his youngest daughter there and she shone as one of its brightest pupils. The Dragon, both progressive and academic, occupies an unusual place in prep school history, and not just for its scholarships to Eton or its roll of former alumni: Old Dragons include John Betjeman and Hugh Gaitskell; Old She-Dragons Naomi Mitchison and Antonia Fraser, who played wing three-quarter at rugger and found the school 'intensely competitive and also genially scruffy'. Its claim to general reverence arose from the fact that other schools aspired to be compared with it. By the 1980s, potential pupils had to be enrolled while *in utero*. John's generation, like every other, produced alumni of distinction: the historian E. P. Thompson, the writer and publisher Richard Ollard, *The Times*'s music critic William Mann and J. R. R. Tolkien's son Christopher.

The school was founded by Oxford dons in 1877, the first year in which college fellows, celibate since medieval times, were permitted to marry. There were no school rules, but the teachers had to be addressed by their daft nicknames, and all female personnel were known as 'Ma'. For decades the school was known as Lynam's, after its eccentric head C. C. 'Skipper' Lynam, eldest of fourteen children of an architect, a passionate sailor who ran the school like a ship, and insisted on being addressed as 'Skipper' not 'Sir'. He was succeeded, by the time John arrived, by his younger brother 'Hum' (A. E. Lynam, who hummed) and G. C. Vassall, known as 'Cheese'; later by J. H. R. 'Joc' Lynam. Most prep-school traditions are parodiable, in the manner of St Cake's in *Private Eye*, but the Dragon was a particularly rich source for John in several plays. For the second televised version of *A Voyage Round My Father*, the school scenes were filmed at the Dragon, with pupils playing themselves, and Michael Aldridge playing headmaster 'Noah' (with sons 'Japhet' and 'Ham'), addressing his pupils as 'ye faithless and hunchbacked generation': speaking, as John said, 'in God's prose, a mixture of Old Testament and Kipling's *Just So Stories*'. Skipper was so keen on Kipling that one of the school houses was called Gunga Din.

Skipper designed the school on the lines of a traditional Victorian board school, with naval overtones. The central hall, off which the classrooms ran, had a high boat-shaped roof and a gallery with ropes and bells: it was variously dining hall, theatre, dance floor, where they learned to foxtrot, and playground, for games with marbles and conkers. Even walking on stilts was allowed, despite the unyielding red-tiled floor. Skipper believed that boys must be allowed to waste time and get into mischief. Every boy learned to swim by being suspended from a rope on a pole and dipped into the Cherwell. They were allowed to take boats on the river, too, and to ride bicycles round the town. John, allergic to any sort of organized sport, was permitted to go to watch Shaw's plays at the theatre in Oxford instead. Aversion to sport was one of John's leitmotifs. 'Sport, as I have discovered,' he would say, 'fosters hostility, and leads the audience to do grievous bodily harm while watching it. The fact that audiences at the National Theatre rarely break bottles over one another's heads, and that opera fans seldom knee one another in the groin during the long intervals at Covent Garden, convinces me that the theatre is safer than sport.'

At the end of term the Dragon staff, smoking pipes and quaffing wine, performed sketches for the over-excited boys. C. L. Tabor, known as 'Box', and C. V. 'Jacko' Jaques played the banjolele and sang comic songs about Captain Brown, who played his ukulele

as the ship went down, and 'Baby has gone down the plug-hole':
the songs John gave the prep-school master to sing in *What Shall
We Tell Caroline?*

Inheriting from Clifford a scorn for the Book of Genesis
('nobody could create a horse in seven days, let alone the world'),
John found school prayers absurd. This impressed his classmate
Richard Ollard, who loathed the school, and shared John's scepticism and his dislike of sport. (John borrowed Ollard's name for a
master, Mr Bingo Ollard, in his play.) John liked to say that
childhood is a great time for lying, and he told Bill Mann, the
future music critic, that he was really the son of a Russian aristocrat,
smuggled out of Moscow in 1917 and taken in by a simple lawyer.
(In *A Voyage Round My Father* it is the schoolfriend who tells this
tale.) When he came to stay at Turville Heath Cottage, Bill Mann
politely refrained from mentioning the discrepancy between the
fable and the reality. The two put on shows for the Mortimer
parents: a one-act play which John wrote, about a pair of ghosts
of young subalterns killed on the Somme, and (using play scripts
from Samuel French) a contemporary revue called *Airy Nothings*
and the musical *Glamorous Nights*. John, flat-footed and tone deaf,
would never fulfil his Fred Astaire/Jack Buchanan fantasy of tap-
dancing down a staircase in white tie and tails. But when there
was no schoolfriend to hand, he performed for his parents scenes
from *Murder in the Cathedral* and Shakespearian tragedies. He later
made countless audiences laugh by telling how he played Hamlet,
having to duel with himself, 'force myself to drink my own
poisoned chalice and make love to myself as my own mother'.

In his last year at the Dragon he developed a crush on 'a tow-
haired boy named Jenks' who reminded him of the 1930s film star
Annabella. Jenks was in fact Evelyn Joll, a popular and good-
looking boy, and the attraction was 'largely unconsummated apart
from a clumsy hug in the school museum'. Although Evelyn
promised to be faithful, John ran into him years later at Heathrow,
by now a distinguished art gallery owner, with his wife and four
children. Later still, Joll's daughter, Charlotte Amory, was standing,
heavily pregnant, beside John at a London party when a woman

asked if she was Mrs Mortimer. 'No, this isn't my wife,' replied John, 'but I was in love with her father at the Dragon.'

Before he left, he had two pieces of prose published in *The Draconian*: an atmospheric description of darkness when the moon is hidden, and a breathless narrative about a night mail-coach into which a loose-limbed stranger clambers and tells ghoulish tales to terrify the passengers, whereupon a bloodcurdling scream is heard, and it turns out that the coach has run over a cat.

But the main excitement was the school play. Each year the Dragon put on a Gilbert and Sullivan opera and a Shakespeare, causing intense competition among the ambitious pupils. Antonia Fraser spoke with pride of giving her Lady Macbeth in 1944. John maintained that no time in his life was as thrilling as the term he won the role of Richard II in 1937. This rankled for ever after with his fellow pupil Mark Ramage, son of the great actress Cathleen Nesbitt. 'Cheese' Vassall had promised the title role to Ramage, who had in the previous year played Shylock to great acclaim, and who duly began learning the part of Richard. Then, during the holidays, 'Cheese' telephoned Ramage at home in Buckinghamshire and told him he was giving the part to Mortimer. Ramage was puzzled, furious and hurt. He was cast as Bolingbroke, deposer of Richard, instead.

In the school's sixtieth year, this production was, as always, thoroughly professional, with splendid costumes and a fourteen-piece orchestra. Saturday 23 January 1937 was the day of John's triumphant stage debut. *The Draconian* published no fewer than four reviews, and there is no mistaking the enthusiasm for his faultless performance. 'Every inch a king,' they chorused. John understood the poetry of his lines and spoke them beautifully. He seemed at ease on the stage and handled most impressively his final death scene in the prison, 'flinging away his life with a careless gallantry that struck just the right note':

Mount, mount, my soul! thy seat is up on high
Whilst my gross flesh sinks downward, here to die.

The most authoritative voice was that of Frank Sidgwick, the writer and publisher. He wrote: 'The School is to be congratulated on having discovered Mortimer and cast him for the king. He looked the part, every inch; stood and moved well, and wore his robes nobly.' Moreover, he had shown a fine appreciation of Shakespearian blank verse, and a rare skill 'in rendering the rhythm, the rise and fall, the pulsations of the long poetical speeches'. Amusingly, Sidgwick found that though Ramage was 'magnetic' as Bolingbroke, 'I felt he was a little too petulant with the crown, orb and sceptre which the King resigned to him with such dignity.' Perhaps, as 'Jacko' Jaques suggested in his history of the school, 'Richard II, of all Shakespeare's heroes, comes nearest to being within the compass of an intelligent thirteen-year-old actor, because he was a king who never grew up.' This may be so, but these encomia do suggest an unusually mature theatrical ability. So it is odd that John never acted again: never even auditioned for a play, at Harrow or at Oxford. But he did enjoy being reminded of his notices, seventy years later, and demonstrated that he could still recite Richard's speech from Act III, Scene ii, beginning:

For God's sake, let us sit upon the ground
And tell sad stories of the death of kings:
How some have been deposed, some slain in war;
Some haunted by the ghosts they have deposed;
Some poisoned by their wives, some sleeping killed;
All murder'd: for within the hollow crown
That rounds the mortal temples of a king
Keeps Death his court, and there the antick sits,
Scoffing his state and grinning at his pomp . . .

Luckily, Clifford was still able to see John's triumph on the school stage.

When 'Hum' Lynam suggested Harrow for John, Clifford 'seemed to regard this as a natural course of events about which nothing could be done – like his own glaucoma and failing eyesight'. Uncle Harold had been to Marlborough, but Hum told

Clifford this was not the right school for John as it was full of bishops, 'but we hear good things of Harrow nowadays'. And if John hadn't gone to Harrow, he might not have made Byron his hero, nor had his escutcheon emblazoned with the motto '*Aestas gliris*', the Summer of a Dormouse, which comes from one of Byron's letters: 'When one subtracts from life infancy (which is vegetation), sleep, eating and swilling, buttoning and unbuttoning – how much remains of downright existence? The summer of a dormouse.'

2. The Clever Boy

Above the Metroland sprawl of suburban villas that were still newly built in the 1930s, the fine old buildings of Harrow School dominate the village of Harrow-on-the-Hill. John Betjeman, a Marlburian who yearned to be a Harrovian, used to say, 'I *did* go to Harrow – in all but fact.' But then Betjeman was enraptured by Middlesex ('our lost Elysium'), excited by the railway lines to Northolt and Rayners Lane, and poetically inspired by the small semi-detached lives of suburb-dwellers in Wealdstone and Wembley, Perivale and Pinner. John Mortimer found it all thoroughly spirit-lowering, with nothing noteworthy in the vista below apart from the gasworks.

In any case Harrow, founded in 1571, was by the 1930s altogether too conventional, too sporty a school to suit him. But he did find congenial friends, and developed his flair for drawing and public speaking. He spent long hours reading in the upliftingly beautiful Vaughan Library, a lofty, light-filled room of ecclesiastical design; like the chapel alongside, it is the work of the great Gothic revivalist George Gilbert Scott. It was in the library that he conceived his enduring passion for Lord Byron, whose dagger, sabre and Turkish slippers, among many other relics, were on display.

Byron was a sportsman and a fighter, utterly unlike the young Mortimer. But in other respects he was an appropriate hero. He was a champion of the underdog, who protected younger boys from being bullied and beaten. He stood up for his right to keep a statue of Napoleon in his rooms. Despite his club foot, about which he was taunted, he distinguished himself, in his own recollection at least, in the first recorded Eton–Harrow cricket match. Like John, Byron was an only child who 'loved and glamorised his father' and declaimed heroic speeches from Shakespeare. Close to the south door of Harrow Church, in a grave that lay unmarked until 1980, Byron's illegitimate daughter Allegra, who died in Italy at the age of five, was buried. Within the churchyard on the brow of the hill, under a tree, lies a tomb marked with the name 'Peachey', where Byron 'lay, lazily lay', as the school song has it, 'dreaming poetry all alone, Up on the top of Peachey stone'. John read Peter Quennell's books on Byron and found him 'so totally different from anything the public school education is meant to produce' that he fell in love with him. He judged Byron's *Don Juan* 'the most sensible poem ever written', and published a rapturous letter to Byron when he was finally admitted to Poets' Corner in Westminster Abbey. What he most admired was Byron's advocacy, in the House of Lords – inspired by the causes of liberty and the rights of man – on behalf of Nottingham weavers facing the savage laws directed at Luddites, and in favour of Catholic emancipation and parliamentary reform.

Writing letters home from Harrow in Byronic stanzas, well schooled in prosody, John could never deny that he was efficiently taught by Harrow's tutors. He was especially grateful to the one he described in his memoirs as 'the rather unctuous cleric, the Reverend Arthur Chalfont'. This was his English master, E. M. Venables, an Oxford man who later became Canon of St George's Chapel, Windsor. Venables introduced him to the Romantic poets, and to Wordsworth, whose pantheism became for John a meaningful and useful substitute for the religion he wanted no part of. Wordsworth's 'still, sad music of humanity' and 'a sense sublime / Of something far more deeply interfused, / Whose dwelling is the light of setting suns, / And the round ocean and the living air . . .' evoked emotions every bit as consoling as those enjoyed 'at Evensong on summer evenings in country churches'. John decided that although Byron despised Wordsworth for snobbish reasons, pouring scorn on his waggoners and pedlars, and even though Wordsworth was short on humour and capable of writing some of the silliest lines in the English language, the old Lakeland sheep was 'by far the better poet'.

John himself was turning out illustrated clerihews which compare well with those W. H. Auden published as *Academic Graffiti* (e.g. 'John Milton/Never stayed at a Hilton/Hotel/which is just as well').

> Henry VIII
> Would like publicly to state
> That he dislikes being thought on
> As an early Charles Laughton.
>
> It is related that Homer
> Fell into a coma
> While reading through
> The Iliad, Book Two.
>
> Savonarola
> Though a demon bowler
> Never had a hope
> Against the Pope.
>
> John Knox
> Had to darn his own socks,
> While his wife went and spent
> The royalties from the 'Monstrous Regiment'.

There was much at Harrow that John thought absurd, starting with the school's nineteenth-century dress of tailcoat, waistcoat, cashmere trousers and a top hat of the type known as a beaver. Any slight departure from regulation costume was stigmatized as 'swagger'. Each summer term entitled a boy to the privilege of leaving undone a further button of his jacket, known as a 'bluer'. After three years at the school he might wear coloured socks and a flower in his buttonhole; he might also put his hands in his pockets. After four years he might sprout a moustache. But no Harrovian of any seniority was allowed to go into a public house or a tobacconist's, or 'stand still on a railway bridge', or walk more than three abreast, or talk to 'persons lounging about the streets'.

Harrow was, like Eton, a 'ruling-class' school, having produced

seven prime ministers. John, incipient socialist, was not temperamentally suited to a one-class institution, its inmates linked only
by parental wealth and obsessed with sporting achievement. He
was unimpressed by a boy who judged a fellow pupil 'common'
because his parents put out side plates at dinner. He never adopted
the traditional assumption of public-school men that anyone who
had been to your old school must be a splendid chap who could
be depended on to do business with. Indeed, he lost few opportunities in later life to make disobliging generalizations about Harrovians as 'dull', 'spivvy', destined to become second-hand-car
salesmen or, in two of his most oft-repeated stories, a butler in
Hollywood ('I heard the words, "New potatoes, sir?" and looked
up to see the unmistakable face of Hugh Derwent, the head
boy') and a chimney sweep who came to do John's chimneys and
remarked, 'Harrow didn't do much for either of us, did it?' These
droll stories, probably fanciful − if true, they concerned non-
contemporaries − entered John's repertoire.

John states in his memoirs that he was, while at his one-sex
school and during 'lonely and isolated holidays', locked into 'a
chrysalis of vague, schoolboy homosexuality'. He revered Auden
because 'he wrote about what we understood: juvenile jokes about
housemasters, homosexual longings, the Clever Boy, the Form
Entertainer and the Show Off . . .' The blessed Byron provided a
precedent for an intense romantic friendship with a fellow Harrovian: he bestowed lifelong devotion on John Fitzgibbon, Earl of
Clare, four years his junior. John writes, in *Clinging to the Wreckage*:
'Years after he'd left school, Byron met Clare on the road to
Bologna and was deeply moved, feeling, apparently, his heart beat
at his fingers' ends.' (The ethos of boy-worship at Harrow, in
Byron's time and after, was underpinned by the classical-studies
bias of the curriculum: 'Horatian' was the codeword for homosexual.) Harrovians' homosexuality was 'dictated by necessity
rather than choice', John wrote. Necessity dictated by inclination
too, surely. He would often blithely say that Harrow was 'a totally
gay world' and referred jocularly to 'the school tart, who could be
had by anyone for a packet of chocolate biscuits'. When a writer

speculated that John Mortimer might have had 'an unpleasant homosexual experience' at Harrow, 'which might explain his life-long dislike of the school, his wariness of men and his adoration of women', I read this out to Sir John. He gave a whinnying laugh and said, 'But I had *perfectly pleasant* homosexual experiences at Harrow!'

In his second year, John found his voice and became a credit to his house, The Grove. On 14 February 1939 he took second prize in the Lady Bourchier Reading Prize, adjudicated by the venerable Sir Arthur Quiller-Couch, alias 'Q', Cambridge English professor and editor of *The Oxford Book of English Verse*. John's chosen recitations were Swift's 'The Honourable Profession of the Law' and Tennyson's song from *The Princess*:

> The splendour falls on castle walls
> And snowy summits old in story:
> The long light shakes across the lakes,
> And the wild cataract leaps in glory.
> Blow, bugle, blow, set the wild echoes flying,
> Blow, bugle; answer, echoes, dying, dying, dying.

'He seemed,' reported *The Harrovian*, 'appreciative of the slender quality of this ever-delightful piece.'

The experience emboldened him to speak, wittily, from the floor at the Debating Society three months later. He supported the motion 'The modern generation believes what it is told rather than thinking for itself'. 'Backchat was once more the order of the day,' reported *The Harrovian*, 'nimbly led by J. C. Mortimer, The Grove, who was consistently amusing.' There are few things so seductive as the sound of laughter caused by one's words. The wit and eloquence of J. C. Mortimer of The Grove having been thus awakened, he took part in every debate in his final year.

In October 1939, in a debate shortened by wartime blackout regulations, he proposed the motion 'This house considers that Man has not yet discovered his purpose', pointing out that if man had done so, the world would not now be at war — a manifest failure of government. Fellow human beings were being 'put into concentration camps, and open towns mercilessly bombed'. How could man have found his purpose when 'the evils of the society and Tatler life, the fox-hunting life, and the Harley Street life' persisted, and 'we are content to sit smugly in the family pew, oblivious of the mine-workers and the factory-workers'? Apart from that fox-hunting reference, the sixteen-year-old's *bien-pensant* polemic presaged that of the octogenarian.

John's memoirs made no mention of his debating successes. But readers may wonder what became of the fellow schoolboys he described, mostly under disguised names, in *Clinging to the Wreckage*. In any school generation, those who display glittering promise often fade into obscurity. So it was with John's Harrovian friends. He outlived most of them – including Christopher Bulstrode, whose usefully über-English surname he later borrowed in several plays and novels. The best friend, 'Oliver Pensotti', the one who was so vague about his mysterious and exotic parents, was in reality Peter Houghton-Gastrell, whose mother lived in Mayfair while his father lived at Cap Martin in the South of France. Houghton-Gastrell remained a friend at Oxford; he became a restaurateur and died in 1960. 'Martin Witteridge' (in fact Michael Whidborne) was John's artistic companion; both were honourably mentioned in the contest for the school's Yate Thompson Art Prize. They would cycle off to paint watercolours of Ruislip reservoir, stopping at a suburban pub for a daring gin and lime. Whidborne remained a friend until he died in 1958. John told a scurrilous story about Whidborne's good-looking younger brother Timothy, who was at Stowe with George Melly: 'During the war, the Whidborne boys' father, Captain C. S. L. Whidborne, had a flat in Sloane Street, from where he would go off to the War Office every day with a briefcase containing a bottle of milk and the *Times* crossword puzzle. When he came back one afternoon he found Timothy Whidborne, stark naked except for his Guards officer's cap, in bed with George Melly wearing nothing but his Able Seaman's hat. Captain Whidborne entered the bedroom and said, "You two boys are a disgrace to His Majesty's uniform."'

And what became of 'Tainton', the disruptive and volatile boy with whom John was made to share a room in the sixth form, because the housemaster thought 'Tainton' needed quietening down? Not even in the divorce courts did John ever come across a cohabitation as violent as theirs, he said. 'Tainton' would hurl chairs across the room and poured green ink over John's Aldous Huxley-inspired novella-in-progress. 'He broke windows, used unspeakable language to the matron, set fire to the *Morning Post . . .*' He was also a heroic masturbator, filling jam jars with the results. This colourful account was highly exaggerated. In reality, 'Tainton' was Richard Wellesley Gunston, son and heir of a baronet and Tory MP, Major Sir Derrick Wellesley Gunston, who was then PPS to Neville Chamberlain. After Harrow and war service, the madcap Gunston joined the Colonial Service, married thrice and, on his return to England, ended up doing good works for the care of churches and cathedrals. He died in 1991, aged sixty-seven.

Gunston's son and heir, Sir John Gunston, told me that in 1983 he was in the Hindu Kush when he heard John Mortimer reading *Clinging to the Wreckage* on the BBC World Service and at once suspected that 'Tainton' might be his father. 'Not for its onanistic content, nor for Tainton's rages,' he said, 'but for the description of Tainton's mother hunting.' 'Tainton' had boasted that his mother gave birth to him on the hunting field, after which she had remounted to be in at the kill. This was just like his grandmother, said John Gunston: she rode with the Beaufort, side-saddle and wearing a top hat, and soon after giving birth to her son – not while hunting but in Chelsea – she took to the field again. Sir John Gunston said he felt oddly grateful to John Mortimer. Although his father had 'the kindest disposition' and no discernible temper, John's description of his Harrow exploits gave him an insight into his father's early years. He had witnessed his grandparents' 'continual bullying of their only surviving child' and suspected that his father 'was most probably a truly disturbed child during the period that he and Sir John knew each other'.

John also referred to 'Keswick', head of his house, who supported the Fascist cause in Spain: 'I knew almost nothing about life, but I knew perfectly clearly that I couldn't stand people like Keswick.' Keswick was probably the late D. C. Rissik, head boy of the Grove. It was through meeting boys of a right-wing persuasion that John's political ideology formed. He obeyed Churchill's nephew Esmond Romilly's exhortation to public-school boys to set up Communist cells, but remained the sole member of his. Even in the 1930s, when the division between left and right was so clear-cut, Harrow remained 'a sea of capitalist enterprise' while John would sit in his room, writing off to the Communist Party's King Street headquarters for copies of *The Worker* and Utopian pamphlets. (He had always sent away for things: invisible ink and fingerprint powder in his Bulldog Drummond phase, cigarette holder and monocle for his Noël Coward impersonations.)

In the view of some contemporaries, John blushed unseen at school. Joe Dean, son of theatrical impresario Basil Dean, was part of John's adult world as a circuit judge, a fellow Bencher and Garrick Club member, but never noticed John's existence at Harrow. Sandy Wilson and his circle considered John a loner, somewhat withdrawn – 'almost disapproving of us, and certainly unhappy'. Wilson, Harrow's top scholar, turned out to be the most famous pupil of their year, as the composer of *The Boy Friend*. There was a moment, around 1960, when the two men were reunited to collaborate on an (aborted) musical. And in 1971, Wilson sat next to John at the preview of *A Voyage Round My Father* at the Theatre Royal, Brighton. He found himself sneaking sideways glances at John and comparing his profile with that of the matinée idol Jeremy Brett, the actor portraying him on stage. But why did John claim in his book that Wilson, while at Harrow, 'took to knitting socks, mufflers and Balaclava helmets, comforts for the troops'? The idea was preposterous and Wilson wrote to tell him so. John strove, as a memoirist, to make his Harrow years sound more amusing. Most writers do. The school's legacy to him was a reasonable classical education, a fondness for Byron and narrative history, and some oft-recalled anecdotes of dubious provenance.

*

In about 1935, Clifford Mortimer went to buy a ladder from Gamages. As he was trying to get the ladder inside a taxi, he struck his head on its roof and the jolt apparently dislodged the retinas of both eyes. (The more picturesque televised version showed him climbing the ladder and striking his head on the bough of an apple tree.) He went to Zurich for a series of painful and ineffectual eye operations that involved removing the eyeball, without anaesthetic. The family's first foreign excursion had been to Nice in 1929, where John got locked in the lavatory in the Hotel Negresco, an experience which left him permanently claustrophobic, with a fear and loathing of lifts; and he claims never to have locked a lavatory door again. But it was while in Zurich, on their walks in the Swiss mountains, that the father and his adolescent son formed 'an alliance from which my mother was thoughtlessly excluded'. Clifford's outbursts of rage, impatience and frustration – 'The devil damn thee black, thou cream-faced loon!' he shouted at a solicitor who had forgotten his documents – were chiefly directed at his wife. 'Kath! Kath! Are you a complete cretin?' he would thunder, if plates were cold or eggs underdone. The abuse was patiently borne, except once, when John saw her walk quietly away, leaving Clifford standing helpless. Kathleen seemed oddly distant to John. He was disconcerted by her, while she was wryly amused by him: a not uncommon feeling between mothers and their sons. But he later found a cache of short stories 'which showed her concern about me and her anxiety, no doubt entirely justified, about what I got up to when out of her sight'.

During his last summer vacation from Harrow, John realized that his father's eyesight had so deteriorated that his mother had to place the toothpaste on the brush and guide it to his mouth. 'Bombs, air raids, bits of food prodded at him, and the edge of the pavement,' as John wrote, 'would, from now on, strike him as equally alarming.' Clifford reported to his sister Gertie in 1939, 'My sight has been steadily getting worse, & just about two months ago, trouble developed in my left eye which necessitated another operation. The oculist expressed satisfaction with the result but there is no getting away from the fact that I am now nearly blind, unable to read or even to find my way about unaided.'

He was still in his fifties. It was a heavy handicap and the outlook was pretty grim, he said, 'though even if the worst comes to the worst and my sight fails altogether there is much to be thankful for. Kathleen spends nearly every minute with me, reading to me and taking me about in the garden, and never grumbles, though the strain on her must be almost unbearable.' He was certainly not depressed or wretched: apprehensive as to the future, but not unhappy. 'Life still holds very much of interest & indeed of positive enjoyment & this trouble has come upon me by such imperceptible degrees that I have had time to adjust myself to it.' He found consolation in listening to recorded books, supplied by the National (not yet Royal) Institute for the Blind. And it was a comfort that they had a competent and knowledgeable gardener. Clifford could remember the location of every plant, and as they faded from his view he would ask for an exact description of the dahlias or the *Viburnum fragrans* ('Paint me the picture' – as in the opening scene of *A Voyage Round My Father*).

Yet Clifford carried on his legal practice as if nothing had happened. In fact, he was busier than ever, as young barristers were called up for military service. He managed to convince witnesses that he could see them shifting and shuffling under his sightless gaze. And at home, in what John called their 'English determination to avoid the slightest embarrassment', the family never spoke of his predicament. They still went to the theatre: they saw Gielgud in *Hamlet* in 1935, and Auden and Isherwood's *The Ascent of F6* at the Mercury Theatre, where a lady drummer named Eve Kish joined the family repertoire of amusing names. They went to Stratford every year, arriving late, after supper, in the middle of the first act, when Clifford, in black tie, would stage-whisper to Kathleen to know what was happening and then helpfully recite the lines seconds before the actors did.

He was planning to get a woman into chambers who would 'come into court with me and prompt me', he told his sister (assuming, probably correctly, that only a female barrister would undertake this self-denying role). But it was Kathleen who performed this task. She drove him the six miles to Henley and accompanied him on the train, reading aloud the evidence for the divorce case of the day. 'The first-class carriage would fall silent as Mother read out, sotto voce ("Speak up, Kath!"), the descriptions of stained bed-linen, male and female clothing found scattered about, or misconduct in motor cars.' To everyone who witnessed them, Kathleen was her husband's shadow, hovering to supply his needs, accompanying him through the long corridors and marbled halls of the Law Courts, leading him into court, sitting behind him and making notes 'with ungrudging devotion'.

This was when John too began to read aloud to his father – Shakespeare's sonnets, Browning, Housman, Eliot – and to guide him about. There is a painting on his study wall, by Jim Holland, of John's tall, lean figure leading his father's more stooped one across Southend Common. The caption indicates that it was done from memory: 'observed 1941; recalled 1995'. John's written account of taking Clifford along the Embankment, his father's hand on his arm, is one of the few moments when he betrays a human irritation at his father's disability. 'I wanted to shake him off, to run away. I had an impulse to let him wander off, hopelessly, among the trams.' (Later in life he confessed to the same temptation when walking in woodlands: 'to escape the loose-skinned hand on my sleeve and run off to a secret hiding place in the bracken', leaving Clifford 'blundering and shouting in the darkness'. He adds: 'But I never left him so.') By the end of 1939, it was still easy to forget the 'half-realised nightmare' of the war, Clifford told his sister. There had been no air raids yet, but Mount Vernon Hospital in Northwood, where he had been for his last operation, was preparing for casualties. He hoped it would all be over before John was old enough to be called up. John, dithering between joining the RAF and signing on as a conscientious objector, mentioned this to his father, who replied, 'Do you think you're brave enough for that?' and advised him to 'avoid the temptation to do anything heroic'.

At Harrow, all boys had to join the school's Officers' Training

Corps. The Grove housemaster, Leonard Henry, a 'gentle English liberal' who had been on the Somme and could not believe it might happen again, had told them war was hell. John and Peter Houghton-Gastrell, whose mother had decamped to the allegedly bomb-proof Dorchester Hotel, wondered if they would die without losing their virginity 'with any sort of lady'. Houghton-Gastrell apparently found himself an obliging ATS girl; the deed was done – this must have been after air raids began, in 1940 – in Clifford's bomb-damaged Temple flat at 5 King's Bench Walk, while John sat among the dust sheets in the next room, drinking port and reading Byron: 'So, we'll go no more a-roving, so late into the night'.

By his last term at Harrow, J. C. Mortimer's light, clipped voice had become familiar, remarked *The Harrovian*, reporting on another debate. But he had not yet learned the vital art of timing. 'He always has much to say: he is so eager to have it all out and done with, however, that he is sometimes hard to follow, and his arguments thus lose some of their persuasiveness.' Proposing the motion that public schools encourage class distinction, John reminded his audience that we are all born equal, and deplored the inevitable class hatred that must spring up between a Harrow boy and the footman who has to serve him. He was defeated by nineteen votes to twelve.

While he was in the History Sixth, the school's literary magazine, *Harrow*, published his poem in six cantos headed 'A letter to Lord Byron', ending:

> When passion seized you, you went forth and sinned.
> We stay home and read Gone With The Wind.

It also published John's short story 'The End of the World', in which a Mr Prendergast dreams that St Thomas More – lately canonized – vouchsafes to him that the world will end in one week's time. He gives all his wealth to charity and continues to perform good works, to read the *Daily Mail*, to believe in God, capitalism and the British Empire (unlike his atheistic *Daily Worker-*

reading cousin Ernest) and waits to be transported to his heavenly resting place. Doomsday dawns, and he is still behind the green curtains in Acacia Road. Perhaps, he thinks, he is expected to take the quickest route to heaven. So he jumps out of his fourth-floor window. The End.

Having been paid ten shillings for this, John was fired with ambition. In *A Voyage Round My Father*, the father persuades the son that a writer sits at home every day, under his wife's feet, in carpet slippers: 'You'd be far better off down the tube each morning, and off to the Law Courts . . . Learn a little law, won't you? Just to please me . . .' Clifford's need for John to learn a little law had now become pressing. He told Gertie he was about to take John away from school and enter him for the Bar, 'so that I can get him in the Chambers as soon as possible and on his feet in case I have to give up'. So John must go to Oxford at once. In the 1930s it was still possible for a well-off parent to decide to 'send' a son to the ancient universities. Clifford chose Brasenose, a college with a legal reputation, where John's housemaster, Leonard Henry, had studied. On 31 July 1940, just after the end of John's final term, Clifford dictated to Kathleen (and shakily signed) a somewhat peremptory letter to Mr Henry:

We have decided to send John to Oxford to read law next October and shall be very grateful if you will use your influence to get him accepted at Brasenose. I myself took the Law Tripos at Cambridge and do not know much about the law examinations at Oxford. I suppose, however, that John had better read for an Honours degree in law equivalent to the tripos at Cambridge. Will he have to take any examinations in general subjects? I should also like to get details of the probable cost . . . I cannot close this letter without thanking you with deep sincerity for the great interest which you have taken in John while he has been at Harrow. He has been very happy and I am delighted at the way he has matured and developed.
    Sincerely yours
    Clifford Mortimer.

After failing to persuade Clifford to let John stay at Harrow another term to try for a scholarship, Mr Henry sent on this letter to the principal of Brasenose, W. T. S. Stallybrass. Stallybrass, born William Teulon Swan Sonnenschein in 1883, had taken his paternal grandmother's name during the First World War, and was known to his friends as 'Sonners'. Mr Henry enclosed a hand-written note to his old college chum.

My dear Sonners,

I hope you won't mind this intrusion into your Vacation. I am writing at the request of a Parent – who, being a barrister, seems to make all his decisions at the last moment! – to ask if there is any sort of possibility of your considering an application for his son, J C Mortimer, who was 17 last April and has just left us, for entry next October. The Father, Clifford Mortimer, with whose name you may be familiar, decided just one week ago that he wished to send the boy to Oxford.

The boy is a good fellow, with courage and something else to him besides: but he is odd, with Bohemian tendencies and mildly anti-nomian views (he particularly hates all games!). He came up to the History Sixth last term when I thought his work showed marked constructive promise, curiously marred by factual inaccuracy. He has done some rather brilliant essay-work for the School Magazine, mainly on Art subjects. I don't think his physique will ever allow him to be accepted for the Army and I think he might do really well in the English Schools – only his Father is apparently determined that he should read Law. I think he ought to be old enough to start next October, but you could judge this best, if you should have time to consider him at all: I think he would be worth interviewing. I hope all goes well with you. We have just finished a splendidly normal term here.

Yours ever,

Leonard Henry

This letter exemplifies the usefulness of the house system in public schools. Mr Henry not only knew John's predilections (art,

English, a loathing of sport) but judged his character astutely: 'a good fellow, with courage, and something else to him besides' is a rather pleasing summary. But he also correctly discerned a leaning to 'factual inaccuracy', bohemian tendencies, and 'anti-nomian views' (i.e. he did not accept religion as the basis for morality). Stallybrass, whose concern was to ensure that college entrants were the right stuff – 'those likely to prove leaders in college life, and add to the prestige of the college' – was nonetheless impressed, or at least not deterred. He sent an entrance form and details of the exam: a general paper, a Latin unseen, and a history paper of John's choice, the sixteenth and seventeenth centuries. Because Brasenose had just been requisitioned by the army, John would be billeted, with 119 others, in another college, Christ Church, always known as the House. As to cost, Stallybrass said, 'A boy who wishes to live in reasonable comfort and is reasonably careful in his expenditure can manage on about £270 a year.' (This was more than the average working man's annual wage at the time.)

Stallybrass added that John could graduate in two years, provided he also served in the armed forces: 'I gather from Mr Henry's letter that your son's physique is not such that he will ever be able to serve, and it is therefore far from clear whether he would be able to take advantage of the special privileges given to war candidates.' To which Clifford responded, 'Although John is at present very thin, there is nothing organically wrong with him and I think that when the time comes he will be able to undergo his military training.'

John claimed that his entrance exam, on 14 September, consisted simply of a Latin unseen, mentioning nothing of history or general papers. As he remembered it, he arrived at Brasenose and was met by a bald old don in carpet slippers carrying a cookery book, who told him to go into the next room and, unsupervised, translate a passage from Lucretius. In the room he found fellow Harrovian Houghton-Gastrell, who had artfully dodged out to Blackwell's to buy a Latin dictionary, which they both made use of. Afterwards they handed in their papers to the slipper'd pantaloon (it was actually Hugh Macilwain Last, Professor of Ancient History, later

to be principal of the college), and the very next day Stallybrass
wrote to tell John that the college had accepted him, adding, 'It
would probably be a good thing if you tried to read some of
Justinian Book I, Titles I–XII and Book II, Titles I–IX in Moyle's
edition before you come up, as your Latin is apparently weak.'
John wrote accepting at once (forgetting to enclose his £1 registration fee) and was assured that, since he was under nineteen,
there was no compulsion to join the Corps. He spent that summer
tutoring a boy at Barrow-in-Furness, and producing a portfolio of
sketches which made his artist mother extremely proud. He still
wished he could switch to reading history. 'How many choices
do we make in a lifetime?' as he later mused. But ultimately he
was grateful that Clifford had put his foot down. The law gave
him a double livelihood – from practising it and writing about it
– for life.

There is another Harrow story which John later repeated endlessly
in his one-man show. The singing of the school songs –

> But the time will come when your heart will thrill
> And you'll think with joy of your time on the Hill!

– was a high point of the Harrovian year. Indeed, this was the
element Betjeman envied above all. John, who left school in July
1940, always said he had been present in December that year, the
famous occasion when Winston Churchill first revisited his old
school to join in the songs he loved. John described the scene:

After the songs were over Mr Churchill climbed with difficulty onto the
stage. He cannot have been more than sixty-five years old, but his ancient
head emerged from the carapace of his dinner-jacket like the hairless
pate of a tortoise, his old hand trembled on the handle of the walking-
stick which supported him and his voice, when he spoke, was heavily
slurred with brandy and old age. He seemed to us to be about a hundred
and three.

Written forty years on, this seemed a graphic description. Yet John's account is at odds with *The Harrovian*'s report of Mr Churchill's visit. The prime minister and his party were already on the platform when the songs were sung. Behind them, a curtain obscured the building work, repairing the recent bomb damage. A new verse had been added to 'Stet Fortuna Domus':

> Nor less we praise in darker days
> The leader of our nation,
> And Churchill's name shall win acclaim
> From each new generation.
> While in this fight to guard the Right
> Our country you defend, Sir,
> Here grim and gay we mean to stay.
> And stick it to the end, Sir.

After a finale of 'Forty Years On', which made him weep, and 'Auld Lang Syne', Mr Churchill (hailed by ecstatic and prolonged applause), told the boys how thrilled he had been by those never-forgotten songs. He then gave a powerfully stirring speech, mindful of the fact that the school had already been under enemy fire and had acquitted itself with courage and decorum. Could anyone doubt, he asked rhetorically, that this generation was as good and as noble as any the nation had ever produced? Herr Hitler, he went on, had recently declared that this war was between those who had been through the Adolf Hitler schools and those who had been at Eton. 'He has forgotten Harrow, and has also overlooked the vast majority of the youth of this country who have never had the privilege of attending such schools . . . When this war is won by this nation, as it surely will be, it must be one of our aims to work to establish a state of society where the advantages and privileges which hitherto have been enjoyed only by the few shall be far more widely shared by the men and the youth of the nation as a whole.'

Churchill, who after 1940 never failed to return to Harrow for the songs every year for the rest of his life, was voicing John's views on social inclusion precisely. But John did not hear him. He was already at Oxford. Had he been there – and not even he could explain why he pretended to have been, except that it made a better story – he might have found the decrepit old tortoise-head's speech quite inspiring.

3. Among the Aesthetes

In October 1940, John took up residence in Meadow Building, overlooking Christ Church Meadow and the River Cherwell. This was the location of Sebastian Flyte's balconied rooms in *Brideshead Revisited*, the novel which created a template for Oxford undergraduate life for several generations. So when Waugh's book came out in 1945, 'Mercury', the fountain in which Anthony Blanche gets ducked and debagged, and Wren's Tom Tower and Tom Quad, were all very familiar to John. Meadow Building itself was mid-Victorian: Christopher Hobhouse pronounced it 'horrific' – 'a vast and prickly pile of brick, well clothed in merciful creepers'. Luckily Hobhouse did not live to see the late twentieth-century excrescences built on to many ancient colleges.

John was allocated Gothic-windowed rooms on the second floor of staircase five, above those of Dr Frederick Lindemann, Churchill's scientific intelligence adviser. There was a panelled sitting room, where John hung his Van Gogh print, and a bedroom, which he exaggeratedly described as 'almost the size of St Pancras station waiting-room'. Fires were not lit until 4.30 p.m., on the wartime ration of one small scuttle of coal per day, so undressing for bed was a hasty business before the dying embers, followed by a dash into the bone-chilling bedroom. Washing facilities consisted of a jug and basin, a can of shaving water being brought by the scout each morning. In a basement along the quad, a bath-house attendant in a Christ Church bowler would ensure that your bath contained no more than the statutory five inches of hot water. What Christ Church in wartime lacked in comforts it made up for in ancient treasures, academic arrogance and high culinary repute. Everyone dined and breakfasted in the portrait-lined hall, where Henry VIII had banqueted: a magnificent, vaulted space with broad hammerbeam roof. But if you arrived a minute after 9 a.m., you would find the head porter at the top of the great fan-vaulted stone stairway, watch in hand, saying, 'Too late'.

Brasenose had two distinctions: sport and jurisprudence. Having zero interest in sport, John was never going to join the college hearties. To underline this fact, he affected a sartorial style of floppy velvet bow ties, purple corduroy trousers, flamboyant weskits and wide-brimmed hat: 'I must have looked ridiculous,' he later wrote. He took to Balkan Sobranie cigarettes and gave every appearance of turning into an aesthete. Study of the law was a minor pastime. There was no Brasenose law don in residence, so tutorials ('tutes') were conducted by 'Wat' Tylor of Balliol, a blind don of acerbic disposition. John attended these with Christopher Sarkis, nephew of the novelist Michael Arlen. But he found Roman Law stultify-ingly irrelevant. 'After a year I knew how to manumit a slave or contract a marriage by the ceremony of "brass and scales",' as he frequently later said, 'skills which I have never found of great service in the Uxbridge Magistrates' Court.' However, he joined the law students' Ellesmere Society, and at the annual dinner in June 1941 played a leading counsel in a mock criminal trial.

At first John shared his rooms with Patrick Freeman, from Tonbridge School, who was reading PPE. In his memoirs John called Freeman 'Parsons', as he was a member of OICCU (Oxford Inter-Collegiate Christian Union), not a twin soul. One night the pious Freeman found himself and a fellow undergraduate having to put an inebriated John to bed after he had consumed pint measures of the buttery's finest sherry, and (John claimed) Freeman fell to his knees and prayed for him. After one term, John requested a move into the set next door, and the sharing of a bedroom ended, to Freeman's relief.

Wartime Oxford was subdued, silent. No church bells rang, the nights were blacked-out and there were no Commem. balls in June. The colleges were half empty, with so many young men away in the forces. The few who remained shared a sense of exile and were obliged, unless excused, to spend two afternoons a week drilling with the Officers' Training Corps. A contemporary of John's wrote an account of quotidian wartime life in Meadow

Building, in which the high point was going out, of an evening, to 'smoke a long pipe' or wandering into St Aldate's Church for a recital by an organ scholar named Wicks. But claret was still to be had, and college dances, Union debates and drama and political societies all carried on.

In his first term, John braved the challenge of the Oxford Union, with a maiden speech that combined serious argument with levity. He lined up with Roy Jenkins and Peter Self (father of Will), both of them eloquent Balliol men, to oppose the motion 'This House believes that the House of Lords in its present form has a valuable influence in the country'. The *Oxford Magazine* said Mr J. C. Mortimer, who 'deplored snobbishness', was among the most promising of the first-time speakers. He also joined a college club of which his room mate was secretary: the Pater Society, named after Walter Pater, former fellow of Brasenose, friend and inspiration to *fin-de-siècle* aesthetes, including Oscar Wilde. The Pater Society's nine members included Robert Runcie, the future Archbishop of Canterbury, who lived on the next staircase. They adopted their own tie and indulged their undergraduate earnestness (at John's first meeting, a member proposed 'that a split infinitive be deleted from the previous minutes' but was defeated) as they discussed matters such as Economics and Christianity, Art and the Cinema, Mr Eliot and *The Times*. John spoke for egalitarianism in their discussion on 'Whither the Universities?' 'Mr Mortimer suggested that the University had formerly existed to supply philosopher kings, [but] that Bevins were ousting the previous élite, making the university functionless and dying.'

A fortnight later John hosted a meeting in his rooms, and read a paper entitled 'Auden on 52nd Street' – a *tour d'horizon* of modern poetry. He revered W. H. Auden (a Christ Church man who later lived briefly in college) as 'a dissecting surgeon to the mind'. He was a poet less exclusive and intellectual than Eliot, said John, who echoed the philosophical quest of his generation; a man influenced by Donne and Hopkins, but who used jazz lyrics and the language of the street. Auden and Isherwood had been much abused by the press for going to America after the Spanish Civil

War. Wars had the effect of making people feel either patriotic in the style of Henry V or cynical, after Siegfried Sassoon, said John. Auden, like Owen, proposed a third way: a remedial view of love surmounting the agony of conflict. 'However, Auden's love ideal is more akin to D. H. Lawrence than to Christ. Sexual intercourse, rather than Agape, is the new uniting principle.' Auden was remote from the insanity of war, and could preserve a vision of truth, beauty and justice 'which are to be the cure for the post-war human rubbish heap'.

The college's Pater Club archive records no reaction to this talk, but notes that members agreed to tip the scout in charge of their staircase 'to the extent of a pint of beer'. Scouts were often the only working-class men these boys came across at Oxford, and the one who waited on John's staircase was named Bustin. Robert Runcie told his biographer, Humphrey Carpenter, that he had once made a remark to Mr Bustin about John's lady visitors. Mr Bustin had replied – and here Dr Runcie adopted his best demotic accent – 'Mr Mortimer, sir, 'e's a man with wot you'd call a troublesome organ.' (John naturally liked this story, and recycled it often, his organ sometimes becoming 'an irrepressible member'.) It is true that John vaguely refers to 'adventures with WAAFs and girls from St Hilda's' and says that the girls he preferred were 'boyish', but these forays into the heterosexual world were, as he says, sporadic. There was a girl named Anne, at the Slade School of Art – exiled in wartime from London to Oxford – to whom he became briefly engaged. 'I think Anne is going to make a great difference to my life,' reads an entry in his Oxford notebook. He couldn't recall her surname, but he always remembered her advice about his drawings: 'Stick to writing.'

It was among male undergraduates that John found enduring friends ('Oxford's greatest gift is friendship, for which there is all the time in the world') who were attracted to his intelligent, entertaining personality. The most valued of these was the good-looking, dark-haired, blue-eyed Michael Fenton, classicist and pacifist. Fenton was, like John, a late-born only son. They stood side by side in the freshers' photograph and became inseparable. Fenton shared John's sense of humour, never taking anything very seriously. His family's wealth came from sheep-ranching in South America. His grandfather, Dr Thomas Fenton, had left County Sligo for what became Patagonia, and was given a tranche of land – at 250,000 acres, bigger than Sligo – for saving the life of the governor's wife. Michael Arthur Fenton (named after his mad Uncle Arthur, who lived like a native Indian in a tent) went to Lancing, wrote pacifist editorials in the school magazine and was such an outstanding Greek scholar that when his son Paul followed him there in 1960, the headmaster called out, 'Will the son of Michael Fenton please stand up? If you are half the boy your father was, you will do well.'

Stallybrass had taken Fenton into Brasenose, just as he took John, at his school's recommendation, though he hated the very idea of conscientious objectors. Indeed, so fond of Fenton did the principal become that he persuaded Oxford's degree board to regard Fenton's civil defence work as equivalent to military service, qualifying him for his wartime degree (normally granted after two years, plus a year of war service). John decided that he too would register as a 'conchy', since Fenton was for him 'a yardstick of moral behaviour'. Like John, he had no religious beliefs: he was 'courageously sceptical, fearlessly agnostic'. But he had a rock-solid dependability that John instinctively admired. He was beautifully mannered, relaxed and pragmatic. Nothing seemed to faze him. It was perfectly clear that when he eventually became a doctor, he would have a gently beguiling bedside manner. The pair stayed up late into the night, talking and drinking and smoking pipes, went punting or took long walks, discussing life, the universe and everything. Fenton also brought music into John's life. Since Clifford didn't see the point of music, John had never learned to savour the lascivious pleasings of a lute. Fenton, who polished his record collection with a velvet pad, introduced him to *The Magic Flute*, to Brahms' Fourth Symphony and W. C. Handy's 'St James Infirmary Blues'. Whole evenings passed listening to the *Missa Solemnis*. John claimed in his memoirs that they lusted after 'tennis-playing virgins', adding, 'There is nothing like sexual frustration to give warmth to friendship.'

Both, John wrote, were 'just emerging from the chrysalis of schoolboy homosexuality'. He also makes the dogmatic statement that 'At Oxford after Dunkirk the fashion was to be homosexual.' This depended on the circles you chose to move in. Certain dons, known to be predatory homosexuals, did behave like relics from *Decline and Fall*; they talked of Firbank and Beardsley and posed as latter-day Brian Howards. John, in his memoirs, wrote: 'By day they lay naked in their rooms, listening to Puccini or to Verdi's Requiem.' (In other reminiscences he cited Charles Trenet rather than Puccini.) In his second year, he began to be adopted into the Christ Church aesthetes' milieu. The man he calls 'Tommy Motte-Smith' was the egregiously camp and affected Freddy Hurdis-Jones, who fancied himself as Oscar Wilde, much given to florid aphorism, and was sent down for his debts. At Westminster School, the dandyish Hurdis-Jones had exploited the school's gay underworld, paying younger boys in tuck. He seemed destined for theatrical glory and played the title role in Peter Brook's London production of *Dr Faustus* in 1942. Brook too had been 'an enthusiastic homosexual' while at Oxford.

Freddy glided into John's life through his acquaintance with another Westminster alumnus, Michael Hamburger. Hamburger was a precocious poet who got the modern languages scholarship at Christ Church in 1941: he had already completed a translation of Hölderlin (at sixteen) which John Lehmann was shortly to publish. He was writing a life of Gérard de Nerval, translated Rilke and could introduce John to Oxford's poets, the blind John Heath-Stubbs and Sidney Keyes, who later met a war poet's tragic death.

Michael Hamburger and John exchanged verses and compliments, sketched one another and hung about as bar-flies in Old Compton Street. Hamburger was already acquainted with the literary and artistic characters of Soho and Fitzrovia: Francis Bacon, George Barker, Oliver Bernard, John Craxton, the 'two Roberts', MacBride and Colquhoun, Paul Potts, Keith Vaughan, the beautiful brown-eyed Sri Lankan Tambimuttu, the old Surrealist painter John Banting and the ubiquitous Nina Hamnett. In the Swiss pub, they always hoped to see Dylan Thomas, whom Hamburger invited to address Oxford's English Society.

Some of John's poetic efforts were published in *The Cherwell*. They tended to strive too painfully for effect, sometimes obscuring all meaning. Here is part of 'Poem', addressed to a girl:

> Greeting with our fingers
> The dead fingers of the railings,
> By the gently academic
> Little jokes of Oxford villas,
> Let's pretend that we can always
> Keep our gyroscopic centre,
> That the cups of tea and kisses
> And the Renoir in the bedroom,
> The young man you met skiing,
> The girl I knew at home,
> Can survive the purging fires
> Of the cruel and jaded morning . . .

In the notebook from John's Oxford days is a poem called 'The Lonely Son', written in autumn 1941. While deficient in grammatical or prosodic structure, it conveys a melancholy wistfulness:

> What help to divide you hand from heart,
> Starting tomorrow on the stairs perhaps.
> Holding, to speak of friends, and when apart
> Thinking I had not met myself at all
> Had not shook my own hand in the hall.
> Had not seen the reflection anywhere before.
>
> Or when the afternoon hangs like a gap
> Gaping in a fluent day, to say,
> Tracing the pencil membranes on a map,
> I shall be happy all alone
> Being the lonely son
> Silent from you, myself or anyone.

Hamburger invited John to his parents' home in bomb-damaged St John's Wood, and took John to meet the sinister, Rabelaisian ex-lawyer and writer E. S. P. Haynes, who lived nearby. Haynes was a collector of decadent and sado-masochistic pornography, which he liked to show to his young men visitors – Evelyn and Alec Waugh among them. According to Hamburger, Haynes beat his dog, and his manservant beat him. John 'got on like a house on fire with this filthy old man', as Hamburger wrote.

The difference between the friends was that Hamburger was drawn towards the war in which he felt he should be taking part. 'The very attractions of the city, the Meadows and gardens, the overhung river, the splendid buildings, seemed like a seduction, an invitation to drop out of the real world.' Resisting this, the dutiful Hamburger enlisted, though the British army was wary of anyone born in Berlin and named Hamburger. (Michael's brother Paul, who changed his name to Hamlyn, was called up as a Bevin Boy, to work in the mines.)

John had now decided to follow Michael Fenton's pacifism. An army medical in March 1942 would excuse him from call-up anyway; and fifty years later he would tell the *New Yorker* he had been rejected for service because he was 'too thin'. But he and Fenton went one day that spring to a cottage called the Butts at Boar's Hill, to be schooled by an Oxford graduate, Charles Dimont, in persuading the authorities of their truly conscientious objection to war. Dimont, who had rebelled against his clerical background, had become a somewhat bibulous journalist, a Reuters correspondent in pre-war Vienna. Now, having convinced Judge Wethered at Bristol that he had an implacable objection to violence of any kind, he was granted unconditional exemption from war service, and worked at the Pacifist Service Unit headquarters. John and Fenton found Dimont at home in a dressing gown, suffering from a cold. As John remembered it, 'There seemed to be a large number of small children about, one of whom was dropping raspberry jam into *The Bible Designed to be Read as Literature*' – a popular book of that period. In a corner of the cottage's main room sat 'a dark young woman of remarkable beauty who said nothing and looked as if she were heartily sick of the tramp of conchies through her sitting-room'. This was Dimont's wife, Penelope. Her daughter Madelon was nearly four and her second daughter, Caroline, was newly born. (Perhaps the childless male regards two children as 'a large number'.) Penelope's own first memory of John Mortimer aged nineteen was that he was 'a nervous boy, thin, with a damp handshake'. John later wrote that he had no idea 'that in some distant peace I would marry the dark, silent Mrs Dimont and bring up her children'. They did not meet again for another five years.

In the meantime, John conceived a romantic infatuation for someone else altogether, with more immediate consequences. Quentin Edwards was, at seventeen, a young man of exceptional good looks and charm. Tall, handsome, with fresh colouring and high cheekbones, he was a boarder in his last year at Bradfield College in the Berkshire countryside.

The spring of 1942 was memorably beautiful. Quentin, whose father was away in Egypt and whose mother had died in 1940, was spending the Easter holidays with his great-aunt and uncle at Rye in Sussex. A schoolfriend, Ronald Cohen, now at New College, invited him and another Bradfield boy to visit him there. Oxford appeared to Quentin a magical world: 'The beautiful buildings, and sunlit empty quads with just a few young men wandering about. There were few cars, and very few people. Ronald's life struck me as marvellous – reading English with Lord David Cecil, living in New College with a sitting room, a bedroom, and a servant to look after him.'

Quentin was put in a commodious New College guest room and Cohen took him to meet his literary friends, Michael Hamburger and John Mortimer. They all went to the theatre and saw Milton's *Comus*, choreographed by Robert Helpmann. Quentin had never seen a ballet before, and he could hardly have been luckier: Purcell's score, arranged by Constant Lambert, stage set by Oliver Messel, and the lost lady, virtuous and unassailable, danced by Margot Fonteyn. The four young men were enraptured, conscious of the gulf between their interests and the pervading military ethos. Wartime heightened such feelings. 'We all knew life wasn't going to be as it had been in peacetime, we were going to have to get into uniform and go into the services,' Quentin told me. 'So we had to show we were different: daffy, airy-fairy, flowery *Yellow Book* aesthetes.'

So this was the background against which John became romantically obsessed with Quentin. Ronald Cohen, who was openly homosexual, resented John's monopolizing his young friend. But the attachment was mutual: John struck Quentin as a thoroughly romantic figure. He took the young visitors out punting, and to a restaurant, where he told them, 'We can have a good dinner because my father's had a well-paid brief.' As they were sitting in the restaurant, one of the party asked, 'What is it you actually believe in, John?' and he facetiously replied, 'Fish, white wine . . .'

Looking back after sixty-five years, Quentin Edwards, QC, by now a retired judge in his eighties, remembered, 'John and I had, I suppose, a crush on each other: it didn't amount to more than that. It was all about nothing! We'd been to single-sex public schools, where people form romantic friendships which are not really quite homosexual. I was not a homosexual, never have been, and neither, the truth is, was John, but he had this idea of romantic friendships. I like to think that what John felt about me was what Tennyson felt for Hallam – elevated, romantic – not what you'd call a homosexual relationship. When we met, it was forty years since Oscar Wilde died, but something lingered in the Oxford air, and Waugh captured that atmosphere very well in *Brideshead Revisited*. We would tell stories about Brian Howard, and Ronald Firbank, who was a great one for pottery rings and long pale hands and floppy ties.'

In his Christ Church rooms John showed Quentin his drawings and paintings, and a copy of *Salomé* with Beardsley's drawings. 'John had a tremendous eye for art. I remember him telling me to observe how the great artist treats the more muted colours, like grey. He was a fast and prolific reader, and I was impressed by the breadth of his knowledge.' Quentin recalled seeing a girl who was said to be John's girlfriend, 'dressed in floating pastel clothes and riding a bicycle', but John refused to introduce them. (Hamburger too recorded that John's girlfriend, presumably Anne, 'served tea but was never introduced to his friends, never took part in conversation'). But John quoted Shakespeare's Sonnet 144, 'Two loves I have, of comfort and despair', and presented Quentin with an inscribed volume of the sonnets. They arranged to meet again in Oxford or Brighton.

Unfortunately in the meantime John wrote several letters to Quentin in his elegant handwriting. 'They were the kind of letters you'd hate anyone else to read, addressed to "My Dear Boy", couched in rather romantic terms, like Oscar Wilde's letters to Bosie, with amusing jokes about undergraduates masturbating in their rooms – they were very funny, rather scabrous letters, and I thought absolutely marvellous. I kept them in a bundle.' As the summer holidays began, in the first week of August, Quentin received a message from his Bradfield headmaster, John Hills, summoning him to the school. He thought this odd, but made an excuse to his great-aunt and uncle, and took a train up to London with his brother, ostensibly to see Michael Redgrave in *Macbeth*, then travelled on to Bradfield. Hills informed him that his housemaster had found one of John's letters lying in his study corridor. So he had opened Quentin's desk to discover the rest of the bundle. Quentin believes there was no such letter in the corridor: the housemaster had, for whatever reason, been rummaging in his desk.

However it came about, John's letters had been read by two schoolmasters, who chose to interpret the florid Wildean phraseology in the worst possible light: that Quentin and John were having a sexual relationship. Quentin denied this strongly, and still believes that nothing in the letters justified their suspicions. But Hills told him that, in the circumstances, he should not return to the school. It was not an official expulsion: having matriculated the previous year, he would have spent only one more term at school anyway. 'I think it was really a question of "You've reached a level of sophistication that makes you an undesirable schoolboy."

The headmaster told me, "I've read these letters. I don't know if you think they're of any literary merit, but I think they're rubbish. You needn't think this man's got any real ability." And of course he was wrong. John has written some wonderful plays.'

If Quentin Edwards was cut adrift from his alma mater, so was John. Hills contacted John Lowe, Dean of Christ Church, a Canadian-born theologian – obviously assuming from John's Christ Church address that he was *in statu pupillari* there, not at Brasenose – and gave him a colourful account of the undesirable friendship between the undergraduate and the schoolboy. 'He clearly insinuated that John was corrupting me,' Quentin Edwards told me, 'and poor old John suffered a terrible penalty, I think. It should have been fairly investigated – but he was sent down without any option.'

Michael Hamburger remained incensed by what happened to John. In his memoirs, although he revealed John Mortimer's name as a fellow undergraduate 'more mature and less inhibited' than himself, he also recounted the scandal, disguising him as 'my friend':

Another friend [i.e. Ronald Cohen], who had been at The Hall with me, invited two boys still at his public school, to Oxford, where we all met. The friend, who I had taken to be heterosexual . . . conceived a violent passion for one of the two boys. In one of his letters to the boy, which had been intercepted by the boy's headmaster, my friend had written: 'Michael Hamburger sends his love'. In the middle of the vacation I was summoned to the Dean of Christ Church and put through a gruelling interrogation.

Hamburger persuaded Lowe that he was an innocent bystander. But 'since he was my friend, I was involved in the disgrace'. What still angered Hamburger sixty-five years later was that Christ Church turned a blind eye to a blatantly homosexual don who would offer freshmen 'instruction in the facts of life'. He offered this to Hamburger's brother Paul, who was bombarded with fond letters from this don after visiting Oxford. 'The duplicity that allowed the College to put up with that ... thinly disguised seduction, and expel a brilliant undergraduate for a single infatuation,' Hamburger wrote, 'was one of the things that made me reject a teaching career at Oxford, when the possibility arose.'

Quentin Edwards – who might, in other circumstances, have proceeded to Oxford himself – was about to join the Royal Navy, but first he went to work on the land on the Berkshire Downs, taking the bundle of John's letters, which had been returned to him. 'The whole episode had had such terrible consequences, and I was so upset, that I felt I'd better burn them, and did, on a Berkshire hillside.' He also erased John's affectionate inscription in the volume of Shakespeare's sonnets. Six years later, both John and Quentin were called to the Bar on the same day. Edwards went on to become a highly respected circuit judge, popular as the side-whiskered, half-moon-spectacled president of the Highgate Literary and Scientific Institution. He and John never resumed their friendship. But they were bound to meet, as lawyers do: Edwards's chambers in Crown Office Row were only yards from John's in Dr Johnson's Buildings.

'Once, in the fifties, in Fleet Street, we met by chance at about six in the evening and he suggested we have a cup of coffee, and I thought: This isn't like John, why doesn't he say let's have a drink? Anyway we did go into the Cock Tavern, and he told me his name had been expunged from the records of his college. He thought that was very hard.' Once, the two men appeared in the same courtroom; in 1972 they were opposing counsel in a blasphemy case brought by Lady Birdwood. John, in old age, exhibited his selective memory when the subject of Quentin Edwards came up. To give me permission to talk to Edwards, he wrote him a postcard which said, 'Sorry we haven't met since our small scandal at Oxford' – seemingly forgetting that thirty years afterwards they had faced each other across Bow Street Magistrates' Court.

So ended John's Oxford days in the summer of 1942. Although the Dean of Christ Church wrote to him, indicating that he should not return to Meadow Building, his letter – of which there is no copy in the chaotic Christ Church archives – must have also reassured John that this would not hinder his entitlement to the wartime degree. On 19 August John wrote to Hamburger from Turville Heath Cottage:

> Dearest Micky
> I enclose the Dean's letter which seems to make everything OK. I am terribly sorry to have got you into all this: but I think you are safely out – I do hope I haven't caused you a lot of worry – I was a bloody fool.
> 　I hope to see you soon, be good,
> 　Love John

John was already seeking work that would count as war service. On 9 July 1942, Dr Stallybrass wrote to the registrar of Oxford, 'There is a young man here who has been in residence six terms. He is exempt from Military Service, apparently on medical grounds, and now wishes to become a preparatory schoolmaster. He seems to be under the impression that he is eligible for a war degree.' Stallybrass – clearly unaware of the recent intervention of the Dean of Christ Church – doubted whether schoolmastering would be recognized, and proposed telling the young man 'that he must come into residence for another 3 terms if he wishes to take a degree'.

The following day, the headmaster of Oxley Farm prep school, Major J. M. Dickson, RA, wrote to Stallybrass to say that one John Mortimer had applied for the post of assistant master:

> I would be very glad if you could let me know in confidence whether you consider he would be suitable to take charge of small boys. His academic attainments are doubtless sufficient, though I cannot understand how he has obtained a 'shortened honours degree' in Law if he is only 19 as he says. I would like to know if you consider he is morally trustworthy and likely to be able to maintain order in class and, if you know it, the reason why he is not being called up.

Stallybrass replied, on 14 July, 'He came to us from Harrow with the reputation of being a leader amongst the "Intellectuals" at that school. He is a man of considerable ability and a certain amount of charm, though he is not cast in the conventional mode. I don't know him well, but he strikes me as a man of lively interests.'

Stallybrass explained that John had come up at seventeen, hence his youth. Although the university authorities did not normally recognize teaching as war service, they might, since John was not called up 'owing to the fact that he suffers from tuberculosis'. John wrote to Dr Stallybrass to confirm that after his medical in March, he had been sent for a TB examination. 'I was then told that if they wanted me I should here [*sic*] within a week' – the word 'here' incurred Stallybrass's scathing pencilled '!!' in the margin – 'but I have heard nothing more: so I presume I am unable to go into the army.' Would some other form of war service count? He added, 'I do hope I am not causing you a great deal of trouble.'

He was certainly causing a great deal of correspondence. On 11 July, the university registrar wrote to Stallybrass 'about your medically unfit undergraduate who wants to become a schoolmaster' and Stallybrass relayed to John his view that munitions factory work would be more acceptable. He added witheringly, 'You say that you were expecting to "here" within a week. Does that spelling especially qualify you as a Schoolmaster? Yours sincerely . . .'

The nature of John's physical unfitness remained vague. He remembered peering myopically at shadowy X-ray photographs of his chest, but whether he was deficient in heart or lung was never explained. He was robust enough to punt his friends up and down the Cherwell. The registrar advised Stallybrass that only government or agricultural work would be approved for Mr J. C. Mortimer. And there the matter rested until 7 July 1943, when John assured the authorities that he had been 'working continuously with the Ministry of Information since the beginning of last year'. So he got his degree.

John's later references to his Oxford days were always offhand

and dismissive. Twenty-five years later, on *Desert Island Discs*, Roy Plomley asked him, 'After school?' 'Well, after school I went to Oxford, but I was there for a very short time', *tout court*. When setting out his Oxford credentials as adaptor of *Brideshead Revisited*, he recalled the *Brideshead* relics in the era of blackouts and rationing: 'the ornate young men who lay naked in their rooms listening to Verdi's Requiem and who were occasionally pitched into the fountain by baying members of the aristocracy'. By 2000, he recalled only one naked aesthete on a sofa in the Christ Church quad, 'listening to the Verdi Requiem' and just one 'distinguished historian' who fell drunk into Mercury.

In his plays, he would return to the theme of a man's passion for another man in youth. It featured in the 1969 *Bermondsey* play from the quartet *Come As You Are*; in the 2001 play *Naked Justice*; and in his 2005 radio play about Byron, *The Last Adventure*.

In 2006, Brasenose College conferred an Honorary Fellowship on Sir John Mortimer, QC, MA (Oxon), which made him smile.

4. Into Bohemia

In midsummer 1942, still only nineteen, John was back home, adrift. His father had been remarkably unfazed when, during one of their walks in the garden, John told him what had happened at Oxford. Clifford responded, 'I think you're very brave to go on doing my petitions and making notes on my briefs, in the middle of all this anxiety.' Which made him love his father all the more.

Clifford had told him that his peccadillo would soon be forgotten. But he saw himself as a young man in a shameful slough of despond ('I am a hermit, a social outcast and generally shat on by the world') when he wrote morosely from Turville Heath Cottage to 'dearest Micky' Hamburger one lonely Sunday evening.

Often as I sit isolated here among a thousand books, smoking and writing my novel into the night, I think of your pale, so nineteenth-century face bent over the yellow, so nineteenth-century paper; among the skeletons, the spidery handwriting, the heavy printed books, the furniture which is all so redolent of your peculiar, fastidious personality. Then I feel so very sad that I can't just cross a bat-ridden quadrangle to see you.

I have devoted myself entirely to writing. I don't move or talk: I just sit here and grind it out. I have broken the back of my book and written about two hundred pages. So for better or worse, it will get finished. If I had some money I would come to London, but I have spent it all on books so I can't move.

Do write to me and tell me about yourself. You are so much, now that everyone hates and despises me and thinks I ought to be locked up, now that I am damned to a tedious and smelly hell with

Mr Haynes, Freddy, Oscar Wilde and Ronald Cohen, you are so
much the <u>only</u> person I like, the <u>only</u> person I want to know.
    And so goodbye.
    And love. And damn the Dean.

And later, John implored, 'Write to me, send me anything you
write. You have genius, my little Michael, and I love you very
much.'

At his jungly fastness in the depths of Suffolk, the poet and emeritus
professor Michael Hamburger looked at John's letters – which he
had placed in his archive at Leeds University – sixty-two years
later. The style, he pointed out, is misleading. 'Anyone reading
these letters, addressed to "My dear Boy" and so on, would assume
that I was John's catamite, that he was in love with me. But it was
just a pose he was affecting at the time. Totally artificial – and one
which I'm glad to say he soon discarded. He was just trying on the
decadent, *fin-de-siècle*, Oscar Wilde persona, to see what it was like,
I imagine.'

John appended little sketches of himself: bony face, floppy hair,
glasses, flamboyant tie. He discussed the novels he had been reading: Gide's *Les Faux-monnayeurs* ('a marvellous tour de force, but
no more . . . you can just hear old Gide congratulating himself,
"what a clever little novelist I am." Still I was very excited about
it. I think the sodomy is rather well done and not much falsified,
but there are some terrible high-life scenes aren't there.'). He sent
verses from Baudelaire. He sent also his own efforts, which he
accurately described as 'my adolescent and orgiastic mumblings in
ill-formed poetry'. He was still fancying himself a poet: he had
sent some poems to Diana Witherby at *Horizon*, the literary journal
edited by Stephen Spender and Cyril Connolly, who had shown
interest. He wanted Hamburger to believe that he too was dedicated to the poetic art. 'To believe firmly enough in your concep-
tions to sit up at two o'clock in the morning driving an aching
hand across the page to form words no one will ever read, that
needs something that we can both pride ourselves on having got,'

he wrote. 'What do you think it is? Lunacy.' In another letter he quoted Proust: 'Proust said that literary success came less from the desire for fame than the habit of being laborious. I think it is so true.'

At the end of September he was still in his hermitage and had almost finished his 80,000-word novel, a rustic yarn with a Henley boatman as protagonist. 'I don't know if anybody will like it or publish it. I don't awfully care, it had to come out and there, very black and fat and important looking, it is. I think it is the best thing I have ever attempted, which is saying damn little. I want you to read it, but not until it is finished, which may be never so it will die unseen.' (It has died unseen, though he later used some of the material in a play.)

Could they meet soon, he suggested, in the corner of some warm little pub and get gently and sentimentally drunk? 'What about next week? About 7 in the Swiss? If you're not playing croquet with T S Eliot, or ring-a-ring-a-roses with Christopher Isherwood.' He recommended Helpmann's ballet of *Hamlet*, 'half charade and half Grand Guignol', and 'a wonderful French film about the whole truth called Gens du Voyage'. He had been reading Flaubert's *L'Education sentimentale*, which

is the story of my life, expensive, pointless and well meaning. In thirty years we shall sit together, you and I, like Frédéric and Deslauriers, having failed at everything we set out to do, having survived the wars and revolutions that thunder aimlessly in the background, and discuss the past. 'Do you remember,' we shall say, 'when we quarrelled about Q [Quentin Edwards] and got drunk and went out to dinner with Ronald Cohen, those were the best days.' And the dreadful thing is that they will have been. I am inclined to think that it is an even greater book than War and Peace; Flaubert realises that the key to life is failure and not a sort of stodgy success.

He said he had fixed a job teaching English in a prep school which would be quite well paid but would probably drive him mad. Or he might go as tutor to a small boy in a castle in Scotland, with a suite of rooms and a footman to himself. 'I am sure if I do, something horrible and Kafka-like will happen. Something to do with whips.'

Before long John's social life in Turville Heath was enlivened by two ladies in a nearby cottage who ran a Henley bookshop and provided good copy for his next letter to Hamburger:

> My spare time I spend with the Lesbians. They are very rich and give me champagne. Their house is full of Marie Laurencins. They remind me of the South of France, of the voitures au cheval, of the Prince of Monaco's aquarium, of the beautiful people on the Côte d'Azur. They wear death's head sun glasses which give, even on the greyest days, an impression of heat. When they give parties they wear black silk men's evening dress. I find in them the culmination of my bisexual desires and am in danger of falling in love, not with them personally, but with their richness, their immorality, a certain sleepy, sophisticated quality in their lives. Also they tell me I write well. I lie on their sofa and purr.

Phyl Duveen and Nancy Morris – 'Miss Baker and Miss Cox' in *A Voyage Round My Father* – were the ladies in question. John was exhilarated by the contrast their sophisticated lives made with the quiet respectability of Turville Heath Cottage. They talked of Paris and the Left Bank and Marlene Dietrich, lent him books and showed him the drawings of Cocteau. John told his father that the two women had known Cocteau, who took opium; whereupon his father made one of his best remarks, about opium's binding effect on the metabolism. Had John never seen a picture of opium-addicted Coleridge? Clifford asked. 'Green about the gills, and a stranger to the lavatory.'

Phyl and Nancy were rather exotic. Phyl, glamorous and Garbo-esque, had been married to the art collector Sir Joseph Duveen. Nancy Morris was the sister of the artist Cedric Morris (at whose school Lucian Freud, lately arrived in England, studied, before setting fire to it); her bull terrier was the subject of a Morris painting. Nancy was tall and rangy and wore men's clothes from Austin Reed's in Reading – cord trousers and jackets with leather patches – until Marcel Boulestin, the celebrated chef and food writer, died and left her his wardrobe, whereupon she would be seen striding across the common in a Frenchman's overcoat with astrakhan collar and patent-leather boots.

What is remarkable is that this small area, no more than a few square miles of the Thames Valley, should have been in the 1940s such a fertile ground in which a young man of metropolitan ambitions might sow various seeds. Here, without venturing far from his parents' house, John found his first female lover, his first wife and his first employers. That autumn, he was able to tell Hamburger that he had landed a job. Just up the road lived Jack Beddington, Balliol man, dynamic head of Shell advertising, much admired for enlisting two other Johns, Betjeman and Piper, to work on his pioneering Shell Guides. Beddington had seen the schoolboy Mortimer's Punch and Judy shows in the garden, and on the strength of these, at Clifford's request, he fixed up a job with the Crown Film Unit, part of the Ministry of Information. So John was now awaiting the call to start at Pinewood.

In the meantime he carried on, in his letters to Hamburger, flourishing his green carnation and affecting the bisexual persona, alternately fey and louche, he had given himself. 'Last time I saw you I was drunk; next time I shall be mad . . . My bed is full of air and my head of old songs, my memory of you who I only love. Being as ill as Tchekov under the green lamp, being as precocious as Proust and as bored as Baudelaire, what should not you and I perform?' He took to writing of fanciful experiences, in phrases laden with nonsensical imagery:

> I have been Feste the Jester skulking in bars to pick up old jokes or beautiful songs, half tight and wholly homosexual I have wandered among the flowers and seen, among red velvet roses, sticky salvia of the Vatican . . . I have kissed a woman and discovered her to be a man, worse I have kissed a man and discovered him to be a man.

I have a black hat like an old curé and a brown hat like Ezra
Pound . . .

And so on and so on. Utter twaddle, says Hamburger. But to
be fair, John was only nineteen, self-consciously seeking a literary
identity, apologizing for his verbal excesses and artifices:

My brain, spunk, everything has gone into the bloody novel and
there is nothing left. I have to write comparative sense for five
hours a day, and so my letters usually turn out like this. Please
forgive it. The novel, is, however, going to be good.

I stood the other day among my things from Oxford, bills,
abortive novels, letters, a little certificate from my tutor to say that
'John Mortimer has passed with a B in Constitutional Law' . . . I
shall go to Oxford the Saturday after next, heavily disguised.

Michael Hamburger left Oxford that Hilary Term of 1942,
expecting to join the army. But they still dithered about accepting
a recruit of German birth, so he waited at his mother's house in
St John's Wood until summoned by the Royal West Kent Regiment in June 1943. He was later commissioned, but his memoirs
describe the embarrassment of confessing to his fellow soldiers that
he wrote poetry. John consoled Michael for the 'tragedy' of getting
into the army: 'I think it may make you happier in a drugged sort
of way. Indolence sharpens the mind to an unbearable poignancy,
work bluntens it to a coma more complete and comfortable than
drugs or drink.' This was cold comfort, he added. 'I can't personally
think of anything more like hell.'

He enclosed a somewhat painful new poem: one extract will
suffice.

> Lavatory paper walls and a wedding group
> A tin of soup poured this unique landscape
> Onto a chicken coup [*sic*].

He was trying, as one who has lately discovered Surrealism might, to startle the reader with unexpected images. Unfortunately they are, like his decadent pose, quite bogus.

Once he had been rescued from solitary introspection and entered the 'very odd surroundings' of Pinewood Studios at Fulmer Road, Iver Heath, Bucks, John's perspective on the world became more rational. Having arrived at the Crown Film Unit, he discovered 'naïve pleasures like getting up in the morning and being hungry: I am even getting a sort of morbid taste for work'.

'I sit here,' he told Hamburger, 'helping to sell the war. I might as well be writing advertisements for laxatives. One of my jobs is to write funny jokes into dire scripts, a most depressing thing to have to do in the mornings. I have some marvellous ideas for a novel but no energy to write. The first novel is very nearly typed so I shall soon be able to celebrate its first refusal.' Weeks later he was telling Hamburger about the rejection slips with their 'few kind words to sugar the pill'.

Living in digs in Slough with an aircraft-fitter and his wife, and listening fascinated to the banter of the film crew, he was getting to know the working class for the first time. John really did not fit in with the tough hired men of the film crew: cameramen, electricians, continuity girls, prop-men. They thought the new second-assistant director was amiable, but looked dim and owlish, and sounded, with his undergraduate voice, quite the wrong sort of person to take charge of a film set. They called him 'Steam-tug', to rhyme with Mug. He constantly retold the story of how his polite, ineffectual calls of 'Ladies and gentlemen, will you please give us a little quiet, PLEASE!' went unheeded, until he shouted, 'Shut up, you bastards!' and the workmen threatened to strike.

Nora Dawson, née Blackburne, who was later to marry the film director Jack Lee (brother of Laurie), was assistant to the Crown Film Unit's great documentary director Humphrey Jennings. She arrived at Pinewood one day to find 'this tall, painfully skinny, bespectacled boy with a rather silly, high, effete voice sitting on a stool in my office, legs crossed, very well dressed in a suit with a waistcoat, who announced, "I've been appointed as your assistant."

I thought: "Oh, Jesus, what shall I do with him?" To get rid of him, I sent him off to do some research on the women with small children whose husbands were prisoners of war. When he came back I looked at what he'd written and thought: "H'm, this ain't half bad." '

He took out a 'hugely desirable' doe-eyed secretary named Mavis, but she talked only of Laurie Lee. Laurie, a published poet, not yet the author of *Cider with Rosie*, had been writing film scripts for the Unit since 1941. Now he was nursing a broken heart because the love of his life, the femme fatale Lorna Wishart, had left him for her new lover, the young artist Lucian Freud. Demented with grief, Laurie just wanted to get out of his Film Unit job. He always claimed that it was he who sent John Mortimer off to Watford Junction to write a script, and that John's tale of a stationmaster's wife having an affair with a GI, inspired by Marcel Pagnol's 1938 film *La Femme du boulanger*, kicked off his career. In later years, envious of John's productivity, Laurie would growl, whenever they met in the Garrick Club, 'I should never have sent you to Watford Junction.'

Twenty-odd years later, in *The Listener*, John reminisced about the Crown Film Unit's documentary style, as seen in *Fire Over England* and *Listen to Britain*:

Though efficient at showing the herring-fleet putting out to sea, or bombers rising into the air to the accompaniment of symphonic music by Vaughan Williams, they were poor at dealing with human motives or dilemmas. Indeed our documentary characters seldom said much except 'Jerry a little naughty tonight' or 'Pass the tea, George.' Humphrey Jennings insisted on using real people, not actors. If a man were to be shown working a lathe, he must work a lathe in real life.

This was indeed Jennings's practice. Nora had the interesting job of meeting returning servicemen, blatantly picking out the best-looking and auditioning the most cine-genic.

The Film Unit's boyish recruit was all the while planning to make use of this material. The malingering and time-wasting of the film crew were eye-opening, like barrack-room blarney to public-school boys in the ranks. After a day as dogsbody on and off the set, John would scribble his notes. Since he had a courteous, self-effacing manner, people talked as if he wasn't there, or told him their life stories. The Film Unit gave him the chance to travel, to see life outside the Thames Valley and 'the way all sorts of people live', in northern mining villages and industrial cities. He was soon writing a novel with the working title *Action*, the word he had so haplessly to call before every take. He cast himself as the naïve protagonist, having a brief dalliance with the director's wife. 'I found myself working with ease,' he wrote later. A satirical style using realistic dialogue came naturally to him. Evelyn Waugh was one discernible influence; lesser novelists Julien Green and Rex Warner were others.

Distilling his Film Unit days into a radio play years after, he described how he had fallen in love with the artifice of cinema. The props department could create convincing Old Master paintings and four-poster beds and royal thrones: 'The pretence and the reality, the falsehood and the truth, the wakefulness and the dream, were confused; seemed like reflections of the same object, in an endless corridor of mirrors. I became filled with thoughts it would take all my lifetime to express, at a time when all we wrote was so unrealistic, and so unreal.'

In July 1943, he wrote plaintively to the Oxford registrar about whether he was now entitled to take his degree, since he was working in a government ministry. And so in October 1943, exactly one year after joining the Crown Film Unit, having taken Mods Law I in 1940 and Mods Law II in 1941, he became J. C. Mortimer, BA. He promised to attend the degree day on 14 October, along with Robert Runcie and P. J. Houghton-Gastrell – but in the event he could not get away and the degree was conferred in his absence.

He would write to Hamburger, under a Ministry of Information letterhead from Pinewood Studios, about the solitary torment of writing fiction, the hours at his desk, chain-smoking, trying to create a scenario that was funny or tragic or grotesque. His new resolve was to change his life, to live alone, without distractions, and to write for eight hours a day. Was the army any more bearable than 'the nameless, intangible horrors of Oxford'? he asked. 'In any case it must be spiritually cleaner to be fighting this war than acting as a little tin trumpet through which the Government blows its brassy propaganda.' In fact, Hamburger was not sent to the fighting, in Italy, until the tail end of the war, and only returned to Oxford to finish his degree in 1947, feeling that he had 'wasted the best years of my youth'.

Hamburger continued to send poems for John's critical appreciation. 'Your great strength,' he told Hamburger, 'is that you write like a human being with an intellect, or an intellectual with human passions, which prevents you writing as much balls as most people.' War, John wrote, brought

> gradual hardening of the arteries, slow chilling of the blood, until horrible things, death, crime, despair become part of everyday life, as unremarkable as the tube journey or the breakfast egg. The crisis does at least deepen the significance of life – although the danger is that the significance becomes too great, one is blinded by the lightning flash and ordinary things, trees, grass and the shape of the land are covered with darkness.

John had embarked on his first full-blown affair with a female lover. Her name was Susan Watson: he calls her 'Sarah' in his memoirs and gives a tender description of her small heart-shaped face and the beret she wore on the side of her head, like a girl in a Jean Gabin film. He met her at one of the parties given by Nancy and Phyl, at the end of 1942. She was twenty-four – five years his senior – and had proved a determined character ever since being born a surviving twin, weighing only two pounds, and with a mild form of cerebral palsy that left her slightly lame. (In his memoirs John refers tentatively to her lameness, which he confesses to having suppressed, much as his family never mentioned Clifford's blindness.) She was also beautiful, with very blue eyes; John attributes 'eyes of two different colours' to her, but the girl with the unmatched eyes was not Susan but her sister-in-law, Judith Stephen, niece of Virginia Woolf. Susan's mother, the vivid, red-headed Wyn Henderson (who had run a Paris bookshop with Nancy Cunard), lived next door to Summer Cottage of John's boyhood, hence Susan's appearance at the lesbians' party.

Susan had been married to a Cambridge don, Alistair Watson, who had left her with a small daughter, Sarah, known as Sally. John appeared to Susan as romantic, slightly dangerous and Byronic, especially when he told her he had been sent down from Oxford. At Nancy and Phyl's they joined in some kind of parlour kissing game; at the end of the party they were discovered in flagrante in a bedroom and were obliged – 'This is not a brothel!' – to continue their lovemaking in the bracken on the common. At the end of this episode, John writes, he went home and read to his father, in a world-weary voice, Shakespeare's Sonnet 129 about lust in action, 'the expense of spirit in a waste of shame'. It was 'the end of childhood'.

Their affair went on for two years, mostly conducted in the Belsize Park Gardens basement where Susan lived, while she worked at a nursery for Austrian refugee children run by Anna Freud in Fitzjohn's Avenue, Hampstead. He took Susan to stay with his parents, but she did not feel she was 'acceptable' to them. John always remembered her with gratitude as eccentric and funny, his 'first great love'. As he said in his memoirs, when people of the late twentieth century talked about the promiscuity of the young, he wondered where they had been forty years before: modern youth seemed dully monogamous, compared with his day, when women 'thought little of packing their overnight bags and fighting their way through the blackout to another shared flat, another tolerant hotel, to keep in touch with a floating and transient population of lovers'. But there was the constant threat of pregnancy: 'Every month brought days of anxiety followed by unexpected relief or incredulous despair.'

Early in 1945, Susan found she was indeed pregnant. The situation seemed all too familiar from the book John was reading at the time, Sartre's *Les Chemins de la liberté*. His reaction, that she should have an abortion, together with his promise that after the abortion he would marry her, was a death blow to their relationship. He could not tell his parents about Susan's pregnancy, and Phyl Duveen, whom he asked, would not help with the necessary money. But the termination was arranged, rather late (more than twelve weeks), and Susan had feelings of guilt about it for years afterwards, because she loved children. (In his memoirs he describes a jaunty girlfriend called 'Angela' inducing her own abortion, by gin and hot baths, 'a decision I was to regret bitterly in the months to come'.)

There is an undated letter to Hamburger, written when living in Hampstead, 'among pointless women and purposeless men', in which he muses on life. He was now 'ambitious, however fantastically, to be a novelist'. 'I have sworn now the whole day and night to my desk, where I twist and swear to produce plays, novels, film stories, anything to fling in the face of a world constantly becoming more obsessed with the refrigerator and the water heater.' Someone had offered to publish his first novel, 'which I have decided to refuse as the thing makes me blush to read. Nevertheless my ambition is by now hysterical and I am determined to produce two more within the next year.'

It is difficult – even with John's help – to disentangle his emotional attachments and geographical displacements in 'that curiously unmemorable period after the war'. He moved constantly around London. There was Houghton-Gastrell's flat in Sydney Street, Chelsea; following the Susan affair, there was a girl called Barbara Tosswell (to whom he gives the name 'Angela Bedwell' in his memoirs, the one who induces her own abortion). For a time he lived in Old Church Street, Chelsea, and for another interlude in Edith Grove at World's End, at a flat belonging to his Oxford friend Peter Newbert's mother; and in a house near Hampstead Heath, with Jean Fenton, former wife of his friend Michael, with whom (Fenton's son assumed) John also had an affair. Like any young man about town, he went to work, to pubs, to parties. His own published account, and the dialogue he recreates, read like a dated 1940s novel, and are dotted with names, some famous – Rodney Ackland, Peter Brook, Richard Attenborough, Jack Clayton; some pseudonymous – Angela, Oliver Pensotti, Mrs Watkins.

In his memoirs he remembered this time as shrouded in despair: 'I had lived twenty-three endless years and what had I to show for it? An unpublished novel, an inglorious war and a disastrous love affair.' But by the end of the century, John would repeatedly say that the years at the end of the war, and just after, had been 'the most exciting period of my life'. 'I had a uniform that said Crown Film Unit and a flat in the King's Road and I was paid £11 a week.' He remembered the alarms of sirens and buzz bombs, and the hiatus of waiting for the bomb to drop on somebody else. 'And then you sort of had another drink,' he said. 'But I was young and going to parties and coming home with the streets full of broken glass and bombed buildings . . .' In a short story for the *New Yorker* called 'The Man Who Loved Parties', written fifteen years later, his wife, Penelope, summed up John's nostalgia for this period, his longing 'once more to sleep on somebody else's sofa, shave with somebody else's razor, cook breakfast for somebody else's wife . . . once more to be young. Is it all over? Must it be over?' In John's 1952 novel, *Like Men Betrayed*, a poet reminisces fondly about the war years. ' "All the girls liked poetry then, and poets. The pickups! Fabulous, I tell you." . . . His eyes were wet with genuine feeling, nostalgia for the silvery barrage balloons in the blue sky, the humming canteen of the Ministry of Information, and his archetype in green trousers with shoulder-length hair and a new copy of Horizon.' John often spoke of driving his father's Morris Oxford in 1945 around the streets of High Wycombe, pulling out the Labour voters, and then waking next morning to the euphoric news of Attlee's landslide victory. 'There was no doubt that all the things we wanted to happen were now going to come to pass.'

But there was no avoiding the doom-laden prospect of reading for the Bar. Like Robert Louis Stevenson, who took on the wig and gown as a sop to his parents but never had any intention of practising, John fell in and enrolled at the College of Law in

Chancery Lane. Unlike Winston Churchill's father, Randolph, who judged his son 'not clever enough for the Bar', Clifford insisted on it. 'It was my father's way to offer the law to me,' the son soliloquizes in *A Voyage Round My Father*: 'the great stone column of authority which has been dragged by an adulterous, careless, negligent and half-criminal humanity down the ages – as if it were a small mechanical toy which might occupy half an hour on a rainy afternoon.'

It was mainly the rainy afternoons that preoccupied Clifford's garden log in 1946. 'A most wet and miserable May' had been followed by 'a most wet and miserable June' and 'the most miserable wet and depressing August in living memory!' But Clifford won prizes for his dahlias and roses, and John's friend Mavis (from the Film Unit) came to stay, and they went to Stratford and saw *As You Like It*, *Macbeth*, *The Tempest*, *Love's Labour's Lost*, *Measure for Measure* and *Cymbeline*. Kathleen took forty pounds of honey from her two beehives, and Turville Heath Cottage was photographed in *Ideal Home* magazine.

   John persisted in pursuing his second-string career. A short story, 'Non Stop', was published in the *Evening News*, and he signed a contract to write the captions for a children's picture book called *Costumes*, published by Puffin, for an advance of £20. (He had always been keen on the history of costume and had met a German artist who asked him to provide the words. So *Costumes* became his first published book, in 1947.) In October 1946 he failed his Real Property exam. Two days later he left for his first visit to Paris. He had found a job teaching English to the models of Christian Dior, so he sat on a spindly gilt chair in the Rue St-Honoré salon, reading aloud Somerset Maugham stories, filled with elation. Staying at the Grand Hotel des Balcons on the Left Bank, he dined on oysters and steak at La Coupole with Freddy Hurdis-Jones 'and his far more masculine mother'. He visited Gordon Craig, the great theatre designer, whose son he had met at the Film Unit. After a month, he returned home to retake the Real Property exam – and found waiting for him a letter from the Bodley Head accepting his first novel, with a £100 advance. He signed the contract, drawn up by the agent Spencer Curtis Brown, on 21 November 1946.

It was 'a very sodden wet November – garden like a sponge', heralding one of the coldest winters of the twentieth century. When the Mortimer family returned from Harold and Daisy's in January 1947, there was deep snow that persisted for weeks. In February there were daily blizzards, the Thames froze at Windsor, and John went tobogganing at Turville with Peter Newbert. Winter was followed by a memorable spring and summer; the scent of the June blossom of Clifford's *Philadelphus* 'Belle Etoile' filled the garden, a barn owl visited nightly and John escaped from his law studies twice, taking a sleeper train to Cornwall to stay with a girlfriend he called 'Cornish Patsy'. A hot July and August brought visitors, including Cornish Patsy, the artist Jim Holland, Anne Duveen and Jane Stockwood. Clifford's roses, sweet peas and pompom dahlias again took prizes at the Henley Show. The glorious weather continued ('never has such a summer been known,' wrote Clifford.) But the Mortimer family's peaceful existence was about to be dramatically transformed by John's falling, at twenty-four, seriously in love.

5. The Penelopiad

At this point, the bewitching Mrs Dimont re-enters the narrative: the dark beauty whom John had fleetingly seen that day when he and Michael Fenton went from Oxford to visit Charles Dimont at the Boar's Hill cottage named the Butts. Penelope, with her ready-made family and her already complicated history, was destined to be the next most significant person in John's life.

Penelope Fletcher was born at Rhyl in North Wales on 19 September 1918. Her father, Arthur Forbes Gerald Fletcher, a cradle Methodist turned C of E clergyman, was one of eleven children, and so was her mother, 'one of the few things they had in common'. Her mother, née Caroline Amy Maggs, a self-effacing but capable woman, was the daughter of a nonconformist Victorian businessman in Wiltshire. When Penelope was born, her father was thirty-nine and had gone off God; her mother was forty-two and had gone off sex. 'My Daddy,' Penelope wrote, 'and I want to add, the poor sod'. She said she inhaled his misery, along with his tobacco smoke, by the lungful. In her memoirs she gave her father's character a masterly summary: he was 'tormented by the sins he hadn't committed and unable to understand the ones he had; tremendously ambitious, without the slightest talent for success; full of urges and yearnings and pains of the soul, frightened and frightening and altogether a mess'. By contrast, in the sequence of vicarages and rectories where they lived, her industrious mother – who had stowed away some tenets of Eastern philosophy – applied her good taste and tireless economy, creating well-upholstered homes and well-tended gardens, quietly taking charge. She even ran a nursery school at home, the Little People's Garden.

Because she was always known as Peggy, and her godmother had given her a box inscribed 'Margaret Fletcher', Penelope was twelve years old before she realized that her name was Penelope –

just as she was being sent away to her seventh school, St Elphin's School for the daughters of the clergy. In the Fletcher family, as in the Mortimers', the approach to children was to send them away; Penelope's elder brother Paul was sent away at four and never forgave his parents.

At eighteen, Penelope escaped: she shared a flat with her brother in London and was deflowered by one of his Oxford friends, an American Rhodes scholar. She took a journalism course, worked for Butlin's publicity office and frequently got engaged. The fiancé she married was Charles Dimont, who had been an exhibitioner in history and a prominent oarsman at Worcester College, Oxford. He was the son of the chancellor of Salisbury Cathedral. To Penelope, the Dimont parents appeared solid and safe, in the cloistered world of Salisbury Close. The wedding took place in the Lady Chapel at Salisbury, the bride dressed in black, her own father officiating. The newlyweds repaired to the groom's flat (their love nest for the past two months) in Dickens Court, off Fleet Street – transformed by Penelope's mother during their honeymoon from a pigsty into a habitable home. Charles, who was working for Reuters, was posted to Vienna at the time of the Anschluss, and Penelope, five months pregnant, joined him in the Reuters flat at Schottenring 35. Mrs Fletcher suggested that she should start writing a diary. 'Not because I am in myself interesting,' wrote Penelope on day one, 'but because I am in Vienna and should, apparently, have some Interesting Experiences.' Indeed she did, observing with outrage the activities of Hitler's stormtroopers; so innocent that she went out in the street in a fur coat and a black sombrero, was taken for a Jewish girl and was menaced in a café until she placed her British passport on the table.

Though a clever and headstrong nineteen, Penelope knew little about life. Charles was not much better informed, and his German wasn't as good as he had claimed; so he was frightened of the job he had taken on, and fearful too of the responsibility of marriage and parenthood. Periodically, he would disappear on benders – he had become a connoisseur of beer while at Oxford – mystifying his pregnant wife. Her Jewish doctor, Paul Singer, was himself frantically trying to get out of Vienna when, in July 1938, her baby – weighing ten and a half pounds – was born. They named her Madelon, apparently after a racehorse.

As the political situation worsened, Penelope took advice from the British ambassador, who admitted that in her place he would leave; so she flew home with the baby. Mrs Fletcher took over the mothering, delighted at the age of sixty-three to have charge of her first grandchild, with the help of an Austrian nurse who washed nappies and pushed the pram.

So Penelope could go off and rejoin her husband, now in Bucharest. As she later said, her mother connived at her reckless approach to childbearing by taking over the babies: 'Through me, my mother had a vicarious family without going through all the unpleasant business. She never took me seriously as a mother, and encouraged me to "run along and play, darling".' There wasn't much play, as war loomed. In Bucharest, Penelope and Charles 'ceased to be happy'. They managed to wangle themselves into King Carol of Romania's entourage on a state visit to England. As Penelope describes it, she and Charles would sit devising fantastic expenses to submit to Reuters, until Charles, threatened with being fired, resigned.

The couple subsisted on his stipend from the Pacifist Service Unit, on Penelope's occasional modelling and published poems, and on ten-shilling handouts from Mrs Fletcher, who had a small allowance from one of her brothers: Will was a prosperous Wiltshire rope and matting manufacturer; Joe inherited the family's dairy business. It was Uncle Joe who underwrote Madelon's school fees from 1943.

When she was just three, Madelon seized Penelope's 'Busy', her infant name for her mother's typewriter (because Penelope, when writing, would tell her 'I'm busy'), and buried it in the vegetable patch. This was at the Butts, a whitewashed cottage rented at a pound a week, furnished with piano and long bookcases containing volumes on Van Gogh and Botticelli. Its garage became a Wendy house for Madelon. When Charles Dimont came home at weekends he would scoop his daughter out of her bath (in the kitchen), walk her up to Mr Hatt the baker's to bring home a lardy cake, and tell her stories of what Mr Hitler, Mr Stalin and Mr Churchill were up to. Penelope, who was not predisposed to play games, created a character for Madelon, 'Mrs Goodhouse who lives in a wooden house': whenever she wanted to write, she would tell Madelon, 'Off you go and be Mrs Goodhouse.'

Penelope's first novel, 'unhappily titled Time For Tenderness', had been rejected. But she was pregnant again, and went home to her parents' rectory for the birth of her second baby, Caroline, born after a stormy night on 12 March 1942. The next month she was back in the Butts, seated in the corner, when Michael Fenton and John Mortimer arrived from Oxford for advice on how to become conchies.

By September the Dimonts had let the Butts, and the family went to live at Wynstones, a Rudolf Steiner boarding school near Stroud where Madelon, at only four, had already spent a term. Penelope took the post of housekeeper/matron, while Charles did approved war work as a hospital orderly at Stroud. The following spring, Charles decided to join the army, a volte-face which took rather more courage than declaring himself a pacifist. He enlisted with the Wiltshires and was accepted by the Pioneer Corps, which gave him a commission; he eventually went to Berlin as a staff officer. But while air raids continued, Penelope took Madelon and Caroline to live with her in-laws at Salisbury, where, she noted, their cook 'seemed to fry everything except trifle'.

So, at the home of her husband's parents, Penelope (a creature of a type not often seen in Salisbury Close, with her godless lipstick and cigarettes) was introduced to Charles's friend Kenneth Harrison. Slight, fastidious and fair-haired, Harrison was a Cambridge biochemistry don working, possibly on chemical warfare, at nearby Porton Down. He had lived his entire life in ecclesiastical and academic circles, first at York, where his father was chancellor of York Minster, and then in Cambridge, where he was lay dean at King's College and author of an illustrated guide to the glorious stained-glass windows of King's College Chapel. An uncompromising atheist, he had also led the college's recently mooted proposal to admit women, despite living the enclosed life of a pre-war bachelor don. He occupied rooms next to E. M. Forster, dined on high table, spent his evenings with books, music and at the bridge table in the senior common room. Penelope used to say Kenneth was so institutionalized he had only the vaguest notion of how to use a telephone kiosk. Yet this sober, intellectual academic fell instantly in love (seemingly the single love affair of his life) with the wife of his absent friend Dimont in the close, a bizarre setting for adultery, in 1944. Harrison found Penelope 'witty, refreshing, elegant'. At weekends, they would cycle off together to visit churches. And after lights-out, improbable though this seems, under the roof of her parents-in-law, he shinned up the drainpipe to Penelope's bedroom. The resulting pregnancy was instantaneous. The baby, a daughter named Julia, was born in a Salisbury nursing home on 30 March 1945. It suited everyone to allow Charles Dimont – who had conveniently been home briefly, on leave – to believe that the child was his.

In May 1945 Penelope took her three daughters back to her parents at Willersey Rectory, near Broadway, in Worcestershire. This house, which is today a hotel, became the nearest thing to a stable, permanent home the girls had known, where they could play in the garden and outhouses. At Willersey, Penelope confessed to Charles that Julia, now aged eighteen months, was not his child. Naturally he was upset, but they were still married when, at the end of 1946, at the Gargoyle Club in Soho, Penelope met a film producer named Humphrey Swingler who worked with her brother at the Film Producers' Guild at Merton Park. Swingler introduced her to his handsome, charming elder brother, Randall. The Swinglers were, yet again, from a Church family: they were the sons of a Kentish rector and great-nephews of Randall Davidson, Archbishop of Canterbury in the 1920s. Randall Swingler, a Wykehamist, had read Greats at New College, Oxford, and co-edited *Our Time* with Edgell Rickword. At the *Left Review* they had published the symposium *Authors Take Sides on the Spanish War* in 1937. Randall had won the Military Medal in Italy, where he had been left for dead, and although mentally afflicted by his wartime ordeal, he became literary editor of the *Daily Worker*, wrote several fine volumes of poems and the libretto for Britten's *Ballad of Heroes*.

Randall Swingler was married to Geraldine Peppin, one of the pianist Peppin twins. She lived with their daughter, Judy, in Essex, while Swingler kept a London flat. By the autumn of 1947, he was Penelope's lover. She was installed in a cottage in the Thames Valley, where he could visit her: it was Wyn Henderson's cottage, 'hung with cobwebs and dead herbs', at Summer's Heath. The baby Julia was left at Willersey in the capable hands of Mrs Fletcher. Caroline joined Madelon at Ballard Point, a happy little dame school at Swanage, Dorset, run by a pair of kind spinsters, Miss Eileen Shean (plump and cosy, with a Pekinese) and Miss Edith Violet Baker (severe and thin, with a dachshund), who introduced the girls to ancient Greek at seven, for which Madelon, a budding classicist, was grateful. So family ties did not get in the way of Penelope's affair with Swingler.

Her apparently cavalier attitude to relationships was not unusual among that hedonistic *galère* of poets, artists and bohemians who hung around the Gargoyle Club in Soho, but she stood out among them with her striking looks. And she was about to be a published author: Spencer Curtis Brown told her in December 1945 that Fred Warburg would offer an advance of £50 for her novel, *Whom the Heavens Compel*, if she would change the awkward title to *Johanna*.

At Phyl and Nancy's that summer John too met Randall Swingler, who began to commission film reviews from him for *Our Time*. John was also having some success in selling short stories to the BBC. 'In the Making' was read on the wireless in February 1947; 'Little Screwball' was read in August. The October issue of *Harpers* magazine carried a photograph of a slim, bespectacled young man with full lips and a flop of wavy hair: 'John Mortimer is a new writer – gay, penetrating, and a stylist – whose novel *Charade*, "an ironic comedy of the manners and obsessions of the film fraternity", comes out this autumn. When he came down from Oxford he joined the Crown Film Unit. Now in the intervals of reading for the Bar he is writing another book.' (His second novel was already accepted, with a £50 advance.)

The writer of this caption, John's first publicity, was Jane Stockwood, lover of Phyl Duveen's daughter Anne. Clifford recorded John's progress as an author in his diary but made no comment. He would not be deflected from his plans for John to join him in chambers. Not surprisingly, John felt no enthusiasm for his Bar finals, which he was due to sit for the second time that October. 'And we hope he has passed this time,' wrote Clifford. By November they heard that he had a conditional pass only. He would have to retake Criminal Procedure on 3 December.

And so it was that on the unseasonably fine afternoon of 30 November, three days before his Criminal Procedure resit, John rode on a small, docile horse past Wyn's cottage and there espied Penelope Dimont, crouched in the garden, painting a coal scuttle. As he tells it, 'I leaned over the hedge and said, "If you want a decent bath, come up to my house." So she did.' (Penelope remembered it differently: she described looking up to see a horse looming over the hedge. 'After a moment's alarm I noticed a young man in glasses sitting on the horse. Presumably he introduced himself, saying he lived nearby with his parents and was a friend of Randall's. I told him I'd run out of bread. He offered to fetch me bread, and trotted away.') She often referred to the misleading impression her husband gave her by his bucolic appearance.

She happened to be alone – as John knew she would be: Randall had told him that the Dimont marriage was breaking up, and that Charles was now in Berlin. The coast was clear for the 'clever, skinny, excitable youth' to start calling on Mrs Dimont. He would collect her in his father's Morris Oxford and they would spend the evening on bar stools in pubs, where John was 'treated indulgently as the young Squire, a bit of a lad, always ready for a bottle of Scotch or can of black-market petrol'. Penelope would advise him in an auntly way as to which of his current girlfriends he should marry – 'Cornish Patsy' the tomboy, who was coming for Christmas, or Siriol Hugh-Jones, who worked on *Vogue* and was coming next Easter. (Siriol became, in time, one of Penelope's few close female friends.)

The Mortimer seduction technique is memorably recorded by Penelope: 'One night he stopped the car on a bumpy track over the Common and said, "What about a quick fuck and then home?"' No consummation ensued, though she had wished it. She writes that she made great efforts to be sexually attractive 'and none whatever to be lovable'.

That she found John attractive is not surprising. They had an exciting link, that both were about to have their first novels published: Penelope's *Johanna*, John's *Charade*. They had the same agent. John was a similar physical type to her husband (tall, bespectacled) and just as much fun, but he was younger and not a heavy drinker. He was also a 'welcome diversion' from Swingler: that affair was 'a solemn business, needing constant analysis'. But she was still in love with Swingler, and when he arrived they would go about as a threesome. The main appeal of John was that he was funny, companionable and knew how to enjoy himself. He made them hysterical with laughter with his impression of a testy old barrister (not having met his father, she did not realize the source). John's generic term for all amusement was 'sprat'. They later wrote a song about it:

> Let's have sprat
> At Cheadle Hulme in Cheshire.
> Let's have sprat
> At Weston-on-the-Sea!
> Let's have sprat,
> Oh Mother where's me hankie?
> Let's have sprat
> It's potted meat for tea.
>
> Dad's in the doghouse – Let's have sprat!
> Mum's in the pantry, cooking sprat for tea.

But just as their sprat began, Penelope discovered that she was again pregnant, by Swingler. (A man had only to hang his trousers over the end of the bed for Penelope to get pregnant, she always said: an explanation repeated by all her family. She never used her Dutch cap and she thought condoms clumsy and ridiculous.) She went up to London to meet Swingler, to tell him the news, and recalled sitting waiting in the Gargoyle Club with Dylan Thomas, who played Incy Wincy Spider with his fingertips up her arm. When Swingler arrived and she told him he was to be a father, he left without a word, and they did not meet for seventeen years.

In John's notebook from that period, containing some practice set-piece scenes, there is a passage of dialogue which appears to describe the evening when Penelope, abandoned by Randall Swingler, met John to discuss what to do. In these paragraphs Penelope is 'Constance', who is driving down to stay with her parents, and wires John to meet her for dinner in a Guildford hotel. Randall seems to have been renamed 'Quentin'.

She came about seven looking very tired. We went straight in to dinner and sat staring at our plates of brown soup. Constance's fingers worked hard on the bread on the cold tablecloth.

'Have you seen about a room?' she said.

'Why, are you staying?'

'I thought we might.'

I steadied myself by drinking some of the Châteauneuf du Pape I had ordered. It was cold, fizzy and very thin, like stale soda water.

'Where's Quentin?'

'At home.'

'Oh?'

'I'm . . . not going to see him any more.'

'Why not?'

'He says not.'

'Oh.'

Far away across the deserted dining room lighter doors led out to a ballroom. A band had started, blaringly but remote, like noisy but distant traffic. I could see RAF officers leaning against the walls and a girl taking tickets.

'You see I'm . . . well it's practically certain now.'

Two very cold looking tears appeared at the corners of Constance's eyes. I gave her my handkerchief to stop them falling into the Windsor soup and she sniffed.

'Oh hell. I'm sorry.'

'Yes. I suppose I shall have to have it seen to.'

'Will you?'

'Tell me. Have you ever got a girl . . . I mean, do you know?'

'Yes.'

'I suppose it happens to everyone sometime.'

'Practically.'

'And does it make you feel, I mean . . . bloody.'

'Terrible. As if the whole universe had been stopped and set going backwards.'

'Oh . . . John!'

She held my hand very tightly under the tablecloth and the waiter brought cod.

'So if you know you can help me?'

'Yes,' I said, 'I know. I can help you.'

John had already had the experience of Susan's abortion: he duly delivered Penelope to a woman in Chelsea. By Penelope's account, she bolted from the house, with John following her down the street, calling out, 'What's wrong? What's the matter?' She would have the baby after all. Penelope may have been wildly irresponsible about her fertility but she loved her babies. She enjoyed the whole business of pregnancy.

She was not yet in love, but John's company was consoling at this bleak juncture, and he made her laugh. And sex during pregnancy can be a heady, high-hormone business. Their relationship turned physical early in 1948, when she was pondering gloomily on the prospect of either returning, pregnant, to Charles or staying with her parents and competing with her mother over Julia. Clifford's diary records that on 9 January 1948, 'John has gone to Willersey Rectory today. We are making Seville orange marmalade.' Penelope records that one day, on impulse, she dressed Julia in her velvet-collared Daniel Neal coat and drove, in the battered

Austin car Kenneth Harrison had given her, to see John at Turville Heath Cottage. John's parents were away in Sussex. She was put, with Julia, in one of the three upstairs bedrooms; early-morning tea was served by the Austrian cook, Hansi, with bread and butter. But she found herself tiptoeing to John's room, leaving Julia asleep. His reaction, she records, was astonishment: 'Whatever else he may have felt, I know he was amazed.' She thought she had high principles about loveless sex. Yet now, as a still-married woman who was newly pregnant with a fourth child by a third man, she had a new lover.

John, sitting in the same house fifty years later, remembered it very well. They had spent the evening indulging in heavy petting. 'We were in the sitting room, and kissing by the fire, and she said "We must stop that, it's terribly *Yank*." She meant we had to go to bed.' Or, as the older lawyers in divorce courts used to refer to complete intercourse, *vera copula*.

Having passed his finals at last, John stood in Middle Temple Hall on Call Night on 26 January 1948, drank a glass of port and was called to the Bar. (As was Quentin Edwards, who had been reading for the Bar since demobilization from the navy in 1945.) And so John began to share his father's dim, dusty room in Dr Johnson's Buildings, 'our ruefully academic cloisters', overlooking a small courtyard with a single plane tree. He later described the scene: 'Staircases that smelt of damp stone, rusting wrought-iron, small criminals' wet mackintoshes. And the white powder of deserted wives. Tall, serious lawyers in bowler hats, with the appearance of never having been young.' The gas lamps were lit by a lamplighter with a long pole an hour before dark. During the week he stayed at 11 King's Bench Walk, the residential chambers Clifford had leased, and supervised the installation of a bathroom. Clifford paid him £5 a week, and began passing on briefs and paperwork, coming to London less often. The clerk 'Leonard' told John, 'We can't expect much work yet. We must wait until a few clients learn to like the cut of our jib.' But the years 1948–50 produced a bumper crop of former servicemen's divorce cases, as men came home and found their wives had flown. On a good day

John could do six 'undefendeds' in a bundle, at a guinea a time. It was, he said, 'like shelling peas'.

Every Friday evening, back from London, John would walk across fields and through woods from Turville Heath Cottage and arrive at Penelope's cottage, 'in a state of over-excited exhaustion to grapple with me,' as she put it, 'as I cooked or washed up or persuaded the children to bed.'

On 18 March, just before John's twenty-fifth birthday, *Charade* was published. For a first novel that was both slender and light, it received heavyweight praise and was a Book Society choice. The *Daily Express* declared, 'His name is new to you. It will become familiar.' Critics were impressed by the young John Mortimer's elliptical, living dialogue (a rare virtue), his uncommon gift for character-sketching, his astringent wit. *The Times Literary Supplement* discerned Proustian idioms and satirical pastiche. Elizabeth Bowen acclaimed his assurance, his lightness of touch and the sharpness of his characters: 'Not for nothing has Mr Mortimer dwelled in the pages of Dostoievsky and Proust – his characters carry worlds of shadow behind them; they haunt themselves and they haunt us.' In this torrent of extravagant praise it is hard to find a dissenting voice; but John never forgot the one which described the young author as 'fumbling beneath the skirts of sex which passes with the suburban mind for sophistication'.

On 19 June 1948, in Henley, at a Catholic nursing home, Penelope's fourth daughter, Deborah, was born, with a cloud of red hair and weighing just over four pounds. An 'over-active sex life' was the reason Penelope gave for the premature birth, and John was the baby's first visitor. Charles Dimont, now in London with the BBC's German Service at Bush House, agreed to assume paternity, so the baby remained Deborah Dimont until she was five. John found a house called Little Barlows, just by the church at Frieth and close to Turville, for £7 a week. Penelope moved in with the two youngest children and John began spending his weekends with them. 'John at Frieth, where the Dimonts have just moved,' notes Clifford, and on 18 September, the day before

Penelope's thirtieth birthday, 'John is today giving Penelope's children a tea-party and treasure hunt at Little Barlows.'

Penelope found it extraordinary that Clifford Mortimer, doyen of divorce lawyers, allowed his son to live with a thirty-year-old married mother of four. She sometimes overheard Clifford berating his son, for an ineffectual performance in court rather than the unsuitable liaison he had formed. She felt protective of John, and angry with Clifford, as she sat on the lawn at Turville Heath, listening 'through an open window to the old man's bellows, occasionally interrupted by moments of silence, which I supposed were John's mumbling defence'. Both parents, though fiercely loving, 'seemed to regard their only child as something of a joke'. And they couldn't understand how a woman with 'her own car and furniture' might see anything in their son. This confrontation made a good scene, where Clifford tries to dissuade Penelope from marrying his boy, in *A Voyage Round My Father*. But in fact the Mortimers liked Penelope. Clifford even became fond of her children, despite the unaccustomed noise and disturbance. They only objected to Smoocher, her Labrador, running riot in the garden.

That summer John and Penelope took the six-week-old baby Deborah for a week's holiday in Connemara. One day they went for a walk, leaving her in her cot, and when they returned found the cottage impenetrably locked, the baby screaming inside, Penelope's shirt soaked with milk. (A version of this scenario, with a child locked inside a holiday villa, was retold by her later in a short story.) But John's main recollection of this holiday was that Penelope became depressed and stood on the beach, tempted by thoughts of death, staring at the sea. This was not a seriously suicidal gesture; it reflected her post-partum turmoil, and the emotional complications of the previous year, when she was ending one marriage and about to embark on another.

Penelope said it took her eighteen months to fall in love with John. 'I could say that he appealed to the child in me,' she wrote, 'or the woman who had never grown up; that I played his forbidden games, shared many of his secrets, relished his sense of naughtiness; that I was at the same time a permissive mother allowing him through the locked door, where games were all the more fun for their spice of incest.' Penelope's maternal qualities had an irresistible appeal for John. She mused later that at this point John might have seen what he was letting himself in for: clearly a life 'full of . . . dramas'. But, as she wrote, 'He was talented, funny, spoiled me in many ways – breakfast in bed, cosseting, treats, presents – and was remarkably tolerant of children.' Apart from her mother, he was 'undoubtedly the most influential person in my life'.

Madelon recalled the summer holidays of 1948 as a happy time, when John and Penelope were writing songs and singing them round the piano. John wrote the words in the style of Noël Coward in his Matelot era, and Penelope wrote the tunes:

Doorstep Kiss

We held hands in the movies but the woman just behind
Didn't seem to care for us.
We tried to gaze at starlight but the glamour of the moon
Didn't seem to wear for us.
Now the evening's over and there's nowhere left, we know,
Yet we can't part, can't leave, can't go . . .

(*Refrain*)
Saying goodnight, and my heart is aching,
Out of the light for a last leavetaking
Can't we pretend that there's still tomorrow
A morning to end this evening's sorrow?

Telling my arms that they will not miss you.
Telling them lies, as I doorstep kiss you.

Limelight Child

Limelight child, I'll turn night to day for you,
Tools of our trade are just toys and play for you,
Dancers are dolls who swagger and sway for you,
Turn every way for you,

Always be gay for you,
Sleep till the last act's done . . .

Limelight child with clowns to care for you.
A mother to swing high up in the air to you,
Over the crowds to do and to dare for you
Sleep till the morning comes.

Your friends and your lovers will be musicians,
Tumblers and jugglers and tired magicians.

Smile as you swing to the farthest star
Brave as a bird on the parallel bar . . .

Hoping to write a musical revue, they played their songs to the
people at the Players' Theatre, under the arches at Charing Cross,
but nothing came of it. Instead, plays and musicals became a feature
of family life, with Madelon and Caroline eventually performing
scenes from Wilde and Sheridan. On Penelope's birthday that year,
in the garden at Frieth, there was a musical play, *The Chickens'
Birthday*, which the programme describes as 'presented by the
Misses Dimont, written by (and the programme illustrated by) J C
Mortimer, who also wrote the words to The Nibbling Song'.

John had been transformed 'from an unhappy young scriptwriter
and novelist into a middle-aged professional man with an overdraft,
a family of four and very little time to wonder if I were happy or
not'. He seemed to relish this sudden immersion in fatherhood
and domesticity. ('I know you had a lonely childhood,' remarked
one friend, 'but haven't you over-reacted?') He cooked the girls'
breakfasts, took them for walks, told them stories, wrote little plays.
Madelon wrote, many years later: 'What an extraordinary thing it
was for this young man, an only child of eccentric parents, to marry
a woman a few years older than himself with four obstreperous
daughters. He was plunged into a world of nappies and cornflakes,
tricycles and wellies, all totally removed from his own sheltered
upbringing. He didn't seem to mind.' On the contrary, he joined
in the family as one of the children. He wrote thirty years later in

Clinging to the Wreckage of the 'feeling of daring and excitement as I left the scene of my lonely childhood and joined what seemed like a great colony of people'.

John had certainly allied his life with that of a family as different as possible from his own. Penelope used this later in her novel *The Pumpkin Eater*: the heroine, Mrs Armitage, tells her shrink that her husband, Jake – based on John – fell in love with her while she was pregnant by her previous husband. 'I think he wanted to join us, that's all. I think he wanted . . . to belong to us. And he was good with the children, playing with them and reading them stories.'

John proposed, Penelope says, over sole Véronique at the Queen's Hotel in Sloane Square, telling her, 'If you marry me you'll have thirty acres' (the size of the garden at Turville Heath Cottage). But first there was the problem of getting Penelope divorced. They made several unsuccessful attempts to supply evidence of adultery. They went to Brighton and stayed in a hotel, trying to draw attention to themselves ('set the bedclothes on fire,' John said), but no chambermaid could be found who had noticed their presence. Finally, up the road to Frieth strode a private detective named Galvin. John carefully moved his dressing gown from its usual hook on the bathroom door to one next to Penelope's on their bedroom door. By the bed reposed a copy of *Rayden and Mortimer on Divorce*. The couple made a confession to Mr Galvin, and in due course Charles divorced Penelope. Charles appeared in court; Penelope did not. 'You're a free woman,' John told Penelope that evening.

In those early months of 1949, John was kept busy in court because Clifford became ill, first with flu, when he was given new-fangled penicillin injections, and then with a blockage in the arteries supplying his left hand and foot, which involved a spell in a nursing home in Reading. But he was back for Easter, for John's twenty-sixth birthday and the publication of his second novel, *Rumming Park*. John, Penelope and the children went to Turville

Heath Cottage for a treasure hunt and picnic tea party on Good
Friday, starting a family tradition.

The reviews for *Rumming Park* did not match those for the first
novel. This one was 'thin, muddled, untidy'. It was set in a Thames
Valley village, where an earnest young parliamentary candidate
from London and his beautiful wife come to live in the father-in-
law's house, among local characters such as the absent-minded
colonel, the vicar and the village moron. At the end the wife dies
in childbirth, at painful length. Reviewers advised him to steer
clear of tragic endings in future. His fan Elizabeth Bowen called it
'a gay novel with a crazy streak'. The *Daily Mail* chided him:
'Anxious not to be direct, he omits to be intelligible.'

Exactly six weeks after Penelope's decree nisi, they were married. Penelope went shopping with her mother in Park Lane and
bought a calf-length tartan skirt with a brown velvet jacket and 'a
sort of doge's hat' and the wedding took place on 27 August 1949
at Chelsea Register Office. It was a low-key affair. 'No marriage I
could possibly have contracted,' wrote John, 'could have been
more inconvenient from my father's point of view. He was the
doyen of the Matrimonial Bar . . .' Only their four parents, plus
Aunt Daisy and Paul Fletcher, were in attendance. There was a
party at 11 King's Bench Walk, 'for which we cut all available
flowers,' wrote Clifford, 'which Penelope arranged with great
effect'.

The newlyweds went briefly to St Malo in Brittany on honeymoon. It was paid for by Aunt Daisy, who also took in the
two eldest girls, Madelon and Caroline. Four months into her
widowhood, Daisy was living in solitary splendour in Sussex with
her hunting dogs, Bruce and Major, which lived outdoors and
expected a treat every time *The Archers* signature tune came on the
wireless. Landed with two girls of eleven and seven, Daisy took
them to the beach at St Leonard's, hiring a bathing hut, and gave
them chequebooks to practise handling money.

When the honeymooners returned on 4 September, they heard
that Charles Dimont, who had been in a depressed and fragile state
(apparently because Penelope refused him access to his daughters,

but still expected maintenance for them), had made a suicide attempt. He sent 'By the time you read this . . .' letters to both Penelope and Sonia Jenkins, a girl he had first met in Germany, where she was serving with the ATS. Sonia had been reunited with him at the 1948 Olympic Games, where Charles was broadcasting and she was working for a famous showjumper. At Charles's bedside in St Stephen's Hospital, Sonia and Penelope met for the first time. As Penelope describes it, she found 'her husband' being slapped back to life 'by a buxom girl called Sonia'. (Penelope places this account in 1948. Sonia Dimont is certain that it happened after Penelope and John's wedding.) Anyway, Charles revived, and very soon he and Sonia were married – a happy union, with three children, ending only with his death in 1993.

Meanwhile, John and Penelope left Little Barlows and moved into 11 King's Bench Walk, their first marital home. Exactly nine months after their wedding, Penelope's fifth child, and John's first, was born: another daughter, Sally Veronica Mortimer.

6. Paterfamilias, *inter alia*

The new stepfather was already adept at amusing Penelope's girls with river trips and play-acting. He now discovered the gratification of real fatherhood: a baby in whom he might recognize something of himself. Sally was much cuddled and loved. As an adult, she recalled that John was more indulgent with her than with her half-sisters. Penelope put her husband's special feeling for his own child into a short story: 'Bessie was his own child, his darling . . . His daughter was everything he loved.' Sally was born at Queen Charlotte's on 28 May 1950, two days after the publication of John's third novel, and the day after Kathleen's birthday. Kathleen too felt keenly that her first grandchild was a *Mortimer*.

And John and Penelope were happy, a fact often later overlooked. 'We were in love, ambitious and in charge of five children: those are the things that motivated our lives,' Penelope wrote. For her, motherhood predominated: 'Work was by no means a priority.' Thanks to the human tendencies to fall out of love and to die, John was handling an increasing supply of undefended divorces and contested wills, guaranteeing income and material to inspire a new novel every year. The future they foresaw was a more glamorous, more spacious version of the present. The Temple flat consisted of a large living room, one double bedroom for the girls, and a sort of cupboard with window, containing nothing but John and Penelope's bed. The new baby's cot stood in the cupboard by day and in the living room at night.

In the gardens below the flat, a Peter Pan statue holds a book inscribed 'Lawyers too were children once', but the Temple was uncongenial to family life, not designed to be festooned with drying nappies, or welcoming to the sound of children's cries. There were complaints from the tenants downstairs, lawyers all, about the rocking of the rocking horse and the soapsuds in the drain. Penelope's next novel would open with a husband being berated by the concierge of their block of flats: 'The management does not like perambulators to be kept in the halls of the flats, sir. It creates a bad impression . . .'

As well as the rent-free flat from Clifford, they enjoyed largesse from others: Charles still paid school fees, while Mrs Fletcher and Sonia Dimont supplied child-care and home-sewn children's clothes. Kenneth Harrison's munificence provided them with a bolthole from the Temple flat. In the summer of 1950 he bought the freehold of the primitive, run-down Burnt House Farm near Dunmow in Essex, for the Mortimers' use at weekends and holidays. Electricity came from a generator, firewood had to be collected from the woods and it was miles from any station, but Harrison also presented them with 'Henry', a Ford V8 station wagon. (He later gave Julia a bicycle, which slightly puzzled the others. Not until Madelon went up to Cambridge did she notice that Julia strikingly resembled the lay dean of King's.)

Madelon had been sent, a scholarship pupil, to board at the Alice Ottley School for Girls in Worcester, of which her father's wife, Sonia, was an alumna. Caroline and Julia became day-girls at the Town and Country, a progressive school in Hampstead. This left Deborah and the newborn Sally at home during the day – and Deborah, they hoped, would be taken off their hands by Granny Fletcher. But it was Sonia and Charles Dimont who took Deborah to live with them in Littlehampton in the autumn of 1951. As soon as the Mortimers had their own house, Penelope took Deborah back, to Sonia's intense dismay.

Madelon, who since the age of four had been informed at the end of each school term where she would be going for the holidays, effectively had two families. In her boarding years she began to feel like a Mortimer family acquaintance, being introduced to the current au pair and the latest dog. Clever, sensitive and imaginative, she was still trying to be Mrs Goodhouse, keenly wanting approval. When John first arrived in the family, she had gone through a phase of thinking she hated her stepfather: she remembered sitting under a rhododendron bush at Frieth, full of angry feelings, then confiding in her gran, who didn't keep the secret and told Penelope. But this was less a feeling against John than a wish to take the side of her deposed father. Now John and Penelope allowed her the eldest daughter's privilege of sitting up and eating supper with them. When she was confirmed, at fourteen, she was surprised and pleased that John, a non-believer as she knew, turned up for the service in draughty Worcester Cathedral, especially since he had a temperature of 103 at the time.

In these years John devised a routine that started before anyone else awoke, allowing two quiet hours to work on his current novel. After breakfast, his long-legged stride would take him up the cobbled lane to his chambers in two minutes, so he arrived before the charwomen. Elderly barristers today relate how touching it was to see John steering his blind old father across Fleet Street from Middle Temple Lane to the Royal Courts of Justice. Penelope typed up the Discretion Statements and found these fascinating: 'Unimaginable brutalities and perversions,' she wrote, 'lurked inside briefs tied in chewed pink ribbon.' (John had a habit of chewing his ribbons, like Skeffington, QC, the libel lawyer in his later novel *Dunster*.)

John always found the paperwork – listing charges and drafting defences – deeply tedious. As he would summarize it: '"Charge of cruelty: flung the toast-rack in 1932." *Everything* was cruelty: talking too much was "incessant nagging"; not talking was "long periods of sullen silence". If you had sex it was "inconsiderate sexual demands". If you didn't it was "wilful refusal to grant conjugal rights" and you had to get a doctor to say your health was affected.'

During that first year of marriage and barristerhood, his dawn lucubrations produced a third novel. 'I have always found it diffi-cult to write directly about myself,' as he wrote in the booksellers' organ, *Smith's Trade News*, 'but the books I have written have all . . . dealt with experiences of my own or had backgrounds from my own life.' John plundered his recent experience in *Answer Yes or No*. It is the tale of a young barrister named Ransom, prone to arriving at court hung-over and ill-prepared, who becomes, while conducting divorce cases, a co-respondent himself. Ransom's sentiments, as he discovers the limits of a lawyer's capacity actually to help people run their lives, were John's. John would go every Wednesday evening to give pro bono advice at a legal aid centre at Bethnal Green, a room smelling of old gym shoes, where he met sad tenants threatened by landlords, and deserted wives with ashen-faced, grimy children. He learned to 'speak client': to remember that a lawyer's lunch is a client's 'dinner', a lawyer's magazine a client's 'book'. A lawyer should curb his feelings and consider cases dispassionately, but Ransom/John felt waves of sympathy and even affection for his East End clients, for the 'old men and dropsical women, their complexions greenish with poverty'. East London seemed 'a great pile of junk, a mess of shops and houses and sprawling, untidy streets which lay an intolerable weight on its inhabitants, pinning them helplessly down . . . Fathers seduced their daughters, wives robbed their husbands, children were tortured for screaming in a room where four people slept to a bed.' Lack of money made them helpless, John realized. He could do no more good than a priest or a psychiatrist; he was just a sympathetic stranger who listened to their woes. How could the law help the feckless, the hopeless, the mad? Where was the wisdom, the impulse to social justice in the legal profession? In *Answer Yes or No*, Ransom listens to venerable old lawyers in the dining hall of his inn, brilliant minds that could sway juries or enthral the House of Lords. 'As a matter of fact my wife is very fond of rice pudding,' one barrister is saying. At the legal aid centre Ransom has been facing a battered wife, asking her, 'Is there anywhere you can go – your mother perhaps?' 'Mother! she's just got the one room, and I've six kids . . .'

Critics were rightly impressed by the assurance and maturity of this young writer, barely twenty-seven. Antonia White, reviewing the book in the *New Statesman*, identified the legal background as John's trump card as a novelist. She would even have preferred 'a little less love and any amount more law'.

★

After two years of Essex weekends, it was time to find a family-sized London home. Jim Holland, who had a semi-detached Victorian house at Swiss Cottage, was separating from his wife. A swap was arranged: the freehold of Burnt House Farm was exchanged for the Hollands' seven-year lease, at a peppercorn ground rent, on 23 Harben Road, NW6. For the next thirteen years, until 1965, this was the Mortimer family home. By the 1980s, one of the routines in John's 'Mortimer's Miscellany' gig was his tale of how he used to leave home every morning in a dishevelled state – chin bleeding, children sickly, baby screaming, au pair tearfully giving notice, piles of bills to trip over on the doormat – and go and advise middle-aged company directors on how to sort out their marriages. There was some truth in this description of mornings at Harben Road in the mid-1950s.

Their house and its three neighbours, a terrace truncated by bomb sites, were about to be surrounded by hideous new blocks of flats, typical of those thrown up everywhere in the 1960s. Number 23 had a sunny south-facing sitting room, across the width of the house, with tall sash windows, a coal fire and a radiogram for their four long-playing records: Judy Garland, Noël Coward, Lotte Lenya singing Kurt Weill, and Ella Fitzgerald. Family meals were taken in the basement, an original Victorian kitchen leading into the garden. But eventually, when the gloomy front dining room was transformed by Terence Conran into a trendy farmhouse-style pine kitchen, the basement became the 'playroom', littered with outgrown shoes and dolls' prams and dead radios, Penelope's 'symbol of the subterranean chaos I longed to sort out'. A small room looking out on a brick wall was variously the help's room and John's study. Upstairs were three light, high-ceilinged bedrooms and one bathroom, a confusion of toothbrushes and rubber toys; the separate loo was piled with bound volumes of *Punch* from around 1900. The attic rooms were occupied first by a lodger, later by teenagers and au pairs.

In a novel later, Penelope wrote a breakfast-table scene.

'I can't find my tennis racquet and if I go without it they will send me home, so where's my tennis racquet?'

'My overall isn't marked and they say if I go once more with an unmarked overall they will send me home, so will you mark it?'

'I have lost my gym shoes.'

'I have lost my French grammar.'

'You stole my pen.'

'I did not steal your pen.'

'I haven't got any socks, someone's taken my socks.'

'I feel sick.'

'I need a loop on my swimming towel to hang it up with.'

'I have lost my library book, will you write a note?'

The racquet, the overall, the gym shoes, the grammar, the pen, the socks, the loop, the library book, the note would all be sorted out, Penelope wrote, whereupon the house would fall silent, 'until the baby cries upstairs'.

For years after she left the Harben Road house, it continued to haunt Penelope's dreams. 'Every drawer is a confusion of knives and cotton reels and spoons and string and skewers and the tops of paste pots.' Revisiting it in a 1974 novel, she explores the basement: 'a tangle of bicycles, some without handlebars, nearly all without chains . . . broken pushchairs and a pram full of rubbish . . . I open a door and a hundred, two hundred, shoes fall down on me: laced shoes, strapped shoes, sandals, slippers, dancing pumps with straps to go round the ankle, muddy shoes, new shoes, Wellington boots, football boots, plimsolls . . .'

Swiss Cottage, after the sterile Temple flat and the primitive Essex farm, seemed to the Mortimers madly cosmopolitan, awash with *mittel*-European refugees and studded with patisseries, delicatessens and boulangeries, and a shop selling every type of coffee. The Odeon still had a Wurlitzer. And on the Finchley Road there was the John Barnes department store with its food hall, haberdashery and shoe department with X-ray machine. In the café the children could have tea, in scalding metal teapots, served by 'tired, kindly women in little pinafores and frilled caps'. The store (now Waitrose) became their village green, their marketplace. The Town and Country was nearby. Previously Caroline and Julia had taken two buses to get there from Fleet Street; now they could walk across the Finchley Road.

Sometimes Julia's father, Kenneth Harrison, would turn up on the doorstep, in three-piece suit and bowler hat, announcing, 'Just coming to see the family.' In the midst of their domestic mayhem, he seemed comically fastidious and proper.

In the summer of 1952, John and Penelope, still very much in love, took a dilapidated wooden bungalow on an island in the Thames, a few hundred yards from Henley Bridge, for the month of August. It was an interlude of sunshine, an adventure. The house could only be reached by boat or punt. John hired a motor launch and cruised past all the houses with lawns running down to the river, to the small stucco Palladian folly, built by James Wyatt, on Temple Island below the bridge. They watched the procession of skiffs with wrought-iron seats, and ancient steamers carrying day-trippers, and attended 'Flannel Dances' at the town hall on Saturday nights. Friends visited, including the political journalist James Cameron (whose daughter was Caroline's best friend), bringing a gross of tinned frankfurters. Every day Penelope would carry her typewriter and a card table to the river bank and get on with her novel, her first for seven years. While she tapped away, John scribbled. His work in progress was his fourth novel, *The Narrowing Stream*. Both novels were set in Henley. Both featured an errant husband.

Meanwhile, life at Turville Heath Cottage remained an imperturbable tableau of domestic and horticultural contentment. 'Two wicker chairs sent out for repair. We bought two coal-hods for the kitchen. Smith has planted the white colchicums which Daisy brought.' At Daisy's expense, they redecorated John's former bedroom, where Deborah and Sally, too young for the perilously river-bound bungalow, stayed. The garden at Turville Heath Cottage became their playground, and when the rest of the family arrived, the dining-room table seated nine, as it rarely had before. That summer there were many teas in the garden: cucumber sandwiches with the crusts cut off, and scones with strawberry jam and Cornish cream, and chocolate cake. Clifford was still a dominating presence; Madelon never felt completely at ease there. Was she holding her knife and fork the wrong way? Despite knowing he couldn't see her, she was disconcerted by the old man's blindness. 'You couldn't laugh at it, you couldn't laugh with it, you couldn't commiserate. You couldn't mention it at all. Everyone pretended it didn't exist. I'd never met a blind person before and it was alarming. I thought perhaps if I kept very quiet, he wouldn't know I was there. But he would ask Kathleen or John to tell him who was there. It was like being summoned into the presence of authority. It was almost as if he had to live up to being the actor-manager of his own establishment.' They became accustomed to his bellows of, 'Kath! Kath! Where are you?' across the lawn. If kept waiting, 'Is there any danger of getting something to eat?' Clifford would demand, glaring blindly about.

Julia, not old enough to be intimidated by Clifford's manner, was happy to clamber on his scratchily tweed-trousered knee as he sat by the fireplace, freshly shaved. She would take out his fob watch on the chain: whenever a child blew on it, its lid would magically fly open, as Clifford pressed a secret button. Julia was allowed to eat his leftover buttered toast, and he taught her to play whist with his Braille cards. All the girls learned to walk the herbaceous borders, holding Clifford's arm, painting the picture for him. 'And he was always spouting poetry,' Julia recalled, 'like Dad.'

Turville Heath weekends were associated for the girls with John's taking them punting (sometimes falling in) and on cross-country walks, and cooking sausages on bonfires. The older girls might stay with Aunt Daisy, who had moved to a house at Benson with a lawn stretching down to the river. John would rouse them with a rhyme:

> 'Come and greet the shining morn!
> Come and greet Aunt Daisy;
> For the child has ne'er been born
> Who could be so lazy.'

When they went back to Harben Road after the holiday, Penelope found 'an indefatigable little woman' who lugged coal and scrubbed floors, enabling her to write. But even with help, she was always occupied. She darned and made the children's clothes, and her own, on an old Singer sewing machine, a wedding present of her mother's from 1910. She collected Deborah and Sally from nursery school, before Caroline and Julia arrived for tea. At 6 p.m. she put the younger ones to bed, balancing her gin and orange on the edge of the bath, listening for John's key in the lock. Sometimes they escaped to the pub or the Odeon. They had no television until 1960, when it was installed in the nursery. John worked at home on his briefs, on his lap, chewing his pink tapes, reading out anything that might amuse them all. Pamela Swingler, wife of Humphrey, was impressed to watch one evening when John arrived home and cooked supper for everyone; but Penelope had 'done all the scullion work' – peeled and chopped the vegetables.

Summarizing their first years of married life, Penelope wrote: 'We make love, we quarrel, we make it up, we quarrel, we make it up, we make love.' Dramatic rows ended in passionate reconciliations. But despite the scenes it witnessed, she felt a visceral attachment to her first London family house. 'I loved the house always,' she wrote, 'and never blamed it for anything that happened there.' Hearing their blazing row one night, Madelon rushed downstairs shouting, 'Stop it stop it stop it stop it stop it' – unable to bear the thought that this marriage might go wrong. In 1953, Penelope decided that a multi-named family was too complicated: all the girls except Madelon became officially the Mortimer girls, and John became 'Dad'.

In that year, John's behaviour changed. He 'began coming home later, making furtive phone calls, being extravagantly affectionate for no reason'. The object of his distraction was Patricia Lyttelton, née Braithwaite, recently divorced wife of the jazz musician Humphrey Lyttelton. John would meet her at the French Club in St James's, telling his clerk he had to leave chambers early. He even brought 'Lyttelton', as Penelope referred to her, home to

Harben Road, as if hoping for his wife's approval. Twenty years later, Penelope tried to analyse this by using it in a novel: 'Even at the height of his uxoriousness, when [his wife] entirely possessed him, he dreamed of asking her permission to go to bed with someone else, of bringing his mistresses home to nursery tea in full assurance of her blessing.' In that novel, *The Home*, the husband starts, after a few years of marriage, 'cautiously realising his fantasies' by having affairs 'which were not wholly consummated until he could present them, shy-eyed and pallid with guilt', to his wife. Empowered by the certainty of his underlying devotion to her, the heroine of that novel would destroy the interloper, so that her husband felt 'afraid of her for doing what he had mutely asked her to do'. But in reality Penelope reacted to the Lyttelton affair with a grief and jealousy that bewildered John. He seemed to feel somehow let down.

During this episode John's fourth novel, *Like Men Betrayed*, came out. The title comes from Wordsworth:

> Action is transitory – a step, a blow.
> The motion of a muscle – this way or that –
> 'Tis done, and in the after-vacancy
> We wonder at ourselves like men betrayed . . .

It was an enjoyable novel but clearly written in haste. On page one a gentlemen's club is described: 'Crammed into furniture seemingly selected at random from station waiting-rooms, his club had never seemed to him a particularly impressive place.' A club crammed into furniture? Did the typist misread his handwriting, 'into' for 'with'? A proficient copy-editor might have excised otiose metaphor – 'Approached by a flight of stone stairs to a doorway that seemed copied from the west entrance of Salisbury Cathedral by a jobbing builder with a squint' – or ugly phrasing – 'Among the plastic curtains, birchwood furniture and built-in cupboards, the Austrian girl stood rubbing the sleep out of her eyes and looking faintly dirty' – which might have been effortfully translated from a foreign tongue.

But the prose springs to vigorous life with the almost Dickensian description of Worsfold, a country village of stone cottages and difficult roads, 'far out of London, too far for the stockbrokers, popular novelists or matinée idols to find cottages, so far that a man would only go there to retire or die'. (It could be Dunmow, site of Burnt House Farm, where this novel was written.) The village 'preserved every discomfort of the English way of life as lived during the closing years of the last century . . . There was not a door in Worsfold that fitted, and the wind usually came from the east; there was not a boiler in Worsfold that worked, and the bath water stemmed from a metallic quarry which made it dark brown as well as cold. Mains electricity, sanitation, water, to these the inhabitants of Worsfold were strangers . . . Only the horses, sleek, fat, every day meticulously groomed . . . only the horses undeniably prospered.' Its cast of well-realized characters, notably the gin-swigging matriarch, Mrs Hume-Monument, were declared by John's publisher, F. T. Smith, editor-in-chief at Collins, to be reminiscent of Graham Greene, Evelyn Waugh and Joyce Cary.

A lifetime of feature articles now opened up, written by journalists in breathless awe of a barrister who 'spends most of his spare time writing', and riveted by the size of his family. 'He lives in a large dilapidated house, has a small dilapidated motor car. His wife is also a writer. He says he works most of the time but occasionally enjoys a little cooking.' He was photographed in bow tie and waistcoat, with Sally, 'the youngest of his five daughters', in *Vogue*. Repeatedly, John described how he wrote early in the morning before the children surfaced, and how he found the profession of the law 'more exciting, dramatic and consistently extraordinary than any other', introducing him to all manner of folk, so he knew how they behaved at times of bewilderment or crisis. 'Now that I am 30 I write because I want to describe the smell, the feel of life as I see it being lived now, in 1953, among the people I think I know.' A writer ought to deal with affairs of the world, keeping his writing as 'a secret vice, a sort of clandestine love affair, for which he preserves his moments of humanity'. Chekhov, for example, was wise to carry on with his medical practice.

But what intrigued the press most was the idea of two novelists writing side by side. To point up this picturesque situation, their two Henley novels came out on the same day in May 1954, when John presented Penelope with a little china house festooned in lilac, with a rustic couple at either side of the door. The double-publication presents a unique opportunity to compare the two as novelists. It is a contest which Penelope's *A Villa in Summer,* a Book Society choice masquerading as her first novel – it was her first under the name of Penelope Mortimer – wins. She grudgingly thought her book was 'just about all right' and professed herself mystified by the enthusiasm of the reviews. 'A brilliantly successful attack on one of the most challenging fortresses of fiction: the spiritual and physical relationship of married life,' said one. 'Masterly in its technical skill and imaginative truth.' Madelon, away at school, read both novels and felt immensely proud of her mother and stepfather, whose sophisticated life was so far removed from the Alice Ottley School for Girls.

A Villa in Summer remains, half a century later, worth reading. It is also a biographical source, since Penelope wrote little that was not based on her life with John. Andrew, the husband, is a divorce lawyer who deals with clients like 'Mrs Travers, whose husband was it seemed a sexual maniac, who had sometimes turned on the light when she was clothed only in her nightdress . . .' The villa, where Andrew leaves his wife, Emily, to cope with the children for the summer while he commutes to London, is a cottage named Hassocks at 'Manningford, near Hamley'. It's the kind of place where film companies seek the soul of Britain, peopled by recognizable characters, including an outspoken mother-in-law named Flavia, who greets them with 'Hullo, you two. Quarrelling?'

Quarrels, followed by craven apologies, punctuate their lives. In writing these scenes, Penelope pillaged her life with John. Andrew and Emily lie in bed together, wakeful and apart. 'She only knew how to be happy with him and they were, she was certain, no longer happy.' She did still love him, and he her: 'Nevertheless, they loved each other' is a refrain. When she flares up at him, he is hurt and puzzled, unaware of any cause: 'Nothing had happened. He had, as far as he knew, done nothing wrong.' She chops wood angrily, ignoring his offers to help; just as, after a quarrel, John would follow Penelope pathetically around the kitchen, saying to any assembled children, 'Isn't Mummy looking beautiful?' while Penelope icily refused to be flattered, and the bewildered children wondered whose side they should be on.

In John's *The Narrowing Stream*, a thriller, the husband's involvement with a woman living on a houseboat (who is found murdered) is not analysed at all. By contrast, in *A Villa in Summer*, Penelope writes with understanding of Andrew, who, while flirting with a girl called Alice, resents the fact that he is giving his wife reason to be jealous. 'He loved her [Emily], but that was beside the point. She stood, determined, possessive, unhappy, between him and the thing he wanted to discover. Alice was unexpected, mysterious, a challenge. He should be free to find out what she was, to explore something new, to add, in some way, to himself. He resented, bitterly, that Emily should stand in his way.' Surely, his wife 'should understand that a man had to investigate, experiment, widen his horizons beyond the small, familiar limits of his wife's body. It didn't mean that he loved her any less. It simply meant that he wanted something else as well.'

When he confesses that he wants to sleep with Alice, his wife is incredulous – 'he was the same man who had been to bed with her last night, kissed her this morning' – and contemptuously flings at him the same question that Penelope hurled at John: 'Are you asking for my permission? Is that why you told me? Do you want me to say go on, have an affair with her, give you my blessing?'

The impression is of a couple locked together, convinced that they cannot live apart, uttering spiteful truths or paralysed in silence. In the summer of 1954, when the Lyttelton affair was finished but had holed the barque of their marriage, the Mortimers set off abroad for a second honeymoon, bent on reconciliation. The children were installed at their old school, Ballard Point in Dorset, with the Fletcher grandparents in charge. Driving across Europe, Penelope managed to overturn the car in a Swiss valley between Besançon and Arona. They stayed five days at the Rome apartment of Nigel Heseltine, an old boyfriend of Penelope's from the 1930s, and dined with the novelist Paul Potts at Trattoria Alfredo. John was preparing a radio talk about Rome, which he broadcast that year, hymning 'the city which raises a golden head amid the neighbouring stars'. Later, Penelope published a short story, 'Second Honeymoon'. It opens in a hotel room, blue sky outside, church bells like gongs. 'Well,' asks the husband, 'how does it feel to wake up in Rome?' 'Exactly as it feels waking up anywhere else,' replies the wife grumpily. 'What's so bloody wonderful about it?' Clearly the problems of the past year had not receded.

In her story they pick pointless quarrels with one another, invent retrospective jealousies. 'I bring you away on a highly expensive holiday,' reproaches the exasperated husband, 'and you behave like a child!' Although she is a woman of exceptional beauty and perpetual youth, her reflection in shop windows reveals 'an un-loved, unloving woman dressed (God knows, she thought, why I bother) in smart linen'. But Penelope gave 'Second Honeymoon' an unusually happy ending, with the couple skipping down the street. And the reality was that in Besançon, that August 1954, John and Penelope enjoyed a fruitful rapprochement: here they conceived their only son.

On 26 April 1955, Penelope was in a nursing home in Avenue Road, St John's Wood, waiting to give birth, writing lovingly to John. She was thinking back over their life together in the shape of a novel. 'The beginning of it was you sitting in Frieth garden with your shirt off & lying on the ants, which makes me smile even now.' She told John how much she loved him, 'because that's what it all comes down to in the end', and

> how pleased & proud, above all proud, I am to be having your baby; and how it's so different in every possible way from ever before, and all life is so different, & me too. And how it's all because of you. If I say this is the first baby I've ever had, the first time I've been in love, married, the first time I've understood even the first thing about being alive, it IS true, because before I must really

have been half-witted, creeping about in a fog. You see all this is only that I love you so, that's all. It's really the beginning & end of everything.

Oh darling I hope when you come you won't look too worried, miserable. I'm just as much in the dark as you, & don't know what to say, only alternate between hopes & fears as the hours trail by, & try to think of it in terms of lives, not minutes. We'll be back in bed together, holding tight, soon, and Toby sleeping independent & good in his own bed, & all the sprat in the world in front of us. I love you darling. Be well and be happy. Pen.

On the morning of 27 April 1955 the baby was born. Their second child and her sixth was not named Toby after all, but Jeremy John Clifford, an exquisite boy with long dark eyelashes and rosebud mouth. The next day, John wrote to Penelope:

My darling Pen: No-one else could have written so beautiful and sweet a letter as yours, and I am lucky to have such a wife, a son and a letter all at once. I agree so much with what you say. I feel that this time, of loneliness and cold grey bedrooms for me and for you, is a great, valuable pause in the curious course of our lives. Like you I don't want to discuss schools or income tax or mortgages, these things seem to me artificial at most times and especially now. There are so many ways of living, but the important things have never really eluded us, even at our most John Barnes moments there is a saving grace in the dark hall, the bed which will never be twin beds, the primitive life in the upstairs rooms. I think, more and more as I read through what you have written, that you are nicer than I am, more integrated, less nervous, more satisfactory in every way. It is true that I have to read Petitions to the blare of Alma Cogan, that I like the inane chatter of people and get up at six in the morning, being too restless to stay in bed. I am consumed with longing, however, for the great excitements, which . . . are concentrated on you – on those very dark nights that are ahead of us and also, and I hope you won't mind it being part of the same thing, a future containing a few bull-fights, some dark olés, a cold, not too comfortable Spanish hotel. Now, with a son, with all we have had and done in the not many years we have been together, I feel so much that we have reached a time when our happiness can be completely, unhesitatingly real for us both – always. In the times we've had there has been so much to worry about – even, perhaps, the worry of will we ever get a boy? Now we've got one, got everything we can ever deserve or want, we must enjoy our luck. All this is to say that I think you are splendid, beautiful, lovely in every way. There is nothing to be regretted in the lonely nights that will soon be over, they have brought a completion to one part of what we hoped for in that field at Frieth when I, no doubt, was behaving with maddening slowness in making up my mind . . . I long for some great adventure, to start out with you for somewhere very old and distant, to know that our son is growing up, every day older. In a way now he is born I feel we are more free to be happy, to love one another, and certain now, free of anxiety, that what we chose was right and we shall be together always . . .'

7. Love and Lizards

In family lore, the longed-for boy is known as an oh–thank–God, as in 'five daughters and then an oh–thank–God'. But Jeremy's arrival, bringing broken nights, was a mixed blessing after the relative freedom of the past four years. 'I was harassed, dull company, trying to write another novel, reluctant even to go to the pub,' Penelope later recalled. 'John, who had spent the greater part of his twenties being a husband, father and stepfather, was restless, uneasy about wasted time and opportunities.'

'Bennies and Dexies', the amphetamines Benzedrine and Dexedrine, alias pep pills or uppers, were handed out like sweeties by GPs in the 1950s. Using them exacerbated John's air of agitation, but gave Penelope 'something I lacked that other women presumably had – frivolity, the ability to adapt, to take life as others found it'. They would leave Caroline to babysit, returning in the small hours, when Penelope would wakefully write. After two hours' sleep she would see the family off to school. Another pill kept her going till mid-afternoon, before fetching the children and awaiting the 'longed-for yet dreaded' sound of John's key in the lock.

Their partying circle included Humphrey and Pamela Swingler, Siriol Hugh-Jones and her husband, the television journalist Derek Hart, the poet James Michie and his Jamaican wife, Daphne, Wolf and Ann Mankowitz, the writer William Sansom and his wife, Ruth, the actress Moyra Fraser and Michael Fenton. They danced to Charles Trenet, Fats Waller, Louis Armstrong. Penelope, slightly older than the other women in their circle, still looked as gamine as Audrey Hepburn. At the Caprice, lunching with Michael Joseph, with Charlie and Oona Chaplin at the next table, she was mistaken for Hepburn by a waiter. Such attention was 'irresistible'.

Penelope's beauty had always suggested an inviolable power

over men. After the Lyttelton affair her self-esteem was bruised and she behaved 'as if she had lost an empire', John said. But she was also being provided with material for the next four novels.

Material: that is what their lives became. 'It's probably as difficult for two writers as it is for two actors to be married to each other,' John wrote in his memoirs. 'Penelope and I were grasping for the same events . . . to write about them as though they were ours alone. She wrote wonderfully, and got great pleasure from describing the awfulness and absurdity of her experiences . . . We lived together dramatically, often sliding to the edge of some dangerous precipice.'

Early in 1956, Penelope slid over the edge. Madelon and Caroline got home to Harben Road one evening to find a distraught John announcing that she was in the Royal Free Hospital and it was 'touch and go'. Madelon's first reaction was shock that Penelope could have said a casual goodbye that day, knowing what she was going to do. 'Also considerable fury,' she recalled, 'that she should cop out like that and leave the baby and the children to John and me.'

John rang his parents and engaged a trained German nanny named Helga, who was sent with baby Jeremy, plus Deborah and Sally, to Aunt Daisy's, while the eldest three stayed at home with John. Everyone agreed that Penelope's overdose was a severe case of postnatal depression. An escape was prescribed. She took Caroline to Igls in the Austrian Alps, where Caroline went shooting down terrifying runs 'like a little insect on the frozen blue slope'. During their talks, Penelope told her about having been in Nazi-occupied Austria. When one day there was no letter from John, Caroline said consolingly that John was 'always full of good intentions'. When John did write, he reported that Madelon (at seventeen) was in love with an aspiring young artist, the son of a psychiatrist, and reassured Penelope that 'I love you to the point of imbecility.' He said, 'I feel sure we are all embarking on a better, saner kind of life.' One solution was more household help: he engaged a cook and a new char. Arriving home, Penelope heard the good news that Madelon had got into Cambridge to read law.

Soon after her return Penelope started having regular sessions with a small moustachioed Freudian psychoanalyst. Yet, despite her ability to express her own feelings with courageous honesty, she was not a good candidate for analysis: her 'sense of the ridiculous got in the way'. Also, she told her diary, 'the probing torch lights up the dark places where words used to come from. Understanding may increase, but – and I'm ashamed to be so corny – poetry diminishes, can only grow in the dark, perpetually fed but always unattended. Oh but what's all this fine talk about poetry? . . . I heartily dislike what I write. Before, it was one of the few things in which I had any pride.' A course of electro-convulsive treatment, then the recommended remedy for depression, was proposed and she sacked her analyst.

One weekend in March, John took his parents the proofs of his latest novel, *Three Winters*: his best so far and the most autobiographical. It related three episodes in a man's life, taken directly from John's own, during the winters of 1935, 1942 and 1956: his lonely childhood, staying with his parents at the grand house of an eccentric uncle and aunt in a seaside town; his wartime youth in the same town, where, unfit for active service, he works in a documentary film unit and falls in love with the local doctor's daughter; and finally, in his thirties, when he has been ten years married. They are in love, but their marriage is a battlefield: the wife is difficult and neurotic, a legacy of her father's abuse of her.

Penelope's father, now retired, had come to live in Cricklewood, north-west London, where he and Gran Fletcher shared a house with their son, Paul, and his new wife, Jay Black. (Clifford had conducted Mrs Black's divorce from her first husband, a doctor described in tabloid headlines as 'the Beast of Lower Beeding'. As John said, divorce judges then liked to label the guilty party with names like 'the Catford Cleopatra', aiming for lurid headlines.) Arthur Fletcher, the sad old vicar, died in May and was cremated at Golders Green. Penelope found herself mourning him more than she had ever thought she would.

A few weeks earlier, Penelope described in her diary the domestic scene on a Sunday evening. She sat smoking and drinking gin and Dubonnet. She imagined an umbilical cord from her chair along the hall, up the stairs and through the bars of Jeremy's cot. She reproached herself for the 'rubbish' women's journalism she had agreed to write, inventing bogus problems and solutions for an agony column. But she was consoled by the prospect of summer. 'The autumn, however prosperous and happy our life, is full of foreboding . . . The secret, awful winter life is over, thank God, for another six months.' But she could not muster the confidence to write. On some days – a classic symptom of depression – she would drive to John Barnes 'and walk round the bales of material, feeling it, touching it; thinking, I know quite well I shan't buy any. I stand in front of the lectern holding a book of patterns; turn the pages thinking, I don't want to buy a pattern . . . Someday I shall write about this.' (Penelope later added the words 'Pumpkin Eater' in brackets here, and readers may recognize the scene from her 1962 novel, in which the clinically depressed Mrs Armitage wanders through Harrods in aimless despair.)

Her latest novel, *The Bright Prison*, written between 1953 and the end of 1955, had not been a success. Her publisher's remedy was to suggest that the Mortimers write a travel book together, about Italy – 'the only way we could afford to go there,' John said – and specifically about holidaying abroad with children, still a daring adventure in those pre-package days. They signed to write *A Journey to Italy* for an advance of £300. Collaboration was not new to them; one of them sometimes started or finished the other's story for a women's magazine.

So at the beginning of August they flew to Naples: a gang of nine including the sterling Helga. On the same flight were the hilariously ostentatious Sir Bernard and Lady Docker and – in the girls' perhaps fanciful memory at least – the Dockers' Rolls-Royce was waiting on the tarmac. (Sir Bernard had lately been sacked from the chairmanship of Daimler.)

The house, owned by a lugubrious painter named Peter Ruta, was 'little more than four small caves in the hillside', 436 steps uphill from the picturesque town of Positano, through which they swarmed, 'dizzy with heat and Chianti and the difficulty of buying cornflakes'. The first night was chaotic – the young slept on Lilos on the terrace, near an old well, and awoke covered in mosquito bites – but the little girls skipped about, loving everything. It was the first time they had all been crammed together for so long, there were still no telephones in Positano, and they felt a sense of wild Mediterranean freedom, far from the tensions of that summer's Suez crisis. John and Penelope both kept diaries, his more meticulous than hers, which became indecipherably blotched with Ambre Solaire. An American family next door were shocked by the Mortimers' casual domestic life – unmade beds, half-naked children cuddling verminous cats, red-headed Deborah getting fiercely sunburnt – while the placid Helga remained in charge: one of a series of women on whom Penelope depended, slightly resenting the dependence.

They adopted Fornillo beach, where Salvatore, who claimed kinship to Frank Sinatra, spread checked tablecloths under the vines and served 'seagull and chips'. They rode a donkey that had carried King Farouk. At the Villa Cimbrone in Ravello they were befriended by the rich American homosexual Arthur Jeffress, who had Tennessee Williams staying, and who later invited them to his palazzo in Venice. Among the English people they met were Peregrine Worsthorne, then a *Times* journalist, with his wife, Claudie, and two children. Penelope, Worsthorne recalled, was then by far the more striking character; John seemed 'shadowy'. The children gathered at a café where Madelon captivated the boogie piano player, Peppino. They went by car to Paestum, to the ruins of Greek temples, to Naples and Pompeii and Capri, which they guiltily loved. They decided that guidebooks to cathedrals and ruins ought to include, for parents, advice on loos and where to get Coca-Cola and ice cream. Penelope made herself a new dress for a party at Nerano, where they got a glimpse of *la vie bohème mediterranée*. They sailed to a great crumbling house on an island with high double doors, ornate glassless windows and bare, cavernous rooms; the hostess was an antique-dealing Austrian widow, married to a young gay Englishman. 'She pressed whisky sours on us, poured out her life story ... offered us a letter of introduction to the curator of Kenwood.' Dinner was served at a trattoria on the beach, 'a glittering patch of jabber in the enormous night'.

Madelon's fine cheekbones and ebullient personality proved alluring to the local Lotharios: Caroline, still known as Titch, was rather disapproving. Madelon managed to resist the amorous advances of Pier-Paolo Piccinato but succumbed to the pianist Peppino. She was too nervous to confide in her mother; and suspected anyway that she wouldn't want to know. In the last few days, in Praiano, Penelope herself discovered a romantic interest: Herman Minner, 'a stocky bow-legged Belgian painter of great charm', with a glinting gold tooth and a gold chain. One day she spent the morning being drawn by Minner, who made her look 'both hard and sad'. As her confidence very much depended on her beauty, she needed reassurance about her attractiveness. She flew home feeling that 'something was left unfinished' – and formed a plan to go back.

While they were away, *Three Winters* had been published, and a telegram arrived at the villa: 'Two outstanding Sunday reviews'. John Wain in the *Observer* likened John to the early Anthony Powell. Elizabeth Bowen called his story-telling 'miraculous', for treating a melancholy theme with humour, and for observing both young and old with understanding. V. S. Pritchett, the most perceptive of critics, praised John's almost deadpan satire at the expense of the middle classes, but he detected a 'moral lassitude' in the author.

For parents of a large family, great swathes of weekend are consumed just in keeping the young occupied, and John was unstintingly dutiful. On a typical weekend after their return in late September, he would leave Penelope at home to work on their book in peace, while he took Gran Fletcher, Helga (succeeded by a new nanny, Isabel), four or five children and one or two of their friends for lunch and tea at Turville Heath Cottage, and a walk in Stonor Park or the Wormsley Valley. Clifford and Kathleen, their lives consumed by the garden, by ailments and household repairs, were always welcoming. On fine days, 'It was very pleasant rambling in the garden and sitting in deck chairs,' Clifford would record. 'Deb & Sally danced about while John played the hose on them and Jeremy tried several experiments.' Sometimes Paul and Jay Fletcher came too. If the girls went alone by train, they would be met at the station – 'At last they emerged trailing mufflers, dropping books, carrying recorders' – and would be supplied with picnic lunches and games of Happy Families, Beg o' My Neighbour, dominoes, crosswords. They might go riding, erect a wigwam in the garden, or pick armfuls of daffodils. One half-term, they drove to Daisy's 'to watch John and Penelope on television, talking about books'.

The Mortimers' Christmas card for 1956 featured a charming drawing by their artist friend Richard Beer of an elephant with the six children on its back, each holding a candle. The three youngest girls spent Christmas and New Year with Clifford and Kathleen, who took them to *Cinderella* and to *The Heartless Princess* in Oxford. They were rather relieved when the holiday was over, but the whole family came back for Clifford's seventy-second birthday, bringing sherry and crackers.

John took over the writing of the Positano book, now retitled *With Love and Lizards*, finessing the narrative with his own embellishments. For instance, the family had not merely suffered the usual blisters, bites and internal disorders, but attracted 'surrealistic disasters'. One day they encountered 'a dwarf on the floor hammering tomatoes into a bottle with a mallet'. On a fishing trip, they landed a fish which 'came out howling like a baby, a long red sausage with numerous waving ears like umbrella spokes'; it was some time before this creature ceased howling and died peacefully in the bottom of the boat. That episode has the distinctive stamp of John Mortimer about it. At the same time he was pouring out short stories, a weekly column in *Punch* about life at the Bar (under the pen name Geoffrey Lincoln), plus a new play, *No Hero*, for ITV, in which a QC returns to his home town to defend a woman charged with manslaughter, gets involved with a local woman, and finds the case providing a parallel with his personal affairs. John's divorce cases, Clifford's diary suggests, could be swiftly dispatched: 'Today Thursday June 28 we went to London for an undefended case by the 10.02 train & caught the 2.25 back.'

Penelope's Muse was dormant. 'Incredible how years & years go by,' she writes on a February night. 'The rain and wind pour outside the black windows . . . The evening comes and John comes home. We worry and quarrel about money. We worry and quarrel about Caroline. We grow older, and aren't awed by it, when we ought to be.' On 26 February 1957: 'Couldn't write, was dreary with John; and the top landing didn't get cleared up, or the carpet cleaned . . . every day is much like this. How can I possibly feel like this with children around?' The second wave of feminism was a decade hence, but Penelope was living out its dilemmas of self-reproach and frustration. 'The sense of despair, which I'm sure comes from not being able to work, can today be coped with by going shopping and then cutting out a pair of trousers for me. Pointless getting through time, squandering a fortune. But this is how most women spend their LIVES, not just the bad patches. And like it. And are gentle and loving and philosophical with it. What's wrong with me?'

Social life seemed an aimless distraction. 'We've been to The Entertainer [John Osborne's new play] & to tea with Miss Ivy Compton-Burnett, who was . . . exactly like an English playwright's idea of an old lady living in reduced circumstances; or a character written by herself. There were doughnuts & cucumber sandwiches in Campden Hill Square & what on earth we were doing there I don't know.' Left alone to write for a day, she would just get started when the family returned. One Sunday evening, John was due back from Turville Heath with the gang. 'It always works like this: at the end of a day alone, thought begins; its first stirring coincides with the key in the lock.'

Jeremy at nearly two 'is perhaps the only man for whom I feel the right things: a desire to sew on buttons and to understand'. She daydreamed of flying away to America to be alone and free. She knew that was nonsense. But the more difficult life became, the more her ambition grew. For the Easter holidays Penelope took the children to a house at Brancaster on the Norfolk coast, leaving John at home, about which she wavered between eagerness and unease. She could write an eighty-guinea story for *Woman's Own*, and would lie in bed on a sun-filled morning, pondering the fact that in thirty years' time she might be dead and 'I really only have 20 more years to write anything in, and what the hell am I doing fooling around with it as though there was a whole lifetime? The woman who missed the bus is me, & will I, at my mother's age, still be running for it under the impression that I'm a promising 80?'

This tendency to be candidly self-critical, even cynical, was deeply ingrained since her somewhat joyless childhood. Her father despised jokes, was unable to recognize irony; and where, Penelope asked, was the *joy* his parishioners were supposed to be filled with? The rooms of the vicarage were 'dense with his unhappiness'. On Sundays, after booming sonorously from the pulpit, he would play some doleful dirge on the piano while parishioners sipped china tea from shallow cups. 'My heart, broken by the bells, bleeds for my father. Sunday is a terrible day.' Penelope had also inherited a puritanical streak. She did not share her husband's fondness for gossip, especially lewd gossip. So she did not laugh much any more at the out-of-court stories John told.

John breezed in to join them all in Norfolk for his thirty-fourth birthday and Jeremy's second, bringing Siriol, daughter Emma and nanny Elfi. As she put Jeremy to bed on his second birthday, Penelope was overcome, 'great sloppy warm tears dripping on him, calmed all through by shallow, warm sentiment about him growing up, and the end of having a baby'. When the family arrived home at Harben Road at the end of the holiday, in May, there was a bottle of Trésor perfume on the mantelpiece and champagne in the fridge: from John.

Penelope was vastly bolstered when Rachel MacKenzie, *New Yorker* commissioning editor, signed her up. Having fallen out with her old agent, Spencer Curtis Brown, she followed John to A. D. Peters, the literary agency in a Georgian house near Charing Cross.

Peters himself lived upstairs, 'with a lot of Sickerts and a blowsy B-movie actress', as John described the scene. Rachel MacKenzie suggested Penelope start with a memoir. She decided to write a story about her father, entitled, 'The Parson' – a project fraught with pitfalls, compounded by the fact that her mother was staying in her house.

It is hard even for a good writer to communicate the difficulty of the process of writing well. 'A hundred things bubble weakly inside, wanting the original force to send them flying,' Penelope wrote. 'I think so long, reject so much, that the ink dries on my pen & has to be shaken all over the sheet.' Then one day – it would have been the old man's birthday – she could write that 'The Parson' was finished, and she believed it was good. 'At first the awful smartness, then suddenly it came – oh I hope.' The *New Yorker* paid a handsome fee: $970.

Looking back, both said that this spring of 1957 marked a significant upturn in the Mortimer fortunes. John had written a radio play, a two-hander called *The Dock Brief*, warmly received by Nesta Pain, BBC drama producer. A dock brief, as John had explained in his *Punch* column, comes about when a prisoner arrives in court unrepresented: he can take his pick of any barrister who is robed. Prisoner and barrister meet in the cells for a hasty consultation, cook up a defence, and the trial begins. John had seen these tattered hack barristers, otherwise unemployed, in the London Sessions, but their archetypes sat in the remoter courts of the Old Bailey, day after day. Their fee would be two guineas, 'which, if the trial lasts several days', wrote John, 'makes the Bar a considerably worse-paid profession than selling evening papers outside the Borough tube station'.

(Judge James Pickles's 1992 autobiography mentioned the ageing, briefless barristers who haunted the Old Bailey 'like the one in John Mortimer's *The Dock Brief* '. 'I heard of one who collapsed through malnutrition,' wrote Pickles, 'and the soles of his feet could be seen through the soles of his shoes as he was carried away.')

In John's play, the defendant is a south London bird-fancier accused of murdering his wife. The barrister Morgenhall is in his sixties, pathetically hoping that this case will put his name in headlines. In the cell they rehearse the roles of judge, jury, witnesses, before emerging to face the rude reality of the trial. But instead of the brilliant address Morgenhall has promised, he is stumped for words, overcome by exhaustion. He longs to be alone in the darkness of his room with a pillow round his ears. His client is convicted, but is pardoned on the grounds of his lawyer's incompetence. As the curtain falls, both men dance out of the cell whistling a happy tune. Morgenhall says what a relief it is 'to go home alone. To undress, clean your teeth, knock out your pipe, not to bother with failure or success' – a poignant understanding of those who just can't make their way in the everyday world, or shine in it.

The Dock Brief was broadcast twice in May, with Michael Hordern as Morgenhall and David Kossoff the defendant. Critics hailed its 'gentle', 'tender', 'affectionate' pathos. 'Occasionally, from the unremarkable flux of broadcast programmes,' said *The Times*, 'a work emerges which makes one profoundly grateful for the medium that called it forth.'

John's success coincided with a family crisis. Penelope had speculated in her diary whether Madelon, still in her first year at Cambridge, might be pregnant, and she was. 'If it was that pleasant Julian (what a bore he'd be as a husband) what would one do, say? Marry him, and in another ten years be unhappy? Probably – and yet it would probably be wrong. In fact it would be wrong. And yet to tell her to get rid of something of her own – no Jeremy?'

Despite her instinctive scruples, Penelope arranged the abortion. A GP and a psychiatrist were required to state that having the baby would endanger the mother's health. The Mortimers' high-principled London GP refused to bend the truth, so Penelope drove her daughter to Gloucestershire to see John's old friend Michael Fenton, now living a contented life as a country doctor, with second wife and two small sons, at Moreton-in-Marsh. Fenton scribbled the necessary formula, a Wimpole Street psychiatrist did the same for a fat fee, and the abortion was duly performed at the St John's Wood nursing home where Jeremy had been born two years previously.

This was not the last time Penelope would have a daughter's abortion to arrange, but she promptly wrote about Madelon's predicament in the next novel, *Daddy's Gone A-Hunting*. It proved to be a faithful account, except that the daughter is a blonde at Oxford rather than a Cambridge brunette, and the boyfriend's scooter is a Vespa, not a Lambretta. Madelon later accepted that this was a book her mother simply had to write. That summer, when it was all over, she remembered lying in the long grass, basking in the sun like a contented cat, then cooking a legendary *gigot d'agneau aux haricots* for the whole family, savouring 'the conscious relief, freedom and light-heartedness'. She could now face the beginning of her second Cambridge year.

That July, in Caroline's O-level summer, Penelope went back, alone, to Positano. Partly, she wanted to see Herman Minner again. But she also vaguely longed 'to recapture something lost in my life: spontaneity, sensuality, anticipation – youth, I suppose'. John was perfectly agreeable. 'He said he was incapable of jealousy and on the rare occasions it came to the surface turned it into something bland and manageable.' She left detailed lists so that John and Madelon and au pair Ellie would run the household smoothly.

She did visit Minner in Praiano, 'but there was never a moment of serious infidelity. I wrote to John every day, saying how much I loved and missed him.' Riding pillion on Vespas, she imagined she was reliving her youth, but longed to be home – 'I even miss quarrelling with you. Without bars, I don't know which way to go' – and felt like crying whenever she thought of Jeremy.

Her letters home were copious, loving, vivid: about fiestas and fireworks, fairy lights and beach parties, about swimming to their little beach, and seeing the characters they had met last summer – the old Marquise 'like a banished old piece of Royalty'; Piccinato, who said if he had any money he would marry Madelon; a black sculptor who was fashioning a head of Aphrodite and 'an unbelievably ghastly man called Asquith'; 'people without work of any kind'. How different from John. 'I think of you in your wig, with your commissions and your Income Tax, and you seem very 3-dimensional, very tough, very real.' It was beautifully hot, but expat parties quickly palled: 'I thought my God, did I come all this way to sit bolt upright with a small gin talking about dogs to a lady from Pelham Place?'

John's letters, written from chambers, were lightly reassuring, just the kind any absent mother hopes to receive. Since he had waved goodbye to her 'sad little face' in the bus, the children were being 'sweet and comforting and companionable', Madelon endlessly efficient.

> Nothing seems very interesting without you, but this is the penalty of being married to anyone as exciting as you: life is dull when you're not around.
>
> Darling I am just going into Court. This is a short note to tell you nothing but that I love you, we are all OK but missing you, and have a wonderful time and come back gleaming brown with no worries about anything. I wish I could take tonight's plane to Naples. Love and so much love; write and tell all. J.

For Madelon, writing to the ever-critical Penelope was 'the most difficult thing', but her letters indicate how much she had inherited of her mother's talent. 'We all wonder how you are and think of you sitting in the Buca with a chestnut tan, tossing down the Fernet Branca and saying firmly "*Non capito*" [I don't understand] to everyone from Paolo to Renato.' Gran Fletcher, she reported, kept telephoning, 'hoping that something dreadful has happened to you so that she can rise to the occasion and refrain from saying "I told you so."' (Mrs Fletcher was always at her best in a crisis.) They had taken a great gang of children punting on the Thames, when one child fell into the river and had to be fished out. 'How much nicer our children are than other people's,' Madelon wrote:

The real torture was the journey home. Going past Hanger Lane, Caroline suggested 'let's have a nice song' and a mighty shout broke forth such as I've never heard, of six children screaming Robin Hood at the tops of their voices, out of tune and out of time. The joy was getting rid of them one by one, tired and wet at their palaces in Golders Green.

Daddy has to keep telling us how miserable he is in order that we should not suspect that he is having a good time being entertained by his friends. But the private detective [hero of his new play] engrosses him. And he is being very nice to one and all and lavish with the money.

The Dock Brief was broadcast again. So was John's new radio play about Mr Frute, whose forerunner, said *The Times*, was the lugubrious investigator in Greene's *The End of the Affair*. Then London turned grey and damp, and fifteen-year-old Caroline, who had starred in school plays as Miranda in *The Tempest* and Eliza in *Pygmalion*, became a student ASM at the Royal Court at £1 a week.

Penelope felt guiltily grateful 'to be sitting here so brown & cool & happy, with a maid to get the lunch', though this holiday was costing less than half her *New Yorker* fee for 'The Parson'. For the first time in years, she felt 'under no obligation to anyone at all and am therefore so calm, so social, so relaxed and sweet and charming that you wouldn't know me. I have cut four parties this week and it's a wonderful feeling . . . Do I sound as though I'm becoming intolerable? I'm not really. Just basking in my own limitations, with no one to shake their heads and say, "WHAT are we going to do with Peggy?"'

She was not having an affair with Minner. ('If Herman has any sex,' she added, 'it is, as they say here, pederast'). But he was painting her. 'It is – I hope you don't object and come flying over with your horsewhip, moustaches bristling – a nude.' (A 'great sprawling nude', her diary said.) 'I'm blissfully remote, and only long, sometimes painfully, for you, and have times of sharp regret at the way I've behaved in the distant, foggy London past, and sharp hope that when I come home I'll be better and easier for you.

'I want you,' she promised, 'and to be someone different with you; my fear is only that back in the sitting-room and John Barnes, even with the beautiful children, I shall again be me.'

The unmistakable sentiment expressed in these letters reflects a decade of shared experience, of each being the other's favourite audience. Most importantly, John cabled Penelope with thrilling news: he had secured the lease of the nursery wing of a Victorian mansion, Cromer Hall, in Norfolk. This was a vast, sham-Gothic castle, built in the 1930s by a railway king, with great halls full of Brobdingnagian antique furniture. Penelope 'danced, whirled with joy, thinking of delicious furniture and the lovely prospect of Cromer and all gone right'. John arranged the removal pantechnicon ('£25, which seems more than you could buy all the furniture for') and dithered about expense: did they really need to carpet the bathroom? But he too was banking on the prospect of Cromer 'with Jeremy in the woods and Sally on the sands and us together, all day and all night'.

'Please let me come back quietly, and no ceremonies,' Penelope told John, in her last letter, longing to clean her fingernails and to work again. 'Just be glad to see me, which is all I want in the world.'

An interviewer who visited the couple at home just before they left for Cromer was told by Penelope that John so loved his work, he wrote all the time, even on holiday; he had no hobbies. 'I go riding on Wimbledon Common,' he offered. 'Oh, John, how long is it . . . ?' protested Penelope. 'I do – I go with Carrie,' he declared. (He did: they were taught by an instructress known as Bottoms-on-a-Plate, from her exhortation, 'Keep your bottom on the plate, Mr Mortimer!') Penelope claimed one hobby: dressmaking. Wherever she went she would buy fabrics and run up instant dresses. They said that they showed each other all their writing – 'If it really stinks he says so. And he's always right,' Penelope added, 'even when it hurts.' (The headline said, 'They Make Each Other Weep'.) But an unnamed friend, who had arrived during the interview, chipped in to say that their problem was, they were both trying to write the same thing. 'John Mortimer smiled pleasantly but impenetrably while his wife protested. "I don't agree at all. That's a most superficial judgement. John's more visual – like a painter. He's good at describing things, things I don't notice. I'm only interested in what goes on inside. Psychology and all that old bunk."'

On their return from Cromer Hall in September, in time for Jeremy to start at the House on the Hill, his Hampstead kindergarten, *With Love and Lizards* was published. Penelope sent a copy to her mother: 'To Mum, without whom none of these people would have existed'. The reviews, Nancy Spain's especially, were appreciative, and it was read on *Woman's Hour*, but the über-intellectual Marghanita Laski in the *Observer* launched a haughty shaft of derision at the entire enterprise. Mr and Mrs Mortimer were serious and clever novelists in the field of literature, but with withering scorn she added, '*With Love and Lizards* is, however, journalism.' Anyone who wrote a book just because it might sell was 'guilty of writing literary journalism' – a rather hilarious view seen from publishers' wildly commercial perspective today. The Mortimers' trivial subject was 'worth no more than an article in a woman's magazine', Miss Laski declared, and, furthermore, family life was not a suitable topic for journalism, but 'a sacred object, to be communicated only as literature or to one's intimates or not at all. One doesn't expose one's children in the market place.'

Three weeks later, *No Moaning of the Bar*, John's collection of *Punch* columns, was published under the pseudonym Geoffrey Lincoln. These timeless pieces on how to become a barrister first exposed his world-weary, irony-laden Rumpolian opinions and jokes. For example, a learned QC says severely to a man he is cross-examining, 'I advise you to answer the questions.' 'The last time I took your advice,' rejoins his client, 'I did twelve months.' Anyone fancying a lucrative legal career was warned that 'crime is falling off, coroners are badly hit by a lack of corpses . . .' In the never-had-it-so-good 1950s, bigamy and bankruptcy, libel and slander were things of the past. Young barristers were mostly, like actors, resting, hedged in by rules 'designed to prevent you running into any danger of earning your living during your first five years of work'. In chambers, they would find 'five very young Old Etonians in Edwardian suits playing cricket in the passage'. Your chambers clerk, 'who can produce hundred-guinea briefs', had to be treated with courtesy and care. 'You call him Arthur and he calls you Sir.' The private detective, unlike Raymond Chandler's lean, solitary and whisky-drinking Philip Marlowe, tends to be 'small, homely and middle-aged, interested in breeding dahlias or collecting matchboxes'. Legal argot must be mastered. For example, 'Are you trying to fence with me, Mr Entwistle?' during cross-examination; also time-fillers such as 'With the greatest respect', 'In my humble submission', 'If Your Lordship pleases', 'I'm much obliged'. He recommends also the useful cue for a pause: 'Would Your Lordship find this a convenient moment to adjourn?' Polite deference to the judge is always advisable, as is appreciative laughter when the judge 'leans back with the sad expression of one about to embark on a joke'. It was perhaps a mistake, writes John, for the advocate F. E. Smith, when a judge said to him, 'What do you think I am here for?' to reply, 'It is not for me, my lord, to fathom the inscrutable ways of providence.'

But it was not an entirely facetious exercise. From his experience of divorce cases, for instance, he frankly described 'the gratified bewilderment of husbands and wives who wonder that years, sometimes decades, of matrimonial disharmony can be severed within such a short space of time. In fact, when they get out of court they are likely to ask, "What happened?" or "When does the case begin?"' *No Moaning of the Bar* so impressed the great advocate Sir Norman Birkett that he quoted from it when addressing neophyte barristers on Call Night at the Inner Temple.

By 21 September, when John and the children arrived at Turville Heath Cottage, he could tell his parents about the astonishing success of *The Dock Brief*, 'which is hailed as a masterpiece', noted Clifford. (Clifford read only *The Times*, where Bernard Levin had that day used the word 'masterpiece' to describe *The Dock Brief*'s 'luminous' translation to television: 'more moving, more funny and more profound than anything I have yet seen by courtesy of the seventh art'.) The BBC fee of £90 had now been paid five times over, with repeats, plus £150 for the TV one; and there had been 280 performances on foreign radio stations. John was already anxious about its successor, but in the meantime *The Dock Brief* won the Prix Italia, so John and Penelope flew to Taormina to receive the millions of lire (about £2,200). Penelope gave her in-laws a vivid account of their Sicilian journey, full of excursions and alarms.

Madelon watched *The Dock Brief* on television in an upstairs room of the Rose pub in Cambridge, where she was working part-time, with her new boyfriend Christopher Booker. She had gone up that term in euphoric mood and Booker's impression was of her bubbly good humour. In fact 'an aura of unalloyed sunlight' seemed to hover over the entire Mortimer family. In the next eighteen months, Madelon made several visits to Knighton House, the prep school near Blandford in Dorset run by Christopher's parents; she went canvassing for John Booker for the Liberals in Salisbury, and was surprised to see that Mrs Booker, a possessive mother, still washed Christopher's hair for him.

Penelope took up her diary for the first time since Positano one Sunday evening when John was meeting the film producer Sydney Box at the Dorchester, and continued the self-analysis she had begun in Italy: 'Now, at 39, I find that it's difficult to live with people any more; that nearly all I want is to be alone and work, organise in small, manageable quantities a hardly perceptible life.' A room of her own, which Virginia Woolf identified in 1929 as what every woman needs, Penelope did not have.

'The house thunders with people. There's not an inch not covered by dust or old socks & newspapers or people. I bought a desk last week & it's invisible under litter. Rain hammers on the window, wind down the chimney.' She would wake up, 'radiant to the thought of a peaceful weekday. I long for it and can't bear it to end – which it does with the key in the lock, "Hullo? What's the plan?'' We must have people in or go out, my room invaded, all routed and nothing left in its place. Of course it isn't my room, and I am bitterly wrong.'

She was, however, producing a stream of lucrative *New Yorker* stories, plundering her life for incidents, 'finding that even the dreariest days contained nuggets of irony, farce, unpredictable behaviour'. Whenever she attempted real, original fiction, Rachel MacKenzie – the 'genius' editor who taught her to be specific, to give the telling detail and to pare down her prose, ditching redundant adjectives and superlatives – would turn it down. At the same time, the *Sunday Times* commissioned her to review novels. 'I was cheeky, opinionated, and totally ignorant of the rules I was apparently breaking,' she wrote. She had fun, oblivious of the hurt she inflicted, making enemies of some and Schadenfreude-minded fans of others. Edith and Osbert Sitwell were admirers; Beverley Nichols wrote, 'I pray you may never cast your steely eyes on any work of mine!'

The women in her stories were of a period type now virtually extinct: 1950s housewives with no paid employment. They were unambitious, pliable stay-at-homes who ferried the children and submitted to their thoughtless husbands. The men were always variations of John. 'Certainly I used writing to get rid of my scorn for some aspects of men in general, but none of them had [John's] positive qualities; none of them were talented, funny or had any charm, none of them were sexually attractive except to girls known in that innocent age as "dollies".'

Penelope's 1957 letters are revealing because what happened later in John's life might seem to suggest that his first marriage had been unhappy, or a mere failure, when it was actually more interesting than that: it was turbulent and volatile, but it contained much that makes life worthwhile. Besides, very few men, and even fewer male writers, have ever had the testing experience of being in charge of six children, as John had, and providing them with happy memories, as he did.

At Christmas, when they all went back to Cromer Hall, Clifford and Kathleen – at a loose end, with no family visit – took it into their heads to emulate their son and to try writing short stories for profit – at top speed. The first was called 'About George', which Clifford posted to John on 21 December. 'My Friend Rawley' was finished by Christmas morning. John rang his parents from Cromer, to be told they were 'busy, writing'. By New Year's Eve, Clifford had finished another story called 'The Dog'. 'John rang to say he liked My Friend Rawley very much. He is going to work on it and send it to his agent. Meanwhile I have finished another story, The Stucco Cherub. John is writing a play called What Shall We Tell Caroline? My new sports coat arrived from the Army & Navy – 44 "portly". It fits well. King went on weeding the south border.' Days passed, more stories were finished. 'John's play I Spy on the radio again and while it was on John rang up. He said he liked my story The Stucco Cherub; & thought it the right length for the Evening Standard. We were much encouraged.' By 9 January 'The Orchid' was finished, 'The Stamp' started. Kathleen started a story of her own, called 'Late Call', On 12 January Clifford began 'My Aunt Lizzie'. John kindly sent two of the stories to A. D. Peters, and it wasn't until February that a discouraging letter arrived from the agent, and Clifford and Kathleen's little foray into literature ceased as suddenly as it had begun.

8. The Media Mortimers

The Mortimers' lives, as Penelope presciently saw, were becoming a performance. Enviably talented and fecund, they were featured – before the existence of lifestyle or celebrity magazines or even Sunday colour supplements – in glossy magazines, which sent photographers to snap the successful pair surrounded by their brood. 'Their large and happy-looking family are frequently photographed,' as *Books and Bookmen* noted, alongside Mark Gerson's portrait of the family gathered round the Wendy house. Penelope's name was invariably tagged 'mother of six'. 'After the peers discuss birth control: a mother replies' was a typical *Evening Standard* headline.

Each generation produces its voice-of-motherhood columnists and Penelope was perfect for the turn of the 1960s. She had an *Evening Standard* column called 'Five Girls and a Boy', presenting a knockabout family life where the parents treated their children as individuals. She wrote about never-ending birthday parties, choosing schools, taking them on aeroplanes and to the dentist, about hiring au pairs and getting through school holidays. Julia aged ten had written a Grand Guignol play; Madelon and Caroline had performed a comic opera 'which reduced us to tears of laughter'. Having children when young 'doesn't keep you young,' she wrote, 'but it does stop you growing up'. She never ventured into the genuine problems she faced: of blending a previous family with a new one, or the chaotic domestic reality, or teenage pregnancy, or a mother's moments of mute despair. Such matters were confined to her novels, in which home-bound wives brood over their children's mulishness and their husbands' misdemeanours. Women's liberation marches and influential neo-feminist books like Hannah Gavron's *The Captive Wife* and Germaine Greer's *The Female Eunuch* were still some years away.

The Mathiesons were . . . an institution. They symbolised a whole way of life. First of all, they had these eight children. Their marriage . . . was continually being referred to by bishops and magistrates and even the occasional High Court judge . . . As though that wasn't enough, they were both fantastically successful writers . . . The energy of those two was absolutely staggering. They wrote novels . . . and television plays and radio plays and stage plays . . . and criticism of practically everything . . . They wrote film scripts . . . They gave amusing interviews to the Press, and if ever a newspaper wanted to find out about children watching television, or the teenage problem, or how to run a house on thirty shillings a week, they got on to the Mathiesons straight away. And the Mathiesons always managed to say the right thing – intelligent, but human – progressive, but somehow cosy. Their children – Sophia, Simon, Emma, Henrietta, Sebastian, Philippa, Piers and the baby, Adam – were not like other people's children. They had great personality and even, in a way, dignity. Well of course this was how their parents wrote about them, and you can't tell much from photographs, particularly in the newspapers. Anyway, they were obviously remarkable children. Being Mathiesons, they could hardly help it.

This extract is from 'Such a Super Evening', a short story by Penelope for the *New Yorker* in 1958. The narrator is a mousy wife who hosts a dinner for the Mathiesons, a glittering media couple. She invites some appropriate guests. But as the evening progresses, the veneer of the Mathiesons is stripped away. The husband, the raconteur, reveals that their eight children are shareholders in their limited company, as a tax dodge. As for his wife's famous energy, he says, 'She does it all on delicious American pills, specially imported, don't you, darling?' Mrs Mathieson, furiously smoking and tapping ash over her uneaten dinner, interrupts with a snort when someone says she has read that Mr Mathieson gets up at six every day. 'You know what time he gets up? Midday. Just in time for lunch at the Caprice.' When another guest expresses admiration for the eight children, Mathieson gives a bark of laughter at the idea that all of them might be his. His wife then erupts in hysterics. Even when other guests begin to depart in embarrassment, the

Mathiesons – oblivious – carry on performing, 'two clever robots packed with enough talk for a week'.

In April 1958 a striking portrait of all eight Mortimers was published in the *Daily Express* entitled 'The Family Behind a Hit'. A double-bill of *The Dock Brief* coupled with John's new play, *What Shall We Tell Caroline?*, had just opened at the Lyric Hammersmith, produced by the young impresario Michael Codron, lately down from Oxford. Codron had suggested pairing *The Dock Brief* with an Ionesco play; John, who claimed he thought Unesco was an organization, promptly wrote another play – *Caroline* – to be put on in tandem instead, only to find himself compared, by critics, with Ionesco.

'I discovered a brilliant new comic playwright last night,' the *Express* critic, John Barber, had announced. 'He is John Mortimer aged 35: novelist, lawyer, and father of six children . . .' and so the image became fixed. In their Norfolk fastness, 'Mr Mortimer of Cromer Hall' was described as a 'local author' by the *Eastern Daily Press*. Now, looking 'portly' like Clifford, he posed for the *Express* as the pleased-as-Punch paterfamilias in front of a grand chimneypiece, thumbs in lapels. Penelope sits cross-legged on a chaise-longue, looking fondly down at the dungareed Jeremy in her lap. Madelon, chauffeured by the *Express* from Cambridge for the photo session, turns her face away from the family; Caroline, soon to start at RADA, looks pensive; Sally and Julia in jodhpurs gaze intently at Jeremy; nine-year-old Deborah is stretched out on the floor. The entire mise-en-scène was a sham: the 'state apartments', as they called them, were not part of their rented wing at Cromer. But Barber referred to 'Squire Mortimer at his improbable country retreat', and said he now understood why John had been so unruffled on his first night: 'After a weekend at Cromer Hall, the mad theatrical whirligig must seem like a dead duck's funeral.' Somehow, he reported, 'the calm fellow with the crooked teeth' managed to write here in his spare time from his legal practice. When does Mortimer write? he asked. 'Well, I get up at six o'clock.' 'Ooh, when?' jeered six voices.

According to John, the Bar fined him a dozen bottles of

champagne for receiving such vulgar and unprofessional publicity.

The dozen curtain calls and prolonged laughter of the double bill's first night were witnessed by Clifford, Kathleen, Aunt Daisy and Mrs Fletcher, seated in their box in evening dress. The *Caroline* play was set in a boys' boarding prep school at Cold Sands on the bleak Norfolk coast and featured four characters: a testy headmaster, his long-suffering wife, a raffish banjo-playing assistant master and the headmaster's silent, nubile daughter of eighteen, who is treated by them like a small child. For the entire length of the play Caroline does not utter a word, until at the end she finds voice to announce that she is leaving home and going to London.

As well as Ionesco, John was likened to Coward, Eliot, Barrie, Anouilh. The Theatre of the Absurd element impressed critics even when it baffled them. Derek Granger of the *Financial Times* discerned 'a rich, Dickensian raciness' with 'characters midway between caricature and human likeness and inflated by a gusty whimsicality'. Milton Shulman was left feeling irritated, 'as one does after being told a shaggy dog story', by comic effects that relied on anticlimax and non sequitur. But the influential Harold Hobson was instantly smitten. He identified John's potential as a dramatist who 'hit with formidable accuracy for one so young'.

Even the theatre programme was applauded. These usually cost one shilling and contained nothing of interest. This one cost only sixpence and featured a manifesto by John. 'Comedy is the only thing worth writing in this despairing age,' he wrote. In drama, and in literature in general, the most important element is the moment of recognition – 'when you realise, sitting in the theatre, with a shock of excitement and unease, that you are watching yourself . . . Parents and children may see their remoteness mirrored, and lawyers and criminals in the audience may even recognise their close affinity.'

The most exciting critic of the day was Kenneth Tynan. Tentatively starting his review with 'I don't want to run Mr Mortimer down', he allowed that John had taken a gallant belly-dive into the tricky waters of surrealist farce. *The Dock Brief* had 'a brisk Dickensian bounce', but he detected 'a forensic pedantry, and an excessive dependence on relative clauses' in the style. These tricks might be used successfully once; but he was alarmed when they turned up again in the second play, which he found 'dismally verbose'. The characters were relics of the 1920s; Mr Mortimer had 'fantasticated' them, and Caroline's muteness strained credibility. 'Precept for new playwrights: what realism can't do, surrealism may. But what realism can do, surrealism wrecks.' John might be labelled 'the brilliant new playwright', but there were dissenting voices who thought he patronized his characters and was both slapdash and too smart by half. 'Mr John Mortimer's reputation has made a rocket-assisted takeoff,' said the *Sunday Times*, 'but is not yet securely in orbit.'

However, the double bill ran for several months and transferred to the Garrick. Meanwhile *I Spy* had moved to the small screen in January, with Donald Pleasence as Mr Frute, the private eye who falls in love with his quarry. *Call Me a Liar* was televised, with Alec McCowen as the Walter Mittyish Sammy Noles, who lives in a dream world, a stranger to the truth, until Martha Heinz, a German mother's help (inspired by the recently departed Helga), enters his life. And in April a dramatization of his novel *Three Winters* was broadcast on radio with Jill Bennett and Basil Dignam. John's understanding of loneliness and human frailty, his fresh and convincing dialogue, and the quiet disclosure of character impressed *The Listener*. The anonymous essayist had wondered whether Mr Mortimer could last the course in a three-act play, and this provided the answer: 'As far as people and their conversation are concerned, Mr Mortimer can keep it up.'

That he could easily keep it up was about to be proved conclusively in his first full-length West End play, which he would write on more realistic lines than his previous work. When he resumed his annual role of locum *Evening Standard* theatre critic that May, he spotted Margaret Leighton in Terence Rattigan's *Variations on a Theme*, as a 'tough, intelligent, racked, elegant, masculine and yet feminine woman'. Miss Leighton, he decided, would be ideal for his play.

The long school summer holidays, coinciding with legal vacations, never daunted John. Possessed of a rare concentration, he could carry on writing in the room where the children littered the floor, while Alma Cogan or Lonnie Donegan blared from the radio, and he was never too preoccupied to make omelettes or give the children a game of chess. Penelope found it impossible to write in these circumstances, so traipsing off to Cromer Hall or a more distant holiday refuge became the norm. The children could ramble down to the beach, and didn't have to be walked in parks or marched round museums. There was a freedom from responsibility. They could 'picnic, improvise, make do'. Mrs Fletcher, delighted to get out of London, ran the household. Also, as Penelope later said, it was only when they decamped to a holiday house that she felt liberated from 'the unknown, invisible someone' who haunted her life at home: John's latest, tiresome 'flirtation, infatuation, whatever they were'. During their bracing bucket-and-spade holidays 'there was always some reason for him to nip off to London, returning with sour offerings of guilt and remorse'. When they began to sail off to more far-flung destinations abroad, the distance from the unknown and invisible mistress gave her a sense of security. But no matter where they went, John would find some theatre-based excuse – meetings with directors, problems of casting – to escape to London.

Penelope's third novel, *Daddy's Gone A Hunting*, starts with the wife seeing her two boys off to boarding school. The summer was over: 'the summer of wet socks, of plimsolls fossilised by salt and sand; of wellington boots and Monopoly, bicycles left out in the rain'. Her husband, Rex, a dentist who supplies gleaming gnashers to a celebrity clientele, has returned with relief to his London flat, after 'the month of anguish and boredom that was known as his holiday'. It had started with strawberries and ended with quarrels. 'And now it was over. The children, the summer, gone.'

Ruth does not hate her husband, but he has changed since his guitar-playing youth. He is forty-five, irascible, overweight. 'In his expensive clothes he still managed to look suave and tidy, to emanate the bitter-sweet smell of money and after-shave.' They live among affluent professionals, men in advertising and films, behind high yew hedges. The smart, bridge-playing, car-driving wives are like icebergs, keeping a bright shining face above the water, though some are poisoned with boredom, or take to drink or go slightly crazy; 'and some are dying from a lack of love'.

Penelope's jaundiced views of men are a foretaste of many feminist novels of the 1960s and 1970s. Ruth's eighteen-year-old undergraduate daughter Angela has gone off with a young man named Tony:

Tony might be a stupid, infuriating bore, a bully and a prig, but this was not at the moment important. He was a man. He had always been a man, lolling in his pram at the age of one, a crack shot with an airgun at seven, an arm-twister and a hair-puller until, at the correct sort of school, he had earned the right to flog little boys. He would be a success . . .'

Loving him, his wife would be driven mad as he became, over the years,

greedy, heavy, his stupidity inexcusable, his crudeness no longer justified by a fancy haircut or an exhibition of boyish charm. He would never understand why the world thought highly of him and his wife hated him. He would never understand that he had lost his only attraction, the quality of offering pleasure . . . He would never understand anything, except that he ought to be loved.

This novel included the daughter's abortion, the wife's nervous breakdown and the husband's affair with a young woman named Maxine, who, being a silly little fool, finds Rex attractive. She laughs at his jokes. As Ruth knows, it is only lies, and reassurance about his youth and sex appeal, that her husband wants to hear. Penelope's knowing and incisive novel – 'pellucid, poetic, tart and compassionate' – was found remarkable, and 'deeply disturbing'.

At Cambridge, Madelon had enjoyed a successful second year. She had acted in the ADC with Clive Swift, directed by John Barton; made a friend of A. S. (Antonia) Byatt, along her Newnham corridor; and got engaged to her clever boyfriend, Christopher Booker. But at the start of her third year, just after *Daddy's Gone A-Hunting* was published, Madelon had 'what was euphemistically termed a nervous breakdown'. In Booker's college rooms in Corpus, she swallowed enough Veganin to require her stomach to be pumped at Addenbrooke's Hospital. Booker, who was not allowed to visit her, not being kin, believed her crisis was due to their separation that summer, and her guilt about the fling she'd had with another man. Madelon did afterwards resume her romance with Booker, but it was 'never glad morning again' for them. And the head of Sidgwick Hall, her hall of residence in Newnham, decreed that she should move out of college and spend her last two terms in lodgings, a curious notion. If she performed badly in her Tripos, Newnham promised that allowances would be made. 'But I got a 2.1,' Madelon said, 'without any bloody help from them.'

Was there not a correlation between the publication of Penelope's novel and Madelon's breakdown? Madelon's view is that there was not. 'It is interesting. But I did not confront Mother, because I tried always to take the line that whenever she felt strongly about anything, she had to write it out.'

Domestic upheavals, in any case, never hampered John's output. On 5 October 1958, the *Sunday Express* published his comical account of taking Penelope, via Venice, to Yugoslavia to spend the earnings he was owed from *The Dock Brief* – a 'short play for which I have already been over-rewarded in various parts of the world'. A payment of £103, his theatre agent Peggy Ramsay informed him, awaited him in Zagreb. But in those Iron Curtain days, it must be collected in person and spent in Yugoslavia. They arrived in Dubrovnik and drove grandly to a five-star hotel. The manageress explained that Zagreb was 300 miles away and there were no trains. Perhaps, she suggested, they could sell their clothes? John looked at his gabardine trousers, bought in Shaftesbury Avenue to give himself 'a dashing, Humphrey Lyttelton, jazz club appearance': they had a crumpled, Devil's Island look. A miserable weekend ensued.

But by Monday his money arrived at the National Bank and

they strode out of the hotel with their riches, into the boulevard with its seventeenth-century houses and pretty archways, full of shops. But there was nothing they wanted to buy. 'We could have bought geometry sets by the dozen. Balls of string, cardboard shoes. Enormous mackintoshes. Fezzes, cigarette holders as favoured by Marshal Tito. Some furtive contraband-looking British dentifrice and a Slav translation of *Finnegans Wake*.'

It was a criminal offence to take dinars out of Yugoslavia and they had 100,000 of them. It took half an hour to drink perhaps elevenpence' worth of Slivovitz. Brandy and cigarettes were dirt cheap. They bought a German airbed and floated about on it, and hired a boat for several hours, but the boatman refused to charge for extra time. They went to an expensive restaurant and ordered the costliest items, lobsters and shashlik, and quantities of Riesling, but when John asked for the bill the restaurateur refused to charge them, as they were guests in his country. On the boat back to Italy, a whisky cost just 50 dinars and you could get a four-course meal for the price of one Venetian sandwich. Finally he found a quantity of Greek filter-tip cigarettes. 'I shall smoke them gasping in the English winter.'

Royalties began to flow in. In November, *The Dock Brief*, *Caroline* and *I Spy* were published in one volume, just in time for Richard Ingrams and Paul Foot, newly arrived at University College, Oxford, to use it for their audition for the university's dramatic society, OUDS. (They played a scene from *What Shall We Tell Caroline?* and both won parts in *Coriolanus*.) *I Spy* was staged in theatres as far apart as Salisbury, starring Timothy West, and Miami, with Hume Cronyn and Jessica Tandy. Ionesco, no less, translated *The Dock Brief* and *Caroline* for their debuts in Paris, where John Mortimer was '*un jeune auteur anglais de la nouvelle génération*', at the Studios des Champs-Elysées. And to round off a successful year, on 19 December 1958, *What Shall We Tell Caroline?* was on *Television Playhouse*.

On New Year's Eve of 1958, Penelope was at home with the sleeping Jeremy, while John was at a party at the home of his old Harrovian friend, the tall, handsome Jasper Grinling, of Gilbey's

Gin. Madelon was 'at Blandford – happy, I hope' with the Bookers; Caroline was leaving for Switzerland; Deborah and Sally were about to go off to board at Knighton House, the Bookers' school. John was happy because he was busy and in demand; Penelope, hemmed in by motherhood, was morose. It was the dawn of a troubled year.

In May, while John was again reviewing theatre for the *Standard* (including Peter Hall's *A Midsummer Night's Dream* at Stratford, with Vanessa Redgrave and Charles Laughton as Bottom), *The Times* announced, 'Mrs Penelope Mortimer, the authoress, is expecting another child – her seventh. She is 40 and the wife of Mr John Mortimer, the barrister and author . . . They live in Hampstead and have five girls and a boy. The new baby is due in December. Mrs Mortimer has just joined the panel which selects books for the Book Society.'

Penelope later recollected the feelings which this late, springtime pregnancy gave her: 'the illusion of cosiness or humanity or dottiness'. But the happiness was short-lived. 'I had a miscarriage in July & the baby was dead anyway, so that was solved. I suppose one day it may appear that a lot was solved.' When John brought her home from hospital, he gave her the news that Caroline had left home, despite his attempts to dissuade her, to live with a bright young actor, Tom Kempinski. With Deborah and Sally now at Knighton House – which Deborah loved, but Sally emphatically did not – only Julia, Jeremy and nanny Rosemary remained at home, and 'the house seemed empty'. Madelon, her engagement to Booker broken off, had finished at Cambridge and moved into the basement. Although she had vaguely expected some help from John at this point, there was no question of a pupillage in his all-male chambers. (He told me, 'I was rather cruel. I didn't help her. I didn't get her into my chambers.') Not that she minded: the awful boredom of Contract and Tort and the Law of Real Property had utterly disenchanted her. Anyway, the barristering idea concealed the fact that she had no notion of what she really wanted to be, except perhaps a famous writer.

Madelon's twenty-first birthday fell that July, and John and Penelope gave a party. Having few London friends, Madelon asked everyone she knew to bring three friends and a bottle. When the parents came home, John joined in the party with characteristic enthusiasm. But in the ensuing weeks, Penelope discovered that it can be difficult to live alongside one's grown-up daughter. One day she rang Madelon at her office and told her coldly that she didn't think she should live at home any more, so she would be grateful if Madelon would make other arrangements. Madelon, mystified, went home to pack, and took a bus to Charles Dimont's flat in Fulham. She suspected it might be because her Cambridge contemporary David Leitch, with whom she had fallen in love, had for some reason become Penelope's least favourite person. Or Penelope may have found a letter to Leitch from Madelon, complaining about her mother. 'The means of communication in our family,' Madelon told me, 'was often to leave private note-books and letters lying around for everyone to read.'

She moved into an all-girls' flat in Aberdare Gardens, Swiss Cottage, until Leitch wrote from Rome saying casually that things were going so well there, why didn't she join him? She resigned from her job and by December she had left for Rome. She went to Harben Road to say goodbye. Penelope presented her with a set of scarlet Revelation suitcases; Madelon would have preferred cash. Only once did she come back to live in England again.

In July, the month of Penelope's miscarriage, a revue had opened at the Lyric Hammersmith called *One to Another*. Eleanor Fazan, known as Fiz, a gamine, elfin-coiffed South African-born dancer and choreographer (later to direct *Beyond the Fringe* and the first London exposure of Mrs Edna Everage, in Barry Humphries's *Just a Show*), devised it by asking up-and-coming writers for short sketches, performed by Sheila Hancock, Beryl Reid, Joe Melia and Patrick Wymark. She was in awe of meeting John Mortimer, but they became friends at once. She had a son of Jeremy's age (four), so they began sharing outings to places like Chessington Zoo. Fiz also introduced John to Tony Richardson, with whom he immediately hit it off. She found John kind, lovable in a brotherly way, a fun companion, 'a bit like a gangly, brainy version of Just William, always ready to laugh and escape'. Fiz had an au pair named Louisa who, if anyone rang up, however important, would say loudly 'IS OUT' and firmly put down the phone. John immediately put Louisa into a sketch for Beryl Reid.

During rehearsals John would sit by the stage making changes to his sketches. Critics agreed that the best were by Pinter and Mortimer. John's sketches included one about a waitress torn between two customers, another about a tycoon on the phone talking to six people at once. These were hailed by Bernard Levin as hilarious, and by Harold Hobson as 'unsettling' and 'close to poetry'. The show seemed to Hobson 'the most original, the most profound, the most intellectually active and emotionally searching revue that London has ever seen'. Today you'd call the sketches Pythonesque.

That summer John and Penelope abandoned Cromer's cold sands, and rented a house at Grasse in the South of France for six weeks. All the family except Madelon went, and Jeremy learned to swim at Eden Roc. This is where Penelope set her short story 'The Skylight' (holiday house locked; little boy is let in through skylight; mother stands helpless outside as silence ensues). She realized later that 'The Skylight' was about her miscarriage. She told her diary she had been taking Dexedrine 'to get through'. 'Also I'm beginning to drink too much. This is painful to write, and I don't know why I make myself write it. I believe that if I could be alone with the small ones (but this might not be true) I would be all right.'

On 18 September 1959, Penelope was alone at home on the eve of her forty-first birthday, and thought she would unlock the cupboard and write in her diary. 'But John has taken the key, on my key-ring – how symbolic can things be? I can't get at my own sordid little secrets. Locked out. This at least is funny – even I can see how funny it is.' Looking back at her life, all she can see is 'years of mums' helps and the children and this house'. Nine days later, her diary for 28 September records that 'John has gone, to somewhere in Wilton Mews'. For the first time, John had decamped, to a flat across town, in Belgravia. He told me he just went out and found himself a flat, and that nobody else was involved. In his memoirs he makes a reference to his agent Peggy Ramsay lending him her flat, once, 'when my life was in turmoil'. Peggy had at that time a flat in SW1. Anyway, Penelope was left with Jeremy and Julia in Harben Road.

Two days later she and John met, 'absurdly', for lunch. He had been sick, he said, all night. They parted like acquaintances. The next day he rang her about his shirts, making her cross, and left for Berlin, where a play was opening. She was writing a piece for *The Listener* about 'Apartness, of all things'. She was in an emotional muddle – feeling John's absence, wanting 'the old myth, the illusion of company & friendliness & support', knowing that 'for the children's sake I must make myself able to live with him, and be liveable with'. The old feeling returned that if only she could restore domestic order everything would improve. 'Like a web, the chaos forms round me.'

John's career was about to take a new turn, as his first three-act play, *North-West Passage* (renamed *The Wrong Side of the Park*) was ready. Bucking the trend of the late 1950s, it featured middle-class people in a middle-class home – recognizably 23 Harben Road, a neglected house with wilting plants inside and out, a dated radio-gram and an 'accumulation of bills, single gloves, postcards sent to the wrong address' in the hall, enclosing the moribund marriage of Elaine and Henry Lee. Dull Henry works at the Ministry, bringing home a briefcase stuffed with buff-coloured PYX42 forms. His parents live with them, as does Elaine's single and pregnant sister, Barbara. On their doorstep arrives a plausible charmer and con man, Miller, looking for digs; he teases out of Elaine the story of her former husband, whom she now sees in a roseate glow (though he was in reality a drunk). In front of Miller, the Lees reminisce about their early days together. Elaine leaves home. In Act III, Elaine returns and, thanks to Miller's diabolus-ex-machina intervention, the marriage is rekindled. The couple embrace as the curtain falls.

The Lees are a childless version of the Mortimers. Their court-ship memories, of flannel dances with 'Hilda Faloon and her

Rhythm Kittens' ('Gladys Falloon' is the name of an old Henley fashion shop) are John and Penelope's. Elaine's sister recalls a time when Elaine 'was laughing all the time'. And Henry Lee's protestation, 'Look, I met Elaine when I was nineteen . . . And now we've been married sixteen years. We've come a long way and landed up on the cold, windy, unsunny side of the park . . .' is certainly John's, as is Henry's exasperated, 'What do you want? I'm only trying to do what you want!' at his wife's complaints. Elaine explains her absence with 'I just wanted to sleep, for a day or whatever it was until I could get away. I never meant to take enough pills to . . .' which has the flavour of Penelope's darkest moments. And interestingly, when Miller says goodbye, he is off to 'the Belgrave Square area', on the right side of the park: precisely where John was now living, in Wilton Mews, Belgravia.

Peter Hall, still in his twenties and newly appointed to run the Royal Shakespeare Company at Stratford, was to direct the play. John had first met Hall, with Peggy Ramsay, in the bar of the Arts Theatre in 1955, during the run of *Waiting for Godot*. Now, in Hall's ornate Montpelier Square house, decorated by his wife Leslie Caron in *fin-de-siècle* style with gilt cherubs, they were discussing John's play when they heard that Margaret Leighton would be their star. When she arrived, with her husband, Laurence Harvey – who was driven about by a uniformed chauffeur on a motor scooter, riding pillion – John noticed how badly Harvey treated his older wife, summoning waiters to 'fetch another drink for my mother'. But Miss Leighton gave as good as she got, and when the marriage foundered the following year, John conducted her undefended divorce.

To play the pregnant sister-in-law, Hall asked John to see a young actress named Wendy Craig, whom he had admired at the Royal Court in Osborne's *Epitaph for George Dillon*. Wendy, aged twenty-four, born in Durham, trained at the Central School, was married to a journalist, Jack Bentley, and the mother of a baby son, Alaster. John met Miss Craig for lunch at a pub in Chiswick. She asked if John would be attending rehearsals and he assured her that he would. On 12 November 1959, the cast was announced:

Margaret Leighton and Richard Johnson as the central couple, George Relph and Joyce Carey as the Aged Ps, Robert Stephens as the dashing interloper – and Wendy Craig as the pregnant sister.

John's forays into the theatre, Penelope realized, 'demanded and supplied a succession of accessible girlfriends'. He did not call them lovers, and therefore expected Penelope to give her blessing; but she could not. She did not resent the sexual infidelity, she claimed, so much as the 'hints and confessions, implausible excuses, furtive muttering on the phone, a flowering of Carnaby Street shirts and medallions'. This comment is anachronistic: Carnaby Street had not yet been created as a hippie mecca, and medallions only erupted a few years later. But what she perceived was that John regarded these amorous opportunities as a compensation for having married so young, missing out on a wild youth.

The Wrong Side of the Park was a tragi-comedy, but it was tame compared with the private drama in the Mortimer household that resulted from his affair with Wendy Craig during the play's run. 'In a way,' John writes, 'that time marked the beginning of the end of our living in the house, because although we stayed on for a number of years we had begun, perhaps unconsciously, to make secret preparations for our departure.'

John was so preoccupied with rehearsals, he let down his parents on successive Saturdays ('We were left with provisions that we had bought in anticipation of John's visit'). Then he arrived, with four of the children but without Penelope, so his parents remained unaware of their problems, or of John's ever having left the marital home. At Christmas Jeremy rode about in his new Red Indian outfit on his new tricycle. John's present to Clifford was a record of Gielgud reading Shakespeare and a fawn woollen cardigan 'of extreme luxury and softness'.

'So ends the year,' wrote Clifford. 'Not a bad year on the whole. We have been free from money troubles and only a little illness, although we were very sorry with Penelope for the loss of her hoped-for baby.'

9. Losing a Father, Gaining a Son

One Monday morning in January 1960, after the coldest night of the winter, Kathleen was up at 5.45 a.m., getting Clifford's tea and describing for him the robins, chaffinches, wagtails and nuthatches in the snowy garden. She put an old coat under the wheels of the car, drove to Henley station, and they caught the 8.43 to London for a contested will case, Seaford deceased, before Mr Justice Karminski. Appearing for the other side was their son. His play, he said over lunch, got six curtain calls at the first Brighton preview. Next day, his parents again braved the snow to get to court for day two. 'To my surprise & chagrin, I lost and John won,' wrote Clifford, 'equally to his surprise I think.'

While Clifford, at seventy-six, fretted about his dwindling income ('At long last a cheque for fees in Beech deceased arrived but alas, the sum is not enough to cover the bank charges, & my indebtedness to chambers') his son was riding a crest of success.

During the pre-London run at Stratford, John had taken Wendy Craig to dine with Michael Fenton and his wife, who at once suspected an affair between the author and the actress. On the day of the first night, 3 February 1960, the *Evening Standard* discovered Mr Mortimer in his overcoat, 'nervously consuming barley sugar' on stage at the Cambridge Theatre. The photograph showed John smiling down upon the seated Miss Craig, who said she was getting a bit tired of playing pregnant roles. 'I've been expectant in four plays now. In *The Sport of My Mad Mother*, I had a baby on stage, if you please.'

'She has it off-stage in this play,' said John.

His parents stayed at the Strand Palace Hotel, and sat in the front row alongside Mrs Fletcher, Penelope, Julia and Caroline. This was the last play of John's his father 'saw'. Clifford's diary recorded, not very illuminatingly, 'We were rather nervous about the play which took a little time to get going but later went across well and there was enthusiastic applause at the end.' The Mortimer women all looked 'resplendent': Julia wore a wonderful dress; Penelope was 'even more resplendent'; Caroline 'even more resplendent still'. 'We saw Harold Hobson who is very small,' noted Kathleen/Clifford. 'The theatre which is enormous was well filled.'

Queen magazine photographed the first-night party: Peter Hall with Leslie Caron; Penelope wearing a pretty tear-drop necklace, its sparkles shrouded in her smoke, with Caroline; Laurie Lee with the sculptor Elisabeth Frink; Margaret Leighton (who had already started an affair with her co-star Robert Stephens) with Laurence Harvey. The next morning John's parents heard their son on the *Today* programme, before joining him and Penelope for lunch at Harben Road. A week later John rang excitedly to tell them of the play's 'almost fantastic' success: the box office took £1,200 on the first Saturday and £5,000 over the week. Even the *Daily Worker* put John 'among the top playwrights of 1960': he appeared to have 'no particular political philosophy' but he did have 'a quality of humanism lacking in his contemporaries'. John kept a wary eye on Pinter, whose *A Night Out*, full of energy, menace and aggression, was televised that spring starring Pinter and his wife, Vivien Merchant; in the ratings it outstripped even *Sunday Night at the London Palladium*.

A successful play creates immediate spin-offs: amateur rights, Broadway transfer, TV. When *The Wrong Side of the Park* was televised, directed by Stuart Burge, it was received as a drama of philosophical and poetic intensity. More radio plays were commissioned. John flew to Paris to discuss a film with Ingrid Bergman. Huw Wheldon's arts programme, *Monitor*, presented *Mortimer's Hampstead*: a portrait, not of the Ur-Hampstead of NW3, but of the coffee bars and bedsits, the schnitzel and strudel shops of Swiss Cottage, NW6. By 7 March, a *Times* headline read, 'Mr Mortimer to Give Up Writing Novels', over a story about John's plan to write one stage play and two television plays a year, preferably featuring characters who were failures. 'It's an attitude I've had since childhood,' he said, 'and in court I was always sympathetic with "the guilty party". When characters become successful, I lose interest.'

Alan Brien, a critic who could be as astute as Tynan, analysed the clever new playwright in the *Spectator*. He placed John Mortimer among those artists (Annigoni, Christopher Fry, Dylan Thomas, L. P. Hartley) who, despite quicksilver talents, never quite produce works of genius. John was for him the Christopher Fry of prose drama 'and therefore probably on the eve of an enormous critical and commercial success'. His style was full of 'quirky insights, unexpected images, persuasive eccentricities and quaint conceits' but these were 'plonked upside-down in the teapot like the dormouse in Alice'. Brien saw his characters' non sequiturs, their tendency to talk without listening – every character speaking in an undifferentiated voice – not as a distinctive theatrical style, but as a flaw. And how could Henry, the deadly dull husband, suddenly turn so charming, sympathetic and perceptive in the last act? John disliked this analysis and, even when Brien wrote warmly of his later work, did not forget.

With prosperity imminent, the Mortimers must obviously acquire a weekend home. House-hunting dominated Sundays at Turville Heath that spring and they gave up Cromer Hall. Despite the thrombosis in Clifford's right leg, it was the parents who viewed potential properties: Gannock Cottage at Nettlebed, Munday Dean Farm near Marlow, Cherry Trees at Northend. They were appalled by the prices.

Meanwhile, Penelope took five children, the au pair and Mrs Fletcher to a house on the cliffs at Lyme Regis in Dorset for Easter. Siriol Hugh-Jones, Penelope's fellow (but more enthusiastic) book reviewer, and equally enthusiastic chain-smoker, arrived with daughter Emma, who was Jeremy's age. Penelope worked on her television play, *The Renegade*, about the time when she ran away from school. She was also writing the *Daily Mail*'s agony column, as 'Ann Temple', addressing readers' problems, until deciding – rightly – that faced with their genuinely agonizing dilemmas, she simply could not advise them without knowing the people concerned.

When John arrived for weekends, Mrs Fletcher 'crept about, trying to be invisible'. Not knowing about his affair with Wendy, Penelope could be the cheerful mother, taking Jeremy on beach walks and to see lambs at a nearby farm. While saying goodnight to the children, helmeted in pink rollers, she was told by Deborah, 'You look so young and pretty – and *happy*.' 'Why spoil this?' she wrote. 'I was. I still am. The magic, or peace, or whatever, is returning. I'm less fraught, more certain what to do. Hush.' On Jeremy's fifth birthday ('John rang,' she notes) she was writing her agony column, moving beds, folding vests and taking Jeremy to see *Tom Thumb*, his first film. 'Six years ago today I didn't, if you look at it one way, have anything.'

Then Caroline arrived with Tom Kempinski and switched on the radio for *Waiting for Godot*, which 'droned on', interrupting Julia's *Pick of the Pops*. The house was bedlam. 'Tom & bevy of children shouting & screaming. Impossible to think or breathe. Rang John, in the hope of hearing a human voice. "It sounds ghastly," he said.'

Suddenly, Sally had to be rushed to Exeter Hospital with acute appendicitis. John arrived, having driven via Cherry Trees, Northend, for which he made an offer, later cancelled. That evening he, Caroline and Kempinski were obliviously 'babbling theatre' when Penelope – provoked beyond endurance by their prattle – crumpled her wine glass in her hand, pouring blood. During the next few days of getting her children, some ailing, back to their various schools for the summer term, she was obsessed and sickened by the execution of Caryl Chessman in San Quentin Prison. Nothing else seemed to matter; certainly not Princess Margaret's 'absurd' wedding to Tony Armstrong-Jones. Madelon was in Rome ('starving,' she wrote, 'send money') and there was a pile of impossible agony letters to read, and Sally to visit in hospital. Only Jeremy ('serious, funny, moving tiny soldiers about in a jungle of daisies and grass') never failed to enchant her. In hospital, now with suspected dysentery, Sally had a letter from a woman called Dempsey. 'In case you don't know who I am,' it said, 'I am your Daddy's secretary.' But no letter from John. ('Get a woman in,' writes Penelope drily in her diary. 'And Sal is so keenly, so really knowing.') Suddenly Jeremy too developed spots and a temperature – it was urticaria – just as Sally was moved to an isolation hospital with jaundice and suspected typhoid. She was put in a glassed-in room and could only be spoken to through a window. But the typhoid scare was a false alarm. On 11 May, Penelope took the family home to Harben Road: newly decorated under the supervision of the housekeeper, it 'looked like a half-finished hotel'.

The Wrong Side of the Park transferred to the St Martin's Theatre in May, and John again became locum drama critic for the *Standard*, reviewing a Wesker trilogy and hailing *The Caretaker*: 'Mr Harold Pinter is a born writer.' He bought a new Jaguar, in which they drove to Turville Heath, where they sat in the garden and discussed the possibility, instead of buying a house, of having a wing built on to the cottage. Clifford and Kathleen wrote next day voicing doubt about the idea, which caused a brief rift: they 'got a nasty letter from John in reply'. Upset, they wrote at once to mollify him and 'were delighted this morning to get a friendly letter from John'.

Like many troubled marriages, the Mortimers' revived for long periods, enjoying 'hectic reconciliations'. A return to Positano, where Madelon could join them, was proposed, but without the young; so Penelope transported Jeremy and the girls and two friends of Julia's, plus record player and transistor radio, to Turville Heath Cottage. 'The girls spend most of their time sun-bathing in bikinis, listening to records (chiefly "pop") & we had little of their company except at meal-times,' wrote Kathleen, mildly disapproving. 'Jeremy was very sweet and kept asking for stories. The girls seemed reluctant to go anywhere . . . and' (when they caught their train home) 'wore the most unbecoming clothes for travelling.'

John made a half-hearted offer on a house near Pangbourne, but it proved to have dry rot and woodworm. Perhaps they should after all build a new house in the orchard of Turville Heath Cottage. The architect Lionel Brett (Lord Esher, founder of the Council for the Protection of Rural England) valued the plot alone at £5,000 and applied for planning permission, which was eventually granted in February 1961.

On 25 June 1960, a Saturday evening, the Third Programme broadcast *Lunch Hour*. This was John's one-act play about a businessman's assignation to meet a young female colleague in a drab King's Cross hotel bedroom in their lunch hour. The couple, played by Stephen Murray and Wendy Craig, are constantly interrupted by the hotel's cockney manageress (and her garrulous son), for whom the businessman has invented an absurdly elaborate tale. He claims that the young woman is his wife, who has travelled from Yorkshire for a serious discussion; they have left three children at an aunt's house, to be alone. The putative mistress goes along with this implausible charade, entering into it so thoroughly that she begins to challenge her 'husband' about his selfishness, and, with shrill indignation, to take the wife's side. So the precious lunch hour ticks away and at the end of it neither of them has removed even an overcoat.

The curious observer might wonder where John had picked up the notion of hiring a hotel bedroom by the hour. From his affair with Wendy perhaps? Since Miss Craig was the mother of a young son, and on stage every evening in *The Wrong Side of the Park*, they needed a venue for their snatched assignations. Clifford noted that he and Kathleen listened to the broadcast of *Lunch Hour*, adding: 'Styrax Japonica in the West Field is in full flower – very striking.'

For six weeks that summer Penelope and John and the three youngest took a house on the Hampshire coast at Emsworth (where P. G. Wodehouse once lived at Threepwood House, adopting these names for key characters). John toiled over the next play, *Two Stars for Comfort*. Without the eldest three – Julia was with Madelon in Rome, Caroline touring in an Agatha Christie play – the summer lacked lustre, and Jeremy had mumps. 'I take Dexadren [*sic*], drink a lot in the evenings; 2 sleeping pills for the nights,' Penelope noted. Dexedrine only increased her depression, since after the high came the inevitable low.

On 23 August, Kathleen rang to say Clifford had had a heart attack. Dr Elliott had arrived at 3.30 a.m. and gave morphia injections; John sped to Henley and fetched a male nurse from the station, returning the following weekend to read aloud his new play to his father. Clifford soon rallied and lost nearly a stone (to 12st 12lb) and they were all taken by Aunt Daisy to Stratford to see *A Winter's Tale*. It was the start of Jeremy's first term at prep school, the Hall in Belsize Park, where he wore a round pink cap 'like a blancmange': his first day there was another milestone for Penelope.

In the week of her forty-second birthday, Penelope's collection of stories, *Saturday Lunch with the Brownings*, was published. Written with her pared-down, unsparing clarity, they illustrate her incendiary determination to scrutinize the dynamics of her marriage. The first review (in the *Sunday Times*) was dismaying: the critic found the married couples in her stories 'trivially embittered, chronically quarrelling about nothing, filled with a fatigued desperation' and asked why they didn't all go to Harrods, buy fifty aspirin and end it all? Reading this, Penelope felt miserable, 'knowing how often, how much worse, I've done it to other people'.

But the *Sunday Times* man could not know how many stories were based on real events: they were supposedly fiction, and not for years did the younger daughters perceive that Penelope had written so closely about their life. In the title story, the father is so besotted with his own daughter, and so irritated by his stepdaughters, that he can turn vicious. 'Get their own father to keep them,' he tells his wife. 'Go on, go and find him. Tell him to keep the lot of you on his five pounds a week.' That story recalled a painful incident when Deborah was told by John not to eat her cherries in the garden, and a flaming row ensued, just before a children's party; whereupon John angrily packed suitcases for himself and Sally. It had happened, some years before, and it had all been smoothed over; but the toxic exchange of words, the husband's 'these delinquent little bitches of yours' and the wife's 'You hit my children!', were founded on a never-forgotten row at Harben Road. Penelope did more than milk their domestic life; her stories reflect how deeply and sympathetically she understood her children and how she also felt a fundamental empathy with her beleaguered, over-burdened husband. In the title story, the husband's hearty homecoming refrain is always (like John's) a breezy 'What's the plan?' He loves amusing company, which children do not invariably provide, and exhibits a helpless bewilderment in the face of all the emotion that gets hurled about within their walls.

Clifford and Kathleen read the book and again refrained from comment. Not commenting was their habit. On 28 September 1960, John was guest of the week on *Woman's Hour*: they listened but said nothing more. On 4 October: 'We listened to John on the Home Service at 9.45. Today has again been showery.' On 7 October: 'We listened to the repeat of John's talk on the wireless. In the afternoon went to Henley, did much shopping.' On 8 October: 'We listened again to John's talk & boxed up some rock roses & potted Spanish gorse – enjoyed the partridge.' But buried in the subtext of Clifford's diary is John and Penelope's literary busyness. One weekend John brought three of the children for a walk and lunch, departing in time to speak in a debate at the Royal Court Theatre; he was also helping Clifford with a brief (Thomson deceased), reviewing a book for the *Spectator* and preparing another play for broadcasting. Penelope was reading one of her stories, 'I Told You So', on the Third Programme. In John's new Jaguar they all went for a spin to Hambleden Lock in the rain, and had a flat tyre; several hours passed before a man from Lewin & Sergeant's in Henley could be summoned. ('Get a man in.')

Every day Kathleen faced new tasks in the relentless garden: labelling dahlias, putting alum on the hydrangeas, dealing with a fallen tree. She made marrow jam, had new leather patches made for Clifford's sports coat and read aloud – at Clifford's request – the new unexpurgated Penguin edition of *Lady Chatterley's Lover*. When Clifford ran up an overdraft because fee cheques, and rental from John, failed to save their balance, Daisy sent a £150 cheque.

Increasingly, it was John alone who brought the children to Turville Heath at weekends, along with other guests – Siriol and

Emma, or the producer Michael Elliott, newly appointed artistic director at the Old Vic, who was to direct John's next West End play – and he would take everyone out for lunch at the Crown, a restaurant in a barn at Pishill. 'Both John & I love Jeremy,' wrote Penelope in December 1960, 'but we don't meet, even with him.' At Harben Road, Mrs Fletcher was installed, 'saving our lazy lives,' wrote Penelope in her diary, 'and I am vile to her'. She later told *Nova* magazine readers how her mother, at eighty, had taken over a household of six children and four flights of stairs, while Penelope 'ran about the world "finding myself",' pursued by Mrs Fletcher's letters with dramatic accounts of the children's coughs, toothache, constipation. In such situations Mrs Fletcher was 'eternally competent, eternally capable, eternally in command'

In mid-December John and Penelope were reunited ('Kill or cure,' wrote Penelope) for a skiing holiday in Adelboden in the Austrian Tyrol. John spent his time writing; Penelope supervised the children.

While they were away, Clifford and Kathleen had driven to Shiplake to view the last of the reject houses: ugly, suburban and depressing. But a week later, on 15 January 1961, they all walked over to 'Southend Cottage', less than a mile away. It was the perfect weekend retreat: two Georgian cottages knocked together, with four bedrooms, and an acre of garden, a lawn tennis court, an orchard with Thames Valley view, and Turville's old windmill beyond. Within a few days John had contracts for two film scripts 'for enormous sums', and since he was also doing Margaret Leighton's divorce, he could buy Southend Cottage from its owner, a Miss Tweed, for £12,500. This decision provoked an unusual comment in Clifford's diary: 'Their visit gave us much pleasure. We had crackers.'

John's stage version of *Lunch Hour* opened on 18 January 1961 at the Arts Theatre, starring Wendy Craig and Emlyn Williams. It was one of a triple bill, along with *The Form* by N. F. Simpson and *A Slight Ache* by Harold Pinter. Mortimer, Simpson and Pinter, 'three of the most brilliant playwrights working today', all got into *Who's Who* that year. John's work was judged the most conventional of the three, and the warmest. (Meeting John for the first time, Pinter found him 'very droll' and 'the epitome of civilisation'.) Emlyn Williams invited the three avant-garde young playwrights to his house at Pelham Crescent for drinks, and was 'wonderfully condescending', telling John, the oldest: 'Well, you just got into the New Wave as the Tube doors were closing!' After the 'sticky' opening night, John's play provoked laughter and good notices from Tynan, Levin ('funny, touching and true'), Harold Hobson and Caryl Brahms.

Within a month it transferred to the Criterion, where Caroline, who was now understudying Wendy Craig, one day walked in on John and Wendy in the dressing room: they jumped guiltily apart as she entered. The photogenic, mini-skirted Caroline was featured in the *Evening Standard*'s Londoner's Diary. What was Caroline's father earning these days? Lord Beaverbrook, the paper's proprietor, always insisted that readers longed to know about people's money. 'The Londoner' (Tudor Jenkins at that time) speculated that apart from his law practice, John Mortimer must be making £20,000 for each of his film scripts, 'and he has another play scheduled for the autumn'. Later it was reported that John was getting £1,000 a week to write a film for Sophia Loren entitled *Shocking*. 'Do you know even a top QC making that?' asked the *Daily Herald*. Wendy Craig's husband, a journalist on the *Sunday Pictorial*, also drew attention to the fortune that smiled on John Mortimer. On 22 January 1961, in his column 'Show Business by Jack Bentley', he wrote in characteristic tabloid style:

I envy barrister John Mortimer. Some of the world's most beautiful stars are clamouring for his services. After a recent trip to the South of France to write a specially-commissioned story for Ingrid Bergman, John last week received a continental call from Sophia Loren. She wants him to write a story for her. There should be a law against such luck!

Magazine photographers continued to descend on 'Mr Mortimer and his authoress wife' and their brood. John's dramatic output, combined with his legal career, was found remarkable: a writer with an interest in 'the real world beyond the footlights'. *Good Housekeeping*, that Christmas, had featured 'The Writing Mortimers' and the *Tatler* sent Mark Gerson to do a series of photos: Penelope seated at a Remington typewriter on her desk, gazing ahead; John standing in front of the bookshelves, gazing at her.

No one would know from John's amenable, publicity-friendly demeanour that momentous things were happening at home. At the beginning of 1961, Penelope had become pregnant again, for the eighth time. She was optimistic. It seemed a good moment. They had Southend Cottage. Jeremy was six, at the Hall; Deborah and Sally were boarding; Julia was doing O-levels at Francis Holland, Caroline was acting and Madelon was in Rome. John's theatre success was assured and he was adapting his old radio plays for the stage. Penelope's indifferent reviews convinced her that she would probably never write another book: this baby would be a compensation.

But her doctor recommended a termination, since she was forty-two – though this was the age at which Mrs Fletcher gave birth to her, Penelope pointed out – and because her last pregnancy had miscarried. And when she asked John what he felt about the new baby, he replied with unaccustomed seriousness: he said that although he had made her unhappy, their marriage was the only important thing in his life and he still depended on a future with her. But in his view another baby would make things difficult, if not impossible. She agreed, at once, to an abortion and sterilization: decisions which brought a curious euphoria, a feeling of having been given back her life. John rang his parents on 26 February 1961 and told them that Penelope would soon be going in for a 'minor operation', for two weeks.

Wendy Craig became pregnant in the same month.

On 4 March, John flew off to Hollywood to stay at the Beverly Wilshire Hotel, to discuss an MGM film for Susan Hayward. That day Penelope went to see her in-laws (with Siriol, Emma, Jeremy, her brother Paul and his wife) and they all called at Southend Cottage. The next day she went into the Welbeck Street clinic.

The day she returned home, 12 March, the wound burst open,

and during Caroline's nineteenth birthday party she was rushed back to Welbeck Street by ambulance. Mrs Fletcher held the fort at home; Jeremy had measles, and, to compound it all, on Saturday night they were burgled. John rang and assured Penelope he would try to get home sooner: he was having a miserable time anyway. (Hollywood, he had decided, was 'indistinguishable from Slough'; and the producer who had lavished praise on your script would then show it to some front office underling, and come back to say it lacked drama, was too literary, contained too many words, etc.)

While Penelope was in hospital, John had written fond letters from Los Angeles 'full of promises and resolutions, planning the miraculous years ahead'. On a sunny spring day, John's parents arranged for a Pickfords van to move their spare furniture into Southend Cottage. Penelope was still in hospital, 'sewn up like a mail-bag', when John came home on 16 March.

A few days later John drove to Turville Heath, taking Caroline, and they went to look at Southend Cottage. Penelope's diary for that day notes: 'See a letter suggesting John has been having an affair with the actress in Lunch Hour.' Which letter? From whom? Wendy had written to John while he was in Hollywood, and letters which arrived after he departed were sent on to Harben Road by MGM. Did Penelope open one, that day when John took Caroline to the cottage, and ring Jack Bentley? Or did Jack Bentley, having got a confession from Wendy, write to Penelope? Either way, Bentley and Penelope spoke on the telephone, and may also have met. At around the same time, Wendy Craig, still appearing in *Lunch Hour*, met John at the Salisbury pub in St Martin's Lane, and told him that her husband had found out; their affair must end. They said goodbye for the last time outside the pub. The drama that followed was stored away as material for Penelope's next novel, *The Pumpkin Eater*.

The preservation of family life takes priority at times of emotional upheaval. John and Penelope kept returning to their cottage, sometimes dropping the children at their grandparents', but more often descending mob-handed. Southend Cottage became the family's social vortex. A chimney caught fire and firemen were called. All the fuses blew and John got a man in. Clifford's diary for Easter Monday 1961 is written in Sally's round eleven-year-old hand, when they had been to the circus in Henley. 'Deb rode on the clown's back and the clown kissed Jeremy it was very cold and the grass was wet. Julia read to me after tea. The four girls cycled to Henley and back the hollow way they were just back after dark very tierd. Little Sally is writing this.' ('Big Sally' was a temporary nanny.)

Newly disengaged from his affair, John became an assiduously attentive son, son-in-law and father. They all gathered on his thirty-eighth birthday, for the unwrapping of presents; and for Jeremy's sixth birthday the next week, when John proudly showed Kathleen and Clifford his garden. He dined with them, admired their rhododendrons and azaleas, lent them books; he took Jeremy on the river with his new best friend Patsy Rance, whose mother, Faun, had been one of John's girlfriends in youth, and who lived in the cottage the Mortimers had rented thirty-four years before. He gave Sally a rabbit for her birthday; inaugurated the tennis court at Southend; and organized a picnic for a gang of children on Watlington Hill.

And these were months of unremitting work. One small success in the theatre, as he later wrote, makes movie moguls reach for their synopses. The Carlo Ponti film for Sophia Loren and David Niven never did get made, but he was also working on *The Innocents*, the film of Henry James's *The Turn of the Screw*, tweaking the screenplay by Truman Capote. He wrote sketches for a new revue, *One Over the Eight*, starring Fenella Fielding. *I Spy* was to be filmed in a Brighton seafront hotel for the TV series *Alfred Hitchcock Presents*. *Two Stars for Comfort* (misreported as 'Too Stark for Comfort') was finished, based on that unpublished first novel, set on the Thames at Henley. A short play, *The Encyclopaedist*, was televised, starring Cy Grant, a former lawyer from British Guiana, best known as the calypsoist from the *Tonight* programme. He played an earnest, bespectacled Trinidadian salesman, doorstepping the beatnik wife of a Chelsea painter. This was a sharply diverting piece, not about race, but about attitudes to learning.

That summer of typically changeable weather – it began with the coldest June day for eighty years, when the pergola fell down in a gale, but midsummer day brought a heatwave – proved to be the final one for Clifford. He was still nipping to the Law Courts ('we caught the 11.30 train and disposed of Kingham before Marshall J in court 8, had tea at Paddington and caught the 4.18 back') and being cheered by the arrival of a cheque: 'Fees in Thomson deceased, much more than we expected'. He welcomed having his routine disrupted by John, calling by to pick some parsley, or borrow their scythe and stone. One Sunday Kathleen noted that John 'seemed rather morose', but there is otherwise no hint that the scenario of *The Pumpkin Eater* was being enacted chez John and Penelope.

Wendy would be four months pregnant by now. When did Jack Bentley tell Penelope about his wife's pregnancy? Her diary reflects low spirits. She had been prescribed a drug called Cavodil, which made her feel 'half dead and quite uncertain'. 'Being pregnant, aborted, sterilised, wounded – it's not surprising, I know, that nothing heals. "Involuntary depression" I read, but don't know what it means. All I want is for it to be over.' The parallels between her life and her later novel are plain. The bitter irony of having herself been sterilized – causing mostly relief, mingled with regret – at exactly the same time as John's mistress became pregnant, explains both Penelope's depression and that of her heroine, Mrs Armitage, in the novel.

Superficially the Mortimers' lives seemed charmed. The first of July was the hottest day since 1947, with a temperature of eighty-six degrees in Henley, and the cottage had acquired a vast blue PVC swimming pool. Most Sundays brought guests. John told Michael Codron that his greatest joy was a gathering of friends at a long table in the garden: Peter Hall, Michael Elliott, Sheridan Morley, Stuart and Caroline Burge, Jack Clayton and his film-star wife Haya Harareet, Derek Hart and Siriol Hugh-Jones all came to Southend. People walking by on a Sunday afternoon, Penelope wrote, might see 'famous actors playing tennis, actresses lolling in the sun, producers and directors sprawled behind newspapers, a dozen children running naked through the orchard'. A scene, as she summarized it, 'of prosperous content'. Nobody would have guessed that Penelope was angry and frightened inside, or that she felt scorn and contempt for John's guests, 'their eagerness to laugh at his often cruel stories'. He in turn found the sight of her illness and misery 'intolerable'. 'His invective was more brutal than he intended – why didn't I just get out, go, I was useless to everyone, I was hideous, why didn't I die?' (The words 'Why don't you die?' were used later in *The Pumpkin Eater*, and Peter Finch in the film managed to say the line without any real malice.) But John would, she felt sure, soon explode, or go mad, or kill her.

One day in July Penelope sneaked into the Law Courts and watched her husband dispatching the divorce of a couple named Evans in Court One. From the public gallery she observed the familiar neck under the yellowing wig, heard him take Mr Evans's part in an 'unfamiliar voice full of authority' with lines like 'She fell out of love with him – physically, that is.' The wife duly lost, and had to pay £50. John departed (after a joking aside to a colleague) from the court. Her conclusion was that the courtroom was 'very like the theatre – a far cry from what really happened, what really was felt'. That evening she went to the recording of *The Renegade*, her TV play about her own schoolgirl escapade. She was played by fourteen-year-old Jane Asher, with Andrew Cruickshank as her father. Cruickshank was quite wrong, she felt, and 'pretty, fragile little Jane Asher' was nothing like 'the dumpy, frightened, ecstatic me'.

They decamped to the country for the summer holidays. But one evening in August, Penelope walked out of Southend Cottage, drove down the A40 to Harben Road and went to bed alone. The next morning she could not get out of bed. 'My brain went round & round, over & over the same things. I couldn't move, couldn't face the day.' Feeling that she was beyond her own control, 'something slipped irretrievably' and she rang John. She wanted to go back – 'to see Jeremy playing cricket, hear Deb's clarinet, hopelessly follow Julia, be in the kitchen, cut off the dead-heads. All that. But I can't do it.' She wrote in her diary: 'I cannot hear once more how he loves or hates me, blames me. I will not be reduced to an uncreative cretin scribbling in notebooks. At last I realise that there's a point beyond which one cannot go.' Caroline, all solicitude, dropped everything to be with her, and Penelope drove her to work at the Playhouse Theatre, 'feeling ashamed & loving & grateful'. After three days she went back, explaining to the bewildered children, half-truthfully, that she'd had to go to Granny Fletcher who was not well.

A little break might be the answer. John and Penelope left for Elba, which was not a success. Their hot twin-bedded hotel room was loud with buzzing flies and overlooked a prison. Penelope was still in post-operative pain. 'The only comfort is to lie on a rubber mattress rocking, like some abandoned aviator, in the middle of the broiling sea.' They returned via Rome on 2 September, in time for the televising of *The Renegade*. John's agent Peggy Ramsay rang to say she admired it. Penelope was briefly tempted to give up on novels and follow John into TV plays.

On her forty-third birthday weekend, she was seized by another whim: to take part in a cause, to join in the historic political demonstration of the moment, the Ban the Bomb rally in Trafalgar Square of 17 September 1961.

I want to be able to say I was there . . . I want tremendously to know how people behave . . . I want, for once, to be in on it instead of sitting in a vacuum tricked out with child-sized 'necessities'. My life has been measured out in meals, socks, little bloody Noddy. I want, anonymous & in my trousers, pill-less & drinkless & uncomfortable & free, to be in Trafalgar Square.

John discouraged her. She stayed at the cottage, fretfully digging the garden as the rain came down. On the news she saw people arrested, 'blondes and beards cheerfully letting themselves be lugged into police vans' – while she was incarcerated in her 'luxury prison'.

Clifford and Kathleen arrived with birthday greetings; John

opened a bottle of champagne and the cork flew out, smashing three glasses. These were the days that led to Penelope's embarking on *The Pumpkin Eater*. As she later wrote, 'extreme despair is often the final stage of gestation'. She could have been among the better writers, she reflected. But 'there's a great weight clamped over my writing hand'.

At Turville Heath Cottage the following Sunday, 24 September 1961, Clifford had a pain in his left wrist, which became swollen, and spent the day in bed. Dr Elliott diagnosed gout. By Thursday that week, he was able to take a bath. 'I sent cheques to the Temple & to Butlers' were the very last words he dictated. On 30 September, Kathleen wrote, 'On September 29th Clifford was very ill and on September 30th at 3.30am he died.' He was seventy-seven. John had sat at his bedside during the long hot night, holding the oxygen mask over his father's face until he had no more need for it. He says he slept solidly for two days following his father's death.

John reflected, at the end of *A Voyage Round My Father*, 'I know what I felt. Lonely.' In long retrospect, he was consoled that his father, who belonged to the age of Empire, missed the 1960s, a decade which would not have appealed to him at all. Clifford's funeral was on 3 October at Turville Church. Though he had never sought the consolation of religion he had a conventional Church of England burial in the churchyard. The next day, Kathleen carried on their diary: 'We had to have a new Simmerstat for the electric cooker. I wrote a great many replies to the very consoling & sympathetic letters which came from members of the Bar & many other people.' On 8 October: 'I have re-started smoking but very few cigarettes.'

Clifford left a modest £3,593. Kathleen sold 'my darling Clifford's law books', six of which went for nine guineas, and his Braille books; two herbal paintings sold at Sotheby's for £25. Later, Mr Simmonds, the Fleet Street bookseller, came and bought Clifford's law reports and some little seventeenth-century copies of *The Iliad*. She planted forget-me-nots and tulips on Clifford's grave. 'I came back and walked round the garden. I was very lonely and could not quench my regrets . . . I cannot believe that Clifford is really gone.' The widowed mother is never a comfortable role, but Kathleen went along with any suggestion, accompanying John to his tailor in Oxford ('unfortunately his car got stuck in the mud outside the cottage and a breakdown outfit came and pulled him out with some difficulty') and Daisy to Oxford Playhouse to see *The Hollow Crown*, wishing Clifford could be there.

On Saturday 4 November, Bonfire Eve, they organized fireworks at Southend Cottage and took Kathleen to the bonfire on the common. On the foggy Monday morning of 6 November, John took the children back to London. It was twenty-five years to the day since Penelope had married Charles Dimont, and she was alone at the cottage. She sat down in the silence, put paper in the typewriter and wrote an opening sentence 'that lit up the dark corners of my heart'. It was the start of *The Pumpkin Eater*, and she wrote non-stop (and dry-eyed) for three weeks. 'Dear world & life that lets me write and speak again,' she wrote in her diary.

Four days later, on 10 November, Wendy Craig's baby, Ross Bentley, was born in a Hampstead nursing home, attended by Jack Suchet. Ross would grow up believing that he was Jack Bentley's son; and John claimed, in old age, never to have known anything about Ross's existence until the summer of 2004 – by which time John had become not only capable of forgetting, but even more adept at self-deception, erasing all unpleasant or inconvenient things from his mind. It seems highly unlikely that he was never told about the baby, even if Wendy kept her secret, just as Penelope had in her first marriage. Unless Penelope kept silence to preserve her fracturing marriage, and unless John wilfully ignored the story of *The Pumpkin Eater*, he would surely have known. His family, and many friends, agreed that he must have had some inkling. In several of his later works (*Edwin*, *Paradise Postponed*, *Felix in the Underworld*, *Hock and Soda Water*), there is a son whose true paternity is in some doubt.

Penelope heard, and told one of her daughters, that 'apparently the child looks exactly like John'. But Wendy always said that

Bentley, on his deathbed in 1994, had implored her never to let anyone know, or talk about it. So it was not until ten years into her widowhood that Wendy – alerted to the fact that her secret was out – came to Turville Heath Cottage for lunch, in September 2004, and told John that Ross, now aged forty-two, was his son.

'Remember way back in 1963, Mr Mortimer. When I was polishin' your floor wearin' me mini-skirt?'

10. Had a Wife and Couldn't Keep Her

The Pumpkin Eater is an extraordinary novel. Its reputation, like that of the Jack Clayton / Harold Pinter film which faithfully adapted it, has endured – despite the book's being out of print for decades and the unaccountable unavailability of the film. The importance of *The Pumpkin Eater* in John's life is that it told so comprehensively his wife's story of what had so recently happened in their marriage. Penelope had written at a crisis point, the kind of crisis that destroys people, and distilled it, with a true novelist's alchemy, into a clear-eyed narrative whose power derived from its profound honesty. It was not 'true', but it was founded on truth. Even the weather she described – 'It was a freak March, they said it was seventy degrees' – is accurate for London in March 1961.

At the start of the novel, 'Mrs Jake Armitage', Penelope's alter ego, sets out the facts of her life to her analyst. (Unlike Penelope, she has no career of her own, but sees herself as 'Mrs Production Limited. I spring from Armitage Enterprises.') After thirteen years of marriage, Jake, her fourth husband, makes £50,000 a year as a newly prosperous film producer and screenwriter. In the driveway stand a Jaguar and a Floride. Financial success has transformed their once child-dominated, kitchen-centred, laughter-filled household. Now they hire interior decorators and mother's helps. They each drive about alone in their cars; the family takes holidays without Jake, while he works.

'Jake doesn't want any more children,' she tells her shrink. They already have a remarkable number, he comments. Does she like her husband? She replies, 'No. Not very much.' But she does love him. She had been pregnant by her previous husband when Jake fell in love with her – instantly, in an afternoon. 'I think he wanted to join us, that's all. I think he wanted . . . to belong to us.' Jake had been an only child. At Christmas he had to wear a dinner jacket and sit with the adults. Their respective fathers had been scathing but pragmatic when they decided to marry. Jake's father had told his future daughter-in-law, 'He'll be a frightful husband. You're bound to be ill for instance. You won't get the slightest sympathy from him, he hates illness. He's got no money and he's bone-lazy.' And Jake would find the children 'tremendously boring'. 'He's out for what he can get,' he tells her. 'Beautiful wife who knows how to cook, ready-made family, plenty of furniture.' (John too later used this scene, with almost identical words, in *A Voyage Round My Father*.) Her own father had been equally mystified: 'For a young man with his life in front of him to saddle himself with a brood of children and a wife as plain feckless as this daughter of mine seems to me lunacy. Lunacy.'

Jake's infidelity is discovered first with the au pair, Philpot (when the children innocently tell their mother that 'Philpot fainted yesterday, and Daddy caught her'), causing a confrontation. Jake insists it was a mere peccadillo. But caught out, he goes on the attack with a tirade:

'You don't care about me, all you care about is the bills being paid and that great fucking army of children that I'm supposed to support and work out my guts for, so I can't even take a bath in peace, I can't eat a bloody meal without them whining and slobbering all over the table, I can't even go to bed with you without one of them comes barging in in the middle.'

He is a normal man, capable of fancying someone else, that's all. Afterwards he's sorry he said all this, he didn't mean it, he loves her and the children. 'You were telling the truth,' says his wife.

When she faints, while wandering through Harrods, bewildered by the lavish displays, Jake is unsympathetic: 'Do you think you're going to get over this period of your life, because I find it awfully depressing?' Eavesdropping on the stairs, she overhears Jake talking to their doctor, man-to-man, over a drink, telling him his wife 'gets mad ideas into her head. Thinks everyone's against her, finds fault all the time.' Perhaps Jake should let her have another child? 'We've got enough children! Good God, we've got enough! I'm sick of living in a bloody nursery!' After the doctor leaves, Jake is heard dialling the telephone and speaking softly to someone.

The narrative is punctuated with press clippings. 'Jake Armitage, one of the highest-paid scribblers in the business, is planning to say "no" at least once a week to movie moguls who are outbidding each other to buy his services.' (Compare the Jack Bentley item from the *Sunday Pictorial* quoted previously.) 'He is currently working on The Sphinx, to be shot in North Africa . . .'

Back from filming, Jake tells his wife stories of life on set, the cheery tales of a gregarious man who enjoys being among people. The few he dislikes, she says, are 'overbearingly sincere, intensely serious and tinged with failure: these he dismissed as bores'. (John's feelings precisely.) Sensing Jake's lowering of spirits at being back home, she suggests they have a party and invite the Conways – Beth, the actress from the film, and her husband. Bob Conway proves to be 'about fifty, squat, fat, with a throttling bow-tie and small, twinkling eyes'. (Penelope's description of Jack Bentley.) Beth's co-star confides that Beth is a bit boring, 'the deadly English Rose type', and has 'the most ghastly breath, have you noticed?' (Penelope at her most poisonous.)

Mrs Armitage becomes pregnant and Jake is frankly dismayed. For years he has been driven by panic in order to support them all, taking on frightful scripts he didn't want to do, accepting everything he was offered; 'destroying, incidentally, his own talent in the process'. And just at this point when he has realized how much he loves her, and they can start planning a better life, enjoy their freedom and broaden their horizons, another child would be 'tragic'. Mrs Armitage is relieved, ecstatic: the abortion will be straightforward to arrange, since she is already being treated for depression.

Penelope was using her novel, not for the first time, as a vehicle for self-analysis. She has produced all these children: why? Who are they, this self-contained army of varying sizes and sexes? Babies have dominated her life, and then they grew up, wanting help with homework, needing food and conversation, 'sitting in a patient row on the sofa preparing to talk to us or play games . . . their eyes restless as maggots, expecting us to bring them up'. And who is this husband she has married? Her previous husbands were all 'peaceful men capable of great physical exertion', whereas 'Jake is a violent man who wears a sluggard body for disguise. Sleepy, amiable, anxious to please, lazy, tolerant . . . this is the personality he wears as a man in the world. His indestructible energy, aggression, cruelty and ambition are well protected.'

A begging letter arrives from a woman who has seen pictures of her in a magazine; a sad woman who has had a hysterectomy and whose husband doesn't make love to her any more. (Just the sort of letter Penelope dealt with in her Ann Temple column for the *Daily Mail*.) 'What should I say to Mrs Evans? "Dear Mrs Evans, I am about to have an abortion and wonder if you could give me some advice . . . I myself am not going to have another baby."' In hospital for the abortion she is also sterilized. Jake's florist sends flowers, from Hollywood, New York, Rome; Jake's secretary brings magazines. With a blood-caked scar on her abdomen, she is full of plans, lists, to sort things out, 'love Jake'.

Then she finds a letter: addressed to Jake, in a mauve envelope. 'Jake baby . . .' it begins. It's from Beth Conway, a love letter. The odious Bob Conway meets her at a café and tells her that Jake and his wife have been having lunch-hour assignations at a pub near the film studio: Jake has, he says, 'been bashing around for years . . . Author's perks. He gets the ones the stars don't want.' He has been sending Beth flowers every day. 'He's crazy about her.' Conway's unstoppable revelations twist the knife. 'You know why you had an abortion? Because Beth's a good girl at heart, she would have left him.' Mrs Armitage flees from this ghastly encounter.

She and Jake quarrel bitterly over how many women there have been. 'Half a dozen. A dozen. I don't know. What does it matter, how many?' She wants to know where the affair happened. 'You mean there are hotels where you can go for some hours, without signing the register?' So it goes on, the circular, lacerating quarrel. Why doesn't she die, why doesn't she leave him? It's all her own fault, he says, 'opening letters, talking to people. You've brought the whole damn thing on yourself.' The knife is further twisted when Conway rings to tell her Beth is pregnant, and it is not his baby. But she is going to have it, 'going to wipe its bottom and stare at its ugly mug for the rest of her young life . . . This kid's going to make her curse Jake Armitage for the rest of her days . . . She's going to hate that kid almost as much as I shall.' So, Mrs Armitage realizes: 'She is pregnant and I'm sterile.' But at least there is some hope for Beth. She may love the child. She may get away from the unspeakable Conway.

Outside her window, the neighbourhood is being demolished. Alone, Mrs Armitage goes to the tower they have been renovating, in the countryside on a hill, and ponders on her unknown future and her lost past as the mother who had 'stood over stoves, stirring things in a saucepan . . . stretched up for the clothes-pegs, hurrying in from the garden, bedouined with washing . . . shook thermometers, spooned out medicine'. Suddenly, up the hill, Jake arrives, with the gang of children in tow. 'I thought I might join you for a while,' Jake says amiably.

This is how *The Pumpkin Eater* ends: on a hopeful – or accepting – note.

Penelope had not only poured her experience into this novel – and it is worth recalling here that John always said that their lives were their 'material', and he thought *The Pumpkin Eater* a 'brilliant' novel – she had also delved into her childhood memories, and added an account of her father-in-law's funeral and her sympathy for her husband's sense of aloneness. 'His father had been the progenitor of Jake's whole world': a man 'sceptical, tepid, suspicious of emotion, contemptuous of the laws he scrupulously kept . . . the only thing that had ever tortured him was boredom' (a fair summary of Clifford Mortimer). The funeral reading is one of Donne's gloomiest sermons, which probably appealed to Penelope's own father, and which Penelope quotes in full, over several pages: 'Let me wither and weare out mine age in a discomfortable, in an unwholesome, in a penurious prison,' it begins cheerlessly, 'and so pay my debts with my bones, and recompense the wastefulness of my youth, with the beggary of mine age. Let me wither in a spittle under sharp and foul and infamous diseases . . .'

Penelope finished writing her novel in the spring of 1962. She marked this milestone in her diary with the chilling line: 'But then, how cruel, everything dies except the writing.'

Quite apart from the emotional intensity, and its revelatory nature, which only she fully knew, it was a remarkably well-written novel. As a purging of personal turmoil, it had been cathartic. Having written, Penelope suddenly began making valiant efforts to re-enter John's world in a wifely manner. She accompanied him to a luncheon for Robert Graves, and to the première of *The Innocents*, Jack Clayton's film of *The Turn of the Screw* – in which Alexander Walker detected 'fey, sinister touches inserted into Henry James's story by John Mortimer and Truman Capote', even though John was not at the time officially credited. And for once, she went with him on location, to Spain, where two of his scripts were being shot: *Guns of Darkness* and Carol Reed's *The Running Man*.

After this therapeutic interlude, Penelope wrote, 'I learned belatedly from Spain that my life's a round hole, all of it, and the reason for so much anguish has been the squareness of me. That Monday when I started the book, it was like writing my own obituary, post-mortem or something. A fortnight among grown-ups in Spain spoiled all that.' (David Niven had proved to be hilariously good company, and John Osborne's current wife, Penelope Gilliat, a congenial companion.)

She also joined her husband on the pre-London tour of *Two Stars for Comfort*, the play set 'in a timbered riverside inn, in the gin and lime belt' in Henley, in which a gregarious publican named Sam propositions a series of Regatta Carnival queens. A group of students act a play, satirizing his dated seduction style and revealing the sad truth about his life, just as Hamlet's players did. Trevor Howard as Sam was the picture of craggy despair, and was often genuinely drunk on stage, causing visible terror in his fellow actors' eyes. Philip Hope-Wallace saw 'the purest Noël Coward' in lines such as the description of champagne as 'white wine with wind'; and Bernard Levin said, 'Two stars? No, give it five.'

The Dock Brief was being filmed for Dimitri de Grunwald at Shepperton, with Richard Attenborough as the murderer and Peter Sellers as the barrister Morgenhall. John found Sellers a riveting study, one of the saddest people he had ever met: a man riddled with imaginary anxieties and terrors, who only came to life when imitating someone else, 'as a shield against, I suppose, the dread of some hollowness within'. To while away the hours on the set, Sellers bought things on a whim; accompanied by John one day, he bought an electric organ, which nobody he knew could play. He was, John said, like the great barrister Sir Edward Marshall Hall: 'a man who stood empty, waiting to be inhabited by other people'.

Penelope had been less than delighted that year when the beautiful Caroline, aged nineteen, fell in love with Leslie Phillips, her co-star in *Go Back for Murder*, who was the same age as John. (John, making light of this later, always said he had a terror of hearing Leslie Phillips calling him 'Dad'.) Penelope was further alarmed when, that spring of 1962, pretty Julia, who had been mutinously unhappy at Francis Holland and had transferred to the French Lycée for A-levels, began associating with someone of whom Penelope disapproved. In desperation, she decided to tell Julia who her real father was. Julia wasn't really surprised, because she had always felt different from her sisters: 'I somehow knew I wasn't a Dimont.' Her real father, Kenneth Harrison, had now left Cambridge to be Professor of Biochemistry at the University of Teheran. Penelope's decision was to put Julia on a flight to Teheran to visit Harrison, a bachelor of fifty. Understandably nervous, Harrison was rather the worse for drink when he met his daughter – hiding her teenage spots, she said, behind a curtain of hair – at the airport. But he put her up at the New Naderi Hotel, and somehow they filled their days for a fortnight. Julia went riding with British Embassy personnel, and Harrison took her to Isfahan, Shiraz, Persepolis in the rain, and to cocktail parties, where he introduced her as his goddaughter. Since the two of them looked very similar, they were undoubtedly the subject of gossip. 'I couldn't really relate to him at first, his interests were so different,' Julia said, 'but he was terribly sweet, and we grew very close.'

The younger children had no suspicion of this. Sally always thought it was clever of her parents to make their disparate brood feel like a single unit. Caroline and Madelon were known to be from the previous marriage; but the revelation of Julia's parentage explained a lot. She had seemed to Sally 'like a princess from another planet'. And although Deborah was so close to Julia in age, she looked distinctively different, with her red hair; and John never indulged Deborah as he did Sally.

Kathleen had spent her first widowed Christmas with Daisy in London, seeing Chekhov and Anouilh plays, exhibitions of Lucian Freud and Francis Bacon, the Leonardo cartoon at the National Gallery, the Pre-Raphaelites at the Tate. She got a television set and saw John Osborne ('rather immature and very slow but he sounded honest') interviewed by John Freeman in *Face to Face*. She recorded every garden incident: 'Pheasants ate the roots of the blue anemone in the far copse that gave us so much pleasure for many years'; 'Swarm of bees settled in bedroom chimney'; 'Four very attractive young people camped in my field at Whitsuntide.' She went with John to Sally and Deborah's school for the end-of-term displays of Scottish dancing on a great lawn beneath the Dorset hills, and Sally's walk-on part in Laurence Housman's *Victoria Regina*. At home she cleared cupboards, discovering portfolios of John's boyhood drawings for theatre sets and some 'quite brilliant sketches of working people in the North' – relics of his tour of mining villages with the Crown Film Unit.

Penelope felt imprisoned that summer, 'in this airless box of a house'. No wonder Julia dreaded coming. 'There's nothing to do except make the time pass somehow – until what? Until in a sudden flare of exasperation I chase the cat out of the room, maddened by the sound of its perpetual washing.' But domestic demands always overwhelmed her during school holidays at home.

'I tell myself I wrote The Pumpkin Eater. But these hundred-weights of girls, this perpetual enquiry, "Mummy?" make it seem very remote. Did I write, work, think, have any sense of proportion? Enjoy myself, be funny, be amused, see curious sights, feel?' It was unseasonably chilly for August, and she struggled to make the cottage comfortable, lighting log fires. 'Up in space, wherever that is, two Russians go round and round.' John, who was to co-produce the film of *Lunch Hour*, had departed for London, to see Maggie Smith as a prospective actress to play the girl.

The following month, they took the four youngest children back to Spain, to the Hotel Miramar in Málaga, and Penelope faced what she labelled 'the Julia crisis'. John again left early for London. Julia was insisting on staying on in Málaga with Ben Sonnenberg, a rich New Yorker of twenty-six, who was renting a farmhouse and drove an Alvis car. John was no help – Penelope hoped he'd 'come out, tackle Sonnenberg, be the heavy father' – but when she rang him, he merely asked where the thermometer was, as he might be getting a cold. This response may not have 'tipped the scales of my reason', wrote Penelope; but it certainly didn't help.

John had gone to see a new prospective girl: Shirley Anne Field. On 29 August 1962, he turned up unexpectedly at Turville Heath Cottage, and gave dinner to Kathleen and Mrs Fletcher at Southend. 'Lunch Hour is to be made into a film,' Kathleen wrote, 'and it was that that made him come back from Malaga.' Off he drove to London, to the Dorchester, to meet Shirley Anne, the sparkling-eyed red-haired actress who had played opposite Albert Finney in *Saturday Night and Sunday Morning*. Robert Stephens, who was to play the man intent on an illicit dalliance with her in the hired hotel room, was there too. Shirley Anne felt that John and Robert Stephens were competing for who could amuse her most, who could be the kindest and the wittiest. She had just been offered a James Bond film; Stephens told her to turn it down. John even offered her 7 per cent of *Lunch Hour*'s gross.

Fame had come early for Shirley Anne Broomfield, who had been brought up in a children's home near Bolton (and did not see her mother again until 1978). She had started as a typist for the Gas Board, posing on cookers for their brochures, and made her film debut as a teenager in the 1950s, moving on to television game shows (*Double Your Money*, *Yakity Yak*) as a decorative hostess. At the Royal Court, Tony Richardson and Lindsay Anderson were looking for someone who could play a working-class heroine without looking or sounding like a barmaid. She was directed by Lindsay Anderson in *The Lily White Boys*, and had played the beauty queen in the film of Osborne's *The Entertainer* with Laurence Olivier. Then Karel Reisz cast her in *Saturday Night and Sunday Morning* – which impressed Reisz's future wife, Betsy Blair, because Shirley Anne's fine-boned looks did not suggest a factory girl at all.

John called her Foxy Face and was soon in pursuit. They embarked on an amorous friendship which remained, if not innocent, unconsummated for several years. But he always referred to her as his girlfriend, 'in the declining years of my marriage'. Naturally he could not resist bringing her to Harben Road to meet Penelope. (He also took her to Turville Heath to meet Kathleen.) Shirley Anne remembered finding out all about the Mortimers' recent upheavals, including the birth of Wendy Craig's son. She was interviewed herself by Jack Bentley, who, she said, told her, 'I got stuck with Mortimer's brat.'

On 6 September, Penelope returned from Spain with the younger children, leaving Julia. They went to Southend Cottage; John collected Jeremy and Patsy from his mother on Sunday and told her he was 'going to London for a meeting at 8pm'. Penelope too left Southend Cottage and drove to London, stopping at a phone box to ring John, and found he was 'out to dinner somewhere' – with Shirley Anne, she suspected. At Harben Road, in a state of acute distress, she let herself into the empty house and took all the Soneril she had, swilled down with a tumbler of neat brandy. She tells what happened next in the baldest terms. 'John came through the front door. I got up & walked into the hall to meet him. Next thing I knew I was in New End Hospital, with a nurse saying "what about all those lovely children?"'

After a day she was moved into Greenways, a nursing home, and was again given ECT. On Monday morning Mrs Fletcher rang Kathleen to tell her Penelope was in hospital. Daisy was mobilized: she and Kathleen took the youngest children to Beaconsfield, to the Tudor house where Ambrose Heal had lived, where there were donkeys, cows and calves, rabbits, geese and a fat cat to amuse them. When John arrived at Southend the following weekend to collect the children, Kathleen wrote, 'John was sad and wouldn't tell me anything about Penelope's illness, so I stopped asking and left soon after lunch feeling rather sad myself.' Julia, in Spain, was shown an English newspaper cutting about her mother's overdose.

An author launching a novel today is cocooned in a web of publicity. Handmaidens arrange interviews and book signings. But in 1962, new novels were simply dispatched without fuss from the warehouse to reviewers and bookshops. Penelope was in no fit state to enjoy the reception of *The Pumpkin Eater*. One day, just before publication date, she was sitting in the garden when Caroline told her that she and Leslie Phillips were off to Turkey on a Rank Organization publicity cruise; why didn't Penelope come too? They boarded the SS *Ackdeniz* at Marseilles. On board, Penelope – skeletally thin and 'still not in my right mind' – started an affair with a good-looking German journalist, Richard Kaufmann. When the ship docked at Genoa, she bought the *Sunday Express* and saw a headline with the words 'Pumpkin Eater' and the sickening story that its author was having a 'nervous breakdown'.

In Rome, Madelon found herself confronted by two unfamiliar couples: her mother with Kaufmann, Caroline with Leslie Phillips. However, she was happy to tell Penelope, 'You're going to be a grandmother' (a pregnancy that miscarried). 'Instantly our nervous, prickly relationship changed and I felt able to relax with her,' Madelon remembered. 'She gave me money to buy a car, and later more or less summoned me to join her in Ascona [where Penelope had taken a flat], one of the most pleasant periods with her I've ever had, almost like a normal mother and daughter.'

The reviews of *The Pumpkin Eater* were deservedly rapturous. The feminist writer Elizabeth Janeway in the *New York Times* welcomed

a subtle, fascinating, unhackneyed novel . . . The heroine has lent us her brain and her eyes and her good sense, vitality, attack. But this is why reading this book is so touching, so moving, so funny, so desperate, so alive . . . Mrs Mortimer is toughminded, in touch with human realities and frailties, unsentimental and amused. Her prose is deft and precise. A fine book, and one to be greatly enjoyed.

One afternoon in Ascona, Penelope received a cable from the film director Jack Clayton: 'Dear Penelope, after months of soul searching have come to the foolish decision that I can make as ghastly a film out of your ghastly book as anyone else.' Clayton asked Harold Pinter to do the screenplay – one of his best, in that fecund period which also produced the superlative screenplays of *The Servant*, *Accident* and *The Go-Between*.

Julia too arrived in Ascona, in a large hat, heralded by reports from the lycée about her 'wildness' and truancy. Then John rang to say he was 'perfectly free this week – Shirley is going away'. He arrived on 9 November and said, 'Let's go to bed and forget all this nonsense.' Penelope arranged to rent a bigger flat in Ascona for Christmas where they would be reunited en famille: John and Penelope, Deborah, Sally, Jeremy and a memorable nanny named Rosemary 'who dyed her hair a remarkably dazzling yellow' and became Jeremy's first passion.

John was due to fly home from Ascona on New Year's Day of 1963, leaving the others to go skiing in Italy. But on 28 December, he had a cable asking him to go back to London for a meeting. 'On the way to the airport,' Penelope writes, 'it transpires that the cable was sent by Shirley Anne Field at his request.' They returned to Ascona, had a blazing row and drove on to the Hotel Zumstein, Macugnaga, in the snow. Here John rang Shirley Anne and 'chaos' ensued. There was another terrible row: Deborah's diary called it 'The worst day of my life'. Penelope recalled 'the bitter mountain

top with no way out'. After one day on the slopes, John appealed
to the children to persuade Penelope not to drive down the mountain in a blizzard; Sally sat in the car with her mother for several
hours. In the end, Penelope flew home with the children and left
John to drive.

Back in London, Penelope spoke to Shirley Anne, who told her
'the affair was all a fantasy'. Indeed, she denied having sent that
telegram. When John arrived home, things were 'all uneasily
patched up'. Penelope, looking back on 1962, called it 'the year
of Spain, and of the beastly sweet Soneril, and the SS Ackdeniz,
of Richard, in Rome and Ascona', and 'the year of Shirley Anne
Field, for heaven's sake'.

11. Queen's Counsel and *Farceur*

'These two people,' said Penelope, levelling her steady gaze at the camera, 'have reached the stage in their married life where nothing else matters but the little room of four walls where the door is locked, they can't get out, where there is nothing except each other.'

It was an extraordinary performance on BBC television's *Bookstand* programme on 22 January 1963. In a white cowl-necked sweater, she stood in her drawing room, with her book in her hand. At first, viewers saw only a back garden, with a child's swing. In voice-over, unseen actors played out a scene from *The Pumpkin Eater*, the confrontation in which the wife asks, 'Why did you go to bed with this one?' 'Out of curiosity, vanity, wanting to keep young!' 'Did you love her?' 'I love you.' 'Didn't you ever, any of the time, try not to?' 'You know I have no self-control.' 'Were there others, before? How many? Who were they?' and so on. The camera then focused on Penelope. She read out the passage which ends, 'Where I had been viable, ignorant, rash and loving I was now an accomplished bitch . . . We should have been locked up while it lasted, or allowed to kill each other physically.'

Closing her book, she explained that the husband in her novel earns more money than he has the maturity to deal with. His wife is protected from reality by her 'great brood of children'. 'He has affairs with little girls around the place, which perhaps mean nothing to him, but which destroy her, because she has no confidence in her own existence without him, and without the children.' She wrote about women, Penelope added, because she was one. To write from the male point of view would take more arrogance than she possessed. The wives in her novels were isolated, 'they haven't yet discovered about being people'. But she disliked talking about writing. 'I think if your means of expressing yourself is writing, you write. I have put into this novel practically everything I can say about men and women and their relationship to one another.'

This was a carefully enunciated, candidly negative evaluation of her marriage, although she maintained that the couple were 'not unique'. She looked serene, elegant, quite composed. Nothing like a woman who had no confidence in her own existence without her husband and children.

The famous white winter of 1963 had arrived on New Year's Eve and the snow lay for six weeks. Every weekend, John took the children and nanny to his mother. Turville Heath Cottage was quite cut off, until three policemen, alerted by John, banged on Kathleen's window at 2 a.m. one night. Southend Cottage, flooded by burst radiators, was uninhabitable.

When the thaw came, Penelope flew to New York for a publicity tour. But after four days she checked out of the Fifth Avenue Hotel, dumped her bags at the air terminal and spent a day drifting through department stores in tearful terror, buying nothing, though she was carrying hundreds of dollars, appalled by the trashy displays of Easter bunnies. It was 12 March, Caroline's twenty-first birthday, 'one of the oddest days of my life'. 'You're a lonesome girl,' a taxi driver told her. 'Lonesome,' she reflected. 'No wonder Dylan Thomas died here.' Her American editor, Bob Gutwillig, found her in Schrafts and took her to the airport for her flight home. Although sympathetic, he didn't try to make her stay.

She had talked boldly of taking a year off in America; now she vowed she would never again try to break out, 'for I frighten myself more than New York frightens me'. So she was back for the rash of spring birthdays: Julia's eighteenth, Sally's thirteenth, Deborah's fifteenth and John's fortieth – which fell on Easter Sunday but was celebrated jointly with Jeremy's eighth on 27 April: a river trip in Jeremy's new inflatable boat. They all spent the summer at Southend, both parents writing, but interrupting their work to join the children in picnics, games, sewing, reading aloud (tales from *The Odyssey*), cooking, walks, tennis. They took them to Morocco at half-term, to France in August. Asked for another play by the BBC, Penelope was stricken with inertia, in the face of the 'unbearable muddle' of domestic life,

the fantasy that one day I shall go through room by room until every drawer & shelf & table is ordered.

There seem to be mountains of half dirty, slightly torn, unwearable clothes; wherever I look a half-finished piece of carpentry or sewing, a bicycle with its wheels off, bits of canoe and lilo. I have a strong fantasy of organising everything, labelling & putting away, making everything clean & tidy & simplified. Like I used to. But I can't.

She feels as if she is sewn inside a sack. It was impossible to think about meals; she found it laborious even to speak, let alone write. Mrs Fletcher organized the garden, read to Jeremy and his inseparable Patsy, and crept about, waiting to be given little jobs to do, sometimes shouted at by her daughter. Telephone calls came in for John from New York as he played tennis with Sally and Deborah.

Unfazed by domestic chaos, he became more prolific and more versatile, and began to regard five projects on the go as a normal working pattern, feeling under-employed with less. Ned Sherrin would ring before breakfast on Mondays and ask, 'Got anything for us?' knowing he could be relied on for satirical sketches for *That Was the Week That Was*, and for its successor, *Not So Much a Programme, More a Way of Life*. His name regularly appeared in *TW3*'s list of credits each Saturday night. He was writing a son-et-lumière for Hampton Court Palace (for the voices of John Neville as Henry VIII, Dorothy Tutin as Anne Boleyn and Michael Hordern as Cardinal Wolsey); Kenneth More was to star in *Collect Your Hand Baggage* on television; and, unlike most playwrights, he was also a reviewer – of theatre for the *Evening Standard* and satirical books for the *New Statesman*. He bought himself a 'totally out of character' Volvo sports car.

His *Lunch Hour* film, starring Shirley Anne Field, was being shot in 'Marylebone Studios', a church off Baker Street. He would arrive hotfoot from the divorce court, tell courtroom tales ('I've just divorced two very strange people . . .'), rewrite bits of dialogue and take Shirley Anne to lunch. She would tell him about her 'other adventures' with various lovers; he became her trusted confidant, and sent flowers and gifts. Shirley Anne was at the height of her success, having made Hollywood films with Steve McQueen and Yul Brynner; and she dined with President Kennedy, who sent her a rocking chair from the White House when she told him about her troublesome back. The *Lunch Hour* film was never released. 'Films evaporate,' as John wrote. 'After weeks of excited work they vanish into thin air.'

The exciting work on *The Pumpkin Eater* was just beginning. One can only marvel at John's sang-froid. Any husband would need nerves of steel to contemplate the public re-enactment of a tumultuous episode in his marriage. But hardly anyone outside the family knew the factual truth of the story. Besides, John admired Penelope for writing it. He could hardly object to her plundering their life: he did the same. And he had told her the book was 'marvellous, brilliant and so on'. When, thirty years later, John was asked whether he regarded *The Pumpkin Eater* as 'a sort of revenge', he replied, 'I didn't, honestly. I didn't really feel I was like the person in The Pumpkin Eater. When I read it, all I thought was that it was a very good book. We all know, what you write about is what's happened to you, so I didn't think it was revenge: you take what's important to you and then write about it. These writings are not deliberate acts within a relationship. They are examples of the writer's solitary way of trying to translate his experience into some form of art.' He was aggrieved only that Clayton had not asked Penelope to write her own script. So was she. When Pinter sent her his screenplay he wrote 'I'm sorry' across the title page. And she was summoned to the Hyde Park Hotel on 1 August 1963, to pose for 'meaningless photos with Conway, that hated character who has become the velvet-voiced James Mason' – a casting that, as John remarked to me, was 'better than Jack Bentley deserved'.

★

A week later, on the car train to Narbonne, headed for Seville, Penelope played a paper game with eight-year-old Jeremy: she wrote half-sentences and he filled in the gaps.

At the moment Jeremy feels extremely itchy
Which makes him very cross with the moscetose
But the MOSQUITOES say to each other Let's make him itch more and they do
. . . Daddy is very odd
Oh. Mummy is very nice
. . . When you were a baby you were A bore
No you weren't. When you are 23 you will be Married
Who to? I DO NOT NO

'Love for my son,' Penelope wrote, 'seems to make everything glow, the dark blue sky, the cold evening, the black trees.' Shy, gentle Jeremy was also bright: his grandmother felt he had 'something admirable about him and I am not quite sure what it is – perhaps concentration'. That year, he was one of the children invited to write a book review in the *Evening Standard*: on *The Buildings of Ancient Egypt*. 'The Egyptians were a bit stupid though,' he wrote, 'because they even praised cats.'

At that summer's Edinburgh Festival, John was participating in Ken Tynan's international drama conference, where Tynan caused mayhem by bringing a naked girl to parade round the MacEwan Hall, later to face the wrath of the Sheriff's Court. On the flight to Scotland, John and Penelope scribbled rhymes to each other.

Penelope:

It's all very well for A Wesker, W Mankowitz, J Mortimer, T Allen, D
    Tutin & J Plowright on this flight
Which gives me such a fright
But personally I am not at all sure that I wouldn't be more right on
The diesel to Brighton.

John replied:

> Very few here, definitely including Miss Tute,
> Is a Novelist of International REPUTE
> And few of them are a bit
> Renowned for their acute
> Observation and disturbing wit
> So why not RELAX?

Penelope went on expressing her nervousness; again John consoled her that she had no reason:

> You are completely real BEAUT
> iful in your golden suit
> (In fact a lovely girl and suit in
> Which you would never see Miss Tutin.)

In the debate on 'Who dominates the theatre of today?', chaired by J. B. Priestley, John supported Wolf Mankowitz's proposals to protect playwrights from textual changes without their consent. But he warned fellow playwrights not to be litigious: they should be grateful not to be working in films, where everybody contributed to the script, including 'all the producer's relatives and the boy who made the tea'. Harold Pinter sent an ecstatic telegram on 3 September from Worthing: 'Your radio excerpt marvellous gust of air your phrase "hostility and indifference" dead on the nail for me worth everything well done grazie merci thank you Pinter.'

Back home, they found the James Woolf/Jack Clayton team from Romulus Films, who had made *Room at the Top*, shooting *The Pumpkin Eater* on location in Turville Heath. Pinter came down one day and met the ravishing Anne Bancroft in her caravan, wearing an alluringly short robe. (Her first marriage having disintegrated, she was about to marry Mel Brooks.) Years later, Penelope told me she found it irritating that *The Pumpkin Eater* attached itself to her name for evermore. Although she admired Pinter – and never told him how closely the novel reflected her recent life – she claimed not to have enjoyed Clayton's film: 'There was Miss Bancroft with her hats and her silk lampshades and matching china

1. Kathleen and Clifford Mortimer, John's parents, in the garden they created together

2. Kathleen, née Smith: an intrepid Shavian 'New Woman', who swam under waterfalls

3. Clifford Mortimer, enjoying an unheroic war: he passed on his bookish preferences to his son, along with much else

4. (*top*) His finest hour: John Mortimer aged twelve, at the Dragon School, 'every inch a king' in the title role of *Richard II*

5. (*left*) The artistic, unsportive and Byronic young Harrovian

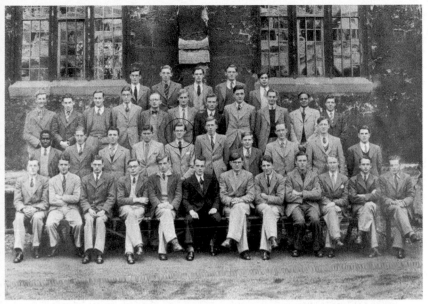

6. John Mortimer (*circled*), Brasenose freshman, 1940, flanked by Michael Fenton, who was to be his soulmate, and (*on his left*) Patrick Freeman ('Parsons'), who tried to save his soul

7. Quentin Edwards in the Royal Navy, 1944, two years after 'our small scandal at Oxford'

8. Michael Hamburger, fellow poet, Christ Church scholar

9. The bewitching Mrs Dimont as a young novelist, soon to become much more famous as Penelope Mortimer

10. The Mortimer family's Christmas card, 1956, drawn by Richard Beer

11. 'Cameramen constantly arrived to photograph the successful pair surrounded by their brood': (*left to right*) Deborah, Madelon, Penelope, Jeremy, John, Julia, Caroline, Sally, in 1959

12. Penelope, mother-of-six, in the garden at Harben Road, 1957

13. 'What most intrigued the press was the idea of two novelists writing side by side': John and Penelope Mortimer at home in Harben Road, 1960

14. Devilish John, with horns, apologizes to his darling Pen, on the flyleaf of a copy of one of his books

15. Posed family scene in the living-room at Harben Road: John, Sally, Julia, Jeremy, Penelope

16. John and Sally, 'his own child, his darling', play chess

17. Wendy Craig, pictured in 1963 with James Fox and Dirk Bogarde, her co-stars in *The Servant*, having given birth to John's son, Ross, in November 1961

18. Shirley Anne Field, John's choice for the film of *Lunch Hour*, pictured in 1968: John was her 'amorous friend' throughout the 1960s

– I mean, these people were supposed to be careless, and *suddenly* rich. If you're married to Peter Finch, smoking his pipe, I can't see what your problem is. She was so *lugubrious*.' (In fact, Bancroft's brilliant performance was rightly nominated for an Oscar, and the point about the couple's sudden change in fortune was extremely effectively made by Clayton. And Peter Finch did not, in the film, smoke a pipe.)

A large surtax demand, caused by payment for *The Pumpkin Eater* film rights, forced John to sell Southend Cottage, a decision regretted ever after. It went for £18,000 to Peter Montagu-Evans, and when they came to clear it out, Kathleen recorded that John seemed 'depressed'. Though she herself was ailing, with fibrositis, 'and old age which one doesn't mention nowadays', Kathleen kept busy: she joined an Italian class, got an inscription engraved for Clifford's gravestone, saw Caroline in a play at Windsor. The family took her to the Battersea Park funfair and to John's Hampton Court son-et-lumière. Was she wise to isolate herself in the country for her last years, she wondered? 'But I know I should miss this cottage & garden which have so much of Clifford about them.' As long as she was weeding, pruning, taking cuttings, sowing seeds, burning rubbish, making mulch, chopping logs, staking roses, clipping hedges, putting Evergreen on the lawn, cutting nettles and brambles, collecting fruit, making jam, bottling figs, attending to the pergola – things she had always done with Clifford – 'I feel as if he were with me almost'.

John too was inspired by memories of Clifford to write his first autobiographical play. He had written in *The Times* about the absence of autobiography in playwrights' work: a novelist can draw on his childhood, and give his views on life, he said, but 'the poor egocentric playwright is apt to find his play finished with most of his ego left out'. So he had devised a memoir play, without a plot, revisiting scenes from his youth. He wrote it for radio, 'the gentlest and least noticed of all media'. *The Education of an Englishman*, with Roger Livesey as Clifford and Max Adrian as the eccentric headmaster, was broadcast in April 1964 on the Third Programme, produced by Nesta Pain, to warm approval from everyone, including

Kathleen. A subsequent version, retitled *A Voyage Round My Father*, had nine-year-old Jeremy in the cast.

In the opening scene the Boy, an only child, is driven off to prep school by his father's chauffeur, an ex-jockey who treats the saloon car like a horse. The Dragon-like school is near Cromer, with a headmaster named 'Noah', his sons 'Ham' and 'Japhet' being teachers. Noah addresses the boys ('O litter of runts'), issuing ever-changing, contradictory advice, and warning the boys about having 'dreams': 'And in the morning you may say to yourself, "You rotter, having a dream like that".' A brisk run, or a cold bath, is the antidote. 'Or supposing a boy from another house may offer you a slice of cake. Go straight to tell the housemaster.'

The friendship between the Boy and his classmate, Reigate, is based on mutual boasting about their glamorous mothers – 'slim as a bluebell, with yellow eyes like a panther' – who go to cocktail parties and wear high heels even at breakfast. Reigate's mother arrives, flat-heeled, nothing like a panther. (Reigate then pretends he was smuggled out of Russia and his real name is Romanoff.) At the Boy's house, they perform plays for his parents, the mother describing the action to the blind father. All these scenes were reprised in John's later stage play. In the radio play, the disruptive room-mate of his Harrow days (Gunston or 'Tainton', now named 'Gunter') appears, hurling chairs about. As the war begins, he and Reigate get drunk together in the cellar of Reigate's mother's Knightsbridge flat. The Boy is now a naval cadet, and although he dreams of coming down a staircase in a white tie and tails, he plans to become a writer. 'My education was over,' the play ends. 'Now, I thought, I might begin to learn something.'

This version of John's early life, his son Jeremy believed, was closer to the truth than subsequent versions, which 'got more refined and fictionalized as time went on'. For Jeremy, who was to make his career in Broadcasting House, the recording of the play in studio 8A was his first visit there.

The Pumpkin Eater was top of the paperback bestseller list when the film had its world première at Cannes. Pinter's scrupulous

adaptation of the book won him the British Film Academy award
for best screenplay of 1964. Clayton's Antonioni-like lingering
over the domestic scene, his ciné-verité use of close-up (particularly of the menacing James Mason in the tea-shop scene, by the
penguin pool at London Zoo), made the Film Critics' Guild vote
it Film of the Year. Clayton had hung lovingly on every flicker of
Miss Bancroft's eyelids, as she walked in a trance through Harrods.
After Cannes, the film was tightened by the editor James Clark
and became 'one of the best films ever made' in the critic Alexander
Walker's view. It included a graphic fight between the Armitages,
with fists flying; it also showed a wife's relief, after being sterilized,
at not having to worry about contraception any more. Birth
control, until recently a cinematic taboo, was usually seen in the
context of unmarried mothers, such as Rita Tushingham in *A
Taste of Honey*.

Madelon had arrived from Rome – looking strikingly like her
mother, Kathleen thought – and Penelope seized the chance to
get Gered Mankowitz to photograph all her six children together.
Gered, seventeen-year-old son of their friends Wolf and Ann, was
to become a photographer of rock groups – the Stones, Jimi
Hendrix. He had long been held up to the younger Mortimers as
an example by John ('Why can't you do a paper round like
Gered?'). Now, in shades and Afro haircut, he photographed the
Mortimer gang like a band, in a studio and in Masons Yard in
St James's – and fell in love with nineteen-year-old Julia. They
married six years later.

   In Edinburgh the previous autumn, Penelope had started an
affair with the playwright David Mercer. He was a genius, she
thought; she loved 'his badger head full of clever rubbish, and his
rare laugh' and he was a refuge from such maternal concerns as
Caroline being cited in Leslie Phillips's divorce. When fire broke
out at Sally's school, Frensham Heights, in January 1965, it was
Penelope who drove to Frensham to salvage her daughter's things.
John, she implied in a piece she wrote about 'The Slothful Husband', left her to manage everything. 'The male Sloth tends to

retire into some cloud-cuckoo-land where he is responsible for nothing. The Sloth's car is always breaking down, his watch doesn't go, his cigarette lighter doesn't work . . . the merest thistledown of a demand on him reduces him to bewildered panic.' As for the Sloth's marriage, it was 'a tragic mess'. Being expected not only to maintain and shelter his wife, and 'understand more or less how the poor little object works', he is expected to love her as well. This need to be loved he finds 'trivial, tiresome and unjustified'.

It was foolhardy of Penelope to disparage her husband in print, because she had taken on a filmscript which defeated her until she enlisted John's collaboration. Otto Preminger had asked her to do the screenplay of *Bunny Lake Is Missing*, a 1950s novel about a child's disappearance from a Hampstead kindergarten. Penelope and John left the younger children at Southend with Granny Fletcher, and flew to Hawaii, where Preminger was making a Pearl Harbor film. Another example, as John wrote, of the absurdity of the movie business. 'In order to write a small film which took place in a nursery school off the Finchley Road attended by our children, it seemed essential to spend three weeks [actually twelve days] on the 25th floor of the Ilikai Hotel, Honolulu in the over-whelming presence of Mr Otto Preminger.' On the long flight they again amused themselves with doggerel exchanges, which shed light on their still interdependent relationship. Penelope's couplet

Ici, à gauche, Chicago.
When are you going to write something approximating to Dr Zhivago?

elicited John's promise to buckle down that summer in Italy:

When I am calm and integrated,
Not underestimated,
Treated as being rather clever
(Which is not to say never),
But
After a certain amount of sweat

Recuperation
Study
And researchio
In San Felice Circeo.

John in turn asked Penelope:

All right, to change the metre,
When are you going to write another Pumpkin Eater?
If only we could stop being bored
If not adored,
And get down to something
Anything
Other than
Eating
Waiting
Drinking
Thinking
Being cross
At a loss
In a mess
Playing chess
Driving
Arriving
Unpacking
Feeling something vaguely lacking
Complaining
Regretting the fact it's raining
Finding the steak deficient
And the cigarette simply insufficient . . .

Penelope:

There speaks my boy –
Distressed and peeved
By joie de vivre,

Miz with Fiz
Surly with Shirley,
Unconvinced by the fibs
Of a million Ad Libs,
Refusing to be enveloped by
Penelope,
A motherless child riled by not being sufficiently wild –
The only thing left not to shirk
Is that super-romantic palliative distraction called
Work.
Talking of which, I shall never write another Pumpkin Eater,
For I am theoretically sick of being a bleater
And would sooner that Peter
Could keep his wife, rather than eat her.

This amicable duologue hardly suggests a couple who know only misery. And in Hawaii, where they observed Preminger being unspeakable to his actors, they managed to collaborate. But the result was more John's work than Penelope's.

San Felice Circeo, mentioned in John's verse above, was their summer holiday destination: the Villa Serafina, on the lagoon, for six weeks, inviting guests including Peter Hall and Clive Donner. They set out with four children. John drove Jeremy and Patsy in one car; Penelope drove Deborah and Sally in the other. At the Italian border, they got separated and Penelope was handed a peevish note addressed to 'Mrs Mortimer, Green Hillman Minx (open)': 'No sign of you in Como and we have now waited for you 2 hours, in heat, at 2 ends of the autostrada. I realise it was a great deal to ask you to wait 2 minutes while we got some petrol . . .' Later John crashed his car; Madelon had to go by Lambretta to pick up the car and drive it to the villa.

After his excursion into radio autobiography, John had signed the first of several contracts to write his memoirs. *My Early Years* by John Mortimer, copyright John Mortimer (Productions) Ltd, was to be delivered to The Bodley Head by May 1965. The advance was £350 on signing, £350 on delivery – but four years later the deal was cancelled, when he signed to do another memoir, again unfulfilled. Instead he wrote a ballet, bizarrely enough, commissioned by an arts festival in Sunderland. 'I don't even like ballet,' he told Terry Coleman of the *Guardian*.

Much more to his taste was writing another slice of his autobiography in radio-drama form. *Personality Split* was the next episode of what later became *A Voyage Round My Father* and was illuminating about what he saw as the wrong turning his life had taken in his twenties. 'Henry Winter', played by John Stride, is wrenched out of his happy job at the Crown Film Unit and steered into the law, as his father (Roger Livesey) insists. Clifford's words of advice – 'It's a very good life in the law, Henry . . . Common sense, that's all you need. Don't confuse your mind with too much damned legal knowledge' – are intercut with lines from John's own poems published in *The Cherwell* at Oxford:

> Be sensible, my darling
> to the way the world is whirling
> While the cruel past is turning
> in the cold and jaded morning.

His father's voice promises: 'You'll have plenty of time for writing' and pleads the case for the law: 'You'll find it can exercise a certain medieval charm. Learn a little law, won't you? Just to please me.' Kathleen listened to the play and, far from disapproving of the family exposure as John claimed, found it 'witty, wise, sad and comic. Clifford would have laughed and appreciated it.'

His one certitude was that he was far more engaged by his theatre and film work than by the law. At Dr Johnson's Buildings were Clifford's gown and other relics, including the blown duck-egg shell on which, in tiny handwriting, someone's will had been proved. John sat there, gloomily wondering why he still needed 'to lead tormented wives or deceived husbands through the maze of the old divorce law. Why should I still be harrowed by cases about the custody of children?' He hated such disputes and questioned judges' strange decisions in favour of one parent or another. He told his clerk, Charlie Crooks, that he was going to leave the Bar.

But there was an alternative: to become a QC, and take to crime, which would free him to write at leisure. His first application was unsuccessful. But along came a big probate case, Fuld deceased, a 2,000-guinea brief 'with plenty of lovely refreshers', as it dragged on for six months from February to July 1965. It changed the legal fortunes of every lawyer involved, as all became silks or judges afterwards: Hugh Griffiths, Richard Parker, John Platts-Mills, Mark Littman, Paul Sieghart and a young pupil, Anthony Lester, who recalled watching John in court, writing screeds of dialogue in longhand on lined foolscap paper, never crossing out a word. What he was scribbling was sketches for *Not So Much a Programme, More a Way of Life*.

Fuld deceased was an unusually diverting case. Peter Fuld's inherited fortune, augmented by his German telecommunications business, amounted to £6m when he died in 1962, aged forty-one. He had arrived in London from Frankfurt in 1939 as a Jewish refugee, read law, and had a house in Little Venice, another in Toronto, in perpetual flight from a dominating, quarrelsome mother who would descend on her son at night and deliver 'long emotional tirades'. He left numerous wills and codicils, some of dubious provenance, signed while he was in the London Clinic being treated for a fatal brain tumour. His mother, his ex-wife Marina, his English mistress Margaret, several other girlfriends, his solicitor, Hartley (the plaintiff), and his physician, the neurologist Dr Tarnesby, were locked in dispute over their claims on his millions. Thirty-six witnesses were called. Judge Scarman had to determine whether 'undue influence' had been exerted. John's sympathies lay with John Platts-Mills, defending Dr Tarnesby. 'I see I'm playing against every member of this team including the referee,' said Platts-Mills, beadily eyeing the judge. Scarman's complex judgement was finally delivered in December. 'Darkness and suspicion are a common feature in will cases,' he said. 'The truth too often is the secret of the dead or the dishonest.' On the strength of this case John applied again to take silk, backed by Scarman, and won the approval of the Lord Chancellor, Gerald Gardiner.

Clive Donner had asked the Mortimers to adapt *Honey for the Bears*, Anthony Burgess's satirical novel about Anglo-Russian relations, to star David Niven and Kim Novak. So during the Easter law recess, John and Penelope sent Deborah, Sally and Jeremy to a hotel at Herm, a Channel Island, and flew to Moscow to absorb the atmosphere. Their joint diary reflects the dreariness of Soviet Russia in Cold War days. The British diplomat who met them at the airport drove them at speed in an embassy car through a 'snow-covered, birch-treed, log-hutted desert' – was he a double agent? Everything was alien and strange. Men, stripped to the waist, stood up to sunbathe against south-facing walls. John found Moscow, 'apart from Red Square, the Kremlin and one old nunnery, the ugliest place in the world'.

After a brush with a hostile Intourist woman in the National Hotel and a three-hour wait for a breakfast of cold hard-boiled eggs and bottles of beer, John was sent out by Penelope into Red Square on a Sunday morning to buy sanitary towels. As they travelled about, having conversations with bureaucrats, John was constantly reminded of Chekhov; he felt a kinship with Chekhov's 'doomed middle class, living an uneventful life in the country, carrying on a daily battle against boredom'. Later that summer, Penelope went back to Leningrad and Moscow with Clive Donner, John being still involved in Fuld. They were given the go-ahead, as long as the film didn't make fun of the Russians. But this film, like so many others, never got made.

A much more inspired commission came from Ken Tynan, now running the National Theatre. He invited John to adapt the Feydeau farce *La Puce à l'oreille*, written in 1907. John had never heard of Feydeau and knew nothing of farce, but discovered it to be a deadly serious business, really 'tragedy played at high speed', in which conventional characters get involved in a series of inexorable disasters after some minor domestic misunderstanding or white lie. It was a form at which he proved adept. The language required, he decided, was not unlike that of Wodehouse and Jerome K. Jerome, and of older barristers he knew. The Comédie Française director Jacques Charon, who spoke almost no English, drilled the cast (including Albert Finney, Geraldine McEwan and John Stride) with military precision, insisting that they must be fit enough to run across the stage in a trice, covering a mile in the course of the play. The breathless pace and split-second timing of exits and entrances through several doors, the bounding up and down stairs, the mistaken identities and surprise arrivals in the hotel bedroom (with a revolving bed by the designer André Levasseur), made *A Flea in Her Ear* 'a jewel among farces'. It was greeted at the Old Vic as the most side-splitting thing in London for years ('You laughed so hard you wondered if you'd survive,' Milton Shulman's wife told me) and John learned much about stagecraft, and comic writing, from it. He remained grateful to Tynan for introducing him to 'a form of drama which seems to me often truer to the facts of life as we know them than many great tragedies'.

Over Harben Road hung an atmosphere more tragic than comic. 'The cracks spread across the ceiling like ever-widening rivers on a map', symbolizing the fissures in the marriage. John had seen many divorcing couples who could not name a single cause for their break-up, as the old divorce laws still required – adultery, desertion, cruelty. He knew 'there is no one cause you can write on the death certificate of a marriage'. Being rival writers in one house was part of their problem, but hardly grounds for divorce. He now understood his clients' reluctance to attribute blame, and their fear of breaking loose: they would soldier on for years in imperfect marriages, half paralysed by the prospect of freedom.

Though he was an even worse candidate than Penelope for psychoanalysis, John went to a shrink in Golders Green, who seemed to spend most of every session arguing with him, and advised him to take up golf. What John thought he needed was a smattering of wild youth, to retrieve the part of his life obliterated by children and overdrafts. In September 1965, the day before her forty-seventh birthday, Penelope took a flat in nearby Aberdare

Gardens. She had already begun carving out an independent life and had been to Rome, summoned by Visconti, about a film. That summer she left John and the family in Mijas, where they had 'a nasty night' with the squabbling Tynans after a bullfight. She flew home and bought Stable Cottage, a small semi-detached house at Steep, near Jeremy's new school, Dunhurst, the prep school for Bedales. Jeremy was ten. When his parents delivered him there in his smart new suit, he told them matter-of-factly, 'I don't want to stay here.' They were 'just dumping' him. On his exeat weekends, John would show up with women other than Penelope, to take Jeremy out. 'Actresses and secretaries who worked for him. It was clear what the relationship was.'

One night, after an evening at the theatre, Penelope went back to Harben Road, looked at the things on John's desk (a postcard to Jeremy, a letter to Sally, bits of work), saw his shoes under the desk, a tea tray on the floor. 'The house was alive; I was alive.' Feeling a surge of happy relief, she crept out again.

It was not until John too had moved out that he finished his new play, *The Judge*. It was about an old judge presiding at his last assizes in his native city, harbouring a dark secret from his adolescence. This seems to involve an aborted child and an archdeacon's daughter called Serena, who is now a raffish old lady keeping a glorified brothel above her antiques shop. With her Gauloises and her memories of Fitzrovia and the Left Bank and Cocteau, Serena is reminiscent of John's lesbians at Turville Heath. Dedicated to the memory of Clifford, this play also featured elements of *A Voyage Round My Father*. In a flashback scene the judge, when young, walks with his father and confesses, 'There is something in this town for which I am responsible. A child helpless, wounded, unprotected. A life dying, dead. A girl screaming in a back room . . . Blood on a newspaper. What can I do?' 'Avoid all temptation to do anything heroic,' the father replies equably. 'It'll blow over. Most people have one small crime in them . . . like the rot in a back tooth, painless if you don't bite on it. Learn to live with it.' (Like Clifford's equable reaction to John's confession about his departure from Oxford.) Perhaps John felt more guilt

about Susan Watson's abortion than he had ever admitted to anyone. Anyway, Peter Hall turned down the play, which coloured
John's low opinion of it.

John felt all the more free to play the field when Penelope
started on another of her 'flirtatious relationships', with David
Adnopoz, a young American screenwriter living in Soho. John's
new girlfriend was Jane McKerron, a bright LSE graduate aged
twenty-six, who lived in a small flat in Primrose Hill and worked
on *Tribune* for meagre pay. First introduced to both Mortimers by
Michael Braun at the Ritz, Jane was much more struck by the
'ravishing' Penelope in a scarlet silk dress, 'that bony, very strong,
almost Red Indian face and the short dark hair', than by John. But
he rang her a few days later, offering lunch. Her *Tribune* office was
near his chambers, 'handy for one's gentlemen friends in Fleet
Street or the law or at LSE'. Jane's instinctive penchant was for
politicians. Her father was the governor of Singapore who had
locked up Lee Kuan Yew – a colonial background that appealed
to John, as did her story that as a child she dyed her Brownie
knickers in coffee beans in the bath at Government House.

They would lunch at the Forum in Chancery Lane, or dine at
dell'Arethusa in the King's Road, where he told tales from the
divorce court in salacious detail. Sex with John was, she said, using
the words of her friend the political commentator Alan Watkins,
'straight up and down the wicket, friendly, and affectionate'. 'We
laughed a great deal, and never had a dark day. He wanted the best
out of life and I've never met anyone who disliked him. He was a
catalyst for fun, for unusual things happening. There was nothing
tortured about him, even though he was a total workaholic, and
would panic about money and declare himself at bankruptcy's
door. He made women feel important, genuinely interested in
how you were feeling, deeply sympathetic if you had the curse.
This was his feminine side; he was one of us really.'

He told Jane he liked 'schmuttery girls', louche types with
ladders in their tights. Shirley Anne, 'who was rather exciting,
having been pursued by Warren Beatty and JFK', was still around.
He introduced Jane to 'little Miss Dawbum', the theatre critic

Helen Dawson (who became John Osborne's fifth wife). And also
to Bobbie, sister of the writer Patrick Seale and the dress designer
Thea Porter, who lived with her American husband, Beecher
Moore, in a flat in the Temple, where they held 'interesting'
parties, otherwise known as orgies. John had found himself there
one evening among people in varying states of undress. 'I went to
the bathroom,' he told me, 'which was covered in mirrors, and
Bobbie entered and suggested that we might have it off. I said,
"Well if you feel like that we'll go to my chambers, away from
your husband," and she said, "What? And leave all my guests?"'

(Some years later, after Bobbie had died, John used this scene
in his play *Collaborators*. One evening, he spotted Mr Beecher
Moore in the audience. 'I wondered anxiously how he would
react when he heard John Wood telling my story about going to
a swingers' party, and the bathroom covered in mirrors, and
Bobbie's line about not leaving her guests. But when the curtain
went down for the interval, Beecher Moore came up and said,
"Wonderful description of our bathroom".')

A good reason for John to rethink his legal future arrived in
November 1965: a brief from Amnesty International to defend the
Nigerian writer Wole Soyinka, later to be imprisoned, exiled and
honoured as a Nobel Laureate. Soyinka was an inveterate opponent
of the despots who ruled Nigeria in the 1960s. The Biafra War was
imminent, and as John was driven along the road from Lagos to
Ibadan, his first vision of an African landscape seemed full of
menace: the dripping rainforest, the burnt-out and riot-wrecked
cars by the roadside, the flash of knives and machetes in the bush.
He found Soyinka calmly reading Wodehouse, smoking Gauloises,
pouring Algerian wine. He asked John to send fond wishes to Joan
Littlewood at Stratford East, where his play *The Road* had recently
been performed. The charge Soyinka faced was robbery with
violence, having entered a radio station and intercepted the victori-
ous election broadcast of the corrupt Chief Akintola with a 'This
is Free Nigeria' message. He was accused of stealing two tapes,
value £2 12s 6d. None of the witnesses could identify Soyinka

and he was acquitted. But John had been vastly impressed by how the British legal system could still function with formality and courtesy in this ill-governed former colony. He decided 'not to abandon the law, but to try and practise it more interestingly in the future'.

12. A Bachelor Life in Little Venice

Moving out of Harben Road in January 1966, John assumed a bachelor life. Number 30 Maida Avenue, Little Venice, overlooks the Regent's Canal, in one of London's pleasantest enclaves. He bought Habitat furnishings and pictures and created a bright atmosphere. Shirley Anne Field remembered it as 'full of stripped pine and flooded with sunlight'.

Jeremy, at eleven, stayed with Penelope, and almost stopped talking to his father. Sally (already one of nature's nurses in John's view) decided that John would need her more. She was preoccupied anyway with a cool school move, to leave Frensham Heights and follow her best friend to Holland Park Comprehensive. Penelope went into Sally's 'dungeon' bedroom on her last night in Harben Road and found her crying. 'What can I do, say? Cry too?'

John had been her 'resident mirror', her 'reaction machine'. Without him, 'how do I know how I'm doing, how I look or am or write? . . . When I begin work, if I ever do, who will it be for, who will read it? Who will understand, say "very good" or "marvellous"?' She had been spoiled, kept in a hot-house by John. She might give a supper for Diana Rigg, Clive Donner, David Mercer; but 'John had a great dinner party with Edna O'Brien & the Tynans & Mellys & God.'

None of the men in her life matched up to the one she was losing, despite the misery he had caused her. She could lunch with them, 'but I gave them nothing, and felt very little for them'. And having affairs was 'like trying to turn a minor hobby into a major occupation'. Derek Hart, whose wife, Siriol, had died of cancer the previous year, briefly brought consolation, but it was just two lonely people comforting each other. She lunched with Sam Spiegel and 'flipped' as she put it. 'Wept and wept into his Kleenex under the lace canopy of his guest bed. His sympathy and warmth and bulk brought it on, his warm and generous clasp, the paternal myth.' Spiegel, already married, proposed to her; but he had a habit of proposing to people.

The Mortimers' film, *Bunny Lake Is Missing*, was released in February: a real oddity, peopled with a gallery of eccentrics. The most original character was the Scotland Yard inspector, Laurence Olivier in a Gannex raincoat, who confides that his policeman father sent him to university in the hope that he would be a poet. 'When I told him I wanted to be a policeman too, he warned me, "You won't have any friends," and he was right.' In a cameo role as an alcoholic poet, Noël Coward tells the inspector, 'No autographs, but you may touch my garment,' while clutching his chihuahua. One day on the set, Coward's dog was yapping incessantly and he told it, 'You're a terrible actor. You'll never grow up to be Lassie.' This became one of John's stock anecdotes. Martita Hunt played the dotty old headmistress of the Little People's Garden (named after the school Penelope's parents ran), but Preminger made Hampstead look alien, Soho a dark down-town area of disturbing menace. The last fifteen minutes were peppered with unsubtle red herrings in a plot undone by sheer implausibility.

John had succeeded Tynan as the *Observer* film critic – a generally reliable one, hailing *The Householder*, by James Ivory, with Ruth Prawer Jhabvala's script; scorning *A Patch of Blue*, in which a blind girl falls in love with Sidney Poitier, for giving 'some of the best laughs since the death of Little Nell'. Kevin Brownlow's *It Happened Here*, in which Germany invades Britain, set him reminiscing (on cue) about the Crown Film Unit; but a BBC docu-drama re-enacting the Lee Harvey Oswald story seemed pointless, since the assassinations of Kennedy and Oswald had been watched, with horror, on television just three years before. 'What in the name of Luigi Pirandello can be the purpose?' It was 'an insult in the terrible face of life'. (Forty years later, reviewing an Oliver Stone film about 9/11 for *Newsnight Review*, John's reaction was almost exactly the same: the reconstruction of recent reality was 'pointless'.)

He would arrive home, Sally remembered, and ask, 'Has the phone gone? Any messages?' Every morning he was up by 5 a.m., littering the floor with briefs and pink ribbon. Sometimes he seemed lonely, cooking a Welsh rarebit for their supper. But there was often a woman's coat hanging in the cupboard. He had given Jane McKerron a key to the flat (rashly, since Penelope sometimes spent nights there), but Jane would never move in. She liked solitude; he 'wanted the place filled with people and lots going on'. He hired girl cooks and invited George and Diana Melly, Joss and Rosemary Ackland, Helen Dawson and Richard Findlater. The high point was inviting Marlon Brando, who arrived hours late and brought a girlfriend and his guru.

The most attractive thing about John, for Jane, was that he made her laugh. She felt she was not really his physical type, since 'he preferred women who looked like boys'. 'One day he was looking at me with no clothes on and said, rather alarmed, "You're very BIG, darling." He spent a whole day trying to buy me a trouser suit [the essential fashion of 1966]. We went all down the King's Road, and to Dickins and Jones, but I was a size 14, with too big a bottom to fit into one. So humiliating. I felt I had totally failed him. He looked good in flowery shirts, kipper ties and flares, having a small bottom and no paunch yet, bounding upstairs on his wonderful long slim legs.'

Jane was the girl he took to the House of Lords on 19 April 1966, the day he put on a silk gown and full-bottomed wig. A Queen's Counsel could make several hundred guineas a day, he had written in *No Moaning of the Bar*, but it was 'a gamble, best postponed until your daughters are safely married, your wife has left you . . . and your sons are doing well in remunerative professions such as managing skiffle groups'. Twenty-two QCs were appointed that day, before Lord Parker in the Lord Chief Justice's Court. The bearded Sir Jocelyn Simon received them two by two as they made their bows 'within the Bar' and knelt in prayer. In second-hand lace jabot, knee-breeches and buckled patent-leather shoes, John stood to be photographed, first with his clerks, Charlie Crooks and Michael Essex, and then flanked by Jane and his mother. Jane had already met Kathleen at Turville Heath and liked her: 'uneffusive, unemotional, self-contained'.

Jane's own mother disapproved of her scandalous liaison with a married man. But within a year John started another affair. Jane introduced him to Liz, an LSE friend of hers, to do secretarial work. 'They were at it behind my back within days. I'm not particularly possessive, but the fact that she was my friend did infuriate and hurt me.' Shirley Anne, too, was sometimes at John's flat, being 'consoled' over her troubled liaisons. However, Jane soon met her future husband, Brian Walden, the Labour MP, and the affair came to an amicable end. 'How could it not be amicable, with John?'

A week after becoming a QC, John went to Stratford on 23 April, Shakespeare's 402nd birthday, to propose a toast 'to the Theatre'. It was the kind of speech audiences appreciated whenever he spoke: wryly urbane, patrician yet anti-establishment, gently bombastic, committed to liberal ideas. A playwright's role in Shakespeare's time was clearly defined by Elizabethan law, he said: common players and playwrights were classed as 'sturdy rogues and vagabonds'. Modern dramatists, still subject to these unrepealed laws, had lost their sturdy-rogue qualities. They had income tax returns to fill in, late-night television shows to appear in, resolutions to draft for the Trades Union Congress. 'If you were alive today,' he said, addressing Shakespeare, 'Miss Jennie Lee would expect you to do useful work for the Arts Council. You'd be asked to explain your more inexplicable plots to Mr Malcolm Muggeridge on television ... Instead of scratching away at *Henry IV Part Two*, you would be hard at work on the tenth rewrite of the film version of *Henry IV Part One*.'

The playwright's life he outlined was his own. His work was constantly re-aired – *Lunch Hour* was back at the Arts, at lunch-times, with a boxed picnic of sandwich, cake and apple for 2s 6d – and he was writing a bold historical television drama, *A Choice of Kings*, to commemorate the 900th anniversary of the Battle of Hastings, imagining a meeting between William and Harold two years before 1066 and all that. He was also protesting against the

Vietnam War in Trafalgar Square that July and taking a stance on other issues. No letter to *The Times*, co-signed by the usual suspects – about the plight of Mikis Theodorakis under the Greek colonels, or British Equity's refusal to perform in apartheid-blighted South Africa, or Ted Willis's Sunday Entertainments Bill – was complete, in the late 1960s, without the signature of John Mortimer.

Most importantly, he was campaigning to abolish theatre censorship. This had become utterly farcical. In *Beyond the Fringe*, the line 'Enter three outrageous old queens. First queen: "Hullo, darlings!"' had been bowdlerized to 'Enter three men of aesthetic appearance. First man: "Hullo, men!"' Even John's inoffensive playscripts had been violated by the Lord Chamberlain's strictures. In *The Wrong Side of the Park*, the old father's line 'With the single exception of your mother, I've never had a woman in my life' had to become 'I've never been with a woman in my life.' Why, John had asked in his Stratford speech, would a nation famed for tolerance and free speech allow Lord Cobbold (who was otherwise in charge of 600 swans, and keeping divorced persons off the Queen's lawn at Ascot, and the granting of coats of arms to the royal marmalade makers) to ban Osborne's *A Patriot for Me*? Playwrights would happily rely on the obscenity laws to regulate them, John told the parliamentary joint select committee, on behalf of the League of Dramatists. Norman St John-Stevas warned that once the comical figure was abolished, intolerant watch committees just might 'make the Lord Chamberlain look like the whitest liberal', and he was right.

As John had hoped, his silken status propelled him into crime. He was sharing his office with Emlyn Hooson, an amiable young advocate who would succeed John Latey as head of chambers. Hooson had already defended the Moors Murderer Ian Brady. He had acquired a vast leather-topped desk that had belonged to Hartley Shawcross (his pupil master on the Wales and Chester circuit) and across it, facing him, sat John. But Hooson, a Liberal MP, was due to open a fire station in his Welsh constituency on the day he was down to defend, at the Old Bailey, a woman who had fatally stabbed her husband. He felt intuitively that this was 'right up John's street' and told Charlie to pass on the brief. Hooson advised John to assert that the brutal, drunken husband had impaled himself on the knife his wife was holding against her chest in self-defence. 'He did it beautifully,' Hooson told me.

Crime was more fun than probate. 'Crime deals with the weakness of mankind, the reality of life on earth, the curse of misfortune and the struggle for happiness,' as a barrister says in one of John's later plays, *Naked Justice*. 'Cases about the human condition. Not some rigmarole about penalty clauses and certificates of completion.'

But it was more fun still to go to Hollywood. In the late summer of 1966 he returned there with his screenplay of *A Flea in Her Ear*. It felt incongruous to be an English writer dictating the plot of an absurd Edwardian French farce to a 20th Century Fox secretary. The secretary cracked not a smile, and then said, 'You're French, aren't you?' 'Why should you think that?' 'Well, you've got a foreign accent.' An American, John concluded, finds England and France both indistinguishably remote.

California was the 1960s hippie epicentre. He was offered pot in Topanga Canyon and LSD on lumps of sugar in the local delicatessen. A cab driver showed him the Watts ghetto, scene of the 1965 riots. 'I got nothing against the Negro,' said the cabbie, 'but to pay him to live with his bastards! That'd really make Marx bitter.' He hired a yellow Mustang and drove to the Bel Air house built by Randolph Hearst for Marion Davies, its swimming pool cracked and dry and full of trees. He went clubbing, to the Galaxy and the Whisky a Go Go, with deafening pop music (pads and pencils provided for conversation). The McCarthy shadow of fear and unease over Hollywood had gone, and writers were no longer driven to drink, like Scott Fitzgerald. He was left alone to work, in tropical heat, by the pool of the Beverly Hills Hotel; down the corridor was Terence Rattigan, as they were filming *Goodbye, Mr Chips*. He dined with Clive Donner and told him, 'Whenever Penelope thinks things are getting boring, she tells another daughter who her real father is.'

Deborah was in Aberdare Gardens, resitting her A-levels, when Penelope decided to tell her that her father was Randall Swingler – who looked rather like Laurie Lee, she said. Deborah wrote a letter to her father at his tumbledown Essex cottage, and they arranged to meet. Randall was euphoric to discover his long-lost daughter. Deborah played the clarinet and Randall, whose wife was now a professor at the Guildhall School of Music, had played the flute. They would meet at Lyons Corner House or the Royal Festival Hall whenever he was in London. Penelope found him 'old & burly, with his watery blue eyes & pretty mouth just the same . . . I can only think of how awful it will be when he dies, and how for Debby's sake I hope he doesn't die too soon.' She knew he had a heart problem and was 'living on borrowed time'. Sadly, just under a year later, Randall collapsed and died of a heart attack – on Deborah's nineteenth birthday, as she was walking with him past the French Pub on the way to Wheeler's. It was a terrible and testing emotional experience. But Deborah was glad to have known her father, however briefly.

Penelope's stability that year was not helped by dealing alone with various problems of her children. Madelon, home from Rome, turned up drunk on her doorstep at Steep; and knowing what drink had done to Madelon's father, Penelope told her that unless she stopped drinking she would have no more to do with her. Sally was in her 'wild child' phase, a pretty, shapely blonde roaring off on the backs of motorbikes. Penelope went to and from Greece, stayed with Diana Rigg and danced with gypsies at Delphi; back in London she shuttled Jeremy between Aberdare Gardens and John's flat, feeling she had no base, 'no chair to sit in, nowhere to hang myself'. At Steep, she agonized over her mental state. Clive Donner's GP, Barrington Cooper, prescribed Ritalin, pentathol, methedrine. 'These pills . . . do nothing, I swear. I must now be saturated in amitriptyline and am no better. If I get really well, then all that remains is to be able to work.'

Despite John's adventures and absences, the bond of the children still held them. When Deborah said she wanted to be a theatre director, he advised her to apply to Hampstead Theatre Club, mentioning 'my stepfather, John Mortimer', and she became a student ASM there (along with Chris Jagger, Mick's younger brother). John took Deborah and Jeremy camping in Greece that summer, Penelope deciding at the last minute not to go. They set out to camp on the island of Rhodes, but after one night plagued by ants, John said, 'No more camping.' They were to come home via Venice, and put the car on a ferry. As it steamed out of the harbour they discovered they were on a cruise to Yugoslavia, so John missed the first week of the new law term. On his return he and Penelope took the children to the cinema. 'We held hands, and kissed,' Penelope records, 'and in the car park the children were divided like Nuts in May & we both drove away to our separate places.' On good days, she felt sane, competent. One night, after taking Jeremy to a film in Leicester Square, over supper at the Angus Steak House, she considered selling her cottage, sending him to a London day-school, 'letting him take the rough & the smooth of me'.

When John recorded his first *Desert Island Discs* at the end of 1967 (he was to be cast away twice more in later years, a record) his voice came from the 1930s: fantastically camp, fast and clipped, with Noël Coward overtones; he sounded glibly pleased with himself, as if everything came easily to him. He said desperation and the need to pay the grocer caused his productivity, that when writing he got up at FOUR in the morning. Having written a son-et-lumière for Norwich Cathedral, he was 'the only person who gets royalties from a cathedral'. Among his records were 'Voi che sapete' from Mozart's *The Marriage of Figaro*, Glenn Miller's *Moonlight Serenade*, and John Gielgud reading Prospero's farewell speech from *The Tempest*. His luxury was a marble bath with piping-hot water and his book was Proust's *A la recherche du temps perdu*. Like Proust, he could only write about his own childhood 'and things that are important to me'. His two new TV plays that year featured a mother preoccupied with reading to a blind father, and small schoolboys telling each other tall tales.

Along with the law, the plays, the filmscripts, the polemic, John could always drop everything for hack journalism. He remained available to newspaper features editors for the next forty years, which annoyed his peers ('Mort's such a tart,' said the acerbic Frederic Raphael), just as envious dons fulminate against tele-historians. Hackery calls for a cavalier, ad hominem approach to opinions; this suited John perfectly. Who was he thinking of when he wrote in the *News of the World* about 'middle-aged delinquency', men of a certain age dressing in Beatle suits and haircuts to attract dolly birds? At forty-three he had grown his hair 'trendily long', and scorned headmasters who forbade their sixth-formers to adopt the hairstyles of Disraeli and Dickens, well over their ears. A writer approaching fifty, he wrote, would once go off to a Greek island and sit in a Panama hat, writing poetry. In 1966, the writer felt 'compelled to stay on the scene, squeezing himself into Carnaby Street trousers, frugging with athletic young girls fresh from the lacrosse field, and swearing off-handedly on television'. Here was the kind of confusion which often muddled his opinion pieces. His tone simultaneously mocked and defended the ageing hippie. The young, he said, were saner, less class-conscious and better-looking than any previous generation. Middle-aged men were 'desperately clinging to the image of the Cavern, and avoiding the shadow of the tomb'. 'What we've lost are the virtues of old age,' he added sagely. Shakespeare had written his calm last plays 'when he'd given up frugging of all sorts'.

The lofty barristerial style, incorporating references to 'frugging', indicated how with-it he was. But John's natural instincts were those of the conservative nostalgist or fogey, better suited to the Panama hat and the Greek island. His age (born in the 1920s, unlike his writing peers, who were children of the 1930s) and his conventional background made his embrace of the pop scene, his Nehru jackets and velveteen bell-bottoms, a touch self-conscious. He had been doing a lot of frugging lately, at the nightclubs which were then the only late-night venues in London – the Pigalle, the Society, the Embassy, the Stork Room, the Raymond Revuebar, Murrays. He was reporting on these for the *Sunday Times* magazine: staying up all night ('at 4.30am the body is weakest, the temperature sinks'), watching strippers, soubrettes in white feathers, conjurors and East End comics.

In more serious journalism he was the consummate professional. He would arrive, dishevelled, at the *New Statesman* office in Great Turnstile, and deliver a 'Centrepiece' essay, for the usual £40 fee, taking a well-informed historical perspective on current events. The departure of John, Paul, George and Ringo to follow the Maharishi Mahesh Yogi in 1967 reminded him of Aldous Huxley's mescalin-fuelled seduction by Sat-Chit-Ananda in the 1930s, which had 'turned his great mind to mystical blotting-paper'. And in *No Armada to Defeat?* he set out the left-winger's disillusion with the Labour government. Britain had been united in a cause in 1945, to get Labour in; the left was united again in the 1950s, to get the Tories out. Today, three years after the Labour victory, the jokes of *TW3* had gone 'horribly flat': even the Tories could not behave more immorally or clumsily than Wilson's government. The left was without a cause. Nobody wanted to bleed at the barricades for the stability of the pound as an international currency. Repeal of the medieval laws against homosexuals and abortion had been achieved in spite of governments. Could not the Labour government take one stand on principle and 'oppose the idiocy taking place in Vietnam'? (Look forward forty years: John Mortimer at eighty-three was polemicizing in much the same vein about the Blair government and the war in Iraq.)

To avoid the embarrassments of a festive season clouded by their separation that Christmas, Penelope and John took Jeremy and Sally to Elbow Beach Club, Bermuda, where John wrote a poem for sixteen-year-old Sally:

> Dropped in the nowhere of a sea –
> Bootlegger's Cave and Spanish Bay –
> We find our harbour guiltily,
> Running away from Christmas Day.
> Upon our left the lovely home
> Of racehorse owner Mrs Jones,

Upon our right the hungry foam
Picks at the flesh off pirate bones.
Oh Sally, love, don't settle down
With Mr Anyone, from Maine;
Buy rum and salt pork in the town,
And say goodbye, and sail again.
Find, if you can, enchanted seas,
Unfathom'd caves, and sabre rocks,
And flee, if possible, white knees,
Bermuda shorts, and long black socks.

'Mr Anyone, from Maine' was in fact an American boy from Queens, New York, staying in the same hotel, whose mother infuriated Penelope by remarking 'what a fun husband you have'. When the Mortimers left for New York on 5 January 1967, Sally and Jeremy went to stay with their new friends in Queens while John met George Cukor, and Penelope flew to Los Angeles, where Clive Donner was in post-production on a kooky Jack Lemmon farce called *Luv*. In Donner's rented house in the Canyon, where even the cleaning lady arrived in a pink Cadillac, she found peace and contentment, spending long days by the pool working on *My Friend Says It's Bullet-Proof*. This was the novel she had conceived, with a sensation of 'radiance', during a trip to Niagara Falls the previous autumn, while in Canada for a literary festival. The interlude had furnished a plot: her heroine, who has just broken up with her long-term partner and is scarred by a recent mastectomy operation, goes on a press trip to America, gets involved with several men and rediscovers her sex life.

The undemanding, equable Donner, at forty, was a classic bachelor – 'austere in his domestic habits, inclined to be fussy' – who after a day's shooting would watch TV in pyjamas rather than go out on the town. They moved to a house with a garden of oleanders and entertained Wolf Mankowitz, Robert Shaw and Mary Ure. She shopped with Penelope Gilliatt (now living with Mike Nichols) in the LA malls. She went to San Francisco with Moshe Safie, a man she'd met in Canada, and to Chicago with the jazz musician Gerry Mulligan. In March she cabled her publisher, Harold Harris, to say her novel was finished. When it came out that October, it was dedicated 'To Clive'.

The play Peter Hall had rejected, *The Judge*, had already been booed when first performed in Hamburg. ('What's the German for "boo"?' John had asked. 'Boo,' they told him.) But now Michael Codron put it on at the Cambridge Theatre in March 1967, with Patrick Wymark playing Judge Chard and Patience Collier as Serena, the guilty secret of his adolescence. Critics were defeated by the improbable scene in which the judge goes berserk and trashes Serena's bric-à-brac shop. Hilary Spurling, *Spectator* theatre critic and a judge's daughter herself, challenged the view that John's legal background gave his play authenticity. 'On the evidence of this scene at least, he can never have seen a demented judge.'

John remained a generous reviewer of others. Peter Nichols's *A Day in the Death of Joe Egg*, the disarmingly funny and courageous play based on the Nicholses' life with their spastic daughter, confirmed John's faith in a comedic approach to everything in life, including disasters. He had left the theatre 'feeling in every way better for having shared the author's experience, and for having, as he also had, the sensibility to laugh'. The two playwrights became good friends.

After two months in America, Penelope came home. Donner had proposed marriage, she claimed, but she felt that to remarry would only confuse and antagonize Jeremy. If only someone would encourage her to go back to John, instead of telling her it would be 'a backward step'. Hunter Davies, whose novel *Here We Go Round the Mulberry Bush* was to be Donner's next film, and Davies's wife, the writer Margaret Forster, spent an uneasy evening with Donner and Penelope. They made a very odd couple, Margaret thought, 'such a contrast, with Clive so soft and limp, and Penelope so stern and full of suppressed fury. She was wearing an ornate dress and looked uncomfortable and defiant. Clive looked like an escort she'd hired: charming and polite and deferring to her all the time.' She couldn't imagine what they were doing together. 'There certainly didn't seem to be any sexual chemistry. The overwhelming impression that has stuck in my mind is that he was being kind to her.' As he undoubtedly was.

John departed for Paris, where *A Flea in Her Ear* was being filmed – and where, coincidentally, *Une heure pour déjeuner* was playing at the Théâtre du Tertre in Montmartre. He stayed at the Plaza Athénée and dined nightly with Rex Harrison and the cast. Harrison was unnerved that the character he played was impotent. His fans would not accept it, he said. 'Couldn't I be just a little impotent, now and again?' 'He niggled away until he got what he wanted – eager to make himself lovable to audiences, at the expense of the film.' (Later Harrison had similar reservations about playing a homosexual in *Staircase*, and later still, about playing John's blind father.) Anyway, *A Flea in Her Ear* could never work on screen, as John knew. It depended on theatrical devices, banging doors and hiding in cupboards, the audience seeing all the compromising encounters and close shaves. Off the set, as John enjoyed relating, a Feydeau farce was playing out between Harrison and his wife, Rachel Roberts, who was learning French and getting drunk every night. One night she leaned across the table and said, in her Berlitz French, '*Cher John, hier soir j'ai fucké le chauffeur de Terence Rattigan dans le Bois de Boulogne.*'

Two of John's girlfriends were by now *hors de combat* as they had dwindled into wives. He was a guest at Jane McKerron's wedding to Brian Walden, who soon became parents of a son, Ben. And when Shirley Anne married Charlie Crichton-Stuart, cousin of the Marquess of Bute, in a grand Roman Catholic society wedding, John's telegram was read out: 'Isn't God lucky, marrying the two of you today.'

But God, of course, did not exist, as John proposed in a BBC debate that June. This was in the series *Your Witness*, staged as a courtroom drama with Ludovic Kennedy playing judge. Quintin Hogg spoke for God, Baroness Wootton for humanism, A. J.

Ayer for philosophy and John for atheism. John argued that man invented God out of his need for consolation, and in an eloquent summing up asked the jury to affirm the dignity of mankind and reject superstitious beliefs. But he was no match for Hogg's advocacy: God won by one vote. Religious belief was a genuine, obsessive mystery to John. When he reviewed Mark Boxer's account of being rusticated from Cambridge for publishing in *The Granta* a poem which called God 'a snotty old sod' (whereupon Boxer staged his own funeral and left Cambridge in a coffin), John was appalled that any university in a free society should ban a student paper for anything it might say on the subject of God.

Wearing his atheism openly on his sleeve, he departed for Rome, with the photographer Eve Arnold, to write about the Vatican for the *Sunday Times* magazine. Madelon organized everything, enlisting from the papal secretariat Bill Carew, a tall, handsome Canadian monsignor with a taste for the good life. They discovered a bar behind the altar in St Peter's, used by priests, amusingly named BarAbbas, and dined on oysters and champagne. The judge in the Sacra Rota, who spent his days annulling marriages, proved to be a genial Scots priest who produced a pack of Senior Service from his surplice and told John, 'Remember me to Malcolm Muggeridge! And Dee Wells!' Vatican personnel, said John, saw no incongruity in living luxuriously in a country of flagrant poverty. 'What surprises the irreligious', he wrote, 'is their apparently total lack of a sense of guilt.' The Pope was 'possibly the only man in the world who is able to believe he's not mistaken'.

Constant travel and work were essential to stave off boredom and melancholia. 'Doing nothing is a strain. Work – the more the better. The more varied the better. Writing is my relaxation,' he told one reporter who visited him at home. He sat 'rearranging his wiry frame, throwing long, unruly legs across an armchair, blinking through thick glasses like an overgrown schoolboy, talking in staccato phrases – eager to please yet likely to wander off at any moment'. He needed to have too much to do, he said. It was not success that drove him on, or the money, 'which is only just enough to keep a good house, send the children to school, and travel when I wish'. His work filled a void of unhappiness and loneliness, he intimated, that began at public school. He had to combine plays and Hollywood films with humdrum days in court – he had just won a contested will case which depended on whether a woman, divorced on the day her husband died, was his widow or his divorced wife – because the law was indispensable to his writing: 'People in crisis speak in a collage of clichés . . . and I use their speech in heightened poetic form. I observe the language barriers, the inability of lawyers and judges to communicate with ordinary offenders. Working in the courts keeps me in touch with everyday drama. It also appeals to the ham in me.'

Disguising his separated state, he said all his children were away at school; the reporter never realized that his wife lived elsewhere, that he was 'on the verge of divorce myself and yet advising others on how to run their lives'. Their divided family life was a mess, horribly inconvenient. Before they took the children for their summer holiday at the Villa Griselda, Nerano, they agreed on another solution: they would live under a single roof again, leading separate lives in separate quarters. So John bought a five-bedroom, four-bathroom maisonette in one of Holland Park's massive stuccoed villas, near Sally's school, and they arranged separate bedrooms at opposite ends of the flat. This was not a happy arrangement. John worked in his dark, ponderously decorated study, with Liz, the secretary-mistress, at his side. By November, Penelope records, John was telling her, 'You're useless as a wife and extremely unpleasant as a companion.'

One rainy afternoon that summer, Michael Fenton, who had been leading a blameless GP's life in Moreton-in-Marsh, had re-erupted into John's life, arriving at Maida Avenue while he was holding a read-through of a play. Fenton had come to ask John's advice about divorce. He had fallen madly in love with a cleaner at the cottage hospital where he worked, meeting her at night in his surgery. He was planning to take the woman away to South America, to his ancestral estate in Patagonia. If she wouldn't come, he hinted, there would be only one solution.

Weeks later, John read what had happened in a tabloid newspaper. As the front page of the *Gloucestershire Echo* on 13 July announced, 'Moreton doctor's body in wood: woman dead in council house.' The body of Pauline Mary Bowden, mother of three daughters, had been found, shot dead, at her home. Fenton's body was found at Spring Hill, between Moreton and Evesham. He had shot his lover and then swallowed all the drugs he had in his medical bag. In his car was his passport, with all his savings.

His suicide note quoted Catullus: 'Odi et amo' – 'I hate and I love'. The next line is, 'I don't know why; I only feel it, and it is agony.'

To his patients, Dr Fenton had been a model of dignity and courtesy: they were astonished to learn about his affair with the cleaner, when 'half the women in Gloucestershire would have jumped into bed with him', as a colleague said. But three months earlier, Barbara Fenton had discovered the couple in flagrante in the flat adjoining their house. The Fentons tried to make a fresh start; but he resumed the affair. There had been an angry confrontation with Mrs Bowden's husband, and Fenton had been practising with a sawn-off shotgun in their orchard.

He left four sons: two teenagers by his first wife, Jean, and two aged six and three by Barbara, who was bitterly angry with John for not forewarning her of Fenton's plans. John had lunch with the poet James Michie, Barbara's fiancé in Oxford days, and they tried to fathom what had possessed their old friend. It was utterly out of character; nothing fitted in with the pacifist they had both so admired. John voiced the theory that there lay the answer: a pacifist locks up his violent instincts and aggressions, and cannot properly express his feelings. Years later, appearing again on *Desert Island Discs*, John told Sue Lawley that Fenton's end remained 'one of the great mysteries of my life'. His best friend from Oxford, a Greek scholar and Mozart lover, who seemed to possess 'the secret of the universe', was a murderer. John was more than ever convinced that anyone can be driven to murder. He thought of Fenton when he called his second book of memoirs *Murderers and Other Friends*.

13. The Defence of Literature

Last Exit to Brooklyn, a collection of stories about New York's violent underclass, had been published in Britain in 1966. Hubert Selby Jr's characters were brutalized victims and outsiders, observed with dispassionate credibility. The book had sold fewer than 14,000 copies when a Tory MP, Sir Cyril Black, was alerted to its most contentious chapter, the story of a prostitute named Tralala whose terrible end, gang-raped to death by thugs who continue abusing her body after she lies dead, was one of the most sickening passages in twentieth-century fiction. Black, a seasoned warrior in the battle for public morality, brought a successful private prosecution before a magistrates' court to have the book destroyed. The Director of Public Prosecutions announced that publishers John Calder and Marion Boyars would stand trial by jury at the Old Bailey.

Patrick Neill, QC, defending, called thirty expert witnesses, five of them professors of literature, including Frank Kermode, who testified that he was greatly moved by the book's originality and its picture of contemporary moral reality. Hubert Selby, in his view, wrote in the tradition of Dickens; and Kermode invoked – as John often did – Shakespeare's blinding-of-Gloucester scene in *King Lear*. But the experts failed to persuade the jury (all male, to protect female sensitivities). A verdict of Guilty was returned in November 1967, seven years after the acquittal of *Lady Chatterley*. Judge Graham Rogers fined the publishers £100, with £500 costs, but Calder and Boyars were at least £10,000 out of pocket. They lodged an appeal, and founded the Defence of Literature and the Arts Fund, with much public and press support, to pay their legal fees. They also wrote to *The Times*, questioning the jury's ability to cope with a work of literature.

John initially hesitated, when asked by Lord Goodman (at Calder's suggestion) to lead the appeal. 'I was never a terrific enthusiast for the book,' he said, 'but I was a terrific enthusiast for freedom of speech.' The appeal was heard in July 1968, before Lord Justice Salmon, Mr Justice Geoffrey Lane and Mr Justice Harry Fisher, who overturned the previous verdict.

Obscenity was (and is even more in the age of Internet porn) a legal minefield, ever since 1868, when Lord Chief Justice Cockburn defined obscenity as that which 'would tend to deprave and corrupt'. This was crucial. 'Judge Rogers had said in the original trial that *Last Exit* was a shocking, disgusting book,' John remembered. 'I said that was irrelevant. I invented an argument, which I developed in other cases later, the "aversive" defence: that the words were so awful they would have the opposite effect. I said that if a description of sex is so off-putting it puts the British public off sex, at least until next Thursday, it is of highly moral and beneficent effect. The Court of Appeal thought that was a good argument. And because the judge's summing up had been flawed, and he had given the jury insufficient guidance, we were able to win the case.'

John's oft-repeated 'at least until next Thursday' is a flip and inadequate précis of his eloquent argument in court. What he said was that Selby's graphic description of the degradation of Brooklyn life was both 'compassionate and condemnatory'. 'The only effect that it would produce in any but a minute lunatic fringe of readers would be horror, revulsion and pity . . . It made the reader share in the horror it described and thereby so disgusted, shocked and outraged him that . . . he would do what he could to eradicate these evils . . . In short, instead of tending to encourage anyone to homosexuality, drug-taking or senseless, brutal violence it would have precisely the reverse effect.' He also submitted that the jury should have been given guidance on the function of literature and the importance of taking into account the times in which a book was written.

When John met Hubert Selby later, he didn't tell him on what basis he had defended his book. 'I just said, "I saved your book" and he said, "Oh yeah?"' The book, lavishly publicized by the court case, began to move off the shelves fast.

The whole case was 'in many ways bewildering to the point of incomprehensibility', Frank Kermode later wrote in the *New American Review*. The expert witness must sell the idea of 'literary merit' to members of a jury who might never have read a book in their lives: 'There is a public which reads, and a much larger one which does not.' *The Last Exit* jury, possibly recalling that the Moors Murderers had committed their crimes after reading the Marquis de Sade, had been impressed by the Revd David Sheppard's claim that reading Selby's book had 'marked' him, and by the aged bookseller Sir Basil Blackwell's testimony that reading *Last Exit* had 'darkened' his life. An obscenity trial, wrote Kermode, is a struggle between a culture and one of its subcultures, transformed by the ritual of the law into something that resembles the real social issue 'about as much as chess resembles war'. Even the appeal judges had admitted being at a loss over the legal definition of 'deprave and corrupt', and over the confusions of Roy Jenkins's 1959 Obscene Publications Act, under which something that was found to be obscene and corrupting could also be 'for the public good' if it had literary merit.

Last Exit remained the last serious work to be prosecuted under the act, and the trial proved that the literary-merit defence was wearing thin. But John was now launched as an apologist for literary freedom, as he already was for an uncensored theatre. It earmarked him for the rest of his career, as he was called on to test the frontiers of tolerance by defending, 'with waning interest', books far less worthy of public esteem.

Among John's lawyer friends, one at least felt he could not have brought himself to 'save' Selby's book. Jeremy Hutchinson, QC, had been John's friend since they had been 'married' in a trial at the Old Bailey, with Hutchinson representing a bank robber and John the robber's wife. John 'put the boot in', said Hutchinson, securing, with 'gentle finesse', the conviction of the robber and freedom for the wife. Hutchinson was briefed for the *Last Exit* defence, and thought he shared John's views on censorship – until he read the book. When he came to the gang-rape chapter, he felt he knew what it meant to be 'depraved, corrupted, degraded'.

Since obscenity cases depended on opinion rather than fact, he decided that the taxi-rank rule (whereby barristers accept whatever case comes along) should not apply. 'It is sometimes painful enough to utter the words of a defendant in a criminal case. But on obscenity, you must convince the jury of your personal view. I could not stand up and read out the account of the rape and say there was nothing corrupting about it. My heart would not be in it. So I suggested they find someone else. It's the only time I've broken the Bar rules in this way, but I felt I was justified.'

John felt equally justified because he believed in the truth of what he was saying. This was 'a dangerous situation as an advocate'. 'The attempts of the law to control the written word seemed to me dangerous and likely to put our Courts of Justice in a somewhat ridiculous light.' The *Last Exit* case had been, he reflected a decade later, 'a notable battle in the long, hard-fought, often serious, sometimes important, frequently farcical, and occasionally trivial, war between the freedom of the written word and our legal system'.

John's most comprehensive polemic about the 'impracticable, ridiculous and positively dangerous' censorship laws was written for *Nova* magazine later that year. Pamela Hansford Johnson, Lady Snow, had argued for censorship, dismissing the Arts Council report on the obscenity laws as 'full of little jokes'. 'Little jokes are the enemies of censors and pornographers,' John replied. 'I defy anyone to study such grave judicial pronouncements as that in the ABC Chewing Gum Case (about the dissemination of 'violent' chewing-gum wrappers in an infant school) without cracking a smile.'

The first point he made remains a valid one. 'It is never, of course, we who need to be censored. The defenders of censorship always assume that the world is full of sillier, weaker, more suggestible people than themselves, who crave protection . . . Censorship builds a hierarchy: the cultured and informed who know best, and the dim, silent majority from whom bad books must be kept.' He cited familiar arguments: that newsreels from Vietnam and Belsen were arguably 'obscene'; that the Nazis were more concerned to clean up art than any other regime; that Dr Bowdler removed the violent bits from Shakespeare, in an era when there was widespread cruelty. Would Miss Hansford Johnson permit the eye-gouging scene in *King Lear*? John's 'blood ran cold' when he read her assertion that critics could 'sort out the rubbish from the rest'. Oh, really? Critics 'insulted the Impressionists, found Keats and Blake lunatic, almost universally condemned Pinter'. They rarely appreciated new departures in art and called artistic experiment 'rubbish'. Would Miss Hansford Johnson like to see her latest novel condemned by twelve honest householders who had never read a book?

'One of America's worst sex murders,' John wrote, 'was done by a gentleman who read nothing but the story of Abraham and Isaac.' John was often to use this anecdotal example of the Bible-obsessed gentleman sex murderer. Better authenticated was the fact that in Denmark, crimes of sexual aggression dropped by 50 per cent after the abolition of censorship. He did concede that 'the pathologically violent person is a different case', but on the whole he was invincibly convinced that 'if our characters and inclinations are formed before we are eight, is picking up a lurid paperback at the age of 32 really going to make much difference?' The obscenity law was inoperable. All it did was send policemen tramping through art galleries and the offices of student magazines, while Soho flourished.

The desire to censor words and pictures comes from a deep reluctance to face the truth about life. Life is dangerous, violent and much of it is difficult to bear . . . It is often living, with all its dangers and difficulties, that corrupts. It is the pride of creative art to be able to face such corruption and speak of it freely and without fear. We do no service to the health of our society when we nervously seek, even for the most honourable reasons, to curtail that freedom.

His authoritative, reasoned tone made it hard for anyone to argue without appearing risibly petty-minded, illiberal and old-fashioned.

★

Argument and advocacy were John's opportunity to play the roles he most enjoyed. He had a theory that we all play roles and give performances all the time in our everyday dealings. In the law, in politics, in the Church, performance counts as much as in the theatre. He had just made a film for BBC2's *One Pair of Eyes* series, *It's a Two-faced World*, with the help of Eleanor Fazan and Robert Stephens, who demonstrated that a trained actor can perform any act more 'naturally' than a real person. Ordinary people, talking about their real lives, behave with stilted artificiality when faced with a camera. He had written on a similar theme in the *New Statesman*. 'Everyone's in Showbiz' was about the audience's 'simple faith' that makes them applaud conjurors more warmly than surgeons. Even at home, we are all acting. 'The place to observe showbiz at its most merciless is . . . on the brightly-lit stage of family life. Teenage children never tire of their performance as teenage children, nor do their parents fail to come in on cue with the necessary feedlines,' followed by the inevitable scene, 'the feet pounding on the stairs, and the banged door which almost brings down the house'.

Rarely a month now passed without one of his plays being produced on television. Getting a bad notice, he wrote, is like being told in the middle of a bicycle ride that you can't ride a bike. You may stumble and get off the bike, but next day 'you're pedalling along again', having moved on to the next project. This was bravado: John minded criticism very much. He would be cast down by disobliging comments. But he did always get back, defiantly, on his bike.

His agent, Peggy Ramsay, had suggested he write a stage play about his marriage. 'You know, how we love each other and hate each other,' he told Penelope, 'and can't live together and all that.' Peggy helpfully offered to lend the Mortimers a tape machine to record their quarrels. He did write the play (*Collaborators*) but it took three years to emerge. Meanwhile, the BBC producer Irene Shubik, who was commissioning for *The Wednesday Play* from John Osborne, Peter Nichols and other writers she admired, had approached John, and he suggested a play about the new divorce laws. *Infidelity Took Place* was about a happily married, high-earning couple (Judy Cornwell and Paul Daneman) who pay tax at 19s 6d in the pound: they would be better off if they divorced and lived together. So the wife, a scatterbrained painter, approaches a seedy divorce lawyer named Leonard Hoskins and presents him with various bogus grounds for her divorce. Hoskins, a lonely middle-aged reactionary bachelor, who lives with his mother and wears shiny suede shoes and a threadbare tie, his waistcoat bearing crumbs of pork pie, was an early prototype of Rumpole.

Among the eight million viewers who watched it on 8 May 1968 was Molly Parkin, the flamboyant, kohl-eyed journalist, painter and sometime restaurateuse of the Red Brick in Chelsea, who had been invited to John's flat to see his play, along with others, including Shirley Anne Field. As the action unfurled Ms Parkin realized that John had plundered the tales she had told him about her first marriage. The heroine was even called Molly. He squeezed her hand throughout, 'as if to say, "don't be cross",' she said. But John regarded his own life and anyone else's as material.

The proposed reform of the divorce laws, he wrote in an *Observer* column that week, would deprive writers of some of their best plots. 'Suffering novels of middle-class life would die away . . . The claustrophobia of marriage, the huddling together on a raft of mutual destruction from the fear of the great, lonely, uneventful sea, is one of the best dramatic situations.' Well, he knew all about that. He had received a letter from Penelope's solicitor about their impending divorce. Yet they continued to huddle together on their raft of mutual destruction. They travelled together to Paris for weekends, and took the children on ever more exotic holidays: Morocco at Easter, a Kenyan safari in the summer. Jeremy remembered barely spending a day at home during the hols. When school broke up, off they flew.

Many years later, a perceptive interviewer asked John whether his 'stormy' marriage had kept going because he knew from the divorce court that people rush into marriage but are far slower to get out of it, since 'any human relationship, however painful and absurd, can seem better than the uncharted desert of divorce'.

'No, I think it was the children really,' John replied. 'And it certainly wasn't stormy all the time. What my clients feared was that they'd rather have the quarrels than be alone; they'd even rather live with people they never spoke to, and just left notes for each other, than be alone. I didn't think I'd be alone, if I was divorced, so it was really the children; and also' (his voice here became very soft) 'there was a lot of affection and emotion too.'

Earlier that year, Penelope had spent three weeks in the Caribbean with Clive Donner. Later she went to Connemara, where Donner was filming *Alfred the Great* at Oranmore Castle, south of Galway Bay, a magical place with views of the Aran Islands. But having arrived armed with a filmscript in progress, Penelope announced, 'I can't work here', and took a taxi to Shannon Airport. She did return to Ireland later that year, with three of the children; but by then, Donner had met his future wife.

As John insisted, what happened between consenting adults in private should be of no concern to others, and he kept his counsel about his own private life, as a quasi-bachelor in an egregiously permissive era. Molly Parkin, girl-about-town between marriages, fashion editor of *Nova* and the *Sunday Times*, found him a kindred spirit: she was keen on sex, a connoisseur of erotic games and devices, and had no objection to adding the famous playwright QC to her collection of lovers. Only decades later did Molly reveal John's penchant, when they fell into bed together after long evenings of ribald laughter and heavy brandy drinking – 'drinking was a big part of it,' she said – for playing 'naughty games' such as being spanked with a hairbrush. (John's later novel, *Summer's Lease*, features an old reprobate character, Haverford Downs, who muses on the Italians' sexual habits: 'They've never known the delights of being shut in a broom cupboard and smacked with a hairbrush by a Nanny whose starched apron crackled across her bosom like approaching thunder.') John defended many spanking magazines, and numbered several spankers and spankees among his acquaintance, including his friend Ken Tynan. But interestingly, when Tynan wrote to John in December 1966, inviting him to write an erotic sketch for his new revue *Oh! Calcutta!* ('*quel cul t'as!*'), suggesting the topics of bondage and flagellation, John did not respond. He did, however, agree to give legal advice on the production, and attended a dress rehearsal. 'Dress rehearsal,' he noted, meant that the cast were quite naked, but were allowed to keep on their glasses, cornplasters, etc. He also found *Oh! Calcutta!* quite devoid of humour.

By now a new girl had sashayed off the catwalk into his life. Ziva was an Israeli fashion model, on the books of the trendy Peter Hope-Lumley agency, which displayed its models' photos on a pack of playing cards. John had stolen Ziva from her film producer boyfriend over dinner in London. She was unusual and larky and almost as tall as he was, a stunning adornment; and he enjoyed telling people that she had been a sergeant in the Israeli army, had stolen a tank, driven to the border and absconded to New York. But Ziva was often away on modelling trips. Liz, who stayed at Holland Park that summer while Penelope was in Ibiza with Caroline and Leslie Phillips, was more available. Her signature witnessed the agreement John signed on 1 July, to write his autobiography for Methuen for a £350 advance. (He had no hope of getting this book written within a year and the deal was cancelled eight years later.)

He was also dancing attendance on Shirley Anne Field again. Having played a naughty nurse in *Alfie* (1966) with Michael Caine, she was now a young mother, feeling lonely, living on the top floor of a West Hampstead mansion block with a four-month-old baby daughter, Nicola. Her husband, Charlie, was out all day training as a pilot. One Friday morning John rang – 'Darling! We haven't seen you, the sun's not shining when you're not around' – and arrived to whisk her to lunch, just as she was about to feed her baby. John took over, cooked the spinach, mashed it and fed it to the baby on the kitchen table. He improvised a carrycot from a vegetable box, draped the box with a shawl, put the baby in it, and took mother and baby to the Barque and Bite in Regent's Park, a floating restaurant on the canal. 'For the next year and a half this lovely man would arrive on Fridays and take me out, with the baby. I looked forward to those days. He gave me an easy, peaceful oasis, made me feel beautiful and unique again, kept me in touch with my business. He was still a would-be lover, romantic and gallant, but more like a father-figure really, affectionate and sweet and generous.'

John did not, fundamentally, want to get divorced. As Penelope knew, he hoped that they could stay married and that she would tolerate the girlfriends. They agreed to put off divorce proceedings until after their safari holiday with Jeremy and Deborah in Kenya at the end of August. In a photograph taken on the beach at Mombasa, Penelope's rictus smile betrays underlying unhappiness. On their return, she had to look for houses for both her mother, now ninety-two, and herself. She took over John's old job as the *Observer* film critic (having hardly seen a film in her life, said John): 'A far cry from real writing, I know . . . but a million times better than nothing . . . All right, once I wanted to be another Virginia Woolf. Now I don't even want to be a superior Margaret Drabble.' On 28 October, Clive told her he was going to marry Jocelyn Rickards. This was a blow. But Donner denied ever having proposed to Penelope. He was never interested in marrying anyone, and had made this clear to all – 'until I met Jocelyn'.

The disaffected Penelope inspired John's next television play, *Desmond*, a monologue. Emma, a clever, bony, chain-smoking journalist, a veteran war reporter, has invited to lunch the nineteen-year-old blonde who has stolen Desmond, her husband. She discovered the affair when Desmond left his chequebook on her bedside table, with the girl's name and address written on the back, and 'I love you rabbit' underneath. She plans to serve her usurper bland nursery fare – 'Builds up the puppy fat! Polishes up the little white milk-teeth!' – and rehearses the confrontation with nervous malice: 'What the hell, I mean what the hell, do you know about life?' The battles between her and Desmond, she will tell this girl, are what keep them going. She needs them, and is convinced that Desmond does too.

This little playlet reflects how fundamentally John understood Penelope's enraged feelings. And it is worth noting how much drama, on stage and screen, was dominated in the late 1960s by the troubled relationships of couples, married or otherwise. The couple in John's next filmscript, *John and Mary*, wake up in bed together after meeting the previous night in a singles' bar and spend the day getting acquainted – flirting, arguing, recalling their old flames. John had already written five drafts of this scenario, based on Mervyn Jones's novel, with Michael Caine and Julie Christie in the frame – until the producers relocated the action from Hampstead to Manhattan. So John left for New York that November, to 'become as familiar with the town as I am with Swiss Cottage and Notting Hill Gate'. 'Entombed' in the Carlyle Hotel, he learned how to pick up a girl in Maxwell's Plum, the gas-lit, Edwardian-style bar on 52nd Street, where John and Mary meet. Mia Farrow was to be Mary. John often mimicked her habit of sitting cross-legged on the floor with a bottle of wine and saying, 'If it's any consolation, I love you, Mozart.' Dustin Hoffman was asked to play the role of the eponymous John. But he needed to be persuaded.

So with Peter Yates, the director, John flew to Philadelphia, where Hoffman was in a play called *Jimmy Shine*. In Hoffman's Hilton Hotel bedroom (while his manager held a noisy orgy in an adjacent room), the three men sat over hamburgers and milk. There was a pool table, so Hoffman played with Yates, urging John to think up a new ending for *Jimmy Shine*, which he found unsatisfactory. So John sat scribbling, until eventually at 3 a.m. the playwright himself, Murray Schisgal, was fetched down from his room, 'looking like the prophet Elijah in rumpled pyjamas', to listen politely to John's ideas for improving his Act Three. 'I wondered how he restrained himself from braining me with a billiard cue,' as John said. 'OK,' said Hoffman. 'I'll do your film.' But he made John explain some essential details: what records did this John character play, what magazines did he read, who were his favourite comics? And why did he cook so much? In America, said Hoffman, only faggots cooked. 'By 5 a.m.,' John later wrote, 'we had convinced him that a man who cooked was not necessarily homosexual,' and Hoffman had to succumb. At 5.45 a.m., as dawn broke coldly over Philadelphia, John and Yates crossed the icy tarmac to catch their flight home.

That Christmas, when John and Penelope took the children back to ski at Adelboden, John left on New Year's Eve and flew to New York for the shooting of *John and Mary* and a luxurious interlude in New York, at the film company's expense. Then, abruptly, he reverted to being Mr J. C. Mortimer, QC, and on 21 January 1969 took a train to Leeds Crown Court, to defend Arthur Dobson, a Bradford bookseller.

Dobson, who had left school at fifteen, was 'a professional purveyor of filth', in the words of Mr Justice Veale. He had been selling *My Secret Life*, by Walter, the eleven-volume sexual diaries of a Victorian civil servant, first published in 1888, and he 'possessed for gain' two books entitled *Bawdy Setup* and *Sex Game*. Walter's *My Secret Life* had been treated as a serious historical document by Steven Marcus in *The Other Victorians*, an analysis of the Victorian underworld, so John called Marcus as an expert witness, along with nine others, including Wilde's biographer Montgomery Hyde and the historians J. H. Plumb and John's old schoolfriend E. P. Thompson. They attempted to justify, on the grounds of historical interest, Walter's accounts of sodomizing a prostitute, and of violating a ten-year-old girl in Vauxhall Gardens. But the jury found Dobson guilty; he was jailed for two years (later reduced), fined £1,000 and ordered to pay £2,000 costs. As one defence witness pointed out, the Obscene Publications Act 'requires from jurors a type of objective reading rare enough among professional critics of literature'.

John maintained that the scrapping of all obscenity law was 'a necessary step to adulthood'. The Arts Council's research found no evidence of a link between pornography and crime. 'I do not think there is anything a human being cannot face and cannot control,' he said. Restraints would come from public opinion in future, which was proper. 'In the end all tastes will be catered for, and I see nothing wrong with that.' He wrote a sketch that autumn for a Royal Festival Hall gala performance, in which the Lord Chamberlain bowdlerizes the 'obscenities' in Mrs Beeton's cook-ery book.

After obscenity, a case with comic potential was an appealing prospect. Home from the family's 1969 Easter holiday in Crete, John went to Wales to defend the Free Wales Army. They had plotted, the previous year, to hire a helicopter and fly over the Prince of Wales's investiture, dropping farmyard manure over the proceedings. The plan was forestalled, but the trial ensued. Emlyn Hooson had declined this brief, believing that the FWA, far from being dangerous men, were a bunch of nutters.

John's client, 'the Goebbels of the group', was a young miner named Dennis Coslett, whose savage dog, Gelert, rode in the sidecar of his motorbike. In Coslett's sock drawer, explosives had allegedly been discovered. 'All the police on the case were called Dai this and Dai that,' John remembered. 'Dai Notebook-and-pencil, Dai Car-parking, Dai Exhibit, Dai Scene-of-the-Crime. When I said I wanted to cross-examine the officer who claimed to have found the explosives, I was told, "Oh, you'll be wanting Dai Plant." And we called the judge "Wee Scruple" because he kept saying, "I have a wee scruple about that."'

John made an excellent final speech, the bit he always liked best. As was his habit, he mentioned recent events in the world out-side, thereby belittling and ridiculing events in the courtroom. 'Members of the jury, since this trial began, men have alighted on the moon . . .' Laughter duly erupted. The Free Wales Army, accused of unlawful military behaviour, wouldn't cause fear in anyone, he said. They were all captains and majors, they had no other ranks. 'I recited the song from *The Gondoliers*: "When every-one is somebodee, then no one's anybody",' John recalled, 'and the Free Wales Army left the dock in fury at my diminishing their importance.' Mr Justice Thompson was disposed to be lenient.

These men, though misguided, were 'lovers of Wales'. He sentenced six of them to short prison terms (three suspended). When John went down to the cells, Coslett told him, 'The day freedom dawns, you will be made a free citizen of Wales,' and presented John with his spare glass eye, as a memento.

During a break from Swansea Assizes in May, John and Penelope travelled together for the last time as a working partnership. Sam Spiegel summoned them to his yacht *Malahne*, moored at Cannes during the film festival, to discuss a script of *The Right Honourable Gentleman*, based on Roy Jenkins's biography of Charles Dilke – another film that never got made. John had to be back in Wales on 15 June, but he joined Penelope at her Hampshire cottage afterwards. 'If only I could pick him up and carry him out of his despair,' wrote Penelope. 'Because I understand his despair.' However despairing she thought him – there was no public sign of despair – he took the family for a month's summer holiday at Grasse in the South of France, staying in Derek Monsey and Yvonne Mitchell's house. En route they picked up an engaging young Irish hitchhiker who joined their house party; the grateful lad remet John twenty years later when he directed a *South Bank Show* film about him. At the Monseys' house were Harold Pinter and Vivien Merchant, Clive Donner with Jocelyn. Joss Ackland and his wife, Rosemary, hired a Jeep and drove over from the Camargue, where Ackland was filming. Invited to lunch, they arrived – after a chapter of accidents, ending with their car in a ditch – at nightfall, and were met with torches. The atmosphere was volatile: 'It was *Who's Afraid of Virginia Woolf?* on ice,' Ackland recalled. One day there was a thrilling forest fire. Nobody realized it, but this was the last Mortimer family holiday.

John's adaptation of a second Feydeau farce, *Un Fil à la patte* (*Cat among the Pigeons*), was another triumph, again directed by Jacques Charon, with a *galère* of stock Feydeau characters, among them Victor Spinetti and Richard Briers, flaunting their mad mannerisms as doors banged, trousers fell and ladies swooned. One particular line, 'You are marrying your lover! What will you do in the afternoons?' brought the house down at the Prince of Wales Theatre. This was just one of many productions John was involved in that autumn.

Harold Wilson's government had abolished the office of Lord Chamberlain and his theatre-censoring powers, a victory for John and the other campaigners, just in time for *Come As You Are*, an evening of four short plays which would otherwise have given the Lord Chamberlain apoplexy. Each play had a different location and featured a different sexual situation: mild fetishism among dentists in Mill Hill; a bisexual love triangle in a pub in Bermondsey; fantasy fulfilment in Gloucester Road; and a kept mistress in Marble Arch whose titled lover dies in flagrante and is removed from the mansion block in a dustbin. The plays' message, John said, was that everyone should relax and be what they are. 'If you want to dress up as Queen Elizabeth or Walter Raleigh when you make love, then that's what you should do. Equally, accept other people with all their faults, for love is not love which alters when it alteration finds.'

The seven-week pre-London run was chaotic. The stage revolve didn't work, and John argued violently with the producer, Alexander Cohen, and the director, Allan Davis, almost coming to blows. Joss Ackland remembered grabbing Davis by the jacket and heaving him down the corridor. One backstage visitor remarked that there was more drama offstage than on. But before *Come As You Are* reached the West End – where one of the plays had an extremely powerful impact – came a much more important play for John's professional future. On 16 October 1969, *A Voyage Round My Father* – a condensed reworking of his radio plays *The Education of an Englishman* and *Personality Split* – was televised.

It was rare indeed to see blindness portrayed on television at all, let alone blindness unacknowledged and ignored, in the person of a powerful paterfamilias. The distinguished Mark Dignam towered over the action as Clifford. Kathleen was played by Daphne Oxenford – a name indelibly attached, for viewers, to childhood memories of *Listen with Mother* ('Are you sitting comfortably? Then I'll begin') – her face showing just a hint of wifely long-suffering.

Timothy Good played John as a boy, prone to inventing tales for his schoolfellows, and Ian Richardson the adult John, hesitant, unable to assert himself in the face of the idiosyncratic father whose affliction must not be mentioned. Arthur Lowe gave one of his inimitable characterizations as the mad headmaster. There was still no plot, just a series of remembered scenes – from home, school and courtroom – but it was instantly hailed as a triumphant end to the *Play for Today* season, and its future as a modern classic was assured.

Writing about his new play, John drew the distinction between memory and nostalgia. One day even 1969 would inspire nostalgia: 'a long hot summer when Granny was a little girl, when life was all tinkling bells and wide velvet trousers . . .' Memory is different: it is part of the present, always with us. Memory can shuffle time like a pack of cards, as film directors do with flashbacks:

Often our distant past, our childhood, remains the most important part for our present actions . . . I have long wanted to write something about my father, not because he recalls my past, but because he is my present and will no doubt be part of my future, and of my children, and in time of their children too. And that, I believe, is the only sense in which we are all entitled to be called immortal.

As Penelope said, his best writing was about his own life, 'and whenever he wrote about his father, his writing was enhanced'.

Nothing – not the television play's success, or travelling with the *Come As You Are* tour – stopped John from appearing in court. He was to be found at Uxbridge Magistrates' Court, unsuccessfully defending the importers of American nudist magazines seized at London Airport; and at Marylebone Magistrates' Court, defending twenty-year-old Richard Branson, whose magazine, *Student*, had violated the Indecent Advertisements Act (1889) and the Venereal Disease Act (1917) by publishing remedies for VD. As John pointed out, in every public lavatory hung a notice offering advice about VD; if Branson was guilty, so was the government. Branson was fined £7, but the legislation was soon amended, and the Home

Secretary, Reginald Maudling, wrote to Branson apologizing for the prosecution.

The film of *John and Mary* opened at Christmas. When Mervyn Jones wrote in the *New Statesman* objecting to the changes to his novel, John replied in self-defence (as 'that despised figure, the scriptwriter'), recalling 'the bleak midwinter evening that Peter Yates and I spent with Mr Hoffman' which 'should make Mervyn Jones grateful for the solitude and serenity of his study'. Lucy Moorehead, journalist wife of the writer Alan, sent off a letter to the *New Statesman* editor. She sympathized with Mr Mortimer's labours, but he had withheld a vital piece of information: 'how much did Mr Mortimer get paid?' The answer is that John, who could command £20,000 for a script, had done this one for less than half that sum, with a slice of the action thrown in. The film – cutely sentimental and witty, using the Mike Nichols–Elaine May formula of voice-overs to show the differences between what a couple say and what they mean – was a hit.

So the end of the 1960s found John Mortimer prolifically successful: a member of the National Theatre board, and one of Harold Wilson's élite 'luminaries of theatre' guests in the gold drawing room at 10 Downing Street on 11 December, along with Laurence Olivier, Margot Fonteyn, Sean Connery, Judi Dench, Trevor Nunn, Janet Suzman, Peggy Ashcroft, Paul Scofield, Ralph Richardson, Peter Brook, Edith Evans, Richard Attenborough, Kenneth Tynan, Michael Balcon, Robert Stephens and Maggie Smith. But he was not a happy man. Penelope, who had resigned from the Dilke film and crashed her car, was still in bed recovering on 30 November when John returned from a trip to Monte Carlo with Liz, and, 'dropping Liz's air ticket in my wastepaper basket', announced that he was moving out. On Christmas Eve in the Holland Park flat, they silently wrapped the children's presents ('We were barely human,' Penelope wrote) and John said he was going to spend New Year in Paris with Ziva. So Penelope gratefully accepted an invitation to take Jeremy to Klosters, joining Jack Clayton and Haya Harareet, Karel Reisz and Betsy Blair, Vanessa

Redgrave and her children. But the Paris trip fell through. John rang Penelope every day 'in a fury of misery, saying he had nothing to do, it was the most wretched time of his life'.

On New Year's Eve, Penelope and Jeremy were at Deborah Kerr's party in Klosters, slithering back over the snow at midnight. That night, as Penelope noted in her Chronology later, 'John meets Penny Gollop at a party in London.' John had rung Jill Rushton, who ran the Hope-Lumley model agency, saying he was at a loose end, did she know of any parties? She said she was having one, at a flat in Edwardes Square.

That evening Penny Gollop, slim, mini-skirted and gaminely pretty, a graduate in modern languages from Exeter University, got home from work at the Hope-Lumley agency, where she was manager of French and Italian bookings. At the Knightsbridge flat she shared with five other girls, each paying £6 a week, there was no hot water left. But she boiled kettles, washed her hair and went along to the party, in a not very festive mood. When a tall middle-aged man in a velvet jacket, with modishly long hair and horn-rimmed glasses, started chatting to her, she appraised him coolly. He introduced himself, and she at once recognized the name of John Mortimer as the *bête noire* of her aunt Marjorie's dearest friend, Sonia Dimont: that frightful man, as the Gollop family saw it, who had run off with Charles Dimont's first wife. They agreed it was a small world, and John invited her to go on with him to another party at Wigs Creations, known in theatre circles as Wigs Cremations, or Wiggers Criggers.

Penny thought that sounded 'rather decadent'. Anyway, she had to work next morning (New Year's Day was still a working day in Britain in 1969), so John drove her home and invited her to lunch next day at the White Elephant in Curzon Street. It was the start of a new decade, a new phase and the end of his 'delayed adolescence'. He claimed in retrospect that he always knew some-one would come along with whom he could settle down and have 'a placid life'.

14. A New Penny Turns Up

On New Year's Day 1970, John picked Penny up from Knights-bridge and drove her to the White Elephant. Penny had never seen anything like the 'White E': 'Plush banquettes, white table cloths, waiters in white jackets, film stars, Tony Richardson . . . Until then the smartest place I'd been was the Bistro Vino.' The agency had allowed her an extra half-hour. John, who was so agitated that he'd backed his car into a parking meter, placed his hand on her knee under the table. 'You can't do that,' Penny said. 'Why not?' 'That's the generation gap.'

John was about to leave for the shooting of a television film, but said he'd send a postcard: what was her surname? She said it began with G. His card arrived: 'Dear Penelope Geranium . . .' Then she saw him on television, in a discussion programme. Three days later, he rang and asked her to *Come As You Are*, opening at the Globe (now Gielgud) Theatre in Shaftesbury Avenue. Backstage, she met the actors Denholm Elliott, Joss Ackland, Glynis Johns and Pauline Collins. It was a new world for Penelope Geranium, but she was sharp enough to notice 'a frisson' from Denholm Elliott's wife, Susan, when they were introduced. Mrs Elliott had been having a little liaison on the side with John during the provincial tour.

He was still living with his wife 'for the sake of the children', he told her, but keeping separate rooms. When they got round to spending the night together, Penny could hardly take him home, as she shared her bedroom with a flatmate 'with piles of clothes and fag ends everywhere, and a loo where you needed an umbrella when you pulled the chain'. So they went to a hotel. 'And at five in the morning John woke up and said, "I've got to get home. If I'm not there for breakfast . . ." and I thought, Oh God, what have I done, I've been to bed with a married man, as old as my father. I shall end up in the gutter.'

That weekend he took her to the Hôtel George V in Paris, where an over-excited John leapt on to the bed and hit the bell-push that summoned maid, butler and valet, who all duly arrived. Clearly they had to find a love nest: he put an ad in *The Times* ('Writer needs flat') and Penny chose a top-floor flat in Campden Hill Square, Kensington, where practically their only furniture was a Bob Dylan album. John summoned his old girlfriends 'to meet little Miss Gollop'. Jane McKerron brought her baby, Ben, in a Moses basket. 'Penny looked like an urchin, an unsophisticated little boy. Very sharp though. I realized there was a powerful attachment, and she seemed to suit him well.' Penelope decided that she too would leave Holland Park. 'Jeremy burst into wild tears. Horribly unexpected.' (It was the end of the marriage, he realized.) She quickly found another house, 134 Loudoun Road, St John's Wood, for which John paid £28,000: a handsomer, older version of Harben Road, with a formal dining room that suggested 'silver tureens and kippers and kedgeree, the reading of the *Morning Post* and the saying of grace, none of which would happen'.

Come As You Are was a hit (though Joss Ackland sometimes had to retrieve Miss Glynis Johns from elsewhere and fling her bodily on to the stage) and the notices were ecstatic. They loved the exchange between two dentists in Mill Hill: 'How do I spot Gerald?' 'Ginger hair. Overweight. Couple of missing percuspids.' But the critics' gaze was chiefly focused on the *coup de théâtre* in the Bermondsey play. *Bermondsey* is set in the back parlour of the dingy Cricketers pub in the Jamaica Road. Bob, the landlord, is having an affair with the mini-skirted teenage barmaid, and – as his wife Iris knows – is planning to run off with her and open a scampi-and-chips diner. But Bob and Iris have invited Pip, Bob's upper-class friend from army days, to stay for Christmas. It emerges that Bob and Pip have been lovers throughout the eighteen years they have known each other. The wife knows this, and exploits it in order to see off the teenage hussy. 'The way I look at it is,' she tells Pip, 'you've kept this family together. You've kept Bob steady. Do you think I'd have had a peaceful home to bring up the children and a good husband and holidays, if Bob hadn't had you as well to keep him feeling young and handsome as a boy of twenty? Why should I object? I knew what Bob was like. I chose him like that, didn't I?' The high point of the evening was when Joss Ackland (Bob) and Denholm Elliott (Pip) passionately kissed, Elliott clutching Ackland's head. It was a first for the West End stage (and a heroic effort for Ackland, who intensely disliked even being touched by another man). This moment 'caused last night's audience to sit bolt upright and gasp out loud, a rare sight and sound these sex-jaded days,' Philip Hope-Wallace – who was gay – wrote. Ronald Bryden found it 'the most civilised treatment of homosexuality' he had seen. John had, of course, been closely observing the example of Denholm Elliott, who was bisexual, and his wife, Susan, who accepted this.

Penny had given notice to the model agency, as she and two friends had a madcap scheme to fly to New York, earn money as waitresses, buy a car and tour America (though Penny couldn't yet drive). Manhattan, they soon discovered, was not like the King's Road, where any pretty young thing could walk into a restaurant and get a job; not having green cards, they slept on the floor of an air hostess friend, and worked as dog-walkers. Penny did one gig as a disc jockey, and had her purse stolen, containing ten dollars, her payment for the night. She ended up with an illegal job, standing on the street enticing people into a seedy pizza parlour, then serving the seedy pizzas.

John, meanwhile, was slumming it in the Hotel Grande Bretagne in Athens with Jeremy, who had just found a girlfriend, so both father and son spent the entire holiday on the phone. Penny had been in New York for six weeks when John rang to say he was coming to take her to Los Angeles: he was to meet Rex Harrison to discuss *A Voyage Round My Father*, the movie. At JFK, the limo was waiting – 'In those days everything was at your disposal in the movie business' – so they were whisked to the Plaza Hotel, and thence on to a first-class flight to LA. Penny had little luggage other than a black Biba miniskirt, a child-sized cable-knit jumper from Harrods and some burgundy jeans. At the Beverly Hills Hotel shop John kitted her out, in *Pretty Woman* style, with more suitable garb for dining with Rex Harrison, Rachel Roberts and Shirley MacLaine at George Cukor's, where Katharine Hepburn still lived in the garden bungalow she had shared with Spencer Tracy. Penny had never heard of Cukor, whose grand drawing room was a famous Hollywood salon.

It was the end of Penny's American scheme. They flew home and took another flat in Blomfield Road, Little Venice, near Kingsley Amis and his wife, Elizabeth Jane Howard, and with trepidation Penny arranged to take John to meet her parents. 'Oh, my God, he's an elderly man,' protested Anne Gollop, who at forty-five was just a year younger than John, 'and Auntie Marjorie says he's a terrible rake.' When Auntie Marjorie heard that the wicked Mortimer was her niece's new boyfriend, she made a frantic phone call – 'Can't we do something?' – to Sonia Dimont.

However, Anne was charmed when John arrived, wearing a respectable blazer with brass buttons. She opened the door in a velvet Alice band, blue eyeshadow and pink lipstick, and issued an immediate challenge to John: she was off to swim in the sea at Whitstable, as she did, naked, every day of the year – why didn't he join her? 'I haven't heard English spoken on a beach for ten years,' he said as he removed his clothes and glasses and stumbled across the pebbles into the grey North Sea. John and his future mother-in-law were equally impressed by one another.

Penny was the eldest of Anne and Bill Gollop's five children. Bill, a *Guardian* reader ('unusual in farming circles', said Penny), had enlisted at seventeen and fought the Japanese in Burma with the Indian Parachute Regiment, until he was shot in the leg and invalided out. The Gollops had started their farm with one pig and a few chickens in their back garden on a new estate in Canterbury, then bought a plot near Whitstable, built a house and developed the farm. Penny grew up knowing about breeding pigs for slaughter, holding the male piglets by the hind legs while Anne castrated them, after which the mother pig would gobble up the little testosterone-producing balls. John would tell everyone that

Penny's mother 'castrates everything in sight, including the budgerigar'. A good story, but they never had a budgie.

Bright and sportive, Penny had sat four A-levels at Canterbury Grammar, playing competitive tennis and badminton at county level. Her three years on Exeter University's new campus were 'the most boring of my life'. 'Girls had twinsets and pearls and the boys tweed jackets with leather patches on the elbows and sports cars, and very few came from north of the Bristol Channel. I wanted some spark.'

The next hurdle was Penny's introduction to John's mother. 'How old are you?' Kathleen asked Penny. When told 'twenty-three', she said, 'You look about sixteen.' As she served cucumber sandwiches, Kathleen remarked to her son, '*Very* jeune fille.' By 26 July, Jeremy too met Penny. 'Jeremy on river with John & Gollop', as Penelope's diary sourly noted. Penelope could not believe that 'Penny G' would be a permanent fixture; and John kept reassuring her with 'Let's forget about this separation' and 'Let's all live together in a commune.' But in long retrospect he would say he fell for Penny because she was such a good, solid person. 'She was a farmer's daughter and they're very sensible, I've always found.' He told an interviewer in 2001 that he had been having a ball in the 1960s, in his bell-bottoms and beads, 'dating all sorts of flaky girls, models and actresses', but 'I knew that there was somebody at the end of the road who was going to be sensible and nice and good and dependable.'

Sally recalled her first glimpse of Penny – at a school quiz, when her father arrived with 'this little girl with long hair' and said, 'This is Penny.' Sally was having such a ball herself – sharing a flat with Jonathan, son of the playwright Pam Gems and a friend of Richard Branson's, riding off on her moped with her boyfriend, Orrin, head boy of Holland Park Comprehensive, on the back, working in an adventure playground – she could hardly appreciate that this girl, only four years older than herself, was not 'just another bird' but her future stepmother.

When John was asked to sit as a judge at Chester Crown Court (which made Kathleen 'shriek with laughter'), he took Penny along to watch while he conducted a nullity case. 'In those days, the question was whether they'd ever had sex, and whether it was impotence or wilful refusal. If it was wilful refusal, the husband could get maintenance from the wife. So you needed evidence of what happened at night. You'd get them into bed, and then you said, "Clear the court." Penny left, and afterwards the clerk of the court told her, "Ooh, miss, the judge says you needn't have gone out, but I'm glad you did. Nice girl like you shouldn't be listening to all that filth."'

John found it no fun to judge. As he wrote, 'Being continually bowed to and asked, if your Lordship pleases? is likely to unhinge the best-balanced legal brain.' To watch in silence went against the grain ('a barrister always wants to talk'). Nobody could possibly decide on custody of two children whose parents lived totally incongruous lives, 'the mother a ballet dancer in Finland, the father a boiler-maker in Brighton'.

That summer John and Penny took a marble-floored, four-poster-bedded house in Ravello for six weeks. Their guests included Jane McKerron and Brian Walden. The house overlooked the Mediterranean, with a view of the white steamer setting off for Positano. So within seven months the new Penny had been taken by John to Paris, Hollywood and the Amalfi coast – not bad for a girl who'd only been to the Bistro Vino. It did not require the services of Penelope's expensive shrink to see that the knife in her emotional psyche was being turned, that her repeated 'relapses' were associated with lonely regret.

She was not the only woman who felt deprived of his company. There is an imploring tone in Kathleen's letters to Sally that summer, begging her to visit, bringing Orrin on their 'motor bicycles', or the children she looked after, or her mother, or her new puppy, Frodo. 'I do want to hear from you, won't you write me a letter or ring me up and tell me how you are getting on with your work at this training centre?' She admired her granddaughter for having the courage and patience to work with handicapped children. But she longed to see her: 'The tulip tree (around which you used to make a fairy ring) is flowering – ten years since it last did this. It's not very showy but like all things (for example your letters) which happen very seldom, one appreciates it all the more.' Gran Fletcher had been to stay. Now in her nineties, Mrs Fletcher had weeded and dead-headed, and 'distinguished herself at Scrabble'. But Kathleen was lonely. In a previous letter to Sally she had written wistfully, 'Before long you will be in Italy with the sun and the warmth and the sea.' John took action: he sent his mother an air ticket to join them in Ravello. It was her first flight. 'I was staggered when I saw my ticket,' she told Sally. 'I really feel wicked that all that money should be used to gratify the whim of an old woman who wants to see her son, and something of Italy.'

John called this Kathleen's Great Escape from his father's house and garden, nine years after Clifford's death. The wariness in their former relationship melted away. He had thought of his mother almost as a stranger, 'totally involved in the supreme sacrifice of her life with my father'. But in the sunshine, in the marble shadows of the house, or sitting under the bougainvillea, drinking cold Caruso wine, 'she giggled, made jokes, wore her long hair down over her shoulders and became a girl again'. Each morning mother and son met in their dressing gowns on the terrace, while the others slept. 'She would smile and say, "Buon Giorno" and we would kiss and plan another day of our great new-found friendship, at ease in a foreign house and a garden where my father had never been.' She was fit enough to clamber down the steep path to the beach, and to sail to Capri; and in the shops she tried out the Italian she'd been learning in Marlow – out of Penny's hearing, because Penny's Italian was fluent.

'The sun shone every day of the fourteen I was there except one when there was a thrilling thunderstorm with lightning flashing over the mountains ending up with a complete rainbow,' she wrote to Sally. 'John was working hard at his script but I am sure the sunshine did him good although at night he got very tired & wanted to go to bed when we wanted to play Bridge.' The villa had the finest view in Italy. 'Virginia, la domestica, was complaining of the poverty and lack of employment among the Italians and when we said "but look at the lovely view" replied "impossibile mangiare la vista".'

Penelope was meanwhile organizing the August wedding of Julia to Gered Mankowitz, at Hampstead Town Hall and a reception at Loudoun Road. Kenneth Harrison came to see his daughter married; John footed the champagne bill. At Turville Heath in Kathleen's absence, Penelope read through Kathleen's diaries:

so sad, naïve, sensitive . . . She is so lonely, has depended so much on John & the children, if not me. She doesn't know or understand anything that happened. I feel a great useless affection for her – much more than for my own mother. She is like a child, and yet is old and feels pain and is frightened . . . I think more & more about old age, & begin to dread it like winter.

She added, 'I think she loves Jeremy. She must see him more often.' (One of the last entries in Kathleen's diary is about longing to see what becomes of her 'interesting' grandson.) Penelope also visited Clive Donner and Jocelyn at their cottage at Speen in the Chilterns, feeling de trop, as well she might: she tended to outstay her welcome, and would stand behind Jocelyn as she painted, until Donner asked her not to.

The novel now mapped out in Penelope's head – A. D. Peters had told her to forget the journalism – was 'weird, probably unforgivable'. Like *The Pumpkin Eater*, it mined her own recent experiences. Eleanor, a mother of five, constructs an uneasy life with her fifteen-year old son after the collapse of her marriage to Graham, a Wimpole street doctor who dispenses drugs to depressed celebrities. He has left her for 'some unimaginable life' with a twenty-two-year-old girl who happens to share her name – Eleanor – but is known as Nell. Eleanor 'cannot take her seriously, least of all her name. Next week it would be someone else.' Graham had adored his daughters, until they 'became older than many of the girls with whom he spent his difficult evenings'. Conscious, again, of its closeness to her own experience, Penelope was both obsessed and 'frightened' by it. She gave pages to Deborah to read, making them both cry.

Kathleen, back from Italy, was pleased to find Penelope using the cottage for writing. 'But you don't really love John, do you?' she said to her. 'I think you've always despised him.' In October, Kathleen stayed with John and Penny at Blomfield Road. She was very sick one night after an oyster supper at the Garrick. Three weeks later, the cleaning lady found her lying on the fireplace at home, having suffered a stroke, and she was taken to hospital in Amersham. She had just written two last letters to Sally. 'Sally darling . . . You are so charming to look at that one longs to see you without those extraordinary rags you put on yourself. There's an art in dressmaking as in any other craft . . . It's not really necessary to be untidy and scruffy to be good.' She remembered Sally at school, 'so smart in grey coat & skirt & great yellow straw hats'. She ended, 'Goodbye dearest Sally from your loving grandmother whom I hope you still love'. Clearly Sally, who already found it hard to deal with her father's new love for a girl only four years older than herself, did not respond well, because Kathleen wrote again on 1 November. 'My darling Sally, I am so very sorry that you were offended – please don't be any longer. If I didn't love you so much I shouldn't bother to risk offending you by being critical. It would be nice to see you again but I suppose I shan't.' She'd seen a TV film about spastic children and said how much she admired Sally for trying to help them. 'It must be heart rending for their mothers . . . My darling Sally, wear what you like but know that your old grandmother always loves & appreciates you.'

These were her last letters. She died on 25 November 1970, the night of the first preview of John's *A Voyage Round My Father* at Greenwich, and was cremated two days later. At her funeral, John read an Emily Brontë poem. Penelope wept ('because I was glad I had known her and in spite of everything she was fond of me; because the children had given her pleasure and she had been loved, and on the whole had a good life. Why weep . . . ?'), but she was drugged with Valium and Lithium. 'My lovely, hateful book is my only hope,' she told her diary, and began writing 'as though I had been given a month to live'.

★

John's play, starring Mark Dignam, who had played Clifford in the TV version, would later transfer to the West End with a different cast and run for two years. On the Greenwich opening night, John gave a dinner for Penny's parents and his friends: Shirley Anne sat on one side, with Penny on the other. He put a hand on Penny's knee and murmured something loving, but she observed his other hand on Shirley Anne's knee. She already knew his compulsion to be 'a naughty boy', his need to keep the love of all the women in his life. She confused this with a belief that he loved women, which is not quite the same thing. He could not say goodbye without leaving the door slightly ajar. He was still reassuring Penelope, promising, 'I'll come back and live with you and have a string of girlfriends', and confided, 'I'm better off with Penny than with Shirley. Less trouble.' Penny had already been with him for nearly a year. 'We are in deadly competition,' Penelope wrote, 'and I must inevitably lose, for I haven't the resources or the will, or really, the wish.'

The notices at Greenwich were good. The anecdotal-biographical format was reminiscent of Peter Nichols's recent *Forget-Me-Not Lane*, another father seen from the son's perspective; and of Robert Anderson's *I Never Sang for My Father*, with a son as author-raisonneur. But John's *Voyage* predated both, in the radio versions six years before. Irving Wardle felt that John had not tried to 'pluck out the mystery of his father's character'. But that is precisely what the title '*A Voyage Round . . .*' was intended to convey. Harold Hobson was struck most by Clifford's refusal to be defeated by his blindness, but pointed out the great cost to his family. Hobson's sympathies were all with the daughter-in-law, who had dared to introduce into the play a moment of truth, asking in exasperation, 'Why do you all pretend that he is not blind, when he is?' 'The house shrank at this,' said Hobson, 'but it was something that had to be said.'

That Christmas Eve, John joined Penelope and their family for the last time at a house in Cornwall. She had finished her novel, 'tiny and dreadful and cruel, a crumb of life'. Deborah arrived on her new moped, and Penelope, following her in the car, had to watch helplessly as Deborah skidded and fell on the icy road, luckily unscathed. Of that Christmas she later wrote, 'I looked at him and thought, how strange, my husband: an overweight, vain, talented man with no idea how to behave or what to do.' Surrounded by his old family, he was constantly on the phone to Penny. Before he left, he had told Penny, 'I love you so much, we must have a baby.' She stopped taking the pill and was pregnant within a month. When she told him, he was stunned. Perhaps, she thought uneasily, he hadn't meant what he said.

On 15 January 1971, Penelope flew to Nairobi with Eleanor Fazan and Nigel Davenport. Fiz had felt so sorry for Penelope in Greenways nursing home a few weeks before, she invited her to join them in Kenya, where Davenport was shooting the sequel to *Born Free*. It was a disastrous interlude. 'She was a pain in the neck,' Fiz said. 'Wherever we went – the most beautiful places on earth, Lamu, Mount Kenya, the Safari Club, with mongooses running around, she was a complete black cloud. Nothing about Africa pleased her. Nigel found her impossible.' She returned feeling worse than ever: her doctor recommended a course of eight ECTs, in Greenways again, to start on St Valentine's Day. On 22 February 1971, she wrote, 'Julia pleaded last night, crying. "Please don't die." So I won't . . . My best moment is when I soar away on the pentathol.' She had only the haziest notion of how many electric shocks she had; her suffering was distressing to behold. John brought champagne, having returned from an interlude in the sun with Penny at Le Nid de Duc, Tony Richardson's hideaway village in the South of France, where, as he wrote in the *Observer*, 'the hills were alive with the twitter of exiled British typewriters'. John had to fly on to Los Angeles, and as Richardson and Penny waved him goodbye Richardson turned to Penny and said, 'Well, if there's a crash you'll be a nice little rich widow, won't you?'

In a later novel, Penelope wrote of being at the mercy of doctors, convulsed with electric volts: 'My body . . . clenched its teeth and writhed in a momentary death throe . . . In the few moments I was conscious (before they put me under again) intense fear was

my main symptom.' They gave her painkilling drugs which made
her scream with pain:

The white shapes hung over me, solicitous . . . They shook their white
heads. If I slept too much, they woke me up. If I was wakeful, they put
me to sleep. If I was depressed . . . they cheered me up. If I was too
cheerful . . . they depressed me again. If I remembered, they made me
forget. If I forgot, they forced me to remember. All in all, I had never
known such unhappiness or such exhaustion.

The only thing that got her through this ghastly treatment was her
powerful determination to survive.

John, meanwhile, was at Bow Street Magistrates' Court for the
Lady Birdwood blasphemy case. Tall, thin Lady Birdwood, with a
penchant for lime-green Edna Everage glasses, was the scourge of
porn magazines on station bookstalls, and of the moral decadence
she saw everywhere. She had brought a private case against a
satirical nineteenth-century play, *The Council of Love*, which
wicked Willie Donaldson produced at the Criterion Theatre. The
play showed an Easter Day orgy involving a cast of randy cardinals,
sexy girls, circus figures and a naked Pope Alexander Borgia, while
God, an old man with matted hair wearing a long dirty robe,
coughing and spluttering and wheezing, looked down. 'This caricature,' said Lady Birdwood, 'came between me and the God I
worship.' On her fourth visit she led a hymn-singing demonstration at the theatre, causing an uproar. She engaged an evangeli-
cal Christian solicitor who shared her revulsion, and accused the
play's director, Jack Gold, and its co-director, Eleanor Fazan, of
putting on a play that 'did violently and ribaldly vilify and ridicule
the Christian religion and did in like manner impugn its doctrines'.

John had told Fiz he would handle the case for her, free. It was
heard by the Chief Metropolitan Magistrate, Sir Frank Milton, a
liberal fellow of cultivated mind and compassionate instincts. Fiz,
sitting very straight in court and filled with fear, was awash with
relief when John arrived with his entourage of juniors, his wig
skew-whiff. He was determined to quash the case at Bow Street,

knowing that the criminal court would spend months defining blasphemy, and the defendants would be landed with impossible costs.

Lady Birdwood's counsel for the prosecution turned out to be Quentin Edwards, now forty-six, a father of three, happily married to Barbara and living in Highgate, a pillar of the Church. This was the only occasion when John and his Nemesis from Oxford days appeared in court together. But it was an abortive trial. Cross-examining, John asked the Criterion's stage manager a leading question: 'You will know that Miss Fazan was away in Nottingham, [choreographing *Lulu*] at the time?' John's evidence – that neither Gold nor Fazan was connected with the production after the first night, or present on the nights Lady Birdwood was there – meant that neither could be held responsible for what happened in the theatre. In short, the case was dropped. Sir Frank Milton said he had no doubt that Lady Birdwood's motives were honourable, but since there was no prima facie case of an offence having been committed by the two people named, the charges against Gold and Miss Fazan must be withdrawn.

Edwards remained convinced that the outcome would have been different if the prosecution had been better handled. *The Council of Love* was 'a scandalous and dreadful play'. 'It showed the Virgin Mary as a blowsy middle-aged whore, and Jesus as a pathetic character in a wheelchair with bandaged head and feet, endlessly whining. It was deliberately performed as an outrage. The language and actions of the play led to no other conclusion.'

John's own new play, a free adaptation of *The Captain of Köpenick*, opened that spring, and was applauded for injecting wit into Carl Zuckmayer's 1931 satirical play. Paul Scofield got a standing ovation and twenty curtain calls for his National Theatre debut as Voigt, the ex-convict who escapes a lifetime of vagrancy by masquerading as an army officer. John discerned that the real hero of the play is the German military uniform itself, conferring authority and dignity on the wearer. In one scene, the tailor's daughter puts on the sky-blue tunic and seduces the wife of one

of the guests, demonstrating its innate sexual power. The play was
a sellout for its short run.

One night John joined Penelope and Jeremy for supper at
Loudoun Road, on the eve of Jeremy's departure for school.
Penelope, just out of Greenways, was cheered by Harold Harris's
message that her new novel was 'stupendous, superlative, marvellous, must win some literature prize'. She offered to drive John
home, and suggested that she might come in and meet Miss Gollop.
Penny – by now three months pregnant – was forewarned by John
and braced herself to meet the 'terrifying' woman. Penelope's diary
records: 'We arrived, I shook a limp hand, admired the flat –
friendly, cosy, lived-in. Penny learning typing so that she can Be
Of Some Use. She seemed to me honest.' (Penny had been learning
to touch-type at Sight and Sound, to save on John's secretarial
expenses.)

Their conversation that night turned to John's parlous finances.
He owed £20,000 in tax, and the only solution was to sell the
orchard at Turville Heath Cottage, with planning permission.
Penelope had already mooted the idea that she might build a house
in the orchard. She turned to Penny: 'John doesn't seem to think
it would be a good idea. Surely you must have some opinion of
your own.' Penny, taken aback, thought quickly and replied that
she wouldn't mind for herself, but wondered, would Penelope
really enjoy living next door to the house she had known as
John's parents' home, with Penny installed? Penelope's impressive
rejoinder has gone into Mortimer family anecdotage. 'Well, that
had worried me,' Penelope agreed. 'I thought that if John was
living with some intelligent, middle-aged, talented, interesting,
articulate woman I would be jealous. But now I've met you, I
don't think I need to be.' 'A brilliant line,' as Penny says, 'and I've
never been able to think of the answer I should have given her.'

When they did invite Penelope to Turville Heath for the weekend it was an ordeal, as Penny had foreseen, and Penelope knew
she was 'plumb crazy' to go. But on other occasions the two
Penelopes got on perfectly well, until Penelope goaded Penny
with remarks like 'I can't imagine what you see in him. He's not

very good in bed, is he?' 'I didn't think there was anything she could do to me,' Penny says, 'dig as much as she liked. But John – I've never seen him frightened of anyone, but he was frightened of her.'

Penelope, who was now in the London Clinic, was told of Penny's pregnancy on 6 May. 'After the first blow, & tears at being hit – Jeremy is released; I am released; a burden removed, situation clarified, independence at last, new life beginning (me or the baby?) hope, change, a sudden strange security.' She went home to Loudoun Road with new resolve. 'I made all cosy for myself so that when I came in, it would welcome.' On 14 May she was able to write, with finality, that she had said goodbye to Greenways for ever. She was vanquished, but determined to enjoy her independence. On 27 May 1971, she wrote, 'Harold Harris thinks the horrible book will be a great success.'

Another ghost was exorcized one night when the producer Neil Hartley invited John and Penny to dine in Maida Avenue. Other guests, including John Gielgud and Tony Richardson, were already there. When the doorbell rang again, in came Shirley Anne, with Michael Rudman. Penny was placed at one end of the table and Shirley Anne at the other, next to John. During the steak and kidney pie, John and Shirley got up and left the room for about ten minutes. (In that interval, John told Shirley about Penny's pregnancy and said he was going to 'stand by her'.) In the drawing room after supper, Shirley sat next to John on the sofa. Richardson, always keen to stir things up, asked which two people in the room had known each other the longest? The answer was Shirley and John. Suddenly, Shirley started removing items of jewellery and stuffing them into John's pockets. When John and Penny left, Shirley came to the door with them, tearful as she said goodbye.

Penny waited until they were walking along Blomfield Road before challenging John about what had been going on with Shirley Anne. His implausible claim that 'the poor darling' was too shy to go to the bathroom on her own made her burst into angry tears. John, who had also been to see Penelope in hospital that day, said, 'Oh, God, my life's so difficult, I've had three women crying over me in one day.'

He was again surrounded by women when he and Penny flew in June to the isle of Hydra, where Eileen Atkins and Helen Dawson had taken a house. Penny, six months pregnant, passed out after the three-hour boat journey. The house proved to have rock-hard beds and, despite having been there for weeks, Eileen and Helen had never found the lavatory, only a doorless outdoor one facing the sea. John found the proper one immediately and began organizing everything. 'He did all the shopping and cooking,' Eileen remembered, 'surrounded by three hopeless women.' She had never met John before and was impressed. 'He looked after us and made us laugh. Early one morning, he got up and went down to the village, found the shops locked, banged on doors to wake the shopkeepers, loaded his shopping on a donkey and came back up to the house – and then discovered that it was only 5 a.m., the sun just rising.'

15. The Wizard of *Oz*

By the beginning of the 1970s all the freedoms for which John Mortimer stood appeared to have been achieved. Theatre censorship had gone, homosexuality and abortion laws had been reformed, a law against incitement to racial hatred had been passed and the death penalty had been abolished under the Labour Lord Chancellor, Gerald Gardiner. Yet the *Oz* trial in the summer of 1971 reflected the mutual scorn and incomprehension that lingered on between youth culture and the traditional old guard.

Underground magazines, representing 'the alternative society', intended to *épater les bourgeois*: *Oz*, *Black Dwarf*, *Red Mole* and the newest, *Ink*, were full of in-your-face sex and drugs and rock 'n' roll, publishing stuff the mainstream papers found unfit to print, tricked out in psychedelic colours that rendered them barely legible. Richard Neville had founded *Oz* in Sydney in 1963 while at the University of New South Wales, and had already been prosecuted for obscenity in Australia, when he was sentenced to six months' hard labour (the verdict quashed on appeal). In 1966 he had arrived, via Kathmandu, in London, where his elder sister, the novelist Jill, lived, and relaunched *Oz* with an edition featuring Germaine Greer's article on Englishmen being useless lovers. In the spring of 1970, Neville and his editorial team of Jim Anderson (a former lawyer from Sydney) and Felix Dennis (a streetwise London lad who had proved an energetic and astute business manager) told readers they felt old and jaded and invited school pupils to take over the editorial content of the magazine for one edition.

It is instructive to take a hard look at *Oz* 28, the 'School Kids' Issue. (I have kept my trophy copy to this day.) The cover retains its shock impact: four dusky naked females intertwined in lesbian embrace, with dildoes and strings – some said rats' tails – issuing from their vaginas. This artwork was not by Martin Sharp, *Oz*'s pioneering artistic genie and Belmondo lookalike, but was filched from *Dessins Erotiques*, published in Amsterdam. The problems of *Oz* 28 might have been reduced had this cover not been used. Within, the editorial content has little enduring merit. Beneath the pink, green and purple typography, most of the school-children's efforts are, like the contents of any school magazine, tendentiously show-off, over-written, tedious and innocuous. Their juvenilia sits uneasily among adverts for penis magnifiers, 'massagers' (dildoes), leather posing-pouches and Swedish porn books, magazines and films.

Across two pages there is a long, turgid review of Theodore Roszak's *The Making of a Counter-Culture*, written by the polemical young Australian art critic Robert Hughes, who is infatuated by Roszak's analysis of revolting youth and its rejection of authority. This review had been commissioned by the *Spectator*, but the editor Nigel Lawson had declined to publish it 'because it consisted of nothing but mindless ranting,' he told Hughes, 'and that is some-thing we are not prepared to publish in the *Spectator*, whatever part of the political spectrum it comes from'. On the letters page, a crocheting hippie from Ibiza rebukes the *Oz* editors for shoving sex ('cocks and cunts') everywhere and ignoring love: 'Where is all the fantastic exuberant joy and optimism from Flower Power times? Love is beautiful: don't vulgarize the only thing every human being longs for and needs so badly.' *Oz* reporters had visited secondary schools and produced sub-literate reports on pupils' grievances. 'They are particularly bugged by the arbitrary punishments meted out by some teachers using violence,' says one such report. 'To the man, they hate exams. Some of the girls complain of the irrelevency [*sic*] of much of what they are taught.'

Among the two dozen schoolkids who volunteered to contrib-ute were some flamboyant young individualists with an eye on the main chance. Afro-haired Charles Shaar Murray wrote a high proportion of the mag's contents. 'T. I. Bradford' was a characterful long-haired hippie from Bradford. A trio of bright sixth-form boys from Latymer Upper School in Hammersmith (which had expelled

Felix Dennis but produced Hugh Grant) went along to the *Oz* office, a basement flat in Palace Gardens Terrace, Kensington, and met the gentle Jim Anderson, who masterminded this issue as Neville was abroad, enjoying a sybaritic spring with his girlfriend in Ibiza. Two of the Latymer boys, Deyan Sudjic and Peter Popham, wrote reviews of books and pop albums. (Both later became, like Shaar Murray, specialist journalists: Sudjic was founder of *Blueprint* magazine and became director of the Design Museum; Popham the Rome correspondent of the *Independent*.) Anderson was generous with his supplies of Afghan black cannabis and Sudjic took a disturbing acid trip at Popham's flat. Sudjic told me the magazine's cover affronted the glamorous Trotskyite girl he was pursuing, even though 'sexism hadn't been invented in those days'. (It had, but he was too young to notice.)

But nothing in the magazine attracted as much attention as the doctored version of Alfred Bestall's much-loved, long-lived children's comic strip Rupert, giving the dear little bear a monstrous erection, which he forcibly inserts into an oddly virginal 'Gipsy Granny'. Fifteen-year-old Vivian Berger had simply cut out Rupert's head and appended it to the notoriously rude figures drawn by the American cartoonist Robert Crumb. Berger (pseudonymously 'Viv Kylastron' in *Oz*) and 'the wildest of the bunch' in Neville's words, was the son of Grace Berger, chair of the National Council for Civil Liberties. His collage might have gone down well if passed around the sniggering classmates at his London school. Discussed at length in the Old Bailey, it gave the trial some of its most diverting moments. As Clive James wrote in an essay, *After the Oz Trial*, 'I have small sympathy for *Oz* in general, and scarcely any at all for the culprit issue no. 28: I laughed like a drain at the priapic Rupert the Bear but found the rest thick-witted and raucous in the usual *Oz* way.'

The obscenity squad had raided *Oz*'s office in June 1970, Detective-Sergeant Frederick Luff carrying off all remaining copies of the offending issue. The *Oz* three – Neville, Anderson and Dennis – appeared dressed as St Trinian's schoolgirls for the preliminary hearing at Marylebone Magistrates' Court in October. Later that

year, the television director Tony Palmer organized a seminar on
the underground press at Balliol College, Oxford, inviting Neville
and Caroline Coon, founder of *Release*, which gave legal advice
to those busted for drugs. Palmer, author of a *Spectator* column
called 'Notes from the Underground', had a huge house in Ladbroke Square which, though only yards from a police station, was
often used as a refuge by Jimi Hendrix, Zoot Money, John Lennon
and the Oz boys, when evading the fuzz. Along with Ken Tynan
and George Melly, Palmer had stood surety for Neville that
December at West London Magistrates' Court – his first sighting
of the policeman Luff.

Neville told his Balliol audience that the School Kids' *Oz* had
been charged with 'conspiracy to debauch and corrupt the morals
of children and young persons within the realm and to arouse and
implant in their minds lustful and perverted desires'. This charge,
unused for 130 years and carrying a maximum sentence of life
imprisonment, was a device to avert the 'public good' defence that
had saved *Lady Chatterley*. Up stepped Geoffrey Robertson, an
Australian Rhodes Scholar reading jurisprudence at Balliol, who
offered to help Neville with his defence. In the ensuing months he
beavered away, along with Marsha Rowe and Neville's girlfriend,
Louise Ferrier, in the Regent Street office of Neville's solicitor,
David Offenbach. They collected statements from 100 potential
expert witnesses – including professors Hans Eysenck, Ronald
Dworkin and Richard Wollheim – willing to suspend their critical
instincts and support freedom of speech. Germaine Greer was keen
to help her old friend Neville, but she was in the USA promoting
her book *The Female Eunuch*. She offered to come home for
the trial, but Robertson suspected that her testimony might be
unhelpful, since she had recently allowed her anus to be photographed for the Amsterdam-based underground magazine *Suck*.

Finding a sympathetic defence barrister was the main problem
for the *Oz* trio. The judge, Michael Argyle, Recorder of Birmingham and failed Tory parliamentary candidate, insisted that the trial
would go ahead on the due date, with or without counsel for the
defence; he would appoint a dock brief for them on the day, if

necessary. Emlyn Hooson, head of John's chambers, had turned *Oz* down, feeling he was too square. Tom Williams, QC (a Baptist lay preacher), backed off after seeing the magazine and Basil Wigoder, QC, also excused himself at the eleventh hour, saying, 'I cannot take the risk.' So John was the fourth counsel to be approached, in the first week of June. Neville had come across John before, in TV green rooms, and at a dinner given by his sister, Jill: John had rung Jill afterwards ('How about I come over and pop into bed?') but her rebuttal caused no hard feelings. Neville was surprised and charmed when John at once agreed to meet him, with Robertson, at a restaurant opposite the Old Bailey. Penny and her sister came too. Over the Parma ham and melon, John asked what the case was all about. Robertson and Neville showed him the Rupert cartoon. Penny laughed, John giggled and said, 'Oh goody, when do we start?' The answer was, in four days' time.

Neville was defending himself, not wishing 'to hide behind the wigs and gowns of the legal profession', so John would act only for Anderson and Dennis. He warned them that he was also involved in the *Little Red Schoolbook* obscenity trial, about to have its preliminary hearing at Clerkenwell Magistrates' Court, so he might be absent on some days. (*The Little Red Schoolbook* was a paperback published by a policeman's son and Cambridge scholar, Richard Handyside, aided by children and teachers. It answered straightforward questions about sex – masturbation, orgasm, intercourse, petting, homosexuality – and warned about drugs, including habit-forming substances such as tea, coffee, tobacco and alcohol. It gave advice about school, society and life in general; but since the tone was left-wing, the voices raised against it, such as Ross McWhirter's, called it 'seditious'. In retrospect John felt that it raised more serious issues than *Oz* did.)

Neville doubted that John would have the time to immerse himself in *Oz* matters, but knew that Robertson, a workaholic and a perfectionist, would make up for that. For Robertson, the trial changed his career trajectory; John became his 'forensic father'.

In the weeks leading up to the trial there was a public circus of agitprop by the Friends of *Oz*: leaflets featuring the *Oz* three dressed as schoolgirls, policemen and City gents were distributed; there were marches, demos and a fund-raising *Oz* Police Ball, with John Lennon and Yoko singing 'God save Oz one and all'. On the Monday morning of 21 June, when *Regina* v. *Neville, Dennis, Anderson and Oz Publications Ink* opened in oak-panelled Court Two of the Old Bailey, there was a carnival atmosphere. The public gallery overflowed with hippies. Penny, aged twenty-four, sat below the dock, her pregnancy now visible, giving the figure of John Mortimer, QC, portly, middle-aged, bespectacled, be-wigged, a link with the age group whose ideals he was to defend. At the back, the press benches being full, sat Tony Palmer, alongside Jonathan Dimbleby, reporting for the *New Statesman*, and Nicholas de Jongh for the *Guardian*. The proceedings were being taped by the film-maker Clive Goodwin, and Palmer astutely realized that if he got hold of the transcripts he could make a book out of the trial. And by the end of week one, Feliks Topolski, the celebrated artist, was there too. The trial was quickly established as the most entertaining show in town. Judge Argyle had repeatedly to threaten to close the courtroom because of laughter, and to admonish the public gallery, 'This is a courtroom, not a theatre.'

The young men in the dock wore long hair, T-shirts, suede jackets and, in Felix Dennis's case, a sharp white suit. All three pleaded Not guilty to three charges, the most serious being con-spiracy to corrupt and deprave the morals of the young of the realm. They were dismayed to see that the jury of nine men and three women (one pregnant woman juror was later discharged) were 'lower-middle-class artisans, of average age about sixty', despite the defence's challenges in pursuit of a younger, trendier panel. Brian Leary, prosecuting, was 'courteous to the point of caricature', said Neville. His voice was gentle and insinuating, his cross-examinations were a lesson in needle-sharp advocacy. His opening speech derided the 'alternative society'. What 'alterna-tives', exactly, did *Oz* propose? 'Dropping out'. Expecting the state to provide, exploiting 'those foolish enough to work'. The worship of sex and 'fucking in the streets'. Cross-examining Neville, Leary flourished the lesbian cover, and read out adverts, lingering over words like 'dildo', 'gang bang', 'rape of virgin', 'male perverts' and an advert for a Swedish contact club 'excellent for masturbations and fuckstimulation!!'

On day three, Wednesday 23 June, John rose just before 3 p.m. His first aim – and his last, in his summing up six weeks later – was to mock the absurdity of the trial by emphasizing the littleness of the magazine, while stressing the importance of the jury's verdict in the annals of justice and liberty. 'I am sure you are all very curious,' he began, pointing at two cardboard boxes containing the magazine, 'to discover what it is that has led us here, people from various parts of London and various walks of life, to consider how dangerous or explosive may be those bits of paper over there in those little sugar baskets.' Cases like this, John told the jury, were about dissent, and 'the boundaries of our freedom to think and say and draw and write what we please'. The accused were challenging the established views of society, anxious to build what they thought of as a better world. We might disagree with their views, but this case was about whether or not they were entitled to disagree with us.

So, in his usual way, John flattered the jury with references that presumed they shared his level of education. The jury might think of 'Dissenters' as Victorian preachers thundering from pulpits in dark chapels, he said (ignoring the greater probability that the jurors had never heard of the Dissenters); but these modern dissenters produced their polemical magazine from a bedsitting room in Notting Hill Gate. Their beliefs included a preference for love and peace over war, for racial tolerance over intolerance, for freedom of expression over hypocrisy, convention and taboos. They might at times have expressed these views childishly. But they stood accused of corrupting the morals of children and young persons. This was exactly what Socrates had been accused of, in the trial that resulted in his death.

John made an impassioned apologia for the unfortunate school-kids themselves – harried by examinations, plagued by questions about drugs and sex, at the mercy of school rules, denied any control over their lives. 'Speaking as a parent,' he added, 'the future of this country we live in depends on the sanity and sense of our children.' School Kids' *Oz* reflected the state of mind of teenagers living in a big city: were we to shut our minds to it, and go on as if the boys thought of nothing but cricket bats and the girls thought of nothing but knitting patterns? Felix Dennis thought it was preposterous to mention Socrates, but the classically educated Neville found it entirely relevant. Tony Palmer thought this speech had star quality: 'John knew that the jury would, by instinct, have these hippies locked up in a trice; but with this eloquent, effortless speech he treated them as thinkers.'

John's first advice to the *Oz* three was to say nothing at all. He would have preferred them simply to present themselves as innocent victims of an unfair law and an unfair system with which they had nothing in common. He was nervous that Jim Anderson would come across as the archetypal fey hippie, that Dennis would shoot his mouth off, and Neville would use the trial as a political platform, which would irritate the judge and bemuse the jury, whose knowledge of the alternative culture came only from the popular press. But Neville, who had (still has) a genuinely messianic, revolutionary fervour about making a better world, did not get bogged down in agitprop. He was impressive in court. He spoke in educated tones, he had a naturally polite manner and seemed thoroughly at ease. He said there had been many themed editions of *Oz*: a gay *Oz*, a flying saucer *Oz*, a Women's Liberation *Oz* (actually labelled the 'Cuntpower *Oz*'). 'At the end of the trial,' he promised the jury, 'we'll invite you to edit a jurors' *Oz*.'

For two days the jury, closeted in their room, pored over the magazine, their appetites whetted by Leary, who told them they would find lesbianism on the cover and 'homosexuality, sadism, perverted practices, and drug-taking' within. Leary appeared to be fixated on Rupert Bear's erection, and virtually demolished the law graduate Jim Anderson – thin, nervous, flaxen-haired – by reading from his editorial, which had hymned Vivian Berger's collage as an example of 'youthful genius'. Leary made Anderson reaffirm his words 'youthful genius' twice over, described the process of sticking together two artists' work and asked, 'Where lies the genius?' 'I think it's in the juxtaposition of two ideas, the childhood symbol of innocence . . .' Anderson began. Whereupon Leary interrupted by bellowing, 'MAKING RUPERT BEAR FUCK?' which had an electrifying effect on the courtroom. Leary later asked Edward de Bono, the lateral-thinking defence witness, 'What do you suppose is the effect intended to be, of equipping Rupert Bear with such a large-sized organ?' 'I don't know enough about bears to know their exact proportions,' replied de Bono solemnly. 'I imagine their organs are hidden in their fur.' Leary persisted, 'Mr de Bono, why is Rupert Bear equipped with a large organ?' De Bono returned the question: 'What size do you think would be natural?' at which the judge reminded him that he was answering questions, not asking them.

Later still, Leary addressed Michael Schofield, psychologist: 'What sort of age would you think Rupert is, to your mind? What sort of aged bear?' 'Oh, I'm very sorry – I'm not up to date with bears.' At which the judge intervened: 'Is Rupert a child or an adult?' Schofield: 'It's an unreal question. You might as well ask me how old is Jupiter!' Rupert's organ continued to fascinate Leary, even after Grace Berger, the mother of Vivian – who had encouraged her son to get involved in *Oz* – gave a lucid and simple explanation. 'It was a joke,' she said. She also assured the court that Vivian's association with *Oz* had done him no harm; what had been far more harmful was that 'the whole thing has been blown out of all proportion'. And in reply to a question from Leary, she confirmed that she had taken her son to see *Hair*. 'Well, just pardon me,' said Judge Argyle. 'Hair? What is it? An article?' '*Hair* is a play,' replied John, with a weary sigh. 'It's been running in the West End for about three years.'

John felt that much that was said in court was trivial and went off along byways and into culs-de-sac that did not aid the cause. The levity and reckless tone of *Oz*'s contents wilted in the literal-minded courtroom atmosphere, under Leary's skilled prodding. There were far too many expert witnesses, even though several had refused to help, because they thought the magazine was indeed obscene, or just not worthy to be defended. At the end of the first week, John feared the case would be lost; he told Palmer his notes would be vital, because it was bound to go to appeal. Argyle would never understand the principle of freedom of speech and, after all, how could Rupert Bear, a wickedly naughty but essentially trivial joke, be defended on Socratic principles? 'There was,' Palmer adds, 'no Aristophanes on hand.' Efforts were made to get rid of some of the experts. John was particularly dismayed that Neville had invited the comedian Marty Feldman to take the stand. Feldman managed to offend everyone and left the witness box muttering audibly that the judge was a 'boring old fart'. And Ronald Dworkin, Professor of Jurisprudence at Oxford, declared that the trial itself was 'a corruption of public morals', which went down very badly with Judge Argyle.

George Melly, another expert witness, was asked to define the alternative society. 'The alternative society is one that tries to invent or evolve its own lifestyle, which is usually in opposition to the official lifestyle,' Melly ponderously explained. 'It has its own press and *Oz* is an organ which seeks to probe and to see what society is about. At forty-five, it's not for me the authoritative newspaper, but I find it interesting and I learn from it, particularly about what people younger than myself are thinking.' In his view, four-letter words were OK, even in front of children. John sat with his head in his hands as Melly floundered, ending with a despairing cry, 'You're trying to make me out the monster of NW1!' (Melly's house was in Gloucester Crescent, the trendiest milieu in London, immortalized in Mark Boxer's cartoon strip 'Life and Times in NW1', caricaturing a neighbourhood that included George and Diana Melly, Dee Wells and A. J. Ayer, Nick Tomalin and his wife, Claire ('the Stringalongs'), Alan Bennett and Jonathan Miller.) There was an even more ludicrous exchange when Judge Argyle asked Melly, 'Well, pardon me, for those of us who did not have a classical education, what do you mean by this word "cunnilinctus"?' (as if it were a cough medicine, Robertson later pointed out). This Melly elucidated for him: 'Sucking. Blowing. Or going down or gobbling. Or, as we said in my naval days, "yodelling in the canyon".' This exchange entered John's repertoire. (And in 1997 the British entry in the Eurovision Song Contest was 'Yodelling in the Canyon of Love'.) 'The whole thing became a charade. It got out of hand,' said Tony Palmer.

One of John's *coups de théâtre* was reading out a list of those who received copies of *Oz* – including 'Mr Kenneth Tynan, Mr Jonathan Aitken, Mr Richard Crossman and Mr John Lennon, a well-known singer'. But Leary went on making fools of the expert witnesses. As John reported, Leary himself had a decidedly camp manner; he would chirrup, 'Give us a kiss, darling,' as he passed John every morning and once, eyeing John's notebook, which had a pattern of dark circles on the cover, remarked, 'Ooh look, arseholes all over your notebook.' After Leary had cruelly cross-examined Anderson – who is gay – about whether the male organ was beautiful, the enraged Felix Dennis decided that the whole trial was a pantomime, and entered into it with all his brash south London confidence, even claiming that *Oz*'s circulation was 'half a million'. When Leary cross-examined Dennis, asking him if he found *anything* indecent, such as 'parading yourself in the nude, in full view of everybody else', Dennis replied, 'It would depend on the circumstances. For example, it would be fantastic to take your clothes off and bathe naked in the sea, Mr Leary, on a beach in Acapulco.' (Dennis knew that Leary often went to Acapulco, notorious for the availability of boys.) At this point Leary switched tack: did Dennis believe there was anything at all which tended to corrupt people? 'Yes, Mr Leary. The object of most people's lives – money!'

By the third week it was plain that grown men and women were exerting energy and intellect to scrutinize, with excruciating closeness, a magazine which, had it not been for this trial, would have gone largely unnoticed. The establishment (the law) could not cope with different approaches to language and the upbringing of children in contrasting classes of home. Anthony Smith, later President of Magdalen College, Oxford, entered the witness box to say he too admired Neville – and that, like Melly, he would not object if a daughter of his wanted to marry Neville. (For a lifelong bachelor this contingency was unlikely.)

Leary later told Palmer he'd grown rather fond of Neville, who remained even-tempered and polite in his well-spoken, upper-class Australian way. And Caroline Coon managed to fluster the prosecution while maintaining both her natural hauteur and a cool command of the subject – drugs – on which she was undeniably an expert. She looked stunning and wore hotpants in court. Leary thanked her for 'lightening a dark and very dull afternoon'.

Leary's closing speech was both admirable and thoroughly manipulative. Reading *Oz* 28, he said, had left an ugly taste in the mouth. 'Let me seek to analyse what that taste was. It's the very epitome, is it not, of the so-called permissive society?' He held up the magazine between finger and thumb, like soiled underwear. Adopting an avuncular tone, he told the jury they must set the public standard of decency. Would they not agree that in the magazine there was 'not one word of tenderness'? 'That's because *Oz* does not deal with love. It deals with sex.' This point struck home with Neville, who later wrote: 'It was true. And strangely so, given that we once claimed that "love is all you need".'

Leary spoke for four and a half hours. John, who followed, spoke for six.

John's closing speech, Neville thought, exuded a weary exasperation, later perfected in Rumpole. 'Ladies and gentlemen of the jury,' he began, 'we have sat here while the best part of the summer has passed us by. Wimbledon tournaments have come and gone, the Royal Birkdale has passed us, and we have almost entered the Common Market, whilst we have turned over and over and over again the pages of a little underground magazine, and done it so often we may feel the Fabulous Furry Freak Brothers have entered our sleeping as well as our waking hours. A huge quantity of public time and money has been spent in the ardent and eager pursuit of what? A schoolboy prank. In pursuit of that prank, ladies and gentlemen of the jury, to squash this rather unsuccessful number of a little underground magazine, to gag a little cheeky criticism, to suppress some lavatory humour and some adolescent discussion of sex and drugs, we have had rolled out before us the great majestic engine of the Criminal Law. The threat to our nation of

forty-eight blurred pages of schoolboy ebullience has been countered by the rolling prose of Count one of the indictment, by the
tireless researches of Inspector Luff and the inexhaustible cross-
examination of Mr Leary, and by the deep, sonorous solemnity of
a great criminal trial. One may be tempted to feel that the prosecution is like some nervous public official who, when a child puts
out a tongue at him in the street, calls out the army.' His Lordship
the judge had rightly outlawed laughter from the courtroom, but
surely *Oz* should be evaluated by those who found it funny?
'When you are laughing, ladies and gentlemen, you are unlikely
to be corrupted.' He could not comprehend how his learned friend
Leary did not see the trial as an attack on freedom of speech.
Moreover, like the defendants, all of us wish to 'do our own thing':
'the stockbroker playing his Saturday golf, the lady in the cathedral
embroidering hassocks . . .'

Richard Neville, as the final speaker, responded courteously to
Leary's question, 'Why have we heard nothing of love?' by saying
they had not been asked. He proposed that the alternative society
was practical and political. They rejected unattainable romantic
myths of love, characterized by Barbara Cartland novels. They
found Bob Dylan's lyrics in 'The Times They are a-Changin''
more in tune with the breakdown of communication between the
generations:

> And don't criticize what you can't understand
> Your sons and your daughters are beyond your command
> Your old road is rapidly agin'
> Please get out of the new one if you can't lend a hand . . .

'Will you lend a hand, members of the jury?' Neville ended, his
hand extended.

The following day, Mr Justice Argyle cleared his throat and
spoke all morning. His summing up was agreed to be, in contemptuous tone and in body language, reprehensibly tendentious.
He referred to 'so-called defence experts' and said, 'If *Oz* was a
window on the hippie world, well – windows sometimes need

cleaning, don't they?' In the Bible, those who led children astray deserved to be drowned in the depths of the sea with millstones round their necks. He asked, 'I wonder how many of you, members of the jury, had heard of fellatio before you came into this court . . . Or cunnilingus?'

The jury retired at 12.45 p.m. for almost four hours. More than halfway through their deliberations they returned to request a definition of 'obscene'. When they came back, their verdict was Not guilty of conspiracy (sighs of relief) but Guilty on the counts of obscenity and indecency. The judge remanded the three defendants in custody at once ('Gaoler, take them down!') for medical and psychiatric reports. (The reports found all three level-headed, courteous and intelligent.) Had deportation papers been served on Neville? the judge asked; they had. When they reappeared for sentencing, each had been subjected to a severe haircut, which caused such protests that Reginald Maudling, the Home Secretary, soon announced that in future people in custody would not be required to be shorn. The judge pronounced sentence. Conscious of Neville's intelligence and character, and Anderson's status as a qualified barrister, he sentenced Neville to fifteen months (with recommended deportation) and Anderson to twelve months. He gave only nine months to Dennis, 'because you are younger and very much less intelligent than the other two'. ('I was just the honest yeoman, who could be given nineteen strokes with the knotted towel,' Dennis reflected thirty-five years on, by which time he was by far the richest of the three.) Outside the Old Bailey a crowd of 300 staged a demo and an effigy of the judge went up in flames.

The previous evening, John's *A Voyage Round My Father* had transferred to the Haymarket; he said it was like having two first nights in a row. Fifteen Labour MPs, including Michael Foot and Tony Benn, put down a Commons motion condemning the severity of the sentences, which 'discredited the English system of justice'.

The *Oz* three languished in their cells in Wormwood Scrubs for the weekend ('sick of being cooped up with each other, sick

of *Oz* and the whole damn thing,' wrote Neville) until the application for bail pending appeal was heard in the High Court on
Monday morning 9 August, when Mr Justice Griffiths granted bail
to all three. Neville was interviewed by David Dimbleby; John
went on television with John Sparrow, Warden of All Souls, who
challenged him to read out a passage from the magazine containing
four-letter words. John declined, saying that there were more
valuable ways of using the programme's limited time.

The six entertaining weeks of courtroom antics were fully
reported in Tony Palmer's *The Trials of Oz* (illustrated by
Topolski), which Antony Blond published with commendable
speed on 21 August 1971; John had advised Palmer to go ahead
with his book, no matter what the eventual outcome, and he
managed to get the trial into early perspective. (It was later
fully recounted in Richard Neville's memoir of the 1960s, *Hippie
Hippie Shake* (1995) and in Geoffrey Robertson's *The Justice Game*
(1998).)

Between the sentence and the November appeal, John still had to
finish *The Little Red Schoolbook* appeal against Handyside's conviction and £50 fine. On 7 October, Penny gave birth to Emily
Kathleen Anne Mortimer, named after both her grandmothers.
Just the day before, John had a tooth capped by an Australian
dentist who played Vivaldi the while, and then met Penelope for
lunch in the sunshine at the Rose Garden restaurant in Regent's
Park. Penelope ordered spare ribs. They talked and reminisced. 'I
remembered the places we had visited, the houses we had taken,'
John wrote, 'the years we had spent writing and reading each
other's words, waiting, in terrible suspense, for each other's smallest
sign of approval.' Then Penelope bit into her spare rib and suddenly
('it was like a freeze-frame in a movie') looked horrified, gathered
up her dog Chloë, her cigarettes and lighter, and rushed from
the scene. John sat, bemused, and eventually took a bite of the
abandoned spare rib. Crack! Immediately he realized he had lost
his brand-new tooth-cap. Then he was summoned to the phone:
it was Penelope, now back home, wanting to explain her sudden

departure. She too had lost the cap of her front tooth when she bit into the spare rib! So the divorcing pair were orthodontically united, at their last married meeting.

At the Cambridge Union in late October, John and Richard Neville faced Lord Longford and Mrs Whitehouse, the motion being 'that pornography should never be forbidden'. The queue of undergraduates stretched down Bridge Street. Arianna Stassinopoulos (later Huffington) presided in floor-length purple with sequins. Steak and kidney pudding was served in Trinity College beforehand; Penny sat next to Lord Longford, who asked her what she did. 'I live with John,' she replied. 'We've just had a baby.' 'Oh dear,' said Lord Longford, aghast. 'Are you engaged?'

John rose, sleek and portly, a man of intellect and substance, voice lightly ironical. 'I would like to be serious in this debate and leave the jokes to Mrs Whitehouse and Lord Longford,' he began. The languid barristerial tones using demotic expressions ('and when the couple came to have it off, as we say in the Old Bailey') won cheers from the excitable student body. The word 'forbidden' in the motion was easy to demolish: 'forbidden' equalled censorship, he pointed out, and pornography is impossible to define. In the US it was once adumbrated, under what became known as the Felix principle, as something which gave Judge Felix Frankfurter an erection. 'And it was noticed,' he said, 'that as the years went by . . . (laughter) and Mr Justice Frankfurter became older and less easily stimulated . . . (louder laughter) the judgements of the Supreme Court became conspicuously more liberal.'

Be aware of the paternalistic attitudes of the opposition, said John. '*We* are never corrupted. Mrs Whitehouse is far too sensible, Lord Longford is much too intelligent. But the world is populated with second-rate, second-class, dim people who must be protected.' He, by contrast, gave human nature the benefit of the doubt; he was willing to treat people as adults. He ended with a not very relevant joke about a woman complaining to the old Lord Chamberlain about the words 'virginity' and 'maidenhead' in a play. 'Madam,' Lord Cobbold replied, 'Maidenhead is a town in

Berkshire where 17,000 people contrive to live without embarrassment.' The wave of laughter turned into a standing ovation; it was
bootless for suave young Michael Howard to argue cogently against
the idea that schoolchildren are incorruptible, and to call John's
propositions 'simplistic, arrogant and irresponsible'. The Zeitgeist
was against Howard, and the vote was 442 for the motion, 271
against. *Varsity*'s reporter was twenty-one-year-old Jeremy Paxman
of St Catharine's College, who thought middle-aged John Mortimer's self-conscious use of expressions like 'hangup' and 'turn on'
was an artificial pose:

If you suspect someone of not being true to themselves, how can you
believe in the truth of their ideas? . . . If we consider the real issues at
stake in the pornography question it becomes apparent how much of
the stand taken by the trendy liberators, and not least by people like John
Mortimer (oh-so-clever with words), is purely a question of fashion.

The *Oz* appeal took place in early November, presided over by
the Lord Chief Justice, Lord Widgery. Neville arrived with a
Provençal suntan. John presented, thanks to Robertson's industry,
seventy-eight grounds for appeal against Judge Argyle's summing
up. 'Geoff is a much better lawyer than I could ever be,' as John
acknowledged, 'and he supplied the legal arguments.' Felix Dennis
believed John's true preferred métier was not wooing juries – 'silly
oiks, vile little people' – but the Appeal Court: 'A man like John
prefers facing his peers.' Lord Widgery agreed that there had been
serious errors, but still demurred, disturbed by the *Suck* magazine
advert in the School Kids' *Oz*: surely a woman's commendation
of the pleasures of oral sex could not be other than obscene?
John and his colleagues waited, despondent. Finally, on the third
afternoon, Widgery emerged from his deliberations with his two
fellow appeal judges, James and Bridge, and quashed the convictions. Rumour had it that James and Bridge had sent a clerk out
to Soho to buy some real hard porn mags, which finally convinced
Widgery that *Oz* paled by comparison. As Robertson later said,
the *Oz* trial was a fig leaf for the Soho porn shops, which, in

cahoots with the Metropolitan Police, carried on regardless. The Obscene Publications Squad ran Soho like a fiefdom, in Mr Justice Mars-Jones's words, 'a vast protection racket', until it was cleaned up in the 1980s by the Met chief Sir Robert Mark.

Three and a half decades on, the *Oz* trial has assumed a totemic status, echoing the *Lady Chatterley* case of ten years before. *Lady C* lasted only six days, while *Oz* dragged on for six weeks, but both drew on academic witnesses and each produced comic soundbites, to be invoked whenever anyone needed to ridicule the fossilized views of the judicial establishment. Mervyn Griffith-Jones, QC's 'Is this a book you would wish your wife or your servants to read?' became the keynote of *Lady C*. Similarly, Brian Leary (after John Peel admitted that he had spoken on the radio about having had VD) asked the *Oz* jury, irrelevantly, 'Is John Peel the sort of person you would be happy to see married to your daughter?' Such prejudiced prosecution views were derided and deplored. The two trials became so confused in people's minds that for ever afterwards John Mortimer was erroneously credited with defending *Lady Chatterley* as well as *Oz*. And what Mrs Whitehouse referred to as 'Mortimer's travelling circus' came to embody the caucus of liberal folk prepared to defend anything, no matter how tawdry and contemptible, in the cause of freedom of speech.

'*Oz* was a pretty nugatory effort, journalistically,' as Peter Popham, one of its schoolboy contributors, said. 'But it was fun to be involved, something one could dine off for ever. I was too young to be a hippie, spent my early teens with my nose pressed up against swinging London, but then along came Richard Neville, like a glamorous rock star in an Afghan coat, wreathed in dope smoke, climbing into Porsches with beautiful women – and he was letting us join in the scene.'

The *Oz* trial had cost around £100,000, the *New Law Journal* reported, and occupied twenty-seven working days of one of the most congested criminal courts in the land. *Oz*'s circulation briefly rose to 80,000, but it soon died from over-exposure. Typically unrepentant, the edition published in May/June 1972 contains a lot of spitting fury in readers' letters: 'Fuck you ripoff artists may you rot in hell', 'Since your trial you seem to be aiming for an exclusive readership of screwed-up judges, MPs and other bourgeoisie.' The cover headline was 'Germaine Greer's Husband Flashes Cock'. (Following the new British *Cosmopolitan*'s coy gate-fold of a naked Paul du Feu, who had once been married to Dr Greer for three weeks, *Oz* promised he would be seen erect – though he only managed half-mast.) Blatant ads still offered the 'finest, strongest and hardest porn in Europe' and pictures of 'pre-pubital' [sic] boys and naked children. By this time Richard Neville had gone legit and was writing a column ('An Alternative Voice') in the *Evening Standard*, edited by Charles Wintour, father of his erstwhile girlfriend Anna. *Oz* went into liquidation with £20,000 debts in June 1973. Meanwhile Jim Anderson went off to write and make films, and Felix Dennis went into the poster and magazine business, made staggering sums of money, bought a house on Mustique and wrote poetry. Neville returned to Oz, to fatherhood, television stardom and global repute as writer, peacenik and eco-guru.

At an *Oz* reunion party in 1990, held at the nightclub which had been Biba's roof garden on top of Derry & Tom's department store in Kensington, everyone – prosecution, defence and defend-ants alike – kissed and made up, including Brian Leary and the unrepentant *Oz* three. Mr Justice Argyle returned his invitation unopened.

Sir Alec Guinness had graced the public gallery of the Old Bailey to prepare himself for his role as Clifford, and *A Voyage Round My Father*'s long West End run cemented John's theatrical esteem just as *Oz* ensured his legal fame. But Michael Codron had to tell Sir Alec that in John's view he was just 'not angry enough' as Clifford. 'But I *am* angry,' replied Guinness. 'I bang my spoon quite sharply on my breakfast egg.'

'Touching', 'delicate', 'civilized', 'affectionate', 'brave' – *A Voyage Round My Father* seemed to reveal the key to John the dramatist. He was his father's son. He came from a family devoted to anecdotes, jokes and stories, in which, as the son's wife crushingly observes, the truth is studiously avoided and 'no one actually says anything'. Interviewed on *Woman's Hour*, John said he thought the suppression of emotion was a much more powerful artistic force than the uninhibited expression of it. 'You get dramatic power when people avoid talking about the important things in life,' he said, 'and you lose it when people shout out exactly what they feel about everything.'

On 14 December 1971, three months after the 'tooth episode' in Regent's Park, Penelope went to court and divorced John, on the grounds of his adultery, citing Penny. The case was, unsurprisingly, undefended. 'You're a free man,' Penelope told him. Did he feel a lingering regret, he was asked twenty years later, about the end of something once precious and loving? 'Yes, I'm sure that's right,' he replied equably. 'There are parts of my first marriage I remember with great pleasure. It was a time of great experience, we were both coming up in the world together, which was quite exciting, often.' Sally, who had acted as counsellor to both parents, encouraging John in the divorce, felt relief that the wrestling match was over. But she and Jeremy, who had been 'left on the back burner for years' while the parents tussled, needed considerable resilience to emerge from it all relatively unscathed.

John married Penny four months later, on his forty-ninth birthday, 21 April 1972. That week, he rang Penny from the Old Bailey to say, 'Look, one of the jury has to go to a funeral, so we've got a day off on Friday. Since we're having my birthday party anyway, why don't we nip down the Harrow Road and see if they can fit us in?' 'Most unromantic proposal you've ever heard,' as Penny said. Guests at the party in Blomfield Road included Harold Pinter and his wife, Vivien, Germaine Greer, Michael Frayn, Peter Cook, Peter and Thelma Nichols, the Amises. Penny, with six-month-old Emily in arms, knew hardly anyone apart from her family, Jeremy (who was best man) and the actress Joanna David, her contemporary, who was newly living with Edward Fox nearby in Maida Avenue. Memory lodges certain snatches of dialogue in the brain; at the end of her wedding party Penny overheard Peter Cook say, 'D'you want a lift home, Germaine?' and her reply, 'No thanks, I fucked you after the last party and you were no good.'

As many divorced men discover, the ex-wife remains a potent presence in the second marriage, and there were few more potent than Penelope. Penny had already endured an unusually testing experience when Penelope's novel, *The Home*, was published in the week Emily was born. In it Penelope had unleashed her acrimony in the person of Eleanor, who faces the future alone while her husband Graham embarks on a new life with young Nell Partwhistle. 'Of course I was Nell Partwhistle,' Penny recalled, 'who sat about all day brushing her hair, and couldn't even cook cheese on toast.' Much of Eleanor's ire centres on money. ('Why should I support you when you're not there to cook my supper?' John had said.) Eleanor's children goad her on in the alimony battle, reminding her that she is entitled to two-thirds of 'the old bastard's' income. There is 'an almost sibling rivalry between money and love,' Eleanor muses. 'No love – no money. It was as simple as that. Graham . . . was not mean. He simply objected to having money extorted from him by law.'

The Home cannot be detached from its autobiographical basis. Penelope told me, when adapting it for television, that it was virtually her autobiography. The couple argue, like John's divorcing clients, over furniture. Graham wants some beds, in case the children come to stay; Eleanor rejoins, 'If you think Philip or Jessie are going to stay with Nell Partwhistle, you're crazy.' 'Why not? She's perfectly harmless.' One daughter has a married lover 'old enough to be her father . . . in his cardigan and grey flannel trousers', like Leslie Phillips. Eleanor lights up, as Penelope did, when she finds a new lover; not just for sex, but for 'the need to have someone at her side, accompanying her out into the world, someone who would be part of that absolutely necessary "we"'. Graham confounds Eleanor, as John had Penelope, with reassurances: 'I could come back and have a string of girlfriends like I did before.' He 'was free of any sense of obligation or loyalty, innocently selfish, naïvely indulgent. Even his cruelty was inadvertent. His mind was excellent, but he could very seldom make it up.'

The Home got admiring reviews, but was 'dismissed by Auberon Waugh in the *Spectator*', Penelope noted. (Waugh's sympathies were invariably with John. Penelope waited a decade before writing a novel which featured a feeble, faithless husband named 'Bron'.) How John really felt about the book is hard to gauge. Newspapers did not then, as they do now, seize gleefully upon such *romans-à-clef* and reveal the feuds played out in print for all to see. John always told anyone who inquired, 'I have never felt disturbed by Penelope's books, she's a marvellous writer. I don't look back on our marriage with any sense of regret or shame.' And he wrote in his memoirs, 'Only she could have turned our lives into such good novels.'

Penelope had given herself ultimata: 'Get a job. Observe other people's lives. WORK.' At the start of 1972 she had gone travelling, visiting Dirk Bogarde in France, driving to Greece with Deborah to meet Jeremy, and on to Rome to visit Bette Davis, '64 tomorrow and kicking off her shoes & sprawling like a 12 year old and drinking like H. Bogart,' she wrote to Caroline. They drove back to London in time for Jeremy to be his father's best man, tall and long-haired, at almost seventeen. A month later, Penelope made her 'debut as the single mother of grown-up children', hosting a party to launch Madelon's impressive first novel, *Darling Pericles*. Madelon had not mentioned her mother's name to her publishers until they accepted the manuscript, and an extract later appeared in *Cosmopolitan*. Penelope, 'proud, satisfied and manless', welcomed Charles Dimont, and they met Madelon's future husband, a 'vast hippopotamus of a man' sitting on the sofa 'beaming goodwill'. L. A. Lee Howard, twenty-stone ex-editor of the *Daily Mirror*, was still married to the *Financial Times* journalist Sheila Black. Even he was quite overpowered, as others were, by the family he had married into.

That July Penelope sailed off to New York to meet Alain Resnais, who might direct a film of *The Home*, with Paul Newman and Joanne Woodward as the divorcing couple. She stayed in people's apartments, befriending their wives and poodles. Bette Davis ('knobkerry legs under the split caftan, toes covered in cornplasters, green headscarf to hide her balding hair') found her a Grandma Moses country cottage in which to write. Penelope had become one of a tribe of single women, new to her. 'Millions of them,' she noted, 'all divorced or deserted, all drinking too much . . . They live alone in their pretty little houses and are faceless, shapeless, sexless, brave . . . Where are their husbands? Off with whom? Younger versions of the same thing, who'll outlive them?' Julia and Caroline arrived to join their mother, the admirable Julia typing up her screenplay, and Caroline 'cool & unimpressed & charming', was there to share the hamburgers cooked by Paul Newman in Westport, Connecticut, 'giving the impression (like John) that cooking was a subtle insult to his wife'. Alas, Joanne Woodward rejected the idea of playing another distressed wife, so that was that; the film of *The Home* collapsed. Later it was reoptioned by Otto Preminger, with Elizabeth Taylor to star, but it was never made.

John, by contrast, carried on his old life with his new Penny, receiving journalists at home in Blomfield Road, which had 'the aura of success': 'Vast rooms overlooking a tree-lined canal, book-lined walls and quicksand carpets,' one reporter noted. 'Pretty wife, pretty baby, pretty uniformed nursemaid.' John was just back from court, shoes off, feet up: 'tubby, bespectacled, a work junkie'. He had written a new play, *I, Claudius*, based on Robert Graves's two Claudius novels – the prelude to a film that was never made – to open at the Queen's Theatre, directed by Tony Richardson, with David Warner as Claudius. Graves warmly applauded John's respectful adaptation. 'Claudius is a lesson in how to survive in an English public school,' said John. 'Harrow was very like the Roman Empire.'

It seems astonishing that John should have been willing, at that stage, to disinter his old marriage. But the play Peggy Ramsay had suggested years before, 'a funny, savage play about the marriage of two writers', was about to open. In it, John came closest to analysing himself as a fallible husband. On 18 April 1973, *Collaborators* (directed by Eric Thompson, father of Emma, and produced by Michael Codron) opened at the Duchess Theatre. It owed nothing to invention: in its way, it was John's version of *The Pumpkin Eater*.

Henry Winter (that name again: Henry Winter was his Everyman) is a barrister and radio playwright with an overdraft, living with his wife, Katherine, in north-west London in a sea of plastic knickers with many small children underfoot. A film producer named Sam Brown (Joss Ackland) arrives to change their fortunes. Sam instantly defines the caustic Katherine (Glenda Jackson) as 'an early Bette Davis ball-breaker' and is astonished by their 'Dickensian' domestic chaos, and by the sight of Henry cooking stew. 'Where I come from only faggots cook,' he says (as Dustin Hoffman had said). Katherine is against Henry's career change. She'd married an 'inexperienced and painfully thin' Henry, who strode up her garden path in gumboots and country tweeds. Now he would be 'someone ghastly', she says, 'with a white Jag and cashmere polo necks and an identity bracelet and a house in Weybridge . . . and . . . a white leather sofa'. With 'Miss Rank-Odeon unzipping her plastic tiger-skin ski-pants'.

Sam asks the couple to collaborate on a truthful film about marriage. 'What keeps a marriage going?' he asks. 'Fear,' replies Henry. To Katherine, their marriage is a collection of 'loaded guns'. Henry calls her 'the Lady Macbeth of Belsize Park', over-dramatizing everything. 'Bring my wife happiness and she won't even bother to unwrap the parcel. She doesn't want happiness. She wants tragedy. She wants war!' She says he never talks, only tells jokes. 'When our children fall over they don't cry, they make jokes, which is what he taught them.'

Everything in the Mortimer marriage was dragged in, including the good times and laughter they had once shared, Gin and Altars, Moby Dick and chips, dancing to 'Eve Tish and her Squad-ronettes'. Later they do a Rogers and Astaire routine to 'I Won't Dance', substituting 'fuck' whenever the word 'dance' occurs. But Katherine tells Sam that Henry now goes off with popsies and floozies, leaving evidence for her to find. They fight and are reconciled; there are screams and tears. Henry goes off to court. (But 'where he goes and where he says he goes,' says Katherine, 'coincide only occasionally.') He arrives home, proud of his speech. ' "Give him justice",' I heard myself say. ' "But let it be justice tempered with that mercy which is the hallmark of the Uxbridge and Hillingdon Magistrates' Court." ' (A line later reused by Rum-pole.) And Henry describes a swingers' party given by a couple named Bottle, when Mrs Bottle propositions him in the mirror-walled bathroom.

Enter a Shirley Anne-like figure named Griselda Griffin. 'I'm afraid of my wife. We all are,' Henry tells her. Griselda suspects that Henry tells Katherine all about his affairs: 'Bring everything home to Mum.' Griselda and Katherine discuss Henry together. Griselda says she was never really a mistress: Henry only took her out to lunch, when the family were with his mother in the country, and she was told that Katherine had put her head in the gas oven – reminiscent of Penelope's overdose, on the night John dined with Shirley Anne. Katherine tells her Henry isn't capable of giving a woman a straightforward brush-off. 'He wants everyone to go on loving him.'

Henry and Katherine are 'a couple of monsters', Sam decides, acting out their dramas in front of other people. 'I'm sorry you find each other so unsatisfactory you have to grab people off the sidewalk for laughs or kicks or whatever the hell it is.' The echoes here are from Edward Albee's *Who's Afraid of Virginia Woolf?* in which George and Martha thrive on their bickering and insults in front of their bewildered guests. At the end of *Collaborators*, Henry and Katherine agree on a loving separation. 'We're stifling each other, choking each other to death. We have to move away so we can breathe. Our divorce will be an occasion for mutual concern. And tenderness.' In the last line of the play, Katherine challenges Henry: 'One day, just for a change – why don't you try telling me the truth?'

A man who has seen his wife cannibalize their marriage in her novels and then does the same thing himself on stage has an unusually robust attitude to self-exposure. John still regarded their lives as material; he admitted that Henry Winter was himself. 'I don't think you can write about anything you haven't experienced,' he told Ion Trewin from *The Times*. 'If I write about Genghis Khan, it is me as Genghis Khan.' Trewin, like most journalists, did not probe further. What struck him most was John's physical rejuvenation, in his rumpled suede jacket: he was like F. Scott Fitzgerald's *The Curious Case of Benjamin Button*. Yes, John agreed, he used to live 'a very middle-aged existence, slogging at the law, keeping all those children. But when I started to write plays my life started going backwards. I've grown younger ever since.' He had just turned fifty – a birthday spent driving Penny under greaseproof-paper skies across the Tunisian desert, staying at a half-built hotel that had a concrete-mixer in the reception, drinking champagne indistinguishable from Eno's Fruit Salts. Meanwhile, *Collaborators* broke records for the Duchess Theatre.

When John and Penny had taken the Porto Ercole house the previous summer, John's old family came too: Jeremy and a girlfriend, Deborah and her TV producer boyfriend Colin Rogers, Sally with her American boyfriend, an artist named Howard

Silverman. John was in his element: 'What's the plan?' his daily mantra, organizing activities, permitting no lazing by the pool. Each morning he would greet Colin Rogers with, 'Have you popped the question yet?' Pop the question he did, and on 24 November 1972, he and Deborah married at Hampstead Town Hall. Penelope organized a wedding for the second time. 'John was affectionate (he said "I didn't start all this, my darling"),' she recorded. 'Penny wore a little woollen hat.' There was supper afterwards for the guests, including the Dimonts. 'So there were 2 husbands, one ex-lover, the legitimate daughter and nephews of Deborah's illegitimate father, all their wives and husbands, Deborah's illegitimate uncle and cousins – my mind boggled. I hurried about through strangers, with a heart – except for Deb's happiness – as leaden as my stomach.' The next morning she found that someone had written 'WE LOVE YOU' in the dust on the back window of her car.

She was loved, and still invited everywhere, alone; she dined at Bernice Rubens's with Sonia Orwell, David Mercer, Fay Weldon; she invited Roald Dahl to dinner. Dahl, in his cardigan, 'made some kind of blurred assignation with me as all seven foot of him eeled into the freezing night'. 'I cook, I entertain, I'm P. Mortimer, self-sufficient, funny, astute. But oh god, when they go. And when they're here. And before they come. The old symptoms.' The artist Daniel Lang, a new American friend, arrived to stay at Loudoun Road. When I asked him about this, Lang recalled, with a certain pride, 'She slapped me on the ass and said, "You're a good fuck."'

Meetings with John, warily polite, took place at their lawyer's office. She still wanted to go off and giggle with him. 'John and I will always be John and I, no matter what else has happened,' but she had to confront her 'diminishing' future. 'Once there was a young man called John Mortimer. Now it's lawyers & hysterectomies [she was about to have a hysterectomy] & John Mortimer distant, tiny, remote, gesticulating at the wrong end of a Fallopian tube.' She was asked to write the screenplay of *The Story of O*, 'my most hated book' (the pseudonymous story of a woman forced by her lover to submit to his sexual torture chamber, whipped, chained, gang-banged, buggered, burned, humiliated. John later named it as his 'most erotic book'). 'Perhaps I could look at it with a new, liberated eye,' wrote Penelope, 'for £X00,000.' But film and book deals fell through. At fifty-four, she needed to work when she wanted; she had no wish to be 'a commercial attraction' at the mercy of mad film producers.

Over lunch before her operation, the divorced pair signed papers about money. Penelope's lawyer rang to warn her not to meet John: too late, she said, he was sitting across the table. 'John said perhaps we shouldn't have got divorced; that he misses me a lot.' He sent flowers in a white vase. For all the 'pain and fury' of their marriage, John was her 'only familiar'; she was addicted. She found him 'so offhand about Penny G. As, I'm sure, he used to be about me.' One day, as she recuperated, painfully and listlessly, they had another angry row about money on the phone. She told him, weeping, 'You should have a hysterectomy sometime':

But I was no sooner in my bath than he rang with profound & abject apologies, and all he could suggest was 'a boozy lunch' and to tell me that I am his greatest friend, the person he likes most in the entire world. But he won't give me half Loudoun Road or a penny for the use and disposal of a womb. I didn't put it like that, of course. But only because I didn't think of it.

Penny, at home with her baby, wanted a sibling for Emily. Alasdair Riley, an old friend from student days, interviewed her about 'Life with John Mortimer', and she told him John was against the idea. 'John was an only child and he wants us to have only one as well,' she said. 'He says an only child gets more love, and more of its parents' time.' John keenly felt that six children had already made enough inroads into his finances. To another reporter he pontificated benignly, puffing his pipe, that the vital thing in raising children is that they should do what they want to do. 'My daughter Sally works incredibly hard at looking after the mentally handicapped,' he said. 'My children aren't particularly conscious of money.' At which point Penny interrupted to suggest that this was because whenever Jeremy's and Sally's cash ran short, their dad was available with a loan. 'Mortimer stopped puffing his pipe,' wrote the reporter, Jeremy Gates, 'and looked hard at Emily, as though the idea was completely original.'

Jeremy, living with his mother, was posing at eighteen as a communist-anarchist, reading Proudhon and Kropotkin. Penelope found him 'secretive, like John'. He rebuked her for her 'smoke-factory' study, and would lie on his bed in furious sulks. Someone should have told her that most teenage boys are like this. Instead she blamed herself: 'I have done it wrong . . . Me and the negligent John together.' Jeremy longed to get away 'to the jungle, or anywhere as far away as possible'. He aimed to go to a new university and read anthropology, but his A-levels were not up to the grades needed for Sussex. The only option was to do Oxford entrance. He was interviewed for New College by Christopher Tolkien and John Bayley, who were eager to hear all about his co-ed schooling, and awarded him an exhibition to read English.

He had already found his future wife, Polly, at Bedales. Polly's father was Harry Fisher, eldest of the six sons of the Archbishop of Canterbury, and one of the appeal judges John had faced in the *Last Exit* trial. Polly, expelled from a Catholic boarding school for rebelliousness, had been removed to Bedales. But when she and Jeremy and two other sixth-formers spent a night, quite innocently, at Penelope's house at Steep, Polly was again expelled. Jeremy was allowed back to do his Oxbridge entrance, but Polly had to do her A-levels from a bedsit in Camden Town.

A spirited girl, she found Penelope 'absolutely terrifying'. 'Intimidating, chain-smoking, withering, deeply unhappy. She made me feel immature, spoilt, airheaded. She would toss feminist magazines at me, a Home Counties seventeen-year-old.' The Mortimers seemed to her hedonistic, with their showy cars, glamorous friends, holidays in the sun; the Fishers took their holidays in Northern Ireland. Jeremy's parents were 'too similar – spoilt, disturbed, brilliant in the same field, both wanting to be the centre of attention. And the children got the worst of it. Jeremy's adolescence was very strange. He was reserved, afraid of betraying emotions. He had lots of dishy girlfriends, he was always brown from holidays in the sun. But Penelope expected him to play the parent, accompany her on holidays. John made a joke of Jeremy not having spoken to him for seven years. I'm sure he felt guilty deep down, he saw the trauma the children were undergoing.' (In fact John was writing a play, based on Jeremy, called *Jackson*, about the problems of a young boy with permissive parents.)

Jeremy went up to Oxford in October, and Polly's father became president of Wolfson College, so Jeremy found a base in the Fishers' house, which was 'full of music and galoshes, books, flowers and the penetrating sound of upper-class women's voices, the antithesis of Jeremy's home life,' Penelope wrote.

Polly, naturally, found Penny a congenial companion, as both of them were entering this complicated family. She observed that Penny had to start afresh in terms of John's friendships, as her husband introduced her into his milieu. Often she was treated like a child. A black-tie dinner at the palatial Hampstead house of Max Rayne and his wife, Jane, with a Henry Moore in the garden, was daunting. 'We walked past the Chagalls,' John told me, 'and gazed at a picture of water-lilies over the fireplace when Henry Moore himself came up and said, "Monet's looking very good, isn't he?"' Penny sat between Jonathan Aitken and Sir Paul Channon, who talked over her head. Another evening, at George Melly's, Sir Freddie Ayer and Dr Jonathan Miller treated her in the same way, so she was pleased when kindly George beckoned her to clamber under the table to sit on his lap.

In the summer of 1973 John and Penny, with Emily, rented a house in Tuscany for the first time — a beautiful old farmhouse near Arezzo, idyllically surrounded by gentle hills, with horses and cows still stabled on the lower floor in the traditional Tuscan way. Jeremy, Caroline, Julia and Gered joined them. One day, a horse escaped and fell into the pool: 'There are few harder tasks,' John wrote, 'than getting a live horse out of a swimming pool.' John cooked, they ate and read by candlelight and gaslight, Jeremy slept

with the cows, everyone was delighted by Emily aged two, and
John fell in love for ever with Tuscany.

'Renting houses abroad is an excellent way of getting to know
people you are never likely to meet,' wrote John the following
year. 'It is, I suppose, like a casual encounter with another man's
wife.' The owners' 'how to get there' instructions invent complications ('After 4 km you will see a dead cypress tree. Ignore it') as
they like to pretend they live in some secret, inaccessible fastness.
'Then you arrive and discover the disconnected telephone, the
refrigerator that either boils the milk or fuses the lights, the huge
crack and the dead mouse in the swimming pool.' It was in this
article that he first broached the themes he would use later in a
novel. One was the villa's undependable water supply: they had to
boil vegetables in San Pellegrino, and order a tanker-load of drinking water from Siena, which was deposited by mistake in the pool.
The other was the mystery of the villa owners' marriage. Disguising
it as 'a house in Greece', John wrote of finding 'a real treasure
trove, a memorandum in which the owner's wife set out her list
of priorities under the heading "The most important things in my
life". The list ran, as I remember, (1) Dr Charides (2) The villa (3)
The dogs and (4) Andrew Cranston. Number 4 was her husband's
name.' He had indeed found such a list. And the house belonged
to an English journalist and his wife, who were understandably
cross when John later reused the list in his Tuscany novel, *Summer's
Lease*, in 1988, and again in his memoirs.

A Voyage Round My Father was being performed across the world,
with Michael Redgrave now in Sydney, and Rupert Davies as
Clifford on tour in Britain. The planned film, to star Rex Harrison,
now seemed to be going ahead. So John and Penny went from
Italy to the South of France to meet Harrison and the American
producer Fred Brogger, who had assembled Wendy Hiller to play
Kathleen and Edward Fox as John. Just as John was leaving the
Hôtel Voile d'Or, the phone rang. 'Rex Harrison here. I want to
tell you one thing before we meet. Are you listening?' 'Yes.' 'Very
well,' the reedy, rasping tones went on, 'what I want to tell you is

that you are a shit. An absolute shit. You are a shit now and you have always been a shit. Do I make myself clear?' A shaken John groped for words to answer this assault; then a chuckle came down the line and he recognized the voice of David Niven, whose Rex Harrison impersonation was his party piece. 'Just thought I'd give you a taste of what's ahead of you, old boy,' said Niven.

At Harrison's house they met Brogger and Alvin Rakoff, the Canadian director: he had been moved to tears by John's play. His own father had just died and he felt *Voyage* spoke for all father–son relationships. Penny and Elizabeth Harrison left the men talking and drove to Monte Carlo in Rex's silver Rolls-Royce, their scarves fluttering in the breeze and the radio playing, when suddenly the car bumped down a flight of steps and was badly damaged, to Harrison's fury. Then Brogger left the hotel, without paying his bill; they would not accept Rakoff's credit card and John had to come to the rescue with cash.

Rakoff did start rehearsals at Elstree, and filmed some moody shots of Edward Fox at Turville Heath Cottage. But Harrison – who had not yet signed a contract – got cold feet about playing a blind man. 'It was the old fear of being unloved,' John said. 'Rex said people didn't want to see plays about blind people. An actor's eyes were his most expressive equipment. The more he rehearsed, the more he wheedled: could he see glimmers of light, perhaps? Or at least distinguish shapes? Finally it got to the point where blindness, a crucial aspect of the film, was as insignificant as a bit of grit in the eye.' But in any case, after shooting the Crown Film Unit scene on the pier at Great Yarmouth, Rakoff had to stop. The finance had collapsed, nobody had been paid, the project was aborted. Rakoff's film was not reactivated until 1982, for television, with Laurence Olivier.

Despite his appearance of prosperity John was still mired in surtax debt, trapped in the 'Booker books' portfolio of authors which had been set up in 1964 by Lord Campbell of Eskan, chairman of the food company Booker McConnell. During a game of golf with Ian Fleming in Jamaica, Campbell had been persuaded by Fleming that a high-earning author could be an investment; he devised a tax-avoidance dodge whereby writers could sell their estimated future earnings in return for a capital sum. Booker soon owned 51 per cent of John and Penelope Mortimer, and of a stable of other writers including Fleming, Robert Bolt, Harold Pinter and Gavin Lyall – all of whom later had to extricate their copyrights from a deal that was not quite as attractive as it seemed. 'At the outset they paid us a tax-free capital sum of about £40,000 each,' John told me. 'We had never touched that much in one gasp before. But they then got half of all our earnings. So I felt I had to run just to stand still.' Penelope too felt she suffered financially from Booker 'or whichever it is that takes 51 per cent of my non-existent earnings and puts the rest (none) on some Channel Island'.

In 1973, John switched accountants and met Phyl Newall – referred to as 'The Exocet' for her fierce attacks on behalf of her clients – who looked after his income, his negotiations and much more for the rest of his life. 'The two most important things to people are their health and their money,' Phyl declared, 'so their relationship with their doctor and their accountant takes prime importance. John is no exception.' The two first met at John's chambers. 'It was a hoot,' Phyl recalled. 'When I sat down, the two arms fell off my chair and then the back fell off. I said, "Is this how you treat criminals?" So we started with a laugh.' They repaired to a Chancery Lane restaurant for a three-hour lunch and discovered that they both shared their birthday with the Queen, and were both stuck on exactly the same clue in the *Times* crossword: an auspicious omen.

Phyl gave short shrift to the Booker arrangement. 'In those days there were many legitimate offshore tax-saving schemes. My view was that clients ended up paying more in fees than they gained: money was moved from country to country and ended up in somewhere like Grand Turks.' In time, John became so dependent on Phyl that he would ring her up for permission to buy a new suit.

The Turville Heath orchard, with planning permission, was sold for £18,000. The Blomfield Road flat was given up and Turville Heath Cottage became John and Penny's full-time home. John felt he 'had no right' to change anything or move the furniture in his father's house, but in time Penny set about repainting walls, spending many hours sewing cushion covers, resigning herself to life as a country wife.

Caroline was starring in her mother's new television play, *Three's One*, in which a couple start an affair, each unknowingly going to the same shrink, to whom they give wildly differing accounts of their relationship. Penelope was 'staggered and moved to tears' watching it; but the following month her film *The Ripening Seed* was televised and she thought it 'quite awful – sub-Lelouch. A sentimental nothing which makes me burn with shame.' Her welcome escape route was an invitation to Yaddo, the writers' colony in upstate New York.

The children hoped that she might find a husband at Yaddo. She didn't, but she finished a novel, *Long Distance*, which was printed *in toto* in the *New Yorker* and remained her own favourite. It was admired by men whose opinion she respected: Pinter, Jonathan Miller, Ronald Harwood. Its stream-of-consciousness passages suggested that she was still beset by images of her life with John. In one scene a king is cross-examined by a bewigged and gowned barrister with sightless stare. The king, accused of being 'brother and father of the children with whom you consort', says, 'I want always to be a little boy and have fun . . . And you can tell me stories about naughty children who have to be spanked when they do wrong.' Auberon Waugh called this passage a 'nonsensical piece of theatre' in a novel of 'ego-maniac drivel' by someone 'who has obviously gone to pieces after her husband abandons her in middle-age'. Penelope was stung into writing Waugh a disdainful letter: 'I am sorry that your well-known flair for satire doesn't enable you to appreciate a rather obvious use of Peter Pan and Oedipus Rex. It's hardly fair to hold writers responsible for the limitations of their critics.'

Sally keenly felt her mother's absences in America, but Penelope was home for Sally's wedding to Howard Silverman in Bristol in January 1973. At the reception, John kissed Penelope (she says) with tears in his eyes. Seeing pretty little Emily, she was reminded of Sally at that age and longed to pick her up. But soon afterwards she wrote a sour column for *Nova* about the charade of weddings, bride and groom in sacrificial costume, making wild promises. If your husband does very well, wrote Penelope, you achieve the image of 'the dazzlingly self-confident and sophisticated Mrs X. Only you know that it's a load of old cobblers. For if you become Mrs Ex, what happens? You sit down for the first time in 20 years, to try and find out what you're really like.' She masqueraded as 'successful novelist, soignée at dinner parties', and drifted, heavy-hearted, through social tableaux, including 'a party where the hostess delivered a lantern lecture on cunts'. She observed Antonia Fraser, 'exquisite as usual, sitting the entire evening on a small sofa, her expression placid, as though about to moo'. After one dinner party she noted, 'This is what the vast majority of people are like. Pleasant, mediocre and dead dull. Is that the human condition? NO, because Mercer isn't . . . Jeremy certainly isn't. John Mortimer, damn it, isn't.'

But she found John's ubiquitous liberal public persona irritating. He wrote speeches for Harold Wilson in the second election campaign of 1974, and was invited to lunch at 10 Downing Street. She watched him debating the Permissive Society on television with Bishop Trevor Huddleston and the *Guardian* columnist Jill Tweedie, talking 'rubbish', 'trembling with sincerity', denying any connection between pornography and gang bangs, declaring that porn was a safety valve, again using the example of the sex murderer who 'exclusively read the Old Testament'. It was a relief to get away from anyone who might mention John, 'virtually everyone, in fact, I had known in the past'. Back in New York, staying in the 54th Street apartment of Kurt Vonnegut, she taught creative writing at the New School, which led to a visiting professorship at Boston University from 1975 to 1977. So apart from sporadic visits home to England, she had at last escaped from what she now saw as 'John's world'.

She also missed the funeral of her mother, who died aged ninety-seven. But she had already published two appreciations of

Gran Fletcher: one in *The Home*, in the portrait of Eleanor's mother, who attends births, nurses sick grandchildren and dispenses wise advice; the other in *Nova*, where she had published a long tribute to her mother's ability to survive alone, placidly cultivating her garden, baking her own bread, beating her grandchildren at Scrabble, dressing each day with 'dainty care'. 'I will never know a more positive personality, a more influential human being . . . Yet she is not formidable,' wrote Penelope. 'Qualities of self-abnegation and intense humility can be as powerful a force as aggression.' ('What rubbish!' her mother had said when she read this piece. 'Why in the world would anyone want to read it?' 'Maybe because I wrote it!' Penelope had angrily rejoined.)

On Christmas Day 1975, when Penny and John gathered their families at Turville Heath Cottage, Penelope was invited too. She brought the young theatre critic John Heilpern (known as 'Hatpin'), whose book on Peter Brook she had edited, and who had become a lover. This, Heilpern suspected, was John and Penny's plan when they introduced him to her, although, he said, 'the author of *The Pumpkin Eater* seemed a little overwhelming to my still quite unworldly self'. It was an altogether awkward Christmas Day: eveyone ended up sprawled on the bed upstairs, watching *The Wizard of Oz* on TV. But Penelope noted in her diary that 'as for P Gollop, whom I must call Penny, she's a sharp warm girl'.

The new Penny was indeed an unusually strong character. She had taken on a famous, prolific, popular and gregarious husband, his complex family, and occasionally his former wife. She could not help but feel like an appendage. Isolated in the country with her daughter, she fretted, at twenty-nine, about not using her brain in some career, as her university contemporaries were. John was often away in court until nine at night; and when at home he was preoccupied with writing – currently adapting Graham Greene for television. At weekends he wanted, as always, to have the table filled with friends, dispensing champagne and largesse. It was still John that people came to see. She might cook lunch for fifteen, but, as she would say, 'All the people he'd worked with in these productions, they terrified me. They didn't want to know me, the pig farmer's daughter.' Gradually, Penny became less inclined to underplay herself and began to invite people she liked. Her distinctive personality, her robust, candid perceptions and her skill in racontage asserted themselves, and she was regarded on more equal terms with her husband; but this took time. For the moment, they mixed mainly with John's friends in a John-centred world: Geoffrey Robertson, the eager young lawyer from the *Oz* trial; David and Hjordis Niven, Edward Fox and Joanna David, Robert and Celestia Fox, Joss and Rosemary Ackland. Another welcome guest was Deborah, who like her husband, Colin, was now writing TV scripts and had moved near Turville Heath with their baby. As Penelope wrote of this friendship, 'John loved people who bounced through life scattering goodwill, undistracted by futile searchings for whys and wherefores.'

But after Emily reached nursery-school age, Penny found another flat in Little Venice, next door to Joanna and Edward Fox, and booked Emily into a Montessori school in Highgate. (Emily loved the school but made John cross when he asked her what she'd been doing all day and she replied, 'Polishing things.') Penny also took up studying law by correspondence course. But when she discovered that it took a year to get through dreary contract law, and was told that this was the most interesting aspect, she decided ('Bugger that') to give up. She had not been thrilled, when eating her statutory dinners in Middle Temple Hall, to find herself well below the salt, drinking vin ordinaire alongside overseas students, and having to bow at the entrance of her husband. As a Bencher, John sat with other grandees at high table, served with the finest fare and all possible pomp.

But soon a deus ex machina arrived in their lives which eventually promised to be the milch cow John was hoping for. He had always wanted to create an enduring character like Sherlock Holmes or Maigret, 'to keep me in my old age'. That character – larger than life, bold, vociferous and amiable – came along when Irene Shubik, the BBC producer, asked John to write an hour-long *Play for Today* which would go out on 17 December 1975. It was called *Rumpole of the Bailey*.

17. The Old Darling

'Horace Rumbold' was the original name. But there turned out to be a Sir Horace Algernon Rumbold, an old Christ Church man now living in Guildford, so 'Rumpole' was substituted. Was John remembering Evelyn Waugh's character Rampole in *Vile Bodies*? Wherever the name came from, it also had a comical echo of Kenneth Williams's Rambling Syd Rumpo. It conjured up a rum character, a substantial, roly-poly, rumpled figure in threadbare wig and frayed gown, ash on waistcoat, claret stains on tie. 'A crumpled fellow,' John said, 'always recovering from hangovers.' Rumpole was, still is, 'an Old Bailey hack', the oldest member of his chambers, who has never taken silk, and boasts only two trial triumphs to his name: the Penge Bungalow Murders and the Great Brighton Benefit Club Forgery. He is married to the dreadful Hilda, known as She Who Must Be Obeyed, daughter of his late pupil master. They live in a dismal mansion flat in SW7, from which he escapes every morning with relief.

Rumpole arrived fleshed-out: born in Dulwich in 1910, son of a clergyman, product of Lancing and Keble College, Oxford. Unheroic war, RAF ground staff. Knows quantities of Quiller-Couch's *Oxford Book of English Verse* by heart. Implacably on the side of the underdog, representing undeserving miscreants under the legal aid scheme. Has an aversion to prosecuting and no interest in boring civil cases. In his first synopsis, John vouchsafed another interesting detail of his history: Rumpole 'got a poor third class degree at Oxford', he told Shubik, 'where he had a tendency to prefer young men'.

John's first choice to play him was Alastair Sim, who was unfortunately dead. Michael Hordern was unavailable (too thin anyway). The director John Gorrie proposed Leo McKern. McKern was only fifty-five, but being portly and jowly, with the face of a battered old prize-fighter – bulbous nose, leathery skin, jungly eyebrows – looked older; he had lost an eye in youth in his native Australia. John had met McKern in 1967, when he might have played the title role in *The Judge*, and found that McKern had an Australian's atavistic disdain for authority, so Rumpole's dislike of pomp came naturally. From the start, McKern's performance was a tour de force, snorting with indignation, puffing on a small cheroot, rolling out mellifluous phrases, as if he had waited all his life for Rumpole. His opening lines, in voice-over, were Wordsworth's 'There was a Boy: ye knew him well, ye cliffs / And islands of Winander!' A great reciter of poems himself, and adept at the *Times* crossword, McKern felt at home in the character ('He's not at all like me but he's got many qualities I admire,' he said), so his acting seemed effortless, instinctive. In the first play, Rumpole defended a young black man charged with attempted murder. Rumpole revealed the defendant's written confession to be a police fabrication, since the boy was illiterate. This slender plot fuelled the eventual change in the rules on police evidence. But it was the personality and pronouncements of Rumpole himself that won over audience and critics alike.

Rumpole's views were John's. Through him, he could scorn judges, question the necessity for certain laws, indulge his ambivalence about his profession. Having given us Clifford Mortimer, Morgenhall in *The Dock Brief*, and Mr Justice Chard in *The Judge*, he had already created several legal figures with a jaundiced view of the law and a penchant for literary quotation. But the gestation of Rumpole, John said, began when he was at the Old Bailey defending the Mile End Boot Boys, sullen-faced soccer hooligans who had stabbed to death an innocent bystander on Charing Cross Station. Appearing with John was the jovial, Pickwickian James Burge, QC, defender of Stephen Ward (who committed suicide during his trial) in the Profumo affair. At the start of the Boot Boys trial Burge turned to John and said, 'As a matter of fact I am an anarchist. But I don't think even my old darling Prince Peter Kropotkin would have approved of this lot.' 'Burge referred to everyone as an "old darling", except his wife,' said John, 'and there I had Rumpole.' (The play's original title suggested by John was *My Darling Prince Peter Kropotkin*, or even *Jolly Old Jean-Jacques Rousseau*, a better-known anarchist: both were mercifully rejected.)

Over time, law gossip suggested other templates for Rumpole: John Gardiner, Micky Bickford-Smith, Michael Rowland Fitch. Some saw Rumpole in the enormously fat, fearless James Caesar Crespi, bachelor and classical scholar, who after a day at the Old Bailey would go by taxi to the Aldwych for tea, to El Vino's for drinks and to the Garrick for dinner, holding court in each venue to an admiring group of young barristers. On the day an IRA bomb went off outside the Old Bailey in March 1973, John was in court, defending a young man accused of attempting to run down a policeman, when the judge was handed a note, which he rather wearily opened, peered at and read out, beginning languidly, 'Ladies and gentlemen of the jury, I have a note here which I must read to you and it says' – and here he leapt from his chair – 'THERE'S A BOMB IN THE OLD BAILEY!' He shot out of the courtroom like a bat out of hell. Later, it turned out that James Crespi alone had been injured in the blast. He said he was so fond of the Old Bailey, 'I felt it was my duty to interpose my body between the building and the bomb.' This incident went into John's repertoire.

'I did use some characteristics of barristers I have worked with,' John said, 'but soon every fat middle-aged barrister in London identified himself with Rumpole.'

'It was some achievement,' as Geoffrey Robertson commented, 'to creat in Rumpole a lawyer the world could love.' English literature prefers legal rogues: Trollope's slovenly Mr Chaffanbrass, defender of the indefensible, who would 'perplex a witness and bamboozle a jury'; Hazlitt's 'fee'd, time-serving, shuffling advocate'. The novels of Dickens, who had plenty of opportunity to observe lawyers at work, are full of loud-mouth barristers pursuing 'the one great principle of the English law – to make business for itself': the case of *Jarndyce* v. *Jarndyce* is predicated on that. Terence Rattigan in *The Winslow Boy* had created a hero of the barrister Sir Robert Morton, but no television attorney or QC has compared in idiosyncratic appeal with Rumpole, who became one of the most endearing, and enduring, characters on both sides of the Atlantic. Only Auberon Waugh ventured to question whether the Bar quite deserved this genial image.

John Mortimer, QC, embellished his own personality through Rumpole. In court he looked increasingly Rumpolian, 'like a stuffed laundry-bag': dishevelled, lank-haired, his bands crumpled and his shirt hanging out, stains on waistcoat, trousers held up by an old tie. The laid-back approach extended to a reluctance to study his briefs in advance, 'but when the case came up,' his clerks observed, 'he would arrive early in the morning and mug it up at speed'. No matter how early colleagues arrived, Radio 3 would be wafting down the staircase of Dr Johnson's Buildings, which meant John was already at his desk. He would get bright junior barristers, among them Michael Grieve and Edward Fitzgerald, to do his donkey work, promising them recompense ('for the usual consideration,' which meant a bottle of champagne, not a chip off his fee) for a comprehensive résumé of the brief. Often they doubted that he would be on top of the case when the day came. 'I would sweat blood,' said one, 'thinking, my God, he has no idea what this case is about, but then I'd be pleasantly surprised in court. He had an inborn ability to speak wonderful English, impromptu. And speeches he wrote in advance were beautifully constructed, in an oratorical style that was pre-war Harrovian.'

John was, in fundamental legal matters, deeply conservative. From 1975 he was a Master Bencher of the Inner Temple and took his duties seriously. Rumpole too described himself as a conservative anarchist, dedicated to the presumption of innocence, and to trial by jury, 'the golden threads of the best legal system in the world'. But he had no aspiration to be a judge, or head of chambers. 'I like to be the one who annoys the head by saying anarchistic things from time to time.' At conferences with clients, John was punctual to start and prompt to finish: when he'd had enough (or got bored), he would gather his papers into a pile, place his hands on top and beam 'God bless!' – the signal for everyone to troop out. Sometimes his hazy notion of the details was plain. When Herman Spielman, a pillar of Manchester's Jewish community and centre of an international child porn ring, pleaded guilty to child prostitution and was sentenced to six years, John was asked to advise on his appeal. Down from Manchester came Spielman's weeping wife, his solicitor, and the elders of the synagogue, for a conference in John's chambers. Twenty minutes before, John rang Michael Grieve: 'You've got to come up and tell me all about it.' Grieve gave him a succinct précis 'in words of one syllable'. Promptly at 4 p.m., in trooped the Mancunians. 'Hello!' cried John. 'Did you have a good trip from Birmingham?' They stared at him. 'Manchester, Mr Mortimer.' 'Manchester! Even worse!'

He was popular in chambers, had time for everyone, never appearing pressured – 'the most easygoing barrister we've ever known,' his clerks agreed. 'He's the same with everyone – relates to people at whatever level.' Unlike some, he was never supercilious with the clerks. At lunchtimes he avoided the Old Bailey's fifth-floor canteen, the barristers' common room. 'Going upstairs, John?' colleagues would ask. 'Urgh no, it's full of barristers . . .' He preferred a local brasserie, where a judge's daughter, who had appeared in *Confessions of a Window Cleaner*, was a waitress, and was reputed not to wear any knickers.

By the mid-1970s, he was emphatically not a cab-rank barrister. 'Do I have to do this?' he would ask John Francis, who arrived in 1974 after the retirement of Charlie Crooks, senior clerk in Clifford's day. Mortimer, QC, recoiled from any case that might bore him. In one of John's staple stories, at the end of a long trial about VAT evasion, he had congratulated the jury on 'sitting through what was undoubtedly one of the most tedious cases ever heard at the Old Bailey'. The judge countered by opening his own speech with, 'Members of the jury, it may surprise you to know that it is not the sole purpose of the criminal law of England to amuse Mr Mortimer.' (This was a line he later applied to Rumpole and others.)

He was, unsurprisingly, suspected of not taking the law seriously.

In his play *Naked Justice*, one judge accuses another, 'Nothing's serious to you, is it? The world's not a serious place. The Law Courts are a delightful tea party, where you can make old jokes and be nice to people . . .'

He was certainly less interested in 'the whole truth' than in opportunities for aphorism. He could always remember the jokes, even when the cases were lost in the mists of his selective memory. He told of one Anthony Sorley Cramb, accused of buggery in the Super Loo in Euston station. Geoffrey Robertson and John had lunch with the judge, who mused, 'Sorley Cramb. Best name for a bugger I've ever come across.' John stowed away this story and used it thirty years later in *Rumpole and the Reign of Terror*, when Judge Bullingham is greeted in his club by a barrister who says, 'How are you, Judge? I'll never forget what a good time we had with that buggery in the Euston Super Loo.' In another case, the prosecution called a doctor to say that certain objects, inserted into the rectum for sexual pleasure, could be dangerous. John unearthed a medical textbook which listed the various things that had been discovered in rectums: 'among them a tin of Brasso wrapped in a duster, a shooting stick, a pepper pot marked Souvenir of Ramsgate, and a small bust of Napoleon III'. This list also entered his roadshow repertoire.

He was not a booming courtroom orator, as Simon Callow found when playing John in the TV drama of the *Oz* trial. His tones were not sonorous but light, high and soft, and sometimes his demeanour was 'resigned'. 'He doesn't have a voice that bounces off the walls,' Geoffrey Robertson wrote. 'But he rises to occasions. Suddenly there'll be a flash of wit, or a sustained metaphor of remarkable beauty.' And there were some notable feats of cross-examination, especially of expert witnesses whose more recondite works he would take care to mention, thereby lulling them into submission. But the final speech to the jury was John's forte. He developed a stock ending for criminal cases, which he passed on to Rumpole: 'This is only a brief interlude in your lives, members of the jury. You'll soon forget about number 3 Acacia Avenue, and the dog food that wasn't eaten. But for my client the

whole of his future depends upon this moment, and your decision.'
When defending blue movies, his final speech followed another
pattern: he would laugh things out of court, inviting the jury to
make light of people hanging upside down with ping-pong balls
in their mouths, etc. He thus beguiled the jury into thinking that
a civilized man was talking to them as his equal, as sophisticated
men and women of the world, as distinct from the prosecutors,
who were Neanderthal men. Sharing jokes made them complicit.
'His humour,' said Robertson, 'could defuse courtroom solemnity.' At Doncaster, defending bondage magazines which featured
clothes pegs attached to women's nipples, he asked, 'Do you think,
members of the jury, that after reading this stuff, a man's going to
come rushing home and tell his wife to come upstairs, saying,
"And don't forget the clothes pegs!"?'

The cases John dealt with in the 1970s, a morally confused
decade, vindicate his unserious approach. He had a genuine aversion to paternalistic legislation: the sort of law that prevented
people from having abortions and insisted on fastening seat belts
in cars and Sikhs wearing crash helmets. He objected to inter-
ference with the freedom to smoke: 'And what for? Another five
years in a geriatric ward in Weston-super-Mare.' He found the
climate of the 1970s, as he did the late 1990s, illiberal, prone to
nanny-state *verbotens*. Like John Stuart Mill, he believed, 'The law
should provide the minimum to prevent people from destroying
or hurting each other.' Besides, if you approve of society telling
people what to do, you too may be told what to do. 'There's an
element of self-protection,' said John, 'in arguing against censorship.' He was implacable about freedom of speech, often pointing
out that 'murder is a crime but authors are free to describe it; sex
is not a crime but authors have often been jailed for depicting it.'

What did seriously need reform was the prison system. 'Locking
people up in a barbarous manner is appallingly destructive, and if
the death penalty ever came back, I'd leave the Bar,' said Rumpole,
who became his mouthpiece for penal reform. 'The reason I only
defend is that I hate the idea of people being locked away with a
chamber-pot.' Prison did nobody the slightest good, and most

prisoners should not be there. 'A hard core of people *do* need to be kept isolated from society,' Rumpole allowed. 'Society must protect itself against the brothers Kray . . . but there are very few of these. Most people in prison get there out of stupidity, or a muddle, or a mistake.' Rumpole did have an alternative solution (now implemented). 'I believe some criminals should be put to social or community work. Everybody knows prison has no curative value whatsoever. It doesn't stop people committing crimes: on the contrary, it consolidates their criminal tendencies.'

Just after the first Rumpole play, John was back in court in a high-profile case, *R.* v. *Hanau*, better known as the Linda Lovelace trial. Johannes Heinrich Hanau, a sixty-six-year-old bookseller with a shop in Old Compton Street, Soho, had imported *Inside Linda Lovelace*, of which 38,000 copies had been sold. Many wondered why a Labour Attorney-General and Home Secretary (Roy Jenkins) bothered to bring a case against this 'scruffy little book' in which Miss Lovelace discovers that her clitoris is in her throat, and has to go round fellating men to achieve pleasure: soft porn by modern standards. *Deep Throat*, the unutterably tedious film of the book, had been a box-office hit (in tandem with *The Devil in Miss Jones*) in the US in 1974. The prosecution team, led by Brian Leary of *Oz* fame, arranged a showing of *Deep Throat* at Scotland Yard, attracting a capacity audience of senior police officers. They were especially amused by the opening scene, in which Linda drives to a suburban Californian house where her flatmate Grace is sitting on a chair with a young stud between her legs, performing oral sex. As Grace and Linda chat, Grace picks up her cigarettes, takes one out and puts it in her mouth, saying to her client, 'D'you mind if I smoke while you eat?'

On the first day, 19 January 1976, John arrived at the Old Bailey from Sri Lanka, where, ostensibly on holiday, he had been writing six television plays about Shakespeare. Among the expert witnesses for the defence, he and Robertson called the journalist Anna Coote, the publisher Marion Boyars, and writers Mervyn Jones,

Jeremy Sandford and Johnny Speight, who would all assert that the book had some sort of integrity. Lovelace's 'confessions', describing her anal and oral expertise, her daily practice with a tubular vibrator and her ability to clench a little finger in a vice-like grip inside her vagina, were alleged later to have been ghostwritten, and Miss Lovelace claimed to have been a wretched sex-slave to her Svengali, one Chuck Traynor. But John presented her account as the candid experiences of a modern young woman, and adopted his most jaunty, mocking tone. 'You will have to ask yourselves,' he told the jury of nine men and three women, 'whether our society is such, having survived two major wars, that it will actually totter to an end because Miss Lovelace cheerfully indulges in all sorts of shenanigans . . . A visitor from Mars,' John careered on in ridicule mode, 'would find us a very wonderful race, at this crisis in our economic existence, that we can spend thousands of pounds of public money and hear thousands of words, all because a twenty-two-year-old has written a book which suggests that sex is a bit of fun!' Miss Lovelace, he said, had explained interesting sexual techniques 'with care, concern and perhaps ingenuity'.

When Leary asked the jury to consider whether they would allow their fourteen-year-old daughter to read this book, John read out, with skilled comedic timing, a particularly absurd swinging-from-chandeliers passage. The whole court, by all accounts, dissolved in laughter, and John was able to say to the jury, 'Mr Leary has asked what effect this would have on a fourteen-year-old schoolgirl. My answer is, the same effect that it's plainly having on a seventy-two-year-old judge.' Judge Rigg too had been convulsed with sniggers. The jury took just five hours to acquit Linda Lovelace's tacky book. Robertson's diary noted, 'We go back to John's home for a celebratory dinner. Ken Tynan calls to congratulate John, who is very happy.'

'If this book is not obscene within the definition of the [1959] act,' said Judge Rigg in his summing up, 'it might well be difficult to imagine anything that *would* fall into that category.' The acquittal of Linda Lovelace, which had preoccupied Fleet Street just as *Oz* had, led to 'de facto decensorship of the word'. Eventually the Williams report of 1979 contended that 'obscene literature' is as muddled a concept as 'obscene music'.

It was a notable victory, but it was not an episode from which the orthodoxy of enlightenment came out well, as Professor John Sutherland later wrote. *The Times* declared that *Inside Linda Lovelace* was 'indeed pornographic', 'an erotic book about a vicious girl written in vulgar language', and such was the backlash against the verdict that a few months later Mrs Mary Whitehouse took on another Cambridge Union debate on pornography and triumphantly won.

But obscenity cases were regarded at Dr Johnson's Buildings as a gravy train. From the moment John proposed Geoffrey Robertson's admission as a tenant in the expanding chambers (which grew in the mid-1970s from twelve members to forty), the pair formed a team. On 5 May 1975 they were at Grimsby Crown Court, defending 'the kind of magazines', as Robertson said, 'that would now be disdained by Richard Desmond'. They often co-defended the Gold brothers, Ralph and David, whose chain of West End shops made them a major force in the British skin-mag industry. In February 1977 they were at Leicester Crown Court, defending *Libertine*. *Libertine* was a journal dedicated to sexual freedom edited by Dr Arabella Melville and Colin Johnson, self-styled followers of the anarchist Kropotkin, who advertised their organ thus: 'Your lady editor fucks Phillip Hodson, Forum's sexiest male editor, we illustrate amazing sexual gymnastics and publish erect cocks.' The jury acquitted in fifteen minutes. In May, they were back at the Old Bailey on behalf of Hayes and Gallagher, video pornographers, who pleaded guilty in return for non-custodial sentences. Another client with reason to be grateful to them was David Sullivan, who now owns the *Star*, the *Sport* and a soccer team. At the Old Bailey on a charge of publishing obscene magazines in September 1975, he had said beforehand that if fined more than £250,000 he 'would need time to pay'; John negotiated a plea bargain with Judge Neil MacKinnon, and Sullivan was fined a mere £50. 'This case was the making of David Sullivan,' said Robertson.

They assembled a team of expert witnesses, writers and pundits on whom they could call: these included the Reverend Chad Varah, who wrote a column in *Forum* magazine, and once challenged a QC, who asked whether this book might tempt people to commit adultery, 'What's wrong with adultery?' QC: 'Isn't it one of the Ten Commandments?' Varah: 'Why are you quoting this ancient desert lore at me? It has no relevance to today at all.' Amenable doctors and sex therapists such as Dr Eustace Chesser, author of *Love without Fear*, and Dr Brian Richards, a GP from Sandwich who specialized in sexual difficulties, would assert that pornography had a therapeutic purpose. If the material was beautiful it was masturbatory, which was a positive benefit; and if it was disgusting it was 'aversive', which would turn people off. These were the experts labelled 'the Mortimer circus' by Mrs Whitehouse. John had an increasing respect for the courage of Mrs Whitehouse, resolutely present at every obscenity trial, like a *tricoteuse* beside the guillotine in revolutionary France, and saying her prayers in the corridor while the jury was out.

Ann Mallalieu, daughter of the Labour minister J. P. W. Mallalieu, regularly acted as John's junior. They had first met in a TV studio when she was just down from Cambridge, where she had been, in 1965, the first woman president of the Union, in whose blonde and comely Zuleika Dobson-like presence visiting politicians melted. Ann was a pupil to Robin (now Lord Justice) Auld, and was renting an isolated Thames Valley farmhouse to which she would rush back from London every day to exercise her horses. The farm was not far from Turville Heath, so she and her then boyfriend, the oarsman Dan Topolski, became regular supper guests at John and Penny's table.

Together Mortimer and Mallalieu defended Gordon Thorne, 'the King of Porn', at Birmingham. They would stay at the Midland Hotel, dine together and laugh over what was said in court, especially when a judge told the defendants they had 'defaced the fair city of Birmingham'. Ann had to read the books, since John refused to read them himself; and when blue movies were shown he claimed he always removed his glasses. Another Birmingham case was the defence of *Toilet Orgy*, a film 'full of nasty lavatorial stuff: there was no way John was going to watch that. The jury were told that if they needed to go out in the middle, the loo was down the corridor.' He and Ann also had 'great fun' at the Old Bailey defending a magazine called *Spank*, when the jurors were instructed, 'Will you please now look at the bottoms at the bottom of page 17.' 'John's speeches were so side-splittingly funny,' Ann said, 'jurors would come up afterwards and ask for his autograph.'

Ann later married Tim Cassel, QC. John had first encountered Cassel when he arrived at the Old Bailey to defend a projectionist of blue films, a man who had been awarded the Military Cross after losing a leg at Anzio. Cassel, son and heir of the slightly mad baronet judge Sir Harold Cassel, was tall, handsome, witty and a diehard Tory. He was thoroughly disarmed when John approached him outside the courtroom on day one of the case. 'Darling, charming, handsome prosecutor,' said John. 'You don't really want to spend weeks and weeks prosecuting this poor, brave, one-legged projectionist, do you?' Cassel, taken aback by John's distinctly camp approach – and aware that the cinema's manager and proprietor were pleading guilty anyway – agreed that there was no earthly public interest in pursuing an expensive case, and withdrew the prosecution of the projectionist.

John always quoted Voltaire's (contested) dictum, 'I disapprove of what you say but I will defend to the death your right to publish it.' He did not enjoy the stuff he defended, but he remained adamant that laws seeking to control what people read or write were inoperable, and only brought the law into disrepute. 'Life is difficult enough for the ordinary citizen without the existence of crimes into which he or she may blunder without any intention of offending.' He saw pornography as 'a useful safety valve if a poor chap can't manage anything better'. What was wrong with aids to masturbation? He had told the Linda Lovelace jury that he himself had enjoyed 'a little solitary sexuality behind the school squash court with only *Reveille* magazine and a picture of Betty Grable for comfort'.

The Mortimer and Robertson 'therapeutic argument' or aversive defense, aided by expert witnesses, hit the buffers late in 1977.

Staniforth and Jordan were booksellers who, having been found guilty, and failing in the Court of Appeal, went to the House of Lords. So, on a wet Monday morning in October that year, John accompanied Robertson to the Lords, where John found himself having 'to lecture five elderly Law Lords on the benefits of masturbation'. He chose to tell them the story of the boy who, warned that masturbation leads to blindness, asked, 'Can't I just do it until I'm short-sighted?' This did not win over their lordships, who decided that experts were not necessary to say whether something was obscene: a jury should decide. So 'pornography as safety valve' was ruled inadmissible.

The defence of porn was a lucrative legal niche, and it suited the 1970s, but it was never going to be, *sub specie aeternitatis*, a noble claim to fame. John had fought for some contemptible pulp fiction and he was not entirely proud of this role. 'I started off defending works that had some value,' he said in 1985, 'but then got down to some pretty worthless things. I found it much easier to defend books if I hadn't read them ... One's only argument could be that people should not be censored.' Only eight years later, John wrote that the argument about pornography was 'no longer of the slightest interest to anyone'.

Today the material available on the Internet is infinitely more dangerous, now that websites give illustrated instruction on 'sexual asphyxiation', etc. The demand grows for ever more explicit and exploitative images, and the view that reading or viewing sadistic pornography has no pernicious effect is rightly questioned. The outcome of the obscenity trials of the 1970s was to benefit porn-peddlers, whose industry flourishes. Ann (now Baroness) Mallalieu told me she had since changed her mind about whether anyone can be depraved and corrupted by watching the material she was obliged to see. 'I never had any desire to look at anything like that in my private life, and felt rather sorry for people who did. The corruption in my case is not that I found the stuff titillating, it's that when you see a great amount of it, you start to think there's nothing wrong with any of it.' Quentin Edwards, too, challenged the view that there is no such thing as corrupting people, otherwise barristers too would be corrupted. He told me he thought some barristers had indeed been corrupted: 'I can think of several examples whose characters were altered for the worse by constantly dealing with horrible things.'

Whenever I asked John about this, he sidestepped the question, reiterating the fact that he never watched the porn films, and (reflecting his out-of-date experience) upholding the old law, which went for the suppliers, not the customers, of obscene material. In 2005 he was asked by Mark Lawson on Radio 4 whether it was ever possible that a book, a play or a film could corrupt or damage an individual. 'I'm not sure about that. The law which we were acting under, the test for obscenity was whether it could deprave or corrupt anybody, and it was very hard for the prosecution ever to find anybody who'd been depraved or corrupted.' Did the libertarian John believe in any boundaries at all? 'I believe in the boundaries of good taste, good sense. Books can be revolting, which we should attack, and not read, and ignore, but I don't believe in censorship.'

LAWSON: So good taste would be a private individual judgement, nothing to do with the law or the state?

MORTIMER: I don't think so. I don't think there should be any censorship or any boundaries on free speech.

John's link with obscenity cases rather obscured the other cases he undertook. At Brixton prison, with Robertson, he drafted the bail application of John Stonehouse, the MP who staged his own disappearance in 1975 (and conducted his own defence, disastrously). He went to Tel Aviv, which he hated, to write a report for Amnesty International when a Palestinian district nurse, practising in Britain and engaged to an Englishman, faced a life sentence after allegedly confessing to links with Al-Fateh. Her family had lived in the small Arab village of Yaffa, outside Nazareth, for a thousand years, John wrote; her family produced doctors and engineers in Britain and North America. He described the feelings of persecution of Arabs in Israel, in a report that was outstandingly fair and full of vivid touches: one prosecution witness was 'a jovial man with a large handlebar moustache which makes him look like the comedian Jimmy Edwards'.

In 1977, John led Robertson in a successful bail application for the journalists Duncan Campbell and Crispin Aubrey, who, having interviewed an employee of GCHQ, were charged under the Official Secrets Act as a danger to national security. In the High Court John ignored the freedom of speech argument and astutely played the class card. Crispin Aubrey was, as his name suggests, well born, and Campbell was 'recently down from Oxford'. 'Which college?' asked the judge automatically. John referred to 'young men of good parentage', Oxford days and student pranks. The pair were released on bail; the working-class ex-soldier whom they had interviewed stayed inside.

In the same year, they were at the Old Bailey defending a Tory councillor named Wyatt, charged with attempting to kidnap and blackmail a member of the South African Oppenheim family, who owned Rio Tinto Zinc. Robertson wanted to stop their indubitably guilty client from going into the witness box, which would sink him, but John insisted. 'You must remember that he faces conviction. It's important that he should not sit in prison thinking, "If only I'd spoken, I'd have got off."' So Wyatt spoke, and was duly convicted. John 'made the best possible speech', said Robertson, 'but it was unavailing' Jacqueline Holborough, a co-defendant caught up in the plot, went to jail and wrote a play about life inside. John later sat on the panel which gave her a young playwrights' bursary, the start of a successful career.

It is hardly surprising that he left the studying of briefs till the last minute. It is amazing that he had time to go to court at all. Currently on his desk were a *Rumpole* TV series; six TV plays about Shakespeare; a musical about Sherlock Holmes; a screenplay for Lew Grade about Rasputin ('Aldous Huxley said he was the only decent character in the Czar's court'); the translation of another Feydeau farce for the National, *Mademoiselle de Chez Maxim*; and an adaptation of Jacques Poiret's *La Cage aux Folles*.

Some of these got produced, some not. Penny, typing a sheaf of handwritten pages every day, was never aware of strenuous research or effort. He rarely betrayed a hint of being pressed for time, but when the *Gay News* trial loomed in the summer of 1977 he said he had so many deadlines he was 'in hysterics'. However, the first blasphemy trial for fifty years was irresistible.

Mrs Mary Whitehouse had instituted her private prosecution against *Gay News* for publishing a long poem called *The Love That Dares to Speak Its Name*. It portrayed Christ, crucified and 'well-hung', as the object of homosexual lust by a Roman centurion guarding the corpse. As John pointed out, D. H. Lawrence had written a short story about Christ having sex, 'The Escaped Cock', that had been in print for decades, 'without any fuss'. James Kirkup, author of the *Gay News* poem, was a Tyneside-born writer who had won the Keats Prize in 1974, had written two excellent volumes of memoirs (*An Only Child* and *Sorrows, Passions and Alarms*) and was now living and teaching in Japan and Ohio. In *Who's Who*, Kirkup's recreation was given as 'Standing in shafts of sunlight'. He was not called to take the stand at the trial; and nor was John's client, Denis Lemon, the 'handsome, intense and rather mournful' editor of *Gay News*.

The judge, Alan King-Hamilton, was clever, quick-witted and Jewish (therefore 'unbiased'), but he was 'shocked and horrified and revolted' by the poem. He at first doubted that he should try the case, but went ahead, reasoning that every other judge would feel the same. During a previous trial of Paul Ableman's *The Mouth and Oral Sex*, King-Hamilton had said, 'We have got on for over two thousand years without any mention of oral sex. Why do we need to read about it now?'

Margaret Drabble, the literary expert in the witness box at the time, hesitated to reply.

'Witness, why do you hesitate?' asked the judge.

Drabble: 'I'm sorry, My Lord, I was just trying to remember the passage in Ovid.'

The *Gay News* trial opened on 4 July 1977. The newspaper was already organizing discos in aid of its defence fund, as Robertson realized when they refused to let him waive his fees: the discos raised £30,000 and 'doubtless facilitated many gay liaisons'. The defence team of Mortimer, Robertson and Grieve were planning to remind the court that mere denial of the truth of Christianity was not blasphemous, as established by Lord Chief Justice Coleridge in 1883; there had to be a wilful intention 'to pervert and mislead', a ruling which had protected Darwin and Huxley from prosecution. So John emerged on the first morning behind a towering pile of law books. 'How long is all this argument going to last?' asked King-Hamilton. 'Until lunchtime,' said John. 'Goodness gracious me,' responded the judge, 'I was hoping the case would be over by then.' John said he was sorry to disappoint his lordship, but they must establish whether the offence of blasphemy still existed.

The prosecuting counsel was John Jackson Smyth, Mary White-house's fellow traveller from The Festival of Light. Smyth called Kirkup's poem 'so vile it would be hard for the most perverted imagination to conjure up anything worse . . . almost too vile for words, even in the Old Bailey'. The jury, who had all taken the oath on the Bible, then had to sit in their room and mull over the vile poem.

After four days of legal argument the judge refused to allow any theological evidence from either side, or the defence's literary evidence. So Robertson introduced character witnesses for *Gay News* itself. Distinguished homosexuals were in short supply, as coming out was not yet in fashion. Lord 'Boofy' Arran's bill to lower the male age of consent from twenty-one to eighteen had been defeated a few weeks before; there were no openly gay MPs, and the Jeremy Thorpe trial was yet to come. Robertson could rally no support even from the two gay members of their own chambers. (In the robing room, one colleague remarked to John, indicating the placard-waving demonstrators outside the court, 'Well, Mortimer, I see you've got your friends from Rent-a-Bum outside.') So they called Margaret Drabble and Bernard Levin. But when Levin declared *Gay News* to be 'a serious and responsible newspaper' he was roundly challenged.

SMYTH: You say *Gay News* is always a responsible newspaper. Look at this review of a book about homosexual lovemaking. It publishes explicit descriptions and illustrations. Is that responsible?

LEVIN: I don't think explicitness is inconsistent with responsibility.

JUDGE: Why should homosexuals need help of this kind?

LEVIN: Because, like everyone else, I suppose, they need to know about sexual techniques.

JUDGE: Well, I don't know why heterosexuals should need help to know how to make love.

LEVIN: Well, the evidence is overwhelming that many of them do.

JUDGE: It's all beyond me, I'm afraid.

Smyth told the jury they were being asked 'to set the standard for the last quarter of the twentieth century'. An acquittal would open the floodgates. But Robertson found another form of persuasion: to go through the poem line by line, explaining how it tried to communicate Christ being the word made flesh. In the hush that fell upon the court, gently and persuasively, he reminded the jury that God loved sinners and homosexuals. He flourished the *Book of Common Prayer* and drew attention to the words of the communion service: 'This is my Body – eat this. This is my Blood. Drink this.' King-Hamilton later wrote that this speech made him realize that there might have been another way of looking at the poem; and even Mrs Whitehouse was impressed: 'a truly remarkable performance', she wrote. But Robertson made a fatal error, later regretted. He left out a section that he could not bring himself to read. After describing Jesus having 'had it off with other men', including Pontius Pilate, John the Baptist, Paul of Tarsus and 'foxy Judas, a great kisser', Kirkup had written:

> And then the miracle possessed us.
> I felt him enter into me, and fiercely spend
> his spirit's final seed within my hole, my soul,
> pulse upon pulse, unto the ends of the earth –
> he crucified me with him into kingdom come.

Robertson read instead the far superior Donne sonnet ('Batter my heart') about a metaphysical union with God which ends:

> for I
> Except y'enthral me never shall be free
> Nor ever chaste except you ravish me.

Robertson's peroration, quoting, 'He dwelleth in me, and I in him,' from the Eucharist, and St Paul's wish to be 'all things to all men', suggested that Kirkup's poem, in a newspaper with a circulation of just 8,000, was not likely to subvert the fabric of society. But the damage had been done. Was the jury surprised, the judge asked, that Mr Robertson had balked at reading aloud those omitted lines, which were the ultimate in profanity?

In John's final speech he pointed out that while the prosecution spoke for 'supernatural forces', he alone appeared for a human being – Denis Lemon – 'who is in the dock, in peril, on this antique charge which has not been used for more than fifty years. The Sermon on the Mount tells us to love our neighbour. But Mrs Mary Whitehouse has put her neighbour in the dock . . .' He recalled the trial of Oscar Wilde in this same place. At this point Judge King-Hamilton, having excused himself for a while, returned and announced, 'It may come as a relief to you during this rather sordid case, members of the jury, to know that England are 210 for three wickets in the test match.' (John, amazed, later gave this line to Judge 'Mad Bull' Bullingham in a *Rumpole* episode, to King-Hamilton's irritation.) King-Hamilton, who wrote in his memoirs that he felt 'the hand of God' aiding him in his final speech, told the jury to forget thoughts of changing history; all they had to do was answer three simple questions. 'Did [the poem] shock you when you first read it? Could it shock or offend anyone who read it? Could you read it to an audience of fellow Christians without blushing?' The reasonable answer, after several hours, from ten of the twelve jurors (two dissented) was yes, yes and no, and their verdict was therefore Guilty. (It almost always has been Guilty, in blasphemy cases.) Nobody asked whether 'shocking to Christians' was a true definition of blasphemy. Lemon got a suspended sentence of nine months. A week after the unsuccessful *Gay News* appeal, Robertson came close to running over Mrs Whitehouse when he drove down a narrow lane in Essex, where she was picking blackberries from a hedge. The two took tea together, and wondered what a coroner's court might have made of the incident, had Robertson mown her down.

As John wrote (and said again, when the Blair government was nervously deferring to Muslim sensitivities), 'We all hold precious beliefs, but unless they can stand against mockery and abuse, they are worth little.' The chief effect of Mrs Whitehouse's successful action was to bring the seventeenth-century blasphemy laws into further disrepute. A lively campaign by humanists failed to abolish the archaic offence, despite support from the 1979 Williams report, and from the Law Commission in 1985. Tony Benn's bill to abolish the law of blasphemy was supported by MPs of all parties, but the anomalous law remains, offering protection only to Christians in multicultural Britain. This had a profound bearing on the 1989 case of Salman Rushdie and his novel *The Satanic Verses*, when Rushdie took initial refuge from the fatwa in Robertson's Islington house. In 1990, John interviewed Dr Kalim Siddiqui, head of the Muslim Institute, about the Rushdie fatwa. Siddiqui greeted John cheerily with, 'Ah! The Rumpole man!' but insisted it was God's will that blasphemers must die. 'The concept of God has no doubt brought many benefits to the world,' wrote John, 'but it's my belief that He should, if at all possible, be kept out of the criminal law.'

James Kirkup entitled his next volume of memoirs with a line from Wordsworth: *A Poet Could Not But Be Gay*. 'I believe in my guardian angel. But I cannot believe in God, who has made such a mess of his Creation,' he wrote. 'Some Christians have told me I cannot write poems and plays on religious themes if I am not a prac-tising Christian, but that is nonsense . . . From what I have seen of Christians, all I can say is, "Save me from heaven!"' By 2007, aged ninety, Kirkup had changed his *Who's Who* recreation to simply 'Living'. Judge King-Hamilton too was still living, aged 102.

18. Lucid Indifference

After the *Gay News* verdict, John got into his car (registration NUD, often thought appropriate), drove to Turville Heath, plunged into his pool and swam several lengths until he 'felt differently about the world'. The next day the *Evening Standard* arts columnist Sydney Edwards arrived at Little Venice: he noted a chess set and a bowl of roses on the table, Schubert Lieder on the radio, Chagall on the wall, friendly tailwagging dog, in an elegant study with long windows overlooking the garden. A civilized, book-lined home, whose owner had been to *Aida* at Covent Garden the previous Saturday night and loved theatre gossip, but seemed careless of his own overweight and long-haired appearance. 'He is formidably intelligent but takes care not to appear so,' Edwards wrote. He seemed insouciant about his prodigious writing projects: his Shakespeare book just out, a play opening at the Garrick, his new Feydeau in rehearsal at the National, his old Henley play *Two Stars for Comfort* reprised on TV for the Queen's silver jubilee. He had written seven Rumpole stories for a Penguin edition, to accompany a possible TV series . . .

With so much writing to do, why did he keep practising law? He could no longer invoke his father's influence. But when he asked his accountant, Phyl, 'Can I give up the Bar now?' she advised him to hang on to the day job. He could command an average of £2,000–£3,000 per hearing at this time, plus daily refreshers and expenses. Anyway, he liked having QC in his passport. He relished the contrast between 'the artificial world of the courts and the real one of the theatre'. And sometimes he said he only felt truly alive and happy when putting on the wig and gown, even if he was heard muttering, 'God I'm bored with this,' during a judge's summing up, and was reprimanded by the administrator of the Inner London sessions.

His book *Will Shakespeare: An Entertainment*, based on his six-part series for television, was an exuberant exercise. All that was known about the world's greatest dramatist 'and most secret and unknown man', could be written on a postcard, as Professor Terence Spencer of Birmingham University had told him, so John turned to the plays and 154 sonnets. As he knew, even a reticent writer cannot avoid self-revelation in his work. When he wrote about Shakespeare, he said – just as he had said of Genghis Khan – 'I'm writing about me as Shakespeare'. There was much to identify with, starting with Will's marriage at the age of eighteen to a woman of twenty-six, possibly 'a shotgun, or at least an arquebus, affair'. And Will too mistrusted judges. John's favourite quotation was 'handy-dandy, which is the justice, which the thief?' He felt completely at one with Shakespeare's 'sense of human absurdity'.

Then there was Will's passion for the 'fair friend' and 'better angel', only begetter of the sonnets, some of them homoerotic. John decided this was Henry Wriothesley (pronounced Risely), Earl of Southampton. Southampton possessed physical beauty, aristocratic wealth, horsemanship, heroism. 'What existed between him and the poet was certainly love,' John wrote in one of many articles at the time, 'although one of the sonnets suggests that it was never physically expressed. It is a question perhaps we have no need to ask.' But in the novel version, Will stays in Southampton's house for three days and nights, fencing and playing cards and billiards and tennis, being awakened from a bed of fine linen to breakfast on cold pheasant, hot bread and white wine. Their love clearly 'surpassed in almost every way the love between Shakespeare and his mysterious Dark Lady,' wrote John. John's invented Dark Lady was Mistress Mary Fleminge, young wife of an elderly judge, who infatuated and tormented Shakespeare. 'He . . . loved her to distraction,' John wrote. 'She moves through his sonnets like an obsession which robs the poet of his reason. But he didn't know how to "shun the heaven that leads us to this hell". Then came the great betrayal. The fair friend, the Earl of Southampton, made the Dark Lady his mistress.'

John's plays were set in the rank and noisome district around the Rose and Globe theatres, in the streets of Blackfriars, Cripplegate and Shoreditch, crammed with 'Dicing Houses, Brothel Houses, Bowling Alleys and other Disorderly Places'. His Elizabethan London was feverishly alive with bear-baiting pits, dogs fighting apes, executions, cardsharps and cutpurses. The action followed Will as he became the principal playmaker, after Marlowe's death in a brawl, and as he mourned his son Hamnet, who died at eleven, with the 'tormented conscience of a far from perfect father'. At his death in part six, the playhouses have been banned by James I, and Southampton has spurned his old companion to become a minion of the king.

Even the caustic Shakespearian A. L. Rowse, who hated novels and plays about his hero ('like putting the most wonderful poetry in our language into Ye Olde Tea Shoppe spelling') was won over by Peter Wood's production, when the plays were eventually televised, with Tim Curry playing Shakespeare. It was Dr Rowse who had fingered Southampton as Shakespeare's 'lovely boy', and insisted that there was no element of homosexuality in the attachment. Naturally Rowse thought Emilia Lanier, the Dark Lady he identified, would have made a better story than John's invented Mistress Fleminge. Anthony Burgess, who could have been grudging, since he had originally proposed to Lew Grade the idea of a Shakespeare film, found John's book 'richly comic', although Will emerged as 'a farcical blunderer with an itching codpiece'. 'Like Shakespeare,' Burgess wrote, 'Mr Mortimer is a popular dramatist.'

The popular dramatist made a *jeu d'esprit*, at a literary luncheon at the Dorchester, of the idea of a playwright whose authorship is disputed. Writing about Shakespeare had meant bombardment with propaganda from the Francis Bacon Society. 'I know Harold Pinter exists,' said John, 'because I have just seen him eating his *poulet à l'Anglaise*.' (Pinter was present, accompanying Lady Antonia Fraser.) But one day, said John, when John Mortimer was in his grave, people might question whether 'an Old Bailey hack', frequently engaged at Uxbridge Magistrates' Court, could possibly have written the books under his name. 'A playwright's life is as fraught as in Shakespeare's day, never knowing where his next *poulet à l'Anglaise* will come from.'

John had described Shakespeare returning to Stratford, buying a fine house, 'pruning of his great vines' and dying in his bed at fifty-two, 'filled with peace, happy in the countryside from which he never, for all his running away, really escaped'. Now that he had reached roughly the same age, fifty-four, John too began to profess his devotion to his country house and the quiet life. He bought more woodland. He yearned, he said, to 'pull up the drawbridge, grow vegetables and never be seen again'.

This hardly accorded with the evidence of his social life. My own voyage round John Mortimer, like most of his acquaintance, consisted of sightings at restaurants, parties and theatre first nights, such as Barry Humphries's new Dame Edna show. He gave a reunion *Oz* dinner for Richard Neville and his future wife, Julie Clark. The expansive Sunday lunches were a fixture, as were the parties for his birthday in April and Penny's in September. In July 1977 Michael Grieve was driven down to Turville Heath in Geoffrey Robertson's open-top Renault with Robertson's current amour, Bel Mooney (Mrs Jonathan Dimbleby), and was amazed to see the sport-hating John swimming in his costly new pool. John said that on a crisp day he could look out of the window and see the steam from the heated pool rise into the air, 'like watching five pound notes go up'. Mark Amory from the *Sunday Times* found him at Turville Heath one Sunday, carving roast lamb and slicing rhubarb pie, looking 'not so much plump or rounded as fat'. Penny was, at thirty, 'a little wisp of a thing', but, as Amory observed, she was 'cool and in the nicest possible way, tough'. An old friend of Mortimer's had told Amory, 'I didn't think she'd last.' 'But she has. She can cope with her husband, and her husband's world.'

With the Old Etonian Amory, John had one of those easy clubmen's chat sessions. But most of his replies 'came winging back to the man he sees as the great influence on his life – his father'. John was planning his memoirs, and had started embellishing the facts. He told Amory the story of Churchill 'appearing about ninety-nine and totally thick' at Harrow School Songs. He claimed, too, that at Oxford he played several minor Shakespearian villains, until he was 'cast as Rosencrantz and stopped going to rehearsals'. Why make this claim? As his daughter Emily later said, 'Dad always tells a lie if it makes things more interesting,' and John often made his own case for the benefits of lying. Perhaps it was wishful thinking or a kind of transference: Jeremy was now involved in Oxford theatre. John took Emily to *The Duchess of Malfi* in the New College cloisters, which Jeremy directed, and a musical called *Orphea*, which he also directed, with David Profumo as a Mafioso and Dido Goldsmith as a vamp. For John, Oxford remained 'the best of all possible dreams . . . honey buns and anchovy toast and listening to the Haydn quartets . . . and making friends who actually do last all your life' in the midst of 'unforgettable architecture'. 'There is no better way of spending three years,' he wrote at this time, 'no finer environment in which to cultivate the private joys of love, friendship and reading books.' He never gave Jeremy any hint of the denouement of his own Oxford days.

But he was soon plunging into Oxford memories. In June 1977 he was back in Positano ('all just like it ever was, beautiful, sunny and friendly,' he wrote to Jeremy. 'We have been on Fornillo beach all day, and are horribly brown & very rested') when he received a call from Derek Granger at Granada Television: would he care to adapt Evelyn Waugh's novel *Brideshead Revisited* as a six-part serial?

John said yes instantly, then panicked. It was not his favourite Waugh novel. He disliked Waugh's attitude to the General Strike and the patronizing of Rex Mottram. But then he read Waugh's preface to the revised 1960 edition, when Waugh found his novel 'infused with a kind of gluttony, full of forbidden luxuries' emerging in 1945 into a world of privation, fuel shortages and rationing. The book had been part of John's life. 'I had grown up in much the same way as Waugh: a middle-class boy, born to hard professional work, educated above our stations slightly, falling half in love, at Oxford, with a more effete and useless way of life.' So he made a start on the adaptation, just as a host of other distractions crowded in.

He had a West End play opening, for a start. *The Bells of Hell* was a version of one of the two religion plays produced at Greenwich in the previous year under the title *Heaven and Hell*. *Mr Luby's Fear of Heaven*, first broadcast with John Gielgud, was a duologue between two men (one saintly, one sinful) lying side by side in the Hospital for Transients and the Urban Poor in Siena, an old palazzo. John had been there, and seen tourists guided through the wards, admiring the painted ceilings while patients lay viscerally coughing or being fed intravenously. Its companion play, *The Prince of Darkness*, was set in a south London rectory, where a farcically trendy vicar named Gavin Faber organizes gay get-togethers, and rubberwear and bondage circles for his parishioners. His wife, Madge (Eleanor Bron at Greenwich, Phyllida Law at the Garrick), learns that the bishop is coming unexpectedly to dinner, with only a kipper and a slice of Mother's Pride in the fridge. Her husband believes in neither prayer nor miracles, but his curate, Bulstrode, having once prayed for rain and received a thunder-storm, prays for food. When Madge opens the refrigerator it is overflowing with loaves and fishes, in time for the arrival of the camp bishop in full canonicals. There was much laughter at this satire on clergy hypocrisy, but never more than on the night in Greenwich when the fridge blew up and the stage caught fire.

These plays, launched between the Linda Lovelace and *Gay News* trials, had a religious message – 'If you abolish the idea of sin you take a lot of fun out of sex,' as John put it. Michael Codron decided that only the church play, renamed *The Bells of Hell*, would transfer, so John had to expand the script – a mistake, he realized. John Osborne had to leap to his friend's defence in print, threaten-ing physical violence against the *Times* reviewer. But there was no critical dissent about the new Feydeau, *The Lady from Maxim's*, at the National. This mad farce of mistaken identity was hailed yet again by every critic as a masterpiece that sparkled like champagne. John, 'the Voltaire of the West End', knew exactly, as he should by now, how to wring a laugh from every line.

With two theatre productions running, and Shakespeare's Globe being built at Elstree for his Will Shakespeare TV series, and Rumpoles overdue, and *Brideshead* just commissioned, it is typical of John that he could say yes – he was pathologically incapable of saying no – when Richard Branson rang with a little legal problem over the Virgin album *Never Mind the Bollocks*. The Sex Pistols, the spike-haired, ripped-leather-trousered punk band prone to drunkenly spitting at audiences (although Geoffrey Robertson found their singer Johnny Rotten 'a polite, studious young undergraduate'), had had their new record banned by the Nottingham magistrates. They invoked the same Indecent Advertisements Act (1889) that had got Branson for his VD advice ten years before. 'What on earth's wrong with bollocks? It's one of my favourite words,' said John when Branson rang. They summoned Professor James Kinsley, head of Nottingham University's English department, to explain that although 'bollocks' was a medieval term for testicles, and had been so used in Caxton's Bible, it had come, in the eighteenth century, after a fictional parson named Bollocks, to mean cant uttered from the pulpit, or rubbish. Professor Kinsley assured the bench that not even a priest would be offended; he himself was a Methodist lay preacher. The case was dismissed, and sales of the Sex Pistols' album rocketed – the abiding effect of all censorship.

The American writer David Solomon, friend of Timothy Leary, the LSD evangelist, also needed John's advocacy. Solomon was one of the Cambridge University drugs ring which had been making millions from manufacturing LSD at a farm in mid-Wales, until rounded up by an undercover police investigation codenamed Operation Julie. Despite a moving mitigation speech by John, Solomon got twelve years. The *Gay News* appeal followed – when the conviction stood, but the judges gave leave for the case to be taken to the House of Lords. The BBC screened a film about the *Gay News* trial, with John played by Norman Rodway. John also advised the Monty Python team when they were threatened with a blasphemy case over *The Life of Brian* film. But behind this apparently effortless and seamless activity, he was beset by anxiety – what was going to become of Rumpole?

The BBC had given Irene Shubik the go-ahead to commission a *Rumpole* series. But the BBC was undergoing a crisis in finance and morale. Discontented staff were leaving in droves, and soon Christopher Morahan, the new head of plays, himself left. His successor said the series would have to wait two years. John, who was then halfway through writing six episodes, 'fell into a decline' when told. 'Poor John,' he whimpered to his producer. 'What am I going to do?'

Shubik suggested taking the series to Thames, where her friend Verity Lambert was now Head of Drama. John brightened: it would be fun there, and they would pay more. His drama agent, Anthony Jones, extricated them from the BBC contract. Shubik left her job at the BBC and threw in her lot with Thames. By May 1977 the series was under way: cartoon graphics were commissioned from Rob Page (in the manner of legal caricatures by Spy) and so was the bassoon-heavy signature tune, from the composer Joseph Horovitz. The Old Bailey courtroom, Rumpole's chambers and his flat were all constructed. An ensemble cast was handpicked, mostly by Shubik.

Rumpole's return to the screen was a triumph. The literacy of the dialogue, the speeches laced with lines from Wordsworth and hymns and Shakespeare's plays ('But me no buts'; 'Seems, madam? Nay, tis') distinguished it from the common run of sitcoms. Viewers gleaned more about the arcane workings of the law from Rumpole than from any other source. They discovered that barristers don't shake hands, that evidence is vital, that the *locus in quo* is the scene of the crime, that habeas corpus is an admirable tenet and that a leading question is friendly, not hostile. They became familiar with Pommeroy's (the name came from F. W. Pomeroy, sculptor of the Old Bailey's statue of Justice with her scales and sword), the wine bar based on El Vino, where Rumpole drinks Château Thames Embankment. They heard Rumpole's view of judges and 'judgeitis', the symptoms being self-importance, intolerance, pomposity and interfering with defence cross-examinations. They discovered that beyond the courtroom, barristers' chambers were hotbeds of egomania and petty squabbling. They got acquainted with the Timsons, John's sentimentalized dynasty of traditional East End villains who beget young villains just as lawyers beget lawyers. 'If you're a Timson, you start off doing small crimes and going to borstal, then bigger crimes and ending up in Dartmoor. That's their way of life, and it's perfectly respectable to them.' The Capulets to their Montagues, the Yorks to their Lancasters, are the Molloy family, purposeful villains with a nice line in GBH. And Rumpole revealed, like his creator, a streak of susceptibility to lady clients: in one episode he became unprofessionally fond of a beautiful hippie, played by Jane Asher, who has a stash of cannabis in her ashram-like pad at Coldsands-on-Sea. John told Jane that this story was true: it had happened to him.

Of course it strained credibility that no prosecutor ever proved a match for Rumpole's forensic talents – like Enid Blyton's schoolboy detectives outwitting the Mr Plods – and Richard Ingrams questioned, in the *Spectator*, Rumpole's assertion that no barrister would defend a client who had admitted guilt to him. But, as John said, if unsure of the absence of guilt, 'barristers are a bit like Roman Catholics over difficult theological matters. We suspend our disbelief. Otherwise 75 per cent of people would never be defended.'

Rumpole was one of the best things in a vintage television year that included Dennis Potter's *Pennies from Heaven*, *The Lost Boys* by Andrew Birkin, and *Edward and Mrs Simpson* by Simon Raven. Jeremy Isaacs, who had initially been lukewarm, immediately commissioned a second series.

But before this could get under way, Irene Shubik and Verity Lambert fell out. Shubik had gripes about working conditions at Thames – a less congenial berth than the BBC – and, just when she was going to America for three months, she was asked to produce the second *Rumpole* series, for a lower fee. Inclined to walk out of the job for which she had given up her BBC niche, she took her plight to John, expecting sympathetic support, but again he did his 'Poor John' act. In mournful tones he said he supposed Thames might not now go ahead with the series. In fact, John accompanied Verity Lambert to Manchester, where

Leo McKern was in *Crime and Punishment*, to persuade him to play Rumpole, with or without Shubik. She never forgave John for this.

Everyone felt sorry for Shubik, who had worked so hard only to discover she was dispensable. Instead, Verity Lambert appointed a new producer, Jacqueline Davis, an eye-catching woman who had first caught John's eye in 1969 on the Thames TV hospitality boat at Teddington Lock. Now, in 1977, they lunched in Covent Garden and he took to her at once: 'a beautiful woman in a white dress, with huge dark eyes and a gentle voice.' 'She's as prone to despair as I am, but often with me it's a device to achieve a result, and with her, a genuine emotion.' (That line about his despair being 'a device to achieve a result' represents a rare access of self-appraisal. John's abject moans about penury, or his career being in ruins, were familiar to friends.) Jacquie, though dismayed about upsetting Shubik ('it was an awful, sad time'), could not give up the chance to produce *Rumpole*, and became John's ally and collaborator. It astonished her that even if he was doing a trial in Birmingham, he would rustle up an extra few minutes of dialogue, if necessary, dictate the lines by telephone and then fall into the rehearsal on the way home.

At the Edinburgh Television Festival that summer, tribute was paid to John Mortimer for creating, in Rumpole and Shakespeare (which had overlapped on the ITV schedules from April to June), 'two fully formed, credible and sympathetically human characters', each 'enriched by Mortimer's insight into the relevant professions of the law and playwriting'.

In the summer of 1978, John and Penny went to Porto Ercole, where the novelist Emma Tennant had rented a house from Lord Bernstein of Granada TV. Penny had been working for Tennant's literary magazine *Bananas* one day a week (for a fiver): a foothold in a working life. Tennant and her partner, Tim Owens, had been invited to Sunday lunch at Turville Heath Cottage in June, where they arrived to the scent of roses, the aroma of roasting meat and then – to Tennant's horror – the sight of John Osborne arriving

with his brand-new (fifth) wife, Helen Dawson. John and Penny
had been among the Osbornes' wedding guests at Tunbridge Wells
some days before. They brought with them Osborne's silent
daughter, the not-yet-disowned Nolan aged thirteen, and a Nebu-
chadnezzar of champagne. Tennant expected Osborne to be belli-
cose, and then provoked him to be just that. Did he know, she
asked, that his famous 'Damn You, England' letter of 1961 had
been written from her parents' farmhouse, La Baumette, near
Valbonne, which he was then renting? 'Dreadful little place,' said
Osborne. 'Sanitation bad. Food disgusting.' He then turned his
vituperation on Emma herself: 'You. I've read about you in *Private
Eye.*' Helen and the Mortimers sat helplessly during his tirade
against Tennant's family (the Glenconners) and her class (upper).
Tennant and Owens left early.

But the Italian holiday was a success: a heavenly house, with a
tame fox that visited every evening at sunset. A pine forest walk
led to a sandy beach, and to restaurants on stilts serving spaghetti
alle vongole. Emma's daughter Rose got on famously with Emily.
John was writing Rumpole, series two. 'This is one of the most
enjoyable holidays I've known,' Tennant wrote in her diary, 'but
John doesn't seem to believe in holidays: up at five in the morning,
he's down at the port with a cognac, a coffee and a croissant by
six and when he returns to our little house in the hills he has
written an episode of *Rumpole* as well as bringing with him a
gleaming fresh fish from the market.' It was, Tennant felt, a proof
of John's liberal character that he never pointed out that he had
made an early start to the day while the rest of the party snoozed
on. 'John is impeccable in this – not a whiff of moral superiority,
no allusion to the morning's stint at all.' He did go to bed early,
however, while the others sat on the terrace under the stars,
consuming white wine and talking 'long after the progenitor of
Rumpole has gone downstairs to bed'.

Editors realized that the playwright-QC was never too busy to
turn his hand to any journalistic exercise. He could fill the Diary
column for the *New Statesman*, fulminating about pernicious

legislation – Official Secrets, libel, Obscene Publications – or the mad decisions of the Arts Council, or the rule banning women in trousers at El Vino's, or the baffling praise heaped on Henry Moore's 'unilluminating' lumps of stone. His strong suit was his legal tales and his digs at judges: 'Our law is administered by human beings as insecure, dominated by their childhood, and alarmed at their own sexuality as the rest of us.' Then Peter Crookston at the *Observer* magazine proposed a series called 'Mortimer's Meals Out', checking out the fashionable diners where Mick Jagger or Bob Dylan might be spotted, now that Alvaro's and the White Elephant were out of style. John always had a weakness, whatever the cost, for eating out at fashionable places full of famous faces. Langan's Brasserie – where the odious Peter Langan would always lurch towards him with 'Hello, you fucking four-eyed git' and then give him champagne on the house – had, John wrote, the timeless appeal of La Coupole; where else could you get bratwurst, hot potato salad and the great sustaining dishes of Alsace? Or hear 'the voice of a gin-sodden old negress singing the blues', which was in fact 'Mr George Melly, doing his act'?

After six weeks of troughing at the *Observer*'s expense John concluded that, although he was still fond of L'Etoile, Mon Plaisir and Khan's in Westbourne Grove, 'London restaurants are over-priced, snobbish and over-ambitious'. Unconvincingly, he said all he wanted now was 'a poached egg in front of the telly'. Harold Evans, editor of the *Sunday Times*, was so struck by these columns that he began wooing John, inviting the Mortimers to dinners in restaurants where, John observed, Harry would dart around taking his guests' orders on a notepad and then hand them to the waiter, until his wife-to-be Tina Brown apprised him of the correct procedure.

It was hard to miss the second series of *Rumpole* at the end of May 1979: Thames TV took half-page ads in national broadsheets. 'Rumpole is back! Rumpole is back!' screamed the *Daily Telegraph*'s headline. 'In this washed-out summer, can there be anything but a joyous welcome for the return of Rumpole?' The first plot was pretty thin stuff – a vicar on a shoplifting charge who, Rumpole discovered, was protecting his menopausal kleptomaniac sister. But again, it was Rumpole's overpowering personality that counted. Hilda, it transpired, had trapped Rumpole into matrimony (which was 'like pleading Guilty for an indefinite sentence without parole'). Rumpole's relationship with the sole fruit of their union, Nicky, was – at least until Nicky became a sociologist – John's with Clifford, father and son allied against She Who Must Be Obeyed, as they walked over Hampstead Heath, playing Sherlock Holmes and Watson.

Court procedures were supervised in scrupulous detail by Jennifer Oldland or Michael Grieve from Dr Johnson's Buildings. Genuine chambers issues were aired, such as resentment about partners' earnings, or disaffection with a clerk. (One partner, Aubrey Myerson, QC, was outraged by John's indiscretions.) Whenever the film crew arrived in the Temple, McKern would stump in to see John's clerks, signing photographs inscribed 'to my much more learned friends'. They had no objection to being portrayed as East End wide boys. 'Clerks always are,' they told me. 'Just as barristers are invariably shown as bumbling incompetents drinking in El Vino's. It was still one of the best take-offs of the law ever.'

Rumpole translated effortlessly to the page. The first story printed (in the *Observer*) was 'Rumpole and the Showfolk', in which our hero goes up north to Grimble, to defend an actress 'whose voice was ever soft, gentle and low, an excellent thing in woman', discovered backstage by the body of her husband with a smoking Smith & Wesson in her hand. Rumpole's former clerk, now in Grimble, asks, 'How are things down south?' and he replies, 'Down south? Much as usual. Barristers lounging about in the sun. Munching grapes to the lazy sounds of plucked guitars.' The first Penguin editions of *Rumpole* appeared, and the *Bookseller*'s resident sage Whitefriar, a.k.a. Eric Hiscock, called him 'one of the major comic characters in literature', already setting him alongside Sherlock Holmes and Jeeves and Wooster. John had found his money-spinner for his old age.

'I like murderers,' Rumpole said. 'They've usually done

whatever it is they needed to do, and they're in a peaceful state of mind, under lock and key, grateful for what I can do for them. I find they're usually rather charming people.' These words were John's own. But just as *Rumpole* took off, John played a part in an extraordinary murder trial in which the defendants could not be viewed in this sentimental way. It was a case of serial killing, the murderous spree by the 'mad butler' Alexander Hall and his accomplice, Michael Kitto.

Alexander Hall was a bisexual Glaswegian con man who worked as a butler for Margaret, Lady Hudson, widow of a Tory minister, in Dumfries. Visited by a former lover named David Wright, who helped himself to Lady Hudson's jewellery, Hall (who had been planning to do the same) shot Wright dead and buried his body in a shallow grave. He then joined the Knightsbridge household of Wright's employer, Walter Scott-Elliott, again as butler, and brought in his girlfriend Mary Coggle, alias 'Belfast Mary', a barmaid and prostitute, as cleaner. Coggle introduced Hall to a footman, Michael Kitto, who became Hall's lover and his accomplice in robbing the Scott-Elliotts' antiques-filled apartment.

The trio, surprised in their robbery by Mrs Scott-Elliott, panicked and smothered her to death with a pillow. The next day, Hall gave the frail eighty-two-year-old Mr Scott-Elliott a dose of drugged whisky, bundled him into a hired Ford Cortina (with his wife's body in the boot) and drove off, with Mary Coggle masquerading as the dead woman in a wig, mink coat and diamond ring. The quartet drove all the way to Scotland, stopping at various banks to clean out the Scott-Elliotts' accounts. Still passing off Coggle as Mrs Scott-Elliott, they rented a cottage on the Cumbrian coast and took the confused old man with them to the pub. In a village near Inverness they unloaded her body from the boot and threw it in a stream, and then strangled poor Mr Scott-Elliott and buried him under rhododendron bushes.

Back at their rented cottage, the two villains turned on 'Belfast Mary': Kitto pinned Coggle down while Hall bludgeoned her over the head with a poker. Her body too was flung into a stream, in Dumfriesshire. Then, when Hall's half-brother Donald, just out of prison, joined them, Hall and Kitto chloroformed him and drowned him in the bath. His body was thrown into the boot and driven to East Berwick.

In a seafront hotel, the killers met their Nemesis in the landlord, an amateur sleuth named Norman Wright. He was suspicious of Hall's claim that he was about to emigrate to Australia, and rang the police just as Hall and Kitto sat down to dinner. The police found Donald's corpse still in the car boot and took the two men to the local police station. Hall escaped, but was recaptured hours later. The pair were tried at the Old Bailey (not in Scotland, where Hall had hoped for a 'not proven' verdict) and when the judge passed sentence – 'You will go to prison for the rest of your natural life, and will never be released unless you are in the terminal stages of a fatal illness' – Hall's butlerish response was to stand erect and say, 'Thank you, sir.' He remained in Kingston Prison, Portsmouth, until his death, aged seventy-eight, in 2002.

John was defending Kitto – who also went to prison – from a seated position, since his leg was in a plaster cast. (At fifty-six, he had had his first fall: sustained when skipping downstairs to answer the door to his neighbour Joanna David, who was, he alleged, coming to confide in him about her love life with Edward Fox.) In defence of Kitto, John claimed that Kitto, a mere footman, had been entirely under the spell of the butler, whose personality was overpowering. But even Kitto clearly did not fit the category of charming, peaceful murderer, or the one in John's favourite Browning quotation – 'Our interest's on the dangerous edge of things/The honest thief, the tender murderer' – from *Bishop Blougram's Apology*.

In the same month he conducted the successful appeal on behalf of Blair Peach, the young teacher who died as a result of a single blow to the head during the Southall Riots of October 1979. John, acting for Peach's family and his common-law widow, appealed to Lord Widgery, the Lord Chief Justice, challenging the coroner's decision to sit without a jury despite strong reasons to view Peach's death as suspicious. This was a noted victory.

John's interest in the law may have been waning, but he was

still willing to seize the chance to perform in an exotic setting, where Penny could join him. So they went to Singapore, where the lone opposition candidate, J. B. 'Ben' Jeyaretnam, was being sued for libel by Lee Kuan Yew, the Cambridge-educated prime minister.

Mr Jeyaretnam's offence was to remark, while campaigning, on how very astute Lee Kuan Yew was in managing his personal fortunes. Lee Kuan Yew saw this as implying that he was corrupt. He had briefed the imposing Robert Alexander, QC, six-foot-six and basso profundo-voiced (who later won Jeffrey Archer half a million pounds in libel damages in the High Court in 1987). Bob Alexander started each day with a game of tennis with Penny, while John, still lame, was borne into court by rickshaw. In court, the two English lawyers faced one another. Alexander said, 'It was pure theatre. You would have to travel many miles and sit in many courts before you heard a contest like it.' John cross-examined Lee Kuan Yew for a whole day, fearlessly refusing to be intimidated, insisting that Mr Jeyaretnam's words could have been a tribute to Lee Kuan Yew's probity and integrity. Lee Kuan Yew was plainly rattled. But that night, the prime minister went home to what had been Government House and recharged his batteries. John and Penny, in celebratory mood, went out on the town and dined well in the company of Desmond Neill – he had played Northumberland to John's Richard II at the Dragon in 1936 – who turned up at their hotel and whisked them off to sample Singapore's night life. Next morning, John was frankly hung-over and not at his best; the refreshed prime minister dominated the proceedings and won easily, being awarded £35,000 in damages from a judge who was, all agreed, in his pocket.

Penelope had returned from her teaching stint at Boston in 1977. In 1979 she won the Whitbread award for her first volume of memoirs, *About Time* – a small masterpiece, covering her pre-John life, her childhood and first marriage, ending with her twenty-first birthday. She was now living in a ground-floor flat near Caroline and Julia in West Hampstead, with a sunny south-facing garden, where we met for the first time in May. At sixty her slender elegance, fine eyes and cheekbones were striking. America had almost claimed her, she said. But she wanted to be near her brood. Besides, she had suddenly seen England as if for the first time. She'd found a cottage in Gloucestershire ('Listed stone cottage in unspoiled village . . . ideal retreat for writer or artist, £26,000'). 'The kids thought, "She'll never settle down by herself," but it's the best thing that ever happened to me,' she said. She'd become an obsessive gardener and could no longer imagine living with anyone. 'I did it all my life,' she said, 'and now I think how awful it must be at my age to have a husband, because you must always be worried about when he'll DIE.' Penelope had continued to visit Turville Heath Cottage: Madelon, who was now living in London, would house-sit there with her husband when John and Penny went away. Penelope quite fell in love with John's thin, brown and singularly affectionate dog, Jackson. Journalists still sometimes persisted in asking John if he was the husband in *The Pumpkin Eater*. To Mark Amory, he had replied. 'Oh yes, I'm the husband all right – and all those other unpleasant husbands.'

'Love, the law, writing. I don't know which has occupied more of my time, although sometimes the three seem to have become inextricably intertwined.' John said this in a radio broadcast in March 1978, before an audience at Henley's little Kenton Theatre. He carried on saying those words for the next three decades. *With Great Pleasure*, the Radio 4 series, had asked him to record his favourite poems and stories, with readings by Isabel Dean and Jane Asher. The programme became the basis of *Mortimer's Miscellany*, the one-man show which he would perform (flanked by two actresses) a thousand times during the next thirty years, hardly altering the format at all.

He opened with John Wilkes's jaundiced view of the lawyer's profession. He then told the story of Churchill (looking '110 years old') coming to Harrow, and his father's tale of having proved adultery solely on the evidence of 'a pair of footprints upside down on the dashboard of an Austin Seven parked in Hampstead Garden

Suburb'. He recounted legal anecdotes, such as the drunken Irish tramp being told by Mr Justice Maude not to have 'even the teensiest weensiest dry sherry before dinner'. Edith Thompson's letter to her lover Frederick Bywaters, William Plomer's 'French Lisette', Rosalind's speech from *As You Like It*, Auden's 'Crack in the Teacup', Browning's 'A Toccata of Galuppi's' and Mrs Millamant 'dwindling into a wife' were all included. He quoted from Camus' *The Myth of Sisyphus*, with the phrase 'lucid indifference', the attitude John regarded as essential in a writer. To illustrate it he read the letter Byron wrote from Rome to his publisher John Murray, describing how he had watched three robbers being guillotined. Byron observed the slow procession to the scaffold, the heavy blow of the axe; the 'great terror and reluctance' with which the first robber died. 'My hand shook so that I could hardly hold the opera glass,' Byron wrote. 'I was close, but determined to see as one should see everything once, with attention.' This, John commented, was 'the perpetual attitude of the writer in the face of experience'. Then he recited Byron's 'So, we'll go no more a-roving, so late into the night'.

The audience gave an audible sigh of recognition when they heard C. P. Cavafy's 'The Barbarians', illustrating our pathetic need to invent barbarians, to maintain our enthusiasm for largely illusory political differences. Finally he came to religion. 'I can't stomach the idea of eternal life; nor can I forgive an omnipotent creator; but there is a religious point of view I can understand – the feeling I have when I am alone in my garden in the evenings, or awake at night, with the wind in the beechwoods and the long empty valley outside my window lit up by a storm, there is an experience which you might call religious, a being at one with nature, a sort of excited tranquillity which Wordsworth understood and is best expressed by Kirilov, the engineer in Dostoevsky's *The Possessed*.' He ended with Thomas Hardy's 'Afterwards', seeing himself as 'a man who used to notice such things'.

He tried out more of his set-piece anecdotes on *Quote . . . Unquote* on Christmas Day 1979. On the panel with Peter Cook, Sue MacGregor and Arthur Marshall, John easily identified lines from Kipling, Auden, Wilde, Wodehouse, Bishop Heber, St Francis of Assisi (Mrs Thatcher's mantra) and Lord Chief Justice Gordon Hewart's 'Justice should not only be done but should manifestly and undoubtedly be seen to be done'. Invited to bring along favourite stories, he related how a judge admonished two gentlemen, caught in a compromising situation under Waterloo Bridge: 'What makes it worse is that you chose to do it under one of the most *beautiful* bridges in London!' Finally he recounted how Emily, aged seven, asked what she wanted to be when she grew up, replied that she didn't know, but 'I know what I'm NOT going to be, and that's a member of the public.'

Emily, destined to be a performer, and decidedly not a member of the public, effortlessly manipulated her father: 'I was shy with everyone else, but a fiend with him.' In the mornings John would fetch her breakfast ('Get my egg, you bugger,' she would command) and drive her to Kensington High School in Upper Phillimore Gardens, where she made him park his red Mercedes round the corner because he was so much older than other dads. 'Children are so conservative,' she said. 'Only later do you realize that it's cool to be different.' He read aloud to her until she was fourteen (when she finally read *Great Expectations* for herself, recognizing her own ingratitude to her father in Pip) and he continued to write her school essays for years. He was indignant one term when she received the report: 'Emily is clearly intelligent, but her essays lack the vital spark of imagination.'

19. 'How are you with God?'

John had delivered his TV adaptation of *Brideshead Revisited* in the spring of 1978. 'I felt it was important that Evelyn Waugh should have his say,' he would later write. 'You may detest Mr Waugh, you may find him snobbish, half-heartedly homosexual and filled with sentimental religiosity. On the other hand, you may bless him as a brilliant and witty writer who faced difficult problems of faith and duty with commendable courage. But as an adaptor you must remain true to him, and that is what I tried to do.'

Brideshead's translation to the screen was long overdue. Waugh went to Hollywood in 1945, when MGM first proposed a film. In 1950 Graham Greene wrote a screenplay, but Waugh was now disenchanted with his novel and rewrote parts of it. After his death in 1966, his agent, A. D. Peters, insisted that a film was the family's preference. But eventually, in 1977, Granada Television secured the rights for £12,000, 'which', wrote his eldest son, Auberon, who had a one-fifth share of the royalties, 'after agent's deductions and income tax at the top rate, reduced this particular orphan's mite to about £700'.

The Waugh estate had the right to choose the adaptor and their choice was Alan Bennett. He agreed, then threw in the towel, daunted by the work involved. Their second choice was John Mortimer, who seemed ideal. He had even spent his Oxford days, like Sebastian Flyte, in Christ Church's Meadow Building. Asked for a 'close and faithful adaptation', John submitted his six scripts with 'a show of collaborative affability'. Then followed months of delay, during which time Derek Granger and the director, Michael Lindsay-Hogg, privately agreed that they were disappointed with the scripts. The first Oxford scenes were reasonably close to the original, but there were sequences of invented dialogue 'in a sub-Coward idiom'; Celia had become a Penelope Mortimer-like

character, and Mrs Beaver from *A Handful of Dust* appeared, deco-
rating Charles Ryder's studio; there was an embarrassing sex scene
where Julia was deflowered in front of the Marchmain fireplace; and Mrs Muspratt was present at Lord Marchmain's deathbed, saying, 'You've been a very naughty boy, Lord Marchmain.'
Sidney Bernstein, Granada chairman, voiced his dismay; and even
the German co-producers asked, 'Where are the Proustian
undertones?'

John was not best pleased when asked to rewrite the six episodes,
but he delivered his 'cursory' rewrites between January and March
1979. But even before this point, at Granger's Kensington flat, he
and Lindsay-Hogg had agreed to jettison his scripts and work
directly from Waugh's novel – that is, 'shoot the book'. Granger
suspected that John had had too much else on his plate (true) and
had polished off the scripts at speed. 'The adaptation of this very
remarkable novel,' in Granger's view, 'required a long, detailed
and time-consuming collaboration between the adaptor and the
creative team.' They hired Martin Thompson, a young writer from
the BBC. Thompson and Granger worked flat out to prepare the
first scripts, so that Lindsay-Hogg could start shooting on 1 May
1979, in Malta and Gozo, the locations used for Sebastian's North
African demise.

Then came a real hiatus. The Granada technicians went on
strike, from 9 August 1979 until 28 October. When the production
was remounted in November, Lindsay-Hogg was committed to
direct in Hollywood and on Broadway, and had to bow out. A
new director arrived, a twenty-eight-year-old Granada trainee
named Charles Sturridge. His television experience had hitherto
been with documentaries and *Coronation Street*, but he was highly
suitable for *Brideshead*: a Roman Catholic, eldest of seven children,
a former infant thespian, educated at Stonyhurst and Oxford, where
he read English. He was entirely in favour of 'realizing' the novel,
as the French say, using Waugh's original words. Sir Denis Forman
of Granada conducted the renegotiations, expanding the series to
eleven episodes (thirteen hours) rather than five episodes (six hours).
'Would you rather have six wooden balls or eleven jewel-encrusted

Fabergé eggs?' Forman asked the Germans, to justify the escalating expense. Obviously, this change rendered John's six-part scripts unusable anyway.

Instead, as Granger said, they 'hugged' the book. It was a conscientious, fastidious and rewarding process and the result was that, with the exception of a few invented scenes, the scripts were by Evelyn Waugh. The writing team could not claim anything for themselves except creative fidelity. The cast occasionally joined in: Diana Quick, playing Julia Flyte, Jeremy Irons as Charles Ryder, Anthony Andrews playing Sebastian and Nickolas Grace as Anthony Blanche could suggest lines from the book.

But if they never used John's scripts, why did John's name stay on the credits? Call it cowardice. Granada's deal had stipulated that the Waugh estate must choose the writer; and since the A. D. Peters literary agency represented both the Waugh estate and John Mortimer, Granger feared that if they turned down John's scripts, the deal would be off. 'Perhaps it was reprehensible of us, indeed morally lax, to have gone ahead with the deception,' Granger said. 'But to have chucked John Mortimer's scripts would, I'm certain, have meant chucking the entire project. We all felt this was too high a price to pay.'

In late summer 1979, John heard that his work was being altered, and his film agent Anthony Jones rang Granger, requesting a viewing of the material Lindsay-Hogg had shot so far. Accompanied by Jones, John had a private screening in Soho. The scenes included Sebastian's demise, shot in Malta; Nancy Tallboys's glamorous party; Anthony Blanche's dinner at Thame; and the picnic scene under the tree at Brideshead, all devoid of dialogue, but with Ryder's voiceover. Granger kept away, fearing an angry reaction. But there was no response whatever. Clearly John approved of what he saw, and made no fuss.

The strike proved a blessing in disguise. Brideshead was a bigger beast than anyone foresaw. Luckily, apart from another hiatus while Jeremy Irons fulfilled his commitment to star in *The French Lieutenant's Woman*, all the key stars remained available: Olivier to play Lord Marchmain, John Gielgud as Ryder's father, Claire

Bloom as Lady Marchmain, Stephane Audran as Lord M's mistress and Mona Washbourne as Nanny. Shooting resumed at stately homes around England, in Oxford, London and Venice, entirely on location; it eventually took nearly two years and cost £10 million, or £750,000 per hour. No expense was spared, down to a Colefax and Fowler canopy, specially woven in Lyons, for a four-poster bed.

At Castle Howard (Brideshead), the ebullient George Howard, BBC chairman-to-be, played honorary props master, delving into a lumber room to rustle up a duchess's hatbox when necessary. Rex Mottram's diamond-studded tortoise and its understudy both went missing on the day they shot the tortoise scene. Sturridge worked to the point of exhaustion and fell in love with his future wife, Phoebe Nicholls (Lady Cordelia Flyte), who had played one of the children in *The Pumpkin Eater*. When the last scenes, shot on the *QE2*, were wrapped, the crew played 'Land of Hope and Glory' and let off rockets and showered Sturridge with Silly String party-poppers.

Brideshead's scale, its luxuriance and opulence, made it a televisual phenomenon. And although John was handsomely recompensed – he was paid for thirteen hours of scripts – consider how awkward it was for him to be on the receiving end of the plaudits, in perpetuity, for a work which in style and substance could have been his, but in fact was not. Whenever *Brideshead* was discussed, he fell into the habit of purring modestly and murmuring, 'It was Evelyn Waugh's script really', or 'I don't feel deeply involved in Brideshead. I think it's all due to Evelyn Waugh if it's a success.' 'It wasn't in any way John's fault,' as Granger emphasized. 'Nobody ever actually told him we weren't using his scripts. And we felt we had to have his name.' By 1994, John wrote in his memoirs: 'Evelyn Waugh remained where he should have been, at the centre of the story. Almost everything in the scripts came from Brideshead.'

The *Brideshead* episode coincided with delays to both John's *Rumpole* series and his Shakespeare plays. So he had turned with relief to something over which he could take sole charge, 'without producers or actors': his memoirs. In April 1980, he repaid the Grove Press's advance of $500 for *My Early Years*, which was ten years overdue anyway. Weidenfeld offered a much better deal: £28,000, payable in four £7,000 instalments, including one 'on producing evidence of progress', for delivery in June 1981.

How to write about oneself without seeming intolerably smug or phonily humble? The classic English memoirists' style, used by T. C. Worsley and Cyril Connolly, features a baffled hero bumbling through life among relations and schoolmasters of Dickensian scale and eccentricity, lightly dismissing personal accomplishments with an engaging modesty. This John adopted. Even modesty, he knew, 'can become a kind of showing off'; but he would deal with himself 'as someone that everything happened to'. *Clinging to the Wreckage*, subtitled *A Part of Life*, was shaped into stories, anecdotes, portraits, only vaguely chronological and, as he admitted, partly fictionalized. He would end the story in 1970, with *A Voyage Round My Father* and meeting Penny. When it came out, he declared that his life up to the age of fifty was now lost to him. He had made himself public property, 'just as I lost my father when I wrote that play about him. You cease to be real and become a character.'

'I'm writing 13 Rumpole radio plays, a couple of scripts, an autobiography. So you see life goes on exactly as usual,' John wrote light-heartedly to Jeremy, who had left his job at the publishers Sidgwick & Jackson to go travelling in South America. John's bulletins, addressed to Quito, Cusco, Bogotá or Bolivia, made John feel he was 'putting a note in a bottle and tossing it over the side of a ship, to drift upon some hot foreign shore . . .' Like any parent writing to gap-year young, he stressed how dull and provincial life was at home, how grim the weather. He envied Jeremy (who now wore a beard and resembled 'a studious Ché Guevara') his adventure in a Graham Greeneish world, his courage to live 'without the drug of boring work'. 'Life slips away quickly in a routine – and you are storing up so many memories and such material.' By contrast, his own achievements were humdrum.

'Unexpectedly I won the Writer of the Year award at BAFTA for *Rumpole* and had to hobble up on the huge stage of Wembley Stadium to get it from Princess Anne, who said, "You must have a lot of material to write lots more."'

Their life, he claimed, was deeply domestic and contented, while the state of the nation induced gloom: 'huge unemployment, a fragmented Labour Party . . . It also rains most of the time and, as usual, it's the worst summer for 200 years.' The siege of St James's Square and the gun-battle to rescue the Iranian hostages in May had turned the police and SAS into heroes. They'd been to *Madame Butterfly*, *Tosca*, *Fidelio* and Michael Frayn's play *Look Look*, which flopped. 'Everyone' was dying: Peter Sellers, Ken Tynan. Penny had stopped working, John reported, and was having tennis lessons. (She had been working for the literary agent Deborah Rogers, a job she was good at, only stopping because John needed her to type what he produced every day. He didn't really want a working wife.) All Penny's girl friends 'seem to be falling out with their husbands', John reported to Jeremy, 'and come to stay in distress.' 'Oh dear,' he added. 'How dull it all sounds.'

His court appearances were now highly selective. One was in a Law Society tribunal, defending a solicitor (who'd done a prison stretch for forgery) from being struck off. He wrote to the judge, asking for a letter saying that the solicitor wasn't so bad after all, and wouldn't do it again. 'And the judge said he'd write what I wanted, provided I wrote a letter congratulating Mrs Whitehouse on her CBE,' John told Jeremy, 'so I had to grit my teeth.'

What John does not mention is that he had a lucrative new commission from the *Sunday Times*: ten pieces a year for 'a terrific lot of money – it would be too like boasting to say how much,' as he later told a reporter. (It was £30,000.) In an era when the newspaper interview flowered, John proved a master of the form. His method was impressionistic – to give an account of how it felt to pass an hour in the subject's company. Among his interviewees, predominantly male and invariably famous, were Malcolm Muggeridge, Graham Greene, Enoch Powell, David Hockney, Laurence Olivier, John Gielgud, Rab Butler, Roy Jenkins, Mick

Jagger, Michael Foot, Ken Livingstone, Arthur Scargill, Cardinal Hume, Archbishop Robert Runcie and Catherine Cookson. Without shorthand or a tape recorder, but armed with a pencil, a playwright's ear and a phenomenal memory, he could pinion people in a single phrase. Here is the novelist Angela Carter: 'A slightly distraught, greying, pretty, high-voiced lady, in her denim skirt, seated at her table in her cluttered Clapham kitchen, smiled at me with a certain tolerance. "Really," said Miss Carter, "I can't see how anyone could fail to like the Marquis de Sade."'

Having found Mick Jagger in a Madrid hotel, he opened with, 'You must have got on well with your father.' 'No,' said Mick. 'Not really.' Jagger's face was 'rutted, deeply lined, like the face of a jockey or a sailor, forever up against a high wind.' He concentrated on Jagger's arrest in 1967 for possession of amphetamines, bought legally in Italy: the judge at Chichester, passing sentence, had quoted the line from *Julius Caesar*, 'You blocks, you stones, you worse than senseless things'. 'Do you believe in immortality?' John asked. Jagger: 'What a question to throw me in the middle of the World Cup!'

John liked politicians to have a cultural bent. Michael Foot recited Byron and possessed all twelve volumes of his letters. Denis Healey collected rare books, knew about opera and Russian films, and was 'one of the few politicians who seems able to make a joke'. (He got chummy with Healey and they remained friends.) He took to Enoch Powell's 'marvellously unpredictable mind' and dry wit. Powell, who pronounced gibberish with a hard g, told him he no longer played the clarinet because 'I don't like things which interfere with one's heart strings. It doesn't do to waken longings that can't be fulfilled.' Georges Simenon, whom he visited at home in Switzerland, agreed with John that 'criminals are ordinary people like you and me' and told him about the hundreds of women he had made love to, and the seventy-two Maigrets he had written, each in seven days flat.

The question John always flung at people, especially at churchmen, was one which genuinely perplexed him: their relationship with God. If God existed, John was sure he wouldn't like him. As

Macduff cried, when his children were murdered: 'Did heaven look on / And would not take their part?' Why would an omnipotent God permit the deaths of children, and the Holocaust? Archbishop Runcie said, 'I am an agnostic about that.' Cardinal Hume confessed, 'In this world I can't understand it.' Muggeridge gave the answer John most approved: that God was a great dramatist, creating tragedy as well as comedy. (But 'to entertain whom, exactly?') Graham Greene reminded John that neither of them would have to wait too long to find out whether God did exist. But for a writer, belief in God was an advantage, said Greene: 'I've always felt it was having no belief that makes the characters in Virginia Woolf so paper-thin.'

In the Stygian gloom of Tony Benn's study, John opened his interview with the question of belief. The ensuing dialogue illustrated Benn's habit of diverting the agenda. 'Christianity?' Benn started. 'You know the bishops banned Tyndale's translation of the Bible. They didn't want the people to read Christ's social message.'

'Yes, but you were confirmed in Westminster Abbey. Do you . . .'

'My father's beliefs came down from the Dissenters,' Benn said, adding, 'My mother is a student of theology.' At eighty-four she had just made a TV programme on the prophet Amos. When the Algerian politician Ben Bella visited Benn, they discussed the socialist basis of the Islamic revival. On went Benn, dropping names: 'Reinhold Niebuhr, the theologian, was a friend of my family,' and so on. At the seventh time of asking, John was blunt: 'So you don't believe in God?' Finally Benn gave in. 'Put it like that,' he replied, 'no.'

Benn's moral fervour, as John said, would exclude him as a future prime minister: the British public would prefer 'some wetter, less formidable, jollier Queen Margaret the Second' (as happened when Tony Blair was elected, sixteen years later). Benn was one of the few surviving interviewees who, at eighty-two, could consult his diary and read me his note that on 1 September 1981 he had met John Mortimer, 'the liberal barrister who has often bravely espoused unpopular causes'; and that he was 'agreeable and friendly'.

With the ancient Lord Denning, John mentioned that he might have stood for Parliament once. Labour or Conservative? 'Oh, I never got round to thinking about that.'

John visited Olivier on the set of *Brideshead* at Castle Howard. A writer on a film location, he reflected, is 'always in the way, standing on a cable, vainly trying to hear a line of his dialogue that no one has bothered to change'. They went to the local pub for lunch. He had tea at the Ritz with Muggeridge, Campari with Runcie at Lambeth Palace, Guinness from the bottle with Hockney. Roy Jenkins told him he drank mostly cheap wine and liked Tesco fishcakes. William Golding poured him Chassagne-Montrachet. Graham Greene offered Scotch in hotel tooth mugs. With Gielgud he had steak and red wine in the Thames TV canteen. Rab Butler said, 'You'd like a little whisky? My wife's not here and I've never really got the hang of boiling a kettle.'

What distinguished him from more merciless newspaper interviewers was that he allowed people's statements to rest without comment, especially if he disagreed with them, however misguided or absurd. It was a courtroom habit: 'exposure without denunciation'; let the witness damn himself. The nearest he came to deliberate damnation was quoting the ghastly lyrics of *Sweeney Todd*, the musical ('how could people possibly like that sort of thing?') and then remarking that its producer, Hal Prince, who wore 'sharply pressed jeans', 'looked frequently at his watch, and as often at the clock on the wall'.

Few subjects turned down the *Sunday Times*'s approach on John's behalf (he hated ringing people himself), but one who did say no was Indira Gandhi, 'which is rather boring and defensive of the old vulture,' he wrote to Jeremy, especially after he and Penny had dined at Stonor with their neighbour, the eccentric Dowager Lady Camoys, along with His Excellency the Nepalese Ambassador, in preparation for their forthcoming trip to India.

John told me at the time that he never spent more than an hour on his interview, followed by an hour forming them into little playlets. (As a rival practitioner who always took rather longer, I found this slightly galling.) He wrote with apparent fidelity to manner and tone, so what appeared seemed verbatim. Magnus Linklater and Don Berry, his editors at the *Sunday Times*, awaited the delivery of each Mortimer interview with undiluted pleasure, as John would flirt with the blonde secretary and tell them gossipy tales about his subjects, their horrible taste in décor, etc. If away on a book tour, he would telephone his interview to a copy-taker, an experience which, as every reporter knows, involves hearing sighs of boredom at the end of the line, or the words 'Is there much more of this?' 'I'd rather face the Court of Appeal,' John said, 'than phone copy over to a newspaper.'

In the summer of 1980 his own travels were, unlike Jeremy's, 'timid': driving through France to a crumbling Nabokovian hotel on a lake in the Haute-Savoie, picking up Emily, who was staying near Toulon with the Craig-Halls, then joining Robert and Celestia Fox at Le Nid du Duc (while Tony Richardson was in America making a film with Jack Nicholson), where the ensemble gathered were a bit too 'Hoorayish' for John's liking. They lunched with Graham Greene in the Félix au Port café at Antibes, before John left to fly to the Edinburgh Festival. At the Assembly Rooms, with fellow playwrights, John spoke against censorship. In the National Gallery of Scotland, he ran into Dr Jonathan Miller. 'He knew everything about every picture, and told me, "Edinburgh is the great centre of civilization, the Venice of the north. Have you read the novels of Walter Scott? Unless you've read *Weir of Hermiston* you can't know anything about Scotland." And I said, "Well, I don't know much about Edinburgh, and even less about Walter Scott, but I do know that *Weir of Hermiston* is by Robert Louis Stevenson." Dr Miller was totally unfazed.'

What took John to Edinburgh was the James McTaggart Memorial Lecture at the Television Festival, when he eloquently defended ITV's controversial 'faction' film, *Death of a Princess*, for which Penelope was credited as 'script consultant' despite having resigned from the project, claiming later in the *New Statesman* that 'rumour and opinion somehow came to be presented as fact' and the audience was 'conned'. The film had caused a diplomatic rift with Saudi Arabia. But deploying his favourite rhetorical tactic, John made light of the offence to Islam and diverted attention from the contemporary case to the historical precedent. Had not the Old Testament, *The Iliad*, the Icelandic sagas and Shakespeare all mixed fact and fiction? Shakespeare had dared to show Richard III unfavourably as a physically handicapped royal, possibly causing offence to the Plantagenet family. Shaw's *St Joan* might have offended the susceptibilities of devout Catholics. And the Inquisition was conducted by men who burned people at the stake from the highest possible motives, 'which we should all respect – particularly if we have valuable trade agreements with the Holy See'. His ringing conclusion was destined for reuse twenty years later in the context of Islamic terrorism: 'In saying that the worst crimes against humanity are committed from sincere religious motives, did not *Death of a Princess*, whether fact or fiction, tell us the truth?'

Having collected Penny from France, he flew on to Florida for the shooting of *Rumpole's Return*. Leo McKern had turned down a third *Rumpole* series – he said Rupert Davies had got type-cast as Maigret and he feared the same would happen to him (as it did) – but he agreed to a single two-hour drama, *Rumpole's Return*. Alongside a newspaper story about McKern's doubts, headlined 'Rumpole – McKern's life sentence?', John scrawled in his scrapbook a bitter annotation: 'Thanks a lot!' with an arrow pointing to the words 'Rumpole, for whom of course John Mortimer *also deserves some credit* . . .' 'People often treated Leo as if he'd invented the character,' John told me. 'And he thought I got too much of the credit. Especially when I got the BAFTA. He always dithered about another series.' 'Leo, old darling, dither no more,' one critic wrote. 'Your viewing public needs you.'

John had already been to Miami that year, at the *Radio Times*'s invitation, to watch televised trials in action. Florida had more citizens on Death Row than any other state. The piece he wrote is one of his funniest and best observed, and it inspired the scenario for *Rumpole's Return*. Rumpole, having lost ten cases, visits his son Nicky in Florida. But he hates the sunshine, which makes him feel like an orange; he is homesick for the rain outside Temple tube station, and rushes back when Phyllida Trant alerts him to a 'lovely little murder' that raises sticky questions concerning blood, his speciality. John and McKern were photographed together, burnished by sun, portly and smiley in a palm-fringed pool. McKern, John said, would make merry with his glass eye, which he would remove and deposit for a jape in the spaghetti bolognese, causing waiters to faint. John's hopes that 'in the mosquito-ridden, geriatric-filled, hurricane-battered Key Biscayne' Jeremy would materialize from the South American jungle were happily fulfilled.

He was soon back on Old Bailey duty, calling Peter Blake as witness when he defended two men on a charge of selling fake Victorian photographs; and conducting his last obscenity cases. One of these depended on whether pornographic videos came within the Obscene Publications Act of 1959, which had been drafted before video technology existed. A Court of Appeal was summoned during the summer vacation, to rule that videos did come within the act. But the case against the video-makers collapsed. The theatre, despite the liberalized censorship laws, still remained vulnerable to Mrs Whitehouse. Howard Brenton's National Theatre play *The Romans in Britain* contained the attempted rape of a druid by a Roman soldier. The Obscene Publications squad stepped in and the GLC threatened to withhold part of the National Theatre's grant. John told the board (on which he had sat for the past eleven years) he was sure the play could not be prosecuted under the Theatres Act 1968: 'It would not induce anything in anybody except feelings of extreme horror and revulsion' – adding, 'Keep right on to the end of the woad.'

But it was prosecuted, its defence conducted by Jeremy Hutchinson and Geoffrey Robertson, before a judge whose expertise was in a branch of Admiralty law known amusingly enough as bottomry. The case collapsed when Hutchinson graphically demonstrated that the prosecution's witness, a Mr Graham Ross-Cornes, might, from the back of the stalls, have thought he had seen an erect penis, when in fact it was merely the actor's protruding thumb. The prosecution was withdrawn (*nolle prosequi*) and the charade had to be re-enacted before the Attorney-General, Sir Michael Havers, who had an eye infection, making him wink uncontrollably: Robertson found it 'hard to tell whether he was trying to pick you up'. Hutchinson's hilarious *coup de théâtre* with his gesturing thumb entered the Mortimer repertoire.

John's workaholic repute was now combined with a serious lunching habit: long, gossipy lunches when he held forth, 'spread out like a benign Michelin Man', like some eighteenth-century figure, the fierce liberal with the red spotted handkerchief in his breast pocket, championing the weak and persecuted, denouncing the prison system, condemning the interfering busybodies of the arts. Journalists queued to hear him amble through his favourite version of his life, from schooldays to wartime – 'the most exciting period of my life. Everyone's husband was away.' He was good company, and good copy.

Penny, in her thirty-fifth year, was at a loss to know why she felt lonely and neglected, and somehow guilty, because on the face of it she seemed to have everything, including a glittering dinner held at the Garrick for her birthday. 'Women always know when things are going on,' she said in long retrospect. From the beginning she had had her suspicions, when John was away in London all day; how, if they were so poor that she had to make curtains and do the typing, was John lunching and dining, and with whom? But whenever she tried to address him about her dark thoughts, she was told she was paranoiac, ridiculous, mad: 'so you begin to think you are'. (Hence her anger when the truth about John's little infidelities emerged, much later.) What was she to make of a phone call from a *Daily Express* reporter, 'We hear your marriage is in trouble'? She knew about at least one old flame, the wife of an actor, because John left his customary trails – a photograph, a note – to be found by Penny in his chambers when she called to collect the mail. And she knew there were rumours – in fact unfounded – about at least one actress in the *Rumpole* series, and about his producer, and anyone whose interest in him seemed to venture further than the professional. It was always John's habit to give lunch to his prettiest associates, enjoying the sensation of the 'possibility of sex' that hovered over such occasions. He described this once to a rather plain young woman journalist, adding tactlessly, 'And you too my dear', gently patting her hand. Wherein, she wondered, lay his famous charm?

In 1981 there was 'the scarf incident', when Penny found in John's pocket the receipt for a silk foulard he had bought for a public relations girl he'd met at the Edinburgh Festival, who had become one of his lunchtime indulgences at the White Elephant or Boulestin. Sometimes, a Penguin colleague would send John home with gifts of children's books for Emily, which Penny flung aside with great force.

Penguin's office at that time was a modern block on the less trendy end of the King's Road, close by the World's End council block where Christine Keeler (shortly to be one of his interviewees) lived. John would arrive in subfusc and take his editors to Alvaro's 'to discuss, over lunch, the finer points of grammar,' as one of them said coyly. 'There is something about the difference between the comma and the semicolon which is very seductive.' John's letters to her, in Penguin's archives, were signed off 'with lots and lots of love' and 'Miss you. J'.

All authors since the 1980s have been summoned to 'away-days', to literary festivals and book signings; and few authors were more amenable to doing the publicity circuit than John. He was uproarious company on these excursions, his fellow author Jilly Cooper reported. He never turned down a request to attend sales conferences where he might woo the reps with his racontage. To York he would go, to Brighton and Le Touquet. In a later novel, John featured an author's flirtatious relationship with a publicity girl called Brenda Bodkin, their long lunches with people from Millstream's (i.e. Waterstone's) bookshops, drinking litres of Australian Long Flat Red, with screams of laughter and the vague promise of post-prandial dalliances, especially when away from home. He adored being flanked by solicitous young women whose duty is to keep their authors happy. John had constantly to reassure Penny with declarations: 'I knew there was a you somewhere, and from the minute we met I knew it was you.' *Au fond*, he meant it. But as he approached his sixtieth birthday, surrounded by willing women, he could resist (like Oscar) everything except temptation. 'I suppose I was greedy,' he replied when asked, 'and selfish.' As he was approaching his sixtieth birthday, the availability of willing women proved irresistible.

Rumpole was fulfilling all John's hopes: he was not a mere tele-character, however magisterially embodied by McKern. Five years after his conception he had been fast-tracked into a literary classic, 'a national institution', 'our modern John Bull'. Lawyers classed the books alongside A. P. Herbert's *Misleading Cases* and Theo Mathew's *Forensic Fables*. David Pannick, QC, placed Rumpole among the great barristers of literature, plying his trade like Dickens's Sergeant Buzfuz, surrounded by wickedly accurate cari-catures from legal London. Judge Stephen Tumim aligned Rum-pole not only with Sherlock Holmes and Bertie Wooster but with Father Brown, Captain Grimes and Flashman.

In America too, Scott Turow extolled the 'renegade spirit' which made defence lawyers the white hats of courtroom drama. American tourists would soon flock to Dr Johnson's Buildings, to be told 'This is where the creator of *Rumpole of the Bailey* sits.' And Graham Greene wrote from Antibes to say he'd planned to read the new Rumpole piecemeal, 'rationing them out for my enjoy-ment', but had devoured it in two days '& have nothing left for Christmas reading. The book arrived at a rather depressing & worrying time & the stories worked wonders on my spirits.'

Rumpole's worldwide impact was gratifyingly obvious when John and Penny made their first trip down under in the spring of 1981. Invited to a conference on porn in New Zealand, and en route to Bali and Delhi, they also took in Sydney, Melbourne and Adelaide. John was fêted everywhere. Oz took to John, and he took to Oz. Richard Neville invited him to his slot on ABC TV. In the green room he watched fellow performers, who included a gurning Bruce Forsyth and a lady who demonstrated how card tables could kill you by snapping shut on your feet. Finally it was John's turn. 'Are you allowed to say orgasm on this show?' he whispered to Neville. 'Oh, yes,' said Neville, 'and clitoris too. But don't be too explicit.' His jokes about judges, it was reported, 'made the ladies in the audience burst into such spontaneous laughter that the flashing Applause signs couldn't keep up'.

Home from Australia, John defended one of his last murderers at Winchester Crown Court. A lorry driver named Asher, who – John told the jury – had been a devoted husband and a loving father, had strangled his wife in the bathroom after she admitted to an affair, and buried her naked body under a road. In Asher's defence John said he had worked seven days a week, often leaving home at 5 a.m. and returning to look after his two children, never taking a holiday, and the couple 'had sex only four or five times a year'. 'There will never be a day in his life when he doesn't regret deeply what he has done to a person he loved,' John declared. He was no danger to anybody else. Mrs Asher's family bore the husband no grudge; his father-in-law had offered to stand bail for him. Asher was duly found not guilty of murder, but guilty of manslaughter. Tearful relatives hugged and patted him on the back when, on 8 June, he 'walked free', another victory.

John and Penny had arrived back at Turville Heath to find their house taken over for Thames TV's filming of *A Voyage Round My Father*. Alvin Rakoff, producer-director, had given Thames a list of three possible leading actors: McKern, Olivier or Guinness, and was told, 'Get Olivier.' So the frail Olivier, who had just died as Lord Marchmain, died again as Clifford – watched by John, as he had watched his father die, in the bed where he now slept, overlooking the garden Clifford had created. 'It seemed to me . . . a metaphor of a writer's life,' John wrote later. 'You live through a terrible private experience which you reinvent for artificial lights and actors and then give it away in public. I don't know if I did justice to my father's memory . . . or whether I diminished it. I really do not know.' The production was destined to enhance the reputations of everyone involved: Olivier, Rakoff and, above all, John.

He wrote, during these years, many more adaptations – Rattigan's *Cause Célèbre* was one – most never seen. But one was screened while he was away: his dramatization of *Unity*, the David Pryce-Jones biography of Hitler's acolyte Unity Mitford. Pryce-Jones thought the film 'quite brilliant'. Shot in Scotland, it dealt with one month in the life of Unity Valkyrie Mitford just before the outbreak of war. Lesley-Ann Down, a great beauty, was memorably loathsome in the part; Julian Barnes said he could imagine her, had she not shot herself, 'running a lampshade factory with the best of them'.

To dramatize characters he found repellent was one thing; to defend them in court was sometimes harder. 'A defence barrister feels protective of his clients,' as John said, 'however ghastly they are.' His next client was a man who worked for the Euthanasia Society, Exit, assisting suicides. 'Their organiser,' John told Jeremy in a letter, 'turned out to be a sinister looking lady in green glasses who apologised for a bad cold. I said I hoped it didn't carry her off before she had a decent chance to commit suicide.' At the Old Bailey John's client in the Exit trial was 'an awful toothless old man in a bobble hat named Lyons who went round with "placcy bags", whisky and sleeping pills. He would tell people, "Hurry up and die because I've got another two to do before lunchtime."' John was amazed that the judge took a liking to Lyons and allowed him bail on the grounds that while he was on remand in Brixton his tapes of G&S operas had been stolen. After a long and depressing trial, Lyons was acquitted, but the Exit organizer went to prison. John did believe that people should be allowed to help others end their lives, he told me, 'if someone is living in inoperable pain and misery. But having done many probate actions, I know how easy it is to victimize some old granny who is just a nuisance; I think it's quite dangerous.'

While John was thus preoccupied at the Old Bailey, *Brideshead* was screened, from 12 October 1981. The effect on John's reputation was predictable. He was forced to stress, time and again, the screenplay's fidelity to Waugh. Just as the Royal Shakespeare Company's ten-hour *Nicholas Nickleby* (which he had lately seen) was not a play but 'a book in the theatre', so *Brideshead* was 'a book on television', he said. He didn't take credit for it. His duty had been to keep himself well out of it, unlike some adapters (he added sniffily), who, having no body of original work, 'think they have a creative part to play in the adaptation. That's always a mistake.' 'Adapting is like being a barrister. You try to do your best for your client. It isn't my work, it's Mr Waugh's, and I hope he has a big success with it.'

A big success Mr Waugh did have. Critics wallowed in superlatives. *Brideshead* was a shimmering, shining, magical, monumental splendour. It made Nancy Banks-Smith wish she could 'watch the whole thing in one disgusting 13-hour gulp and be satisfyingly sick'. She added, 'All have done well and all will get prizes but I am particularly grateful to John Mortimer for his remarkable fidelity to Waugh.' *The Times* hailed John for being 'writer enough himself' to retain Waugh's prose: 'a triumph of beauty, fidelity and relevant embellishment'. 'He has cut a little, rearranged some more, but complete passages of dialogue and description are transcribed verbatim,' wrote Peter Ackroyd. 'This was not laziness: it was art.'

Evelyn Waugh's son Auberon, or Bron, took 'an almost physical pleasure in the lavishness and expense' – exactly the feeling the novel was intended to produce. He could not object to a syllable of John's 'slavish' adaptation. (He demurred only at the prettiness of Anthony Andrews, who reminded him of a California bumboy.) But Bron, commissioned by a US television magazine to write a piece ('He Who "Wrote" Brideshead'), subjected John to a long cross-examination over lunch at Boulestin in Covent Garden. For American readers Bron introduced this 'genial, easygoing man with a cheerful, almost amateurish manner', at the pinnacle of three professions, who commanded record fees. How much John was paid for *Brideshead*, Bron did not inquire. 'All concerned with that production had watched in horror as the budget soared above its original target . . .'

Behind Bron's inquisition was puzzlement. His father's High

Tory Catholicism was worlds away from John's beliefs. John was devoted to comedy, and took the side of the underdog, with an aversion to 'imposing a code of behaviour upon individual and unpredictable human beings'. A beautiful philosophy for a lawyer, Bron declared, but how did a liberal atheist reconcile this with admiration for Waugh's 'textbook of Catholic High Toryism'? 'I don't see it like that,' replied John. 'I see it as a sort of *Cinderella* story, like *Jane Eyre* or *Rebecca*.' John added that he found Ryder's father very sympathetic, 'rather like my own father'.

'Whenever John Mortimer talks about himself,' wrote Bron with some exasperation, 'or about Rumpole or almost any of his characters – the conversation always returns to his father, who died nearly twenty years ago. I wanted to steer him back to *Brideshead Revisited*, if possible.' It was impossible. Bron tried again: Evelyn intended the Catholicism in *Brideshead* to be seen as an ultimate truth – surely just the system of 'established rules' that John Mortimer deplored. 'Oh, I like the religious aspect,' breezed John. 'I think the religion is very interesting and moving.' Which part? persisted Bron. 'Any belief which makes you give up what you want in life. I find that very sympathetic.'

At this stage, Bron recorded, his guest was tackling the roast duck in its own juice with 'gratifying cries of delight'. Had he often given up what he wanted in life? 'Very rarely,' replied John, 'very rarely.' (Here John gave one of his 'engaging giggles'.) Perhaps it was the idea of a man's giving up a woman that appealed? 'Like Rumpole, Mortimer regards those of his fellow men who err on the side of male chauvinism with an indulgent eye.' Charles Ryder was a terrific male chauvinist, John agreed, 'which I don't mind, I don't mind at all.' John's first wife, Bron reminded readers, had pioneered the feminist novel about housewifely angst and maternal depression. 'Anybody who has read Mrs Mortimer's novels may understand why Rumpole spends so much time at the wine bar.' Afterwards John left Bron with the Boulestin bill for £92 and motored off to Bristol. (But he wrote to Bron later, saying he was appalled at the price of their lunch and he hoped the magazine had paid up.)

There was another matter which exercised commentators – what Peter Ackroyd called the 'oblique but real homosexuality' in *Brideshead*. Were Sebastian and Charles lovers? Jeremy Irons replied yes. John (who had told Bron he had had to conceal his girlfriend at Oxford, homosexuality being the fashion) gave the same answer as he had about Shakespeare and the Earl of Southampton: he didn't believe that Charles and Sebastian were involved in a homosexual relationship, 'though I do believe they are in love. Certainly Charles Ryder is not inherently homosexual any more than Evelyn Waugh was. They were just going through that English process of growing up.'

'Apparently,' John told Bron in his letter, 'Lord Sebastian look-alikes are being judged in the streets of San Francisco; an event which your father could hardly have foreseen.'

Ten million viewers had been transfixed by a television milestone guaranteed to win awards, including one, received by John, from the American Alliance for Gay Artists.

20. No More Moaning of the Bar

In the second TV version of *A Voyage Round My Father*, Lord Olivier, aged seventy-five, was – like McKern as Rumpole – utterly in character as Clifford. Olivier was quite frail, and could be cantankerous and forgetful. But doddering about in straw hat drowning earwigs, delivering advice to his son about sex ('pretty uphill work, if you want my opinion'), making random comments ('After you've been troubled by a wasp, don't you love a fly?'), he was remarkably convincing. He brought mischief and danger to the role: the sort of man who can weep with laughter at his own jokes but also erupt, at the slightest provocation, into an imitation of King Lear abandoned in the storm, at once tyrannical and vulnerable.

'I've seldom had any real success,' John said, 'that hasn't been to do with the law or my father or both.' A view borne out by the two works which emerged in the spring of 1982: *Clinging to the Wreckage*, John's most widely read volume of memoirs, came hard on the heels of *A Voyage Round My Father*, watched by a television audience of millions for the second time on 2 March.

Elizabeth Sellars was docile, anxious Kathleen; Jane Asher sharply intelligent and iron-willed as Penelope; Alan Bates respectful, reflective (if too handsome) as John. Madelon wrote an article about how vividly the film brought back her childhood visits to Turville Heath Cottage, all the more so for being filmed in the actual setting. Miss Sellars was so uncannily like Kathleen, 'that patient, devoted, much-abused lady', that she had rubbed her eyes with disbelief. At the film's launch, Madelon approached John, who broke off from holding court and embraced her. She explained to those nearby that she was John's 'ex-stepdaughter'. 'His face crumpled and he said, "NO! Not ex-step! We are *family*!"'

But a line had been drawn under his former life with the four stepdaughters when he dedicated *Clinging to the Wreckage* 'to Penny and Sally, Jeremy and Emily Mortimer, the survivors'. The title came from a bearded yachting type who told him over lunch at the Garrick Club how to deal with a female crew member in a Force 10 gale: 'Stun her with a blow of the fist, so she won't be swept overboard.' The sea-dog had never learned to swim himself, so if he fell overboard, he would cling to the wreckage until rescued. 'That's my tip, if you ever find yourself in trouble, cling to the wreckage!'

His favourite Camus quote, 'Everything begins with lucid indifference', underpinned John's approach to memoir-writing: to write with vivid perception, but also with insouciance. There were colourful evocations of Dragon and Harrow days, a moving analysis of his passion for Byron, and a droll anecdote on every page. The glimmers of self-examination were almost inadvertent. His first novel had been published without long years of rejection. 'The troubles came later,' he wrote, 'in years when my writing seemed to be advancing nowhere, when I felt myself bumping painfully up against my own limitations, when I despaired and thought that the voice in which I had once spoken was lost for ever.' A rare admission.

He greeted interviewers with the genial air of having all the time in the world. Everyone marvelled that he wrote so prolifically, yet his life appeared effortless. He worked, he told Stephen Fay of the *Sunday Times*, with 'the guilty energy of a lazy man' – that is, only with a deadline, when he would get up at 3 a.m. It was only rumoured that he worked hard, he said modestly, because the result 'comes to people's attention'. He'd been lucky to be well rewarded for merely 'using words and arranging my thoughts'. He knew his capabilities. 'I'm like a painter whose work you can always recognize. I don't have great periods like Picasso. I'm more like Daumier.'

The self-deprecating façade made him immensely 'agreeable', an adjective which stuck. Unlike Pinter or Osborne, he was never combative, tetchy or affronted with the press. Despite his convictions, his politics were woolly. 'Stands on the fringes of the establishment; is a bit limp about his socialism; and even his liber-tarianism is defective,' wrote Fay. He accepted the unions' closed shops, for instance, because as a barrister he lived in one. He felt vulnerable about his privileged life and the 'champagne socialist' question: 'I send my daughter to a private school' (Emily had got into St Paul's, the hotly academic independent girls' school). 'Well, we live in a rat race. What alternative have you got?'

Stephen Fay was one of the few to question him about his private life. In the memoir, his sexual confessions ended with 'Angela Bedwell' at twenty-three. 'That is the point at which I became the person I have become,' said John enigmatically. So Fay asked Clifford's favourite divorce court question. 'Is there anything you have done in the course of your married life of which you are thoroughly ashamed?' 'Yes.' 'What?' 'I've been married twice. I don't think I can say any more.'

Clinging to the Wreckage shot to the top of the bestseller list and was celebrated with one of Lord Weidenfeld's grand dinner parties at his Chelsea Embankment flat. Critics were disarmed, enchanted by its yarns, without being duped into believing they were getting a reliable, straightforward narrative of his life. Bron Waugh chose it as a book of the year, for its 'funny anecdotes . . . such as one might hear from any entertaining drunk in any saloon bar. I do not believe a word of it, but thought it a jolly good read.' The only malcontents were the po-faced who regarded John Mortimer as 'the enemy, the soft-liberal progressive-permissive' who was '*pas sérieux*'; and those who felt he had invented tales, such as Sandy Wilson – who denied ever knitting socks for the troops at Harrow ('the very idea!') – or Michael Fenton's wife, who had been obliged, when forewarned by John about his book, to tell her young sons for the first time about their father's suicide. Some discerned 'behind the thick spectacles and the Hapsburg chin' a man who felt 'much bewilderment and some pain'. He was a cagey memoirist, said the astute Professor John Carey: he had inherited his father's detachment and 'adopted insincerity as a barrister's professional necessity'. So, 'those who like autobiographies torn damp and throbbing from the soul's hidyholes may find this one hard to size up. Ironic and discreet, it is the kind of life you might expect from an unusually astute Cheshire cat.' Victoria Glendinning agreed: 'Mr Mortimer is, intellectually and emotionally, very well defended.' A most perceptive comment.

The relationship between truth and memory is notoriously unreliable. Everybody, consciously or not, improves their stories – particularly writers, even more so autobiographers. 'A writer's autobiography is a lived fiction, a literary act,' said Elias Canetti. Then there is the great left unsaid. 'Much more happened that I cannot tell or remember,' John wrote at the end of *Clinging to the Wreckage*. This was only 'a part of life'. I reflected on this when rereading the book twenty years afterwards, by now aware of some unwritten parts of his life. But even when reminded of episodes left out, John's reaction was to give his usual shrug, a little light laugh and a display of ignorance: 'Did I? Was I?' Certain things had been shelved, like all unwelcome or embarrassing matters, in some 'never to be mentioned' recess. Easier to pretend to have forgotten. But why should he divulge more of himself? He was much happier 'to put all the colouring in the surrounding characters'. Every autobiographer is master of his own history, setting in stone a version of his life for public consumption, crystallizing events which might, by others, be recalled quite differently.

The public's appetite for John Mortimer seemed insatiable. His moon face and plump jowls, photographed somewhat threateningly by Lord Snowdon, became ubiquitous. Though he faced his sixties obsessed with time ('too many months have been wasted writing rubbishy filmscripts'), he was infinitely approachable, infinitely available. No editor hesitated to commission another interview with John Mortimer, and he never apologized for rehearsing an old anecdote. Not only did newspapers not tire of him, but he never tired of himself.

When Christopher Howse, the intelligent, wildly bearded young *Catholic Herald* journalist, went to the Little Venice flat to cross-examine him on 'Mortimer's Faith', he discerned contradictions in the 'tall bulgy man': the *Brideshead* atheist, the dramatist who defended murderers, the non-believer obsessed with God. Death's finality, said John, made life absurd: 'We have these great powers and potentials and dreams and it all ends. That is why I think comedy is so important.' After considering Waugh's Catholicism, he preferred Graham Greene's; it gave Greene's writing strength and power, but was almost indistinguishable from atheism. He would hate to see England without churches, or to live in a world without religion. He found his churchgoing friends – Osborne, Ingrams, Muggeridge – 'more sympathetic than agnostics or *Guardian* readers or women's libbers or whatever . . .' But we should, he proposed, judge the beliefs of men like Ian Paisley and the Ayatollah Khomeini by their actions. His own atheism was an act of faith: 'I think I'm a lapsed Catholic atheist.' When Howse asked what made John happy, he replied, 'Oh, God – what makes me happy is to have finished a bit of work.'

Few people questioned John's merry picture of himself, but a personable young man named Edward Whitley, researching a book about Oxford graduates, did. Why was John's book so light-heartedly unrevealing? John said he had no desire 'to probe down into the great innermost secrets of my life'. Whitley suggested that these memoirs approached fiction, and John agreed, since he regarded fiction and autobiography as one and the same. He saw himself, and everyone he knew, as a fictional character. He had made Clifford a character in a play. Being a writer involved 'experiencing life and then trying to translate it back into words, into some sort of entertainment. I can't distinguish between fact and fiction.' When Whitley persisted in inquiring whether he had in fact made love to 'Angela Bedwell' while married to Penelope, John removed his glasses, reducing his interrogator to a distant blur. 'Now, whether that happened or whether that didn't happen, that's how I wanted to end that story. Because it's an unexpected ending.' The truth of it didn't matter. 'I was thinking of making the character of "me" into a character who would be interesting to read about.' It was not 'confessional'. 'I don't do much confessing.'

Whitley, earnest and disingenuous, was not prepared to accept John's well-rehearsed lines unexamined. Roy Plomley was much more malleable. When John did his second *Desert Island Discs* that summer he could effortlessly shimmy, in his high breathy voice, through all the old stories – from Sloane Square Wolf Cubs through growing watercress in his Harrovian topper, to teaching English to Christian Dior models. He was offhand about every turn his life had taken. For instance, 'By this time I had about five children by some strange quirk of fate' (a remark guaranteed to enrage Penelope) 'so I had to keep turning out novels.'

Those who saw him in convivial places met only bonhomie. But he sometimes mentioned getting depressed in the afternoons, which 'usually lasts until the first drink in the evening'. This was a transient melancholia, accidie, ennui, an egotist's reaction to being enveloped by solitude at the quietest time of day. He needed solitude to write, but was too gregarious to stand it for long. Sunday lunches bolstered his spirits: with Geoff Robertson and his latest girlfriend (currently the quick-witted Irish actress and writer Jeananne Crowley), or his neighbours the artist John Piper and his wife, Myfanwy. Awards and new projects buoyed him: Best Single Drama award for *A Voyage Round My Father* from the Broadcasting Press Guild; contracts signed for a *Rumpole Omnibus* and a book of *Famous Trials*; Yorkshire Post Book of the Year award for *Clinging to the Wreckage*, presented to him in Leeds by James Herriot.

'John Mortimer at home: like an actor playing a barrister speaking lines written by himself', read a newspaper caption. And for the next twenty-five years, the self-portrait and the quotations became interchangeable, typified in 'A Room of My Own' in the *Observer* magazine. The room was his study, in what had been Clifford's garage, and the former cooks' or au pairs' quarters. This was John's sanctum sanctorum, with adjoining book-room and bathroom. There was no distracting view of the glorious garden. On the walls were framed caricatures of himself, photographs of the many children, and posters of his old plays, to reassure him that he might have a theatre success again. On Uncle Harold's desk was a mug reading 'Old lawyers never die – they just lose their appeal'. Beside the desk was the old barrel-organ which had housed his father's first radio. By his chair stood the blue and white umbrella-stand holding Clifford's walking sticks. He still smoked a pipe. The house was 'unpretentious', the word often applied to his childhood home, although by now there was the handsome conservatory kindly left behind by Thames TV. Whenever he got paid, he would buy a lithograph or print, 'the sort of thing you can buy without being a millionaire'. He had crossed the world to see the Taj Mahal, but his heart lifted at the sight of his house. He loved food shopping in Henley and would cook himself 'a little pheasant in the evening, a fresh trout for lunch'. Like most writers he found innumerable things to do rather than write. But once started, he wrote at speed: ten pages of handwriting, 2,000 words, he considered a good day's work; Penny was the only person who could decipher them.

It was plain now that John was reluctant to 'maintain a servile posture before judges'. But he had to kowtow to the only female High Court judge of the day, Rose Heilbron, when he took on the defence of Erin Pizzey. Pizzey, pioneering founder of Chiswick Women's Refuge, the haven for battered wives, met John on BBC Radio 4's *Any Questions?* panel. She expected 'a rumbustious extrovert' and was amazed to find 'a quiet, private man'. But that was in the green room. Once the microphone's light went on, he changed as always into a polished raconteur. 'He had the audience in the palm of his hand, and his encyclopedic knowledge kept him way ahead of the rest of us.' Afterwards, Pizzey told him about her pending court summons. She had aided and abetted a battered wife to snatch her three children from her husband, who had been given their custody, arranging for her to flee with her children to Ireland on the night boat. In court, Pizzey had lied under oath about the children's whereabouts. Months passed before the fugitive family was found. Pizzey, a grandmother with three foster-children, was charged with contempt of court. John listened sympathetically as she rambled on and promised to help her. As she was indubitably guilty, all he could do was argue in mitigation, persuading Mrs Justice Heilbron not to send her to jail. Michael Grieve drafted the affidavit, setting out all that could be said in

Pizzey's favour. 'I do not believe the court has ever been so scandalized in its history,' said the judge. John meekly agreed with her. In an account of her trial (illustrated by Mark Boxer's excellent caricature of John), Pizzey extolled his virtues as an advocate. In his final speech he said, 'Imagine, if you will, the clang of the iron prison gates behind my client's back.' Though she was inevitably convicted, the sentence (a £1,500 fine instead of nine months inside) could be managed, with some fund-raising by the Chiswick Women's Refuge.

Pizzey had formerly seen him as 'a multi-faceted genius with a curious ability to be all things to all men', which might suggest a sly, devious, chameleon-like nature. Now she had witnessed the powerful charisma: 'He can suck a person, a court or a theatre into his world. They find themselves enthralled by his magic. In spite of a volcanic temper if crossed, he has a truly gentle side to his nature that supports the underdog and more particularly a woman in distress.' That 'volcanic temper if crossed' referred to a sticky moment during the conference in his chambers, when one of Pizzey's acolytes had begun voicing her own opinion, to be briskly rebuffed by John with, 'Are you conducting this conference or am I? Because if it's you, I'm leaving.'

The truth was, he could be as disagreeable and tyrannical as any man with too many commitments and a public profile to maintain. Privately he was anxious and pessimistic, horribly impatient in restaurants (rude to waiters, prone to sending things back) and sometimes impossible at home, where Penny bore the brunt of his demands, maintaining their household, endlessly typing, organizing the lunches, the travel arrangements. He was 'sometimes sadder than he allows himself to appear to the outside world', one profile had it. Only the agreeable side was on show. Reviewing the first collection of his interviews, *In Character*, I too fell into the descriptive cliché, 'agreeable': 'What could be more agreeable than to accompany Mr Mortimer in these revealing encounters?' Other critics – among them Terence de Vere White in the *Irish Times* and Richard Ingrams in the *Spectator* – declared that none of his interviewees was remotely as interesting as Mortimer himself.

Ingrams was still editor of *Private Eye* when John defended the magazine in the Desmond Wilcox libel case. This was a long and complex action that began when Wilcox, head of BBC Features, had been the credited author of a 1975 book, *The Explorers*, which had in fact been stitched together by two ghostwriters from the scripts of the series. The writers had been awarded compensation of £54,000 in 1980. Mr Justice Jupp accepted that the *Eye*'s accusation was justified, but said it was 'guileless plagiarism': he approved Wilcox's account of having had the book thrust upon him, in the face of his ethical scruples. But while investigating another story attacking Wilcox, concerning a series called *The Jews*, *Private Eye* had again called him a plagiarist. At the conclusion of *Wilcox* v. *Pressdram* on 6 May 1982, after a fifteen-day hearing, Wilcox won £14,000, plus £40,000 costs awarded against the *Eye*. Ingrams had found John somewhat unimpressive at first, uttering tentative remarks in a soft voice, giggling frequently. But he worked hard in court, and Ingrams described him as 'a natural optimist who believes, sometimes a little too much so, in the basic goodness of his fellow men'. John dedicated a later Rumpole book to Ingrams 'in memory of our days in court' and Ingrams always called him 'Rumpole'. They became fast friends, often meeting with their mutual friend John Piper, with whom Ingrams played piano duets, and wrote a book, *Piper's Places*.

John's sixtieth birthday was celebrated with Piper's eightieth in June 1983: a supper party in the glowingly colourful garden of the Pipers' 'magical' house, Fawley Bottom, with long white-clothed tables, many children scampering about, and fireworks, designed by Piper, set off at 10 p.m., emblazoning the words HAPPY BIRTHDAY JOHN AND JOHN across the sky over the Chiltern hills.

Fifty miles to the west, Penelope contemplated her garden at the Old Post Office at Chastleton in Gloucestershire. The garden was almost too alluring, too tempting, to allow time to write. To get on with a novel, she devised a solution: she advertised in a gardening magazine as 'a middle-aged, anti-social writer who needs to get on with a work in progress' seeking 'house-room and regular meals'. In the home of kindred spirits, she finished *The Handyman*, a fine novel about ageing and loneliness, in six weeks. One of its characters was a vivid self-portrait: the reclusive novelist Rebecca Broune, a brusque, chain-smoking divorcee. There was a bizarre aftermath, when the imaginary events in the novel began to take place. A local problem family she referred to as 'the Starkadders' used their muckspreader to cover her garden in slurry, and even moved her hedge, while she was away, by three feet. Despite these disturbances, she pronounced herself, at sixty-four, to be happy: 'I just feel lucky to be here. It's so peaceful.'

John's courtroom days were coming to an end. At the Old Bailey he defended a 'likeable' man known as 'The Bull of Waltham Cross'; the case involved bare-knuckle fighting (affray, with a fatal outcome) in an aerodrome by night. Lesley Garner, in the press gallery, remembered John's cross-examining a woman witness who said, 'They keep saying I was the biggest 'ore in Brentford, but everyone knows I never come from Brentford.' To Garner, John appeared cynically detached, intent on extracting amusement from the bizarre events. 'His approach,' she said, 'was that of a writer rather than a lawyer.'

His final High Court performance was in May 1983, when he took up the case of Turville's little Church of England school, threatened with closure by Buckinghamshire County Council. John's parents never entered St Mary's Church in Turville (until their funerals) but John always attended Midnight Mass on Christmas Eve, just for the ritual of it. Otherwise his only link with the school was that Deborah's son Ben had been a pupil. Now all six little church schools in the beautiful Hambleden valley were shrinking; the roll at Turville was due to drop to sixteen. John tried to prove that the council had acted unlawfully, but Mr Justice Woolf dismissed the application for a judicial review. (He refused to award costs against the applicants, which was a small victory). The school became a *cause célèbre* in John's and Penny's lives. They saw it as an ideal holiday centre for disadvantaged urban children who would otherwise never see the countryside. Other Turvillites, such as the philosopher and former Master of Trinity Anthony (Lord) Quinton and the writer Alistair Horne, who both lived much closer to the building than the Mortimers, were appalled by the idea: what would these city kids do in the evenings without discos or slot machines? But a trust was formed, a loan raised to buy the school for £220,000 and Penny threw her considerable energy for the next fifteen years into fund-raising projects for the school.

Getting up to speak in court was a kind of addiction. Perhaps this was why John agreed to mount so many podiums and address audiences: the Granada Guildhall lecture; a Royal Television Society debate at Cambridge; a lecture at the New York Museum of Broadcasting, about how privileged television writers were in Britain, with their huge audiences and showcases for new writers. And he was the obvious candidate, in October 1983, to speak at the St Martin-in-the-Fields memorial service for his friend David Niven, who had died of motor neurone disease. A frail Olivier read the lesson. John recalled that the suave, elegant Niven had been a stylish actor and a witty writer, but his greatest performances were at restaurant tables, telling stories which 'improved with repetition' to an audience of friends, whom he made to feel, as Oscar Wilde did, more alive for being in his company. Before Niven died, unable to speak, he had written to John: his letter was typewritten, because 'My arm seems to have gone over to the enemy.' Poignantly, he wrote, 'Perhaps it's because I have talked too much all my life that this has got me now.'

At the service, John saw Shirley Anne Field after many years and told her, 'Penny's gone and got pregnant again.' This had not been a surprise conception; they had undergone a succession of fertility tests and Penny, at thirty-seven, had had a hysterosalpingography. The prospect of a late-born child was clearly the moment for John to rethink his future. When Penny was three months pregnant, in January 1984, he went to Singapore for a second time, to defend again the irrepressible Ben Jeyaretnam, still the lone opposition MP to Lee Kuan Yew. Later John would always say he

decided to leave the Bar when he arrived jet-lagged at the Singapore court, and the lady in charge of the robing room greeted him
with, 'Ah! Lumpore of the Bay-ree!' He had intended to give up
the law the moment he could be self-sufficient without it, and
Lumpore of the Bayree was his escape route.

Mr Jeyaretnam was now accused of fiddling his party's funds, a
charge carrying a mandatory jail sentence of up to seven years.
The Chinese judge, Michael Khoo, one of a partnership called
'The Singing Khoos' who entertained at children's parties, was
'terrifically on my side', John said. Judge Khoo acquitted the
defendant on most of the charges, imposing only a small fine. On
the day of the acquittal John had lunch with David Watt, the
correspondent from *The Times*. Over roast beef, John told him he
felt like giving up. He said he had lost two recent cases, including
the *Private Eye* libel. He had hated having Mr Jeyaretnam's future
in his hands. He had enough writing projects to keep him busy
for years. 'And the next morning,' said John, 'it was in *The Times*.'
'Rumpole retires with relish' was the headline. Watt referred to
'Mr Mortimer's Rumpole-like sojourn in Singapore with its exotic
gastronomic delights'. 'I thought, well, if it's printed in *The Times*,
it must be true. So that was the last case I did.'

(As soon as John had left Singapore for San Francisco to publicize
Rumpole, Mr Justice Khoo was sacked, and poor Mr Jeyaretnam
was retried, convicted and imprisoned. When he appealed to the
Privy Council, they abolished the Privy Council. So much, said
John, for Singapore's English system of justice.)

To leave the Bar, he told me, all you have to do is not show up
in chambers any more 'and they can't drag you there'. But solicitors
were still requesting his services and Lord Hooson, head of chambers, was dubious. 'One should treat John Mortimer's statement
with the same degree of scepticism as one would treat Rumpole's,'
he told *The Times*. 'His name will remain up at the door.' Sightseers
who might formerly have visited Fleet Street to see Dr Johnson's
house or the office where Dickens once worked now flocked to
see Rumpole's name painted up on the list (among sixty-four
others by now) at the chambers entrance, and to be shown the

'Rumpole Room' with its cartoons and photographs. Butter-worth's annual Law List for 1985 contained a new entry. Between Rumfitt, Nigel, of Essex Court, and Rundell, R. J., of Lincoln's Inn, is 'Rumpole, Horace', at '3 Equity Court'.

John's chambers held a farewell dinner, at which Michael Grieve in his speech pointed out that 'at the end of every Rumpole series he seems to be bowing out, but in the next series he's back again. Let's hope it is the same with John.' But he would not be tempted. He would miss being able to take refuge in rehearsal rooms if he had lost a case; or distracting himself, if his writing went badly, by taking another case. 'I have nowhere else to go now.'

He had always been ambivalent about the law: he had felt like a doctor trying to cure or prevent disease – trying to get people out of trouble as painlessly as possible. The responsibility for defendants' lives, their possible imprisonment, made it 'a terrific relief' not to have to do it any more. He said he had now only one ambition: to write well. The theatre was the 'more rational' world that he loved and trusted.

There is a whiff of self-persuasion about these statements. But he had high hopes of a new play, *Edwin*, previously broadcast on radio with Emlyn Williams and Michael Gough. On 29 April 1984 it went out on Channel 4. Alec Guinness played Sir Fennimore Truscott – a crusty, pedantic old judge, now retired to a Norfolk country house named Gallows Corner and reduced to trying the wasp that lands on his marmalade, or his dog Haversack on a charge of digging up plants. He then puts his neighbour, a potter, on trial, on the charge that 'You, Thomas Marjoriebanks, feloniously and unlawfully did roger Lady Margaret Truscott'. Truscott is convinced that the potter's illicit union with Lady Truscott, consummated among the maidenhair ferns in the conservatory, resulted in the birth of the Truscotts' son, Edwin, now grown up and (like Nicky Rumpole) working in computers in California. Truscott and Marjoriebanks taunt each other with rival paternity claims.

Then, unseen by viewers, Edwin arrives. He turns out to be a health-obsessed vegetarian wimp who drinks only fruit juice, to the horror of both judge and potter. Would either wish to claim paternity of a man who turns down a glass of claret for fear of heart disease? The two now compete furiously to deny Edwin's fatherhood. When saintly Lady Truscott is put on the stand, the codgers are astonished to discover that neither of them was in fact the daddy. It was an adroit inversion of the English literary preoccupation with parentage. (And, as it happened, John's secret son, Ross Bentley, had recently been told by his godmother about John being his father. Now in his early twenties like Edwin, he was living with his parents ten miles from Turville Heath Cottage, at Cookham.) John hoped that the play, Rumpolian and hyperbolical in flavour, would translate to the West End stage. 'Fingers crossed for *Edwin*!' Alec Guinness wrote.

I sometimes observed John as paterfamilias that year, presiding over his Sunday lunch table that included Jeremy and Polly, Deborah and Colin and their children. John and Penny were unfazed by large numbers: even our family, with four children under seven, were welcome. The grandchildren were expected to take part in adult conversation and sprang up to clear plates in a highly civilized manner. Spending weekends in Henley at that time, we ran into John one rainy Saturday night with Emily and her friend Araminta Craig-Hall in the long queue outside the Regal, the only cinema for miles, to see the new James Bond. The Regal, with its mighty Wurlitzer, was shortly threatened with demolition by the even mightier Waitrose. John was among local showbiz luminaries who campaigned to save it: *Mortimer's Miscellany*, in aid of the Regal, was a sellout at Henley's pretty town hall.

As a father, Emily said, John was 'always on my side'. When she was not instantly offered a place at St Paul's but put on the waiting list, John had eventually telephoned Mrs Brigstocke, the headmistress. A catty Paulina in Emily's class said, 'You only got in because your father's John Mortimer,' and Emily, blessed with a sunny, modest nature, suspected that, oh, God, she might be right. But John told Emily she was one of those racehorses that move up stealthily on the inside. (She had faced a sad blow, not long before, when her best friend Lucy Hoggett, granddaughter of John and Myfanwy Piper, was run over and killed. Twenty years later, on her wedding day, Emily laid her bridal posy on Lucy's gravestone in Turville churchyard.) With Emily installed in her new school, they had exchanged their London base, 24B Maida Avenue, for a more spacious flat nearby at 15 Park Place Villas, bought by Penny at a knockdown £70,000 from the Church Commissioners. At St Paul's Emily developed into the perfect teenage daughter: unrebellious and conscientious apart from the odd late Saturday night at the Mud Club.

On 14 June 1984, Rosamond, the longed-for last child, was born: the cause of much congratulation for John at sixty-one, and also for Penny, who had had a difficult birth. When the vivacious Lois Sieff, who sat next to John on the National Theatre board, told him it was her sixtieth birthday, he said, 'And what have you got to show for it? I've got a baby.' From Queen Charlotte's Hospital, John took Emily to a Chinese restaurant and she contemplated her new status, at thirteen no longer an only child. John too pondered on this late blessing. Was it intolerably selfish to be an old father? 'Men who become fathers after sixty may not be there at their child's twenty-first birthday party. So should there be a law against it?' John wrote this ten years later, by which time he misremembered being sixty-two at Rosie's birth. He determined to enjoy her company for as long as possible. 'For me life becomes insupportable, and inoperable pomposity is liable to set in, unless there's a fairly young child about the place.'

Among those who sent congratulations was Graham Greene, who wrote from Antibes, 'I hope she is not keeping you awake too much at night!' (So even great writers are at a loss to find anything original to say about babies.) In fact they were suffering far more than wakeful nights. That summer John tripped over a telephone wire and became lame again. 'I've just fallen over twice, pulled muscles in leg and hobbling around + stick,' he wrote to Geraldine Cooke, his editor at Penguin. 'All very dramatic and boring. About all that's happened to me lately except work!' His

19. (*top*) John out on the town with his new Penny, 1971

20. (*left*) John and Penny with Emily, 1974

21. (*above*) Penelope, with her family gathered about her, 1978: *left to right, back row*: Colin Rogers, Polly Fisher, Jeremy Mortimer, Sally Mortimer, Gered Mankowitz; *middle row*: Deborah Rogers (with son Tom on knee), Penelope (with granddaughter Jessica on knee), Julia Mankowitz; *front row*: Madelon Dimont, Penelope's grandson Ben Rogers, Caroline Mortimer

22. (*left*) Jeremy, Oxford undergraduate, and John, photographed by Lord Snowdon for *Vogue*, 1977

23. John with Laurence Olivier, the director Charles Sturridge and the producer Derek Granger on location outside Castle Howard, the setting for *Brideshead Revisited*, in 1981

24. (*above left*) John with David Niven, on location for *The Running Man*, in Spain in 1961

25. (*above right*) Rumpole and his creator: John with a bewigged Leo McKern, 1980

26. (*left*) John with Sir John Gielgud on location in Siena while making *Summer's Lease*, 1989

27. (*top*) Turville Heath Cottage when Clifford built it – 'I would be Master of a Small House and a Large Garden' – in 1934

28. (*middle*) Turville Heath Cottage remained untouched, except for the addition of a conservatory, by 1985. In this picture Penny is retreating from the camera, with baby Rosie in her arms and King Charles spaniel Tizzy at her side

29. (*bottom*) John in the splendour of the Turville Heath Cottage garden – his 'solace, and a kind of drug'

30. (*top*) John, proud to have become a father again at sixty-one, and his last-born, Rosamond, always known as Rosie

31. (*left*) John at Buckingham Palace, getting his knighthood, 1998, flanked by Penny and Emily

32. John and his 'best friend' Kathy Lette, mistress of pun and provider of fun: 'We talked until our lips fell off'

33. Geoffrey Robertson, QC, 'a better lawyer than I shall ever be', arrived with the *Oz* trial and became John's accomplice in defence of freedom of speech

34. Ann Mallalieu, QC, John's favourite partner in crime when at the Old Bailey defending the kings of porn

35. Joanna David, neighbour and steadfast friend: John's sidekick for innumerable *Mortimer's Miscellany* performances

36. John presided over a splendid table at La Rufena, the Ingrams' house in Tuscany, every summer for twenty years

37. John's 'Heavenly Twins': Jackie Paice and Vicky Lord, Deep Purple wives and providers of cures for all ills

38. 'The Mortimettes': John is serenaded on his seventy-ninth birthday with 'The way you wear your hat . . .' by, *left to right*: Jackie Paice, Margo Buchanan, Marsha Fitzalan-Howard, Phyllida Law, Joanna David, Penny Mortimer, Candida Lycett Green, Kathy Lette, Clare Francis, Vicky Lord

39. John takes the microphone at the wedding of his
newly rediscovered son, Ross Bentley, in 2005

40. John leads the way in the Turville Heath Cottage garden, 2007, in his battery-
operated Sun-Gift tricycle. *Left to right*: Sam, son of Emily, in the arms of his father,
Alessandro Nivola; baby Iris, in the arms of her father, Ross Bentley; and Emily

Achilles tendon had snapped and the eventual operation to repair
it caused a deep vein thrombosis in his other leg. So began his
intermittent dependence on a wheelchair. Even worse, for Penny,
was that Rosie, at only five months old, became mysteriously ill
with a life-threatening digestive disorder.

The anxiety was exhausting enough. The doctor called daily.
John was no help. One day Penny was delivering Rosie to the
Portland Hospital to be put on a drip, just as John emerged in
plaster, taking a taxi from the London Clinic. Rosie had chronic
diarrhoea for eighteen months and underwent further tests every
week. At the same time their cleaner (who had worked there since
Kathleen's day) had to give notice. On Christmas Eve of 1984,
Penny ironed twenty-four bedsheets. On Christmas Day, Jeremy
pushed his father in his wheelchair to the copse to make his
customary bonfire of the wrapping-paper (John had been addicted
to bonfires since his childhood, when Clifford burned the rubbish
every single night; and once managed to fling his best trousers,
plus a short-wave radio, into the flames). Penny decided they must
get away, so they set off over frozen roads to a hotel in Wiltshire,
with John in plaster and a mass of equipment for sickly Rosie.
During Sunday lunch in the dining room, John choked violently
on a piece of beef and stumped around the room on his one leg,
roaring and retching, alarming fellow guests, until Jeremy thumped
him on the back so the meat shot out of his mouth.

It was the end of a bleakly memorable year. They had hardly
noticed when John's fourth adaptation of a Feydeau farce, *A Little
Hotel on the Side*, opened at the National, the Olivier theatre's epic
scale magnifying the familiar slapstick humour. 'Seldom,' wrote
the New York critic John Simon, 'has human misfortune been
purveyed so blissfully.' Human misfortune was all too prevalent at
home, but eventually, after several more months, Rosie began to
recover.

Perhaps it was to cheer John along that the Penguin chairman
Peter Mayer proposed, in February 1985, a 'John Mortimer Month,
in which we knock ourselves out to *get attention for John Mortimer
in all media* [my italics] based on his new book, the television series,

all his old books, his strong public stance, his engaging manner in many areas of British life'. They reprinted two of his early novels, *Charade* and *Like Men Betrayed*. *Charade* in particular stood the test of time as a satire on the film world, in which critics found no trace of 'a literary novice'.

Did his public image need bolstering? There had been a disappointment when his screenplay of Graham Greene's *Dr Fischer of Geneva* was rejected by (again) the director Michael Lindsay-Hogg. But his TV adaptation of John Fowles's *The Ebony Tower* was a small triumph. Fowles's story, set in a rural idyll near Limoges, was another splendid vehicle for Olivier as the vigorous, opinionated, rascally old painter Henry Breasley. A young art critic arrives, to find two nubile English girls known as the Mouse (Greta Scacchi) and the Freak (Toyah Willcox with punk pink hair), basking in the sunlit meadows, seemingly spellbound by the old man: 'We don't deny him the bit of love he can manage.' John's excellent script played out the arguments about modern art dividing the young critic and the old artist (John himself was decidedly on the side of art being 'difficult'; his own favourite painting was *An Old Woman Cooking Eggs* by Velázquez). The director, Robert Knights, lovingly photographed the lush river banks like a Monet painting. John took Penny and Emily to the shoot. In an interview, Toyah Willcox suggested jocularly that John had been ogling the girls in their naked swimming scene. John demanded and got an apology for this allegation. Soon afterwards Ms Willcox became one of his *Sunday Times* interviewees, 'because I am of a forgiving nature,' he said.

But he had to resist Bron Waugh's invitation to adapt *Scoop!*, one of his favourite Evelyn Waugh novels (William Boyd did it instead), because he was just too committed: a TV series, a novel, the interviews, a script of Chesterton's *The Man Who Was Thursday*. 'My legs have given out,' John wrote to Bron, 'otherwise I'm more or less intact.' In February 1985 he and Penny took a restorative holiday, the first of many, at the sybaritic La Gazelle d'Or, in the Atlas mountains near Marrakesh, where roses bloom in January and there are open fires in the bedrooms, acres of orange groves, cool terraces and tented dining rooms. At the Gazelle d'Or, as on all his holidays, John wrote every day. Each morning Rashid, a slim figure in long white gown and backless slippers, would help him to a table under an acacia tree by the pool, where he could write until lunchtime. He was finishing a novel, his first (Rumpole stories apart) for thirty years.

21. The Politics of Paradise

Paradise Postponed was not his idea. Bryan Cowgill, managing director of Thames TV, had suggested 'something about England from the 1950s to the 1980s' for a drama series. John thought of Coward's *Cavalcade* and demurred. But then he pondered. He'd observed fifty years of social history in his village, from post-war days to the present. And as *Voyage* and *Wreckage* had proved, his own life resonated with the public. Every major event of his life had happened around Turville. The bodgers' cottages might now belong to merchant bankers and ad men, who added granny flats and car ports, but there were still secret woods and deserted valleys in this privileged fastness in 'the more fortunate half of England' which had suffered no hardship worse than butter rationing and dried egg. No research would be necessary. He could survey the Aldermaston marches, the Profumo scandal, the Vietnam demos, the Wilson years, Greenham Common, the Falklands War, the miners' strike, and show 'how we set off to create a new Jerusalem and ended up with Mrs Thatcher'. Thames wanted twelve scripts, with a nice fat novel thrown in. (For the novel alone he got £75,000 from Viking, in four instalments, and from Viking US an advance of $100,000.)

By the time of Rosamond's birth he had defined the political credo behind the novel. In 1945 he had believed Paradise had arrived. But forty years on we had 'the nastiest society I can remember' (obliterating from his memory the 1940s, when he had seen for himself the East End's slum children with rickets and women toothless crones at thirty-five). Britain had become 'deeply unpleasant, mean-spirited, grasping'. The Tory Party no longer represented an altruistic noblesse, landed gents like Macmillan, Churchill, Butler; Mrs Thatcher appealed to the lower middle classes, the deeply conservative Alf Garnetts, a much bigger constituency. 'It grieves me very much,' John said. 'She's a woman without the saving grace of a sense of humour, which makes her both dangerous and absurd.'

Paradise Postponed opens in May 1985 with a deathbed scene, a funeral and the reading of a will. A classic formula: the mystery bequest. The late rector, Simeon Simcox, a Canon Collins-style socialist and CND marcher, has left his £2 million of shares in the family brewery not to his two sons but to one Leslie Titmuss, a creepy Tory Cabinet minister, who was born the son of a housemaid and a humble clerk in the Simcox brewery. The story was told in flashbacks because, as Kierkegaard said, 'Life must be lived forwards, but it can only be understood backwards.' Through Titmuss and the Simcoxes, John could unfurl a social and political panorama of England, 1948–85. As a youth, Titmuss had been roughed up and dunked in the river by jeering toffs at the Conservative Ball, because he wore a clip-on bow tie. (Don Berry, John's editor at the *Sunday Times*, had told him about his own clip-on humiliation – without the dunking – at an Oxford May Ball. 'It was some consolation,' he said, 'to see it turned into art.') Titmuss, bent on vengeance, shrewdly marries the squire's rebellious daughter, changes his accent and rises in the Tory hierarchy.

The disinherited Simcox brothers, Henry the show-off novelist and Fred the good country doctor, represented two sides of John's own character – the divided self of which he had been conscious since childhood. Or perhaps John/Michael Fenton. Could Henry have been fathered by someone else? John knew about such secrets. To Nicholas Shakespeare, who came from *The Times*, he said he could not write about anything that hadn't happened to him, even family secrets: 'All the important things in my parents' life were kept quiet. My mother's father shot himself. She was never told.' (Here John was ignoring factors of class and time. Before people started picking at their family's scabs and attributing blame for imagined trauma or real misery, suicide was normally regarded as a matter for family reticence.)

Every reader could recognize Titmuss, whose progenitors included Norman Tebbit, Peter Walker, Cecil Parkinson. They might also see in Henry Simcox, the leftie writer turned professional Blimp (whose politics 'had once been as red as his hair', but who now fulminated about the menace of the left and the moral disintegration of Britain), a Paul Johnson, a John Osborne. The local GP, Humphrey Salter, is reminiscent of Penelope's parson father: he blows smoke rings over ailing patients while telling them not to bother to cling on to life: 'Don't want to hang about in this vale of tears, do you? Death is the most effective painkiller there is.' Dr Salter's daughter Agatha is Penelope, with her 'expression of sad superiority', repudiating Fred's advances with, 'I hate heavy petting, it's Yank.' 'Is it?' 'Terribly Yank.' Penelope's very words in 1947.

'Hartscombe' was a thinly disguised Henley, the 'Rapstone Valley' the Thames Valley with great houses (Stonor Park, Wormsley), an ugly town (Reading, renamed 'Worsfield') and ungentrified villages such as 'Skurfield' (Skirmett) with unweeded cottage gardens where prams, motorbikes, paraffin stoves are dumped. Henley's Leander Club became the 'Hellespont Club'; even the diminutive gravestone on Henley's Fairmile commemorating 'Jimmy, a tiny marmoset', got a mention, with Jimmy renamed 'Harry'. The Garrick became the 'Sheridan Club', serving overdone roasts and jam roly-poly to lawyers, writers, actors, publishers – 'the sort of Englishman who has never totally recovered from an emotional relationship with his nanny'. Across this landscape John could hit satirical targets – the law, C of E sermons, Hollywood screenwriting, scheming politicians – and people his narrative with Dickensian names: Nubble, Doughty Strove, Tom Nowt, Benjamin K. Bugloss.

In March 1985, Alvin Rakoff began shooting *Paradise Postponed* in the pretty village of Ewelme, a mile and a half from Turville Heath, using the old rectory, with a solid cast including Michael Hordern, Annette Crosbie, Zoë Wanamaker and David Threlfall. It took thirty-two weeks and cost £6.5 million. Despite its vast panorama, the novel's plot was thin for twelve one-hour episodes. 'Thames,' Rakoff said, 'had been hoping for *A Voyage Round My Father* multiplied by twelve.' So John's scripts needed heavy work by Rakoff and the producer Jacqueline Davis, who fell out. Jacquie had been Rakoff's production secretary at Thames and was now his producer. 'It takes a big man to get over that,' Rakoff confessed, 'and I'm just not big enough.' In their angry exchanges, he made Jacquie cry. Producers, Rakoff felt, should not cry in public. But John wrote that Jacquie could 'win the hearts of that most brutal and intractable of bodies, a film unit on location'.

During the shoot John had his leg operation, when the deep vein thrombosis developed. Yet he kept on producing interviews for the *Sunday Times*, going to Birmingham to see Billy Graham, to Constable country to see Ruth Rendell, to Edinburgh to see the reformed murderer Jimmy Boyle. On Sunday 13 June 1985 – the weekend of Rosie's first birthday, and a party at Turville Heath – his subject was Lauren Bacall, found on a hot afternoon in her dressing room at the Theatre Royal, Brighton. This prompted an affectionate letter from 'Your devoted Larry O' in West Sussex: 'I write only to say Bravo Bravo Bravo (underlined once, twice, thrice)' and to ask for La Bacall's phone number. Olivier too was immobilized by a leg injury, confined to bed, obliged to 'bore myself to death in intolerable obedience'.

When the novel was launched, a year before the TV series, in September 1985, John spoke of the writer's insecurity, his embarrassment about past work, or trepidation that he would never write as well again. So when Bron Waugh found it 'a thoroughly English, good-hearted book that made the reader feel better' – he disliked the flashback formula but would 'let Mr Mortimer off with a warning this time' – John wrote to thank him: 'I was in a great state of nerves about doing a novel after so long, and your tolerance and understanding came as a huge encouragement and relief.'

The *Observer* profiled him as a Chesterton or Belloc *de nos jours*, 'the epitome of the good-natured man'. He might feel a bit low in the afternoons, but at the Garrick he never seemed in a hurry, greeting everyone with, 'My dear, how lovely to *see* you. How *are* you?' He was 'that peculiarly English phenomenon', a rebel who was tolerated and approved of, an old Labour Party man who helped Wilson 'and entertains the Kinnocks'.

Entertaining the Kinnocks was a recent development. He had gone to interview Neil Kinnock for the *Spectator* at the House of Commons, but disliked having a press secretary sitting in, taking notes; Kinnock said, 'OK, John, come back to our house and chat properly.' John took to Kinnock in his Marks & Sparks suit and second-hand Cortina, describing him as everyone's favourite best man; but he wondered whether he would ever win the hand of the British public. At the Ealing house, he took to Glenys even more – they laughed at each other's jokes – and he named a character 'Glenys' in *Paradise Postponed*, which Neil selected as his book of the year. The friendship was sealed when the Kinnocks were staying in San Gimignano while the Mortimers were in Tuscany the following year. 'What I appreciated,' Glenys said, 'is that I was just a teacher at the time, but if we met at a party John wouldn't be glancing over your shoulder, like some people, looking for someone more important to talk to.'

Paradise Postponed, with theme music from Elgar's Cello Concerto, was soon required viewing on Mondays at 9 p.m. It was shown in the US simultaneously, so John went to Hollywood in July to promote it. That the drama took wing was largely down to David Threlfall's brilliant performance as Titmuss. Threlfall, a Manchester lad and a socialist, had played the heart-rending Smike in the RSC's *Nicholas Nickleby*, yet John had at first been dubious about this casting and wanted him sacked. But he had to admit that Threlfall was perfect, bringing 'a cold, classless, carefully ironic voice, pale intensity, unremitting tension and moments of sarcastic delight'.

Interviewers trooped down to see the real village. John drove in his red Mercedes to meet them in the Bull & Butcher over a glass of Brakspear's Best Bitter, brewed in Henley, the original for Simcox's Ales of Hartscombe. They were shown the Norman church in Fingest, the village shop in Hambleden. They met the local vicar, Paul Nicholson, former champagne salesman, and the local poacher on whom Tom Nowt was based.

Wasn't John, the champagne socialist, a snob, disdaining Titmuss's efforts to better himself? Yes, he confessed to Alan Franks of *The Times*, there was snobbery on his part. He felt a sentimental regret about the loss of parliamentary toffs and 'gents' – Foot, Benn, Healey. Franks asked if the committed leftie shared Mrs Simcox's feeling that 'the working classes should be running this country, but she wouldn't want to have them to tea'. 'That remark,' John admitted, 'was the most brutal attack I could make on myself.' In the criminal courts he had met all sorts, but had never had his clients to tea. 'I am middle class. I believe in middle-class virtues. I think the middle class produces not only the best literature but also the best revolutionaries.' He was a committed leftie in the same way that Graham Greene was a committed Catholic. 'In other words, you'd hardly notice it.'

But the interesting thing is that John gave to his 'obnoxious' new Tory an adoption speech in which he made a cogent and sympathetic case for Thatcherite arriviste conservatism. Leslie Titmuss spoke of his hard-working parents in their council house, with salad cream on the table. They were true Tories, he said, who were 'tired of being represented by people from the City, or folks from up at the Manor. They want one of themselves. The people who know the value of money because they've never had it. They are the backbone of the country. They aren't Conservative because of privilege or money, but because of their simple faith in the way we've always managed things in England.' Having set out to write an unspeakable monster John made Titmuss both credible and sympathetic, very much as he did in his real-life interview with Norman Tebbit. 'Although I loathe everything that Norman Tebbit stands for, I had a sneaking fondness for him, much to my surprise.'

Melvyn Bragg was given the full Monty tour around John's garden, with pale rhododendrons in bloom, for his *South Bank Show*. John's leg had recovered enough for him to stride alongside Bragg, guiding him to his father's old chambers at 1 Dr Johnson's Buildings, which had become 'very radical', and through the Turville churchyard, and into the Bull & Butcher, and across the lush, timeless landscape of the Thames Valley. 'What kind of village is it?' Bragg asked John at one point. Bragg liked what he saw and twenty years later he bought a cottage at Turville Heath – one reason being that John lived there.

John admitted to Bragg that his store of experiences had been seriously depleted by writing *Paradise Postponed*. It had left him rather empty. 'It's a frightening amount to use. I need a great new intake of experience.' 'Really?' asked Bragg. 'Yes, I need to think of something. Yes. At the moment I'm writing Rumpoles, which I do easily. I hope more accidents will happen to me' – laughing – 'I need more experience.' But even if John had never left home again for the rest of his writing life, his output would have been much the same. All his material was around him, and in his mind. Why look further? He produced two further Titmuss novels, just by observing developments under Thatcher's long reign. Indeed, he became, from this point, a notable commentator on politics. In the House of Commons a Tory industry minister, John Butcher, denounced him as 'an upmarket punk who has made money for fifteen years by ridiculing the values of Conservatives'. And Brian Walden defined the middle-class intelligentsia's attachment to the Labour Party, giving it a respectability it would otherwise lack, as 'John Mortimer syndrome'.

In an exhaustive tour he filled theatres from Cheltenham to Newcastle with his urbane platform presence. Only occasionally did a (generally youthful) interrogator complain that he couldn't get anywhere near the man. From *Blitz* magazine came a young writer, Paul Morley.

'Who do you think John Mortimer is?'

'I don't think about it an awful lot.'

'When you think about it, who do you think he is?'

'A moderately talented old fart, trying to keep going.'

'He plays the part of the chuckling, vulnerable, wise old fool,' wrote Morley.

'Mortimer presents a carefully edited version of himself,' wrote Jonathan Rugman, then an undergraduate at Churchill College, in *Varsity*. After one of his story-telling performances, John looked 'dazed and tired' but poured champagne for Rugman and retold more old stories. He didn't think he would be remembered as a great barrister – 'I've killed that' – or a great writer. He just wanted to be popular, with a big audience; to be 'remembered for what

I'm proud of: *Clinging to the Wreckage* is the best thing I've done.'
His epitaph would be 'The defence rests'. As 'a rich socialist', he
was also essentially conservative. He wanted to conserve the traditions of Dickens and liberal egalitarianism, the English countryside, village schools, the Authorized Version. 'I'm totally Christian
about everything except belief in God.'

What most typified John's willingness to adopt any side of an
argument was his journalism, which has always blown where it
listeth. Not long before he wrote *Paradise Postponed*, he had written
a passionate polemic in the *Sunday Times* on 'Why I don't accept
the nightmare view of Britain', deriding the views of 'Mister
Christopher Booker – "a distinguished social commentator" according to the *Daily Mail*'. Booker had written a bleak why-oh-why on
social disintegration, the erosion of family life, heroin addiction,
video nasties, etc. Well, John's family life had not disintegrated,
John was glad to report. He lived among preserved woodlands,
with badgers and deer. His London street was like a well-kept
village. He worked among dedicated people in British television,
the best in the world, and with 'young, underpaid editors in
publishing who don't count their hours or withhold their enthusiasm'. Let us celebrate all the good things about Britain today!
cried John, and feel 'proud of having left the worst aspects of the
Victorian age behind us' in 'the most beautiful, most tolerant and
most politically mature and . . . the most peaceful of countries'.
Not quite the nastiest society he had ever known, then.

Ultimately, John decided, the political pendulum was irrelevant
to important things: birth and death, the consolations of art and
religion, the pursuit of happiness, the fulfilment of work, all of
which go on irrespective of politics. As Dr Johnson wrote:

> How small of all that human hearts endure,
> That part which Laws or Kings can cause or cure.

He dedicated his second collection of interviews, *Character Parts*,
to Don Berry 'in memory of life before Wapping', a dig at Rupert
Murdoch's coup in removing News International's operations

from Gray's Inn Road. This collection included Lord Hailsham, the Lord Chancellor, son of a former Lord Chancellor and there-fore 'born into the law', like John. Hailsham's admission that during the longueurs on the Woolsack in the House of Lords he would mutter 'Bollocks!' to the bishops became one of John's stories. Much funnier was Hailsham's self-description, beginning, 'I was academically exceptionally gifted, and being intensely ambitious and competitive by nature, made full use of this gift.' As usual, John got along with his subjects; any damning was self-inflicted. 'Were your parents snobs, would you say?' he asked Lord David Cecil. 'Not in the least. They hardly needed to be, did they?'

He took one last swipe at the obscenity laws. With Kingsley Amis, David Attenborough, Michael Frayn and John Schlesinger, he spoke against the Tory MP Winston Churchill's 'silly, ill-thought-out, unnecessary and destructive' Obscene Publications (Amendment) Bill, which would extend the act to cover radio and TV. Any portrayal of the listed subjects could be prosecuted: cruelty to people or animals, sodomy, masturbation, lewd exhi-bition of nudes, cannibalism, bestiality. David Attenborough said, 'The praying mantis does at least three of these simultaneously.' John adopted his familiar rhetoric: 'The listed subjects occur in *King Lear, Titus Andronicus*, the Bible. It will bring the law into contempt. It goes against the principles of British justice established in Magna Carta.'

When Jeffrey Archer accosted him at a book fair and told him, 'Kill Rumpole! It'll make a terrific story,' John was most indignant. But in the third series, the old boy appeared to breathe his last, falling to the courtroom floor in an apparent coronary seizure. The sad tidings were greeted with no great show of grief by his colleagues, who proceeded to scramble for his desk, umbrella stand, etc., before agreeing to send a modest floral tribute from the petty cash. Then Rumpole astonished everyone by reappearing at the Old Bailey, bewigged and large as life, claiming 'a Biblical prece-dent for this kind of thing'. Conan Doyle may have tired of Holmes and pushed him off the Reichenbach Falls, but John had not yet tired of Rumpole.

And no matter how strenuously Leo McKern tried to withdraw his services (even re-emigrating to Australia) he did return, and did six more series before 1992. He was not to be seen at a Rumpole launch party at El Vino's, but then, unlike John, he avoided all public appearances, speeches and dinners. Nor did he share the antipathy to Thatcher, and changed a critical reference to her in the script to 'the PM'. But through Horace Rumpole, John could revisit all his old courtroom dramas: defending the opposition leader in a former colony, investigating an art forgery and taking the cause of a porn bookshop selling titles like *Schoolgirl Capers* and *Manacle Me*. 'I deplore that rubbish,' declared Rumpole. 'But I will defend to the death your right to read it!' Each episode followed a formula: two or three interwoven plots, in four locations – chambers, El Vino's, the courtroom and Froxbury Mansions, where Rumpole sometimes seemed quite fond of She Who Must. 'Hilda,' he would say, pouring her a glass of wine, 'would you care to fade away with me into the forest dim?' And in one episode, John himself was glimpsed, Hitchcock style, in the background in the Taste-Ee-Bite breakfast bar.

In breaks from a book-signing tour from Glasgow to Guernsey (taking in 'the Gnome bookshop', run by Richard Ingrams's wife at Wallingford) he collected various awards. An honorary Doctor of Laws degree was conferred at Exeter University, where the public orator began, 'Always scribble, scribble, scribble! Eh, Mr Mortimer?' The orator could find little new to say, except that Mrs Mortimer was an Exeter graduate in French. In Toronto he got an honorary DLitt from the University of Susquehanna. And he went to Buckingham Palace, having been appointed CBE in the Queen's Birthday Honours. He already knew he had one royal admirer in the Queen Mother, who had sat next to him at dinner at Woodrow Wyatt's. She had written from Clarence House, in a note full of charm, to say she was 'simply delighted' to have *The Rumpole Omnibus*, 'so stuffed full of wonderful entertainment and wit', and was taking it away for the weekend.

*

Penelope's view of the Queen Mother, indubitably the nation's best-loved matriarch, was sharply at odds with the general reverence. That year, Penelope had published an acerbic and courageously partial biography, *Queen Elizabeth*. It was a tough assignment, hacking into the carapace of a living 'national treasure' aged eighty-six. Macmillan had commissioned it, but rejected it; Tony Lacey of Viking picked it up. 'Granny-bashing', one reviewer called it. A fellow writer remembered seeing Penelope get a slow handclap from an affronted audience at a *Yorkshire Post* lunch. As Frances Donaldson had written, biography is always 'a desperate enterprise . . . a hundred times worse when the subject is a member of the Royal Family'. Nothing better illustrated Penelope's fearlessness than this undertaking, and she paved the way for future, franker royal biographers.

As for John's version of their life together, she had watched Jane Asher playing herself on television and read John's memoirs. 'I don't know if the "marriage ending" cards were dealt when we first stood on the beach in Ireland and Penelope was overcome with thoughts of death,' John had written in *Clinging to the Wreckage*. 'In time a new hand would be dealt to me . . . There would be years of unlooked-for happiness, another marriage, another child . . .'

'It was rather a surprise,' Penelope said, 'to open one's *Sunday Times* and find the end of one's marriage all over it.' But she would feel free, in time, to respond to that, and to tell their story in her own uncompromising way.

22. Summer's Leases

'As grey dingy day follows grey dingy day in England, with an occasional delivery of snowflakes to become slush, in a winter that seems to be lasting for ever, I'm kept going by the thought of Tuscany in July.' John wrote this after eighteen successive summers in Chiantishire, 'home of the world's greatest paintings, beautiful cities, simple cookery', where he and Penny had lit upon their favourite house in 1987.

Renting other people's houses among vineyards and olive groves was John's favourite form of holiday, despite the irritations of familial togetherness ('Holidays can be brutal occasions: husbands and wives . . . forced into each other's company for twenty-four hours a day'; teenage daughters unpacking suitcases full of 'old dresses bought from barrows, ratty bits of fur, crumpled and disorderly history notes', and then, deprived of London friends and Soho discos, collapsing on their beds in terminal boredom, listening to Beastie Boy tapes, or narcissistically monitoring their tans: 'How's your watch mark?' 'Brilliant.').

In the mid-1980s John and Penny had rented a house near Cecina. It wasn't available the next year, but one of their guests, Judy Astor, happened to sit at dinner next to Leonard Ingrams. He was Richard Ingrams's brother, owner of Garsington Manor, the Oxfordshire opera house with Bloomsbury connections. Judy mentioned John's quest for a holiday house in Italy. 'As a matter of fact I have a house,' said Ingrams. This was La Rufena, near Gaiole, a converted *casa colonnica*, fifteen miles east of Siena and next to the Castello di Brolio, source of the Ricasoli family's Chianti wine, which, John said, 'can be drunk in large quantities with no ill effects whatsoever'. The house proved congenial, with its long table on the terrace and old-fashioned kitchen with hanging pans and herbs and log fire. The room where John wrote had been

converted from stables into a music room, with a Bechstein piano
on a platform (where Georg Solti performed one summer), and
had french windows opening on to steps down into the garden.
Unadorned by luxury loungers or poolside umbrellas, La Rufena
was a slightly shabby, lived-in family house, like Turville Heath
Cottage. It became the Mortimers' Tuscan retreat every July,
where they entertained a variable house party of family and friends
for the next two decades. 'If I didn't consider myself stuck for life
in my father's house,' he wrote, 'that corner of Italy is where I
would choose to live.'

Radda-in-Chianti, the nearest small town, could supply the
finest provisions ('a grocery and deli to rival Fortnum's') and sea
bass and mussels on Fridays. Radda also has the Bar Dante. Guests
often puzzled over John's devotion to the Bar Dante. It stands on
the corner of the main road to Poggibonsi, hard by a petrol station,
with lorries thundering past, so you have to shout to be heard.
'Yet it's one of the places in the world where I feel entirely happy,'
John proclaimed. Try as she might, Glenys Kinnock could not
fathom its appeal – 'Here we are on a beautiful Tuscan hillside,
yet we're sitting on a main road, deafened by motorbikes.' She
embarked on a running joke, eulogizing passing pantechnicons. In
later years John would be wheeled to his usual table, pointing out
that at least the happy old men in the Bar Dante were not locked
away in old folks' homes.

The place he most loved to watch the world go by was the
Piazza del Campo in Siena, 'the most beautiful town square in the
world – a place of medieval beauty which is alive, energetic,
humming with activity', from which to see not only the brutal
bareback Palio horserace, but every Sunday morning a procession
of medievally costumed 'knights' twirling flags and beating drums.
He loved the paintings in the Palazzo Pubblico: Martini's solitary
horseman and the infant Christ carried over the river by
St Christopher, and paintings about 'good government' and 'bad
government'. Behind the Palazzo is Le Logge restaurant, where
they would dine al fresco, flanked by a floodlit church wall,
enjoying Gianni Brunelli's own wine and pasta and listening to

him singing 'Ciao, Bella', a song of the communist resistance. There would be trips to the opera at San Gimignano, to Arezzo to see the Piero della Francesca frescoes, to Piero's birthplace, San Sepulcro, or to the ducal palace at Urbino.

But the centre of operations was La Rufena's veranda, with John presiding over long lunches and dinners, followed by charades, word games and card games, singing and dancing. Jacquie Davis, Peter and Thelma Nichols, Ann Mallalieu and her husband, Tim Cassel, both now QCs, and their daughters Cosima and Bathsheba, were among their earliest regular guests. John had encouraged Ann's marriage to Tim, despite Tim's right-wing views. He was the ideal stooge to John as they retold old Bar tales. In their first year at La Rufena they all went to the Gaiole Ball, hosted by the communist mayor, where John found himself dancing cheek to cheek with a German boy, and Emily aged fifteen pinched a policeman's bottom, and Cassel drove the wrong way up a one-way street, pursued by police sirens.

At La Rufena in 1987, John finished his novel *Summer's Lease* – from Shakespeare's sonnet 18:

> Rough winds do shake the darling buds of May
> And summer's lease hath all too short a date . . .

The setting was not La Rufena but the Tuscan house he had rented earlier, near Arezzo, with its thrillingly bat-infested tower and its big wooden table scrubbed 'white as a bone on a sea-shore', which he had first described in the article on villa-renting in 1974. The heroine is Molly Pargeter, whose husband, Hugh, is a weak, unreliable solicitor. He is having a lunchtime 'affair' with an elegant lady client and gets caught by Molly sending her a surreptitious postcard (a familiar experience to John), whereupon a row erupts which is reminiscent of *The Pumpkin Eater*:

'So what did you do after lunch?'
 'Nothing.'
 'What do you mean, nothing?'

'I mean nothing in particular.'

'Oh yes. And where did you do nothing in particular? In a sleazy hotel bedroom? Or did someone at the office lend you his flat? Men do that don't they?'

But these warring spouses are totally dwarfed by Molly's father, Haverford Downs, who has inveigled himself into their holiday. John described Downs as 'a lecherous old journalist, author of an appalling column called Jottings, which he fills with random and frequently pretentious thoughts'. He had been a fond father, once, who would make Molly a witch out of his knotted handkerchief (this was John's way of entertaining his infants, making 'Little Miss Witchie'), but as an old rake he is disappointed in his stolid, ample-breasted daughter, his preference being for gamine girls with 'the tip-tilted noses of impertinent page-boys'.

Haverford Downs was the undoubted star of the novel, launched in London with a party at Meridiana on 27 April 1988. He was also my Nemesis. Reviewing the book in the *Sunday Times*, I commented that the amusing Downs was 'an amalgam of Clifford Mortimer, Rumpole and Alistair Forbes'. I had barely met Forbes, but it was well known (I thought) that the septuagenarian hack, who lived in Château-d'Oex, Switzerland, wrote long-winded pieces for the *Spectator*, forever dropping the names of exiled European royalty and obscure contessas. Oh dear. Forbes made a considerable income from litigation by plunging editors into libel cases. He had even sued Bron Waugh's impoverished *Literary Review*. Now he decided to sue me.

In May, with *Summer's Lease* the number one bestseller, the *Sunday Times* editor Andrew Neil and I received writs alleging that we had brought the plaintiff, 'a well known man of letters', into 'public scandal, odium and contempt'. The combative Neil engaged Geoffrey Robertson, QC, who, striding restlessly round his chambers, impressed us with his dynamic optimism. We must go for a defence of fair comment. 'From what John Mortimer tells me, the plaintiff was not in fact in his mind,' he added. I rang John. But to my dismay John did not leap at the chance to take the witness stand in my defence. It was foolish of me to suppose that he might (Jacquie Davis had the same experience when he witnessed her slight car crash: he would not testify on her behalf). No lawyer volunteers to appear in court as a mere civilian, least of all John. 'I'm sorry, darling,' he said in a curiously enfeebled voice, 'I really can't help you. Sorry. Goodbye!' So I gathered in evidence Forbes's articles (which read exactly as if written by Haverford Downs) and, over many months, alternately fretted and chortled over the ludicrous apologies suggested by Forbes's solicitor, Lord Goodman. The threat dragged on until March 1989, when the case was settled out of court with a payment of several thousand pounds to the pestilential Forbes. We heard later that he was crowing about his haul over lunch in the Beefsteak Club.

This was tiresome, but John was under his own black cloud. One bad review cancels out a hundred good ones, as many authors know, and the veteran Tuscan expat Lord Lambton (who had been at Harrow with John) had written a poisonous review of *Summer's Lease* in the *Spectator*. 'An indigestible lump of tourist journalism,' Lambton called it. He found all the English characters (except old man Downs) dull and uninspired, and the Italian characters were 'exactly what I would expect from a professional-class, left-wing parlour pink who has for years courted the company of millionaires'. The novel was repetitive and tedious about wine, and inaccurate about every aspect of Italian life – 'How could Mr Mortimer have produced such trash?'

Some suspected a subtext behind this vitriol. Might Lambton have been the secret lover referred to in the tell-tale list of 'Important Things in My Life' found in that Tuscan villa in 1973? John had just compounded his original indiscretion (though only those in the know would notice this) by inserting another such tantalizing list in *Summer's Lease*. He had also written about it in the *Telegraph* in April, when he had described a rented villa where the couple were 'clearly not getting on'. The wife had left her typewritten list beside the telephone, headed 'My Assets', which began 'Extreme physical beauty'. 'She had also made a list of "What is important in my life",' John wrote, 'in which the house itself came first, someone called Gaston second and the rest of the family also ran.' Whatever Lambton's motive for his vituperation, it wounded John. He did not greatly enjoy even light-hearted mockery. That August, at La Rufena – where we went to lunch – I showed John what I thought was a witty 'Afore ye go' column in the *Spectator* by 'Wallace Arnold' (a.k.a. Craig Brown), proposing a heartfelt toast to 'The CHARM of Mister – John – Mortimer!' Obviously it was intended ironically. But John did not smile. 'Who *is* Craig Brown?' he asked coolly. (The two later became good friends.)

His 1988 scrapbooks, unsurprisingly, contain no trace of Lord Lambton or Craig Brown. Instead, on page after page John is pictured, beaming, often barefoot, champagne glass in hand, on a Lloyd Loom chair in the dappled shade of the snowy-blossomed *Cornus kousa* tree in the Turville Heath garden. On another nation-wide book tour, flanked by publicity girls, John kept everyone amused. Over lunch in the Shelbourne Hotel, Dublin, he admitted to a difficulty in thinking up plots: the playwright Charles Wood, he said, planned to have his gravestone inscribed 'A plot at last'. John's smiley, well-fed face was everywhere – 'It is a shock to look at an old photograph and find that he once had a jawbone,' wrote Catherine Bennett in the *Sunday Times*. 'Odder still, that he was once described as "wiry".' The words 'national treasure' were not yet used, but, 'If anyone has inherited the mantle of the late John Betjeman as the nation's favourite uncle, it must be John Mortimer,' Richard Ingrams wrote. 'He has the same love of England, the same determination to be cheerful and to make people laugh and above all the same simple faith in humanity.' This cuddly encomium added that Mortimer also shared Betjeman's deceptive appearance, shuffling along, smiling absent-mindedly, languid of voice and prone to giggles – disguising an industrious approach to work.

Like Betjeman, John had turned into a caricature of himself. *Private Eye*, whose editorship Ingrams had just relinquished, par-odied the clichés of every John Mortimer interview under the Glenda Slagg byline: ' "Would you like some more champagne?" beamed the brilliant barrister turned bestselling author and playwright. We were sitting in his delightful 17th century Oxfordshire oasthouse on the river near Henley, discussing the new series of Rumpole. "He's quite a dear, isn't he, old Rumpole, don't you think?"' and so on. When a journalist named Jody Tresidder was told by the Viking PR that John was too busy to meet her, she rang John directly. John Mortimer too busy for an interview? Certainly not. They met next day in the Groucho Club, between his lunch with Griff Rhys Jones and a dinner-dance given by David Dimbleby at Kew Steam Museum.

The ceaseless exposure had continued during his second trip to Australia ('my new-found-land') the previous year, when he and Penny went back to Canberra, Brisbane and Sydney. John gave his *Mortimer's Miscellany* at Sydney University's law school, and met Malcolm Turnbull, defence lawyer in the Peter Wright *Spycatcher* case. They saw their old friends David Hunt (a High Court judge) and his wife, Marg, Rosie's godmother, and Jack Lee, Laurie Lee's film-director brother. At the Great Barrier Reef island of Bedarra it rained every day; there was nothing for it but to drink his way through every bottle in the hotel room. But he had five years' worth of writing commissions in hand: the Tuscany novel, another Rumpole, prefaces (to *Little Dorrit, Bleak House,* a Ronald Firbank novel, a life of the advocate Edward Marshall Hall) and an adaptation of Strauss's *Die Fledermaus* (with a new translation written for him by Miriam Gross) for Covent Garden. He also hosted and organized, with Gawn Grainger, Olivier's eightieth birthday celebrations in spring 1987. And he was plotting a second visit to the Rapstone Valley, in a novel called *Titmuss Regained* – based on the Tory minister Nicholas Ridley's recent 'Nimby' problems over a development near his home.

That year he had stopped interviewing for the *Sunday Times*. 'I might go back,' he said. 'My moral positions are always dubious, vague and subject to a certain amount of contradiction.' He had an atavistic attachment to *The Times*, Clifford's daily paper: the crossword, the gardening column and the law reports were his father's 'Matins'. Clifford had done some *Times* law reporting, before becoming the star of law reports himself. At school, John had taken *The Times* while more brutal boys opted for the *Morning Post*. When publication of *The Times* had stopped for a year (1979–80) it was 'like the death of the past'. On *The Times*'s 200th anniversary, 1785–1985, John had written the introduction to a celebratory volume. He had spent a day in the Gray's Inn Road office in September 1984, the day suicide bombers attacked the US embassy in Beirut. He sat in on news conferences, watched the letters being selected, and called on the literary editor Philip Howard, who told him Dickens always got terrible reviews from *The Times*, and on the obituaries editor, who told him the policy was to be 'broadly favourable to the corpse'. 'No, you can't read your obituary,' he was told. 'Nobody can.' John was dismayed to find that the nearest thing to lunch, at the *Times* office, was a machine in the corridor offering sandwiches, Kit-Kat and orangeade.

Two years on, the Wapping revolution had happened and Don Berry, his favourite editor, had resigned to join the *Daily Telegraph* under its new editor, Max Hastings. Why not come too? Berry suggested. John demurred: 'I want to write for papers my friends are likely to read.' But his agent Pat Kavanagh briskly fixed a deal: twelve monthly pieces (at £3,000 a time plus 60 per cent of any syndication), entitled 'John Mortimer's Calendar', starting in April 1987 on the front of the *Telegraph*'s new *Weekend* section. His first excursion was a pilgrimage – by chauffeur-driven Rolls – to Canterbury, 600 years since Chaucer's *Canterbury Tales*. He was accompanied by a verray parfit gentil knight named Sir Christopher Foxley-Norris, retired Battle of Britain pilot, and a nun, Sister Incarnata. They set off from the George at Southwark, stopping for lunch at an Egon Ronay-recommended restaurant, where the nun chose a 'health-giving citrus fruit cocktail' and the knight said, 'Count me out of anything labelled health-giving.' The knight still had nightmares about being in his Spitfire; the nun said she never dreamed at all.

Max Hastings, a rebarbative fellow, sometimes resisted a Mortimer interview, on the grounds that he found John 'too generous'.

He was generous; but he did find some people less than congenial, among them Woody Allen, who 'thought about each question seriously, and made no jokes'. John tried to persuade Woody that Chekhov called his plays comedies, that life was indeed short and unsatisfactory and it was comedy that confronted the truth. But Woody was cheerless, despite having just become the father, in his fifties, of a baby named Satchel, who lay in the arms of a jet-lagged Mia Farrow. When the *Telegraph* contract ended, John signed up with the *Mail on Sunday*, for the same fee, £3,000 per piece. So journalism would remain a lucrative diversion. He got $4,000 to write about the Thames Valley from the American Express magazine; a dollar a word for 2,000 words on the Old Bailey from *Condé Nast Traveller*. And he continued to review for the *Sunday Times*, and sometimes still to do interviews: with Kingsley Amis, for instance, who famously shocked John by telling him he never was really angry, 'except when I hit *my son* with a hammer'. The Amises had a good laugh about this. John had misheard; what Kingsley said was 'my thumb'.

The book reviews were, with the interviews, his best journalistic work (yet he did not value them enough to keep them; his scrap-books were reserved for pieces about himself). Many authors were grateful for his judicious comments; his name would endorse the paperback and readers gleaned from them a good sense of whether the book was worth buying. His views carried authority: 'What I believe we need now are barristers who care passionately about injustice, and who can feel for the outcasts, unfortunates and victims of our society' (reviewing Peter Rawlinson's memoirs). He had a good eye for a witty line, like the novelist Christopher Hope's description of Pretoria, 'a city with one foot in the nine-teenth century and the other in Woolworths'. He admired Lord Hailsham's ability to describe, movingly, the unbearable grief of flying home from Sydney with the body of his wife, who had been killed in a riding accident, in the aircraft hold. And when writing about Nigel Dempster's life of Christina Onassis (who inherited $50 million a year, and was found dead at thirty-four in her bath in Buenos Aires), John commented, 'Her story is a drab and

unhappy one, but it will have served a useful purpose if it encour-
ages old age pensioners to splurge their savings before anything
passes on to their children.' John's accountant Phyl was an early
advocate of 'skiing', spending the kids' inheritance, and would
discourage John from his plan to leave his children comfortably off
'in order that they would go on loving him'.

One evening in May 1988, the Mortimers were having dinner
with the Pinters. They talked of politics: the Official Secrets Bill,
Clause 28, the cuts in welfare, the fact that people were sleeping
rough on the streets ('even in Bayswater,' said Antonia Fraser; 'I
see them at the back of Catholic churches'). John remarked on the
low level of political discourse, now that old lefties like Paul
Johnson had gone over to Thatcher and nobody in the *New
Statesman* wrote inspiringly from the left. 'All we had believed in,'
John wrote, 'was dismissed as dangerous or absurd or both.' At this
Pinter threw out a challenge: 'What are we going to do about it,
then?' They couldn't just do nothing. 'If we tried,' Antonia
reasoned, 'we can at least tell our grandchildren that we tried.' It
was decided that at 52 Campden Hill Square – where during her
former marriage to Hugh Fraser, Antonia had previously hosted
political gatherings of the all-male Conservative Philosophy Group
– they would be At Home to a discussion group of writers opposed
to Thatcherism. The venue bestowed 'a Marie Antoinette feeling'.
    At the first meeting, on 20 June 1988, an excellent fork supper
was served, after which Anthony Howard, *éminence grise* of political
journalists, former editor of the *New Statesman* and of the *Listener*,
gave a lecture on the inconceivability of Labour ever winning
another election. Listening to his words were Salman Rushdie (not
yet imprisoned by the Ayatollah Khomeini's fatwa) and his wife,
Marianne Wiggins, Germaine Greer, Margaret (later Baroness) Jay,
Ian McEwan (whose fortieth birthday eve this was), Angela Carter,
Margaret Drabble and her husband, Michael Holroyd, Emma
Tennant, the Labour MP Mark Fisher, Peter Nichols and his wife,
Thelma, and David Hare who had not yet written his Labour Party
play, *The Absence of War*. Penny and Thelma Nichols were to take

minutes. They called themselves the 20th of June Group, and soon expanded to include, as members and/or speakers, Melvyn Bragg, Lord Williams, Geoffrey Robertson, Denis Healey, Jonathan Porritt, Barbara Castle, Ben Pimlott, Sir Denis Forman and Anna Ford. On the first evening, a date was fixed for the next meeting in September, and Harold insisted on secrecy.

Fat chance. The story leaked out within days. Frank Johnson revealed its existence in the *Sunday Telegraph* and the group woke up to find themselves 'ridiculously newsworthy' and the butt of much scorn. Even the political columnist Peter Jenkins suggested that the idea of the socialist intellectual had become absurd: 'reactionary chic' had now replaced Tom Wolfe's 'radical chic'. The novelist D. J. Taylor asked, 'Does the left really need a write wing?' Another novelist, Paul Bailey, an old Labour voter, declared his revulsion at rich writers, enjoying vast advances, ungraciously expressing anti-Thatcher views. Antonia protested, 'Mrs Thatcher does not write my books nor pay my royalities. I think I am responsible for my own prosperity.' Anyway, as the daughter of Lord Longford, she said, she had no sense of embarrassment when mocked. But since the Pinters' house was now marked, later meetings were held at the Groucho Club, at Ruth and Richard Rogers's Chelsea house, or at Ruth Rogers's River Café.

'The storm of press hostility enlivened us and made me feel we were justified,' Ian McEwan said, looking back. 'It spoke a lot about the times we were living in. I found the meetings stimulating.' They were not, he conceded, remotely like a Russian dissident group. Indeed, their views were, in the world of the arts, entirely orthodox: nobody in the arts supported Mrs Thatcher. But they forged a link with Labour Party policy-makers, and John Smith, the Shadow Chancellor, addressed them impressively about what he wanted to do in government. They were too diversely divided as a group, however, ever to publish a manifesto.

There were internecine squabbles. One night, the journalist Duncan Campbell proposed a ban on smoking, but John in the chair declared that smoking was a matter for individual conscience. Angela Carter argued with Peter Nichols over Salman Rushdie's apology for *The Satanic Verses*. John pointed out that the workers at Penguin Books, Rushdie's publishers, were in equal danger and without police protection (while Rushdie had SAS guards at £1,000 a day). John's memories of the meetings tended to feature Harold Pinter's explosive outbursts. On 1 March 1989 John arrived at the River Café in a van, out of which rolled two beer cans, 'with *two women*', as a newspaper reported: Penny and Ann Mallalieu. That night Harriet Harman read a paper, heckled by Charles Williams ('Come off it, Harriet!', 'Airy-fairy claptrap', etc.). Ann was provoked into saying why didn't they all stop talking and do something? Harold, in the chair, grandly asked, 'Madam, I don't even know why you're here, as you weren't invited.' Penny piped up that Ann was her guest. Antonia said she wasn't on the list; Penny said she was. Later Harold apologized to Penny and said, 'I'll never act as chairman again. I only behave like a ruffian.' (Peter Nichols commented, 'We prefer the ruffian Pinter to the would-be gent.')

'I was at my worst that evening,' Pinter recalled. 'Regrettably. But she did say something very aggravating. She was a newcomer, and I was chairing and should have asked the speaker to respond. Instead I said, "Who the hell are you anyway?" which was unfortunate.' Next day Ann received a brief note: 'Dear Ann, Sorry I was rude – Harold.'

On another evening the Mortimers were in a Notting Hill pub with the Pinters, discussing 20th of June matters, when Penny mentioned having seen the film *Scandal*, about the Profumo affair. Pinter took exception to the film. Penny responded bravely that she thought no subject in art was taboo. At this Pinter exploded ('Oh, art, is it?') and Penny went on recklessly to say that having been a child (seventeen) at the time of Profumo, he was a historical figure to her, 'like Henry VIII'. Pinter snapped back, 'Henry VIII! That puts the tin lid on it! I won't sit here and be told that Profumo is the same as Henry VIII.' At which point, belatedly, John was moved to say, 'Oh, piss off, Harold,' and the Pinters swept out. He and Penny ordered champagne and sat gloomily, feeling it was all over – but soon the Pinters were back, explaining that they felt sensitive about the *Scandal* film because they feared that one day such a film might be made about them. In time, the Pinters left the 20th of June Group, and John felt that the meetings now lacked an essential element of dramatic tension. Mrs Thatcher, anyway, was eventually toppled by the machinations within her own party.

Nearly twenty years later Pinter told me why he thought the 20th of June Group 'didn't quite work out'. 'I hold two factors responsible. One was me. I was extremely neurotic at that time. I can see that. I was very, very edgy. And John's equilibrium was admirable. I was a kind of disruptive force. I'm not proud of that at all. I was sort of uncontrolled. I was so incensed about Thatcher, I just couldn't control it. Which was clearly unfortunate. The other factor is that the media were totally against us, and tried to take the piss out of us right, left and centre. A lot of people wrote that they thought we were pretentious: what right had fucking writers to speak at all about politics? And mockery being the British weapon, they made life very, very difficult, actually. At the same time, I have to say it was an admirable enterprise and a great deal of it was due to John, and where it was at its best was where he was at his best. There were some excellent people concerned. But it wilted and finally collapsed, and the final irony was that we all wanted a Labour government, and what a fucking shit-house that has turned out to be! I mean, give me Thatcher every time! At least she wasn't a hypocrite. And this is the irony of it.'

For John, the 20th of June Group was vastly enhanced by the arrival of skittish, fast-talking, mini-skirted Kathy Lette, who became his 'best friend'. The ebullient and pun-crazed Australian novelist breezed in one night with Geoffrey Robertson, whom she was shortly to marry, attracted by his 'child-bearing lips'. John at once took to her, and to her puns. Kathy was one of four daughters of a Sydney optician known as 'Optic Merv'. 'I still spoke with irritable vowels,' as she says. 'I was a surfie girl. I left school at fifteen. When I arrived here, everybody was horrible to me. How could the gorgeous QC dump the gorgeous domestic-goddess-to-be [Nigella Lawson] for a loudmouth colonial nymphomaniac? And I'd say please! don't call me a loudmouth. When Geoff brought me into the 20th of June Group – I'm sure it didn't help my case that I bounced in like a kangaroo – they were paranoid about the media getting in. Harold said, "Who's she? You can't bring partners!" Antonia said, "And who are you?" And I said, "Well, who are you?"

'I felt I'd landed in the Borneo jungle. Who were these awful English people with a condescension chromosome, who had plucked their highbrows and looked down on me, even those who were shorter than me? They didn't know what my intellectual calibre was (which is nil). But then in the midst of this snobocracy sat John Mortimer. I sat next to him and he explained them all to me – he was like a David Attenborough who could introduce me to the species. We started talking that night and carried on till our lips fell off.

'He could do the wordplay – wordplay is foreplay for females! – he was so mischievous and wicked, and he laughed at my jokes and could trade my awful puns.' John also introduced her to Byron, fuelling more puns – 'Byron couldn't abide a woman with no redeeming vice.' She would always call John 'a babe magnet' who made every woman feel like a sex goddess. Even the 20th of June Group had to admit that Kathy Lette made them laugh.

Five years later Bron Waugh, reviewing John's memoirs, discerned that John had been bruised by the 20th of June Group episode. 'He does not really understand why at the age of 65 he suddenly became a figure of obloquy and derision.' John had blamed the press reaction on 'reactionary chic', but 'I am afraid he is wrong,' said Bron. 'Chic has nothing to do with it. Champagne Socialists are detested by New Britons – for their class.' John might call himself a socialist, but he was really a liberal, humane bourgeois of the old guard. And if the left shed the humane bourgeois trappings John represented, things might be even worse. 'Let us thank our lucky stars,' Bron concluded (this was 1994), 'that pretty Tony Blair at least went to public school.'

John wrote to Bron:

Although we approach politics from different angles I'm sure we agree in finding political life ridiculous, and there was plenty of absurdity in the 20th of June group. I also entirely agree with you about the danger of political correctness, the arch-enemy of all freedom, taking over the Labour party. Sanity can only be preserved while politicians have people like you to laugh at them.

Four-year-old Rosie had started school. Influenced by Glenys Kinnock, they decided that she would attend a state primary school at Radnage, followed by middle school at Stokenchurch with Cosima, daughter of Ann Mallalieu. But when she was eleven, John discovered they weren't teaching her any Browning or Tennyson, so he whisked her off to the Dragon at Oxford, where she thrived. He was convinced that she had the makings of a future novelist, and often told the story of how, when he was sitting in the bath with her one night, Rosie said, 'I don't love you, Dad.' 'Don't you?' said John. 'That's very sad.' 'Yes, it is sad,' she replied. 'But it is interesting.' Emily was about to leave St Paul's. In her teens she had become obsessed by the tackier side of showbiz, by Torvill and Dean, the figure-skating champions, anything with exotic dancing girls in feathers and sequins, in whom she found 'a great tragic dignity'. 'That's what made me want to be an actress – not the posh actors or writers who came here,' she said.

Since John was a famously indulgent dad, it was left to Penny to inject any discipline. Emily was also much influenced by her grandmother, Anne Gollop, and would often stay at the farm with her many cousins. 'When we drove the pigs to the abattoir, granny always insisted the pigs loved having a day out.' She would help to squish the sausage meat, cycle along the front at Herne Bay, and rootle through the antiques, fur coats from jumble sales, beads and baubles that Anne stored in her barn. There were often 'difficult' children staying there on country breaks. Penny was eventually able to do the same for deprived children, through the Turville School project. Children from the Blackbird Leys estate in Oxford would arrive twice a week during the summer to swim and have lunches and evening barbecues at Turville Heath Cottage.

Emily's place at Lincoln College, Oxford, to read Russian and English took her to Moscow in her gap year. It was the year of glasnost and perestroika and the failed coup against Gorbachev. A poet named Denis, whom she had met at a London poetry reading, invited her to his birthday party and, at seventeen, she fell in love. She stayed with him in a composer's house full of bearded poets and singers practising their arpeggios, 'feeling I was in a black and white film with subtitles'. One night when Denis was asleep, she shaved off his moustache. 'I was halfway through, when he woke up and cried, "In Russia we have a saying that kissing a man without a moustache is like eating an egg without salt."' She rang home to say she wanted to stay in Moscow and marry Denis. 'I had the idea that my life would be living in garrets and ironing poets' shirts.'

John and Penny insisted that Emily should take up her place at Oxford. There, Denis showed up again. On Christmas Eve, he arrived in time for Midnight Mass at Turville Church, and the contrast in their lives was painfully obvious. Denis lived with his mum in a twenty-five-storey block on the outskirts of Moscow; now here he was, among 'our hundreds of presents and the tree and the ridiculous excess'. Then there was the Deep Purple concert. Denis had already been thrilled by the fact that Emily's father had defended the great Sex Pistols. Now they went to a gala benefit at the Kenton Theatre to save the Regal cinema, and Deep Purple (two of whose musicians lived in the Hambleden Valley) were playing. 'In Russia, Deep Purple were bigger than the Beatles,' said Emily, 'and suddenly, there they were, in this sleepy little English town. Denis couldn't believe it.'

John was now a grandfather (and step-grandfather) to a growing dynasty: Sally in Bristol had two boys, Gus and Joe, and there was Felix, son of Jeremy (now a BBC radio producer) and Polly, who had married in London in 1987. Their long relationship had known many vicissitudes since their schooldays, including Polly's absence in New York as nanny, lodging with the family of Sienna Miller, and her period of acute bipolar disorder. Jeremy was the rock in her life throughout, and their wedding reunited John and Penelope, who organized the flowers for the reception at Lauderdale House, Highgate Hill. Within four years, Jeremy and Polly had three children.

At the end of the 1980s John was indefatigable. He held a visiting fellowship at Dartmouth College in New Hampshire, where the students were greatly exercised by the need for a law against 'spousal abuse'. Underpinning John's life of travelling, writing and performing was Penny. She undertook all the letter-writing and organization of the 20th of June Group. She dealt with the fundraising for the village school. All matters pertaining to the family were left to her. In her mid-forties she had become an accomplished horsewoman and joined Ann Mallalieu and Tim Cassel at hunt meetings in Berkshire and on Exmoor, where she later bought a cottage; there were six horses in their Turville Heath meadow. And there was ceaseless entertaining, for which she took charge of guest lists and invitations. Like the Osbornes at their house in Kent, who opened up their garden every summer to a vast crowd of thespians, writers and neighbours, the Mortimers invited a similar crowd. The champagne flowed and guests would include the Kinnocks, Jeremy Irons and Sinéad Cusack, Barbara Castle, Michael Green, David Hare, Drue Heinz, Sir Peter and Lady Parker, Eileen Atkins and Bill Shepherd, Anthony and Catherine Storr, the Osbornes, the Stoppards, Michael Frayn and Claire Tomalin, Ann and Tim Cassel, Peter and Thelma Nichols, Edward Fox and Joanna David.

Summer's Lease was filmed for television in June 1989 and John went out to Italy again. Colin Rogers, husband of Deborah and John's great admirer, was the producer. He and John and the director Martyn Friend shared a house just outside Castellina and took turns to cook in the evenings. John Gielgud, John's revered childhood Hamlet, whose photo in rakish hat he had pinned to his wall at Harrow, was absolutely perfect as Haverford Downs, 'his blue eyes bright with curiosity' and still smoking at eighty-five. He was always the best subject of theatre people's stories, and John had never forgotten that when Emily was a baby, he and Penny had taken her in her carrycot to a dinner party. When the Mortimers arrived, Gielgud eyed the cot and said, 'Why have you brought your baby? Are you afraid of burglars?' During the *Summer's Lease* shoot he had to be flown home for a prostate operation, but returned even brighter-eyed and more smoking, to regale the company – who also included Rosemary Leach, Leslie Phillips and Michael Pennington – with stories. They filmed the novel's party scene all night in the garden of the pink-washed, floodlit Villa la Vignamaggio near Greve in Chianti. Gielgud was reading a book about Lord Lucan and asked John if you could really get a hit man to murder someone for £3,000. 'Donald Wolfit would have paid that to get rid of me.' He sent John a Christmas card that year, with 'thanks again for giving me that splendid part'. In 1991 he got his first Emmy for it.

There was one genuinely poignant moment during his return to Italy for the filming. John discovered, eighteen years later, that while he had sat in the Piazza del Campo in Siena, having a drink with John Gielgud, a young man nearby was observing them. The piazza is like a vast theatre set. The young man who sat, with a friend, eyeing John was Ross Bentley, Wendy Craig's tall, slim, bespectacled son. Ross was working in Italy that year, running a hotel in Lucca. He had by now been told by his godmother about his real father, but he had never set eyes on John Mortimer before. Suddenly, there he was, at a café table with Sir John Gielgud! Should he go over and reveal his existence? 'I was tempted. I thought about it,' Ross told me. 'But my immediate concern was the repercussions on his family, and mine: Penelope was still alive, my dad was still alive. Ninety-nine per cent of me thought it would be so nice to speak to him – but I simply lacked the courage.'

23. Scribble, Scribble, Scribble

'Sooner or later, great men turn out to be all alike. They never stop working,' wrote V. S. Pritchett, in his essay on Gibbon. 'They never lose a minute. It is very depressing.' It may be depressing, said Pritchett's biographer Jeremy Treglown, but it is also reassuring. Pritchett said the same about Virginia Woolf: 'She worked harder than ever when she became famous . . . what else is there to do but write?' These were John's sentiments exactly as he approached seventy. He was fired with a *furor scribendi*. 'How else would I occupy my time?' he said. 'I don't play golf, and I'm too old for love affairs that occupy the day' (or even the lunch-hour).

His prodigious creativity, within the half-decade of his seventieth birthday, brought forth three novels plus their screenplays, three Rumpole volumes plus TV scripts, a volume of memoirs, two anthologies about criminals and great trials, two opera librettos, two plays for radio and TV, much journalism and a monumental stage adaptation of Dickens's *A Christmas Carol* for the Royal Shakespeare Company. He campaigned for penal reform, fund-raised for the theatre, chaired three committees and performed his *Mortimer's Miscellany*. He was repeatedly likened to J. B. Priestley, to Dr Johnson and to Chesterton. But he was, in many ways, Dickensian.

The addiction was chiefly to writing, but also to attention. He would be cast into a slough of despond if he wasn't reviewed, reviewing, interviewed or interviewing, in one of the Sunday papers every week. Not even bronchitis stopped him from setting off to promote the new novel, *Titmuss Regained*, in the spring of 1990. He embarked on a world publicity tour of America, Canada and Australia. His walk was a shuffle and he wore an expression of 'bovine resignation' as he met a young lady from the *Scotsman*, Colette Douglas Home, in March. 'Another night, another town, another interview,' she wrote. 'The price of being top of the bestseller list.' He said it was nice to get out and meet people. 'It's very lonely, writing, and it's cold. My feet get very cold.' But what, she wondered, do we not already know about John Mortimer? She appealed to him to think of some anecdote that had not already been published. 'I will try,' he said, sinking on to a sofa. 'Might be difficult. Shall we have a drink? Let's make it champagne.'

By June he was in the Blue Mountains outside Sydney, visiting Richard Neville at his gloriously isolated house named Happy Daze. Despite a bad asthma attack, he continued his punishing round of appearances, in tartan trousers and flamboyant tie, the charm struggling to emerge between coughing fits. Usually Dr Greasepaint would kick in as soon as he faced an audience, but ten minutes into his talk at Adelaide town hall his voice gave out. 'I was with a very nice publicity girl whose boyfriend was a barrister in Adelaide,' he said. 'I said I'm sorry, my voice has gone, and she was very sad, but then she brightened and said, "At least we won't now have to postpone our bondage party! We hold it in a Scouts' hut, because the ropes are already there."' Perth had to be cancelled.

When he got home, Penny organized a vast midsummer party, and they set about producing the three-part TV version of *Titmuss Regained*, with the irreplaceable David Threlfall. Television networks were now abandoning expensive drama for cheap quiz and game shows, so Jacquie Davis, John and Penny had formed an independent company, New Penny Productions, and John was free to cast whomever he liked. He managed to secure Kristin Scott Thomas, whom he had admired in Waugh's *A Handful of Dust*, to play the second Mrs Titmuss.

Penny had hitherto classed herself, along with the other playwrights' wives Helen Osborne and Thelma Nichols, as 'The Wash-Out Wives', acronym WOW, as an antidote to the frenetic fame of Tom Stoppard's wife Miriam, doctor and writer. This disguised, disingenuously, the fact that none of their helpless husbands could have written anything without the support of the wives who ran their lives. Certainly, John's summers in La Rufena could not have happened without Penny doing the donkey-work, collecting or delivering guests at Pisa airport, raiding the Radda supermarket, supervising beds and meals for ever-changing numbers. She was aided, from 1991, by the cook Jo Elwin, who produced legendary feasts, twice daily: polpette of veal with lemon risotto; brasato of beef; rolled scallopine of veal stuffed with smoked pancetta, Parmesan and sage; Tuscan salsiccie with red onions and porcini and John's favourite mash; pear and almond tart, and sorbets and poached fruits from the orchard. (Glenys Kinnock said she put on half a stone in two days at La Rufena.) Guests saw Penny as 'a superwoman, resilient, energetic, the anchor of the family'. It was no longer just John's show. She was, everyone agreed, 'a great girl' and John was 'bloody lucky'. She was also confident about inviting people *she* liked, defined by Emily as 'anyone who was fun and unstuffy and had spirit and added to life'.

Kathy Lette and Geoffrey Robertson started joining the party in 1991. 'La Rufena was a human minestrone,' said Kathy, 'with a dash of politician, a soupçon of pop princess, a Roman Catholic priest, plus those of thespian tendencies, all kept going on the high level of alcohol. You had to be hospitalized from hilarity after lunch.' Jeremy Irons and Sinéad Cusack would arrive by Harley-Davidson. Anna Ford, after the death of her husband, Mark Boxer, in 1988, was invited with her two daughters for summer after summer, as was the newly widowed Myfanwy Piper. In a way, John was emulating life at Tony Richardson's Le Nid du Duc in the South of France. He had been bewitched by Richardson's lavish hospitality, his cast of guests that might include Rudolf Nureyev and Jack Nicholson, his fiendish games of get-the-guests. Games at La Rufena became increasingly mischievous. Once, a guest was put on trial because he mentioned buying a Versace dress for his wife; she denied this, and everyone realized that he'd bought the dress for another. 'We mounted a mock trial. Neil Kinnock played the policeman giving evidence, Geoff represented the husband, John was the judge, and it all got a bit dangerous.'

On another occasion a lady novelist was asked by John who of all her lovers was the great love of her life – famous actor, writer, politician? Under John's cross-examination she divulged his name (a former Cabinet minister) within minutes. Charades lampooned people's foibles. Guests agreed, 'It was like living in a play.'

John was in his element, surrounded by female attention (women always outnumbered men), flattering them all. 'Darling,' he would greet a child, 'you must be the most wonderful girl in the world. Why am I surrounded by such beautiful women? I'm so lucky.' The children loved him because he became one of them, 'slightly naughty'. There was a motorcade each year to the opera in San Gimignano: there was a memorable *Rigoletto*, under a dark blue sky, the full moon rising behind. Most evenings there were singalongs, Neil Kinnock's Elvis Presley imitations, a bit of jiving, Trivial Pursuit for the children, and verse-writing contests in which John would suggest a first line: for example, 'Christopher Bland had a one-night stand.' But the main obligation was telling stories. They all went to visit Dame Muriel Spark for lunch at her house, a converted church near Arezzo, then she and her companion, Penelope Jardine, drove over to La Rufena for dinner.

John relished Muriel Spark's advice on writing novels: 'You are writing a letter to a friend. Write privately, not publicly; without fear or timidity, right to the end of the letter, as if it were never going to be published.' He also relished Miss Jardine's story about her father (a wartime army commander in West Africa), who had been offered the chance of a meeting with Hitler. He devised a plan which would dispatch the Führer: he would take a box of Swan Vestas packed with yellow fever germs, and during their talk he would strike a match to light his pipe, releasing the germs. The Foreign Office told him not to be silly: to kill Hitler like that 'wouldn't be cricket'.

One year Edna O'Brien, trying to finish her book on Yeats, found the noise insupportable and took refuge in the house next door. Since La Rufena was not available that year, they were in a substitute house. It was slightly suburban: immaculate, but just not the same. 'The owners left a cat to be fed,' said one guest, 'and I remember John kicking it. Edna sat downstairs with her typewriter on the ping-pong table, John upstairs, writing by hand. Her tapping drove him absolutely mad.'

In 1994, Richard Eyre recorded, they all visited the Soltis near Grosseto, and found Georg Solti wading in the sea up to his thighs, 'wholly absorbed, silently conducting the Tchaikovsky he was about to do in Salzburg'. Luciano Pavarotti had lately been to the Soltis' and cooked supper for them. He had used, they reported, 'a litre of olive oil, a litre of wine and a kilo of Parmesan'.

Those who travelled to Italy with the Mortimers witnessed the hysterical panics John could get into when boarding an aircraft, even standing up and screaming, 'There's going to be a crash!' He hated flying, so it was odd that he flew so much. But when he arrived at La Rufena, all anguish departed. The king was in his *castello*. Early-rising guests would find him out on the terrace at 6 a.m., making tea, humming to himself, listening to the radio, about to start work.

The novels he was writing in the 1990s were entertaining, well-observed middlebrow social history, with some prescient themes. *Titmuss Regained* opened with Gerard Manley Hopkins's lines:

> O let them be left, wildness and wet;
> Long live the weeds and the wilderness yet.

The weeds and wilderness of the Rapstone Valley are threatened by a proposed new town, with a theme park carved from natural woodland. Leslie Titmuss, now the prosperous Minister for Housing, Ecological Affairs and Planning – but still avenging the heartless toffs who pushed him into the river – confronts the battle between local conservationists and developers. Since his first wife was killed protesting at Greenham Common, he has bought the Fanners' great house, where his mother used to be in service, and woos the Fanners' beautiful daughter Jenny, widow of an Oxford don ('We have so much in common – both married to dead people') to be his trophy wife. When Titmuss's palatial house is threatened by developers, he clandestinely funds the protesters.

Ten years into the future, an epilogue foresees the Rapstone Valley turned into Fallowfield Country Town, with pedestrian shopping precincts and multi-storey car parks. There is global warming, and in what is left of the countryside, the harvest mouse is an exotic rarity. England is in the grip of market forces, merchant bankers, avaricious builders and perfidious locals, lured by the prospect of making a fast buck. As A. N. Wilson wrote, 'This is the drama of modern political life which Anthony Trollope would have written, had he been alive.'

In the Thames Valley, a new town was indeed proposed. John, by now a considerable land-owner and president of BBONT (Berkshire, Buckinghamshire and Oxfordshire Naturalists' Trust), conserving the wild woodlands, found himself supporting Michael Heseltine, Tory MP for Henley. Heseltine asked him to kindly keep quiet about it: 'Words of praise from you will ruin my future in the Conservative Party.' The new town, near Thame, was stopped. 'Of course there should be more building,' said John, 'but why not build on some waste site in Cowley? It's ridiculous to tear down churches and build on green fields.' He was already suspecting that Titmusses might emerge in the Labour Party, 'carrying briefcases and portable phones and personal computers and Filofaxes'. There would be 'a bright young Gordon Brown type . . .'

The fearless defender of *Oz*, the good-hearted liberal *bien-pensant*, had always been at heart an old fogey. Fogeyism was now much more desirable than radicalism in newspapers and John's Bah! humbug commentaries on modern life ('Thirty-five television channels and nothing worth watching') exhibited healthily Blimpish views on the dreary sameness of English high streets, all chain stores and leg-waxing salons, and the ghastliness of international hotels, where he frequently made crotchety scenes. In a San Francisco hotel bar, having ordered a beer, he asked the waiter, 'Do you think it could be put back in the horse?' After weeks on the book-signing trail, he wrote a why-oh-why about modern inventions that make life worse: hotel reception desks ('a bored girl tapping silently, staring at a screen, unable to unlock the secret of where one's room is'); supermarket bar-codes; airport check-ins; ATM machines that swallow your cards; telephones answered by robot voices. Who could write a decent novel on a word processor? Dickens's manuscripts reveal a mass of crossings-out. 'If Dickens had had a word processor we should know nothing about the working of genius.'

Change and decay in all around he saw. Everything seemed to deteriorate during one man's lifetime, as Fred Simcox said in *Titmuss Regained*. 'The summers got worse, the music noisier and more senseless, the buildings uglier, the roads more congested, the trains slower and dirtier, governments sillier and the news more depressing.' Perhaps it was a stroke of mercy by divine providence, 'because when he came to the end of his allotted span in a world so remote from the one he had grown up in, the average citizen was quite glad to go'.

He wrote a 'Happy Birthday, Ma'am' to Her Majesty when she reached the age of sixty-five, on the same day as he was sixty-eight. They were both, he said, from 'an endangered species' (the monarch and the socialist). 'Many people no doubt would like to see us abdicate. I believe we should soldier on.' And when the Prince of Wales declared that Shakespeare must remain on the school curriculum, John poured out his Shakespearian heart, alongside a photograph of himself as Richard II at the Dragon. He could still while away time in airport lounges, 'inviting myself to sit upon the ground and tell sad stories of the death of kings'. Why limit children to studying *Lord of the Flies* and the socio-political aspect of soaps? In Shakespeare they would find sex and violence and rude jokes, and plays still relevant and accessible enough to fill theatres where, 'unlike at a football match, you are unlikely to get kneed in the groin'.

As the father of an eight-year-old he had no time at all for modern children's books with bright illustrations of 'mischievous little aeroplanes and playful dragons'. In an essay in *The Pleasure of*

Reading, Antonia Fraser's anthology for the bicentenary of W. H. Smith, he said it would be no loss if no more children's books were produced. There would still be *Alice's Adventures in Wonderland*, *Treasure Island*, *The Hound of the Baskervilles*, *The Thirty-Nine Steps*, *Good Morning, Jeeves*, and *The War of the Worlds*, 'as satisfactory to pensioners as they are to ten-year-olds. The same cannot be said of *Ted the Naughty Little Tractor*.'

His next novel was launched with a party at the Ivy. The eponymous *Dunster* was another version of Gunston / Tainton / Gunter, his Harrovian room-mate from hell. Dick Dunster is the adversary, ever since schooldays and Oxford, of Philip Progmire (alliterative heir to Piers Plowman, Peregrine Pickle, Paul Prendergast), a timid accountant. Cocksure Dunster, who panned Progmire's undergraduate Hamlet, now writes caustic theatre reviews, and has stolen Progmire's wife. So their lives – like those of David Copperfield and James Steerforth, or Amelia Sedley and Becky Sharp – continue to be intertwined.

Progmire works for silver-haired Sir Crispin Bellhanger at Megapolis Television. Dunster is writing for Megapolis a series on war heroes. Investigating a Nazi massacre of Italian civilians in 1944 in the Appenines, he discovers that this might have been a terrible error by Allied soldiers – commanded by Sir Crispin, DSO, MC. They had blown up the village church, full of praying villagers. 'We will have to say the Germans did it,' Sir Crispin had allegedly said. Was he a war criminal? And are people responsible for the sins of their former selves? Is their guilt still punishable fifty years on? The resulting libel action, *Bellhanger* v. *Dunster*, provides the novel's riveting climax, a long blow-by-blow account of proceedings in Court Five of the Royal Courts of Justice, presided over by an unusually fair-minded judge. It would have made a splendid television drama. An American reviewer wrote his review in mock heroic couplets, ending:

> And so just one thing's left to guess –
> Will this too be on PBS?

(John did write the filmscript, but *Dunster* never made it to the screen.)

A Labour victory in 1992 had seemed entirely probable, until the misplaced triumphalism of the Sheffield rally a week before polling day. But long before the election, it was widely suggested that John might become Lord Chancellor in Kinnock's Cabinet (there was little competition in the form of Labour lawyers). The *Independent* even suggested that if Britain ever looked for a playwright to be its president (like Vaclav Havel in Czechoslovakia) the choice should not be Havel's friend Harold Pinter, 'a man of gloomy, taciturn mien', but 'Lord Mortimer of Turville as he will soon become'. He had stayed loyal to Labour, 'but like all the best socialists, he is profoundly conservative at heart, favouring the good old days when the squire was in the manor and there weren't any beastly yuppies about the place'. Titmuss's adoption speech about the Toryish aspirations of the working class was relayed to the Shadow Cabinet, to illustrate the social challenge facing Labour in the election. But John Major won, and Kinnock's attempt to get John into the Lords failed. 'It was a great pity,' said Ann Mallalieu. 'He might not have been there for voting night after night, but he could have been useful on identity cards, terrorism, civil liberties. By the time there were slots for working peers, it was too late – he'd started to be over-critical of the party.'

As the novelist Allan Massie wrote in a fulsome tribute in 1995:

Politically Mortimer is like Betjeman. He thinks back sentimentally to a golden time after the war when he imagines that all classes were bound together by brotherly sympathy, when the rich did not grind the faces of the poor, and the poor did not envy the splendour of the rich. It is bunkum of course, but in Mortimer's case it is at least honest bunkum. The truth is, he is politically a dilettante. He loves everything that is old and familiar and English and comfortable: and this is one reason why he arouses such affection.

His continuing allegiance to the Labour Party after 1992 was sustained principally by his loathing of the new Tory Home Secretary, Michael Howard. 'Really – I cannot speak about the man in temperate terms. We now imprison more people than Turkey.' The Howard League for Penal Reform, which John chaired, became for him 'the Penal League for Howard Reform'. (He had gone to the Home Office in 1991, to discuss the problem of fifteen-year-old boys hanging themselves while on remand. The then minister had breezily chatted to him about opera, and 'shrugged off' the problem by saying, 'You're right, it's terrible, we're looking at this, keep up the splendid work.' 'By the time anything is done,' said John, 'another twelve will be dead.')

He now had so many London commitments, they decided to sell the Little Venice flat, for £300,000, and Penny found a bigger one just off the Portobello Road, an astute move. The redoubtable Phyl stepped in and discovered that the freehold was in jeopardy (the company that owned it was bankrupt and hadn't made a tax return). She suggested that Advanpress (John's company) bought the freehold, for a mere £5,000, so she could collect £7,000 from the other tenants. John, who had been hesitant about this deal, later said, 'Wasn't it a good idea of mine to buy that freehold?' At last, Phyl said, John had realized that he wasn't broke, and that £1,000 on a suit was well spent. In the new portrait of him by Tai-Shan Schierenberg, unveiled at the National Portrait Gallery in March 1992, he exuded prosperity in his expensive tailoring. But nobody could resist calling the portrait 'Rumpolian'.

'*Timor mortis*, like arthritis and failing eyesight, sets in around seventy,' John wrote later. He had always recoiled from thoughts of death: 'Noël Coward said he believes in life before death and I think that's a good attitude.' A radio interviewer who had the temerity to offer to show John his obituary, which he had prepared for the BBC, was given short shrift. But every newspaper 'morgue' was now prepared: Geoffrey Robertson wrote an obituary for the *Guardian*. The anonymous one then on the stocks at *The Times* (long since replaced) began: 'Although best known as a droll comedian, John Mortimer was in some respects a tragic figure.' He had 'ended his life depressed by a more and more rigorously conformist and dirigiste society'.

But a real glimpse of *timor mortis* had set in one day in 1992, when he was at Pearson's, on the panel deciding which young playwrights should win bursaries. Suddenly, half the room was plunged into darkness and the faces on his left vanished into the gloom. The retina had left one eye, as had happened to his father. The next day he was on the operating table at Moorfields Eye Hospital, and faced the prospect of following Clifford into total blindness. The night after leaving hospital he dined with Barbara Castle and had to apologize for spilling wine on the tablecloth because he couldn't see out of one eye. Lady Castle told him he was bloody lucky, she was going blind in both. Her cheerfulness (and her undiminished ability to deliver a knockout speech) impressed him. A letter came from the DVLA in Swansea, offering to renew his driving licence but asking if he had any disabilities. He replied that he had only one eye, couldn't judge distances and added for good measure that he had never been a very good driver. Back from Swansea came a new driving licence and a note saying, 'Happy motoring!'

Determined to ignore the eyesight problem, he had much to celebrate on his seventieth birthday. He was on the top of the bestseller list with *Dunster* and the BBC rescreened the original Rumpole play. There was a big party at Turville Heath Cottage, with dancing, combining John's milestone with Emily's twenty-first, so the marquee was full of beautiful bright young things from Oxford. Jacquie Davis held a women-only birthday dinner for him – Eileen Atkins, Joanna David, Kathy Lette, Genevieve Cooper and, by telephone, Sinéad Cusack – because 'his closest friends were women'. John regarded few men as real friends, having an aversion to 'locker-rooms and sweaty gymshoes and the traditional masculine preserve of sport'. He told Sue Lawley later, 'I've been quite good at friendships with women in my life but no good at best-buddy male friendships.'

*

The Rumpole Society of America, 'honouring John Mortimer and the Rumpolian concept', began to descend regularly on London. John had addressed 400 society members at a dinner in San Francisco, and discovered that a large proportion were distinguished American lawyers. But their only aim was to have fun. They visited the 'Rumpole sites', the Old Bailey and the Temple, met John for drinks at El Vino, and visited the TV studio to meet the cast. They produced a Rumpole cookbook and held blind tastings of Dodo Mackintosh's Cheesy Bits, She Who Must Be Obeyed lookalike competitions, and golf contests, chipping balls into wastepaper baskets. Their motto was 'Lunch! I'm particularly fond of lunch.'

John had been vastly relieved when Leo McKern had finally agreed to do a sixth TV series (for £100,000) in 1991. McKern's daughter Abigail joined the cast as Rumpole's junior, the thoroughly modern Mizz Liz Probert. As usual, in one episode, 'Rumpole and the Tap End' – in which Peter Bowles played the judge horrified to hear about a wife who made her husband sit at the tap end of the bath – John could be spotted, on a table full of judges, under a horsehair wig.

It was rumoured that Rumpole was among the programmes offered for sponsorship by ITV. Surely not, said Nancy Banks-Smith. 'Rumpole projects an air of down-at-heel but indomitable integrity. The state of his weskit defies description, but his hands are perfectly clean.' They did find a sponsor: Croft Port. But the seventh TV series proved to be the last.

When Leo McKern could no longer be persuaded to play the old darling, he was revived on radio, with Maurice Denham (and later by Timothy West, with Prunella Scales as Hilda), and John carried on writing the stories anyway: 'Much simpler: a novelist's freedom suddenly seemed intoxicating.'

But with or without television, Rumpole's immortality was sealed. One evening at a party given by Hatchards (supplier of books to Buckingham Palace) John was talking to the Queen when Prince Philip, passing by, said, 'Regina meets Rumpole.' Rather bright, John thought.

*

Some writers take to drink, others to audiences, said Gore Vidal. John, like Dickens, took to audiences, performing *Mortimer's Miscellany* at least once a month. In the hall of Lincoln's Inn, he proposed the toast at the Trollope Society's annual dinner. He starred in a Folio Society debate: 'Fictional crime is more interesting than the real crime we read about.' P. D. James proposed. Murders today were sordid, crude, lacking emotional depth or mystery and committed by uninteresting people from obvious motives. John countered with his tales from the courtroom, proving that 'truth was more entertaining than fiction'. John won, but his tales were actually 'two decades old,' said one lawyer in the audience. P. D. James was probably right, but John's advocacy had won, as it so often had, on laughter.

'There is nothing nicer than giving away other people's money,' John wrote. As well as being on the Pearson's young playwright bursaries panel, he was, as president of the Royal Society of Literature, one of the judges awarding the biennial £30,000 David Cohen Prize, bigger but lower-profile than the Booker, given for lifetime literary merit by the philanthropic Cohen. With Eleanor Bron, Seamus Heaney, P. D. James, Michael Holroyd and Penelope Lively, he awarded the prize to V. S. Naipaul. His RSL role also involved 'spinning out our tenure of the lease at Hyde Park Gate with tremendous lawyer's skill,' said Claire Tomalin, 'until in the end everyone felt sorry for the owner'.

Max Stafford-Clark invited him to apply his chairing skills to the Royal Court Theatre. He had never had a play on there, but at the Royal Court playwrights, not actors, had their names in lights. Backstage the building was rotting and so were the wooden posts underpinning the stage. The roof leaked and the tube roared underneath. It was a fund-raising job, and John sent out begging letters to putative benefactors. Would Peter Mayer, his name misspelled Meyer, make Penguin Books a corporate member, at £1,000 a year? Mayer replied with a cheque for £500. As he explained to his colleagues, this was a gesture in 'straitened times', 'as John is one of our major authors but also one of the nicest of men'.

★

Every winter they went back to the Gazelle d'Or, now joined by Anna Ford and her children, who found John every morning writing by the pool under the acacia tree, until noon, when he would stop for a gin and tonic. In 1992 Bob Geldof, one of John's recent interviewees, was there. They were all sitting round the log fire when Geldof's record manager said it was his birthday. 'So everyone did a performance. Paula Yates juggled with tennis balls, Penny did a dance, Emmy did Helena from *Midsummer Night's Dream*, and I did my Richard II speech about the deaths of kings.' The Geldofs joined the Mortimers' regular guest list. They met Michael Portillo there too. He impressed John because Rosie had a pet chameleon, and when John said, paraphrasing Hamlet, 'Does he eat the air – the chameleon's dish?', Portillo instantly furnished the next line: 'You cannot feed capons so.' On New Year's Eve one year 'half the French government' turned up at the hotel, and Anna Ford's daughter kissed Valéry Giscard d'Estaing at midnight. For John it was 'all part of life's wonderful entertainment'.

In the autumn following John's seventieth birthday, Penelope published her second volume of memoirs, *About Time Too*, in which she wrote about the break-up of the marriage, a great deal less tactfully than John had. While acknowledging the elusiveness of biographical truth, she had done her best to achieve it. She was unable to resist divulging the flippant comments John made to her about his new girlfriend Penny when she came along. Penelope sent John a copy of her book, but having received no reply, she followed up with a fax.

Penny recalled this as 'one of those moments in your life that are as clear as a bell, like a film. I was in the sitting room when John came through. "I've just had this fax from Penelope, I think you'd better read it." It said: "I sent you my book three weeks ago, and I haven't heard from you. Why not? The press are getting rather interested in what I said about you and Penny, so I think the best thing would be if we all had lunch somewhere very public, to show that we're all still friends."'

PENNY: 'What does she mean? What book?'
JOHN: 'Oh, I don't know, I put it in a cupboard.'
PENNY: 'Go and get it!'

'I opened the book and saw the bit about going into his chambers and his gown "smelling of sweat, semen and eau de cologne", and I just threw the book on the fire. It's the only book I've ever burnt.' John did not reply to Penelope's fax.

The fact that it was acclaimed as a memoir written with unsparing honesty, respected by critics and greeted with excitement by newspapers, was lost on John and Penny.

Penelope wrote to me:

The Press reaction so far is inevitable, I suppose, though it seems curious that such ancient history can be made scandalous in 1993.

I can only assume John's negative reaction. Perhaps it's naïve of me, but I hoped that he was confident enough now to take the book in the spirit in which it was written. This saddens me, but there's nothing I can do about it. A grave pity.

Even after so long together, she did not really know her husband at all. He had no such confidence.

She had almost finished writing volume three, but Weidenfeld dithered over it. They might reconsider if there were more 'tremendous' reviews. 'I rather hate them all,' she said. It never was published. John made no public response, but six years later – by which time Penelope was dead – he told Ginny Dougary of *The Times* how hurt he had been, Penny even more so, by her 'really nasty book about us'. It was fine for novelists, he said, to plunder their own lives ruthlessly – he too had done it – but in his view different rules applied to non-fiction. Did he think he had been a shit? Dougary asked charmingly. 'Well, I was not a perfect husband, that's true,' replied John. 'But then she was unfaithful.' Did they have an open marriage? 'No, not at all. We had the worst of both worlds.' He supposed Penelope had depended on him and had 'felt terribly rejected'. His own memoirs, volume two, which he was writing when hers came out, made no mention of Penelope at all.

Instead he went in search of his more distant past. He took a twelve-day trip to South Africa in September 1993, in search of his ancestors, and Jeremy joined him. Aided by Bill Bizley of the University of Natal, who arranged their trip, and by John's cousin Graham Pechey, now an academic in England, assorted aunts, uncles and cousins were assembled to meet their famous relation. Good liberals all, one of them recalled visiting John in Harben Road and being asked by John, 'How many black people have you had to dinner lately?' in his 'smug north London pinko' phase. John and Jeremy were shown family albums and Mortimer gravestones, and went to a game reserve to see black rhinos, giraffe and wildebeest. They learned to call Clifford's boyhood city 'Maritzburg', and saw the old Mortimer house and the old Pechey house, now part of St Anne's School, where Kathleen had been art mistress in 1915. At the Victoria Club, which still had the air of a last outpost of empire, they met a tortoise presented to the club in 1914 by a British army captain, as a brass plaque nailed to its shell declared. It was a bonding trip for father and son. They talked more than they had for years. The diaries written by his grandfather John Mortimer III, who had emigrated to South Africa in 1871, proved useful in *Murderers and Other Friends*.

This was an unconventional autobiography. Facing old age, he dipped randomly, in no chronological order, into the people and events he had known: the *Gay News* trial; the 20th of June Group; the Rumpole saga; John Gielgud; memories of Tony Richardson and Le Nid du Duc. He went into detail about the extraordinarily complicated process of translating opera libretti (he'd recently done *Die Fledermaus* and Mozart's *Zaide*), finding the right number of syllables to fit each musical phrase, with the accents or emphases on the appropriate notes. He wrote of Sally's work supervising the care of special needs children in Avon. 'Walter Sickert said that the world can be divided into patients and nurses. Sally is, like all great nurses, an extraordinarily efficient organizer . . . She becomes, I sometimes think, more interested in me as my handicaps increase.'

And he wrote about Emily. Emily had become a star of Oxford theatre: John had seen her in his own version of *A Flea in Her Ear*, and while in Kafka's *The Trial* (which sent Penny's parents to sleep) she had fallen for another actor, Tom Ward. When they spent a year at the Moscow Art Theatre, John went to see her. He had already been back to Russia once, in 1988, reporting hilariously on the National Theatre's Shakespeare tour to Moscow and Tbilisi, with Peter Hall directing Tim Pigott-Smith, Eileen Atkins and Geraldine James. Now he wrote a TV play set in post-glasnost Moscow, with a part for Emily.

He also wrote more candidly in this book about the relationship of his parents. His father's rages, though 'grossly inflated and easily punctured', had once made Kathleen walk out. Clifford was distraught. She came back an hour later

carrying a pair of whited antlers she had found in Stonor Park. He was on his knees, begging her forgiveness and she helped him up, anxious that he shouldn't appear pathetic and ridiculous in my eyes . . . I think it was then I realized that most women are better, calmer and more civilized than most men – a view I have never forsaken, despite occasional evidence to the contrary.

As for the murderer friends, readers already knew about Michael Fenton. Here John told of killers he had defended. The book began and ended with John's recurring nightmare: of running down the marble corridors of the Law Courts wearing unsuitable garb (pyjamas, or beach shirt and shorts), quite unprepared for the case in which he is to take part. When he reaches the courtroom door, it is locked. Did this betoken a deep-seated terror that had afflicted him throughout his Bar career, or was it a commonplace anxiety? (Quentin Edwards said he had the same dream too.)

One odd thing is that he yet again included in his book, for the fourth time – as if obsessed – the Tuscan villa-owner's typewritten list headed 'What is important in my life', in which the house came first; her husband also-ran. The couple who had rented him their villa twenty years before were still married, but the wife was 'mortified' to see her confession in print again.

A doughty ally joined the battle for the village school project when Jeremy Paxman became one of their nearest neighbours. Penny had run into Paxman in Tom Conran's deli in Westbourne Grove, and he told her he and his partner, Elizabeth Clough, who had just had their first child, wanted to move to the country. When an old farmhouse between Turville Heath and Stonor was being auctioned, Penny told Paxman, and he got it. He was enlisted in fund-raising for the school, hosting barbecues for the city children when they started to arrive. He and Penny also shared a passion for fly-fishing, so her country sports interests expanded. 'Lurching from one lost cause to another,' John wrote to Bron Waugh in 1994, 'we have undertaken to convert the Labour Party to foxhunting.' This cause was never going to make it on to the Labour Party's agenda, but the outlawing of hunting with dogs was already a real prospect under the Tories and John's first piece on the subject was written with passion, although he had never hunted in his life. 'Our stinking and broken-down prisons are already full to bursting. Must they now make room for the Master of Foxhounds and the children from the Pony Club too?'

John was just back from a Canadian tour at Christmas 1994 when his adaptation of *A Christmas Carol* was performed by the RSC at the Barbican. It was a dazzling adaptation that owed a debt to David Edgar's haunting *Nicholas Nickleby*. Apart from the technical originality of John Gunter's staging, which achieved a panoramic vista of London rooftops and Scrooge touring the earth, John was faithful to Dickens's prose in every detail. It took him just four weeks to write, he said, 'as Dickens had done all the hard work'. The descriptions of the shops stocked for Christmas, and of the Fezziwigs' ball with its groaning tables, were divided up for the cast of twenty-two, so that everyone took part in telling the story of Scrooge's redemption. As John said, Dickens's most passionate philanthropic sentiments sometimes lie in the narrative, not the dialogue; the fierce denunciation of poverty in *A Christmas Carol* rattled the audience's bourgeois comfort. In the last scene, a shower of snowflakes fell on rooftops and cast. It was an unforgettable production. John said he felt an affinity to Dickens: 'He was definitely a Champagne Socialist.'

24. Penny Tells It Like It Is

To turn fifty, have a hysterectomy and lose one's mother in the same year, as Penny did in 1996, might be regarded as an excess of rites of passage. John, who rarely expressed his appreciation of her in writing, sent her a poem on her birthday, written as they lunched with their two daughters in a Dorset hotel, near Rosie's new school, Bryanston.

> 'Glamour,' they'd say, 'with attitude':
> Penny the mother, Rose and Em –
> To live out half a life with them
> Is the supreme beatitude.
> They meet in Blandford's one hotel
> For lunch and, if the truth be told,
> None is too young, none too old
> To cast the magic young-girl spell
> Upon the wondering odd man out –
> Who thanks his stars he's lived to be
> Part of their bright-eyed company.

The poem ended:

> And you, I met first of the three,
> Gave life to them, and life to me.

'Penny is a woman who knows no fear,' John wrote. 'She has hunted in Ireland, where the horses jump over barbed wire or scramble up walls and land on piles of rocks. She has swum with sharks and laughed at death threats from hunt saboteurs.' Having overcome the nerve-jangling that strikes everyone who rides to hounds ('They do you a very good death on the hunting-field', as

Dr Salter says in *Paradise Postponed*, a line now in *The Oxford Dictionary of Quotations*), country pursuits had claimed her. She went shooting, trout fishing, stalking in Scotland. Field sports became a mission: hence the fringe meeting on fox-hunting she boldly organized at the Labour Party conference in September 1996. And the Turville School project, on which she had set her mind, now drew sixty children each summer from east London, Birmingham, and the Blackbird Leys estate, Oxford, 'where they steal your car and set it on fire,' John said, 'and they've never even met a sheep or cow'. The protesters were silenced – and indeed, some offered hospitality to the children.

When her mother first had a stroke, Penny rushed to her bedside. Emily drove her to Victoria station and heard Penny's cry of 'Oh, Mum, please don't die.' Anne seemed to be recovering, but while they were in Italy she died, aged seventy-two. At her funeral John spoke movingly about his life-enhancing mother-in-law 'and made everyone cry'.

Like Anne, Penny was a coper. At seventy-four John had increasing needs, now that his leg had developed ulcers and he was sometimes wheelchair-bound. Their two daughters' behaviour was, to put it mildly, irritating. The best illustration of Penny's approach to their chaotic upheavals is the diary she kept, for her own and her friends' amusement, when they all went to Australia for Christmas in 1997. Under Penny's charge were her ageing husband (needing to have his ulcers dressed daily), her equally ageing widowed dad, also with wheelchair after a leg operation, her actress daughter Emily, who was having a wild affair with the actor Paul Bettany, and Rosie, who at fourteen had become as mulishly monstrous and monosyllabic as a teenager could be. They had rented a house on Palm Beach near Sydney, next door to Kathy Lette and Geoffrey Robertson.

The narrative begins at 6.30 a.m. on 14 December, in the kitchen at Turville Heath Cottage, the two old men vying with one another over who had the least sleep last night. John (despite taking Temazepam) had slept for only one hour, 2 a.m. till 3 a.m. 'Round one to John,' writes Penny. She has to wake Emily and her lover from the pile of cushions and bedspreads on the floor. Emily asks to borrow a bra and knickers, as she has forgotten to bring any underwear. Penny has to pluck up courage to rouse Rosie from under her duvet 'for fear of Kevin-like verbal abuse'. Rosie starts to pack, grabbing a random selection from the piles of jumble outside her room, twenty minutes before their departure for the airport. Emily starts to cook Paul a full English breakfast. Penny dispenses 'little blue pills' to John, whose asthma is bad, and Emily. Emily and Paul are locked in a passionate farewell embrace and Penny is shouted at for asking them to get a move on.

She summons wheelchairs at the airport for the two dads, who are in the lounge with coffee and brandy by 9 a.m. Rosie and Emily go off to do their Christmas shopping in the duty-free and Rosie gets lost. Onlookers are amused by Penny's attempts to marshal her troops. When all are aboard, three minutes before take-off, Emily shoots out of the door of the plane and up the gangway into the airport, minus her boarding pass, to ring Paul. Back aboard (by sheer winsome charm) in the nick of time, she orders champagne and falls into a deep slumber. Bill Gollop hails every passing steward to tell them about farm subsidies and how he acquired his gammy leg in Burma.

At Bombay airport Penny rounds up their seven suitcases; Emily is still unconscious, draped over a luggage trolley. 'I am a cross between Cinderella and the wicked stepmother; there are two beautiful sisters (who can both pull very ugly faces when something displeases them), John is Prince Charming (always in search of a shoe, or his black bag) and Granddad is Buttons, always good-natured, always getting the wrong end of some stick.' In the hot Indian night, the princesses switch on the television in their luxurious hotel and call room service.

They spend a few days on Goa's palm-fringed beaches, where John nearly drowns when knocked over by a succession of big waves. 'He is finally beached on all fours with his bum in the air and his ancient M&S swimming knickers round his ankles, helped ashore by three kind Indians.' Emily phones Paul constantly on Penny's BT charge-card, or searches for phone boxes in remote jungle villages. 'Only mild Delhi belly all round.' Each morning they are wakened by a medley of 'Jingle Bells', 'Rudolph' and 'White Christmas' blasted out from a Catholic church. It is thirty-five degrees centigrade. John and Granddad are photographed on either side of a signpost reading 'Home for the Beautiful Aged'.

On Sunday 21 December they face the drive to Bombay and a long flight to Sydney via Singapore. Penny can't find Granddad's Australian visa. 'By the time we get to the Bombay hotel, I could cheerfully murder most of the party.' In the hotel restaurant, after quantities of champagne and vodka, Emily is 'copiously but elegantly' sick. 'Perhaps it would be rather pleasant to spend Christmas at Turville Heath next year.' Penny spends hours telephoning Delhi and Canberra about her dad's visa, and gets their procession of wheelchairs and trolleys to the Qantas check-in. At Singapore, they have to unload everything and then reload. Emily is reunited with Paul and, once airborne, the pair entwine themselves in the seat next to John, until a steward asks them to move back to steerage 'as they are embarrassing the other passengers'. Paul declaims, 'This is how they did for Romeo and Juliet!' 'When will this ghastly journey be over? Next Christmas I shall find a Trappist monastery on a remote Hebridean island.' As the plane descends into Sydney, Granddad finds his visa – in his wallet.

On 23 December they are in their house on Palm Beach, awoken at 7 a.m. by hammering, drilling and loud Australian pop music. Houses are under construction on either side – 'but the noise of the waves breaking on to the shore over the road is wonderful'. Feeling nauseous and with a splitting head, Penny shops with Kathy in Woolies, two suburbs away, among Aussie men in shorts and Santa Claus hats, filling three trolleys: 'Shopping with jet lag is a hallucinatory experience.' She collects their hired car, driving back on her own, and falls asleep at traffic lights. 'I feel socially irresponsible. Dicing with death on the highways of the southern hemisphere.' Emily hires a car too but has brought no money and her Visa account is unpaid, so John pays up. Later, Emily loses the car keys and the camera Paul gave her for Christmas. They go to a party where Rosie is so mutinously silent she is assumed to be deaf and dumb, and people offer her cake in sign language. The host is Mike, who has a radio show and is recently divorced:

His ex-wife Kerry is there. It turns out that Kerry left Mike because he was having an affair with someone called Sherry. But this was an excuse, because Kerry was having an affair with Terry. But once Kerry had left Mike, Terry decided to stay with his wife and moved to England. Meanwhile Mike had finished with Sherry. But Kerry and Sherry and Mike and Terry are still all good friends.

On Christmas Day they meet all Kathy's 'relos' – three charming sisters, husbands, nephews, nieces and her parents, Optic Merv and Val. Everyone goes surfing; Penny surfs the Internet for 'Foxman' in America, 'someone I've been after for ages. So I'm thrilled.' 'The crocks' now swim daily. 'Not so great is to hear John doing his morning retching routine, which he insists is an integral part of his asthma.' Rosie tells Emily that if she has a baby, she wants to be present at the birth, 'because I'd like to see you in terrible pain'. 'When granddad asks me what I'm thinking about, I say "Being alone for quite a while in my cottage in Devon".' Penny has recently seen *The Addams Family* film and, 'funnily enough, it keeps popping into my mind'.

On 29 December Granddad wakes with one side of his face swollen like a balloon. He has an abscess on a back tooth and Penny has to find a dentist, missing most of a lunch with their old friends David Hunt, High Court judge, and his wife, Marg, Rosie's godmother. Rosie sulks and won't eat any of Marg's delicious food. Next day Cate Blanchett, who has just played Elizabeth I (with Emily as her lady-in-waiting), comes to supper. Penny orders Thai noodle salad from a deli, where the man says he'll 'run a few prawns through it'. 'A chap called, believe it or not, Bryanthon Oldfield rings up, and after a minute or two asks me what part of Australia I'm from. Strewth, I must watch it!'

By New Year's Eve, when they see *Così Fan Tutte* at Sydney Opera House, the old crocks are fit enough to walk to the pool and John's asthma has gone. At a party they meet Paul Keating, the former prime minister. He tells Penny that the last time he was in London a cabbie said, ''Ere, aren't you the geezer what put his hand on the Queen's bottom? What was it like?' What did he reply? asks Penny. 'Oh, quite a nice old bit of stuff.'

On 2 January there is a party at the Robertsons', where, Geoff tells them, are gathered 'the cream of Sydney society'. Penny meets the author Tom Keneally, 'a jolly, rotund little man with a gnome's beard'. Emily and Paul go off to the Blue Mountains and 'it's a treat not to have to listen to Rosie's shouts of "I hate you, Emily!"' 'John is happy because he got three "G'day, Rumpole!"s at the pool today. Also an offer of free swimming lessons from the man who teaches the small children. This is because he hasn't actually been swimming in the pool, just walking up and down making swimming motions with his arms.'

The Sydney episode culminates in John's two performances of *Mortimer's Miscellany* at Sydney Opera House, with Emily and the Australian actress Tara Morice. Penny, Rosie, Paul and Granddad travel there by sea-plane: it is 'an exercise in contortional dynamics' to get Granddad in, and a feat of strength and ingenuity, by Paul and the pilot, to get him out. 'It seems inevitable that they are all three going to fall into the harbour.' Paul and Penny finally find a restaurant where 'joy of joys, we can smoke! Every time we take out a fag a passing waiter lights it for us with his Zippo.'

John's performances are a sellout, with queues stretched round the bay. Afterwards in the bar Penny is bored witless by two of John's long-lost relos from Tasmania, 'one of whom describes in detail all her menopausal symptoms'. Optic Merv pronounces the show a success, so Kathy says it must be mega: Merv never gives unqualified praise. At a lunch afterwards they meet the Gough Whitlams, and the young man who wrote *Strictly Ballroom*, who looks all of sixteen, and David Williamson, 'who must be the tallest playwright in the world'. There are only two days to go. In a 'piss-elegant' restaurant John has a prickly encounter with a Basil Fawlty-like head waiter, Emily is told to put on her shoes (she hasn't brought any) and Kathy casually mentions that a great white shark has been lurking off Palm Beach ever since they arrived. She didn't tell them before, in case it deterred them from swimming. Finally, John opens an exhibition called *Convicts' Love Tokens* in Sydney: 'This is as interesting as it sounds.' They meet Richard Neville and Christopher Hitchens, who is writing 'an in-depth article on Australia for *Vanity Fair* – in five days'. The flight back is on 8 January; Emily and Paul are booked on a different flight but will probably miss it. 'I couldn't care less,' writes Penny. 'I'm writing this on the plane home.' During the trip she had often thought 'Never again' but, now that it was over, she realized she'd enjoyed it. 'But then, the Hebrides does sound enticing. I'll reflect on it for a while.'

Australia was bound to love John Mortimer, Kathy said. Apart from the fact that Rumpole was played by an Australian, 'John loves convicts, and we've all got a bit of convict in us. There was serious talk of putting his head on a stamp! I said, "John – what job satisfaction – you get licked all day."'

The Oz trip rounded off a year with two things to celebrate: their twenty-fifth wedding anniversary, followed by the Labour victory. On election night, 1 May 1997, John and Penny went to see *King Lear* at the National, John removing his glasses when Ian Holm removed his clothing ('I didn't want to intrude on his privacy'). He felt the last line of Edgar's speech was particularly appropriate: 'Speak what we feel, not what we ought to say.'

'We hadn't been allowed to say what we felt for so long,' said John. (This is arguable. Nobody was sent to the Tower for criticizing Margaret Thatcher or John Major.) Across the river they went, to join the *Daily Telegraph*'s election party at Christopher's in Covent Garden, cheering loudly as the Labour gains became a landslide. John suspected that the Tories present were equally pleased, but the *Telegraph*'s managing editor, Jeremy Deedes, and fashion editor, Hilary Alexander, found the Mortimers' cheers extremely irritating. Hilary approached and said, if they thought Tony Blair was so wonderful, why didn't they go and drink his champagne? 'You can't come here and drink *Telegraph* champagne and gloat.' So they departed for the Royal Festival Hall to join the dancing, whooping party faithful, and 'our leader came down from the skies' – Blair arrived by helicopter from his constituency. When they got back to Portobello Road 'all the taxis were hooting with joy'.

The Labour victory had already lost its lustre six weeks later, when John and I talked over China tea in the library at the Garrick. The Blair government was 'footling about with things that don't matter a twit', succumbing to authoritarianism and political correctness, 'wanting to send people to prison just for doing something you don't like'. He was watching Jack Straw carefully. 'If liberty means anything,' John said, 'it means tolerance of people who do things you don't approve of, like smoking and foxhunting. Intolerance always backfires. You only have to ban something to make it really popular – viz. Prohibition. Like "leave your car at home day", yesterday. Did you notice? There were more cars on the road than ever.'

But John's disaffection with New Labour – which would furnish the plot for a final Titmuss novel – had long been fermenting. He was a Kinnock man, and Kinnock represented the old ideals of the Labour Party of Attlee and Nye Bevan. He felt no emotional pull towards Blair's lot. Peter Mandelson had danced an elegant jive with Penny at her fiftieth birthday party in the Turville Heath garden. But any friendship with the new prime minister and his wife was short-lived. They were invited to dinner at Chequers and, during drinks on the terrace, Penny asked if she could smoke. Cherie grimaced and replied, 'You can have just one, if you must. But it's a disgusting habit.' At dinner Penny sat next to Philip (later Lord) Gould, Blair's master of polls and focus groups. He observed the doddering John, whom he had not met, and said, 'He's getting really old, isn't he? Why do you stay with him? Is it love or duty?' For the second time in her life Penny was so taken aback she was stumped for an answer. Gould denies uttering those words, but John reported this story in his next book, and reflected, 'What was it that made my mother stay with my blind, irascible father? Was it love or duty that made her dress him, cut up his food . . . lead him round and describe the slow progress of every shrub and hardy perennial?' Penny, he pondered, had married 'a middle-aged QC still capable of standing on his hind legs for anything up to six hours in the Central Criminal Court'. Now she faced his 'bad temper and failing joints'. 'Is staying on to put on another person's socks the mark of a truly heroic character? I would say undoubtedly yes.'

Penny had helped Ann Mallalieu to set up the Labour pro-hunting pressure group Leave Country Sports Alone. They had enlisted impressive names on the letterhead, including Denis Forman, Melvyn Bragg and Jeremy Isaacs, and Penny lost no opportunity to speak about hard-working local people whose livelihood depended on the hunt and to squash the myth of the 'red-faced, red-coated toffs who ride roughshod over the peasantry in a frenzy of blood-lust'. When a reporter from the *Independent* told her they were 'Labour toffs' she said, 'Listen, young man, I've just had my family history investigated and I come from a long line of scavengers.' It became uncomfortable for any anti-hunting friends in their circle, including the Kinnocks, who had to skirt around the subject. One who found herself the lone dissenting voice at their La Rufena table alongside eleven pro-hunters said things had become emotional: 'They couldn't bear it that I didn't agree with them and it was quite unpleasant.'

But most of their close friends had country lives, and among their allies were the Prince of Wales and Camilla Parker Bowles. On 2 November 1999, after John had written a polemical leader page for the *Daily Mail*, Prince Charles wrote to him from St James's Palace.

Dear John,
As I never read the horrid newspapers I had missed your splendid article in the dreaded *Daily Mail* . . . I just wanted to say how heartening it was to read such good sense on a subject that seems to have become submerged in astonishing/prejudiced hysteria. The awful thing was going out hunting that day and being able to

predict accurately, in advance, exactly what these ghastly media people would do and say.

'As far as I'm concerned,' John wrote, 'anyone is perfectly at liberty to detest fox-hunting . . . and seek to persuade hunters to give it up. What is ridiculous is to turn it into a criminal offence.' His support for this cause, which took him into Whitehall bearing a placard on the first Countryside March – alongside Norman Tebbit, 'a charming companion' – was entirely libertarian. He had never caused the death of an animal in his life since he had shot a rat with an airgun when he was 'about fifteen' (actually he was twenty-two; it's in his father's 1945 diary, 'John shot a rat.'). His life continued to be centred on matters urban and literary. He was regularly in America, dining at the Harvard Club with Sherlock Holmes devotees, and performing his readings, attracting large crowds – 'lawyers mostly,' he said. 'If you want to write a book that's successful in America, write about lawyers. Every other American is a lawyer.' They naturally sought his views on the O. J. Simpson trial, during which Rumpole had been cited in court, twice. 'As Rumpole would say, it all comes down to the blood,' the prosecution lawyer said. And Simpson's defence lawyer, Gerald Euelman, told Judge Ito, 'I was watching *Rumpole of the Bailey* last night and I am going to borrow a line from him. He suggested in the case he was litigating that there was "a real danger of premature adjudication" .' John, who had watched the Simpson trial razzmatazz on television, said it would strike a death blow to any plan for televising trials in the UK. The participants in the case commented nightly on the trial's progress: 'In England they'd all be sent to jail for contempt of court.'

Of the two novels John wrote in these years, *Felix in the Underworld* (1997) was the most interesting, and it was this we met to discuss at the Garrick. Felix is a middlebrow writer living in Coldsands-on-Sea, haunted by the words of Trigorin in Chekhov's *The Seagull*: 'We will talk about my splendid, bright life. Well, where shall we begin? I am haunted night and day by one persistent thought. I ought to be writing. I ought to be writing. I ought . . . What is splendid and bright about that, I ask you? Oh, it is an absurd life!' 'Felix is like me,' said John (as I suspected), 'in the Trigorin thing, the guilt, the feeling that he must write, write, write . . . And the terrible thing for him is, at the end, people will say "he wasn't as good as Turgenev".'

There were several fanciful aspects to this novel. One was that, since Felix finds himself sleeping rough on London's streets, John had to do a bit of research. He had gone out to visit the homeless beggars in cardboard boxes behind the Savoy, not too far from the Garrick, and safe in the company of John Robinson, the Queen's chaplain from the Savoy Chapel, and the homeless police team from Charing Cross, 'who know all the regular sleepers and look after them, 102 of them between Lincoln's Inn Fields and Shell-Mex House'. The homeless, John discovered, were largely 'nice, gentle people who guard their territory and set out their possessions as carefully as sailors or monks'. Apart from the young drug addicts or prostitutes, and a few 'totally mad old women', they tended to be 'confused middle-aged men who just can't cope after some family trouble – disputes, divorce or death – or ex-soldiers, so institutionalized by the army that they can't look after themselves, can't boil an egg. One businessman I met couldn't face the back tax he owed; he could have been rehoused, but he dare not have an address, or he'd have to pay the back tax. He sleeps in the doorway of the Inland Revenue in Kingsway.'

They could make £30 a night, begging, 'and if they spend it on six-packs of lager I don't mind. I certainly never found them at all threatening, although the dog-owning drug-dealers are a bit alarming. I'm very much in favour of giving money to beggars. I feel no moral outrage. It's a perfectly honourable profession. I beg the entire time. For the Royal Court I'm holding out my hand for £5 million.' He had wanted, in Felix, to show how a middle-class man could be reduced to living among people 'outside the stockade'. 'The great mistake of all politicians is their belief that inside the stockade are decent, property owning, law-abiding people who educate their children, and outside are ravening hordes of alien beings who have to be kept at bay. I wanted to say we're all the same people really, to show how Felix could be reduced to living among them.'

I had found the book sad, and said so. 'Well,' said John, 'Felix does end up with the little boy, who's not his.' This was yet another of his plots that involved the paternity (or not) of a mysterious boy. I had not noticed this at the time, but in the novel the publicity girl from Felix's publisher gets wildly excited when Felix is accused by a woman of having once made love to her on a Coldsands beach, thereby fathering her son, Ian, who is now aged eleven. This will do wonders for his flagging sales, cries the PR, Brenda Bodkin: 'FAMOUS NOVELIST'S LOVE-CHILD! Wicked! I think Lucasta Frisby on the *Meteor* would be *very* interested. When Helena Corduroy's husband went off with another man, she got the centre-spread in the *Meteor*.' Seven years later John's life would affirm his fiction: there were similar headlines when Ross Bentley – whose father Jack was now dead – was revealed to an unsuspecting world.

But at the time, John and I discussed only the relationship between a writer's experience and what he writes. 'The demarcation line between truth and fiction is very shaky,' he said. 'We write stories to interpret events. The trouble is, you sit at your desk and nothing ever happens to you. You've got to have more experiences, in order to write about them, which is time-consuming and an awful nuisance.' As it happened, I had just interviewed David Hare on his fiftieth birthday and he had said the same: 'As a young playwright you go out into the street. Then you don't go out on the street any more.'

John had been, the night before, to see Hare's new play, *Amy's Choice*, and had told Hare he found it 'irritatingly good'. 'Ah, envy,' said Hare. 'That's the best tribute you could pay me.' 'I'll give you envy,' said John. He hankered for another theatre success, but had 'almost forgotten' how to write a play, after twenty years. In the previous two years there had been tours of *The Dock Brief* and *Edwin* in a double-bill, and of *A Voyage Round My Father*, which was seen at the Oxford Playhouse by a house stuffed with famous names, including Salman Rushdie, still flanked by his bodyguards. A new radio play, *Summer of a Dormouse*, starring the glittering names radio plays can attract – Paul Scofield, Alex Jennings, Joanna David, Gemma Jones and Imelda Staunton – was about an old man in Coldsands-on-Sea, obsessed by Byron's letters and journals and the regrets of his youth. Retitled *Hock and Soda Water*, it arrived on stage (at Chichester) in 2001.

Compared to plays, which demand crafted dialogue full of conflict, film-writing – short visual scenes and few words – seemed the simpler option. A film for Franco Zeffirelli, about his childhood and wartime youth in Florence, looked like an attractive prospect. Zeffirelli, the illegitimate son of a dressmaker, was brought up by English ladies in Florence, who taught him about Shakespeare, Elizabeth Barrett Browning and P. G. Wodehouse. 'The ladies rather liked Mr Mussolini, but he interned them all in San Gimignano,' John told me, 'and they saved the towers of San Gimignano when the Germans were going to blow them up.' To work on the script (the latest of several writers to do so), John was summoned to Zeffirelli's house in Rome, where he felt imprisoned. One evening Zeffirelli informed him, after several glasses of Cacchiano wine, that 'the pyramids of Egypt were not built by human beings but miraculously appeared in the desert by some supernatural force'. (Rather like the time Robert Graves informed John that Jesus Christ lived to be eighty, went to China and discovered spaghetti.) *Tea with Mussolini* took several years, but one summer Zeffirelli came for a day to La Rufena. 'Franco was utterly charming and we were all completely in awe,' said Anna Ford. 'But it was clear that John was getting a bit irritated with Franco reinventing his life, because Franco didn't think it was interesting enough, and John said, "Well, it's your life, you dictated it to me." I think he found collaborating quite tiresome.' Eventually, Joan Plowright, Maggie Smith and Judi Dench were signed up. Shirley Anne Field was in California, heard about the film and rang John at the Beverly Hills Hotel. He invited her to lunch and said he'd love to give her a part in the film; but it was not in his gift.

New Penny Productions had produced, with Colin Rogers, John's *Under the Hammer* for TV, a six-part series about a smart art auction house named Klinsky's, and the fakery, forgery, looted masterpieces and misattributions behind the scenes. A resting-actress friend of Penny's who worked at Sotheby's, where John had just bought a Jacob Epstein drawing, furnished him with plots. Richard Wilson – not John's choice – starred as the art expert, and the props department created some amazing likenesses of works of art. At the end of the shoot, in an old nursing home near Heathrow, they auctioned these, and the bidding rose to dizzy heights.

His next adaptation, of Trollope's *Orley Farm*, never got to the screen, and nor did his TV serial of Jessica Mitford's *Hons and Rebels*. John had often dined, when in San Francisco, with 'Decca' and her lawyer husband, Bob Treuhaft. But around this time, Decca rang her sister 'Debo' Devonshire to say, 'It's a bugger, but I'm going to die in four weeks.' At her London memorial, where a tape was played of her ineffable singing (with Maya Angelou) of 'Maxwell's Silver Hammer', John addressed the packed Adelphi Theatre, as did Christopher Hitchens and Polly Toynbee.

He was able to revive the work of another old friend when Laurie Lee died in 1997 and John, having spoken at Laurie's memorial, was chosen to write a new TV adaptation of *Cider with Rosie*. Down in the Gloucestershire village of Slad, Kathy Lee told him Laurie would have been pleased that his old protégé was doing the script. It was shown on Christmas Day 1999, with Juliet Stevenson as Mrs Lee and Emily Mortimer ethereally haunting as mad Miss Flynn, who drowns in the village pond.

Emily's acting career had taken off, ever since an agent spotted her at Oxford in *The Trial*, which led to her first TV part in Catherine Cookson's *The Glass Virgin* in 1994. Without pausing to go to drama school, she was rarely without some film or TV role after that, starting as Sean Bean's girl in *Sharpe's Sword*, filmed in the Ukraine ('We lived in this ghastly sanatorium with no running water and cholera in the next village – great fun, a bit like a school trip'). By 1999 she was playing Hugh Grant's 'perfect girl' in the film *Notting Hill*. Like John, Emily was destined to talk about her father ('the best company in the world') in every interview she gave. 'He thinks all his children are clever and wonderful and you end up believing it. But you need a cutting edge, and that was my mother.'

John never hankered after public office, but he had become one of the great and the good. In 1998 Chris Smith, Blair's culture secretary, appointed him 'Lord of the Plinth'. What statue should adorn the empty fourth plinth in the corner of Trafalgar Square? For a century, Lord Nelson and his Landseer lions had been surrounded by two military heroes, Generals Napier and Havelock, and two kings, Charles I and George IV. John's natural preference was to put Charles Dickens there, but Dickens had vetoed any statue in his will. So his plinth committee agreed that there should be a series of temporary exhibits, starting with *Ecce Homo*, Mark Wallinger's stark and touching white statuette of Christ. John was surprised to discover that such statues today are not hewn and chiselled as by Michelangelo or Rodin, but formed from caking a real body in plaster. He retained 'an old-fashioned feeling that art should be more difficult'.

The new Royal Court building was now under way, aided by Arts Council and Lottery money. While they were seeking the last few millions, John performed his cabaret at a fund-raising dinner in Notting Hill where everyone was given a square inch of wood from the boards of the dismantled old stage. The half-reconstructed theatre, a building site, proved a dramatic setting that July for a gritty American play, *The Lights*, a hellish vision of a city in the near future, with Emily playing a fragile girl called Lily. The final £3 million came from the Jerwood Foundation – but they wanted the name 'Jerwood' on the front. By subterfuge, John got Jack Straw to confirm that Her Majesty would never permit another person's name to go in front of the word 'Royal', though the Royal Court had nothing to do with royalty. When writing to Straw, John 'steered clear of mentioning Labour's threat to jury trials, or displacing the burden of proof, or cancelling habeas corpus . . .'

Under John's chairmanship the Howard League had at least managed to ensure that prison cells now had lavatories. He hosted a lunch at Wormwood Scrubs, where grandees paid £200 to eat with the inmates. (Addressing the prisoners, John assured them it wasn't his fault that any of them were inside, because he hadn't practised as a barrister for over ten years – prompting a shout of 'The lifers are upstairs, John!') One Sunday, Barbara Castle offered him the chance to 'have a go at' Jack Straw, who was coming to lunch with her at Hell Fire Corner, her house at Ibstone, across the Hambleden Valley. It was hard to have a go at a chap – Straw was a former barrister too – over a sunny Sunday lunch. But he did 'put a toe in the murky waters of rape cases'. 'You lawyers!' said Straw. 'You want to blacken the character of some unfortunate woman and yet you keep all the details of your client's past a secret from the jury!'

Straw had a good point. I recall a particularly horrible multiple-murder case in 1984, when a family had been butchered by an axe-man named Hutchinson, who broke into their house after a wedding party. The only survivor was Nicola, the eighteen-year-old daughter, who had been raped by the axe-man after she discovered the bodies of her murdered parents and brother. In court, Hutchinson's counsel, James Stewart, QC, had accused Nicola of inviting Hutchinson into the house for sex. Writing about this at the time, I appealed to John to agree that it was appalling for the defence counsel, who said he knew his client to be a liar, to utter such things in open court about a girl whose life was already in shreds. But John was implacably on the defence lawyer's side. 'However horrible, the criminal must be defended. And the more horrible, the more important the principle is. Even if it causes the witness pain and embarrassment.'

The public-spirited pro bono efforts bore fruit. His seventy-fifth birthday present from the nation was his knighthood, bestowed by Prince Charles – though it was rumoured that the honours committee had had to persuade Blair to sanction it. 'Sir John Mortimer' sounds very well, and when he was summoned to the

Garter King of Arms at the College of Heralds, he was told he was entitled to a coat of arms too. 'Choose a nice animal,' 'Garter' advised. So he chose a dormouse, perched on a shield and drinking a glass of champagne; and the motto '*Aestas gliris*', the Summer of a Dormouse. His actual birthday coincided with a *Mortimer's Miscellany* in Brussels, with Joanna David and Sinéad Cusack. The Kinnocks, now installed with the European Commission, hosted John's birthday party after the show, at their home in the Rue Van Kampenhaut. Kathy Lette, Geoff Robertson and Jeremy Irons were there, and after 'quantities of champagne' the festivities descended into a crazy Kinnock party, 'everyone behaving in ways inappropriate to their age', cavorting about (except John) as an improvised skiffle group with mops and brooms. John's musical preference was far removed from skiffle. On Radio 3's *Private Passions*, or (yet again) on *Desert Island Discs*, his selection was sublimely classical, with Fred Astaire singing Cole Porter his one concession to the modern age.

His journalism was more catholic. Articles by John only rarely sprang from a burning desire to pontificate. He did produce a scholarly and lyrical essay on Byron's little-known play *Cain*, but usually he wrote whatever any features editor suggested. Hence his venture in search of the vox populi when Princess Diana's mourners thronged the Mall. 'Go away,' one of them told him. 'I don't talk to the paparazzi.' On Pooh's seventieth birthday, he could shamelessly write a 'three cheers for Pooh' piece for the *Daily Mail*, declaring the bear 'a fat hero in the line of Falstaff, Micawber and Billy Bunter'. And at £1,000 a time, why not?

His last political satire, *The Sound of Trumpets*, in which Lord Titmuss aids the rise of a Labour politician of the Blair/Clinton type, did better in the US than in the UK. With asthmatic cough and leaning on his walking cane, he was back in New York and Washington, addressing the Supreme Court, being given a tour of the Senate – and being quoted everywhere: 'Political life today is like the food you find in international hotels; it doesn't really taste much of anything.' At home, he was at seventy-five 'still beautifully naughty,' gushed Deborah Ross of the *Independent*, promising 'no hanky-panky' when they stayed in the same hotel at Fowey in Cornwall, but assuring her that they would have 'lots of fun and champagne'. But after the gig, he was in a more reflective mood. 'While I've written good novels,' he said, 'I've never written a great novel.' A glimpse of something behind the performance, said Deborah Ross, 'but it doesn't last long'.

The new Lady Mortimer had been away for her birthday in 1998, fishing in Scotland. So John sent her a nostalgic fax.

> I remember a girl with long hair, peering expectantly, there to meet me at John F. Kennedy airport. I remember her curled up like a ball, hungry for sleep, in an almost unfurnished flat high up in a square. I remember her wonderfully pregnant in a bikini, irritating the habitués of a gay bar in St Tropez. I remember her twice risking her life to produce the two most beautiful, remarkable, occasionally impossible children in the world. I remember her smoking and giving up smoking, saying 'do I drink too much?' without reason. I think of her fondness for newspapers and the telephone, doing all she does well, seeing through me when I need seeing through. I know I was never properly happy until I met her that New Year's Eve. And now, on a birthday which has made her no older, many happy returns and all my love, darling Pen.

This access of uxorious sentiment suggests that he had been cogitating on his life as a husband. Penelope, the original 'darling Pen', was now ill. Her lung cancer had come back – one lung had been removed – and the emphysema was worse. She lived with a wheelchair and an oxygen pump. John went to see her in her flat in Willesden Green, three doors from Peter O'Toole, looking out on to her lovely garden. Her little white Bichon Frise dog, Coco, was frisking about and making her laugh. At eighty she was still beautiful. 'We discuss the children, those we have in common and those fathered and mothered by others,' he wrote. 'We spend an hour behaving with the politeness of strangers.' Penelope had become a devotee of the stand-up comedian Eddie Izzard, and was surrounded by his tapes, videos and signed photographs. She told the family that any memorial was to say: 'Penelope Mortimer – Writer, Gardener and Eddie Izzard fan'.

On 19 October 1999, Penelope died. Since her eighty-first birthday a month before, she had been having palliative care at the St Charles Hospital in Ladbroke Grove. She made it clear to the family that she did not want any mention of 'after a long illness, bravely borne'. She hated the whole business, Jeremy said, and death, when it came, was certainly a release. The obituaries were prominent and perceptive, with photographs of her beautiful younger self. They gave due recognition to her achievements in fiction, biography and gardening; and to her spare, unflinching prose. 'Yet she is likely to be remembered as the ex-wife of John Mortimer, the flamboyant socialist barrister and author . . .' said *The Times*. 'She had never made it easy to separate her life from her work.' Her novels' honesty, and precision about 'the suffocating tensions of domesticity, the fragile hopes and agonized betrayals of disintegrating love', made the conjunction of her life and work 'too telling to ignore'. Her former literary agent Giles Gordon wrote that she hated being complimented: 'Nearly all writers are difficult but Penelope was impossible.'

Her funeral was at the West London Crematorium on 26 October 1999, with all five daughters and son, and all the grandchildren, present. Her dog, Coco, sat in the front, on Madelon's lap. John was wheeled in by Emily. I sat beside Dee Wells, Lady Ayer, a writer as spiky and a smoker as inveterate as Penelope. An Eddie Izzard tape was played, but it was almost impossible to hear his jokes, only the bursts of audience laughter. We sang 'For all the saints who from their labours rest'. The daughters read extracts from Penelope's diaries – quite different passages from those she had used in her memoirs:

May 16, 1980. This has been one of the happiest weeks of my life. I've done exactly what I like, the sun shines, everything looks beautiful. I discover new things about the garden all the time . . . The robin hops round, follows me, flirty . . .

September 9, 1982. A young hedgehog came. I gave it a saucer of milk, which it drank like a kitten, then it tottered away.

Afterwards John joined Jeremy, Sally and his four step-daughters at Penelope's flat. He did not say anything about how much he had loved her, or how much she had influenced his life. But he seemed moved when Madelon and Caroline sang 'Limelight Child', the song he and Penelope had written in their happy youth. 'The time when we sang that seems near enough to touch.' Also, he wrote:

It's hard to believe that so much talent, anger, humour, dash and desperation could be shut in a long and slender box . . . Sitting there, I can only remember the best of times. The day I saw her kneeling in the garden of the cottage, when she was living with another lover, carefully painting his coal scuttle for the improvement of his home. The evenings when I walked through the woods and across the fields to visit her in Turville . . .

No doubt Penelope was difficult, sometimes, as a wife and mother. Her life, she once told me, had been divided by newspapers into three phases. In the 1950s and 1960s they asked, how on earth do you manage with six children? In the 1970s they only wanted to know about the break-up of her marriage. And from the 1980s it was always the garden. The last time I had seen her was in that garden, a winding progress among secret resting places, and the scents of box, lavender and rosemary. She had stood, smoking, slim as a girl, giving laconic horticultural advice, half-amused by one's ignorance. Anna Pavord, the gardening writer, said Penelope's garden was 'like a protecting cloak that she drew round herself'.

Unlike John, she never found happiness with anyone else, and there was no doubt that John was the love of her life. Clive Donner, who still visited Penelope till the end, told me he had heard that John had read a wonderful paean of love to Penelope at the funeral. I told him this was not so.

Days later, I watched John performing at the Cheltenham Festival, as he did every year. He chaired the festival's key event, a debate between the *New Yorker* and the *Independent*, during which Howard Jacobson hijacked the evening by ridiculing Simon Schama's suggestion that in Rembrandt's painting of his mistress bathing in a river, the girl was examining her reflected pudenda in the water beneath her skirts. Before we voted, John instructed the audience to exclude this matter from their minds and said 'you can try it for yourselves at home later'. The laughter, applause and hilarity were too much for Sally, who accompanied her father to the dinner afterwards. Her mother had just died and nobody, least of all John, seemed to want to acknowledge this. After John had left the table, Sally became hysterical and was led from the dinner, to be consoled by the headmistress of Cheltenham Ladies' College.

The emotion felt by the older girls was predominantly an overwhelming relief. As Caroline said, she had done her mourning for her mother years before. Penelope had been intending to leave her flat to Madelon, a serious gardener like herself, but Madelon, who lived in France, told her she had no wish to spend the rest of her life in Willesden. Anyway, to pay for what the family referred to as a 'bod', a carer, Penelope had to borrow against the value of her flat. In her will she left £85,000 to Madelon, now widowed for the second time; the others, all comfortably established in domestic twosomes, got the residue divided equally among them. Jeremy and Julia were the executors. Penelope had made detailed lists stipulating who should receive which of her thousands of books.

Her children bequeathed to John her useful gripper-stick for picking up things. 'So, after so many years of love, adventure, rivalry, disputes and separation,' wrote John that year, 'we share the services of a stick with a claw for picking up the things we are too old, or too idle, to reach for.'

25. Nothing Like a Dormouse

It is a key rule of scriptwriting that the action should speed up towards the end. Or so John wrote. In the lives of most writers nearing eighty, there is a natural diminuendo. John was different. He saw in the new millennium at Robert Harris's old vicarage, with songs around the piano played by Richard Ingrams. The next day, *Mortimer's Miscellany* was broadcast on Radio 4 and he got back to work on his new book, an account of 'a year of growing old disgracefully'. In *The Summer of a Dormouse* he found, at seventy-seven, an endearing voice: wise, sensitive, wryly nostalgic, gathering together the strands of his remarkable life.

The caricature on the cover showed him in his wheelchair at a stand-up-and-shout party, condemned to sit at child-height while conversation sparkled and glasses chinked above him. Cunningly conflating the past three years into one, he gave an impression of a schedule even more crowded than it was – shuttling to Rome to see Zeffirelli, to Tuscany with the 'laughing, squabbling' Kinnocks, to New York and Sydney, Edinburgh and the Everglades of Florida; leading the wheeled contingent on Countryside Alliance marches, attending his first wife's funeral, and performing on platforms from Blackpool to Bristol to Brussels. He took up arguments about hunting, the jury system, the scandalous fact that farmers were going bust and committing suicide, while the government squandered millions on the ludicrous Millennium Dome. He told excellent new stories about his friends, illustrating the self-importance of Roy Jenkins, the accident-proneness of Joss Ackland and the undiminished energy of Muriel Spark. Dame Muriel wrote to say she was 'busting with pride to be included in such a lovable book'.

It ended with a lyrical account of his birthday picnic in the bluebell woods, family and friends driving past the ailing horses in the meadow, unloading the Moroccan panniers, John seated in his battery-charged 'Sun-Gift' tricycle, surveying, 'like some absurd Canute', the scene: scampering grandchildren, half a dozen dogs, haze of bluebells. 'I feel neither old nor in any way incapacitated. Everything is perfectly all right.'

'How engagingly he grows old,' wrote Fay Weldon in her review, 'and with what benefit for the rest of us, this clever and once notoriously randy young man.' 'As to that empty plinth,' wrote Humphrey Carpenter, 'isn't it time they put a statue of him on it, wheelchair and all?' Anne Chisholm recognized the book's artfulness: 'Sadness and fear lurk beneath the jaunty prose.' Perhaps she detected what John's Oxford contemporary, the novelist Francis King, perceived: 'How difficult it is now, to believe that half a century ago this breezy man of the world was once the awkward, sometimes discouraged, often pensive author of innovative novels that made one think he might become another Henry Green.' Ah, shades of Trigorin.

The great book, the great novel, the great play: that chimera eluding so many writers who cannot know, however long and productive their lives, whether immortality or oblivion awaits. It was possible that this book, stuffed with wit and wisdom, might be John's last. It wasn't – far from it – but he had chanced upon some lines in Shakespeare when looking something up for Emily and the page fell open at *Henry VI Part Two*, Act III, Scene i:

This devil here shall be my substitute,
For that John Mortimer, which is now dead . . .

The devil referred to is Jack Cade, who led the peasants' revolt of 1450 using the grander pseudonym of John Mortimer. 'Was there a terrible warning in the chance opening of a book?' John reflected. 'I have never had a doctor pronounce a sentence of death after a fixed term of years, but I can imagine that such a grim verdict might almost come as a relief, adding a magical value to the time remaining . . . I find it in a single cold moment, strangely stimulating.'

But following Clifford's example he would not be confined by his dependence. It was a pleasure to sail through airports ahead of the queues. 'Partial immobility has few terrors for writers,' he wrote. 'The writer lives in a sedentary state.' He did admit to being unable to put on his socks. A kind couple in New Zealand sent John their patented 'Soxon' machine, which involved inserting the leg into a sort of cage containing the sock. 'Unhappily, having few mechanical skills, I find the leg, once in, difficult to extricate.'

Timor mortis was superseded by *timor descendi*. At Clifton Nurseries, while buying red hot pokers, he tumbled down the stairs to the Gents. In a Sydney hotel, on a slippery marble bathroom floor, 'I pirouetted down the steps, across the wet floor to crash into a set of glass shelves . . . I fell amongst splintering glass and a hailstorm of cotton-wool buds . . .' So he now had torn ligaments in his knee, as well as his painful and debilitating ulcerated leg. The consolation was his first encounter with 'the Heavenly Twins'. John had first met Jon Lord, Deep Purple's keyboard player, when they were photographed with George Harrison in the showbiz line-up to save Henley's Regal cinema in 1984. Next, they had met wheeling trolleys in Waitrose, where Lord was struck by the great author's feet, encased in 'huge, unlaced Reeboks'. Then, when nothing seemed to improve John's ulcers, Penny heard about Jon Lord's wife, Vicky, and her identical twin sister, Jackie, who lived at Hambleden and possessed a black box with magical healing properties: a box apparently invented for Russian cosmonauts which, applied to eczema or to arthritic joints, could achieve miraculous results. John was sceptical. But into Turville Heath Cottage breezed the twins, frizzy suntanned blondes in floating white clothing, to kneel before him and apply their box to his leg. Very soon even the conventional nurse who came to change his dressings had to admit that the wounds were healing. And John fell quite in love with his Heavenly Twins. Vicky Lord and Jackie Paice, formerly the Gibbs twins from Birmingham, stars of the Speakeasy Club in the 1970s, live out their identical lives under New Age principles (crystals, yoga, meditation) in handsome country houses near Turville. With their Deep Purple husbands

Jon Lord and the drummer Ian Paice, they at once joined John's close inner circle. Jon Lord, with his grey ponytail and black suits, his keenness on classical music and poetry, became John's new 'best friend'.

Most people start to lose friends as they near eighty. Not John. With Penny he collected a new, younger set, which included Frida of Abba, Betjeman's daughter Candida Lycett Green, and the Prince of Wales and Camilla, who invited John and Penny to Sandringham at Easter 2000. En route, John grumbled about the enforced pause in his work schedule. But by Monday he was loath to leave. He loved the fact that his valet, Clive, was married to a gym teacher named Miss Plimsoll. Penny was greatly cheered when greeted on arrival by Phyllida Dare, the Prince's secretary. 'I don't suppose we're allowed to smoke here,' said Penny. 'Of COURSE you are,' said Phyllida. 'Have one of mine!' So a relaxing, smoke-filled time was had by all. And soon Penny was invited to go grouse shooting with the Prince in Scotland and riding in Tuscany with Camilla.

Among other new friendships in the 1990s were the journalist-turned-author Robert Harris and his wife, Gill Hornby, whose grand Gothic rectory on the canal is an hour from Henley. They met through the Turville School project. Jeremy Paxman and Penny weren't doing too well from writing begging letters to potential donors, so Paxman's friend Gill suggested holding a quiz, for which she would devise the questions. It started at St Mary's Church in Paddington, but then one contestant, Ruthie Rogers, offered her River Café as a venue – and so the annual River Café quiz, at £100 a head (quizmaster J. Paxman) took off. The quiz could raise £18,000 in an evening, won in successive years by the tables of John Gross, Sir Tom Stoppard, Nick Hornby and – aided by a Mastermind winner – Piers Morgan.

Their circle further expanded when the Anglophile philanthro-pist Sir Paul Getty and his third wife, Victoria, came to live at Wormsley (the great house with Civil War connections and 2,500 acres), where Getty created a woodland of 90,000 trees, lakes and grottoes, a splendid cricket ground with thatched mock-Tudor pavilion and a medieval-style baronial hall housing his fine library of antiquarian books. John had first met Victoria when she lived with the painter Timothy Whidborne, brother of his Harrow friend Michael. John, having designs on Victoria, took her to lunch at the White Elephant, 'but she went off to Italy with Alexander Londonderry'. In Rome, Victoria met Paul Getty II, who eventually married her in 1994. 'I hadn't seen Victoria since our lunch in the White E,' said John, 'when she and Paul came to live over the hill.' It transpired that Getty, benefactor of many English institutions, such as the National Gallery and the Tory Party, was a great admirer of Rumpole. Soon John and Penny were back on Hydra on the Getty yacht, and Paul took the cricket-hating John to a Test match at Lord's, where he met John Major. After Getty's death in 2003, the witty and spirited Victoria remained a good friend.

These relationships were not about intimacy. 'I don't think John ever wants a serious conversation, and certainly nothing personal,' as one of the older friends said. But such friends guaranteed a cheering social life with lavish lunch and dinner parties close to home. There was always fun when John was present. 'He lights up the table,' Gill Hornby said. His fund of anecdotes seemed inexhaustible. He might recount the time he arrived in Boston to find his hotel room chaotically unprepared. He asked the desk clerk to get him the manager at once. The phone rang and a small polite voice said, 'Mr Mortimer, sir?' 'Forget the sirs! This room is a tip! It's the most disgusting mess I've ever seen! There's blood on the towels, used glasses under the bed, ashtrays overflowing . . .' There was a pause. 'I'm really sorry about your troubles,' said the voice. 'But I'm the director of the Smithsonian Institution in Washington. Just ringing about your talk . . .'

Or he might tell the well-worn joke about the visitor to Boston who was hoping to try the local delicacy, a fish named scrod, so he asked the cab driver, 'Where can I get scrod?' Driver: 'That's the first time I've heard that word used in the pluperfect subjunctive.'

A new wave of journalists came trawling for confessions. Forty years after *The Pumpkin Eater* he was still being asked whether he was Jake. 'The polite way of putting it,' he replied once, resignedly, 'is to say I was then more aggressive and more a pain in the neck than I am now.' Sometimes their persistence verged on inquisition, on matters he had long ago determined not to answer, such as how he could have encouraged Penelope to have an abortion to save their marriage, when he was having an affair. To this question (from Andrew Billen) John murmured vaguely about 'a sort of seemliness by which you can live your life, without having great moral principles'. So Billen delivered his 'killer question'. Given John's view that character was immutable, why should we believe that he was any more faithful to his second wife than to his first? John's response to that was to look young Billen in the eye and tell him he would have made a good cross-examiner. Billen never wrote up this interview. By the next time they met, Penelope was dead, so John could speak of her beauty, her danger, her large family, their 'long stretch of really quite good life together' before success came and things got 'a bit ropy'. Billen elicited a rare moment of self-appraisal when he asked about John's afternoon glooms. Didn't the public's 'eternal love' lift his spirits? 'But I don't think that what they think they love is what I really am,' John replied. If readers witnessed his post-lunch slump, they would say, 'Oh, Christ, gloomy old bugger, moaning about having to write another eighty pages of Aesop.' (He was now adapting *Aesop's Fables* for TV.)

'All worthwhile projects are investments in the future,' John wrote. 'After you're seventy, it's probably too late to establish another career . . .' He finished new screenplays (of books by David Niven and Eric Newby), but what he most wanted was to revive his success as a playwright. His hopes centred on two plays produced in 2001. *Naked Justice* (from Auden's 'In the burrows of the Nightmare / Where Justice naked is / Time watches from the shadow / And coughs when you would kiss') opened at the West Yorkshire Playhouse, with Leslie Phillips in the lead. But John was dissatisfied and decided to rewrite the whole thing. Then on 14 November 2001 *Hock and Soda Water* (the former radio play *Summer of a*

Dormouse) opened at Chichester. Joss Ackland had to withdraw from playing the lead when his wife, Rosemary, one of John's favourite people, was stricken with motor neurone disease. The new title was again from Byron:

> I would to heaven that I were so much clay,
> As I am blood, bone, marrow, passion, feeling –
> Because at least the past were passed away –
> And for the future – (but I write this reeling,
> Having got drunk exceedingly today,
> So that I seem to stand upon the ceiling)
> I say – the future is a serious matter –
> And so – for God's sake – hock and soda water!

It was a play about ageing and memory. In the garden of the vicarage at Coldsands-on-Sea, an old journalist, Henry Troutbeck Pottinger, watches his younger self and himself as a boy. Within minutes Pottinger is warning his twelve-year-old self, 'The time of your life will come . . . when you'll hear a voice from the sky thundering, "From this day forth thou shalt not be able to put on thy socks"!' He also warns of the effort required to heave oneself out of a chair. (People were often alarmed by John's 'Japanese war cries' and 'Sumo wrestlers' yelps' as he levered himself up from the table on his almost-useless legs. Even worse was manoeuvring oneself out of the bath: 'You'd have less trouble rising from the dead.')

But Pottinger's chief regret is having let a girlfriend slip through his fingers – a woman named Mavis, whose career has outstripped his, as she left Coldsands and turned into a Martha Gellhorn-style foreign correspondent. They meet again in Coldsands, forty years on. Mavis refers to her early Fleet Street career, 'when I had my little boy'. How old was her son? Henry asks. Mavis: 'What if I said he was born . . . exactly nine months after I left Coldsands?' His name is Nick . . . The possibility that he was Pottinger's son is left hovering. Just a possibility. John was once more dropping a heavy hint.

The play, disappointingly, did not transfer to London.

*

John had always given the impression that his writing was effortless: the lined foolscap pages handed over to Penny, typed, submitted, published. This changed in the summer of 2001 when, in the Piazza del Campo in Siena, Robyn Davidson presented him with a blank notebook with pretty endpapers, inscribed 'to John, the darling knight'. So on 7 August he started writing a diary: 'Muriel [Spark] came. Muriel writes notes, but doesn't look at them when she starts to write a novel. So what would be the note for Lie Down Comic?'

This was the first indication that he was writing a play about Penelope in her dying days. 'The central character is a woman like Penny the first,' he writes. Her name will be Jo (as in *The Pumpkin Eater*). The comedian with whom she is obsessed is 'Matt Mendoza'. 'He is the devil, the angel of God, the Star. What it needs is the story. Dock Brief changes of roles? They play parts . . . She's dying. He's there to entertain her. She entertains him. He may die the death on stage?'

John handed me this notebook with the words: 'It was mostly written in the Bar Dante, saying "I'm very depressed".' (On 23 July 2002, he notes that the Bar Dante 'now keep a special chair for me, with arms'.) To me the book was a revelation, written evidence – at last – of doubts and unease behind his prolific output. 'So what are we looking for?' he would write. 'An idea for a play. Must write (1) the play and (2) the new Rumpole.' It was also an outlet for grouses about La Rufena guests: 'X is the mother from hell: she cannot leave her children alone . . . If you talk to her she stops listening, interrupting everything to give instruction to her children; she never sits down to a meal, rushing into the kitchen to get other things she orders them to eat.' The children, he adds, are 'charming'.

At times the notebook deteriorated into illegibility, with pages of repetition. 'So what should I write. Not another Rumpole book – enough of that for a year. So what should I write. Not another Rumpole book. Not yet anyway. Not another Rumpole book. Not yet anyway. Of course I want to write a play. But can I? Well I can try can't I? . . . Lie Down Comic not perfect.' His mind goes in circles, his handwriting (once fine) often indecipherable. What is discernible is self-reproach – 'My prose rhythms don't seem as good as they were' – and the need for reassurance: 'On Friday I deliver 38 pages of book which is either good (Penny has said) or pompous garbage.'

A new Rumpole was published in October 2001: *Rumpole Rests His Case*. Ginny Dougary of *The Times* arranged to see him, apprised that this would be the last Rumpole. John was annoyed to hear this. He was not about to kill off Rumpole; he still needed him 'to say what I think about the world'.

On 6 January 2002, he took up his Siena notebook again:

Deep depression. Up to Xmas everything exciting. Going well. Perhaps too well. Amazingly good notices for everything – Rumpole book, King's Head perfs. Then Rumpole radio plug on Xmas day. Xmas spoiled by family spats. Rosie in a mood. No one really happy. I'm grumpy and Em says so. I feel a general breakdown, especially of my relationship with Em. Then the dark empty days between Xmas and New Year.

On New Year's Eve they had been to Robert Harris's old vicarage, with its lofty oak library and cedar-shaded lawns and all the trappings of Harris's literary success. 'Am I jealous?' he asked himself in the notebook. Penny had left for her Exmoor cottage, 'tired out, exhausted by this awful effort of Xmas. Then I go back to what seems suddenly a very lonely house . . . Deep freeze . . . frosts. I work frantically on the translation of the Bald Prima Donna' – an adaptation of Ionesco's satirical masterpiece of English suburban life.

'. . . I also work on my play which I can't really like and feel very nervous about . . . it's not a truly inspired bit of absurdity like Ionesco, but a not altogether successful revue sketch . . . of course I don't want criticism. Who does? And who shall escape whipping?'

A page later he asks himself:

Haven't I written all I can, said all I have to say, made what I could of my talent. Should I pack it in? Not if I'm to go on living as I want (a) the money and (b) the pleasure of writing, the admiration (c) if I don't write, nothing will happen and I shall live out these lonely days, reading as well as my eyes will let me, and sleeping too long in the afternoons.

Then:

So what's in hand? First and most likely to relieve boredom, the read-through & first rehearsal of Naked Justice. I don't like the play nearly as much as the Chichester play, but audiences liked it . . . What ever it is, it is something happening, which is a great deal better than nothing happening. Must leave at 8am to get to the rehearsal room – my favourite sort of place.

Apart from the new short play and *Lie Down Comic*, there was 'The book. This is a big worry. So let's start worrying about it.'

'The book' was his version of Lord Chesterfield's letters to his son. 'Reasons for doing it: I must do something; also money. Also people I trust – Pat K, Tony [Pat Kavanagh is his agent and Tony Lacey his publisher] – think it's a good idea. So what is this book? Whom am I writing to? Not anyone real. An unknown grandchild. Am I doing Summer of a Dormouse again? That book had a simple subject. It also said where I stood . . . So now let's have a go at it. Or cook some lunch (it's only 10 o clock.) Or go stark raving mad . . .'

On Monday 7 January 2002 he was driven to London through fog and heavy traffic to a rehearsal of *Naked Justice* in the Arch-bishop's Diocesan Institute, next door to Lambeth Palace. 'Met by very kind young man – could be Sir Galahad in a Pre-Raphaelite painting. All assemble in a huge room and I look at the set. Back to childhood, designing model theatres.' Leslie Phillips was unhappy about the end of Act One, and even walked out, declaring John's rewrites to be 'rubbish'. But he came back. And John's winter gloom lifted slightly as he signed contracts for another Rumpole (£45,000) and the Lord Chesterfield book, eventually called *Where There's a Will* (£75,000). 'I've also found the one-act play to go with the Bald Prima Donna at Watford: Full House. Very nervous about this. It may fall flat on its face and not be funny at all.' (He was right.) He had just unearthed the old Harrow notebook containing his clerihews and a long poem in the style of Yeats's *The Tower*, 'which disturb me by being good – as are several pieces of prose. Was I a better writer then? Have I misused my talent, such as it was? Whatever, it's far too late to worry about this now.'

Naked Justice reopened at Birmingham Rep on 12 February 2002. Since it concerned three judges sharing their obligatory residence on circuit, John could reuse some favourite stories, such as the one about the judge who tells the court that he has spent all weekend preparing his judgement but unfortunately has left it in his cottage in Wales.

COUNSEL: 'Fax it up, My Lord.'
JUDGE: 'Yes, it does rather.'

Not knowing John's history when I saw (and enjoyed) *Naked Justice* at Oxford, I did not appreciate the significance of an important strand of the plot: the threatened blackmail. One of the judges harbours a guilty secret from his youth. Keith is a self-righteous, prim figure who carries his own mahogany lavatory seat with him on circuit and is appalled that his two fellow judges, Fred and Elspeth, dare to go out to a pub. Elspeth then brings a guest, her boyfriend Roddy, a dodgy accountant, into their lodgings. Keith and Roddy are left alone, and the following exchange takes place:

RODDY: I never thought we'd meet again. After Saint Tom's.
KEITH: No.
RODDY: I never thought our paths would cross again.
KEITH: It seemed extremely unlikely.
RODDY: An outside chance! But it came up. A bit of luck.
KEITH: Was it?

RODDY: For me. I hope so . . . Dear old Saint Tom's College . . . You
know. Now I come to look at you, I can't think how I ever came to
fancy you! . . . You remember our times together at old Saint T's
don't you? You do remember?

What becomes clear is that Keith, now so strait-laced, had been,
for a brief interlude in college, Roddy's lover. Roddy had been 'a
bit of a show-off' who 'wore purple corduroy trousers and swung
both ways'. Keith had been 'a pale young schoolboy with an
interesting profile', a 'damp-handed stripling', fascinated by the
purple trousers. After a drunken afternoon, Keith, with 'eyes full
of terror and desire', had confessed, 'I've been wanting to say this
all year. I do love you, Roddy!' So Roddy obliged with 'an act of
absurd generosity' which he now hoped had paid off, because he
wants Keith to remember this when he judges a forthcoming
criminal case in which Roddy is implicated.

RODDY: You will help me, won't you, Keith darling? Otherwise . . .
KEITH: Otherwise what?
RODDY: I might start talking about the old days . . . So you'll do it for
me, won't you, darling?
(Roddy moves towards Keith and kisses him . . .)

This play, which dramatically brought together almost every
comment John had ever made about courtroom conduct – the
presumption of innocence, the malignant disease of judgeitis, the
manipulation of juries by flattery – was well received, and Leslie
Phillips was the ideal Judge Fred. But Duncan Weldon decided
not to bring it into the West End.

John's quasi-theatrical lifeline was *Mortimer's Miscellany*. It was by
now a highly polished performance. Leslie Phillips had taught John
the technique of perfect comic timing: every anecdote had fixed
pauses for laughs, building on previous laughs until reaching a final
crescendo. It worked every time. He would tell of a Mrs Scott, of
Southsea, whose husband made seven attempts to kill her – even

poisoning her and eventually driving his car straight at her. ' "At no point," said the trial report, "did Mrs Scott feel that the magic had gone out of her marriage." ' Or the tale of Mr Thirsty from Edinburgh, who, accosted by a robber in the street, shoots his hand up his wife's skirt, detaches her wooden leg and bludgeons the robber to death. 'Well,' John would end, 'that could happen to anyone.' He decided that he was an actor manqué: 'All I ever wanted to be was a strolling player.' Except that he could no longer stroll. 'I hobble on, supported by an actress and a stick, and sink heavily into a suitable chair.' One of his team of regular actresses, Rohan McCullough, had introduced John to Clive Conway, musician and impresario. Conway's company, Celebrity Productions, put the show on a more sophisticated and businesslike footing – offering *Mortimer's Miscellany* or *An Evening with Sir John Mortimer* to regional theatre companies – just as he did for Tony Benn's and Alastair Campbell's road-shows. John could rely on a rota of willing co-performers, including Joanna David ('I will go anywhere, any time, for John'), Sinéad Cusack, Gabrielle Drake, Marsha Fitzalan-Howard, Jill Freud, Geraldine James, Louise Jameson, Nichola McAuliffe, Lisa Goddard, Celia Imrie, Angharad Rees and Phyllida Law. The venues got bigger and further-flung; they no longer found themselves performing, as they had once, in a church hall on a stage improvised from a billiard table. Twenty years after leaving the Bar he had found 'a more satisfactory way of performing'.

'The adrenalin beforehand, the relief when it's over, no drug could produce the sensation,' John wrote. 'This particular narcotic killed Dickens and polished off Dylan Thomas . . .' The best bit, the irresistible high, would kick in when the performance was over. 'Back we go in the car drinking warm champagne from the bottle and eating petrol-station sandwiches.' At the wheel of his Mercedes was the reliable Peter Hayes. Peter looked, as John would point out, like a junior Tony Blair. He was the son of their former gardener, and nephew of their former cleaner, and had joined the Mortimers' staff at sixteen as under-gardener and woodsman. Now he accompanied John everywhere as chauffeur and chair-pusher: a deceptively slight figure, tirelessly patient. John had once asked Peter if he ever read while he waited in the car outside venues and Peter replied, 'Sometimes I have a look at the *A–Z*.' One night John fell asleep in the car home, put his hand on Peter's knee – thinking he was Penny – and said, 'I do love you, darling.' 'Thank you, sir,' said Peter.

It had occurred to Penny that John might not see his eightieth birthday. So she conspired with her husband's fondest admirers to make his seventy-ninth memorable: a triumph of organization. Two hundred friends were sworn to secrecy and invited by email to dine on 21 April 2002 at her friend Suzanne's vast barn at Wheeler End. In the weeks beforehand, Penny would tell John she was going to Pilates classes when she was in fact rehearsing with John's harem to form a line-up of chorus girls called (Vicky Lord's idea) 'The Mortimettes'. After the birthday dinner, on to the stage stepped Penny, Marsha Fitzalan-Howard, Joanna David, Phyllida Law, Candida Lycett Green, Kathy Lette, the novelist Clare Francis, the Heavenly Twins and their choreographer, Margo Buchanan, all decked out in fishnet tights and toppers, high-kicking, and singing Cole Porter's 'The way you wear your hat . . .' ('They Can't Take That Away from Me'), pointing at John, who beamed and basked in his chair, his Fred Astaire fantasy finally fulfilled. Jon Lord played his specially composed 'Sir John his Galliard' and presented it to John in a leather-bound book. Captured on video was John's beatific reaction. 'All John wants,' as Ann Mallalieu said, 'is to be surrounded by female company, smiling on him.'

That summer in Tuscany, he got a call from his old friend Joss Ackland. It was, as he feared, to tell him that Rosemary had died. The *Daily Mail* asked John for an 'In Memoriam' tribute to Rosemary, whose life had been a catalogue of 'disasters surmounted and tragedies overcome'. When she was expecting their sixth child, the Acklands' house caught fire one night. She fought her way upstairs through the flames and threw five children down to wait-ing neighbours, then jumped twenty-five feet, breaking her back. In hospital, she refused painkilling drugs to protect her unborn child. She was told she would never walk again – but she did, and had a seventh child. Through many misfortunes that ensued – a car crash in a Sicilian thunderstorm, a roadside telephone struck by lightning while Joss was talking on it, a car door that fell off so they arrived at the Mortimers' with Rosemary held in by a rope – she remained the lively centre of the Acklands' life at their Covent Garden flat and their holiday house in Italy, 'full of children, babies, friends, champagne and laughter . . .' And when their eldest son died of a drug overdose, Rosemary formed drug awareness groups throughout the country.

John wrote: 'Anyone who, like me, suffers from slight disabilities (hard to walk, difficult to see) should remember Rosemary Ackland – living life to the full, loved by a huge family and dismissing all physical troubles with cheerful impatience.' When John emerged at lunchtime having written this charming piece (earning £1,000), two of his *Daily Mail*-hating guests were so annoyed they vowed never to return to La Rufena. But Ackland, who had told John that his house, 'though filled with family, now seemed empty', was deeply grateful and asked John to speak at Rosemary's memorial service.

Gratitude for John's eternal willingness to perform also came from the Prince of Wales, when John chaired a workshop at Dartington Hall on 'Literature and Human Values'. The Prince thanked him for his 'typically amusing contributions'. I too was grateful when, needing yet another interview, I arrived at Turville Heath Cottage that autumn, to find him available as usual in his stifling study ('I deplore fresh air') despite four writing projects on his desk. Through the closed door to the dining room we could hear Penny and several friends volubly discussing the arrangements for Emily's wedding. This was another of Penny's heroic feats of complex organization, with half the guests travelling from the US and needing accommodation. 'Arranging a daughter's wedding,' said John, who footed the £40,000 bill, 'is like putting on a West End play, but with no box-office returns.'

Emily had met her stunningly handsome Sardinian-American bridegroom, Alessandro Nivola, when both appeared in Kenneth

Branagh's film of *Love's Labour's Lost* in 1998. Now a hot Hollywood property, Emily was often compared, as Penelope had been,
to Audrey Hepburn. Not only did the camera adore her, and
filmgoers warm to her (especially in *Lovely and Amazing*, in which
she was just that – and was subjected to a prolonged naked appraisal
by Dermot Mulroney, who advised her to 'trim her bush'), but
interviewers did too. This refreshingly un-actressy actress, deceptively scatty, chatted without minders or PRs and phrased her
thoughts with originality. 'I'm a people-pleaser,' she would say. 'I
used to worry whether the bus conductor thought I was nice or
not . . .' What one magazine called 'The effortless charm of Emily
Mortimer' could move mountains, John always said; she once
arrived at Sheekey's and persuaded a waiter to fax her column over
to the *Telegraph*. This column, mostly about the absurdity of an
actress's life, once became a weighty polemic questioning the
necessity of sending Jeffrey Archer to prison, curiously echoing
almost verbatim her father's sentiments. (When John helped her
with her Oxford dissertation, she flung it back at him, saying, 'It
reads like something for the *Daily Mail*!') Ever since Oxford, she
had talked of writing a biography of Chekhov's wife, Olga
Knipper, and confessed to 'falling asleep in libraries all over the
world', but it remains unwritten.

The nuptials called for superwoman skills from the mother of
the bride. John described the scene in the kitchen one night when
Penny was being driven crazy by Emily and her wedding plans.
'Fudge', Alessandro's mother from New York, had come to stay,
and Rosie had just broken up with her boyfriend, Kieron, who
was distraught. Penny was cooking dinner while Fudge gushed
over John ('Your use of words is so wonderful'), when Rosie
announced that there was a mouse in her bedroom. Kieron caught
the mouse, but let it go; the cat chased the mouse round the
kitchen and the Jack Russell terrier, Heather, pursued the cat.
Penny seized a wooden hammer used for tenderizing steaks and
made to kill the mouse, to a general uproar of protest on the
mouse's behalf. At this moment Elizabeth Clough arrived from
the Paxmans' house and asked if anyone had any stuff for cleaning

contact lenses. 'Family life, far from being dull and secure,' John wrote, 'is a constantly unfolding drama.'

On 4 January 2003, after days of grey rain, there was bright sunshine over Turville Church and a fleet of 'karma cars' lined with mirrors and aromatic with incense arrived from Notting Hill. Jon Lord had composed, and played, the organ music; Sam Brown (daughter of Joe Brown of the Bruvvers) sang Irving Berlin's 'I'm Putting All My Eggs in One Basket'. Emily and Alessandro emerged in a shower of confetti, surrounded by stars. There was supper (fish pie) in a marquee on the terrace of the cottage and dancing to a Mexican punk band from Los Angeles; there was limitless champagne, and a firework display. Alessandro's witty speech referred to the fact that John kept calling him Alfredo. John, scattering his wine and notes, spoke from his wheelchair, contriving to be funny and kind and loving to his whole family. 'What came through,' said one guest, 'is how much he adores Emily.' The honeymoon couple departed for Cliveden and instantly conceived their son, Sam, born in September 2003.

Two months later another disrupting force descended on Turville Heath Cottage: the filming of a birthday profile for Alan Yentob's BBC *Imagine* series, 'John Mortimer Owning Up at 80'. All the children and grandchildren were interviewed and the closest circle were filmed with cake and candles in the garden. The film opened with Fred Astaire tap-dancing, juxtaposed with John bowling down the lawn on his tricycle, telling Yentob that writing was his way of saying, 'Look at me, I'm dancing.' Yentob called him a 'legendary Lothario'. Richard Eyre said he was 'a hero for our generation' and that, if taken hostage, he would rather be stuck in a cellar with John than with anyone else on earth. Jeremy Paxman said, 'He stands for freedom of expression, whether you agree with him or not.' Geoffrey Robertson pointed out that Rumpole had changed the law on police evidence, which since 1984 had been recorded on tape, not in unreliable notebooks; his wife, Kathy, said John was 'God's gift to womankind'.

The programme was not entirely hagiographic. Yentob used the footage of Penelope's 1963 *Bookstand* programme, with painful clips from *The Pumpkin Eater*. Penelope's good-looking middle-aged daughters – articulate, thoughtful – spoke forthrightly: 'It was obvious that he was screwing half London,' said Caroline. Julia said, 'My mother had the wrong sort of husband. He was rather a coward, and needed to get away.' The children of John's first marriage came across as sturdy survivors of the wreckage. Penny too perceived her husband's susceptibility with merry insouciance – 'He'd like to be Pope, with women at his feet and kissing his ring.' Everyone remarked on his desire to be admired and reassured; Ann Mallalieu mentioned his woe-is-me cries of 'My career is at an end!' The impression emerged of an old man blessed in his family; also one who couldn't abide criticism, and who, like King Lear, needed shows of affection. The affection was genuine, but the need could be irritating.

The film was structured around soundbites from the new book, *Where There's a Will*, a collection of anecdotes, disguised as advice to a grandchild. It began with lines from Yeats's *The Tower:*

> It is time that I wrote my will . . .
> I have prepared my peace
> With learned Italian things
> And the proud stones of Greece,
> Poet's imaginings
> And memories of love,
> Memories of the words of women,
> All those things whereof
> Man makes a superhuman
> Mirror-resembling dream.

Much of the advice he proffered, in the manner of Sydney Smith's much-anthologized letter to Lady Georgiana Morpeth, listing rules for life, was sound. Being really drunk, he advised, is not a pleasant experience. Being cornered by a drunk is almost as bad as being drunk, and drunk scenes in plays and films aren't funny. Yet there is something 'strangely depressing' about lunch with people who drink only water.

Learn poetry by heart, as nutrition for the mind. John suggested Browning's *Bishop Blougram's Apology*:

> All we have gained then from our unbelief
> Is a life of doubt diversified by faith,
> For one of faith diversified by doubt:
> We call the chess-board white, – we call it black.

He admitted to lying, and recommended it. 'Lies can be used to brighten an otherwise bleak and underpopulated life. They often reveal more about the liar than what emerges when he or she is telling the truth.' A fiction writer must have a confused view of the truth. He advised 'the occasional use of kindly deception'.

Most of his advice had a universal application: always give money to beggars; write in plain and simple prose; light fires ('In England there are too many empty grates'); heed John Stuart Mill on the tyranny of majorities, and the sovereignty of the individual over his own body and mind. Don't be duped by 'consumer choice', a dubious benefit: in television channels as in restaurant menus, more means worse. His advice about preferring the company of women – 'Women have the greater gift for friendship. It is always better to sit in a restaurant with a woman' – was tempered with Robert Graves's coda from 'A Slice of Wedding Cake':

> Or do I always over-value woman
> At the expense of man?
> Do I?
> It might be so.

He told his grandchildren that if they became writers they would be 'a maddening if not impossible person to live with'. They would be threatened by Trigorin's terror that the public's eventual verdict will be that his writing is charming and clever, but not as good as Tolstoy or Turgenev. (John had long resigned himself to the categorization of his fiction in the middle rank: 'I straddle the chasm,' as he said, 'between Jeffrey Archer and Salman Rushdie.')

Where There's a Will is a patchy work, studded with real insights. Any earnestness is relieved by jokes, sometimes cruel. On the happenstance of fate he cited the story from that recent summer when the South of France was ravaged by forest fires and helicopters were used to scoop water from the sea to douse the flames. 'An innocent and harmless man was happily snorkelling, when he was scooped up by an aeroplane, carried off and dropped into a blazing inferno.'

If John's grandchildren were to find this book useful, they would have to acquire a copy for themselves. The book was dedicated to the children of Sally and Jeremy – 'Gus, Joe, Felix, Dora and Beatrix'. Unfortunately it did not occur to John, until Sally suggested it at the book's launch party, to send each of the children their own copy.

Penny had said in the Yentob birthday tribute that if John couldn't write he would die; and he had said he hoped to die with his hand still moving across the page, like Henry James. One Saturday morning in June, Penny found him sitting at the lunch table, burbling incoherently. She rang the Paxmans, friends in need. Elizabeth came and at once said, 'He's had a stroke.' The doctor sent for two female paramedics, who put an oxygen mask on John's face, whereupon he revived instantly and said, 'What are all these lovely women doing here?' That night Penny got him to bed only with Paxman's aid, and the next day, at the family's insistence, he underwent an MRI scan, reluctantly. There was evidence – two little white spots on the edge of his brain – of two 'mini-strokes'. New pills were prescribed, and he resumed his usual life. But he looked suddenly very much older, his once-plump face quite sunken.

Lie Down Comic was broadcast on 2 January 2004. Having just been invited to write John's biography I was struck, listening to this play, by the understanding he showed for the dying Penelope, whose voice – played by Sinéad Cusack – came over with clarity and candour as she bridled at her dependence on a bubbly young carer known as 'Tickety-boo'. Sickert's words 'Patients and nurses

– that's the great divide in the world, not the rich and the poor'
(used in *Paradise Postponed*, later applied to the caring Sally) were
now given to Penelope, an instinctive nurse obliged to be a frac-
tious patient. 'Jo' is at first prickly with the Eddie Izzard-like
stand-up comedian who has been persuaded to visit her. But as
they talk, he confesses that he is afraid of 'dying' on stage, that his
forthcoming show will be a flop. The twist in the tale is that his
show is a success; but when he comes to tell Jo of his triumph, she
is already dead.

It is August 2004. I have been seeing John regularly ever since
his eighty-first birthday in April, and I had been to Tuscany and
joined the table that July at La Rufena, along with the Usual
Suspects and their uproarious laughter. Shortly after his return
from Italy, John rang me in some excitement: he would have a
Big Secret to tell me on my next visit. I knew at once what this
would be. When I arrived he greeted me from behind his desk
with arms spread wide: 'Wonderful news,' he said. 'I have a son.'

26. The Family Reunion

As Ross Bentley discovered, it is a fine thing to meet your famous father for the first time when he is a merry old soul and you are an upstanding citizen in middle age, adolescence long over. This was to be a father-son relationship without tears.

John and Penny were at La Rufena when Wendy Craig telephoned John to say she urgently needed his advice. It was their first conversation (apart from glimpses across crowded rooms) since 1961. Wendy was coming to lunch next week, John said. Penny left the old lovers alone to talk in the study; then all three sat down at the kitchen table. Penny noticed that Wendy talked a lot about her younger son, Ross, how sensitive he was, and how he had not got on too well with his father. Finally, after almost an hour, Wendy said, 'So of course, I had to tell Ross who his father was.'

'Hang on,' said Penny, 'who *is* his father?'

'John, of course.'

'John sat there,' said Penny, 'not saying anything. So I said, "Well! Gosh, we'd better meet him."'

Ross did not wish to intrude on their lives, said Wendy; but they urged otherwise and things moved swiftly. Ross telephoned John, then spoke to Penny. He said, 'Penny, do you realize I've spoken to my father for the first time in my life.' When he arrived at the cottage, Penny opened the door, said, 'Welcome to the family,' and led him into John's study, where the two exchanged a manly British handshake. Ross spied the signed photo of Fred Astaire, given to him by Emily, said, 'I have an album of Stacey Kent singing Fred Astaire songs, *Let Yourself Go*. I was listening to it before I came,' and 'John pressed the play button of his stereo – and he had the same CD on!' Photographs of Ross taken that day revealed that he looked more like John – and even more like Clifford – than any of John's other children. He was the same height, had John's timbre of voice, the Mortimer eyesight and the Mortimer jaw.

Wendy, the wholesome mother-figure of TV sitcoms, was 'a bit afraid that this will ruin her image', John told me, and she had become a born-again Christian. 'But she keeps ringing to say how lovely it all is, and that Ross is a new person.' What made John feel guilty, he said, was that Jack Bentley had been unkind to Ross. 'But Bentley made Wendy swear on the Bible that she would never talk to anybody about it. On his deathbed he made her swear again.'

Within days, Ross met his half-sisters Rosie and Emily in the Bonaparte pub in Notting Hill. At a Sunday lunch, Emily's baby, Sam, met his new cousin, Ross's baby, Iris, both born in 2003. Ross and his partner Kate Forster, whom he had met when she arrived to cook at his Lucca hotel that summer when Ross spied John in Siena, had been together for thirteen years. They were already booked to go to the Colombe d'Or, in the South of France, where Ross had planned to propose to Kate. So there was a wedding, combined with Iris's christening, in February 2005, bringing the family together at the candlelit Grosvenor Chapel. Wendy and Penny read lessons. Jeremy made an endearing speech as best man; Ross's brother Alaster played the oboe, his niece the flute. Iris was baptized by the elderly American priest. A double-decker bus carried everyone to the reception. John made a short, touching speech, looking very frail, mentioning his plea-sure at being reunited with Wendy. There was, Ross said, not a dry eye in the house.

Since no effort was made to keep Ross's existence a secret – John was known in the family as 'Radio Mortimer' – the story broke immediately. My advice was that he should offer to write his own story – 'My long-lost son – fatted calves all round' – but that would have meant divulging more than he cared to about 1960–61. The headlines ('John Mortimer's secret love-child') were uncannily similar to those he had written in *Felix and the Underworld*, seven years before. But then most tabloid headlines are formulaic, and the secret love-child is, along with the battling granny and the mindless thug, one of the regular dramatis personae. The stories were anodyne: Ross was happy, John was happy, the resemblance was obvious, Penny was fantastic, the half-siblings were affectionate and welcoming, it was a happy ending. John and Wendy's affair was said to have been brief (not so: it lasted eighteen months) and John was quoted as saying it had come to an abrupt end 'when his wife [i.e. Penelope] found out and told Miss Craig's husband'. This was something he had never vouchsafed before.

Few discordant notes were struck. Vanessa Feltz, absurdly, upbraided Wendy for 'depriving Sir John of the joy and responsibility of sharing in the upbringing of his son'. A *Telegraph* columnist, Tom Kemp, said John Mortimer had just one facial expression: 'a great big rubbery smile of self-satisfaction'. He had plenty to be pleased about – Rumpole, and his 'lightweight, snobbish, middle-brow' novels. 'But when footballers or politicians are caught deceiving their wives, the tabloids call them love-rats. When Sir John's marital sins come to light, this only goes to show what an all-round good egg he is.' A *Daily Express* editorial praised John's 'grace and good manners'. Nothing, groused Kemp, about his failure to connect his affair with the birth of Wendy's son, or his having escaped the expense of bringing up Ross. 'At the age of 81, he is presented with a perfectly formed son ... and dares to congratulate himself on how nicely the boy has turned out. No wonder the smug git smiles so much.'

'Relationship psychologists' were called on to comment. John had joined a glamorous fraternity of famous fathers of love-children – from Jonathan Aitken to Mick Jagger to Martin Amis. Michael Fenton's son Ben, a *Telegraph* reporter, wrote authoritatively: 'Anybody who knew Sir John Mortimer in 1960 would not have been surprised to know that the adventurous playwright and novelist was being unfaithful to his wife, Penelope.' After a weekend on the telephone fielding press inquiries, John was quite 'wrung out' and told me he hoped the story would now blow over. What he really feared was being thought to be at fault.

Sally and Jeremy summoned all their resources of filial tolerance

and loyalty and accepted their father's 'astonishment' without challenge. But his stepchildren were sure he had known about Ross
all along. Penny believed he was telling the truth, but said, 'If John
doesn't want to know something, he doesn't know it.' Sally, before
meeting her new half-brother, told me the newspaper stories had
'stirred up long-buried feelings of hurt/loss and being abandoned
(as I saw it as an eight year old)'. She said it didn't matter if Ross
was 'so nice, so sweet', as everyone said. What mattered was 'to
feel some connection, and for there to be a future'. Sally, who
had long tolerated hearing John refer publicly to his 'two lovely
daughters', seemingly forgetting her existence, was determined
that the junior Mortimer clan's ability to hang together in un-
shakeable amity – there were nine of them now, the four step-
daughters and the five children of John Mortimer – should
continue. In mid-September, I met John at Sheekey's for dinner,
when Ross and Jeremy both came too – the half-brothers' first
meeting. Two tall, gentle-voiced men aged forty-two and fifty,
fraternally united by their old dad, who wanted everyone to be
happy. For Ross's next birthday in November, Jeremy gave him a
1961 recording of Wendy in the BBC radio version of John's
Lunch Hour.

The story did not blow over. Shirley Anne Field got in touch with
the *Mail on Sunday* and revealed that of course John had known
about Wendy's baby; he had talked to her about it at the time, and
she said John had received menacing phone calls from Bentley.
John was cast down by her treachery, as he saw it – 'I can't raise
any enthusiasm for continuing with life,' he told me – and even
instructed the solicitors Peter Carter-Ruck to send a stiff warning
letter to the *Mail on Sunday*, which made him no less miserable.

The astonishing thing is that instead of going to ground and
really letting it all blow over, John the interview-junkie agreed to
see Emily Bearn of the *Sunday Telegraph* the following week. (He
had, after all, *Rumpole and the Penge Bungalow Murders* to promote.)
When Miss Bearn rang him, his voice sounded like an old lady's.
She found him 'rather frail for such an onslaught'. He was barefoot,

in a dirty white shirt with buttons missing, drinking from a mug emblazoned 'I deny nothing'. She asked him if he had been 'a rotten husband', and the piece she wrote – duly pasted into his scrapbook – was headlined 'Rumpy-Pumpy of the Bailey'.

A year passed before I sat down alone with Ross, now aged forty-four and completely absorbed into the Mortimer family. For more than twenty years he had carried around Bernard Levin's review of *The Wrong Side of the Park* ('Move over, Mr Coward, we now have John Mortimer'), mentioning 'how well suited Mum was to delivering Dad's lines'. He was reluctant to attribute blame to anyone, but he had become depressed in his late teens, partly because he felt so different, physically and temperamentally, from Jack Bentley and his older brother, both musicians. 'A baby monkey, given a barbed-wire monkey in an experiment, will accept it as its mother. You accept your parents.' After enjoying his boarding school, St Paul's, he lacked academic confidence and Reading University 'made no impression'. When told at twenty, by his godmother, that John was his father, 'I only thought, how reassuring. It explained so much.'

Jack Bentley had been his mother's Svengali, twenty-five years older: a trombone player in the Ted Heath Band before turning to journalism. 'He was extrovert, gregarious, made friends with Sinatra and Sophia Loren. He liked bawdy. He was a macho father. Not a sensitive man,' Ross said. 'I'm sure he thought I was effete and gay at school. I was closer to Mum, and to Mum's outlook and temperament. I think Jack was jealous. I don't think he liked seeing the two of us together alone.'

When the family moved to Cookham, on the Thames in Berkshire, Ross had felt an affinity to the area, knowing it was Mortimer-land. 'I spent a lot of time in Turville, cycling on picnics, walking the dog. The subtext was always the hope that I might bump into him.' When Jack died of cancer at eighty, Ross had felt a sense of liberation, 'freed of the burden of this person who resents you'. Meeting John at last had been like the solving of a mystery. 'The angst dropped away years ago, but there was always a residual melancholy in not having met him. I'd loved *A Voyage Round My Father* on television, I could relate to it. I yearned to know him.'

So when the press posse arrived on the doorstep of his Paddington mews house in September 2004 – Ross had gone to fetch the milk, and found a siege of paparazzi, as in the film of *Notting Hill* – he was more than willing to tell the world at last. He told the reporters he would meet them in an hour in Caffè Nero. 'They expected me to be shocked, but I said I felt incredibly happy. It's been terrific, not just finding a father, but Penny and a fantastic extended family who are all kind-hearted and welcoming and the best company. Plus there's something we share in common, our father. We've assimilated so seamlessly.' Wendy had been reunited with Caroline, her understudy in *Lunch Hour*. Ross was soon spending a weekend in Madrid on location with his new half-brother-in-law Alessandro, and even employing his new nephew, Sally's son Gus, in the company he runs, which sets up IT programs for film producers on intellectual property rights.

The following summer, Ross joined the Tuscan holiday, and he and John went together to the piazza in Siena, 'which closed the circle'. 'To be with him, at that villa so rustic and simple, with the Heavenly Twins and Jon Lord and Frida and Father Joe [an ebullient Jesuit priest] and my sister and brother – sometimes eighteen of us for dinner, sitting up till two in the morning – was just wonderful. Jon Lord and I ended up playing the piano – I played in a band called Thrombosis – and everyone sang.'

Ross told me, 'I don't think my mum and dad ever fell out of love. Mum said she still loved him. It must have been so hard for her to end the relationship.' The 'if only' for Ross was that, had he known about John earlier, he might have had someone to direct him academically. But he felt no resentment towards his mother. 'Work was important to her and it was too high a price, for an icon of middle-class, family-values propriety. For an actress, work is image.' Finding John had changed his attitude to fatherhood. 'My only experience of fatherhood was Jack. I hadn't been desperately keen to become a father. But I love seeing Iris with her grandfather, he's so good with little children, and she's so like him.

Now I'd be happy to have a von Trapp family.' Ross and Kate's second child, Beau, was born in 2006.

Ross arrived on the scene when I had spent six months voyaging round his father, navigating John's crowded diary. On weekdays Peter would still drive him into London – for lunches and dinners with literary editors, agents or one of his children; for publishing parties, awards ceremonies, theatres, a Prom, the opera, the cinema. He went regularly to Bristol, to take Sally, and soon Ross too, to opera at the Old Vic. At weekends he was chronically sociable in his local circle, or inviting old friends like Ludovic Kennedy. At least once a week he was driven off to a *Mortimer's Miscellany* gig, now accompanied by Jon Lord on piano and 'the barefoot cellist', Samantha Rowe, a schedule booked months ahead for Portsmouth, Pitlochry, Winchester, Great Yarmouth, Lincoln, Grimsby, Ilkley, Cork. They filled St Alban's Cathedral, but in another holy venue, a Baptist chapel at Bury St Edmunds, the authorities were so shocked by John's salacious stories that he was banned from returning. On Sunday nights there might be a fund-raising gala – at the Oxford Playhouse, for instance, in aid of Helen House children's hospice, where John did his cabaret and they auctioned Johnny Depp's knickers and Jude Law's sweatshirt.

Any literary festival – Oxford, Hay, Cheltenham – was a welcome diversion from what he dared to describe as his 'lonely author's life in solitary confinement, longing for an interruption'. So was any speech: an encomium for Peter Hall at a Garrick dinner, a plea to save Henley's cricket ground at Remenham ('We must raise this trivial sum of £445,000 – it wouldn't even buy you a chicken-hut in Turville Heath'); an address to the Byron Society; a tribute to Henley's Kenton Theatre on its centenary; a toast to Talking Books for the Blind (invented the year Clifford lost his sight); a eulogy for Graham Greene's centenary at Berkhamsted. He popped up on *Breakfast with Frost*, *Front Row*, *Quote . . . Unquote*, *Newsnight Review*, Ned Sherrin's *Loose Ends* and Andrew Neil's *This Week*, fulminating against the Blair government: 'What is Rumpole's verdict on this week?' 'I find it Guilty as charged.'

He was filmed at home, brandishing a champagne glass: 'Here am I, smoking a small cigar – though I gave up smoking years ago. I've been married to people who smoked, my children smoked and I've reached eighty-one without passing out. The NHS has become a tyranny: it's not there to dictate our way of life. And I'm terrible on a horse, but if this hunting nonsense goes on I'll have to get on a horse again. As for obesity – silly word, call them fat people, "let me have men about me that are fat: sleek-headed men, and such as sleep o'nights" – here we are killing thousands of people in Iraq, and we worry about people eating fish and chips And they're going to stop us from having a bottle of wine with lunch on a long train journey! As a champagne socialist I hugely object to that.'

Maintaining this life demanded a dedicated support team. There were Penny, and Peter, and gardeners, and domestic staff: Maria, the housekeeper, living in a little house in the yard, told me she was 'far more than a housekeeper' – she would cook, drive, shop, look after the animals and run the whole place when they went away. Phyl the Exocet accountant too told me she was 'far more than an accountant'. All bills, receipts and statements were shoved in a Jiffy bag and sent weekly to Phyl in Swansea. She fixed John's budget, and dealt with every negotiation, however footling – even road tax disc renewals. She filled out the insurance claims when a stampeding horse or stag brought down its hoof on the bonnet of the Mercedes. When a dry-cleaner lost John's trousers and would reimburse only the price on the ticket, Phyl took the cleaners to the cleaners. 'Phyl is rude to everyone on my behalf,' said John. 'Sends thunderous letters – and once sent another accountant a copy of *Accountancy for Beginners*.' She waged war with Thames Water when they billed him for a local farmer's field-watering. If one of John's children wanted help to buy a car she would tell them sternly, 'That ten thou has to come out of John's taxed salary.' If he felt a bit low, John would ring Phyl and ask, 'Are we all right?', to hear his solvency cheeringly confirmed, or her warning, 'Yes, John, but don't put too much jam on your bread.' 'I get between him and everyone else, so he can stay on friendly terms with them,' she said. 'But sometimes he rings in a little whimpering voice and says, "Phyl! I'm stuck. My writing days are over . . ."'

Whenever I arrived at Turville Heath Cottage he was at his desk, foolscap pad before him, felt-tip pen in hand. There would be a symbolic glass of champagne on the desk, often untouched. He had finished the new Rumpole and a screenplay of *Così Fan Tutte*, set in a country-house opera. He was adapting Barrie's *The Admirable Crichton*, and writing a film about Edmund Campion 'for a producer who has eight children and lives in Wagga Wagga', and another about Benny Hill. That May, he signed the contract, £50,000, for a non-Rumpole novel on a topical subject, the mentoring of released prisoners. 'A burglar, just out of Wormwood Scrubs, is given a posh young mentor, a bishop's daughter. The burglar explains to her why he enjoys the criminal life: breaking into a sleeping house at midnight is more thrilling than downhill skiing or bungee-jumping. She goes with him one night, discovers the thrill and takes up burgling. He is affronted, and trains as a probation officer. It's like Colin MacInnes's *Mr Love and Justice*,' John said.

Lunch would be set out – smoked salmon, salad, white wine – in the kitchen, warm from the Aga. In the adjoining vine-hung conservatory, housing an enormous fridge and stacks of boxes of Pedigree Chum, were four snoozing dogs: Snowy the black Labrador, Heather the Jack Russell, Bubbles the tiny spaniel, and Poppy, the product of Bubbles and a visiting black Labrador (Bubbles had produced nine Labradors, all twice the size of herself). On fine days we sat in the garden among scarlet poppies, white lilac, blue ceanothus, the fantastic azalea from Stonor, the 'Nelly Moser' clematis. John had no snobbish preference for all-white gardens in the Sissinghurst mode: he liked riots of colour. Our conversations were punctuated by the cries of red kites, introduced by the Gettys. He would complain about the herds of errant deer from Stonor, which galloped through the garden at night, devouring camellias. In the garden the phone would ring, and he would stop to discuss last night's terrible Hamlet – 'to me he seemed like a tiresome teenager' – with Anna Ford.

He would report to me on Penny's latest fishing, stalking or shooting excursions, the pigs she bred and the splendid sausages they made for the barbecue. The Royal Poulterer would be arriving from Highgrove, bringing 'the Royal Cock' to service Penny's superior hens. She held a fund-raiser for her Romanian orphanage, raising £3,000 with the help of John and his Lord and ladies. She attended, with Frida, a royal gala performance of *Mamma Mia*, where Camilla greeted Vicky Lord with, 'I know who you are – a Heavenly Twin!' and HRH was agog to hear about the healing of John's ulcers. Penny's charitable expeditions – cycling down the coast of Jordan, for instance – had long been familiar, because she would appeal for sponsorship or write about them. Now her adventures were even more exotic. She was flying off in a private jet to go bone-fishing in Cuba, thence to New York, thence to Cannes, where Emily's new film was nominated; or flying in Frida's jet to Germany for an Ayurvedic detox, or to a spa near Haut-Brion, or to visit Emily on location in Vancouver.

Penny had written, that spring, one of her occasional diaries in the *Sunday Telegraph*. 'I haven't had a great week so far. I am lying in bed in an NHS ward in Reading with a temperature that keeps trying to hit 40°C.' Her husband, she said, seemed to regard her illness as a deliberate attempt to deprive him of full care and attention. He could be heard on the telephone wailing, 'My wife is ill! My daughters are both away! I might as well die!' 'I am afraid there is no cure,' wrote Penny, 'apart from the full recovery of the wife.'

The children of her Turville school project would be arriving soon, in five batches, twelve at a time, through the summer. 'Some of them are amazed to find out where their breakfast milk comes from.' It did occur to her that these children, some from 'horrific' backgrounds, 'come for a week, see how the other half lives, and are then dumped back into a wretched world'. But at least while there, they could swim, visit farms, take river trips, run wild through fields and woods, and get an idea of 'a better life to aim for'. (John would entertain them – making up rhymes about their names – between their swim and their barbecue lunch.) She braved the Oxford Union, speaking in a debate on class, opposed by Jeremy Clarkson and Nicky Haslam. On her side was Mrs Ronnie Kray, who arrived with her consort, Razor. Penny's account of her conversation in the loo with Mrs Kray was one of her party pieces.

Kate Kray: 'The whole time we were married, he was in Broadmoor.'

Penny: 'Did you actually sleep with him in Broadmoor?'

'NO, darlin', he was a homosexual.'

That June, Adam Tyler-Moore, a young London solicitor omniscient about cinema and theatre, who had unearthed for me a video of *Bunny Lake Is Missing*, suggested that he and the designer Nicky Haslam might come to Turville Heath one day and we could watch the film, and hear John's Hollywood tales. A Saturday date was arranged. When they arrived Nicky began unpacking lavish hampers of 'simply wonderful wine' and 'the best chicken salad in the world'. John joined us, hobbling on his stick, with cries of, 'How exciting! What excitement! The excitement is intense!'

For the next three hours, prompted by Adam the film buff, John and Nicky regaled us with non-stop racontage. It was like a name-droppers' convention, as each capped the other's stories – the kind of company John most enjoyed. Tales were told of (*inter alia*) Rex Harrison, Peter Sellers, Woody Allen, 'Princess Pushy', Mia Farrow ('Frank Sinatra had a model railway in their bedroom and he got angry with her for standing on Forest Lawn station'), Carol Reed, Brando, Dietrich, Gielgud, Tony Richardson, Larry O (who had told John, 'I gave Ken Tynan the National Theatre because I thought he was homosexual, and homosexuals are always terribly nice to me – then I discovered that far from homosexual he was a rather dirty form of heterosexual!'), Alec Guinness, Terence Rattigan, Maggie Smith ('who got stuck with Kenneth Williams's voice for life'), Julian Slade, Margaret Leighton ('Isn't Margaret Leighton an anagram of "malnutrition"?') and of course Noël

Coward. Nicky: 'We were all staying in Château-d'Oex and Ali Forbes said, "Goodbye, Noël! Go with God!" and Noël said, "I did once, dear. Disaster!"'

About a year after this, John rang me and asked, had I seen the *Evening Standard*'s list of 'the most charming people in London'? 'I came second,' he said. 'Nicky Haslam came third.' Who came top? 'David Cameron.'

This was the world into which Ross Bentley was adopted, joining the team of his father's companion / chair-wheelers as he went out and about – to Peter Hall's new Rose Theatre at Kingston, or the Much Ado bookshop's literary luncheon at Alfriston, Sussex. At Christmas 2004 he and Penny flew to New York to spend the holiday on Long Island with Alessandro's family. They were home for New Year, then off to the Gazelle d'Or in January. Back in time for John's gig at the Royal Court, the entire family in attendance, including the new contingent, Ross, Kate and Wendy; and so the 'Jennifer's Diary'-like whirl continued. One weekend, after the Dorset wedding of Emilia Fox to Jared Harris, where 1,000 white butterflies were released like confetti, and there was dinner and dancing till midnight, they got home at 3 a.m. and faced Sunday lunch next day at Turville Park with the Sainsburys and the Braggs.

A long-hoped-for revival of Rumpole on TV never materialized. Albert Finney and Jim Broadbent were approached to step into Leo McKern's shoes, but the producers wanted to appoint a new writer – and besides, there was now a new generation of TV lawyers, like Judge John Deed. John was aggrieved about this, but already on his desk was a writing pad bearing the title: BYRON. John's Byron play, *The Last Adventure*, would be about Byron going off to Greece to fight in the Greek war of independence and dying at Missolonghi in the fevered swamps. 'Everybody betrayed him, let him down, cheated him, but he kept working for the cause,' said John, 'and died for it.' The play was directed for Radio 4 that summer by Jeremy. The launch of his novel *Quite*

Honestly meant another round of literary festivals, 'the pleasure of meeting other writers, and the rivalry over the lengths of their queues at book-signing tables'.

'Work' was John's prime recreation in *Who's Who*. 'Working is what I enjoy doing most,' he said. 'It's my chief pleasure. Every day I get up and work. That's what I enjoy.' He had already signed to write another novel in 2005, *Rumpole and the Reign of Terror*, in which Rumpole defends a Pakistani doctor accused of being a terrorist. This would be his big attack on the Blair government's curtailment of civil rights, which he hoped would irritate 'everyone at the Home Office and in the new, unnecessary Department for Constitutional Affairs'.

The general election on 5 May 2005 was the first in which John abandoned Labour and voted Lib Dem. That night, his friend Bob Marshall-Andrews, the maverick Labour MP and QC, was certain he had lost his seat – which would have delighted Tony Blair – and then, moments later, found to his dismay that he had won after all, by 200 votes. In the BBC studio the cry went up, 'The old rogue is back! Rumpole is back!' 'Rumpole' had become the sobriquet for any amiable iconoclast from the legal world.

John's journalistic output still outstripped that of many journalists. Give him a subject and he'd summon his views – about his father on Father's Day, or seduction for *Vanity Fair*, or 'My heart breaks for our children condemned to a world where reading is redundant', or his memories of VE day ('one huge orgy') on every Second World War anniversary. Why shouldn't Kate Moss be allowed to take cocaine? Is it possible to put a cash value on a good sex life? ('What attracts unlikely couples to each other is a matter for perpetual wonder – not a subject for actuaries.') He wrote in fury when Walter Wolfgang, Old Labour activist, was manhandled out of the Labour Party conference. He abandoned his lunch at the Wolseley one day when told that Marlowe's *Tamburlaine* was being bowdlerized by the RSC to avoid offending Muslims. He sat writing at the restaurant table until 4 p.m., then Penny read his words over to the *Mail*'s copytakers. Only twice did I hear him turn down a job. When asked to take part in *The Moral Maze* on

Boris Johnson's extramarital scandals, John, for obvious reasons, declined. And when the *Mail* asked for a piece about olive oil, even he had to concede defeat at stretching his Tuscan raptures to 1,200 words on olive oil.

On his eighty-second birthday the stepdaughters were summoned to the bluebell picnic, to meet Ross and Kate for the first time. 'It gives John a feeling of belonging, even to those people to whom he no longer belongs,' said Madelon, 'to be at the centre of an ever-expanding gang of people who will always be interconnected.' It had taken considerable planning to get all the families together on that April day, but just four days before the gathering Caroline's husband, the actor John Bennett, died very suddenly. (This was only two years after the death of their son Sam, not yet twenty one, from a rare bone cancer.) Caroline, as ever admirably stoical, did not want to let everyone down, and she went along to John's party. But John did not mention her husband's death. (He did, however, go to John's funeral, and heard Jake, Caroline's elder son, who has Down's syndrome, speaking beautifully and heroically about his father.)

This shying away from mentioning death to the bereaved was a failure of sensitivity others noticed in John. At the *Evening Standard* drama awards he sat next to Drusilla Beyfus, wife of the recently deceased Milton Shulman who had been a friend and reviewer of all John's plays. But John did not mention Milton to Drusilla, even when the Milton Shulman Award was announced. The only question he asked her was, 'How are you with God?'

He did amuse her by telling her 'how unbelievably ghastly' Rosie had been as a teenager, 'but how she has become everything one could ever want'. Rosie, absent from this narrative since her sulks in Australia in 1996, had indeed been a troubled and challenging adolescent who refused to be impressed by anyone and caused her parents great distress when she walked out of Bryanston one day and, despite her excellent exam results, scorned the idea of university. 'Rosie got taken hostage by her hormones,' as Kathy Lette put it. At La Rufena she was always terminally bored by the adults' conversation. But she was now twenty-one and making her name as a model. So John, who had so often been photographed with 'the Mortimer girls' forty-five years before, now had his Mortimer girls Mark II, perpetuating the image of a man surrounded by youth, glamour and beauty. Rosie at twenty-three became his favourite theatre companion.

Wheezing asthmatically, John told me in February 2005 that Penny was ill, in the London Clinic: 'I am surrounded by catastrophe,' he wailed. But both were well again in time for the royal wedding in April, and could enjoy the privilege of the disabled, sailing past the other guests queueing for buses at Windsor Castle. Camilla told them that when she got up that morning, her sister had told her she looked like death warmed up ('but she looked wonderful'). In the Queen's speech, when Her Majesty announced that Hedgehunter had won the Grand National, and congratulated the happy couple on getting past Bechers Brook and the Chair; John had 'turned down money' to write about it.

His life, taken at the face value of his announcements to me, was a catalogue of triumphs, reported in the manner of a child who got ten out of ten and a gold star in the class test. 'I had a full house at Richmond – we raised £25,000', 'My name was in lights outside Portsmouth Theatre Royal', 'One man thought I was God and came to kneel at my feet', 'At Robert's party I had nothing but adulation. At the House of Commons, a policeman pushed me miles down the corridors, and when I said thank you he said, "It's a small reward for the great pleasure you have given me throughout my life."' The pleasure of John's company was sometimes auctioned for charity: a Japanese lady paid £1,500 for lunch with John and Kathy Lette; someone else paid £7,000 for John alone. At a Foyles lunch at the Dorchester, a note was passed to him by the Dutch ambassador, from Lord Snowdon: 'My dear John: you are just the funniest genius ever.' One night he ran into the son of Mrs Maroo, his junior counsel in Singapore (who, in one of his favourite tales, had asked him, 'Are you taking Mrs Mortimer to Bangkok? Coals to Newcastle, sir!') 'Mrs Maroo's son is now a banker in London,' John reported. 'He saw us in the Wolseley and said, "You were such an inspiration to us all in Singapore. And you did it with such enormous charm!"'

So, in the summer of 2005, John was extremely pleased with life. Then, he came home from Tuscany and what he had dreaded came to pass. An unofficial biography was published, *The Devil's Advocate* by Graham Lord – the writer from whom John had withdrawn cooperation and hoped to forestall by appointing me. Lord's research had, in fact, already done the Mortimers a great favour. It was, after all, his sleuthing that had prompted Wendy to contact John the previous year, so the happy advent of Ross was thanks to him. There was nothing unconcealed about John's infidelities during his first marriage. But Lord's tales of John's continuing infidelity during his marriage to Penny predictably dismayed John, and caused Penny – however suspicious she had been – to feel hurt, angry and betrayed. At first, John had told her the book was 'all complete lies'. She challenged him to sue Lord, if so. But he said he could not do that. 'I suddenly realized,' Penny said, 'how much he had lied.'

Her pain was understandable. There had been years when he didn't consider her happiness at all. 'He tells me, "I've always loved you, you know that." But he admits he behaved in both marriages as if he wasn't married. In his first marriage he looked on his stepchildren as brothers and sisters – he was a big child, a big naughty boy.' Seventy-two-year-old Molly Parkin's wicked recollections of their shenanigans forty years before caused a further display of abject despair. 'Oh, God,' John said. 'I shall just have to live through this – or die.' He lived through it. Shortly afterwards, Richard Ingrams and his girlfriend, Debby, went to dinner at Turville Heath Cottage. Penny couldn't resist suggesting to John, 'When you die, we'll put a hairbrush on your coffin, don't you think?' and Debby said, 'H'm, yes, how about a nice little wreath of Mason Pearsons?'

The friends rallied round both, but particularly around Penny. She now had a trump card, Kathy Lette told her, and advised her to play it. 'I said OK – it's jewellery and guilt-free travel for you from now on.' John went to Bond Street and bought diamonds, and threw a birthday party for his wife in September, where Penny made a speech. 'Well,' she began, 'it's been an interesting FUCKING summer.' No longer could John make her feel guilty when she left on her travels. No longer could he object – 'You've already got a winter coat!' – if she returned from a designer warehouse in Italy with a beautiful Max Mara cashmere coat.

In any case, Kathy said, 'I think we should all be a little more French now, about these liaisons.' (François Mitterrand's famous response, when reporters challenged him about his illegitimate daughter, was '*Et alors?*') John's adulteries were in the historic past. As he said, 'Fidelity doesn't present a problem when you can't walk.' But some women in their circle were not so ready to forgive. One said, 'He claims to love women, but has to be judged by his actions. He thinks it is unfortunate that he was found out: he doesn't, fundamentally, think there is anything wrong in pursuing your natural instincts.'

John would admit, 'Penny was devoted, and I was terrible.' But as Penny said, 'Whatever my life with John has been, at least I've never been bored. If I hadn't met him, I'd probably have married an accountant in Surrey.' Convivial, Falstaffian jollity can always see a man through embarrassment and guilt. As Melvyn Bragg said, the mere sight of him made you want to call him good Sir John, merry Sir John; he could carry on, with a little help from his friends, playing the Lord of Misrule.

Does John get emotionally engaged by anything? I asked Penny. 'No,' she replied, 'I don't think he does. The girls love him, and he has been a good and adoring father. But they both feel for me. And I don't want them to hate him.' Anyway, as she well knew, the only thing that really mattered to him was his work. 'If we were all killed in an accident, he would be desolate,' said Penny, 'but he could still write.'

In public, John wore a mask of insouciance. Mark Lawson, in a *Front Row* interview, said, 'Your first wife, Penelope, wrote novels in which you can be detected quite easily. You've been written about a lot. And now you are the subject of an unofficial biography. Have you read it?'

'No.'

'Has it affected you?'

'Well, it's really affected me not at all.'

But Emily felt both her parents were affected. It had been a 'bracing' episode. 'It's as if Mum is armed with all the information she needs now. It's liberating, in a way. And he seems just a tiny bit meeker. Who would have thought he'd have a huge scandal in the papers in his eighty-third year, and be a celeb! I think it's cool.' Her mother, she felt, now had a valid escape clause. 'Anyway, as long as you can still have fun and make each other laugh, nothing else matters very much.' Emily has a daughter's confiding and intense relationship with her mother, wanting to help her cope, wanting her to be happy. 'With Dad – I feel implicitly he understands and forgives me, and I understand and forgive him.' Sometimes, meeting him for dinner or theatre, she would plan to confide something – but then, what she had planned to say would seem 'unnecessary and silly, just part of the absurd cycle of life'. 'When you're with him you forget everything else, and you know you're definitely having more fun than anyone at the other tables in the restaurant.'

Being married with a child herself now, she felt sympathy for her mother, and a need to be protective, which Rosie shared. 'But we can't imagine them ever not being together. There is something right about them. There has been pain, but they are a match for each other. My mum has that straight thing of saying how it is, and he's the opposite, never saying how it is. I think it's quite a sexy relationship even though they haven't, God knows, been to bed for years. It doesn't amaze us that he slept with other women, or had another child. It doesn't shock us at all.'

Then she added, 'I wish I had his capacity to breeze through without much self-recrimination, and let himself off the hook.'

Coda

Scene: the Polish Hearth Club in Queen's Gate, October 2005; the publication party for *Rumpole and the Reign of Terror*. Enter Sir John Mortimer, on wheels. To compound his newly enhanced reputation as an old roué, a bevy of his favourites flock round him: Frida, Kathy, Ann Mallalieu, Binnie, his blonde-haired helper, the Heavenly Twins, a pretty publicist and several girl gossip-columnists hungry for quotes. He tells them, 'I'm just hearing about how brilliant I was as Richard II' (I am reading to him extracts from his Dragon School reviews, having just been to Oxford to retrieve them), and proceeds to recite from memory the familiar speech about sitting on the ground and telling sad stories of the death of kings.

Then George Melly stumps over in his loud striped zoot suit and black eyepatch. This party is also the launch of his memoirs, *Slowing Down*, a book which John has glowingly reviewed. The two one-eyed octogenarian relics greet each other with expansive bonhomie.

'I've got a son!' cries John.

'You old dog!' says George.

'From an affair with Wendy Craig! I didn't know about him till last year.'

'I had that sort of experience once,' says George. 'I had a baby with my first wife but she denied it for years – and then owned up when the girl was twenty.'

John introduces George to the Heavenly Twins.

'Love all the wild hair,' leers George. 'If I took off my eyepatch I'd see FOUR twins.'

And they chat about old Jack Bentley, who used to play with the Ted Heath Band at Ronnie Scott's, and about good old Molly Parkin.

'Molly Parkin broke up my marriage,' says George, without rancour.

The story ought to draw to a close here, but – John being John – there were further ambitions to be fulfilled in his eighty-fourth year. A West End revival of *A Voyage Round My Father* opened in June 2006 at the Donmar Warehouse, starring Derek Jacobi, the fourth theatrical knight to play Clifford. Playwrights are not invariably welcome in rehearsals, but the young cast needed John at their run-throughs in an Islington chapel, to explain what was now very much a period play – Clifford and Kathleen essentially Edwardian figures, school scenes from the 1930s, Crown Film Unit operating in wartime. So John watched Thea Sharrock, aged twenty-eight, her four-month-old son in her arms, directing Joanna David as Kathleen ('I would have died to play that part,' Joanna had said), and Natasha Little who, although she knew nothing of Penelope Mortimer, brought her beautifully to life. Penelope's refusal to play along with the family charade of ignoring Clifford's blindness ('Why do you bother with all this gardening when you can't see it?') had lost none of its impact. The critics were even more rapturous than they had been in 1970.

I saw the first preview from the front row, with John alongside in the aisle, on the same level as the stage. A few feet in front of us sat Jacobi in an old fashioned basketwork wheelchair. John appeared quite moved as he watched Jacobi breathing his last. The audience seemed to share the sense of bereavement because Clifford, dominating the stage as he tapped about with his stick, remained a powerfully affecting figure.

In his review of the original production, the critic Harold Hobson – who was wheelchair-bound himself – had pointed out what Clifford's stoicism really meant to his family. 'I am the last person in the world to underestimate the difficulties of the handicapped,' he wrote. 'But the real, searing penalty for disablement is paid, not by the disabled, but by their wives and husbands and families . . . who, with constant patience, see that they are not bumped into in the street, who help them up stairs, who stage-manage their public appearances so that they are seen to least disadvantage.' All John's family were by now accustomed to this penalty.

The play transferred to Wyndham's, a jewel of a theatre, and ran until Christmas. During the summer John and Penny invited the entire cast, including the six schoolboys and their families, and the babies of Thea Sharrock and Natasha Little, to a picnic at Turville Heath Cottage. The little boys ran through the garden in search of earwigs, but couldn't find any, so they brought John two grasshoppers, and a toy dog labelled 'A MOST LUGUBRIOUS HOUND', as in one of the stories Clifford tells his grandchildren in the play.

'You started as a playwright with Harold Pinter, John Osborne, Tom Stoppard,' Mark Lawson had said to John in the recent *Front Row* programme. 'Do you have any regret that you haven't had as substantial a stage career as they did?'

'Yes, well, perhaps I do regret that,' said John, who had always felt an undercurrent of rivalry with Stoppard in particular. 'Perhaps I would have liked to have written more for the stage, because I do love the theatre.' He added, 'I might still.'

Asked about his legal career, John had no regrets except to wish he had left the Bar earlier. When Lawson commented that he had sometimes defended 'artistically inferior work', notably Linda Lovelace, John's view was unrevised: the sole issue was freedom from censorship. He applied the same intransigent principle to what he saw as the Blair government's curtailment of free speech in the name of anti-terrorism. 'It means that the whole of my youth, which was spent saying how wonderful the Free French resistance were in the war, has got to be outlawed.' Lawson politely ignored this *reductio ad absurdum*. It was a habit John had got into by his eighties. Asked about 9/11, he would reply that the Blitz had been exciting: 'When I look back to those days of bombs falling on London, it was rather a happy period of my life.' Challenged about the need to curtail incitement to racial hatred, in particular the murderous rantings of Islamic extremists, he would reply that he didn't mind, when in Australia, being called a

whingeing Pom. Apart from the constraints against libel and con-
spiracy to commit a crime, people must be allowed to say what
they like, in his view. And to see what they like. The proposal, in
2007, to outlaw the downloading of Internet images of women
being sexually tortured, he found ominous: 'I think it's quite
dangerous, to make a law that prevents you from looking at things.
It was never a crime to read pornography. To criminalize the
audience would be a big legal step. Where do you stop – are we
not allowed to see Gloucester's eyes being gouged out in *King
Lear*?' He conceded some doubt about paedophile contact via the
Internet; but then he added, 'I am hopelessly unconnected to the
Internet.' Censorship, for John, was incontrovertibly wrong. His
association with such cases was ruled by the Zeitgeist of the 1960s
– very different from the culture of the twenty-first century.

His father had been a scholarly barrister who loved to ponder
on the most arcane and complex corners of the law, 'as in the
doctrine of the renvoi in the cases on domicile, or of "dependent
relative revocation" in Probate'. Clifford regarded the law as enjoyable, like the *Times* crossword. To John, the law was essentially 'a
sort of maze through which a client must be led to safety'. 'The
basic morality on which law is founded has always seemed to me
crudely inferior to those moral values which everyone must work
out for themselves,' he wrote, 'and the results of even the best
laws, when consistently applied, are bound to be intolerable in
many individual cases.'

As for his political stance, John had told audiences that his
socialism was based on an essay by Oscar Wilde, 'The Soul of Man
under Socialism'. 'Oscar says the great thing about socialism is that
it will look after everyone, and we can all stop feeling sorry for
people ever again,' he said. 'If socialism takes care of everyone, we
can get on with enjoying ourselves. That's Wilde's view.' Once
Blair was in power, he was excused from taking politics too seriously. 'If the Prime Minister represents the priggish tendency in
the Labour Party, Sir John Mortimer represents the whiggish one,'
a *Daily Telegraph* leader had declared. 'Sir John combines liberal
opinions and conservative instincts with enviable ease . . . Even

his socialism arises from his own unabashed enjoyment of the good
things in life – the bar and the Bar.'

Producing a book every year ensured a relentless round of appearances and signings, of which John never tired, ringing his literary
agent almost daily with 'Hello, darling, how's my career?' He
badgered his publisher for sales figures, and his publicist about
garnering more reviews. Critics had always been good to John,
but a prolific output presents a problem to literary editors, striving
to find reviewers who have not already had their say the previous
year. Penelope Lively, tackling *The Penge Bungalow Murders*, wrote
candidly that Rumpole devotees would be rewarded, 'but perhaps
a trifle thinly'. The novel was set in the 1950s, but she felt Rumpoles were always located firmly somewhere around 1930, in the
same never-land inhabited by Dornford Yates and P. G. Wodehouse. 'The humour is very much of this vintage . . . If the legal
profession is like that in real life, heaven help us: the frivolity would
be bad enough but the conversational style deserves prosecution on
its own account.' In America, reviewers were far more positive.
'In 190 pages [of *Rumpole and the Reign of Terror*] Mortimer packs
more wit, social observation and truth about life than most authors
do in 500.'

The California Bar Association descended on London on 10 July
2006, on the eve of his departure for Tuscany, and John addressed
them from the judge's throne in Court 28 of the Royal Courts of
Justice. Four barristers had bundled his chair up the steps to the
bench, where he sat with Penny at his side, telling old stories of
his father and Rumpole. Afterwards they presented him with a
framed diploma, and he was asked about the difference between
English and American courts. He could have dredged up memories
of the O. J. Simpson trial – but he made no real attempt at an
answer; he liked to stick to his own agenda. When he did an *Oldie*
literary lunch every year, bets would be laid about which dozen
of his familiar stories would be re-aired. The ones that always got
the best laughs were Lord 'Boofy' Arran, and the sleeping juror.
Boofy had steered two bills through the Lords: one, to reduce the

homosexual age of consent to eighteen and one for the preservation
of badgers. 'I can't understand it,' said Boofy as he lay dying.
'Hardly anyone showed up for the badgers' bill. When we passed
our buggers' bill, the place was packed.' 'Have you never considered,' he was asked, 'there are very few badgers in the House
of Lords.' The sleeping juror story is told by Richard Eyre in his
published diary:

A woman was giving evidence in a sexual harassment case, but she was too
shy to say out loud what had been said to her. 'Write it down,' said the
judge. So she wrote it down. It read: 'Do you want a fuck?' This was passed
around the court, eventually ending up with a dozing juryman, who was
sitting next to an attractive woman. The woman prodded the juryman
awake and handed him the note. He read it, looked at her, smiled, folded
the note and put it in his pocket. The judge asked for the note to be
returned to him. 'Merely a private matter, my lord,' said the juryman.

John's energy seemed unflagging. He had to go to Dublin, where
his *A Christmas Carol* was staged for the third time at the Gate
Theatre. He attended the première of Emily's Woody Allen film,
Match Point (a lovely performance by Emily in a dire film). He
read a Betjeman poem in the televised Betjeman centenary celebration in 2006; he read 'Death in Leamington Spa', while the Prince
of Wales read 'A Subaltern's Love Song'. He was made an Honorary Fellow of Brasenose in 2006. He still popped up on television,
reminiscing about his advice to the Monty Pythons about the
possibility of a blasphemy case for *The Life of Brian* in 1978–9. In
a programme about H. Rider Haggard, he told viewers that whenever men asked him to sign a Rumpole book, they requested the
dedication 'To She Who Must Be Obeyed'.

He often encountered Wendy – at the opening of the Unicorn
Theatre, or a garden party at Clarence House, for instance. At a
Bonfire Night party, he met Lincoln Elias, a record producer who
had bought the old John Piper house. When Myfanwy Piper had
died, John had noticed in the catalogue from Maggs the booksellers
that they were offering for sale all the Pipers' books, including

those signed copies John had given them over the years. So Lincoln Elias had gone marching into Maggs. 'They looked askance at him' (Lincoln is black) 'but, he said, "In the end I made them wince" – as he bought up the remaining Pipers' books, and has put them back on the shelves at Fawley Bottom.' At one of John's country gigs in Gloucestershire, who should turn up in the audience but 'Parsons', alias Patrick Freeman, his pious room-mate from Meadow Building, who John claimed had prayed for him when he got drunk. Freeman too was now in a wheelchair, with Parkinson's disease. Hearing about their encounter, another Brasenose contemporary, John Browning, asked me, 'And did wheelchair speak unto wheelchair?'

Penny was in the Western Highlands for her sixtieth birthday party in 2006, at her friend Caroline Tisdall's turreted house on a great loch. John was wheeled on to a landing craft, and as they approached the jetty on the other side of the water, a boy piper wearing a kilt sounded a welcome. Being among mountains, and writing an *Observer* piece about this experience, John was prompted to launch into Wordsworth's *Tintern Abbey*, summarizing his own feelings:

> . . . Therefore am I still
> A lover of the meadows and the woods,
> And mountains . . .
> well pleased to recognise
> In nature and the language of the sense . . .
> The guide, the guardian of my heart, and soul
> Of all my moral being.

'On the whole I'm not in favour of writers who don't do jokes,' John wrote, 'but jokeless Wordsworth is among my favourite poets – and Rumpole's. Speaking of his wife Hilda's cooking, he said that her baked jam roll was "an emotion best recollected in tranquillity".'

★

At the beginning of 2007, the King's Head pub theatre in Islington asked John to fill a three-week season in February, which would mean performing eight times a week, including Saturday and Sunday matinées. Everyone was aghast. Penny said it would kill him – and John replied that he couldn't imagine a better way to go, like Dickens. He thrived on the daily exposure, and the show was as fresh and funny as ever, with a revolving rota of actresses including his stepdaughter Caroline. I went three times, and watched amazed as Dr Greasepaint exerted his magic. Before going on stage, John would sit inert, like a limp rag. Once on stage he would spring to animate life. One Saturday he was sitting in the tiny dressing room between performances when the actress Lily Bevan arrived equipped with pink fluorescent scissors and Evening Primrose hand cream, and proceeded to manicure John's grubby fingernails, while he told her the tales of the various rings he wore: one was a ring he had given to his mother when he was a school-boy; the dormouse ring was a gift from Penny.

The sound of the King's Head applause after John's recital of Byron's 'So, we'll go no more a-roving, so late into the night' was heard on Radio 4 when Peter White talked to him for his series *No Triumph, No Tragedy*. Why, the engaging White (himself blind from birth) wanted to know, did John still do these performances, when almost blind and unable to walk, and approaching his eighty-fourth birthday? 'It can't be the money' (£100 a night).

A truer motive – as one of John's actresses' husbands put it to me – was that John was 'a Chekhovian egotist'. What John said to White was, 'I have a determination to go on as I am, really.'

'So is that the Mortimer plan, to go on doing what you're doing?'

'Oh, absolutely. As long as possible. Try and fill the day with work you enjoy. My religious beliefs, if they can be called that, are just the importance of the individual moment, in the present. That's the valuable, the precious thing.'

At the start of White's interview John had been heard calling out to Binnie, 'Binnie! Bin! Where's my Guinness?' I wished that John had made a point, in the programme, of thanking his wife and the team of half a dozen people who made his life possible, including Binnie. It is noble to be stoical, and he clearly still gave pleasure to audiences wherever he went: but his was not a solo act. Indeed, several listeners contacted the BBC to point out that the contented wheelchair life was 'all very well for rich authors with lots of paid help'. John had apparently failed to imagine the unbearable reality of other, similarly afflicted, lives. His perspective was a privileged and protected one. Sometimes, sighed one friend, 'I wish he would try living in a wheelchair on a Peckham housing estate on fifty pounds a week.'

He had admitted to White that he did sometimes have regrets that his writing 'isn't better'. He was still prone to glooms, and some were surprised to find he was not always the cuddlesome roly-poly Rumpole. I found no real distinction between the private and the public man. But his family, and selected close friends, witnessed his ability to turn suddenly coldly angry – 'and even quite frightening' – in arguments. 'It's deadly for anyone trying to argue with him. He can become quite poisonous. It doesn't happen often, but there is a part of his brain that is acutely analytical, and that is working all the time.' They felt rather sorry for the victims of his demolition arguments. 'The appearance of vulnerability is part of the charm offensive,' as Jeremy said. 'He does desperately need the love and attention. Which can be tiring for everyone. But he hardly feels alive without it.' At the end of February a recording was made, for posterity, of *Mortimer's Miscellany*, with Emily joining Joanna David as his two readers, before an invited studio audience. Everybody present must have heard the show a dozen times before, but the laughter and applause were enthusiastic. He was bathed in glory, surrounded by adulation.

About ten days later, while walking from study to kitchen, John fell. His right leg was rendered useless, and he had bruised a shoulder, but he still turned up to record *Quote . . . Unquote* that week, at the Drill Hall in Bloomsbury. Two days later he flew to Glasgow with Penny and Joanna David to watch a Scottish actress, Alison Peebles, playing the Penelope part in *Lie Down Comic* in the Oranmore Theatre, part of the Glasgow Comedy Festival, with the comic Sandy Nelson. Marilyn Imrie, who directed the piece, said John was visibly moved by Ms Peebles's performance, which he said was 'so like Penelope'.

A few days later the National Film Theatre's Lesbian and Gay Season included a screening of his *Bermondsey* play – the version televised in 1973. This superb production starred Dinsdale Landen and Edward Fox, whose sudden kiss had lost none of its shock value over the years. John, wheeled into the auditorium by Jeremy, was applauded and cheered. Once again he was able to tell this heavily partial audience that he had won an award from the American Alliance for Gay Artists 'for the most tasteful representation of a gay love affair, in *Brideshead Revisited*'.

The next week, it was painful to see him, in obvious discomfort, being manhandled up the Simpsons stairs in his chair, by two strong waiters (he was terrified of lifts, hence this undignified operation). He was propelled into the restaurant, to sit on top table at the Oldie of the Year lunch, alongside Sinéad Cusack, Peter O'Toole and Leslie Phillips. Immediately after the awards, Penny took John to Harley Street, where his leg was found to have a fractured tibia. So for two weeks he had been travelling about, even flying to Glasgow, and sitting for hours (on the road and in theatres) with a broken leg. He was in hospital in St John's Wood for just one night, and as he came out of the anaesthetic, having had the bone set, he was singing softly, 'Little man you've had a busy day'. He would be in plaster for three months, yet he would not think of cancelling a single engagement. After he sprained his right wrist when levering himself into his car, a new car with a ramp arrived. For a short while, writing became impossible. Now that he really had something to be self-pitying about, he uttered not a word of self-pity. 'We have little choice but to go along the road Fate has chosen for us,' he said, 'and try not to complain.'

Age and physical debility reduce all men to powerlessness. They must rely on their wits – and John's mercifully were intact. His hearing, too, was unimpaired (though Penny recalled that he had once become suddenly deaf and a specialist found a pencil lead embedded inside his ear). His memories remained vivid. He could recall, half a century before, meeting E. M. Forster, who showed him all the toys he'd kept from childhood, 'including a kaleidoscope where rats went into a person's mouth when you turned the handle'. He remembered Olivier confiding his method for finding the right scream for Oedipus Rex – by imagining the agonized cry of an Arctic ermine, trapped by salt sprinkled on ice, so that its tongue, licking the salt, is welded to the ice. His old friend James Michie said, 'If locked in solitary confinement, John could – like me – cover the walls with lines from Shakespeare.' Whenever John went on *Quote . . . Unquote*, by far the oldest of the regular contestants, he knew all the answers. He knew which poet entitled one of her books *A Good Time Was Had by All* (Stevie Smith) and could add, 'She looked like a little wet rat, but she was extremely funny and a marvellous poet.' He used to move, he said, in her bohemian circles; Stevie had been a friend of his first lover, Susan Watson. At his eighty-fourth birthday picnic among the bluebells in April 2007, he was serenaded with 'Little man you've had a busy day'.

John's life has been in my hands for three years. I knew that embarking on this voyage round John Mortimer would test his attitude to biography. In one of our interviews, seven years before, John had told me he had just reviewed a biography of Chekhov. 'Chekhov couldn't make love to any woman twice,' he said. 'He was like a cheetah, they always need to get another cheetah. But I didn't really want to know that.' He added that he 'absolutely worshipped' Dickens, 'but I don't need to know that he nailed up the door to his wife's bedroom and kept a mistress. It's quite interesting, but it doesn't really add any insight.' I totally disagreed. Our understanding of Dickens, our appreciation of his writing, were enhanced by knowing the details of his life, in my opinion. 'You think Chekhov's work might be obscured by this stuff about cheetahs,' I said, 'but is it, really?' And John said, 'It's true, I still love Chekhov just as much, after reading this book.'

At the revival of *A Voyage Round My Father*, one critic had astutely remarked, 'This is a voyage round a man who remains elusive, not a voyage to his centre. Maybe Old Mortimer's flippancy was defensive, a way of preserving his privacy. Maybe it was his response to a world he thought essentially absurd. Or maybe it was a sign that he had no centre at all.' This comment reminded me that when I first embarked on this enterprise, Penny had said, 'I wonder if you'll get to the bottom of John? Sometimes I wonder if I've got to the bottom of him.' Then she added, 'Maybe there's no bottom!'

It was strange to confront a writer with no 'papers', just scrapbooks. He did not keep his reviews of others' work, or his illuminating interviews. But he kept every tiny snippety review of his books, including those from the *Youngstown Ohio Vindicator* or the *Sacramento Bee*. What mattered was the praise, not who bestowed it. His archives, lodged with American universities, contain nothing but manuscripts. He kept no sentimental billets-doux, no charming scribbles by his children. Of his legions of friends, not one, outside his immediate family, could show me a single letter from him since 1944 – 'only postcards saying thank you, about which he is punctilious'. (The longest postcard I had from him came in 1994, when, in a radio review, I had misattributed a short story to Deborah Moggach. 'I am glad you enjoyed "The Other Girl",' wrote John plaintively. 'Alas, it was not written by Deborah Moggach, but by your old friend John Mortimer.') As for letters he received, his 'Important letters' file contains no more than a dozen brief notes from people such as the Queen Mother's lady-in-waiting and Sir John Gielgud. Unusually for a writer, he kept no journal. So, apart from the Siena notebook, there was scant evidence of his terror of neglect, opprobrium or oblivion.

The need to support a large family only partially explained what kept him at his desk every morning. (Alan Coren suggested a title for this book: *Clinging to the Royalties*.) But far more important than royalties, I realized, was the need for praise. 'You're wonderful,' he constantly said to others, and, 'You're so kind': a way of willing people to bestow praise on him. He basked whenever he was approached in a public place: I can recall a City solicitor coming up to say that he gave all his young apprentices a Rumpole video, 'which would show them more truth about life in the law than they get from *Chitty on Contract*'. Whether people were 'nice' to him was John's defining judgement. If they weren't they were summarily dropped. When the *Big Issue* magazine asked him to confess his worst fault, he said, 'Wanting people to like me.'

As he wrote, writers often invent their personalities. 'Evelyn Waugh invented that person, and performed it – and then the wind changed and he was stuck with it.' Dickens 'invented himself as a commonsensical, decent, home-loving family man, although he was an unfaithful husband capable of elaborate deception'. John too had created his own mythology. He had written of 'the writer's gluttony for material, his habit of eating his life as a caterpillar consumes the leaf it sits on, and spinning it out changed and perhaps unrecognizable'. 'Writing down events is the writer's great protection, his defence and his safety-valve. Anger and misery, defeat, humiliation and self-disgust can be changed and used to provide a sense of achievement as he fills his pages.' His autobiographies, blurring fact and fiction, were masterpieces of non-revelation, written to amuse, to exorcize misery and failure, and to obscure his real feelings, leaving 'a sense of achievement'. 'Every one of us, reinventing our pasts,' he wrote, 'is a mythmaker to a certain degree.'

Michael Holroyd said it is the biographer's difficult task to try to explain how the magician's rabbit got into the hat. But John's dearest friends would admit to being unable to fathom his legerdemain. Penelope, with whom I felt an instinctive bond, had quoted Frances Donaldson on the biographer's task: 'to seek out and represent as faithfully as possible the human being behind the history'. This was almost impossible with the Queen Mother, who was 'protected by a carapace of praise more impenetrable than the walls of the Royal Vault'.

John's 'national treasure status' formed a similar protective carapace. His legendary charm and popularity were beyond question, to all but a very few refuseniks. Sir Alistair Horne, for instance, found John implacably hostile after their dispute over the village school. 'Certain characters possess, to the British nose, an intrinsic fragrance,' as Bryan Appleyard wrote. 'They are, almost irrespective of what they do, national treasures.' Of course the term has been debased by over-use: *The Times* recently called the playwright Caryl Churchill a national treasure, though she has no mass audience. John might appear open and expansive: 'Ask me whatever you like, how can I help you?' But I had seen how the campaigner for freedom of speech could get on the phone to Carter-Ruck if he felt threatened by unwelcome exposure. He would call for diversionary champagne – 'Shall we fill up our glasses?' – whenever I ventured into territory not already dealt with in his own published versions of himself.

If irritated by my persistent presence he never showed it. And even at the dark moments all biographers know, when they feel condemned to a life sentence, I always looked forward to seeing John. I totally shared his view that laughter must be sought above all things, and there was much laughter. To me, the most human element in his superhuman image was that he remained the centre of an affectionate family: Madelon in France, Julia and Caroline in their neighbouring houses in Willesden, Deborah in Cornwall, Sally in Bristol, Jeremy near my own home in north London, Emily permanently in transit between the US and a film location, Ross and Rosie in west London. Gratifying the needs of a large family is demanding, and there were inevitable internecine resentments, but John could be depended on when a crisis arose, as Sally found when she had to undergo chemotherapy in 1997 for breast cancer. 'He was dependable when I needed him. We got the closest ever to talking about life and death.' He also did a *Miscellany* to raise money for the breast scanner at Sally's hospital. And when John was in need of an extra nursing hand in 2007, while Penny was away on safari in Kenya in February and he was enslaved by the King's Head performances, Sally came to his aid.

★

May 2007: John, still unable to wield his pen, composes a verse for Sir Denis Forman. Forman, himself nearing ninety, has written John a little verse to commiserate about his broken leg. It is rather touching to see this exchange of doggerel, by two ancient knights, each in a shaky and myopic hand.

To Sir John Mortimer, On the occasion of his experiencing a bout of ill-health, From his old friend and fellow knight, Sir Denis Forman:

> Broken leg, failing eyes and sprained wrist:
> This must be Fate's cruellest twist
> And if there's a God
> The lazy old sod
> Must be sleeping, or dormant, or pissed.
>
> I know that you'll face this ill-luck
> With your usual indomitable pluck
> But I send you this letter
> To keep up your pecker –
> Just keep cheery and don't give a fuck.

Sir Denis, who lost a leg at the battle of Monte Cassino, and spends half the year on Goa, had stayed with the Mortimers in Tuscany. John recalled that when Sir Denis parked his car in Siena, he would leave his spare wooden leg on the bonnet, to repel the carabinieri. So John replied:

> Go break a leg, actors say –
> A phrase I've often heard.
> Unhappily, the other day
> I took them at their word.
>
> I stumbled through an open door –
> It isn't bad, it could be worse:
> But nothing could delight me more
> Than a friend's letter, couched in verse.

I'm not heroic, as *you* are
But one day I will write a sonnet
On how you used to park the car
And leave a spare leg on the bonnet.

From Opera House to Goa's beaches,
By way of Brideshead's golden serial,
The lesson that your great life teaches
Is that legs are immaterial.

10 May 2007: We are in the picturesque seaside village of Fowey, Cornwall. On the centenary of Daphne du Maurier's birth, the Fowey Literary Festival has invited Sir John to do the opening event, and I am to be his interlocutor. Over dinner the night before, we do our best to recite Matthew Arnold's 'Dover Beach', a poem we both love. The next morning we meet as arranged. I am listening on my Walkman to Melvyn Bragg's *In Our Time* on Radio 4, which is discussing Victorian pessimism; by coincidence, Bragg recites 'Dover Beach'. But John does not hear this: he has fallen asleep in his chair before the smoky wood fire in the hotel drawing room. His foot is encased in a great plastic boot which has valves to maintain comfort and rigidity. His other foot is encased in a sock. Minutes before we are due to go on stage, in the dressing room, John is sound asleep again. The rain is beating down on the dripping marquee. But Dr Greasepaint gets to work again. The expectant audience waits. John wakes up, brightens and is wheeled on stage by Peter. I begin by asking, did John ever meet Daphne du Maurier? No, but he recalls a limerick about her father:

There was a young lady named Gloria
Who was screwed by Sir Gerald du Maurier,
Jack Hylton, Jack Payne,
Sir Gerald again,
And the band of the Waldorf Astoria.

Later he tells another story of how Basil Dean, the unpopular impresario, who wanted to get into the Garrick, had been black-balled. He made one final effort to apply for membership, then sat waiting at home. Gerald du Maurier was deputed to go and give him the result. Du Maurier said, 'I'm afraid it's bad news, Basil. You didn't get in.'

'Were there many black balls?' inquired Basil sadly.

'Well . . .' du Maurier replied. 'Have you ever seen sheep shit?'

How the audience laughed. And queued afterwards, to have their books signed.

This story is unfinished. On this July morning, I have watched the dawn over Hampstead Heath, knowing that at Turville Heath Cottage John will also be up, and already at his desk, in the house where his father and mother died. He has plenty of cheering prospects ahead: lunch today at the Wolseley with a fan who bid for him in an auction; the promise of Tuscany; a new writing project, a potted history of Durham Cathedral for the university's 150th anniversary later this year, to accompany Jon Lord's concerto for Northumbrian pipes; and two of his plays, *Edwin* and *The Dock Brief*, are going to open at Bath, in the autumn of his eighty-fifth year. He has just made an excellent speech at Westminster Abbey, for the centenary of Olivier's birth. He is finishing another novel, *The Anti-social Behaviour of Horace Rumpole*. At this moment, he will be looking at the blank page in front of him and thinking, with Trigorin, 'I am haunted night and day by one persistent thought. I ought to be writing. I ought to be writing . . . Oh, it is an absurd life!'

Notes

Chapter 2: The Clever Boy

p. 38   **W. T. S. Stallybrass**   Stallybrass was a popular college character who kept up a correspondence with many old BNC undergraduates in PoW camps and left his entire estate to Brasenose, including 6,000 negatives of his photographs, many of soldiers, indexed and named. He died suddenly in 1947, falling from a train near Iver, having opened the carriage door mistaking it for the lavatory (though speculation persisted that he had been pushed out by a rival).

Chapter 3: Among the Aesthetes

p. 45   **organ scholar named Wicks**   W. A. F. Brister, *The Brazen Nose*, Vol. 33, 1999, p. 30.

p. 48   **'an enthusiastic homosexual' while at Oxford**   From an interview with Peter Brook in *The Times*, 7 February 2006.

p. 50   **E. S. P. Haynes**   Selina Hastings relates in her biography of Evelyn Waugh that while Evelyn was at Oxford in the 1920s, he and his brother Alec went to lunch with Haynes. The three men got through a bottle of burgundy each, plus two different kinds of port and some 1870 brandy, which they swigged out of tumblers. Later, Haynes acted for both Waugh brothers in their divorces, and Evelyn used Haynes in *Work Suspended*, as part of the basis for a character named Plant, a painter who lives alone in St John's Wood and dresses in *Yellow Book* style.

Chapter 4: Into Bohemia

p. 68   **Susan Watson**   She went on to take a job looking after George
         Orwell's son in Scotland and then in Canonbury Square. Forty
         years on, she was very upset by John's memoirs, in which he
         changed her name to Sarah – her daughter's name. But when
         Sarah wrote to tell him of Susan's death in 2001, he wrote back
         touchingly, saying 'after all, she was my first great love'.

p. 69   **Wyn Henderson**   She introduced Dylan Thomas to Caitlin,
         was a mistress of Havelock Ellis and finds her way into several
         Fitzrovia and Bloomsbury biographies. Late in life she met a
         young Dominican monk, Benet Wethered, who visited her in
         hospital; he promptly fell in love, left his order and married
         her. Wyn typifies the interconnected characters who erupted in
         John's life in this period in that small group of Thames Valley
         villages.

Chapter 5: The Penelopiad

p. 91   **Sonia Jenkins**   Sonia saw Charles through his drinking epi-
         sodes, which soon stopped. Dimont carried on writing for radio,
         and contributed to *History Today* and other specialist journals.
         He won an award in 1965 for agricultural reporting, having
         begun by knowing nothing about farming. But his first passion
         was rowing. Schooled by Steve Fairbairn, an Australian rowing
         coach with a revolutionary mind-over-matter approach, Dimont
         became rowing master to the oarsmen at Emanuel School,
         Wandsworth, and the driving force behind several London
         regattas. Since he and Sonia and their three children lived a few
         hundred yards from the Thames at Putney, he became a familiar
         duffel-coated figure on the towpath to everyone using the river,
         until his death, just before his eightieth birthday, in 1993.

Chapter 8: The Media Mortimers

p. 140   **The Wrong Side of the Park**   John's play contains references, revived in later plays and novels, to 'Gin and Altars' for wartime black-market communion wine and 'Moby Dick [whale steaks] and chips' (see page 270).

Chapter 11: Queen's Counsel and *Farceur*

p. 182   **treats the saloon car like a horse**   This is curiously reminiscent of John Betjeman's *Summoned by Bells*, published in 1963.

> William our coachman who, turned chauffeur, still
> Longed for his mare and feared the motor-car
> Which he would hiss at, polishing its sides . . .'

In fact there are many striking resonances between Betjeman's blank verse memoir and John's play – and many parallels between the two men's lives overall. A lonely childhood as an only son; an afflicted father (Betjeman's dad was deaf, and he too wanted his son and heir to follow in his footsteps); attending the Dragon School and enjoying its eccentricities; disliking public school (though John B. wished he had gone to Harrow) and hating games; fellow-travelling with the Oxford aesthetes; getting unjustly sent down; getting a job with Jack Beddington; stormy and unfaithful marriages to wives named Penelope, plus many shared friendships; and ultimately, achieving 'national treasure' status through an addiction to public performance.

Chapter 14: A New Penny Turns Up

p. 235 '. . . **boiler-maker in Brighton**' This was John's hypothetical example, but in 2006 the case of twelve-year-old Molly Campbell opting to live with her Pakistani father in Lahore rather than stay with her Scottish mother in Stornoway pointed up the futility of judicial intervention in such cases – even more so before the High Court's Family Division, and the Children Act, came into existence.

Chapter 17: The Old Darling

p. 285 James Crespi was taken to Bart's Hospital, where they decided not to attempt to remove the bits of bomb from his vast bulk. But he lived another twenty years.

p. 302 The nine-month sentence on Lemon was later lifted on appeal. And when, later still, the question of *mens rea* (a guilty mind) was taken to the House of Lords by Robertson and Louis Blom-Cooper – as John was away at the time – the conviction remained.

Chapter 18: Lucid Indifference

p. 320 **Edith Thompson's letter** Edith Thompson (29) and her lover, Frederick Bywater (20), were hanged on 9 January 1923 for the murder of her husband, Percy Thompson.

Chapter 20: No More Moaning of the Bar

p. 348 **the handsome conservatory** John and Penny also built a guest cottage by the back door which was eventually to become John's sleeping quarters. They found the same green tiles for the roof and gave it the same white walls and yellow window frames. It has two bedrooms, a small kitchen, a bathroom, and a sitting room – Penny's computer room – lined with books.

p. 354 **Marjoriebanks**   The name came from Edward Marjoriebanks, half-brother of Lord Hailsham and author of the life of Edward Marshall Hall – a book and a subject greatly admired by John.

Chapter 24: Penny Tells It Like It Is

p. 418 **John had to do a bit of research**   The idea that John might go out and talk to the homeless on the streets of London was suggested by Virginia Bottomley, the Tory MP. They met one night over dinner at Michael and Sandra Howard's, when Mrs Bottomley told John that the problem of persuading the homeless to move off the streets and into hostels was an extremely complex one. She urged John to accompany her that very night, at midnight, to the Embankment: she would introduce him to some cardboard-box dwellers who would explain why they preferred to remain where they were. John demurred. But later, when writing *Felix in the Underworld*, he was emboldened to venture out, with the chaplain and the police officers, to see for himself.

p. 424 **On Radio 3's *Private Passions***   4 June 1995, John was sandwiched between Toyah Wilcox and Chad Varah. Michael Berkeley, who normally records the programme at his home, went to Turville Heath and found John looking wonderfully 'Rumpole-like'. He chose Placido Domingo singing 'E lucevan le stelle' from Puccini's *Tosca*, Mozart's *Sinfonia Concertante* (finale), the third movement of Brahms's Symphony no. 4, 'How sad it is' from *Die Fledermaus*, the 'Dies Irae' from Verdi's *Requiem*, 'Beim Schlafengehen' from Richard Strauss's *Four Last Songs*, Cole Porter's 'Let's Face the Music and Dance', and 'Una voce poco fa' from Rossini's *The Barber of Seville*.

Chapter 25: Nothing Like a Dormouse

p. 445   **'John Mortimer Owning Up at 80'**   Yentob had left a great deal of overmatter on the cutting-room floor and Sally felt that John should see it. The following February she brought the tape to Turville Heath Cottage and suggested they watch after dinner. He lit a fire, but as soon as Sally began speaking, he fell asleep. But when Yentob asked Sally how Penelope felt about John, and she replied, 'Well, I think he drove her absolutely –' John suddenly woke up, and filled in the word 'mad'. He did watch the footage of his grandchildren discussing him. When Sally's son Gus said it was the childish part of his grandfather's character that kept him young, John murmured, 'You got it, Gus.'

Chapter 26: The Family Reunion

p. 466   **in a *Front Row* interview**   Sir Richard Body, QC, recalled a solicitor bringing in a client with a dispute over a divorce settlement. John asked, 'What is your employment?' and on receiving the reply, 'Assistant executioner,' turned the client away. John often told this story, whenever asked if he had ever refused to defend anyone. Body, who witnessed the episode, says John's colleagues were not surprised by his action, but they did wonder if he was right. And in 2005, when John related this tale on Radio 4, Mark Lawson challenged him: 'So you would defend a murderer, but not a hangman?'

List of Works

John Mortimer

fiction

Charade (Bodley Head, 1947)
Rumming Park (Bodley Head, 1948)
Answer Yes or No (Bodley Head, 1950)
Like Men Betrayed (Collins, 1953)
The Narrowing Stream (Collins, 1954)
Three Winters (Collins, 1956)
Will Shakespeare: An Entertainment (Hodder and Stoughton, 1977)
Rumpole of the Bailey (Penguin, 1978)
The Trials of Rumpole (Penguin, 1979)
Rumpole's Return (Penguin, 1980)
Rumpole for the Defence (first published as *Regina v. Rumpole*, Allen Lane, 1981)
Rumpole and the Golden Thread (Penguin, 1983)
Paradise Postponed (Penguin, 1985)
Rumpole and the Age of Miracles (Penguin, 1988)
Rumpole's Last Case (Penguin, 1988)
Summer's Lease (Viking, 1988)
Rumpole à la Carte (Penguin, 1990)
Titmuss Regained (Viking, 1990)
Dunster (Viking, 1992)
Rumpole on Trial (Viking, 1992)
Under the Hammer (Penguin, 1994)
Rumpole and the Angel of Death (Penguin, 1995)
Felix in the Underworld (Viking, 1997)
The Sound of Trumpets (Viking, 1998)
Rumpole Rests His Case (Viking, 2001)

Rumpole and the Primrose Path (Viking, 2002)
Rumpole and the Penge Bungalow Murders (Viking, 2004)
Quite Honestly (Viking, 2005)
Rumpole and the Reign of Terror (Viking, 2006)
The Anti-social Behaviour of Horace Rumpole (Viking 2007)

non-fiction

as 'Geoffrey Lincoln', *No Moaning of the Bar* (Geoffrey Bles, 1957)
with Penelope Mortimer, *With Love and Lizards* (Michael Joseph, 1957)
Clinging to the Wreckage (Weidenfeld & Nicolson, 1982)
In Character (Allen Lane, 1983)
Character Parts (Viking, 1986)
Murderers and Other Friends (Viking, 1994)
The Summer of the Dormouse (Viking, 2000)
Where There's a Will (Viking, 2003)

edited by

Famous Trials (Penguin, 1984)
Famous Trials of Marshall Hall (Penguin, 1989)
The Oxford Book of Villains (Oxford University Press, 1992)
Great Law and Order Stories (W. W. Norton, 1992)

stage plays

The Dock Brief (1957)
What Shall We Tell Caroline? (1958)
I Spy (1958)
Lunch Hour (1960)
The Wrong Side of the Park (1960)
Collect Your Hand Baggage (1961)
Two Stars for Comfort (1962)
The Judge (1967)
A Voyage Round My Father (1970)
Come As You Are (1970)

I, Claudius (adapted from Robert Graves, 1972)
Collaborators (1973)
The Fear of Heaven (1976)
The Prince of Darkness (1976), renamed *The Bells of Hell* (1977)
Edwin (1982)
When That I Was (1982)
Hock and Soda Water (2001)
Naked Justice (2001)
The Hairless Diva (adapted from Eugene Ionesco, 2002)

stage plays adapted by

A Flea in Her Ear by Georges Feydeau (1965)
Cat Among the Pigeons by Georges Feydeau (1969)
The Captain of Köpenick by Carl Zuckmayer (1971)
The Lady from Maxim's by Georges Feydeau (1977)
A Little Hotel on the Side (from Feydeau's *Hotel Paradiso*, 1984)
A Christmas Carol by Charles Dickens (1994)

ballet scenario

Home (1968)

opera translations

Die Fledermaus (1989)
Zaide (1992)

radio plays

Like Men Betrayed (1955)
No Hero (1955)
The Dock Brief (1957)
I Spy (1957)
Call Me a Liar (1958)
Three Winters (1958)

Education of an Englishman (1964)
Personality Split (1964)
My Luby's Fear of Heaven (1976)
Edwin (1982)
The Summer of a Dormouse (2000)
Lie Down Comic (2004)
The Last Adventure (2005)

TV plays

The Dock Brief (1957)
I Spy (1959)
What Shall We Tell Caroline? (1959)
David and Broccoli (1960)
Lunch Hour (1960)
The Encyclopaedist (1961)
Twenty-Four Hours in a Woman's Life (1961)
Collect Your Hand Baggage (1963)
The Choice of Kings (1966)
The Exploding Azalea (1966)
The Head Waiter (1966)
A Flea in Her Ear (1967)
Infidelity Took Place (1967)
The Other Side (1967)
Desmond (1968)
A Voyage Round My Father (1969)
Married Alive (1970)
Only Three Can Play (1970)
Alcock and Gander (1972)
Bermondsey (1972)
Gloucester Road (1972)
Knightsbridge (1972)
Marble Arch (1972)
Mill Hill (1972)
Swiss Cottage (1972)
Rumpole of the Bailey (1975)

Shades of Green (adapted from Graham Greens, 1975)
Special Duties (1975)
Unity (adapted from David Pryce-Jones, 1978)
Rumpole's Return (1980)
Dr Fischer of Geneva (adapted from Grahame Greene, 1982)
Rumpole for the Defence (1982)
The Ebony Tower (adapted from John Fowles, 1984)
Edwin (1984)
Urania Cottage (1994)
Cider with Rosie (adapted from Laurie Lee, 1998)
Coming Home (1998)
Don Quixote (2000)
Love and War in the Apennines (adapted from Eric Newby, 2001)

screenplays

Ferry to Hong Kong (1959)
Lunch Hour (1961)
The Innocents (additional dialogue to screenplay of Truman Capote and
    William Archibald, 1961)
The Dock Brief (*Trial and Error* in USA, 1962)
Guns of Darkness (1962)
The Running Man (1963)
Bunny Lake Is Missing (with Penelope Mortimer, 1964)
John and Mary (1969)
Something Wicked This Way Comes (1982)
Tea with Mussolini (1999)

Penelope Mortimer

as Penelope Dimont, *Johanna* (Michael Joseph, 1947)
A Villa in Summer (Michael Joseph, 1954)
The Bright Prison (Michael Joseph, 1956)
with John Mortimer, *With Love and Lizards* (Michael Joseph, 1957)
Daddy's Gone A-Hunting (Michael Joseph, 1958)
Saturday Lunch with the Brownings (Hutchinson, 1960)

The Pumpkin Eater (Hutchinson, 1962)
My Friend Says It's Bullet-Proof (Hutchinson, 1967)
The Home (Hutchinson, 1971)
Long Distance (Allen Lane, 1974)
About Time (Weidenfeld & Nicolson, 1979)
The Handyman (Allen Lane, 1983)
Queen Elizabeth: A Life of the Queen Mother (Viking, 1986)
About Time Too (Weidenfeld & Nicolson, 1993)
Queen Mother: An Alternative Portrait of Her Life and Times (Andre Deutsch, 1995)

Bibliography

In addition to Penelope Mortimer's and John Mortimer's own works, which are listed on pages 491–6, I have found the following books most useful.

Ackland, Joss, *I Must Be in There Somewhere* (Hodder and Stoughton, 1989)

Branson, Richard, *Losing My Virginity* (Virgin, 1998)

Carpenter, Humphrey, *Robert Runcie: The Reluctant Archbishop* (Hodder and Stoughton, 1996)

Croft, Andy, ed., *Randall Swingler: Collected Poems* (Trent Editions, 2000)

Dimont, Madelon, *Darling Pericles* (Heinemann, 1972)

Eyre, Richard, *National Service* (Bloomsbury, 2003)

Fay, Stephen, *Power Play: The Life of Peter Hall* (Hodder and Stoughton, 1995)

Fleming, Anne, with an introduction by John Mortimer, *Bright Darkness* (Nottingham Court Press, 1983)

Gathorne-Hardy, Jonathan, *The Public School Phenomenon* (Hodder and Stoughton, 1977)

Hamburger, Michael, *String of Beginnings* (Carcanet, 1973; reprinted by Skoob Books, 1991)

Harrow School: Existing Customs (1931)

Hattersley, Alan F., *Merchiston: A South African School, 1892–1953* (A. A. Balkema, 1953)

James, Clive, 'After the *Oz* trial', in *The Metropolitan Critic* (Faber, 1974)

Kirkup, James, *A Poet Could Not But Be Gay* (Peter Owen, 1991)

Laborde, E. D., *Harrow School Yesterday & Today* (Winchester Publications, 1948)

MacCarthy, Fiona, *Byron* (John Murray, 2002)

Neville, Richard, *Hippie Hippie Shake* (Bloomsbury, 1995)

Palmer, Tony, *The Trials of Oz* (Blond and Briggs, 1971)

Robertson, Geoffrey, *The Justice Game* (Vintage, 1999)

Shubik, Irene, *Play for Today: The Evolution of Television Drama* (Manchester University Press, 2000)

Sutherland, John, *Offensive Literature: Censorship in Britain 1960–1982* (Junction Books, 1982)

Thwaite, Ann, ed., *My Oxford* (Robson Books, 1977)

Tynan, Kathleen, ed., *Kenneth Tynan: Letters* (Mandarin, 1995)

Walker, Alexander, *Fatal Charm: The Life of Rex Harrison* (Weidenfeld and Nicolson, 1992)

Webster, Richard, *A Brief History of Blasphemy* (Orwell Press, 1990)

Wellwarth, George E., *The Theatre of Protest and Paradox: Developments in the Avantgarde Drama* (MacGibbon and Kee, 1965)

Wheen, Francis, *The Sixties* (Century, 1982)

Whitley, Edward, *The Graduates* (Hamish Hamilton, 1986)

Acknowledgements

The pleasure of writing this book, apart from spending time with Sir John Mortimer at Turville Heath Cottage and elsewhere, was becoming better acquainted with his family. Lady Mortimer – Penny – was already a friend, but she proved a stalwart and sturdy supporter. John's step-daughters, Madelon Dimont Burk, Caroline Mortimer, Julia Mankowitz, Deborah Rogers and her husband, Colin, were all – Madelon in particular – enormously helpful, as were John's own children, Jeremy Mortimer (Penelope's literary executor) and his wife, Polly, Sally Silverman (keeper of family archives), Emily and Rosie Mortimer, and Ross Bentley. I thank them all.

I could not have written this biography without the testimony of the poet Michael Hamburger, who died in the very week I finished writing. There is nobody I would rather have sent my manuscript to than this gentle, wise and scholarly man. I am indebted again to Pat Kavanagh for suggesting John, a fellow client of hers, as a subject. I was pleased to work again with Tony Lacey at Penguin, and with Annie Lee, and to meet Lesley Levene, inspired copy-editor of Trojan industriousness. The beady-eyed Douglas Matthews was, as ever, the nonpareil of indexers. I owe thanks to Robert Thomson, editor, and Keith Blackmore, executive editor, at *The Times*, for giving me the months of freedom required to write. The unexpected bonus of the last three years is that in 2005 my husband lost his heart to another lady, the lovely *Deglet Nour*, of a vintage just two years younger than mine. She is a traditional gentleman's cruiser, built of wood, and lies in that beautiful stretch of the Thames not far from Henley Bridge. On long summer evenings we can gaze across John Mortimer's hill from the deck of our *pied à l'eau* and toast him in appropriate champagne.

Among John's army of friends, the following were particularly invaluable and kind in sharing their memories: Joss Ackland, the late Robert Alexander, QC, whose widow, Marie, allowed me to see his diary, Jim

Anderson, Dame Eileen Atkins, Don Berry, Christopher Booker, Lord Bragg, Tim Cassel, QC, Michael Codron, Clive Conway, Geraldine Cooke, Sarah Cox, Joanna David, Jacqueline Davis, Felix Dennis, Sonia Dimont, Clive Donner, Quentin Edwards, QC, Michael Essex, Sir Richard Eyre, Shirley Anne Field, Anna Ford, Sir Denis Forman, John Francis, Lady Antonia Fraser, Derek Granger, Michael Grieve, QC, Sir John Gunston, Sir Peter Hall, the late Michael Hamburger, Patricia Hodge, Lord Hooson, QC, Anthony Howard, Lord Hutchinson, QC, Marilyn Imrie, Glenys Kinnock, MEP, Verity Lambert, Nora Lee, Kathy Lette, Jon Lord, Vicky Lord, Ian McEwan, Jane McKerron, Baroness Mallalieu, QC, James Michie, Nicholas Mosley, Richard Neville, Phyllis Newall, David Offenbach, Tony Palmer, Graham Pechey, Harold Pinter, Alvin Rakoff, Geoffrey Robertson, QC, Irene Shubik, Lois Sieff, Pamela Swingler, Alexander Waugh, Sandy Wilson.

Other helpful informants included Charlotte Amory, Jane Asher, Tony Benn, Michael Berkeley, Elizabeth Boardman (Brasenose College), Sir Richard Body, QC, Arthur Bone, Eleanor Bron, John Browning, Tony Cash, Richard Cohen, Wendy Craig, John Croft, Peter Crookston, Hunter Davies, Jonathan Dimbleby, Jo Elwin, Jennie Erdal, Sir Richard Eyre, Stephen Fay, Margaret Forster, Edward Fox, Patrick Freeman, Lesley Garner, Margaret Gaskin, Rita Boswell Gibbs (Harrow School archivist), the late Dr Howard Gotlieb (Boston University), Haya Harareet, Peter Hunter (Harrow School), Howard Jacobson, Martin Jarvis, Susanna Johnston, Francis King, Margaret Knight (Harrow School), Sue Lawley, Prue Leith, Lord Lester QC, Magnus Linklater, Mark Littman, QC, Professor Eva Lomnicka, QC, Hilary Lowinger, Carol MacArthur, Tim McBennett, Angus McGill, the late George Melly, Margo Miller, Edna O'Brien, the late Richard Ollard, Vita Palladino (Boston University), Molly Parkin, Jeremy Paxman, the late Tom Pocock, Peter Popham, Diana Quick, Mark Ramage, Nigel Rees, Amelia Richards (Christ Church, Oxford), Jill Rushton, Richard Savage, Ned Sherrin, Paul Sidey, Christine Stone, Charles Sturridge, Gay Sturt (Dragon School), Dr Tom Stuttaford, Deyan Sudjic, Judy Taylor, Emma Tennant, Martin Thompson, Claire Tomalin, Adam Tyler-Moore, Peregrine Worsthorne.

Permissions

Index

JOHN MORTIMER

SUMMER'S LEASE

It's high summer, and high comedy too, when Molly drags her amiably bickering family to a rented Tuscan villa for the holidays. Molly is sure that the house is the perfect setting for their three-week getaway, but soon she becomes fascinated by the lives of the absent owners - and things start to go horribly wrong ...

'She is saddled with her randy old tease of a father, a lawyer husband suspected of feeble infidelity and three daughters ...With a cosy fluency of wit, Mortimer charms us into his urbane tangle of clues' *Mail on Sunday*

'Part social comedy and part adventure story-cum-murder mystery ... Mortimer's wit never stalls' *Guardian*

'A book of enormous delights and subtle shifts of tone, atmosphere and narrative pace' *Time Out*

'Amusing, entertaining ... and a cracking good read' *Sunday Express*

JOHN MORTIMER

THE ANTI-SOCIAL BEHAVIOUR OF HORACE RUMPOLE

'Is football a crime nowadays?' asks Horace Rumpole

Apparently so. For twelve-year-old Peter Timson – of the London family of petty criminals – has been served with an ASBO for playing the game in the street. Pretty soon, however, Rumpole realizes that there's something fishy about the Timson case. Why are Peter's neighbours pursuing a vendetta against him? Could they have more sinister reasons for wanting him off their street? And could it be connected to the death of a prostitute, in which the prime suspect is a hapless young bachelor protesting his innocence – a second call to arms Rumpole can scarcely ignore?

As if all that weren't enough, Rumpole's colleagues are up in arms about the cigars and glasses of wine he occasionally enjoys in Chambers. The way things are going, Rumpole himself will be getting an ASBO …

'Very funny about the old dinosaur's attempts to fit into the depressingly clean modern world' *The Times*

'One of the fictional immortals, right up there with Sherlock Holmes and Bertie Wooster' *Daily Telegraph*

'Hugely entertaining, very funny … classic Rumpole' *Herald*

JOHN MORTIMER

RUMPOLE AND THE REIGN OF TERROR

**Justice isn't blind –
it's just a little short sighted and weak around the knees …**

His wig may be yellowing and his gown might be in tatters, but Rumpole will not give up the good fight – not while there's injustice to battle.

When a distressed Tiffany Timson (of the infamous South London clan of petty criminals) tearfully explains that her husband Dr Kahn has been arrested on suspicion of terrorism, Rumpole knows that to take on this case will mean not just defending one man – but squaring up to the very notion of modern British justice.

With She Who Must Be Obeyed mysteriously shutting herself away and fellow-members of his chambers just plain scared, it seems that Rumpole must stand alone against the Establishment. But that is precisely the position any defence barrister worth his salt relishes most …

'A fine comic creation. A figure who represents something important: the defence of liberty against the arrogance of power' *Scotsman*

'Written with Mortimer's customary aplomb and an infectious enjoyment' Elizabeth Buchan, *Sunday Times*

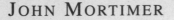
JOHN MORTIMER

THE FIRST RUMPOLE OMNIBUS

Who rose to enduring fame on Blood and Typewriters, told the pregnant Portia of the Chambers it would come out in the end, advised Guthrie Featherstone, Q.C., to adopt a more judicial attitude, returned in the tender gloaming of each evening – via Pommeroy's and a glass of Château Fleet Street – to She Who Must Be Obeyed?

The answer is Horace Rumpole whose legal triumphs, plundering sorties into the *Oxford Book of English Verse* and less-than-salubrious hat are celebrated here in the first omnibus edition.

It brings together three volumes:

Rumpole of the Bailey

The Trials of Rumpole

Rumpole's Return

'I thank heaven for small mercies. The first of these is Rumpole'

Clive James, *Observer*

'A fruity, foxy masterpiece, defender of our wilting faith in mankind'

Sunday Times

John Mortimer

THE SECOND RUMPOLE OMNIBUS

Horace Rumpole turning down yet another invitation to exchange the joys and sorrows of life as an Old Bailey hack for the delights of the sunshine state, where Senior Citizens loll on beaches and the sarcastic tones of the Mad Bull (Judge Roger Bullingham) are heard no more, settles instead for the beaded bubbles of Château Pommeroy's ordinary claret, the domestic chill emanating from She Who Must Be Obeyed, and his role *extraordinaire* as Defender of the Faith: 'Never plead guilty.'

This omnibus brings together three volumes:

Rumpole for the Defence

Rumpole and the Golden Thread

Rumpole's Last Case

'Rumpole is worthy to join the great gallery of English oddballs ranging from Pickwick to Sherlock Holmes, Jeeves and Bertie Wooster' *Sunday Times*

'Rumpole has been an inspired stroke of good fortune for us all' Lynda Lee-Potter, *Daily Mail*

He just wanted a decent book to read ...

Not too much to ask, is it? It was in 1935 when Allen Lane, Managing Director of Bodley Head Publishers, stood on a platform at Exeter railway station looking for something good to read on his journey back to London. His choice was limited to popular magazines and poor-quality paperbacks – the same choice faced every day by the vast majority of readers, few of whom could afford hardbacks. Lane's disappointment and subsequent anger at the range of books generally available led him to found a company – and change the world.

'We believed in the existence in this country of a vast reading public for intelligent books at a low price, and staked everything on it'
Sir Allen Lane, 1902–1970, founder of Penguin Books

The quality paperback had arrived – and not just in bookshops. Lane was adamant that his Penguins should appear in chain stores and tobacconists, and should cost no more than a packet of cigarettes.

Reading habits (and cigarette prices) have changed since 1935, but Penguin still believes in publishing the best books for everybody to enjoy. We still believe that good design costs no more than bad design, and we still believe that quality books published passionately and responsibly make the world a better place.

So wherever you see the little bird – whether it's on a piece of prize-winning literary fiction or a celebrity autobiography, political tour de force or historical masterpiece, a serial-killer thriller, reference book, world classic or a piece of pure escapism – you can bet that it represents the very best that the genre has to offer.

Whatever you like to read – trust Penguin.